THE WHICH? GUIDE TO

SCOTLAND

THE WHICH? GUIDE TO
SCOTLAND

Andrew Leslie

CONSUMERS' ASSOCIATION

Which? Books are commissioned and researched by
Consumers' Association and published by
Which? Ltd., 2 Marylebone Road, London NW1 4DF

Distributed by The Penguin Group:
Penguin Books Ltd, 27 Wrights Lane, London W8 5TZ

First published April 1992
Revised April 1994, June 1996

British Library Cataloguing in Publication Data
A catalogue record for this book is available from the British Library.

ISBN 0 85202 628 5

Typographic design and line illustrations by Paul Saunders
Cover photograph by Still Moving Picture Company
Maps by David Perrott Cartographics

Text by Andrew Leslie with contributions from Deborah Buzan
Editor for *Holiday Which?*: Anna Fielder

Additional research and assistance (first edition): Morag Aitken,
Ben Hall, Helen Oldfield, Polly Phillimore, Nick Riddiford,
Caroline Sanders and Lucy Smith; (this edition) Lorna Dean,
Helen Oldfield, Liz Piccin.

> For a full list of Which? books, please write to Which? Books,
> Castlemead, Gascoyne Way, Hertford X, SG14 1LH

Typeset by Hewer Text Composition Services, Edinburgh

Printed and bound in Great Britain by
Richard Clay Limited, Bungay, Suffolk

CONTENTS

ABOUT THIS GUIDE

THIS guide to the whole of Scotland is the culmination of a long tradition of reporting on the country's regions in *Holiday Which?* magazine. It aims to combine the best in travel writing with solid advice and recommendations, as well as an informed insight into the country's past and present.

The 13 chapters that follow the general introduction and history cover all the mainland regions as well as the islands; the general map of Scotland (see page 28) gives an overview of how the regions relate to each other. Within each chapter is an easy-to-follow gazetteer of the region aided by a map and two boxed sections that give travel planning information and advice on good bases – highlighted by a black strip on each map.

WHERE TO STAY

Our recommended hotels – all inspected by *Holiday Which?* or its sister publications, *The Which? Hotel Guide* and *The Good Bed & Breakfast Guide* – have bedrooms with bathrooms or showers en suite and most serve evening meals. The price categories are based on the cost, per night, of a double or twin-bedded room in 1996, including VAT and breakfast. Tariffs quoted by hotels sometimes include dinner – check when you book. You can expect to pay £12 to £20 for a set meal in a simpler hotel, up to £35 in a luxury one.

£ – under £70 per room per night
££ – £70 to £110 per room per night
£££ – over £110 per room per night.

WHERE TO EAT

Our recommendations for places to eat at were compiled with the help of *The Good Food Guide* (published by Which? Ltd) and many are featured in the 1996 edition. Hotels featured in this section are particularly recommended for their food. A ★ marks a place that is particularly good value for money.

OPENING TIMES

We give 1996 opening times, in brackets, following the name of each sight – but always double-check, particularly if you intend to visit early or late in season. Bear in mind that opening times vary from year to year and that at many sights last admission will be 30 to 45 minutes before closing time.

HS, standard times means Historic Scotland's standard opening times: Apr to end Sept, Mon to Sat 9.30 to 6.30, Sun 2 to 6.30 (last ticket at 6); Oct to end Mar, Mon to Sat 9.30 to 4.30, Sun 2 to 4.30 (last ticket at 4).

NTS means that the sight is run by the National Trust for Scotland.

For more details about these organisations, see pages 24 and 25.

INTRODUCTION

THE best reason for choosing to go on holiday to Scotland is this: it is one of the last places inside the crowded and frenetic European Community where it is possible, indeed easy, to be alone in empty countryside. This is not to say that Scotland, like everywhere else, does not have its tourist traps, its crowded roads or its popular beauty spots. It is merely to stress that it is easy to escape from them. Nor is it to imply that Scotland is a deserted wilderness – it has its great cities, its country hotels and its many festivals. But again, if you wish, it is easy to get away from them.

In fine weather, Scotland is one of the most beautiful countries in the world. The quality of the light is not to be matched further south, while the variety of vegetation and landscape makes for constant change. At every season of the year, except in bleakest November or March, the Scottish landscape is an extraordinary blend of subtle colours. Blues predominate – in the sea and the lochs or in the distant hills. Green and white add their shades in spring, lilac and purple in summer, and, perhaps most magnificent, the tans, caramels and russets of autumn, with, by the sea lochs, the intense orange of the seaweed. A frosty winter's day in sharp white, grey, black and intense blue shows a landscape less subtle, more magnificent. The way in which these hues change over a single slope of hill as trees give way to patches of grass, heather, moss or bracken, broken by outcrops of rock, is worth contemplating in detail. It does not much matter whether it is mountainous coastal scenery or a quiet Border valley – something of the same richness will be found in both.

Curiosity alone may lead you to Scotland. For a thinly populated mountainous country on the fringe of Europe, it has had a disproportionately large impact on the world. The Scot abroad, whether as a mercenary soldier in the European wars of the sixteenth and seventeenth centuries, an explorer, a missionary, a Hong Kong merchant, a New World statesman or a football fan, has long been a distinctive figure. Equally, Scottish inventors, philosophers and scientists have been responsible for many of the ideas on which our understanding of the world is based. The tensions which have turned the Scots into a paradoxical mixture of hard-headed realists and sentimental patriots, which have drawn them to be tempted by idealism and self-interest alike, or which have made them into a nation of reluctant emigrants, can best be understood by going there.

It is a mistake to think that Scotland is merely an extension of England. Indeed, no attitude is capable of causing greater offence. The Scots successfully resisted English attempts at domination for seven hundred years, and the mere fact that the two countries now have the same monarch, parliament and currency does not mean that visiting Scotland is much the same as visiting the Lake District. Many differences between the countries remain – in law, culture, education, church and language, not to mention politics. Scotland's history, traced in its castles, battlefields, ancient trading towns and folk museums, in its cultural and architectural links with France, Flanders and

Scandinavia, is distinct. This is again a reason for coming to Scotland – to learn what life looks like on the other side of an old frontier.

To enjoy Scotland to the full, you must enjoy being out of doors, and not just in fine weather. For the naturalists, the anglers, the walkers, the golfers or the rock-climbers who are sometimes prepared to suffer for their hobby, the country is a delight. It is a delight too for those who are happy to track down Neolithic sites, old castles, old hill roads or interesting geological outcrops across rough and sometimes boggy country. To those who are, for one reason or another, tied to their transport, a holiday in Scotland is a more chancy affair. As a country to tour through it can be magnificent, but much depends on the weather, and the weather is unpredictable. This is not necessarily a cause for despair. Edinburgh and Glasgow, Stirling, Perth or Aberdeen have enough attractions to provide solace in a rainy spell and are even better in a fine one. Both Edinburgh and Glasgow deserve better than to be tacked on to a general Scottish holiday. Both are ideal short break cities: Glasgow for its energy, its wealth of galleries and its shopping habit, Edinburgh because it is one of the most beautiful cities of Europe and has a host of sights – historic and otherwise.

IRRITANTS

Wet weather
It does not always rain in Scotland, far from it, but to prepare yourself, mentally and physically, for a spell of wet, possibly windy, weather is vital. On a damp, drizzly day, with low cloud shrouding the mountains to their feet, the Scottish countryside is about as interesting as the inside of a cardboard box. It is impossible to predict what sort of weather you will meet, so be prepared for the worst. If a week of blue skies and high temperatures is your reward, so much the better.
● Take waterproof clothing – trousers too if you intend to walk much – and a pair of wellington boots.
● There is often a difference in weather between the western and eastern sides of the country. If the west is wet, head east; if the east is cold, the west may be warmer.
● If you are going self-catering, make sure you will have enough space to be able to endure each other's company in wet weather.

Midges
In all the swathes of literature pumped out to encourage visitors to Scotland, there is seldom any mention of the humble midge. This is unfair, for midges rank close to bad weather as the greatest barrier to the full enjoyment of an outdoor Scottish holiday, and they are at their peak in July, August and September. Midges are a menace everywhere in Scotland, but they are at their worst in the Highlands, where the damp ground provides ideal breeding territory. Midges are tiny (but not invisible) blood-sucking insects, and they descend upon warm-blooded humans in swarms. Their activity seems to be governed by light: the dim conditions of early morning, evening, or overcast days bring them out in thousands, while sun, strong wind or darkness makes them vanish.

Except to the few people who suffer strong allergic reactions to them, midge bites themselves are little more than an itchy irritant. What is intolerable is the attack itself, for the insects get into hair, scalp, eyes, ears and on to every exposed piece of skin, until the itchy prickle of their biting provokes frenzy in the most patient of creatures. Activities such as bird-watching or fishing, which require stillness, are most easily disrupted by midges. Picnics are vulnerable too, as are evening walks. But it is probably the innocent camper who chooses a sheltered site who will suffer most. Few tents are truly midge-proof, and there are few experiences more awful than attempting to eat breakfast while the midges are eating you.

- Take plenty of repellent.
- Wear light-coloured clothing for preference. A hat helps too.
- Seek the company of a smoker.
- Regard the wind as your friend. Do not camp or attempt an evening picnic in sheltered, dimly-lit places.
- If camping, take a can of insecticide or a mosquito coil.

Trees

Sooner or later, someone must decide whether forestry or tourism is more important to Scotland's economy. From the point of view of the visitor, the wholesale planting of spruce in the Scottish uplands has been little short of a catastrophe. The attraction of the Scottish landscape lies in the sweeping panoramas over hillsides rich in colour and light, so there is little pleasure in contemplating a countryside of monotonous green of which you quickly tire. Whole tracts of Scotland have been ruined by forestry. Galloway is smothered, the high Liddesdale hill routes impenetrable, Loch Tummel irreparably damaged, and much of Sutherland besmirched. The Forestry Commission does its best to make its plantations more attractive to visitors – other commercial enterprises do not have to be so public-spirited. Whoever owns the trees, the point remains: commercial forestry plantations are two a penny throughout Europe; the Scottish landscape is unique.

If you want to see what a Scottish forest can be like at its best, head for the fragments of the old Caledonian forest at Rothiemurchus, or the Black Wood of Loch Rannoch, or even some of the man-made plantations of Scots pine round Nairn. These pinewoods are places of light, colour and birdsong, in contrast to the barren darkness of the spruce plantations. Whenever you see the pattern of lines on the slope of a hill, which denotes a new plantation, look carefully at the view. You won't see it again for the better part of a century.

Gift-wrapped Scotland

Walter Scott started it with *The Lady of the Lake*, the poem which brought the first tourists flooding to the Trossachs. Since then, the Scotland which has been assiduously sold to visitors is a soft-focus land of high romance, full of fierce but noble chieftains, tartan-clad clansmen and the drama of lost causes – ideals popularised in recent Hollywood films. To this the twentieth century has added bad jokes about haggis, the kilt and the cult of Nessie, the Loch Ness Monster. Much of this kitsch may be enjoyable, and a good way of selling kilts, bottles of whisky or cuddly monsters, but it bears little relation to the truth about Scotland, past or present.

SCOTLAND'S HISTORY

Scottish history is often baffling to the visitor. It is seldom taught beyond the borders of the country, so few outsiders have any idea of what went on before the union of the parliaments in 1707. However, some knowledge of it is useful, not simply for visiting castles, but because it helps to explain modern Scotland and some of the tensions within it. Scottish history, read from one angle, is a litany of dashed hopes: the silence into which the Declaration of Arbroath fell in 1320; the long sequence of military incompetence at Falkirk, Halidon Hill, Flodden, Solway Moss, Pinkie, Dunbar and Culloden; the gradual realisation in the sixteenth century that the 'Auld Alliance' with France was a double-edged sword; the sense of having been abandoned by the later Stuart kings; the terrible failure of the Darien colony and the discontent felt after the Act of Union. Add to these the devastation of the Highland way of life in the eighteenth and nineteenth centuries, the destruction of the Lowland heavy industry in the twentieth, the failure to achieve any degree of administrative independence from England and the increasing sense of being once more isolated on the edge of a continent whose centres are Strasbourg and Brussels, and it would be surprising if there were not some truth behind the old clichés about the insecurity and touchiness of the Scottish character.

Looked at from another angle, the Scottish tendency to divide into factions or to put self-interest first can be held to blame for most of the country's past troubles. The endless squabbling between powerful barons and kings trying to exert their authority went on longer in Scotland than almost anywhere else. The religious sectarianism which plagued seventeenth-century Scotland was an outbreak of the same tendency. It can be argued that almost every failed enterprise undertaken by the Scots has been doomed from the start by argument and failure to work in unity. It is perhaps no surprise that Wallace and Robert the Bruce, who managed to provide Scotland with a brief flicker of united endeavour, are two of the most revered of Scotland's heroes.

UNITY

Romans

The difficulties of communication over Scotland's mountainous, boggy and sea-loch-riddled terrain long made the establishment of an effective centralising authority difficult. The Romans were the first to try, moving north from England in at least three separate campaigns between AD 81 and AD 208, defeating the inhabitants of Caledonia at Mons Graupius in AD 84. Only the area south of the Forth and Clyde was subdued for any length of time. Gibbon describes the Romans as giving up in disgust, turning 'with contempt from gloomy hills assailed by the winter tempest, from lakes concealed in a blue mist, and from cold and lonely heaths, over which the deer of the forest were chased by a troop of naked barbarians'.

Picts, Scots, Angles, Norsemen and Britons

The sixth century saw what is now Scotland parcelled up into four kingdoms, three of them inhabited by Celtic peoples: Picts, Scots and

Britons. The Picts, in central and eastern Scotland, held the greatest area of territory, the Scots (from Ireland) had formed the kingdom of Dalriada in what is now Argyll and the Britons held Galloway and Cumbria. The Angles, from their power base in Northumbria, had extended their rule northward into Lothian. In the ninth century, the Norsemen added to the brew by extensive coastal raiding and by establishing themselves in Shetland, Orkney, the Hebrides, Sutherland and Caithness. Warfare between the rival kingdoms was constant, the battle of Nechtansmere in 685 (when the Picts defeated the Angles) being particularly notable because it stopped Anglian expansion northwards. Marriage brought some kind of unity between Picts and Scots under Kenneth MacAlpine, King of Scots, around 843 and by 1034 the old kingdoms of Britons and Angles had also been absorbed.

Malcolm Canmore and William the Conqueror

Several bloody conflicts took place before Malcolm Canmore emerged as king in 1057, killing Macbeth in the process (here at least Shakespeare is accurate). Two important events occurred during his reign – his marriage to Margaret, the English princess, who was a refugee from the Norman invasion, and the act of homage which Malcolm paid to William the Conqueror in 1072 at Abernethy (see Independence and Religion below). Malcolm, often seen as a big barbarian married to a cultured and holy wife whom he adored, spent much time trying, and failing, to establish Scotland's southern frontier along the River Tyne.

David I and the Norman incomers

There was no Norman conquest of Scotland – the Scottish kings did the job themselves. Malcolm's successors, holding lands in England and with increasingly strong ties there, encouraged Norman families to settle in Scotland, granting land and promoting the building of castles. Many of the most famous names in Scottish history have Norman origins. David I (1124–53) hastened Norman-style feudalism by the establishment of abbeys and cathedrals and the system of royal burghs. Under David, Scotland began to develop an administrative system to match that of England, while the authority of the king was much increased.

Last of the Norsemen

Under the improbably named Magnus Barelegs, the Norse settlers in the Hebrides had forced the Scottish crown to concede all the western islands to them (and Magnus shiftily added Kintyre to the list by dragging his boat across the Tarbert isthmus). The Norse-Hebridean chiefs were a menace to the Scottish kings, supporting rebels and making forays of their own. Somerled, ancestor of Clan Donald, was a particularly forceful character in this respect. In 1263, King Haakon of Norway assembled a huge fleet for an attack, but was routed at the battle of Largs. After this defeat, Norway gave up all her Scottish possessions apart from Orkney and Shetland under a treaty of 1266. A royal marriage with Norway in 1468 brought Orkney and Shetland to the Scottish crown.

Highlands, Lowlands and Islands

For centuries, the clans of the islands and glens continued a law unto themselves, sometimes allied to the crown, sometimes hostile to it. It could be argued that they never became fully part of a united Scotland. Despite expeditions mounted by various Scottish kings, it was not until the defeat of the last Jacobite rebellion at Culloden in 1746 that the power of the clans to act independently was broken. There is still a division between Highlander and Lowlander today – sometimes exaggerated, sometimes glossed over.

INDEPENDENCE

If there is one theme that infects Scottish history, right down to the present day, it is the independence of the nation, and in particular, independence from England. In the 1992 general election, 21.5 per cent of Scots voted for the Scottish National Party and its independence platform, a substantial proportion for a country that has been unified with England for 300 years.

The Wars of Independence

The conflict between England and Scotland really started in 1290 with the death of the child-queen Margaret, 'The Maid of Norway'. The blame for it must be carried almost entirely by Edward I of England, popularly known as 'Hammer of the Scots'. Edward had a clear idea that he was feudal overlord of Scotland, and was able to point to the homage done by various Scottish kings to various English kings to make his point (though what, exactly, they were doing homage for is still disputed). Edward's chance came when he was asked to judge between 13 rival claimants for the Scottish throne. He made his judgement in favour of John Balliol, but proceeded thereafter to treat this weak-minded man as such an underling that even 'Toom Tabard' (empty coat) as he was known, was forced into revolt in 1296. Edward's response was to sack Berwick, invade Scotland, plunder the stone of Scone on which Scottish kings were traditionally crowned, depose John Balliol, and set up a government similar to the one that he had already imposed on conquered Wales. Scotland was to be a little-regarded province of England.

Revolt started almost at once, especially among the small land-owners who had no holdings in England to put in jeopardy. William Wallace defeated the English at Stirling Bridge, but was defeated in turn at Falkirk in 1298. He was captured in 1305 and executed as a traitor in London. Scottish resistance collapsed and Edward set up a new, less repressive government.

In 1306, Robert the Bruce, grandson of one of the claimants to the Scottish throne whom Edward had rejected, killed his Comyn rival in a church, thus laying himself open to charges of murder and sacrilege. His reaction was to have himself crowned King of Scotland at Scone. Edward immediately swore that he would never rest until Scotland was conquered and set about defeating Bruce. Bruce's deliverance came in May 1307 with the death of Edward, whose son, Edward II, turned back from the Scottish campaign.

Bruce proceeded to defeat his Scottish enemies, then turned on the English-garrisoned castles, until, by 1314, only Stirling remained in

English hands. The Battle of Bannockburn (page 272) put the seal on Bruce's triumph and made his kingship undisputed, but it was not until 1328 that Scotland's independence was recognised by the English king.

Further Wars with the English
The conflict did not end there. By 1333 everything that Bruce had achieved had gone. John Balliol's son, with the support of Edward III of England, invaded, defeated the Scots at Halidon Hill, and promptly paid homage to the English king. His reign did not last long, but it set the pattern for the following centuries. English kings claimed feudal overlordship or supported discontented Scottish nobles, and occasionally invaded. Scottish resistance, usually marked by internal strife and military weakness, was sporadically successful, but owed its survival to the fact that English kings had more pressing tasks than subduing Scotland, notably that of maintaining their claim to France. Scotland's worst defeat by the English was entirely self-inflicted when James IV invaded England on behalf of his French ally. The result was the terrible battle of Flodden in 1513.

Henry VIII and the Rough Wooing
James V of Scotland, the nephew of Henry VIII of England, was not inclined to follow his uncle in throwing off the Pope's authority. Rather, he chose a French bride and kept faith with the Vatican. In 1541, Henry summoned him to confer at York but James chose not to go. Henry dispatched an army northwards and James replied by sending one south, only to have it defeated at Solway Moss in 1542. James died soon afterwards, leaving the infant Mary Queen of Scots as his heir.

Henry saw his chance of bringing Scotland into his orbit by arranging for his son, Edward, to marry Mary. There were enough Protestant (and hence anglophile) lords in Scotland to make this attractive to the Scots, and a treaty was even signed at Greenwich to confirm it. But a putsch by those in favour of the old alliance with France led to Scottish rejection of the match. Henry, typically, overplayed his hand by replacing diplomacy with force. The burning of the south of Scotland in 1544 and 1545, ironically called the Rough Wooing, merely strengthened Scottish determination. Defeated at Pinkie in 1547, the Scots spirited the young queen to France and agreed to her marriage with the French dauphin, the future François II.

A French Province?
The mother of Mary Queen of Scots, the redoubtable Mary of Guise, was now regent of Scotland and her response to the English invasion of the country was to bring in French troops to defend it. A military stalemate resulted, but Scotland found itself increasingly governed by French administrators. When, in 1559, a group of Protestant lords rebelled, they did so as much to rid Scotland of the French as to promote their religion. After the death of Mary of Guise in 1560, the matter was sealed: the French left.

The Neglected Outpost (1603–1707)
When James VI, son of Mary Queen of Scots, inherited the throne of

13

England in 1603 and travelled triumphantly south, he promised his Scottish subjects he would return every three years. He did not keep this promise. For a brief period during the conflict with Charles I (see Religion below), the Scottish parliament asserted its independence, but the invasion of Scotland by Oliver Cromwell in 1650, the enforced, if temporary, union with England, and the absolutist policies of Charles II after the Restoration left Scotland with little independent voice. The hesitation in Scotland after the Glorious Revolution of 1688 had deposed James VII from the British throne was brief – the Scottish crown was offered to William and Mary only two months after the English.

The Union of Parliaments (1707)
In the years before the final union of Scotland and England, the relationship between the two countries was extremely frayed (see page 128). To many Scots, union with England seemed to be the only way of avoiding bankruptcy and war. When the Scottish parliament voted itself out of existence it seemed the end at last of an independent Scotland.

The Jacobites (1715–1745)
The uprisings of 1715, 1719 and 1745, which sought to restore the Stuarts to the British throne, were not in any sense a popular struggle for Scottish independence. While the unpopularity of the Union was a factor that led some people to join the Jacobites, Lowland support for the Jacobite risings was patchy at best, and Highland support was far from solid. Nor were the ambitions of the 'Old Pretender' (James VIII) or his son, Prince Charles Edward Stuart, confined to ruling Scotland – the invasion of England in 1745 was undertaken with the purpose of gaining the British crown. Nevertheless, the uprisings showed that the old link between Scotland and France and the loyalty of many Scots to the person they saw as their legitimate king had not been entirely destroyed by union with England.

Home Rule Movements (1920–1979)
The first serious attempts in modern times to regain home rule for Scotland were made between the two World Wars, at a time of economic depression and, on Clydeside, left-wing radicalism. The nationalist movement was given added fuel by the 'Scottish Renaissance' literary revival, led by Hugh MacDiarmid. All attempts to attain a measure of self-government for Scotland came to nothing, except that they eventually resulted in the formation of the Scottish Nationalist Party (SNP) in 1934. Hampered by factionalist infighting for years, the SNP made something of a breakthrough in 1974, winning seven seats and polling 21 per cent of the vote, largely because the discovery of 'Scotland's Oil' held out the prospect of independence in wealth rather than penury. An extremely confused period, in which the word devolution came to mean many different things to different people, ended in a controversial and inconclusive referendum of 1979 when a proposal for a form of devolution was rejected by a majority of the Scottish electorate, an abstention being held to count against. Since then, the issue of home rule has, if anything, become more prominent, and seems unlikely to disappear, whatever temporary solutions to the problems of Scotland's government are found.

RELIGION

The Celtic Church

The first Christian missionary to Scotland was St Ninian, who, from a base in Galloway, set out to convert the southern Picts around AD 400. He was followed, in 563, by St Columba, whose foundation at Iona became a centre of learning and spirituality which was to have enormous influence throughout Scotland. The Celtic church, its gospel spread by missionaries whose names still crop up in remote place-names, eventually made contact with the Roman church, whose doctrine, brought to England by St Augustine, had spread up to Northumbria. In various conflicts over practice (the date of Easter was one point at issue), the Celtic church gave way. Its influence was weakened by Norse raids on Iona and the Roman doctrine gained increasing hold.

The Norman Period

Just as the Anglo-Norman settlement of Scotland established feudalism, so it placed the Roman doctrine on a firm basis. The remnants of the Celtic church, many of whose priests were not celibate, could not exist within the new system. Malcolm Canmore's wife Margaret, who founded the monastery at Dunfermline, rebuilt Iona but was firm in suppressing the erroneous ways of the older church. By the time dioceses and parishes had been established, continental monastic orders invited in and great abbeys founded, the church in Scotland was almost identical in practice to that in England. The Celtic church, except perhaps in the Highland fastnesses, had vanished.

Church and Crown (1153–1560)

Just as the English kings claimed jurisdiction over Scotland, so did the English church – but in this case the Scots had an easier victory, for the Pope recognised the Scottish church as directly responsible to Rome in 1192. In 1472, St Andrews became an archbishopric. During the Middle Ages, the church, wealthier than the king and wielding immense influence, was a strong force for stability in the face of recurring crises. However, in common with the church in so many European countries before the Reformation, it grew fat and lax. When the Lutheran doctrines began to be heard in Scotland, they found fertile ground, although reformers were burnt – notably George Wishart in 1546. The energetic Cardinal Beaton, doing his best to counter the anglophile, Protestant party, was murdered in his turn at St Andrews in the same year. The regency of Mary of Guise, during the time when the young Mary Queen of Scots was in France, saw open warfare, when Protestant lords, aided by the English, confronted the government.

Reformation (1560)

In the brief period between the death of Mary of Guise in 1560 and the return to Scotland of Mary Queen of Scots in 1561, the Scottish Reformation took place. The preacher John Knox laid before the Scottish parliament a Confession of Faith, which was accepted; the authority of the Pope was denied, and the mass declared illegal. Scotland achieved, in one

15

step, a radical transformation of her church. At the same time, the principle that the church was independent of state control was laid down and the basis for Presbyterianism established. This essential difference between the reformed Scottish church and the Church of England was to cause much anguish. The Confession of Faith was followed by the Book of Discipline, which laid out not only how the new church might be organised but envisaged a complete scheme of education from primary schools to university, astoundingly in advance of its time.

Mary Queen of Scots

In 1561, Mary, a Catholic queen, returned to a country in the first uneasy aftermath of a Protestant revolution. Fear of a reimposition of the old faith was strong, and the Catholic powers of Europe encouraged Mary to undertake a counter-revolution. The religious tolerance with which Mary attempted to rule was no solution to the polarisation of attitudes within Scotland. Although she suppressed the Catholic Huntly family, she did herself no good by marrying the Catholic Darnley. Part of Mary's tragedy is that she attempted to steer a middle course between two extremes. The nobles who rebelled against her did so largely out of self-interest, but religious concerns were not far beneath the surface.

Absolutism and Civil War (1567–1689)

The turmoil which gripped Scotland throughout much of the seventeenth century was the result of monarchs attempting to impose their will on a church unprepared to accept interference in its affairs. James VI succeeded in reimposing bishops upon the reformed Scottish church, thereby gaining a means of exerting authority, but he achieved this only after long struggle. Charles I, in attempting to dictate particular forms of worship, went too far. The signing of the National Covenant in 1638 led indirectly to civil war in Scotland, England and Ireland, to the throwing off of the king's authority in Scotland and to the appearance of a temporary theocracy, which crumbled in the face of Oliver Cromwell's invasion. After the restoration, Charles II re-imposed bishops and let loose troops to persecute the Presbyterian extremists who refused to be reconciled to his policies. The 'Killing Times' round the year 1685 saw the worst of the unequal contest. The accession of James VII, himself a Catholic, led to another swing of the pendulum. Extreme Presbyterianism would not be tolerated in Scotland, but a Catholic monarch was not acceptable in either country. The Glorious Revolution of 1688 deposed James and made way for the Protestant William of Orange and his wife, Mary.

Disruption

The Reformed Church of Scotland, now once more in the ascendant, was an austere body, with the authority to enforce its discipline at the 'repentance stool' in church if need be. One major point of dissent remained – the issue of lay patronage, or whether or not congregations had the right to choose their own ministers. Conflict over this matter led to the withdrawal of more than 470 ministers from the established church in

1843, an event known as the Disruption. During the nineteenth century, other branches of the Kirk split and rejoined. The Church of Scotland remains strong throughout the country; more extreme Presbyterian churches are found in some parts, notably Skye and Lewis.

HOLIDAY CHOICES

● **Self-catering** Self-catering properties range from traditional croft cottages to chalet complexes and caravans and are found everywhere. Having a place of your own to return to for drying your clothes and spreading yourself in can make a lot of sense but remember that the local shops in remote areas will probably only stock essentials. The Scottish Tourist Board publishes a book, *Scotland Self-Catering*, and regional tourist boards have their own lists too. Other sources worth trying are: Blakes Cottages (01282) 445096; Character Cottages (01282) 445300; Country Cottages in Scotland (01328) 851155; Country Holidays (01282) 445095; Hampster Cottages (01899) 308775; Hoseasons Holidays (01502 500500); Mackay's Agency (0131-225 3539); National Trust for Scotland (0131-226 5922); Summer Cottages (01305 267545).

● **Caravanning** There are caravan sites in abundance in Scotland, many of them well positioned on the coast. Do not expect every site to have masses of facilities; some may simply be a field which is put to other uses out of season. The Scottish Tourist Board publishes *Scotland Camping and Caravanning*, or, if a member, you can contact the Camping and Caravanning Club (01203 694995), the AA (01256 20123), the RAC (0345) 331133 or the Forestry Commission (0131-334 2576).

● **Bed and Breakfast** Large numbers of Scots offer bed and breakfast, and moving round the country staying in one home after another is an extremely popular way of touring. The Scottish Tourist Board operates an advance booking service and publishes *Scotland Bed & Breakfast*; all regional tourist boards have lists of those bed and breakfast establishments who are members. But a number of households are not members, and they may be just as good.

● **Island-hopping** Only masochists will try to reach as many Scottish islands as possible in the course of a holiday. But choosing to move in a leisurely fashion between one island and another is a different matter. You will have to plan and book in advance if you intend taking a car on ferries during high season; you will have more flexibility if you can do without. Island-hopping by aeroplane, using hired cars on the ground, is a good alternative if you can afford it. Caledonian MacBrayne (CalMac), the main ferry operator, offers unlimited travel island rover tickets (with or without a car) which are valid for eight or fifteen days. Ring (01475) 650100 for details.

● **Hotel-based touring** The days when you had to exist on white bread and tinned vegetables in remote areas are long gone. Several hotels miles from anywhere, ranging from the luxurious to the relatively simple, are purpose-made for a comfortable holiday in the wilderness. In the cities there is less of a range: your best chance here is to look for off-season or weekend rates at one of the more modern business hotels or to spend time in seeking out a guesthouse that pleases you. Small-town hotels away from the most popular tourist areas are apt to be unmemorable, though not necessarily bad value. The tourist boards operate an advance booking system for all hotels and guesthouses which they grade (for telephone numbers see the useful directory in each chapter). Fishing hotels are a Scottish speciality. Usually with water of their own, and with ample understanding of anglers' needs, they make an ideal base from which to foray out in pursuit of trout or salmon. Seek out a copy of *Scotland for Game, Sea and Coarse Fishing* (Pastime Publications/STB, 0131–556 1105).

● **Packages** There are package holidays to suit most tastes and most activities. The Scottish Tourist Board (see page 23) has details. Write or telephone, explaining what kind of holiday you are looking for.

BIRDWATCHING

The many different habitats make Scotland a superb place for bird-watching. Areas most favoured by birds include the Highlands and the myriad islands. You can also spot birds in the central lowlands and southern uplands, by the large firths and other coastal waters. The specialist birdwatcher visits Scotland in spring and autumn for migrants and in winter for coastal waterfowl and abundant geese; May, June or July are good for watching seabirds thronging the cliffs and for moorland and mountain birds – but do not disturb breeding birds.

Birds of prey are particularly abundant in the Highlands, from the frequently encountered buzzard to the merlin, a small dashing moorland falcon. Cruising along mountain ridges may be the king of the Scottish skies, the golden eagle. Lochs in the vicinity of pine forests may attract an osprey. Scotland's most celebrated conservation success, ospreys are now widespread, though Loch Garten remains the main sighting spot. The area around Loch Garten is excellent for other birds too. The ancient Caledonian forest, with its native Scots pine, hosts some spectacular birds including the capercaillie, a turkey-sized forest grouse.

In more open woodland, you may spot the smaller black grouse, while the trees support crested tits and the Scottish crossbill, its strangely shaped beak a perfect tweezer for extracting seeds from pine cones. Various rare birds live on mountain tops, including the ptarmigan, a grouse which dons white plumage in winter. On bleak moorlands you can hear the melancholic call of the golden plover. A walk through the heather may provoke an explosion and a whirring of wings as a covey of red grouse breaks cover. Upland lochs and lochans are home for a number of birds, including elegant divers, with their eerie, wailing calls in the half-light of summer nights.

It is well worth taking binoculars on a visit to the islands as their cliffs host some of the most impressive seabird colonies in Britain, especially the rows of enchanting, comical puffins along the clifftops in June and July. Many of the islands have their own special birds such as corncrakes in the Hebrides, white-tailed eagles recently re-introduced to Rum, Fetlar's red-necked phalaropes and, on a number of islands, skuas prepared to attack unsuspecting visitors in defence of their moorland nests.

You can spot birds anywhere, but, especially for trainee birdwatchers, the protected areas offer the best opportunities. The Royal Society for the Protection of Birds (17 Regent Terrace, Edinburgh EH7 5BN; 0131–557

3136) has 52 reserves in Scotland. You can write (enclose an s.a.e.) for the comprehensive booklet on reserves. Facilities vary; RSPB members get in free where a charge is made. Other organisations with responsibility for natural areas include Scottish Natural Heritage; 0131-447 4784), the National Trust for Scotland and the Scottish Wildlife Trust (for addresses, see 'The support system' page 23). Fair Isle has a bird observatory, open May to Oct, (01595) 760258 which provides hotel-standard accommodation and the opportunity to learn more about breeding and migrant birds. There is also an observatory offering a choice of guesthouse and dormitory accommodation in a new wind and solar powered building, on North Ronaldsey in Orkney (01857) 633267.

● **Useful books** For identifying birds: *The Shell Guide to the Birds of Britain and Ireland* by James Ferguson-Lees, Ian Willis and J. T. R. Sharrock (Michael Joseph). For the best places to visit: *Where to Watch Birds in Scotland* by Mike Madders and Julia Westwood (Christopher Helm). For background information: *Birds in Scotland* by Valerie M. Thom (Poyser).

GOLF

Scotland has the oldest golf courses and golf clubs in the world. Although the first rules were not formalised until 1744, there are records of bets on a game of golf in 1504. The home of the Royal and Ancient Golf Club which administers the game is in St Andrews overlooking the first tee and eighteenth green. For the holiday golfer there are over 400 courses to choose from; the most famous five play host to the British Open. Not surprisingly it is hardest to get a game on these courses. If you are less concerned with emulating golf's great players, there are an exceptional number of other superb courses where the casual visitor has a better chance of getting a game. Fees for the open championship courses start at around £30 a round, although £20 or so will get you a round on some of the others which are equally picturesque and challenging. For the real holiday hacker there are municipal courses where you pay £5 for a round. If you are setting out to play the championship links, arm yourself with a valid handicap certificate (preferably showing a reasonable level of competence) and settle down with the phone early in the year to book your start times. If you are planning a golfing holiday you should avoid the peak months of July and August.

The Open Courses

● **St Andrews Old Course** You need to book months in advance to be assured of a tee-time, or you can put your name down for the daily ballot. Two-thirds of all start times are allocated by ballot. To be included, contact the starter before 2 on the day before you wish to play. Handicap certificate or letter of introduction required; handicap limits are 28 for men, 36 for ladies. (01334) 475757, closed Sunday.

● **Carnoustie** Like St Andrews, Carnoustie is a public course. Demand for tee-times is not as heavy as at St Andrews but you are still advised to book at least a month in advance. Handicap certificate preferred. Visitors not allowed before 1.30pm Saturday and 11.30am Sunday; handicap limits are 28 for men, 36 for ladies. (01241) 853789.

● **Muirfield** Home to the Honourable Company of Edinburgh Golfers, this course has some of the highest green fees in the country. Handicap certificate required; handicap limits are 18 for men, 24 for ladies; ladies can play only if accompanied by a man and are banned from the clubhouse. (01620) 842123.

● **Royal Troon** This course has limited start times for visitors – the main days are Monday, Tuesday and Thursday. Fees are quoted per day and include two rounds and lunch. No ladies are allowed on the Championship course; a handicap certificate is required; handicap limits are 22 for men, 26 for ladies (on the Portland course). (01292) 311555.

● **Royal Turnberry Hotel** This course is Japanese-owned and visitors take second place to hotel guests in the allocation of start times – only residents play in summer (01655) 331000

The Best of The Rest

● **Royal Aberdeen** Handicap certificate required; handicap limits for play on the championship course are 18 for both men and ladies. Book in advance. No visitors before 3.30 on Saturday and Sunday. (01224) 702571

● **St Andrews Dukes Course** Newly opened in 1995 and managed by the Old Course Hotel. No handicap certificate needed. Book at the pro shop in the hotel or call (01334) 474371.

● **Blairgowrie** Handicap certificates are required. Advance bookings required on Monday, Tuesday, Thursday and Friday, but not at weekends or Wednesdays (01250) 872622

● **Cruden Bay** Handicap certificates required; no visitors after 11am on Tuesday or before 3.30pm on competition days. (01779) 812285

● **Royal Dornoch** Handicap certificate required; handicap limits are 24 for men, 35 for ladies. Advance booking advisable. (01862) 810219

● **Nairn** Advance booking advisable. (01667) 53208

● **Prestwick** No visitors at weekends. Handicap certificate required; handicap limits are 24 for men, 28 for ladies. Advance booking necessary. (01292) 477404

HILL-WALKING IN SCOTLAND

Scotland's mountains are not to be treated lightly. They are not especially lofty – there are few over four thousand feet – but they are both northerly and close to the sea, which means that the weather can turn foul very rapidly and kill the under-equipped or inexperienced walker who has got into difficulty in a matter of hours. A mountain which looks easy to tackle in bright sun can become a death-trap if the clouds come down suddenly and you are left without a map, compass, or other essential equipment.

As a minimum, wear proper boots, pack extra layers of clothing, take a map and compass and know how to use them, and make sure someone else knows where you are going and your estimated time of return. It is sensible to add some high-energy food, a first-aid kit, a lightweight survival blanket, a torch (with spare batteries) and a whistle to your equipment.

There are hills and mountains in Scotland to suit every taste and every degree of experience. With the exception of the Black Cuillin on Skye, which demand rock-climbing ability, most are within the reach of the experienced rock-scrambler or hill-walker. If you do not enjoy heights or rocks, excellent walking is still to be found on the Cheviots, the Pentland or Ochil Hills, or on the gentler slopes of the Perthshire or Angus mountains.

You may come across the 'Munro-bagger', the walker who is aiming to climb every one of the tops over 3,000 feet listed in the tables compiled by Sir Hugh Munro. There are 279 of them, and working through them can become something of an obsession for many. You may well find fewer people and gain just as much satisfaction if you make for the mountains which do not reach the magic three thousand foot level. There are two long-distance walks, the West Highland Way, which takes an easily managed 95-mile route along valleys from Milngavie to Fort William, and the much tougher Southern Uplands Way, which runs from coast to coast, 212 miles over exposed lonely hills from Portpatrick to Cockburnspath. A 42-mile section of the Speyside Way, from Tomintoul to Spey Bay, is also open. The *Good Walks Guide* (Consumers' Association 1995, £25) includes 18 walks in Scotland – detachable and fully mapped.

● **Access to the countryside** Most landowners are tolerant of walkers on their land, particularly in moorland and mountain areas, although there is a law of trespass in Scotland. If a path is defined on the ground you can usually assume that you may follow it. In fields, keep to the edges. Many walks take advantage of rights of way, defined in Scotland as routes between public places that have been in use for more than 20 years. Rights of way are not officially registered as they are in England and Wales, although the planning departments of local authorities may keep records and maps. Rights of way are not distinguished from other paths on Ordnance Survey maps, although they are often signposted. For more information, contact the Scottish Rights of Way Society (0131-652 2937). During the stalking and shooting seasons in the Highlands (usually August to October) access to private land may be restricted – check your intended route with the local tourist office.

WHEN TO GO

The Scottish tourist season is short. Outside Edinburgh and Glasgow, many sights do not open before May, and some close at the end of September. Yet Scotland is arguably at its most attractive in October, when autumn colour is beginning to suffuse the hill-sides and the woods and when the first frosts sharpen the air. June is also an attractive month. The midges have not got into their stride and the wild flowers of the Hebridean machair beaches are stunning. There is generally less to be said for July. August is redeemed by the coming into flower of the heather, which transforms the Scottish moorland into a wide brush-stroke of purple. November can be a good month to take a short break to Edinburgh or Glasgow: hotels may have off-season rates, those sights that remain open will be peaceful, and there will be warm spots to shelter in if the weather turns nasty. In winter, when there is a spell of clear weather with snow on the ground, Scotland can be fabulously beautiful. Otherwise, it is best avoided between December and early April.

Every region of Scotland has its own local festivals, games or sporting events. Tourist offices compile local lists and the Scottish Tourist Board publishes the yearly free *Events in Scotland* booklet.

TRAVELLING TO SCOTLAND

● **By air** From south of the border you can fly direct to Aberdeen, Edinburgh, Glasgow and Inverness from London (Heathrow, Gatwick or Stansted) and several regional airports. Airlines flying these routes include British Airways, British Midland, Air UK, Gill Aviation and Business Air. Loganair, one of the main operators in Scotland, has been taken over by British Airways; its services within Scotland, including inter-island, now operate under the name of British Airways.

● **By train** There are InterCity services to Scotland from 93 stations in England. Sleeper services operate between London Euston and Edinburgh, Aberdeen, Inverness, Fort William and Glasgow. APEX fares are available on many routes – these must be booked at least seven days in advance and offer considerable savings. Scotrail also has a range of rail passes. For information, call 0131-556 2451 or 0171-387 7070 (British Rail).

● **By coach** National Express (0990) 808080 is the main coach operator running day and night services between the main English and Scottish towns. Fares are cheaper if you book a week in advance on some services. Scottish Citylink (0990) 808080 operates services in Scotland.

SHOPPING

● **Tartan** The whole elaborate mythology surrounding tartan dates from only 1822, the time of George IV's visit to Edinburgh, when Highland dress suddenly became fashionable. Tartans were probably originally associated with districts rather than individual clans, so the whole process of finding the tartan that goes with your name (and most shops have lists) need not be taken more seriously than you want. Tartan travelling rugs, scarfs or headsquares are all good buys.

● **Tweed and knitwear** Shops all over Scotland specialise in these, but you are likely to find the best bargains if you look for mill shops or individual weavers and knitters. The textile towns of the Borders, especially Hawick, Selkirk and Galashiels, are fertile hunting grounds and there are mill shops too on the southern fringe of the Ochil Hills. The bargains you find on Harris, source of the renowned Harris tweed, may not actually cover the cost of getting there, but you can have the satisfaction of watching the cloth being woven by hand. Garments made from high-quality Shetland wool are sold all over the country, but the best bargains are to be found on Shetland itself. The Fair Isle jumper, with its distinctive patterns, is often imitated. The genuine article, knitted on Fair Isle, is rare. You can order one, or visit the island and see if you can persuade a local producer to put you top of the list.

● **Smoked produce and other foods** Smoked salmon, trout and venison can be found in shops or in the many smokeries which dot the Highlands. Many will post your order. If you can get them home fast, or can cook them on the spot, Scottish kippers, especially the lightly smoked Loch Fyne ones, are delicious. Look out too for Arbroath 'smokies'.

Oatcakes – dry, sustaining oatmeal biscuits – are easily found and easily transported. So is Scottish shortbread, sweet and crumbly. Cheese-making in Scotland is undergoing a revival and there are a number of varieties, including Lanark Blue and Bonchester, worth looking out for. Buy a black bun for New Year – highly spiced dried fruit and peel are packed into a thin pastry casing which will keep almost indefinitely until opened. Dundee cakes, light fruit cakes with a handsome topping of golden almonds, are extremely filling, good for a long day on the hill.

● **Silver and semi-precious stones** There is a big market in small silver items. Scottish silver-work has a long tradition behind it, and you can buy contemporary silversmiths' work in craft shops up and down the country. If you are feeling rich, a silver 'quaich' (a traditional flat drinking cup more usually made in wood or horn) makes a good present for someone. The best-known Scottish gemstone is the whisky-coloured 'Cairngorm'.

FOOD AND DRINK

Scotland produces some of the best fish, seafood, meat and game in Europe, has a long tradition of baking and confectionery, and grows some of the best soft fruit in the world. Aberdeen Angus beef and Border hill lamb are both renowned. So of course is Scottish salmon (though eat wild fish rather than farmed if you have the choice). If you are in Scotland during the raspberry season, make sure you find a plateful somewhere. The reputation of both porridge and haggis has suffered at the hands of comedians. Porridge should be made from oatmeal which has been steeped overnight. Purists insist it should be eaten with a horn spoon, standing up, and never adulterated with sugar (salt is all right). Haggis is made from minced sheep's 'pluck' (usually heart, liver and lungs), mixed with oatmeal, suet and spices and stuffed in the sheep's stomach. It is very much more tasty than this description may suggest. Haggis is traditionally eaten with mashed potatoes and puréed turnip (called bashed neeps, and known further south as swede).

If you want to buy whisky, you can choose between a blended whisky, a de luxe whisky (a blend of particularly old or fine whiskies), a single malt whisky (see box on page 366) or a whisky-based liqueur, such as Drambuie or Glayva. There is considerable variation in flavour and 'smoothness' between the various brands of both blended and single malt whisky. Island malts (from Islay and Jura) are fiery and smoky; Speyside malts are lighter and smoother. If you have not developed your own preferences in malt whiskies, a bottle of Glenfiddich or Glenmorangie will appeal to most tastes.

THE SUPPORT SYSTEM

On your travels you will run across various organisations which manage sights, can provide you with information, or specialise in some activity.

● **The Scottish Tourist Board (STB)**, 23 Ravelston Terrace, Edinburgh EH4 3EU (0131-332 2433). The STB has a network of fourteen Area Tourist Boards (as of April 1996). At local level, there is a network of Tourist Information Centres (TIC), over a third of which are open all year, the rest only open seasonally (see opening times in our useful directory sections in each chapter). The STB has publications of general or specialist interest to visitors. The regional boards can provide lists of accommodation and usually a gazetteer of things to see or do, as well as their own publications. In local offices you will also often find town trail leaflets, or descriptions of walks in the area as well as a range of other publications. The size and efficiency of the local TICs varies, as does the quality of the leaflets they provide, but in general they are excellent.

Although many hotel owners, tourist attractions or owners of local businesses are members of the tourist board, some, for one reason or another, choose not to be, so the accommodation lists, for example, may not be comprehensive. Excellent hotels and guesthouses exist which have chosen to go it alone.

The STB pioneered the 'dual rating' system, by which hotels, guesthouses, bed and breakfasts and self-catering accommodation are classified according to the facilities they have and separately graded for their quality. Only establishments that are graded and classified are listed in STB publications – some choose not to join and therefore will not be listed (which is a weakness of the system).

Facilities are shown by crowns, and there are six steps, ranging from 'Listed' for simple accommodation to five crowns for a place with all the trimmings. The quality of the accommodation (which has nothing to do with the facilities) is shown in four steps by the words 'Approved', 'Commended' and 'Highly Commended' and 'Deluxe'.

The scheme can cause confusion if you forget how it works and take the number of crowns to be an indication of quality. In general, we have found the quality gradings useful, but rather limited. Establishments carrying the 'Highly Commended' award usually deserve it. 'Commended' covers a wide range, rather too wide a range for one award. The 'Approved' award is defined by the STB as 'acceptable'. In our experience, this can mean anything from perfectly adequate to fairly dingy. It is hoped that the fourth step recently introduced by the STB in its grading system ('Deluxe') will allow for finer discriminations.

Apart from the publications mentioned in the relevant sections above, useful free publications produced by the STB include *Scotland Short Breaks*, *Practical Information for the Traveller to Scotland*, and *Scotland Home of Golf*.

● **Historic Scotland (HS)**, Longmore House, Salisbury Place, Edinburgh EH9 1SH (0131-668 8600). This is a government agency responsible for the care of Scotland's historic buildings and monuments. Most of Scotland's prehistoric sites, ruined castles, abbeys and cathedrals are looked after by Historic Scotland. Its custodians are often experts on the building in their care, and while they manage not to be obtrusive, they are well worth chatting to, especially if you want to know something obscure that is not in the guidebook. They keep the lawns round their monuments in first-class condition, too. If you are going to visit a number of ancient buildings, the 7- or 14-day 'explorer' pass, allowing you free entry to all their sights, will probably save you money. For details, ring 0131-668 8800. Historic Scotland also produces an excellent range of books on aspects of the country's past (ring 0131-668 8752 for details).

● **The National Trust for Scotland (NTS)**, 5 Charlotte Square, Edinburgh EH2 4DU (0131-226 5922). Like its sister organisation in England, the NTS is a charity, independent of government support, charged with the preservation of the properties in its care. It looks after over one hundred of these, including castles, historic sites, gardens and tracts of Scottish land. Of its many responsibilities, the NTS is particularly good at maintaining and running its gardens. Its duty to preserve the buildings in its care sometimes leads to short opening hours, especially out of season. NTS houses gleam with polished furniture, and guides are enthusiasts, if not experts. But despite attempts to give them a lived-in feeling, houses are inclined to lack the personal touches or downright eccentricity you may find in visiting those which are still privately owned. NTS membership allows you free entry to its properties in Scotland, and to those of its sister organisations in England and Ireland. NTS also organises conservation holidays, working in such places as Fair Isle.

● **The Forestry Commission**, 231 Corstorphine Road, Edinburgh EH12 7AT (0131-334 0303). The Forestry Commission manages over 500,000 hectares of woodland in Scotland. Visitors are allowed to walk on forest roads, and there are trails for cyclists and horses too. The Forestry Commission picnic site, with its wooden benches, is a common occurrence throughout the country. Individual Forest Districts publish leaflets with details of walks and facilities.

● **Scottish Youth Hostels Association**, 7 Glebe Crescent, Stirling FK8 2JA (01786) 451181. The SYHA runs 83 hostels ranging from cottages to Highland castles, and organises various activity holidays, including skiing, sailing, walking and pony-trekking (ask for the *Breakaway Holidays* leaflet).

● **Scottish Wildlife Trust**, Cramond House, Kirk Cramond, Cramond Glebe Road, Edinburgh EH4 6NS (0131-312 7765). Nearly half of the SWT's 100-plus wildlife reserves are open to the public and the Trust will advise best times to visit, special events and any restrictions. There are visitor centres at Loch of the Lowes, Dunkeld (osprey), Falls of Clyde, New Lanark (badgers, woodland), Montrose Basin and Montrose (migratory birds). Publications include *Scottish Wildlife* magazine.

HINTS AND TIPS

● The local government reforms which came into effect in 1996 replaced the previous system of regions and districts with 29 new 'single-tier' authorities and 3 Islands Councils. The giant region of Strathclyde, which included Glasgow, Ayrshire and Argyll, has disappeared, to no one's regret, as have the uninspired Tayside and Central regions. The upheaval in local government boundaries over the past half century has, however, left many people wondering what to call the part of Scotland they live in. You may run across names of vanished counties (Inverness-shire), old regions (Grampian), the new councils (East Dumbartonshire) or even older district names such as Lochaber or Mearns. The area tourist boards have different boundaries and different names too.

● In the Highlands and islands, many of the smaller roads are single-track with passing places. Driving on them demands a slow speed and awareness of cars coming the other way. There is no rule of precedence at passing places, though the satisfaction of getting polite waves from other drivers is motivation for being the first to give way. It is very useful to have a tow rope in your car, in case you come across a driver who has been gazing at the scenery and has put a wheel in the ditch, blocking the road to all traffic.

● Scottish beer comes in many varieties, but is generally stronger, darker and sweeter than its English equivalent. Draught beer is traditionally either 'heavy' or 'export'. Asking for 'bitter' may cause puzzlement.

● The one-pound bank note is still widely used. There is seldom any problem in getting them accepted south of the Border.

● Scotland does not share the same public holidays as England and Wales, and on Scottish public holidays usually only the banks and perhaps some chain stores close. Instead, towns will have their own local or 'trades' holidays. It may be worth finding out when these are, especially in cities.

● In the far north, London newspapers may not arrive until late in the day. The three main daily Scottish papers are *The Scotsman*, *The Herald* and *The Aberdeen Press and Journal*. All are worth reading. Local papers flourish and are a valuable source of information on local events and attractions.

● October is a favourite holiday time for Historic Scotland's custodians, so check that the smaller sights will be open before you visit them.

BACKGROUND READING

GENERAL HISTORY
Arnold Kemp *The Hollow Drum* (Mainstream, 1993)
Michael Lynch *Scotland – A New History* (Pimlico, 1992)
J. D. Mackie *A History of Scotland* (Penguin, 1991)
John Prebble *The Lion in the North* (Penguin, 1973)
T. C. Smout *A History of the Scottish People 1560–1830* (Fontana, 1985)

SPECIFIC HISTORIES OR HISTORICAL NOVELS
John Buchan *Montrose: A History* (Greenwood Press, 1992)
Antonia Fraser *Mary Queen of Scots* (Mandarin, 1989)
George Macdonald Fraser *The Steel Bonnets*, a companion to border warfare by the author of the *Flashman* books (Collins, 1989)
Eric Linklater *The Prince in the Heather*, Prince Charles' wanderings after Culloden (Hodder & Stoughton, out of print)
John Prebble *The Highland Clearances, Culloden, The Darien Disaster* and *Glencoe* (all Penguin, 1969/70/78/69)
Sir Walter Scott's *Waverley*, about the 1745 rising (Penguin, 1995), and *Old Mortality*, on the Covenanters (Penguin, 1975), are worth trying.
The Wallace (out of print) and *The Bruce Trilogy* (Hodder & Stoughton, 1985) by Nigel Tranter add colour to Scotland's medieval history.

MEMOIRS
Lord Cockburn *Memorials of his Time* (post-Enlightenment Edinburgh) (Mercat Press, 1971)
Elizabeth Grant *Memoirs of a Highland Lady* (Canongate, 1992)

Johnson and Boswell *Journey to the Western Isles of Scotland* and *Journal of a Tour to the Hebrides* (Canongate, 1996; Houghton Mifflin, 1989; Penguin, 1984)

NOVELISTS OR POETS FOR PARTICULAR AREAS

Poems by Robert Burns (South-West)
Robert Garioch (Edinburgh)
Lewis Grassic Gibbon (Aberdeenshire)
Alasdair Gray, William MacIlvanney and Neil Munro (Glasgow)
Neil Gunn (Caithness and the far north)
George Mackay Brown (Orkney)
Sir Walter Scott *Heart of Midlothian* (Edinburgh) and *Rob Roy* (the Trossachs) (Everyman Classics)
Robert Louis Stevenson's *Kidnapped* (World International Publishing), Compton Mackenzie's *Whisky Galore* (Penguin) and Derek Cooper's *Hebridean Connection* (Fontana) (West Highlands and Islands)
David Thomson *Nairn in Darkness and Light* (Arrow Books)

Maps

The Michelin map of Scotland (1:400,000) covers the whole country; the Ordnance Survey Routemaster series (1:250,000) would be good for those on touring holidays; walkers will need the Landranger maps (1:50,000).

INTRODUCTION TO THIS EDITION

IN the four years since *The Which? Guide to Scotland* was first published, there has been steady, if slow, progress in making Scotland even more attractive to visitors. The changes range from small things such as better signposting, and ever-increasing numbers of audio-visual or interactive gadgets at sights, to more substantial ones, such as continuing improvements in standards of accommodation and food. You will find this reflected in our Where to Stay and Where to Eat sections, which contain many more recommendations than previously. There has also been a change of emphasis in the way Scotland is marketed, with more stress correctly placed on the isolation and beauty of its landscapes and less on haggis and tartan. More needs to be done now to offer the kind of all-inclusive 'green' holidays which will actually help visitors to get out into the countryside. Scotland's tourist season remains short: dreams of making it a year-round destination outside its big cities still run up against the hazards of short opening seasons, and public transport which is not always fast or convenient. Nevertheless, Scotland remains, as we have stressed all along, one of the best countries in which to unwind in the middle of a landscape that can be matched nowhere else in these islands.

KEY MAP OF SCOTLAND

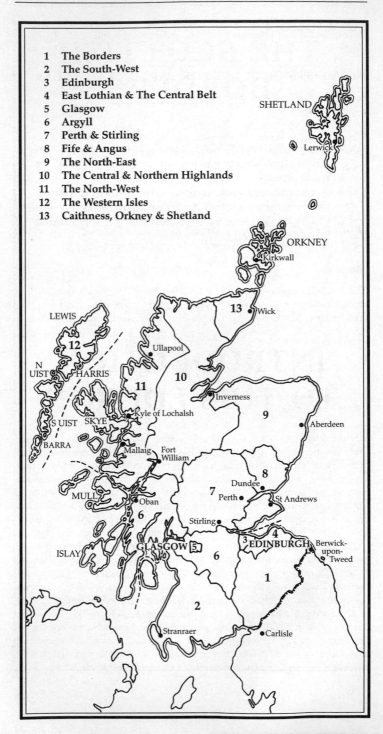

1   The Borders
2   The South-West
3   Edinburgh
4   East Lothian & The Central Belt
5   Glasgow
6   Argyll
7   Perth & Stirling
8   Fife & Angus
9   The North-East
10 The Central & Northern Highlands
11 The North-West
12 The Western Isles
13 Caithness, Orkney & Shetland

SHETLAND

Lerwick

ORKNEY

Kirkwall

LEWIS

12

N UIST   HARRIS

13   Wick

Ullapool

11   **10**

S UIST   SKYE

Inverness

Kyle of Lochalsh

9   Aberdeen

BARRA

Mallaig
Fort William

MULL

8

Oban   **7**   Dundee

6   Perth   St Andrews

Stirling

ISLAY   SKYE

GLASGOW **5**   EDINBURGH **3**   Berwick-upon-Tweed

6

1

2

Stranraer

Carlisle

THE SCOTTISH BORDERS

- An exceptionally varied landscape, ranging from windswept sheep pasture to fertile woodland or rocky coast
- A fascinating, violent past, which has left castles, abbeys and a rich folk tradition in its wake
- Compact, ancient burghs, all different, surrounded by unfrequented countryside

Jedburgh Abbey

For the better part of three centuries, between the first invasion by Edward I of England in 1296 and the union of the crowns of England and Scotland in 1603, the Borders were the battleground for two warring nations. Those three hundred years of constant invasion, counter-invasion, siege, burning and plunder have shaped the land and its people more significantly than anything that has happened since. They left the countryside scattered with ancient fortresses, with the ruins of once-great abbeys, and with small towns which may have seemed in the twelfth century to have a prosperous future ahead of them, but which were to be burned and burned again, while trade and influence moved elsewhere. They also left an obsession with riding, a fierce local pride and a vivid folk-culture – the ballads.

For the inhabitant of those times, on both sides of the frontier between England and Scotland, nothing was worth possessing which was not portable. Horses, weapons and cattle were the currency of the Borders, and 'gear' was accumulated by raiding, not by trade. This was the age of the reiver – the horseman with his lance and his steel bonnet riding secret hill routes by night, descending in a flurry of violence on village or farmstead, driving his slow, mooing plunder homewards.

The predation was by no means a simple question of Scots against English. Constant feuding between families, cross-Border connivance, protection rackets and bribery by the agents of one or other government meant that the Borderer was accustomed to putting his own interest before that of his neighbour, and was as ready to steal the cattle next door as to rustle those across the frontier. The frontier provided an easy refuge for those on the run and, for both the Scottish and English authorities, attempts to impose order were a nightmare. Over the years a whole canon of frontier law involving a degree of cross-Border co-operation came into being. It was enforced by the six Wardens of the Marches, three on each side of the frontier, with varying degrees of success. Yet it never succeeded in stopping the raiding; it took the Union of the Crowns in 1603 to do that. Sixty hours' hard riding brought Robert Carey from London to Edinburgh with Queen Elizabeth's coronation ring to hand to her successor, James VI, King of Scotland, and the frontier disappeared for ever.

Today, crossing from England into Scotland, it is hard to believe that the frontier ever existed. Only on the high pass of Carter Bar across the Cheviots, with its sudden panorama of the Tweed Valley beneath, is there any sense of climax. Indeed, the history and culture on either side of that old frontier are so intimately bound together that the Borderers of Scotland and England can be said to have more in common with each other than with the rest of their respective nations: to confine your exploration to one side is to see only half the picture. We cannot cover the whole English Border country in this guide, but we have included Berwick-upon-Tweed. The town was part of Scotland for four centuries; it is the logical place to base yourself if you want to explore the east coast, and its football team still plays in the Scottish league. So, for the purposes of this book, we are bringing Berwick home.

Border country

It is surprising to anyone who knows the area that the Borders are the least visited region of Scotland; less than five per cent of Scotland's tourists stay here for any length of time. Most people pass through on their way to better-known areas further north. If you choose to go against the trend, you will find your enterprise well rewarded.

The region's pleasures are subtle, for the hills are lonely rather than dramatic, the towns quirky but unassuming, the coastline rugged but not wild, the people hospitable but reticent. Yet in all of Scotland there are few other regions with such a mixture of landscapes; bleak moorland lies only a few minutes' road journey from thick beech woods and lush pasture. The character of the countryside changes with a peculiar rapidity, often between one river valley and the next.

In the Borders, the past intrudes on the present with an equal suddenness as you come across a ruined tower half concealed by trees, spot a place name from a sixteenth-century ballad, or see the outline of Iron Age ramparts on the crest of a hill. It pays to become a little obsessive about the past here. Tracking down old castles will lead you from end to end of the region, but you can equally well pursue Roman remains, old churches, drove roads, Iron Age settlements, eighteenth-century bridges or the relics of the once-magnificent railway network, whose stark embankments and broken bridges bear witness to the most recent vandalism inflicted on the region.

There is a final consideration: in foul weather the Scottish Borders are much less depressing than the wilderness areas north of the Highland Line. There is more to be seen under

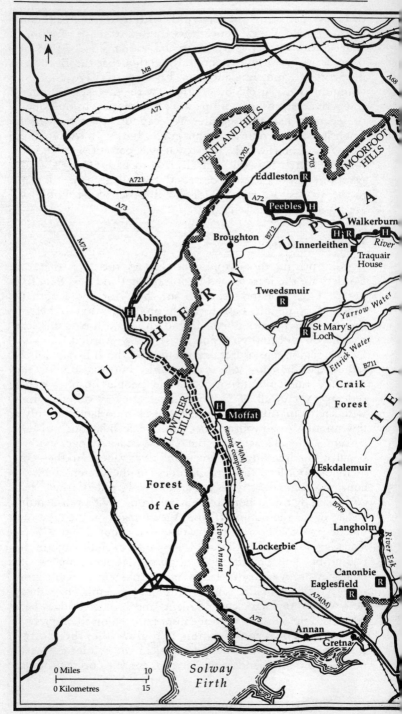

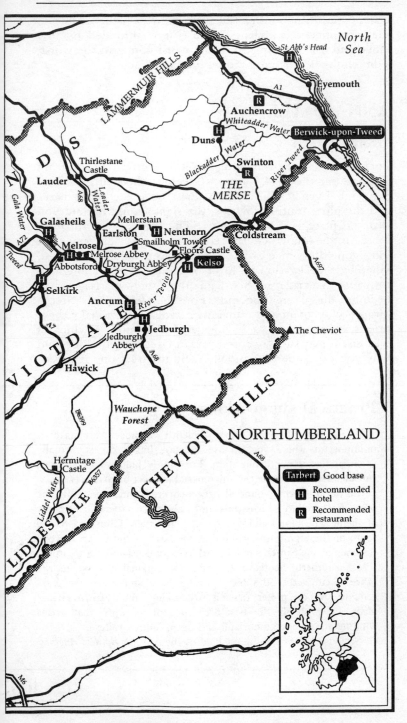

cover; you do not suffer the frustration of being unable to see magnificent landscape because it is shrouded by low cloud and driving rain and, if the worst comes to the worst, Edinburgh and Glasgow are within easy reach.

ANNANDALE

Gretna Green

For many visitors travelling up the western route from England on the A74, Gretna Green is their first taste of Scotland. Even if you did not guess from the coach parks and the piper touting for tips, the signs would remind you that the place is world-famous. The romance of runaway lovers is the draw: Gretna Green owes its celebrity to a long-gone difference of law between England and Scotland, whereby a declaration in front of witnesses was enough to formalise marriage in Scotland after such marriages had become illegal in England. For the self-styled Gretna 'priests' elopement was a lucrative trade. Traditionally these priests are supposed to have been blacksmiths – which is why anvils play such a central part in Gretna mythology, and why you can undergo a mock ceremony over one if you so

Practical suggestions

The Scottish Borders are sufficiently compact to make it unimportant where you choose to stay, but a car is virtually essential for proper exploration. For family holidays by the sea, consider **Eyemouth** or the tiny coastal outpost of **St Abbs**.

Border hills are rounded, grass-covered and lonely. In the south-west, round **Liddesdale** and **Eskdale**, conifers cover many of them. The best walking areas are either the **Cheviots** to the south or the high, bleak ground at the head of the River Yarrow. Sections of the **Southern Upland Way**, a coast-to-coast footpath across southern Scotland (a guide is obtainable from tourist offices), cut across the high ground here and make for good walking. If you prefer driving to walking, the **Lammermuir Hills** are probably the best area to explore, with small roads winding across open moorland and deep, hidden valleys.

Serious anglers should get hold of the *Scottish Borders Angling*

desire. In its modern incarnation Gretna Green is a sorry tourist trap. The Old Smithy, apart from its anvil and a collection of coaches, is otherwise a large gift shop glittering with brass, and its more genteel rival down the road, Gretna Hall Hotel (with another anvil and a bridal chamber), has plenty of selling space too. The most incongruous object in the whole place is a modern statue called, pretentiously, Smith God – a human figure struggling to escape from the spears, swords and bits of old iron into which he seems to have fallen. Gretna Green thrives on cash, though endearing graffiti with hearts and arrows show that some people are still somehow determined to get their money's worth.

The Debatable Land

Head east from Gretna on the back roads towards Canonbie and you enter one of the bloodiest parts of the Borders. The landscape is now innocent, rolling farmland, but for more than three hundred years it was a no man's land between the Scots and English, claimed by both but subject to the rule of neither, a haven for those who lived by thievery. In 1552 it was divided, with the French ambassador acting as referee. A dike was dug, cutting the land in half. Its line is still clearly marked by a plantation of trees. **Canonbie**, on the Scots side of the line, is the site

---

Guide, available from the Scottish Borders Tourist Board (for address, see page 66).

Bargain-hunting round the mill shops of the region's textile factories is a favourite occupation. **Hawick** is the place to go for woollens, **Selkirk** and **Galashiels** for tweeds or tartans. **Walkerburn**, in the Tweed Valley, is another possibility.

Borders life is at its most vivid at the rugby grounds and at the Common Riding festivals. Rugby (especially the 'sevens' variety) is a Borders obsession. April is the month to catch these tournaments, the Melrose Sevens probably being the best known. The Common Ridings mostly take place between May and July. Almost every sizeable town has its local celebration, some with a tradition extending back hundreds of years, others more recent creations or revivals. Those in the central Borders are firmly horse-centred and may combine a riding of the town's old boundaries with pageantry associated with heroic events of the past. They are serious and deeply felt occasions, not just put on for the tourist.

of an old priory, and now boasts a good place for lunch at the Riverside Inn, beside the Esk.

In the squelchy morass of Solway Moss near Gretna a few hundred English Border riders shattered the Scottish army of James V in 1542 as it ploughed southward into England. The defeat ushered in the destructive campaigns of the 'Rough Wooing', when Henry VIII of England tried to persuade the Scots to marry the infant Mary Queen of Scots to his son by indiscriminately burning and looting southern Scotland.

Good bases

● **Moffat** This small town was once a spa, and retains the atmosphere of an early Victorian hill resort. Poised between hill country and the lowlands leading down to the Solway Firth, it is in an ideal position for exploring the western edge of the Borders, for touring into Dumfries and Galloway, or for travelling up to the Clyde Valley and Glasgow. There is plenty of accommodation here, mostly bed-and-breakfast.

● **Peebles** An ancient royal burgh, fortuitously placed among some of the best of Tweed Valley scenery, Peebles is a thriving one-time county town and a bustling centre for day excursions from Edinburgh and Glasgow. There are notable things to see in the town itself, some interesting shops and a large range of hotels and guesthouses. The best sights in the Tweed Valley are only a few minutes away by car, and good walks abound.

● **Kelso** The most appealing of all the Border towns, thanks to its graceful square, the ruined abbey and the River Tweed which flows round it, Kelso is well placed for exploring the central Borders, especially the abbeys and stately homes. The Cheviot Hills, with their intricate valleys and fine walks, are about 20 minutes' drive away. Accommodation in Kelso is sparser than in Peebles or Moffat, for the town is less obviously on the holiday trail, but there is a reasonable range.

● **Berwick-upon-Tweed** The town has been English since 1482, but Scotland laps up to its doorstep. Once an important port, now a quiet river-mouth town, old Berwick is enclosed by sixteenth-century ramparts and has streets lined by elegant eighteenth-century buildings. You will find old coaching-inns within the walls and plenty of guesthouses outside. Berwick is a logical base for exploring the east coast up as far as Edinburgh, or down into Northumbria.

The Romans were here too, leaving, at **Burnswark**, a kind of assault course for attacking hilltop forts. The climb up the hill above the earthworks of the old camp is short, but gives you good views of the Solway estuary to the south and the hills above Moffat to the north.

Thomas Carlyle, one of the graver of Scotland's Victorian sages, was born in the skittish-sounding **Ecclefechan**. 'One life – a little gleam of time between two Eternities,' he wrote. The village, a quiet place of trees and harled cottages, seems unsuited to such a weighty sentiment. The **Arched House** (NTS, open end Apr to end Sept, Fri to Mon 1.30 to 5.30), where he was born, was built by his father. Inside it is more like a shrine than a museum – and the custodian is primed to make a convert of you if you show signs of interest.

Lockerbie is now irrevocably linked to the tragedy of December 1988, when a fully laden aircraft, blown apart by a terrorist bomb, descended on the town. At the far end of

THE BORDER BALLADS

We can only guess at the reasons why the bloodstained Borderland produced the stirring poetry it did. Sir Walter Scott, who first started collecting the old ballads which had been handed down for generations, put it down to a link between a wild society and the wild violence of poetry. Whatever the case, reading the ballads while touring the Borders gives immediacy to the history. Among them you will find the tale of Thomas Rhymer's journey into fairyland, the rescue of Tam Lin from enchantment, the battle of Otterburn where Douglas and Percy met in a fierce night–time encounter, the slaying of Lord Douglas and his seven sons, and the lament of the Border Widow. Four of the best ballads come from Liddesdale, among them the tale of Kinmont Willie's rescue from Carlisle Castle, and the raid suffered by Jamie Telfer in the Fair Dodhead and how it was avenged.

A compact edition of the ballads is *Border Ballads* (edited by James Reid) published by Gollancz.

the town's graveyard (out on the Dumfries road) lies a garden of remembrance, and a simple memorial to those who died, the majority being from the United States. It is a corner of a sad America in a sad Scotland.

Moffat

Where the Southern Uplands close in on Annandale lies Moffat, reached in a couple of minutes from the M74 yet happily out of earshot of it. It seems a town of unlikely size and dignity until you realise it was once a spa and even had the distinction of its own branch railway line from Beattock. Its huge hydro hotel burned down early in the century, but it is still possible to visit the two mineral springs where Moffat's health-seeking visitors used to gather before breakfast. The stench of rotten eggs and the skeins of white gunge in the water are hardly tempting. Today, Moffat is bed-and-breakfast land – its sedate Victorian villas are thick with signs. It has everything you need for a couple of days – good walks close by, a broad, sedate High Street with shops selling woollens, antiques and sweeties (especially the renowned Moffat toffee), a little local museum, and the best of the sun if there is any. It also claims the narrowest detached hotel in Britain. Where most towns have statues of local worthies, Moffat's High Street boasts a huge sculptured ram. This is prosaically supposed to symbolise the links between the town and the woollen trade, but it is more fun to think it might be a fertility symbol.

Round Moffat

Moffat is backed by the high, bleak hills which separate the valleys of Annan, Clyde and Tweed (the sources of all three rivers are within walking distance of one another). From the town you can drive and then walk into the **Devil's Beef Tub**, a huge and gloomy declivity in the hills, at its best in mist. This is the best-known of the many 'beef tubs' in the Border hills, where stolen cattle could be hidden and easily guarded. Eight miles up the narrow valley of the Moffat Water, on the A708, you reach the **Grey Mare's Tail**, a waterfall which drops from a hanging valley. This is a popular spot for outings, though the crowds seldom reach oppressive numbers. Beware of coaches on the narrow road. To see the waterfall, you must walk a short distance from the car park on a slightly vertiginous track (the most dangerous section is now barricaded off).

Alternatively, a longer, steeper walk on the northern side of the Tail Burn leads you to the top of the fall, and eventually to Loch Skeen above it, set in some of the wildest country in the Borders. There are usually feral goats in the area, although they keep themselves to themselves – unlike the local sheep, which have learned that tourists are a soft touch. On this road, just outside Moffat, **Tweedhope Sheep Dogs** is run by a veteran of *One Man and his Dog*. There are displays at 11 and 3, when you can see the dogs rounding up reluctant sheep. There is also a Shetland pony.

Another good, and unfrequented, walk near Moffat is along **Glen Wamphray** (take the minor road south towards Boreland to reach it), where a burn of limpid clarity boils in rock cauldrons among the trees. Well-engineered duckboards and steps save you from the bogs.

The Kagyu Samye Ling Tibetan centre is also within easy reach (see page 41).

LIDDESDALE

Liddesdale, valley of the Armstrongs, was for centuries the most piratical, the least law-abiding, the worst (in the eyes of the authorities) of all the Border valleys – and from Liddesdale have come the most stirring ballads: *Jock o' the Side*, *Jamie Telfer*, and *Dick o' the Cow*. All are scattered with Liddesdale place names such as Mangerton and Pudding-Burn.

Detour down to the iron bridge over the river at **Kershopefoot**. The English border runs away from you up the burn opposite, into the outlying conifers of the Kielder forest. The junction of burn and river was one of the meeting places for the English and Scottish Wardens of the Border Marches. On designated days of truce, both sides would meet at places like this to settle cross-border disputes under the complicated procedures of the law of the Marches. They were tense occasions, more than once degenerating into fights. It is curious to think, sitting on the peaceful banks of the Liddel, that this place was once a hair-trigger frontier.

Somewhere round here the refugee Earl of Westmorland, after a failed rebellion in support of Mary Queen of Scots, changed clothes and swords with Jock o' the Side, and it was near this ford, if we are to believe the ballads, that the Captain of Bewcastle was shot through 'the left ba' stane'. Now it is all farmland and forestry. There is no heritage centre at Kershopefoot yet, so you will need your imagination, and preferably a copy of George Macdonald Fraser's *The Steel Bonnets*.

There are two heritage centres at Newcastleton. A little way up the valley, at the **Clan Armstong Trust Centre** (open Whitsun to Sept, Tue to Sun 1.30 to 4.30), the Armstrongs will tell you all you could ever want to know about their clan. **The Liddesdale Heritage Centre** (open Easter to Sept, Wed to Mon 1.30 to 4.30) is a tiny affair in an old kirk, with information about the valley and its violent history. From Newcastleton a back road leads to Langholm, crossing the Tarras Moss. This bleak stretch was an invaluable refuge for the inhabitants of Liddesdale whenever the law tried to catch up with them, and if you cross it you can see why.

If you need a picnic spot, wait until you get to the valley of the Tarras Water, where the landscape suddenly softens.

Hermitage Castle

(HS, standard times, weekends only in winter)
This is the most menacing castle in Scotland, once the stronghold of the Keeper of Liddesdale. It is a great square lump of virtually windowless masonry, pierced on two sides by flying arches like sharks' mouths – a cross between prison and frontier fortress. The massively thick walls are stained algae-green where the light does not reach them and nothing in the remains of the interior suggests comfort, least of all the horrible pit prison.

Throughout most of its early history the castle changed hands between Scots and English and was held successively by Douglases, Dacres and Hepburns, with plenty of plotting and cross-border treachery revolving round it. One of its earliest lords, William de Soulis, supposedly dabbled in demonology within the walls until he met his fate (according to Leyden's ballad) by being wrapped in sheets of lead and boiled alive in a cauldron at the nearby stone circle of Nine Stane Rig.

In 1342, Sir Alexander Ramsay, rescuer of Black Agnes at the siege of Dunbar Castle (page 165), was starved to death in the pit prison by Sir William Douglas, his torment horribly prolonged by a trickle of grain from a storeroom above. In 1566 Mary Queen of Scots rode the 40 or so miles from Jedburgh and back again in a single day when her future husband James Hepburn, fourth Earl of Bothwell, was lying wounded at Hermitage after a tangle with one of the local villains, 'little' Jock (wha daur meddle wi' me?) Elliot. It was an unfortunate journey for the Queen, who lost her watch in a mire (see Jedburgh, page 43) and caught a fever from which she nearly died.

Hermitage Castle was restored in the early nineteenth century, extremely effectively in view of its current air of nastiness. Although it has played no part in history since the union of the crowns, it is one of those places you sense to be dormant, not extinct.

ESKDALE

Langholm is the southernmost – and perhaps the most fanatical – of the Border rugby-playing towns. Situated at the meeting of three valleys, it is full of bridges and people on their way to somewhere else.

The best approach is from the east down from the Tarras moors (see Liddesdale, page 39). From this road, you will see a piece of sculpture, shaped like an open book pierced by cut-outs, which is a memorial to Hugh McDiarmid, Scotland's greatest modern poet, whose childhood was spent in Langholm. The memorial's appearance, its siting and its very existence aroused huge local controversy (McDiarmid not having been at all popular with some elements in his home town), and the fact that it ended up in this little-travelled spot in the moors can still arouse the ire of Scottish literati.

The village of **Eskdalemuir** is surrounded by miles of trees, but is worth visiting to see the **Kagyu Samye Ling Tibetan Centre** (service 1.30 to 3 daily – visitors welcome; office closes at 6). Prayer flags flutter outside an old shooting-lodge, whose brightly coloured window frames provide another clue that the building has departed from its original purpose.

At the back, hidden from the road, lies the largest Tibetan temple in Europe. In this high, bleak landscape it is an astonishing burst of colour; inside, the red and the gilt dazzle, while rows of Buddhas gaze contemplatively down at you. The centre runs residential courses on aspects of Buddhism (write for a brochure to Eskdalemuir, Dumfriesshire DG13 0QL).

TEVIOTDALE

The A7 between Langholm and Hawick is not the most attractive of roads, running for most of its distance in a trench between undistinguished hills. However, it is certainly the most convenient route from the west coast to the centre of the Scottish Borders.

It is easy to miss Teviothead, which is just a few scattered cottages beyond the watershed where the burns start to run north-east to the Tweed. A craft-shop with a totem pole outside houses the **Museum of Border Arms and Armour** (open all year), worth stopping at to pick the brains of its knowledgeable curator about the weaponry on display and how the Borderers used it to slaughter each other. Teviothead is also where the notorious raider Johnnie Armstrong was 'convicted of common theft' and strung up by his King, James V. 'What wants yon knave that a king should have?' said James, seeing Armstrong's finery. Legend rapidly turned Johnnie into the betrayed patriot; 'I am but a fool to seek grace at a graceless face,' he is supposed to have said, before meeting his fate. Whatever the truth, the memorial in the old churchyard here is firmly on Johnnie's side.

Hawick

This is a busy textile town, with none of the gentility of Melrose or the county-town atmosphere of Kelso. It is grey, grainy, and has enough bleak-fronted mills left to remind you that woollens, especially stockings, have long been its *raison d'être*. Mill shops with bargain bins offer splendid opportunities for a rummage.

Shopping apart, there is an excellent reason to visit Hawick on a grey day: the Teviotdale Leisure Centre, with its steamy tropical pool. In Wilton Park, the local museum's displays are in need of an upgrade, but there is plenty of fascinating material about the hosiery industry and the working conditions of a previous century. Perhaps the most notable exhibit is the jumper which established the world record for the time taken to produce a garment from the back of a sheep — a feat accomplished in four hours and thirty-five minutes.

In the High Street, one of the few old buildings left in Hawick, **Drumlanrig's Tower** (open Apr to end May, daily 10 to 5; June 10 to 6; Jul, Aug 10 to 7; Sept 10 to 6; Oct to Mar 10 to 5, in winter call 01450 377615) has been restored as a modern museum bringing the town's history to life.

Jedburgh

Jedburgh is a long, thin town, running along the Jed Water in a steepish valley, and is the first you will reach in Scotland if you come up the A68 over Carter Bar. Only ten miles from the frontier and in the heart of Teviotdale, it has seen plenty of violence in its time; its inhabitants gained a reputation for obstinate independence, and for playing football with Englishmen's heads — the streamers attached to the ball in today's festive version represent the hair. Jedburgh has lent its name to the Jeddart axe (one of the most common Border weapons) and to Jeddart justice (hang first and try later). The Jeddart snail (a curly peppermint) ranks alongside Hawick Balls, Berwick Cockles and the Galashiels Soor Plooms in the list of Border confectionery, and was apparently invented in the eighteenth century by a bored French prisoner. Jedburgh was once a textile town, with a polluted river and a huge rayon factory, but all industrial dereliction has been swept away and the main road now runs past open spaces fringed by modern housing.

Jedburgh Abbey

(HS, standard times)
The excavations of 1984 and the opening of a small visitor centre have allowed Historic Scotland to make a first-class job of interpretation here. The plainsong in the visitor centre, the scale model, the helpful explanations at view-points within the site and the clear, concise guidebook make Jedburgh the best starting point for exploration of the Border abbeys.

It is an austere ruin, much of its architecture being Romanesque and some of it dating from the fifteenth century, when repairs were made after English raids. There are plenty of architectural curiosities for enthusiasts. Jedburgh, like other Border abbeys, was founded on the initiative of King David I in 1138 for a community of Augustinian canons, and, like the others, suffered not only from the depredations of the English but also from the eventual diversion of resources into the pockets of commendators – officers appointed by the crown, usually with only the most spurious religious qualifications – shortly before the Reformation of 1560. The abbey church at Jedburgh remains remarkably intact despite this, but most of the surrounding buildings have not survived above their foundations.

Jedburgh Castle Jail

(Being refurbished and scheduled to re-open late 1996. Call 01450 373457 for information.)
The jail is well worth the steep walk from the town centre. There is nothing left of the old castle: it was long ago demolished by the Scots to stop the English using it. A jail was built on its site in the eighteenth century on the lines of the best contemporary model, and remains complete. The old cell blocks, the governor's office and the kitchen are sufficiently unchanged to give you a good idea of what life was like for the prisoners.

The first floor contains a local museum with plenty of insights into Jedburgh life.

Mary Queen of Scots House and Visitor Centre

(Open mid-Mar to mid-Nov, Mon to Sat 10 to 4.45, Sun 10 to 4.30)
There is something a little unsettling about this museum. The late sixteenth-century fortified house is lovely but it is not entirely certain that Mary stayed here when she was in Jedburgh, though the guidebook does not admit to any such doubts. This would matter less if it were not that the museum chooses to plunge you into a kind of Shakespearean tragedy rather than tell a straight story. Mary's life is split into Prologue, Drama and Epilogue, all linked (we are told) to Mary's motto 'in my end is my beginning'. Early music echoes through the rooms and snippets of text are displayed on engraved glass panels: they are so hard to read that they have to be repeated on printed cards.

The highest point of this high-minded kitsch is the empty white chamber which 'symbolises the full circle of Mary's drama', but is a more telling symbol of the size of the house

BORDER CASTLES

One hundred and forty-seven castles are listed in Mike Salter's gazetteer *Discovering Scottish Castles* (Shire) in the area covered by this chapter. Half-crumbled into the fields, hidden by trees or restored and converted into homes, they are everywhere. The biggest, such as Roxburgh or Jedburgh, were too vulnerable to being taken and held by the English and were often demolished by the Scots themselves, so the ruins that remain are usually simple rectangular towers or 'peles', mostly dating from the sixteenth century. They are simple structures, usually with a vaulted ground-floor room, the main hall directly above, and a further one, or perhaps two, storeys. Entrance was on the first floor. Much of the life went on outside the tower in the surrounding enclosure called the 'barmkin', where cattle could be sheltered in times of trouble. Pele towers were designed to hold off small raids. They did not catch fire easily and could act as a rallying point and defensive centre whenever a raid was threatened. Even so, they were not entirely invulnerable – there are records of raiding parties climbing the walls and breaking in through the roof – but they did give some protection to humans, even if the cattle were rustled from under the walls.

Most of the ruined towers are still on private land, and you should obtain permission before exploring. The ruins are often precarious, so you venture into them at your own risk. As well as the castles mentioned in the text, look out for:

● **Cessford** (near Jedburgh), stronghold of the Cessford Kerrs, now a riven hulk of red stone, easily visible from a nearby road.

● **Ferniehurst** (near Jedburgh), belonging to the Ferniehurst Kerrs and open to the public on Wednesdays, May to late Oct, 1.30 to 4.30.

● **Fatlips** (near Minto), an inaccessible jagged ruin perched on top of Minto crags near Jedburgh.

● **Whitton** (near Morebattle), a ruin in a farmyard, surrounded by hens.

● **Gilknockie** (near Langholm), now restored, may have been the hold of Johnnie Armstrong, the notorious raider. You can see around by making an appointment – call 01387 371876.

in comparison to the small number of genuine exhibits. By far the most intriguing object in the place is the French watch unearthed by a mole in 1817 on the route of Mary's ride to Hermitage. You may come away with a lot of odd ideas about Mary, but the house and the watch are certainly worth going to see.

Near Jedburgh

Down by the Teviot, off the B6400, the **Harestanes Visitor Centre** (open Apr to end Oct, daily 10 to 5) has a series of pleasing walks centred on the steading of an old estate. Much imagination has gone into providing original puzzles, games and exhibitions – all about, or using, wood.

Off the A68 to the south of Jedburgh, at Mervinslaw, you will find the **Jedforest Deer and Farm Park** (open May to end Aug, daily 10 to 5.30; Sept to end Oct, 11 to 4.30), which is refreshingly unpatronising and is good for families. For picturesque villages, try Ancrum or Denholm; for views, climb Rubers Law. For excellent smoked produce, visit the Teviot Smokery, just beyond Eckford, and for drives through splendid Border scenery, the patchwork of roads round Oxnam and Hownam (a short stretch on the line of the Roman Dere Street) is recommended.

SELKIRK

Selkirk would have had its own abbey if the Tyronensian monks had not been moved to Kelso in 1128. They may have been grateful, for Selkirk's position on a steep hillside is rather exposed. The long High Street has a statue of Walter Scott at one end and one of Mungo Park, the explorer of the Niger, at the other. Here, too, is the fierce Flodden Memorial by Thomas Clapperton, who was also responsible for the magnificent war memorial in Galashiels. Of all Border towns, Selkirk seems to have taken the terrible battle of Flodden in 1513 most to heart. **Halliwell House** (open Apr to late Oct, Mon to Sat 10 to 5, Sun 2 to 4; July, Aug, daily 10 to 6; Nov to mid-Dec, daily 2 to 4) is one of the best local museums in the Borders, with a complete ironmonger's shop and much well-presented information on the growth of the town; here you can see the Flodden flag, brought home by the town's sole survivor of the disaster, while the centrepiece of the town's Common Riding ceremony is a re-enactment of the wordless casting down of that tattered standard five centuries ago. This battle, in which Scotland lost one of her best kings (James IV) and 10,000 men, turned one of the most promising periods in Scottish history back into the more usual course of internal strife and misery.

The old **courtroom** (open Apr to end Oct, Mon to Sat 10 to 4, Sun 2 to 4) where Sir Walter Scott once dispensed justice as Sheriff of Selkirk has recently been restored and opened as a small museum, with an audio-visual display providing the background

Directly beneath the High Street, Selkirk's textile mills are gathered in a solemn row by the river. A number are deserted (and make good subjects for atmospheric photography), but there are still enough working for this to be profitable hunting ground if you are looking for tweeds and tartans. The visitor centre at **Selkirk Glass** is well worthwhile. You can get really close to the glass-blowers. Seek out a Selkirk bannock before leaving the town – this sweet, sultana-packed variety of bread tastes addictive.

Ettrick

A drive up the Ettrick takes you through the whole range of Borders scenery. At first, you travel through rich farmland, with cows chewing the cud in the fields and a large mansion (Bowhill) distantly glimpsed through the trees. The river is wide and alluring, with hardly a bridge. Ettrickbridge, a tiny village, marks the start of the sheep country, the river narrowing and flowing faster through defiles, or flattening into shingly stretches, the haunt of oyster-catchers. Higher still, the village of Ettrick is just a few houses and a red sandstone memorial to James Hogg, the 'Ettrick Shepherd', who is better known today for his psychological novel *Confessions of a Justified Sinner* than for the poetry that originally made him famous. A new (and welcome) exhibition about him is to be found at the restored **Aikwood Tower** near Ettrickbridge, home of Sir David Steel MP and his wife Judy (open Easter to mid-Sept, Tue, Thur and Sun 2 to 5). Now the road becomes single-track and the hills close in, forming barriers so that it is hard to see where the valley is going to turn next. However, at the very head of Ettrick, once one of the most unspoilt and beautiful places in the Borders, the landscape has been ruined by spruce plantations. It is a depressing climax to a lovely drive.

Yarrow

It was in the flat ground between Ettrick and Yarrow, just upstream of Selkirk, that Montrose fought the disastrous engagement of Philiphaugh – his first major defeat by the Covenanters (see page 136). The victory was stained by massacre: in accordance with their battle-cry of 'Jesus and no quarter', the zealots slaughtered Montrose's camp-followers in the courtyard of Newark Castle nearby. You can reach the atmospheric remains of this stark tower above the Yarrow through the Bowhill estate.

Bowhill and beyond

(House open July, daily 1 to 4.30; country park open end Apr to end Aug, Mon to Thur and Sat 1 to 4.30; Jul 12 to 5) The family of Scott of Buccleuch was once among the most prominent of the Border 'riding families', and since the days of 'Bold Buccleuch', who replied to Elizabeth of England's accusation of presumptuous daring with 'What is there that a man dare not do?', the family has tied itself to the Douglases, the Montagues, and the Royal Family too. Many of the treasures they have accumulated over the centuries now rest at this mansion hidden in the trees a few miles west of Selkirk. It is not the most elegant of houses, for its simple lines were considerably altered during the nineteenth century, but the quality of what lies inside makes it essential visiting for those who like stately homes; nearly all the best Scottish portrait painters, French furniture masters, miniaturists and makers of fine porcelain are represented. The Raeburn portrait of Sir Walter Scott with Hermitage Castle in the background and the extraordinary painting of George IV in Highland dress are, in their separate ways, wonderful. So too are the Venetian scenes by Guardi, the early Lorrains and the portrait of Lady Caroline Scott by Reynolds. There are monstrosities too – particularly the silver candelabrum weighing 13 stone – and the unconsecrated chapel given over to relics of the Duke of Monmouth (who married a Scott) is a little too like a shrine. Perhaps the most intriguing object in the house is the Pittenweem-made clock of 1775, which, in good Presbyterian taste, plays tuneful airs six days a week, but ceases on Saturday and does not start again until the Sabbath is over.

Above Bowhill, the valley of the Yarrow is less beautiful than that of the Ettrick, though more celebrated by the ballads. The two roads which run over the hills to Ettrick have much to commend them as short diversions to obtain good views of both river valleys. The river starts at **St Mary's Loch**, a well-known beauty spot, apt on fine weekends to become a little too filled with the sails of yachts and sailboards to be called tranquil. The centre for most of the activity is the equally well-known **Tibbie Shiel's Inn**, once a convivial meeting place for Scott, Hogg and fellow writers, and equally convivial, if not quite so literary, today. Over the watershed beyond St Mary's, you come eventually to the Grey Mare's Tail, and so down to Moffat (page 38).

THE TWEED VALLEY

The run down the Tweed from the watershed north of Moffat is the classic Border tour. The landscape is gentle, with heather replacing grass on many of the hills; the castles and houses are grand or imposing, the towns prosperous and sunny. The river itself, moving from upland shingle runs to deep salmon pools, is consistently lovely.

The Upper Tweed Valley

At **Tweedsmuir**, a detour on the minor road through the hills past the Talla Reservoir to St Mary's Loch takes you straight into the high, bleak and isolated country which fringes the Tweed to the east. If you stay on the A701, the valley begins to open out near Drumelzier. Here you are in Arthurian country, for at **Drumelzier** lies Merlin's grave. King Arthur fought his seventh battle (in the wood of Caledon) at Cademuir Hill above Peebles, and Merlin met St Kentigern at the 'altar stone' at Stobo. Such, at least, is the tradition.

At **Broughton**, you come to the boyhood haunts of John Buchan, author of *The Thirty-Nine Steps* and other tales of derring-do. A converted church, the **John Buchan Centre** (open May to mid-Oct, daily 2 to 5), holds an excellent museum celebrating his extraordinary career. Buchan was not only a novelist but Governor-General of Canada too, and the museum has photographs, mementoes and books in plenty, as well as knowledgeable curators happy to answer all questions. If you are in a mood to visit more museums, drive over the regional boundary to visit Biggar (see page 184), where there are another four.

Dawyck Botanic Garden

(Open mid-Mar to late Oct, daily 10 to 6)

The arboretum in this estate on the banks of the Tweed, just off the B712, is now an outstation of the Royal Botanic Garden in Edinburgh. Among the redwoods, Nootka cypresses and Douglas firs are many specimens over a century old. Most of the older planting runs along a small burn, where rhododendrons, azaleas, meconopsis and rodgersias lend colour in spring and autumn. A chapel sits in the middle of the wood; it was designed by William Burn, doyen of the Victorian version of the Scottish Baronial style, as was the house nearby. The gardens seem to be populated largely by enthusiasts – tracks are worn through the long grass where visitors have detoured to read the labels. Nevertheless, this is a good spot for non-gardeners too.

Peebles

Not many towns are the subject of poems by kings, but James V wrote one about Peebles, describing the bustle and raucous excitement of the town's Beltane festival, which still takes place in mid-June. Peebles was a hunting base for Scottish kings, a former county town, and is a popular place for a day trip from Edinburgh. It has also been blessed by the perfect marketing slogan, uttered by a resident returning from abroad: 'Give me Peebles for Pleasure'. The town's pleasures are gentle ones – golf, fishing, walking, and above all excursions into the scenery, for it is well situated in the best of Tweed Valley countryside. It is an excellent place from which to tour: historic houses, castles and gardens lie nearby, and it is easy enough to lose the crowds by striking out a short distance into the hills.

The High Street fills up fast at weekends: buyers of gifts, antiques and woollens contend with people in town to do the Saturday shopping. There are craft-shops, and old weavers' cottages beyond the ancient Cuddy's brig. There is no shortage of hotels, of which there is a good range, though they have to live in the shadow of the enormous Peebles Hotel Hydro, a vast, much-altered nineteenth-century spa hotel which sits in cheery splendour on the edge of town, host to family holidays and conferences alike.

In and near Peebles

Prominent on the High Street lies the **Chambers Institute** (open all year, Mon to Fri 10 to 1 and 2 to 5; Apr to Oct,

Sat 2 to 5). This philanthropic foundation by the epony-mous publisher comes in three parts – the Tweeddale museum, an art gallery and the Secret Room (in fact merely a gallery off the main stair), which is an unusual survival of the high-minded Victorian idea that a museum should uplift and enlighten its visitors. Quiet greys and clarets are the background to two large classical friezes – one a copy of a section from the Parthenon, the other the Alexander Frieze, done in similar heroic style by nineteenth-century Danish sculptor Bertil Thorvaldsen. It is worth a peep for the incongruity and the atmosphere of quiet erudition.

In Innerleithen Road, you will find the **Cornice** (open daily in summer, weekends spring and autumn), subtitled the Scottish Museum of Ornamental Plasterwork. This is a recreation of a plasterer's workshop from around the turn of the century, closely associated with an old local firm, L. Grandison, whose work you will see in the restoration of Thirlestane Castle (page 59). There is a jumble of patterns for flowers, fruits, geometrical abstracts and faces of nymphs or cupids. Explanations are rather vague, but it is possible to puzzle out the techniques of moulding work and of building running cornices with laths and templates. You are sometimes allowed to play at plastering on a wall; wellies and apron are provided.

Just outside the town, a little way upstream off the A72, **Neidpath Castle** (open Easter to end Sept, Mon to Sat 11 to 5, Sun 1 to 5) stands above a dark and swirly bit of the Tweed. This is a good, atmospheric ruin, with massively thick walls, tiny windows and a gloomy pit prison, in which you are invited to deposit your children. More seriously, Neidpath is an excellent place for learning about castle-building techniques, for the fourteenth-century triple-vaulted structure is clearly visible beneath the seventeenth-century alterations and the interior is bare. You can prowl right through the castle up to the roof, for most of it remains remarkably well preserved. Above Neidpath a waymarked path runs up either bank of the river, giving a round walk of six miles (a leaflet is obtainable from the tourist office).

For picnics or a view of gentle scenery, try the Meldon Hills or the valley of the Manor Water, both within easy reach of the town.

Traquair House

(Open Easter week to late Sept, daily 12.30 to 5.30; July and Aug, 10.30 to 5.30; Oct, Fri to Sun 2 to 5)

Traquair is one of the most rewarding houses to visit in Scotland. There are plenty of sound historical reasons for coming here, as Traquair is the oldest continuously inhabited house in Scotland, possibly dating in part back to the tenth century. Twenty-seven monarchs are said to have visited over the centuries, and there are connections between Traquair and many of the best-known figures of Scottish history. Mary Queen of Scots was here with her young son; Montrose may have been betrayed by the second Earl before the battle of Philiphaugh, while Prince Charles Edward was made welcome by the staunchly Jacobite household. The 'Bear Gates' on the main avenue were closed behind him as he left, and they will not be reopened until a Stewart sits on the throne again. Traquair also has the romance of having been a Catholic house in hostile country, with a priest's room where the incumbent could escape by a secret staircase.

The history, though, is somehow incidental to the charm that Traquair powerfully exerts on its visitors. What you remember is the odd yet harmonious shape of the house, which is mainly seventeenth-century and looks as if a large *château* had been grafted on to the back of a smaller one in similar style, the whole turned into a stage setting by the addition of side wings and iron gates. Part of the strangeness comes from seeing it at an angle as you arrive – for a Windsor is on the throne, and you come in by a side road.

This is an ancient house, not a stately home. The steep stone stairs, thick walls and small rooms are tortuous rather than elegant, and certainly do not distance you by their grandeur. Everywhere lies an array of objects, some ancient, some mysterious, others merely endearing.

The cleverness of the Traquair style, established by Peter Maxwell-Stewart and now continued by his daughter, is to recognise that museum-pieces are not all that visitors want to see. Consequently, a chest of musty documents, perhaps labelled merely Bundle XXVIII and tantalisingly unreadable, is displayed with the same degree of prominence as the fragile collection of Jacobite glassware or the rosary which belonged to Mary Queen of Scots. The tale of the house is brought right up to date with a modern letter from a firm of solicitors justifying a bill. Each has its place in the tale of the house and its family, and visitors are encouraged to speculate as well as to admire (and occasionally have their leg gently pulled too). Do not leave without sampling some Traquair ale, brewed on the premises, and taking a stroll round the craft workshops in nearby buildings.

Innerleithen

Peebles was given a poem by a king, Innerleithen a novel by Sir Walter Scott – *St Ronan's Well*. It was by turns a spa resort and a textile town and you can still sample the waters at the **St Ronan's Well Centre** (open Easter to Oct, daily 2 to 5). Do not miss **Robert Smail's Printing Works** (NTS, open Easter to end Oct, Mon to Sat 10 to 1 and 2 to 5, Sun 2 to 5) at the eastern end of the High Street. This little family business, whose technology, in the words of the guidebook, was 'as obsolete as the steam engine', was saved with all its equipment and business records intact in 1986. Excellent, imaginative work by the National Trust for Scotland (all the information is printed on the firm's machines, for example) allows a close-up of the life of a jobbing printer from the early nineteenth century onwards. The machines still run and you can practise setting type by hand or simply leaf through the guardbooks that are packed with the work done over a century or more – advertisements for sales, announcements of concerts, business cards, hymn sheets, menus and postcards.

Galashiels

Gala, as it is called, is home of the Scottish College of Textiles, centre of the tweed industry and the largest town in the area, with a rash of housing estates and light industry extending towards Melrose. Galashiels is one of the few towns in Britain that is worth visiting just to see the war memorial: under the clock-tower, a Border reiver astride his horse seems to shout brave defiance across the centuries. Information about the sculptor, Thomas Clapperton, is on view at Old Gala House, on the hill behind the High Street. There is an excellent little historical display about the woollen industry in the **Lochcarron of Scotland Cashmere and Wool Centre**, where you can also see the modern machines at work (formal tours twice a day, but ask anyway).

Abbotsford

(Open mid–Mar to end Oct, Mon to Sat 10 to 5, Sun 2 to 5) This is the house that Sir Walter Scott built (most of it around 1822), and an odd one it turned out to be. It stands beside the B6360, and is well signposted. Few people would call its turreted, corbelled and battlemented architectural mish-mash pretty, but it is certainly intriguing. Inside, Abbotsford is less a literary shrine than a high–class junk shop. Most people would not have salvaged a door used by condemned criminals on their way to execution and set it into their own house, or hung the skull of an elk dug out of a Roxburgh bog in their entrance hall, but Scott loved curiosities such as these. The whole house is stuffed with a jumble of objects, many of them reputedly once belonging to the most famous figures in Scottish history. On show is a model of Robert the Bruce's skull, Montrose's sword, Rob Roy's sporran purse, a pocket book belonging to Flora Macdonald, plunder from the battlefields of Waterloo and Culloden, and more. Much was given to Scott by admirers, but most of it, including the collection of about 9,000 books, he assembled himself. It is in bad taste to ask how many of the relics are genuine: a wry grin is about all you will get by way of a response from the guides. Scott drew sightseers during his lifetime, but in nothing like the numbers that flock to his house today. Abbotsford was not constructed with coach parties in mind, and you can feel like a herring in a barrel if you go round when visitors are at their thickest. But Sir Walter's descendants and their staff cope cheerfully, and there is ample space in the ground and gardens (which contain their own curiosities).

MELROSE

The rugby ground and abbey car park are about the biggest things in this quiet red sandstone town, but its attractions are remarkably diverse. As well as the abbey, there is the wonderful **Melrose Motor Museum** (open Easter to mid-Oct, daily 10.30 to 5.30), housed in an old garage down beyond the abbey. Almost all the cars and motorcycles on display were locally owned, and each has its snippet of history attached. The star is the 1909 Glasgow-built Albion, with massive coachwork and a speaking-tube through which to give the chauffeur orders. There are shelves and cupboards stuffed with ancient accessories, from 1930s motoring coats to a stove to heat your 'motor-house'. Children are kept off the most precious exhibits, but are allowed to romp on the 1943 Jeep. Alternatively, **Teddy Melrose** (open all year, Mon to Sat 10 to 5, Sun 2 to 5), a museum dedicated to toy bears, could prove a draw.

Railway enthusiasts (and others) should not miss seeing

the graceful spans of the **Leaderfoot Viaduct** which carried the old railway across the Tweed east of Melrose. It is one of the most delicate bridges to be found in the Borders.

Priorwood Gardens (NTS, open Apr to end Dec, Mon to Sat 10 to 5.30, Sun 1.30 to 5.30; shop also open Jan to end Mar, Mon to Sat 12 to 4), near the abbey, specialise in flowers suitable for drying, and are much nicer than this bald description suggests. The flower-beds are small (but well-labelled) and the displays of preserved flowers and of preserving techniques persuade you to think what a pleasant hobby this might be. Beyond the garden, a quiet orchard, ideal for a picnic, is laid out to show the history of apple-growing from Roman times.

Melrose lies in the shadow of the **Eildon Hills**, a triple-peaked volcanic plug visible from all over the central Borders, and the focus of many legends. Michael Scott, the wizard who lies buried at Melrose, instructed the Devil to split the hill into three, and King Arthur's knights are said to sleep in its fastnesses. The Roman fortress of Trimontium was built beneath the Eildons too (a pillar marks the site) and there is a good display of finds at the **Trimontium Exhibition** in Melrose (open all year, Mon to Sat 10 to 5, Sun 2 to 5). Views from the top of the Eildons are all you might expect: the climb up starts just south of the by-pass off the B6359.

Melrose Abbey

(HS, standard times)

Melrose Abbey was thrust into prominence by Sir Walter Scott, who used the combination of moonlight, a wizard's grave and the old ruins to good effect in his poem *The Lay of the Last Minstrel*, and sent many people, as he later confessed, 'needlessly bat-hunting' to savour the gothic shivers for themselves. More prosaically, Melrose is widely agreed to be Scotland's finest Gothic building, with stone carving to rival the best in the United Kingdom. The first impression the ruins give is of delicate precariousness. Flying buttresses, reduced to a single course of stone, hang perilously between ruined masonry, while the east window, its internal tracery missing, is divided by pencil-thin columns of stone, ready to be blown down by the slightest wind. Scott chivvied the Duke of Buccleuch into preserving the crumbling remnants.

The interior would be quite lovely, even in its ruined state, if it were not for the hideous remains of the seventeenth-century parish kirk which was built inside the nave after the Reformation. Where there was once soaring fifteenth-century vaulting (the original twelfth-century building was almost entirely destroyed by the English), there is now a tunnel like a stone Nissen hut. To see what Melrose must once have been like you need to make for the presbytery and the north transept, where some of the vaulting has survived the fall of the tower. The elaborations of stonework here, fragmentary though they are, are wonderful. Under the east window an embalmed heart in a casket was discovered in 1920 – perhaps that of Robert the Bruce.

The best views are from the outside, for here the seventeenth-century intrusions are not visible and the harmony of the architecture is undisturbed. The remains of the old cloisters (copied by Scott for the Abbotsford garden) are especially worth spending time on. Lawns fill the spaces between the

SIR WALTER SCOTT (1771–1832)

If one man can be said to be responsible for starting tourism to Scotland, it is Sir Walter Scott. At the height of the early nineteenth-century passion for the Romantic, his poems (especially *Lady of the Lake* and *Marmion*) thrilled readers with their tales of passion and legend among stirringly described scenery. When he gave up poetry (recognising the superior talent of Byron) and turned to writing novels drawn from Scottish history – *Waverley*, the first, was published in 1814 – the impact was just as great. The novels were at first published anonymously, though many guessed Walter Scott to be the author.

In his childhood, staying with his grandparents in the Borders, Scott became infected with the passion for history and legend which informs his writing. Called to the Bar in 1792, he travelled extensively through Scotland, and there is scarcely a sight on today's tourist trail that he does not seem to have visited. From the valleys of the Borders, where his work as Sheriff of Selkirkshire took him, he collected the songs and ballads which had been handed down over the centuries and published them as *Border Minstrelsy*. With the money from his poems and novels he bought land by the Tweed and built Abbotsford, for Scott, a Tory by inclination, loved playing the country gentleman. Prosperous, admired, granted a baronetcy and at the centre of a legal and

foundations of the old abbey buildings, and although the on-the-spot explanations are not up to the standard of nearby Jedburgh, it is altogether a more rewarding place in which to linger. The Commendator's house (mostly built in 1590 with stones from the abbey church) now contains fragments of stone, allowing you to see details of carving and construction in close-up. Melrose Abbey finally fell victim to the English during the Rough Wooing in 1545, though some of the Cistercian brethren lingered on, denied money to repair the building, well into the Reformation.

Dryburgh Abbey

(HS, standard times)
This is the best positioned of the four Border abbeys, virtually surrounded by a bend of the Tweed near St Boswells and set

---

literary circle, Scott's happiness seemed assured until the sudden bankruptcy of his publisher in 1826 left him with debts of £116,000. Determined to pay these off, he flung himself into his writing and eventually succeeded in doing so, but at a cost in mental and physical health which are only too well charted in his *Journal*. He was 61 when he died.

How his contemporaries felt about him is best symbolised by the magnificence of the Scott monument in Edinburgh. He had single-handedly restored the nation's pride by pointing out and popularising the richness of its past. He was responsible for the rediscovery of the long-forgotten crown jewels of Scotland, had stage-managed the first royal visit to Scotland (George IV in 1822) since Charles II, and had created, in the historical novel, a new literary form.

It is difficult, even today, to escape the influence of Sir Walter Scott. His poetry may remain largely unread and his novels be too tortuous and prosy for today's taste, but the Romantic Scotland he created, with its fierce passions, its unyielding scenery and its gallery of noble or villainous characters, is still happily sold to the modern visitor. He left a more solid legacy, too, for he was assiduous in encouraging the preservation of the past. It is largely thanks to him that Melrose Abbey is not more ruinous, that the Border Ballads are not lost and that Mons Meg (see page 124) draws visitors to Edinburgh Castle.

round with fine old trees. You reach it via a spur from the B6356. Dryburgh, the home of White Canons (Premonstratensian monks) from 1150, never quite achieved the magnificence of Kelso or Melrose. Today, there is little left of the abbey church, apart from the transepts, but the surrounding buildings are well preserved – there are even the remnants of painted walls in the chapter house. Most of what is visible dates from the thirteenth century. On a sunny day, the cloister is an extremely peaceful haven. Like Melrose, Dryburgh was more or less finished off by the Rough Wooing in 1545, though religious activity lingered on until the end of the century. Since then its buildings have been used as a house, a cow byre and as a romantic folly. Sir Walter Scott is buried here, squeezed into the north transept among other Scotts. Earl Haig, the British Commander-in-chief on the Western Front from 1915–18, lies here too.

LAUDERDALE

The valley of the River Leader runs north from the Tweed near Melrose and is followed by the A68, the fastest route from the Borders to Edinburgh. Many drivers hurry through, but the valley has its attractions.

Just behind the filling station on the southern outskirts of **Earlston**, a crumbling, ivy-clad heap of stone is all that remains of **Rhymer's Tower**, said to have been the home of Thomas of Ercildoune, or True Thomas, the Border country's best-known prophet-poet. Taken into fairyland after boldly kissing the queen of the fairies, Thomas returned gifted with second sight, prophesying, among other disturbing intuitions, that 'Kelso Kirk would fall at its fullest'. No one knows whether a relatively harmless collapse of the roof in 1771 was what he meant, or whether there is worse to come. Earlston straggles away from the main road, and is one of those large villages that seems about to become picturesque, but never quite does.

One of the best-hidden sights of the Borders is **Legerwood Church**. To find it, take the minor road east off the A68 at Birkenside. Legerwood itself is merely a few cottages around a crossroads; its church lies behind a farm-steading about half a mile further on the road towards Corsbie, and is hardly signposted at all. Once you have discovered it, read the framed history in the porch, then go in to be amazed by the beauty of the pinkish sandstone Norman archway which stands between you and the chancel – a thing of sensuous magnificence in an otherwise bare kirk. Its colour, its carving and its warmth have the intriguing quality of a revealed secret and indeed the arch was hidden behind a wall for centuries. Before you leave, thumb through the visitors' book to see how widely the parish has scattered its sons and daughters.

Lauder has not expanded much beyond its medieval boundaries, so is a good place to discover the typical layout of an old Scottish burgh. A single High Street was bordered by strips of land called tofts, tenements or burgages extending at right angles to the town walls, with closes or wynds running between them and perhaps further linking streets at the back. Lauder is where several unfortunate favourites of James III were hung from a bridge by Archibald 'Bell-the-Cat' Douglas, the leader of a baronial faction discontented by the King's policies.

Thirlestane Castle

(Open Easter week, May, June and Sept, Mon, Wed, Thur and Sun; July and Aug, daily; castle 2 to 5, grounds 12 to 6)
Just south of Lauder, the pinnacles, turrets and ogee-roofed tower of Thirlestane stand strategically over the River Leader, looking like something from a peaceful French landscape. Many of the more ornate details are Victorian, but done in keeping with the work of Sir William Bruce, who transformed the original keep in the 1670s. Thirlestane was once the seat of the first (and only) Duke of Lauderdale, Charles II's Scottish Secretary – an unscrupulous man who made the most of his powerful position. His second wife stripped the castle of 14 cartloads of furniture for her London house. The last cart was turned back by outraged locals.

This is a very friendly stately home to visit. Part of it is still lived in by the Maitland family, who have held Thirlestane since the thirteenth century. Each of the long sequence of rooms has its own attendant, many of whom are locals and will fill you in on the history of both family and house, from the photographs taken by the fourteenth Earl of Lauderdale early this century to the magnificently ornate plasterwork on the ceilings of the state rooms. The restored nursery wing has splendid dolls' houses and Victorian and Edwardian toys, as well as a rocking-horse, masks and a dressing-up box for children to use. Some of the out-buildings contain exhibitions of Border country life, with various rural implements rather stolidly displayed.

KELSO

Although, according to a local historian, Kelso was more important before 1500 than it has ever been since, it is nevertheless the most attractive of the Border towns thanks to its eighteenth-century square, which gives it the air of a French market town. The ruins of the abbey close to the town centre, the sweep of the Tweed past the backs of houses and on through green parkland and Rennie's elegant bridge across the river contribute to the easy atmosphere. Add some good shops, some interesting domestic architecture and the relaxed bustle of an agricultural centre, and it is plain why Kelso is a good base. It does not have as many places to stay as either Moffat or Peebles, but there are enough.

It is worth exploring the strange octagonal parish church, the old Cross Keys coaching-inn, and the fine Georgian Ednam House as well as the small streets running down to the Tweed. The local museum (open mid-Mar to end Oct, Mon to Sat 10 to 12, 1 to 4.45, Sun 2 to 4.45) provides the background, or, for more details of local history, you can arm yourself with a copy of Alistair Moffat's *Kelsae: The History of Kelso since Earliest Times* (Mainstream Publishing) which you can get at the local Tourist Information Centre.

Kelso Abbey

(HS, open at all times)
There is less left of Kelso Abbey than of the other three abbeys nearby – in fact, not much more than a stump is visible – but what does remain shows the monumental scale of what is now thought to have been the biggest and grandest of the Border abbeys. A document discovered in the Vatican suggests that it had towers and transepts at both eastern and western ends, making it one of the most impressive Romanesque buildings in Britain. The Rough Wooing put an end to that in 1545 despite the resistance put up by monks and townsfolk, and all that remains is part of the west galilee and the north-west transept with its turreted façade and its 'surprising disregard for the structural prudence of placing arch above arch, solid above solid'. The memorial cloister of the Dukes of Roxburghe is modern and not particularly attractive.

Floors Castle

(Open Easter weekend, end Apr to end Sept, daily 10.30 to 5; Oct, Sun and Wed 10.30 to 4)

The seat of the Dukes of Roxburghe, this is a huge folly of a palace. For some years Vanburgh was thought to have had a hand in it, but now it seems that William Adam and William Playfair were dually responsible. If you come upon it from the side, your eye is immediately caught by the roofscape – dozens of little turret caps like columbines and forests of chimneys and finials, which look more like an aerial pinball table than anything else. Once past the gift shop and café, you enter the castle proper, feeling suitably humbled by the grandeur. The interior, however, is on a much more human scale, with ducal views across the policies down to the Tweed and to a yew tree which marks the spot where James II was killed by a bursting cannon while besieging Roxburgh.

The quality of the items on view is not, in general, as good as at Bowhill (see page 48), though there are fine tapestries, a small collection of post-Impressionist paintings and some Chinese porcelain. There are also some strange collections – very solid stuffed birds, whole cases of snuff-boxes, minerals, coins, robes, potties and carriages, which leave you feeling you have visited a gigantic magpie's nest. In the old walled garden the good play area will keep energetic children happy, and there is a garden centre too.

Smailholm Tower

(HS, standard times)

Of the many simple sixteenth-century fortalices known as pele towers which litter the Border landscape, Smailholm is the best preserved. It has the advantage of a superb setting on a craggy outcrop above a small loch, making it frequently photographed for calendars and postcards. As a child, Sir Walter Scott stayed with his grandfather at the adjacent farm of Sandyknowe, and later set his ballad *The Eve of St John* at the tower. The approach, signposted from the B6404 or the B6397 to the north-east of Kelso, leads you through a farm with the stone tower looming above. Once inside, you are confronted with Historic Scotland's restoration. The modern flooring, the atmospheric music and the displays of dolls and tapestries illustrating various Border ballads may grate on the purist, but they do not spoil the strong sense of the past with which the fort is imbued. From the guard–post on the roof there are views down the Eildons and the Cheviots, and you can readily imagine the raiders from Tynedale storming the crags and making away with the cattle.

For a contrast to Smailholm, seek out **Greenknowe Tower** (HS, open at all times) on the A6105 just west of the dull village of Gordon. Built in 1581, the red sandstone ruin marks how the Scottish tower house grew out of the defensive keep, for Greenknowe was built more to impress the neighbours than for defence. A nasty gun-loop, placed to emasculate unwanted visitors, is, however, a reminder that the times were still uncertain.

Mellerstain

(Open May to end Sept, Sun to Fri 12.30 to 4.30) Signposted from the A6089 north-west of Kelso, Mellerstain is, for many, the most beautiful Adam house in Scotland. It was started by William Adam, who was responsible for the wings, and finished by his son Robert in a style which approaches the perfection of neo-classicism. The exterior of Mellerstain is severe and uncompromising, but the interior, with its sequence of breathtaking ceilings, its fireplaces, its Adam-designed side tables, mirrors and cupboards, is a place of light and harmony, created for gracious family living rather than for stately processions. The library is the most perfect of the public rooms, where the eighteenth-century bindings on the shelves are complemented by the figures of Teaching and Learning.

After the splendour of the ground floor the bedrooms seem distinctly ordinary, though the main staircase is again wonderful. At the very top of the house Adam designed a ceiling for the magnificent long gallery, but unfortunately it was never put into execution.

Visitors to Mellerstain tour in the usual stately home fashion. Roped-off routes lead from room to room, while you long to relax in one of the armchairs and put your feet up in front of a roaring fire. Do not become so engrossed in the architecture that you overlook the family portraits. The strength of the Baillie-Hamiltons (Earls of Haddington) lies in the women they married – you can see it in their dignity and power. One in particular – Grisell Baillie – spent a legendary childhood dodging government forces to help her covenanting father. She later became mistress of Mellerstain and left meticulous household records from the early eighteenth century, some of which are displayed in the long gallery. Mellerstain's landscaped gardens are also held to be among the best of their kind, though there are too few flowers for modern eyes, and the lake looks better from a distance than from its boggy margins.

THE MERSE

The flat, richly agricultural basin of the lower Tweed north-east of Kelso does not make for interesting touring, although there are several curiosities hidden away in among the narrow lanes peopled by tractors and horseboxes. Wherever you travel you will see the planned agricultural cottages and hollow square farm-steadings of the eighteenth-century improvers, who helped usher in the agrarian revolution.

The knobbly outline of **Hume Castle**, off the B6364 north of Kelso, is a distinctive landmark. The old stronghold is long gone, and the walls on a craggy outcrop are a romantic folly. Even they are crumbling, but the views you get from beneath them are first class.

Duns, tucked under the Lammermuir hills on the A6105, lacks character, though it was once the county town of Berwickshire after Berwick was lost to the English. Its nature reserve, in the grounds of Duns Castle, has the unhappy name of Hen Poo. Stop at the **Jim Clark Memorial Room** (open Easter to end Sept, Mon to Sat 10 to 1 and 2 to 5, Sun 2 to 5) even if you are not a motor-racing fan, for the memorabilia of the former farmer turned world champion are extensive and moving. There are 122 trophies on the shelves, and photographs and letters from all over the world.

Just to the east of Duns, **Manderston House** (open early May to end Sept, Thurs, Sun and public holidays 2 to 5.30) bills itself as the swan-song of the Edwardian country house. Most of the ideas for this early twentieth-century statement of wealth came from an earlier age – imitations of Adam work in particular. However, the silver staircase – which must be dismantled and polished now and again, is unique to Manderston. Keep an eye open for the collection of biscuit tins – the present owner is a member of the Huntley and Palmer dynasty. Another stately home nearby is **Paxton House** (open Easter to Oct, daily 12 to 5), a Palladian creation with Adam designs, and a wonderful picture gallery.

If you follow the banks of the Tweed downstream from Kelso you arrive at **Coldstream**, from where the regiment of guards which now bears the town's name marched south to aid the restoration of Charles II. Coldstream is a quiet place away from the main road, and it is easy to find your way down to the river bank and gaze at the dark swirls of the Tweed. A new museum outlines the history of the famous regiment, and of the town. Just outside the western edge of the town, the grounds of the **Hirsel**, seat of Lord Home, are open daily and make a good spot for Sunday walks or dalliance beside the lake. An old steading has been turned into a craft centre and estate museum. Dundock Wood – reached from the A697 – is generously endowed with rhododendrons and azaleas and is extremely colourful on a bright spring day.

The Lammermuir Hills

Forming a natural boundary to the northern edge of the Merse, the Lammermuirs are a low, heather-covered range. Several small roads run across them into East Lothian from Duns, all of which make good drives. It is worth looking out for **Edinshall Broch**, one of the most southerly of the curious Iron Age towers which are found nowhere else but Scotland. The walk to the broch is pleasant, and there are enough stones still on top of one another for you not to feel your time has been wasted. **Abbey St Bathans** is a tiny village tucked into the depths of the Whiteadder valley. The road leading up towards the Whiteadder Reservoir is wooded and grassy by turns, finally rising up on to the treeless moor, with long views across the hills.

BERWICK-UPON-TWEED

If you have been touring the Scottish Border towns, Berwick may not seem particularly different at first, until you notice that the banks are English, and the tourist literature carries a rose on the front cover. For 400 years of its history the town belonged to Scotland, and was a Scottish royal burgh while Glasgow was still a village. During the twelfth and thirteenth centuries (a time of comparative peace), Berwick was Scotland's chief port, trading with the Low Countries and the Baltic. It is a measure of Berwick's importance that, when Edward I of England decided to make an example of it, he seems to have found 12,000 inhabitants to massacre.

It was Berwick's misfortune to be in the worst possible

position during the ceaseless wars between Scotland and England. It changed hands 12 times and was finally seized for England in 1482. Even so the town did not legally become part of England until 1836, and used to be separately referred to in charters. While the loss of Berwick was a disaster for Scotland, it had even worse consequences for the town itself. From a flourishing port it turned into an isolated frontier fortress; the massive Elizabethan fortifications show how much England felt it to be under threat. These fortifications are the only complete sixteenth-century example in Britain. For the military historian they are a delight, for here are the bastions and flankers which replaced stone walls as a defence against artillery, intact and built with no expense spared. For the layman the ramparts make a magnificent walk round the perimeter of Berwick, with glimpses of the Tweed, the sea, the Scottish hills and of lovingly tended back gardens.

Berwick makes an excellent base for exploring the eastern half of both the Scottish and the English Border country, and it is an attractive town into the bargain. Behind the ramparts the buildings are eighteenth- and nineteenth-century, with some fine Georgian houses. The modern developments at Berwick are all outside the ramparts, so you feel that you are living in a small, rather old-fashioned county town. There are plenty of places to stay, ranging from town-centre coaching-inns to bed-and-breakfasts on the outskirts.

The Barracks (open Easter to late Oct, daily 10 to 6; rest of year 10 to 4, closed Chr and 1 Jan) are the earliest purpose-built barracks in the United Kingdom, dating from 1721, and are now in the hands of English Heritage. The Berwick local museum is here, too, as is a display about the life and times of the British infantryman. The most surprising thing in the museum is Berwick's very own Sir William Burrell collection (open Easter to end Sept, Mon to Sat 10 to 12.30 and 2 to 6, Sun 11 to 1 and 2 to 6; rest of year Tue to Sat 10 to 12.30 and 1.30 to 4), hardly a rival to the one in Glasgow (page 218) but well worth a visit. The wealthy steamship magnate and art collector Sir William Burrell lived in Berwickshire for much of his life and made a number of gifts from his collection to the town, including some works by Degas. The museum is laid out in a quirky fashion (a promenade through the bowels of a dragon, for example) which will not appeal to everyone, but which certainly enlivens the atmosphere.

USEFUL DIRECTORY

Main tourist offices
Scottish Borders Tourist Board
70 High Street
Selkirk TD7 4DD
(01750) 20555

Dumfries and Galloway Tourist Board
Campbell House, Bankend Road
Dumfries DG1 4TH
(01387) 250434

Northumbria Tourist Board
Aykley Heads
Durham DH1 5UX
0191-375 3000

Tourist Board publications Very useful: annual *Visitor's Guide* (Dumfries and Galloway; Scottish Borders – everything listed, from site opening times to golf courses and cycle hire). Special interest: *Scottish Borders Angling Guide*, *Scottish Walkabout* leaflet; guides on walking, including the *Southern Upland Way Guide*. Postal or credit card phone orders from the above addresses.

THE BORDERS COAST

The Tweed at Berwick is not in fact the frontier between Scotland and England, despite the Royal Border Bridge which crosses it. You must follow the A1 northwards for about two miles before you reach the edge of the old liberty (lands belonging to the burgh) of Berwick, where the Border signposts appear.

Eyemouth

Where the main road veers inland, the coastal A1107 brings you to this mixture of fishing port and seaside resort. Eyemouth is a larger place than you might expect, with fish-processing industries on the outskirts – not such a romantic trade as the smuggling for which Eyemouth was once

Local tourist information centres
Berwick-upon-Tweed (01289) 330733
Coldstream (01890) 882607 (Apr to Oct)
Eyemouth (01890) 750678 (Apr to Oct)
Galashiels (01896) 755551 (Apr to Oct)
Gretna Green (01461) 337834 (Easter to Oct)
Hawick (01450) 372547
Jedburgh (01835) 863435/863688
Kelso (01573) 223464 (Apr to Oct)
Langholm (01387) 380976 (Easter to Oct)
Melrose (01896) 822555 (Apr to Oct)
Moffat (01683) 20620 (Easter to Oct)
Peebles (01721) 720138 (Apr to Oct)
Selkirk (01750) 20054 (Apr to Oct)

Local transport
Carlisle and Berwick Railway Stations (01345) 212282
Lowland Scottish Omnibus (covers the Borders) (01896) 758484
Western Scottish Omnibus (covers South-West Scotland)
(01387) 253496
Northumbria Buses (01289) 307283

Timetables and bus guides available from the Director of Roads
and Transportation, Borders Regional Council – (01835) 823301
– or from any Tourist Information Centre.

notorious. Kegs of contraband liquor came straight into the
harbour and were stored in the warren of caverns lying
beneath Gunstone house, an innocent-looking Georgian
building standing on its own above the fishing boats. Ploughs
have been known to vanish from the fields as the roofs of
old underground passages caved in. The higgledy-piggledy
layout of the old town was ideal for smugglers on the run;
much of it has been rebuilt in modern fishing village
vernacular style. A respectable semi-circle of sand fringes the
bay beneath the sea front and there are seaside resort touches,
such as the buckets and spades sold in newsagents.

Start your exploration of Eyemouth at the recently
renovated museum (open Easter to end May, Mon to Sat 10
to 4.30; June, Mon to Sat 10 to 5; Jul to end of Aug, Mon to
Sat 9.30 to 6, Sun 1 to 5.30; Sept, Mon to Sat 10 to 5, Sun
2 to 3.30; Oct, Mon to Sat 10 to 4) in the Old Kirk near the

harbour, which also houses the Tourist Information Centre. Central to the museum is the tapestry stitched locally to commemorate the tragedy of 1881, when 129 local fishermen were drowned within sight of land. There is also much well-displayed information about Eyemouth's fishing connections. The town trail leaflet takes you through some of Eyemouth's streets, down to the harbour, and up to the bluffs north of the town where Scots and English both had forts at different times.

You need only bother with **Coldingham Priory**, north of Eyemouth on the A1107, if you are an expert on church architecture, for although it was once rich and important the Rough Wooing almost destroyed it and Oliver Cromwell finished it off. Only part of the old Norman choir remains, roofed over, extensively rebuilt and turned into a barn-like church. If it is a fine day you will have more fun at Coldingham Bay, where there is sand.

Sheer cliffs, stained white by seabird guano and echoing to the raucous shouts of nesting gulls, mark **St Abb's Head**, now a National Nature Reserve (NTS and Scottish Wildlife Trust, open all year), which is reached by turning off at Coldingham. The cliffs are less inaccessible than those of many seabird colonies and are consequently popular with bird-watchers. A half-mile walk from the car park takes you to the clifftops, and there is a network of paths along them. There are fine views from the cliffside paths, interesting flowers and an offshore Marine Reserve (called the St Abbs and Eyemouth Voluntary Marine Reserve; there is a special car park for divers). Wardens organise guided walks in both reserves throughout the summer – information from the Eyemouth tourist office or Borders Regional Council (page 67).

Fast Castle

This presents a good, if rather dangerous, goal for a short walk. One and a half miles of narrow road lead from the A1107 to a row of farm cottages. After that you take to your feet for a further 20 minutes across the clifftops until the path plunges down and you see fragments of stone decking a headland which is little more than a large rock. A path across a narrow isthmus, barely protected by some very ancient chains, takes you to this rock, into what was one of the most remarkable fortresses in the area.

There is nothing much left now except for grass-covered heaps and the odd wall, but there is enough to show how hard it must have been to build here, how intolerable it must have been to live here, and how difficult the castle must have been to besiege. Despite this, it seems to have been captured and destroyed with the usual frequency. Walter Scott may have used it for Wolf's Crag in The *Bride of Lammermoor*, but he certainly described it with a lot of artistic licence. It is a splendid, rather scary spot, with seabirds wheeling and mewing all round the cliffs in the breeding season, and there is a legend of buried treasure to go with it (one of those who searched was John Napier, inventor of the logarithm). It is not a place for children or those who cannot stand heights.

WHERE TO STAY

£ – under £70 per room per night, incl. VAT

££ – £70 to £110 per room per night, incl. VAT

£££ – over £110 per room per night, incl. VAT

ABINGTON
ANCRUM
Ancrum Craig Guest House
Ancrum, nr Jedburgh TD8 6UN
TEL (01835) 830280
Two miles from Ancrum, this house enjoys fine views. The interior retains many original features. Comfortable bedrooms.
£ April to Oct; 3 rooms; games room; credit cards not accepted

GALASHSIELS
Woodlands Country House
Windyknowe Road, Galashiels
TD1 1RG
TEL/FAX (01896) 754722
Imposing baronial mansion with architectural curiosities. The cosy bar sports a tartan carpet; good food in the formal dining-room. Comfortable bedrooms.
£-££ All year; 10 rooms

INNERLEITHEN
Caddon View Guest House
14 Pirn Road, Innerleithen EH44 6HH
TEL (01896) 830208
Beautifully kept gardens and a well-cultivated vegetable plot surround this large stone house, set back from the main road on the edge of town. Breakfast is served in a smart dining-room; dinner and packed lunches are available by arrangement. The owner's son has a small restaurant at the rear of the house which is open at weekends.
£ All year exc last two weeks Jan; 5 rooms; credit cards not accepted

The Ley
Innerleithen EH44 6NL
TEL/FAX (01896) 830240
Lovely guesthouse above Leithen Water, accessible via winding road past a golf course and set in 30 acres of garden and woodland. The drawing-room is full of antiques and comfortable sofas and food at the Ley is delicious. Spacious, elegant bedrooms contain luxury extras such as sherry.
£-££ Mid-Feb to mid-Oct; 3 rooms; credit cards not accepted

69

JEDBURGH
Hundalee House
Jedburgh TD8 6PA
TEL (01835) 863011
Georgian manor in grounds above
Jed Water. Country-house
splendour predominates. Enormous
Scottish breakfasts served. Modern-
style bedrooms
£ *Closed Nov to Mar; 5 rooms,
credit cards not accepted*

The Spinney
Langlee, Jedburgh TD8 6PB
TEL/FAX (01835) 863525
A modern bed and breakfast two
miles from Jedburgh. The interior is
spotless and the sitting-room restful.
Bedrooms have and flowery prints.
£ *Closed Dec to Feb; 3 rooms; credit
cards not accepted*

KELSO
Bellevue House
Bowmont Street, Kelso TD5 7DZ
TEL (01573) 224588
After 1860, this house was the home
of a celebrated local poet and angler.
Recently taken over, the hotel is
now partly refurbished. Guests use a
comfortable lounge; evening meals
are served by arrangement in the
dining-room and packed lunches are
available. Bedrooms are comfortable;
some share a bathroom.
£ *All year; 9 rooms*

Ednam House
Bridge Street, Kelso TD5 7HT
TEL (01573) 224168
FAX (01573) 226319
Guesthouse by the Tweed dating
from Georgian times. Most of the
guests are anglers, and reels and rods,
stuffed fish and angling prints offset
original cornicing and plaster reliefs.
There are two bars and three lounges;
food is traditional. The bright and
airy bedrooms are well furnished.
£-££ *All year exc Chr and 1 Jan;
32 rooms; drying-room*

Sunlaws House Hotel
Heiton, Kelso TD5 8JZ
TEL (01573) 450331
FAX (01573) 450611
Part of a ducal estate, Sunlaws is a
friendly hotel in 200-acre grounds.
An octagonal tower dominates the
building. Ancestral portraits hang in
the formal Green Roxburghe room;
the drawing-room and conservatory
are elegant. Excellent food, with a
good Scottish cheeseboard. Spacious
bedrooms, decorated in country-
house style.
£££ *All year; 22 rooms;
drying-room; fishing; tennis; shooting;
croquet; health and beauty salon (See
Where to Eat)*

LONGFORMACUS
Eildon Cottage
Longformacus, nr Duns TD11 3PB
TEL (01361) 890230
A grey house with dormer windows
and a pretty garden, Eildon Cottage
doubles as the village post office. It is
near the Southern Upland Way,
popular with walkers. The cottage is
comfortable and pleasantly decorated;
meals are served at a round table in
the bay window of the sitting-room
and packed lunches are available.
£ *All year exc Chr and New Year; 3
rooms; credit cards not accepted*

MELROSE
Burt's Hotel
Market Square, Melrose TD6 9PN
TEL/FAX (01896) 822285
Traditional hotel with friendly
service and good food. The smart
dining-room has a fishing
decoration scheme. Imaginative
suppers in the popular lounge bar;
tasty food in the dining-room.
Excellent breakfasts. Simply
furnished bedrooms, well equipped.
££ *All year; 22 rooms*

MOFFAT
Alba House
20 Beechgrove, Moffat DG10 9RS
TEL (01683) 220418
Charming terraced house on the
outskirts of town. Collections of
pottery and pictures decorate the
rooms. Packed lunches are available.
Spacious, comfortable bedrooms.
*£ All year exc Chr; 3 rooms; credit
cards not accepted*

Beechwood Country House Hotel
Harthope Place, Moffat DG10 9RS
TEL (01683) 220210
FAX (01683) 220889
Excellent service at this country
house set in 12 acres overlooking
town. Guests enjoy pre-dinner drinks
around a crackling open fire.
Enjoyable cooking, with delicious
puddings and a good Scottish
cheeseboard. Bedrooms are
comfortable and well equipped.
*£ All year exc 2 Jan-15 Feb; 7 rooms;
drying-room*

Ericstane
Moffat DG10 9LT
TEL (01683) 220127
Working farmhouse in attractive
countryside outside Moffat. Simply
decorated with paintings and prints.
Breakfast only is served; packed
lunches are available. Large,
comfortable bedrooms.
*£ All year; 2 rooms; credit cards not
accepted*

Fernhill
Grange Road, Moffat DG10 9HT
TEL (01683) 220077
Hospitable guesthouse set in
elevated position overlooking the
Annan Hills. The large sitting-room
is decorated with pictures and
mementoes; breakfast only is served
in the pretty dining-room.
Comfortable bedrooms.
*£ Apr to Sept; 3 rooms; credit cards
not accepted*

Thai-Ville
3 Dundanion Place, Moffat DG10 9GD
TEL (01683) 220922
Small, modern bungalow in a quiet
residential street with a warm and
welcoming air. The owners' Thailand
travels inspired the name of the house.
Breakfast only is served, but a
complimentary supper tray is placed
in guests' rooms in the evening.
*£ Mid-Mar to mid-Nov; 2 rooms;
credit cards not accepted*

Well View
Ballplay Road, Moffat DG10 9JU
TEL (01683) 220184
FAX (01683) 220088
Carefully run Victorian house. Tables
in the pastel blue dining-room are
highly polished; food is inventive. The
cheerful bedrooms have co-ordinated
furnishings.
*£-££ Closed 2 weeks in Jan and
Feb; 6 rooms (See Where to Eat)*

NENTHORN
Whitehill Farm
Nenthorn, nr Kelso TD5 7RZ
TEL/FAX (01573) 470203
A Victorian farmhouse on a working
farm in the Cheviots. Visitors can
walk around the farm. Inside the
large sitting-room has an open fire.
Evening meals are served by
arrangement. Spacious bedrooms.
*£ All year exc Chr, New Year and
variable periods; 4 rooms, most with
wash-basin*

PEEBLES
Cringletie House
Peebles EH45 8PL
TEL (01721) 730233
FAX (01721) 730244
Set in beautiful gardens, this
baronial house boasts wonderful
views over the hills. A family-run
country-house hotel with delightful
service, it has a book-lined library
bar and choice of lounges. Food is a

blend of traditional and modern. Cheerful bedrooms, some with fine antiques.

££ Closed 2 Jan to 8 Mar; 13 rooms; drying-room (See Where to Eat)

SELKIRK
Philipburn House

Selkirk TD7 5LS
TEL (01750) 20747
FAX (01750) 21690

An Austrian feel prevails at this Georgian house. The bar has heart-motif furniture; a split-level dining-room looks out over the swimming-pool. The slate-walled sitting-room is cosy. Menus utilise a range of traditions and there is a children's tea menu. Bright bedrooms furnished in pine.

££ All year; 2 cottages; 14 rooms, most with shower/wc; drying-room; badminton, outdoor heated swimming-pool

ST ABBS
Castle Rock

Murrayfield, St Abbs, Eyemouth TD14 5PP
TEL (01890) 771715
FAX (01890) 771520

All the bedrooms at this isolated Victorian house on cliffs above the harbour have sea views. Evening meals include a vegetarian dish. Well-equipped bedrooms.

£ Easter to end Oct; 4 rooms

WALKERBURN
Tweed Valley Hotel

Galashiels Road, Walkerburn EH43 6AA
TEL (01896) 870636
FAX (01896) 870639

Unpretentious country-house hotel enjoying glorious views over rolling hills and the Tweed. Rustic and generally old-fashioned, it has a large fishing clientele. The bar and lounge area are welcoming; there is a Wedgwood-blue ceiling in the smart dining-room. Floral bedrooms.

££ All year exc 25-26 Dec; 19 rooms; drying-room; sauna; solarium; mini-gym

WHERE TO EAT

Key: A ★ marks a place that is particularly good value for money

AUCHENCROW
Craw Inn ★

Auchencrow, Berwickshire TD14 5LS
TEL/FAX (01890) 761253

Child-friendly pub in a small hamlet not far from the coast and the A1. The tiny bar is balanced by a spacious dining area; standard pub fare on the menu, yet quality ingredients, a fresh approach and super puddings lift the cooking out of the ordinary. Wonderful value Sunday set lunches. Straightforward bargain wines and some good real ales. A real gem.

Open for food 12 to 2, 6 to 9 (midnight Thur and Fri); exc dinner Mon to Thur Jan to Mar

CANONBIE
Riverside Inn ★

Canonbie DG14 0UX
TEL (01387) 371295

A civilised country inn close to the border. Skilful cooking; with clever

use of seasonal produce; cheeses and breads are excellent. Fixed-price dinners served in the restaurant. Super wine list, good ciders and exemplary real ales.
Open for food Mon to Sat 12 to 2, 7.30 to 8.30; restaurant Mon to Sat 7.30 to 8.30; closed 2 weeks Nov, 25-26 Dec, 1 Jan, 2 weeks Feb

EAGLESFIELD
Courtyard ★
Eaglesfield DG11 3PQ
TEL (01461) 500215
This well-run pub-cum-restaurant serves good value meals and welcomes families. Good home-made puddings. Decent wines and beers.
Open for food Tue to Sun 12 to 2, 7 to 9; restaurant Sun 12 to 2, Tue to Sat 7 to 9

EDDLESTON
Horseshoe Inn ★
Eddleston EH45 8QP
TEL (01721) 730225
Victorian coaching-inn with traditional bar and restaurant. Imaginative blackboard specialities and a good children's menu; reasonably priced wines and good ales.
All week 12 to 2.30, 6 to 10, Sun 12.30 to 10.30, winter 12.30 to 9

INNERLEITHEN
Traquair Arms ★
Traquair Road, Innerleithen EH44 6PD
TEL (01896) 830229
Good food at this village inn-cum-hotel, where standard dishes are augmented by a good selection of vegetarian meals. Impressive selection of beers.
Open for food summer 12 to 9, winter 12 to 2, 5 to 9; restaurant Wed to Sun 7 to 9

KELSO
Sunlaws House Hotel
Heiton, Kelso TD5 8JZ
TEL (01573) 450331
FAX (01573) 450611
Steak, lamb and game are patriotic choices at this Borders mansion. Seafood is good; the Scottish cheeseboard is excellent.
All week 12.30 to 2, 7.30 to 9.30 (See Where to Stay)

MOFFAT
Well View
Ballplay Road, Moffat DG10 9JU
TEL (01683) 220184
FAX (01683) 220088
This repertoire at this gracious Victorian house is wide-ranging, the cooking inventive on a modest scale. The popular five-course dinners are created with prime ingredients and utilise recipes from all over the world. Laudable wine list.
All week 6.30 to 8.30, Sun to Fri 12.30 to 1.15 (See Where to Stay)

PEEBLES
Cringletie House
Peebles EH45 8PL
TEL (01721) 730233
FAX (01721) 730244
A well-stocked kitchen garden helps supply this Victorian mansion with fresh produce. Excellent traditional cooking enhanced by modern flourishes results in a fresh and varied menu for the four-course fixed-price dinner. Super puddings, both rich and refreshing. The wine list is praiseworthy.
All week 1 to 1.45, 7.30 to 8.30 (See Where to Stay)

ST MARY'S LOCH
Tibbie Shiel's Inn ★
St Mary's Loch TD7 5NE
TEL (01750) 42231
Afternoon teas, dinners and bar meals all keep this bustling and

popular inn busy. Soup with home-baked bread and good old-fashioned puddings rank among favourites. Decent wine list and plenty of malt whiskies.

Open for food 12.30 to 2.30, 6.30 to 8.30, afternoon teas 3.30 to 6

SWINTON
Wheatsheaf Hotel ★

Four Seasons, Main Street, Swinton TD11 3JJ
TEL/FAX (01890) 860257
Friendly and informal country inn with French-influenced Scottish cooking. Seafood and game well treated, as are vegetables. Rich, comforting puddings. The international wine list is well priced.

Tue to Sun 12 to 2.15, Tue to Sat 6 to 9.30; closed 2 weeks end Feb, 1 week end Oct

TWEEDSMUIR
Crook Inn ★

Tweedsmuir ML12 6QN
TEL (01899) 880272
Claiming to be Scotland's oldest licensed premises, this inn has served some famous names over the years. A fairly standard pub menu, with enlivening modern Scottish flourishes. A fixed-price menu is offered in the restaurant. The good value wine list includes some unusual Scottish wild infusions. Fine malt whiskies.

Open for food 11 to 10; restaurant (residents only) 6.30 to 8.30

THE SOUTH-WEST

- A rocky and, in part, marshy coast surrounding an often lonely interior of moor or pastureland, tree-covered hills and isolated lochs
- A past of religious and political turbulence, well illustrated by Christian monuments and fortified castles
- Robert Burns' home country
- A good variety of towns and villages, most of them tranquil and neatly kept

Statue of Robert Burns

Dumfries and Galloway, divided into ridges and valleys by south-flowing rivers, take up most of the broad bulge of land of south-west Scotland. Nearly a quarter of the country is covered by trees, mostly Sitka spruce plantations, and further vast tracts are barely inhabited moorland. Merrick rises high out of the compact central group of mountains that dominate the Galloway Forest Park.

The coastline dithers between ragged and smooth, the shoreline between murky brown mudflats at the eastern end of the Solway Firth, and rocky or sandy beaches at the wilder western end where smugglers once beached contraband. This is not an area plagued by mass tourism, and you are less likely to find ice-creams and postcard stands than to come across solitary birdwatchers lurking beside the mudflats, or waiting for rarities in the coastal nature reserves.

The Ayrshire coast to the north-west extends from near Stranraer in the south to the mouth of the Clyde and Glasgow's outskirts in the north. Here are long stretches of beach (often monopolised by Glaswegian weekenders) and some of the least expensive golf courses in Scotland. Nearby islands decorate the horizon, so the seaward views are frequently splendid. One such island, Arran, is only a short hop by ferry from Ardrossan, and provides a rugged contrast to the gentle farmland of the mainland. Inland, Ayrshire is strewn with small, once prosperous coal or weaving towns from the eighteenth and nineteenth centuries.

Most visitors come to the South-West on the trail of Robert Burns, who was born near Ayr and died in Dumfries, and the figure of Scotland's most famous poet is apt to eclipse the region's other claims to fame. Burns trails, sights, souvenirs and postcards are inescapable, but this corner of Scotland had influence long before the 'Ploughman-Poet' was born.

Galloway was the site of the earliest Christian settlement in Scotland, for St Ninian founded his *candida casa* here in the early fifth century, and the region has some important early Christian monuments, and three fine abbeys from later centuries. During the persecution of Covenanters following the Restoration of Charles II, this part of Scotland became the last refuge of the most extreme Presbyterian sects.

Galloway gets its name from the Gall-Ghaidhil, the stubborn Norse-Gaelic peoples who kept the South-West a thorn in the flesh of the Scottish kings until the thirteenth century. When the region had been assimilated into feudal

Scotland, it became the fief of powerful families, among them Bruce, Douglas, Maxwell and Johnstone. Their rise and fall can be traced in the ruined strongholds of the region. The many planned villages of the eighteenth century tell of a more peaceful life.

DUMFRIES

Unlike other villages and towns along the Solway coast, many of which are built of dour granite, Dumfries is largely reddish sandstone. Its handsome Georgian and Victorian buildings are set along tidy streets, and the broad River Nith has a weir, wide banks and bridges of every dimension and age.

The old town nestles within a bend of the river. The wide esplanade, Whitesands, once teemed with cattle on market days; nowadays, it is cars and buses that are nose to tail. One of Scotland's oldest streets, Friars' Vennel, leads from the river up to the now pedestrianised centre of the town.

Almost certainly an important Roman settlement, this gateway to Galloway was made a royal burgh in the twelfth century. Edward I seized the castle (now gone but commemorated by a street name) in 1301. The weightiest event in the town's history came five years later when King Robert the Bruce murdered his rival, the Red Comyn (see the box on page 82). Dumfries suffered at the hands of the rampaging English several times during the fifteenth and sixteenth centuries, and little of the medieval town remains.

Most sights concern the poet Robert Burns, and all are listed on the *Burns Heritage Trail* leaflet available from the Tourist Information Centre. The town is the best touring base on the Solway coast, with good shopping facilities, and accommodation and restaurants ranging from simple to fairly grand.

In and near Dumfries

The slightly listing **Midsteeple**, in the High Street, was built in 1707 to provide more prison space, a town council meeting house, a courtroom and, almost as important, the town's first steeple. A table gives distances to far-flung cattle markets, and a relief map shows Dumfries as it was in Burns' time. Burns' favourite howff (tavern), the **Globe Inn**, further along the High Street, is a long, whitewashed pub,

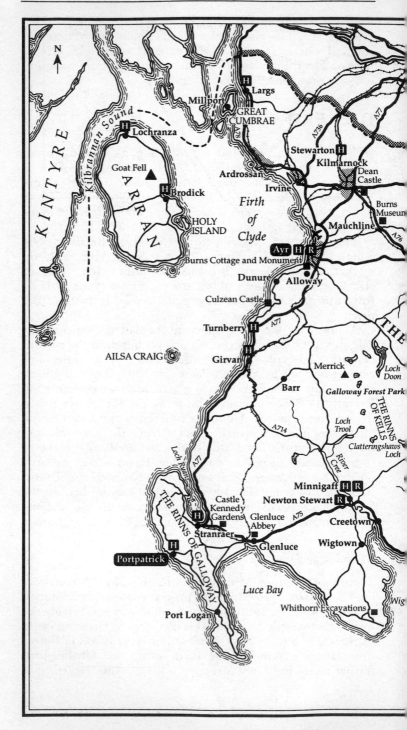

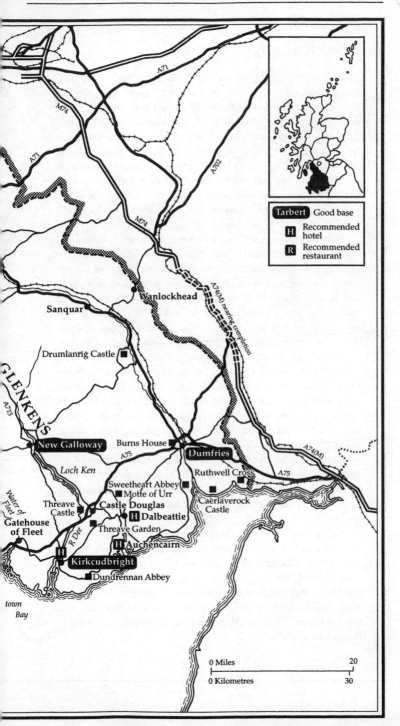

Tarbert — Good base
H — Recommended hotel
R — Recommended restaurant

A71
M74
A71
A702
M74
A74(M) nearing completion
Wanlockhead
Sanquar
Drumlanrig Castle
GLENKENS
A713
New Galloway
Burns House
A75
Dumfries
A74(M)
A75
Loch Ken
Ruthwell Cross
Sweetheart Abbey
Motte of Urr
Caerlaverock Castle
Water of Fleet
Threave Castle
Castle Douglas
H Dalbeattie
Gatehouse of Fleet
Threave Garden
R Dee
H Auchencairn
H Kirkcudbright
Dundrennan Abbey
town Bay

0 Miles — 20
0 Kilometres — 30

Practical suggestions

Many people have been through Dumfries and Galloway. From England you must cross it to reach Stranraer or Cairnryan for the ferries to Northern Ireland. And you must drive through part of it to reach the Highlands and central Scotland. Comparatively few come for a holiday, which, as tourist offices are eager to point out, gives it that desirable 'undiscovered' status. The South-West is also sparsely populated, so you can expect space and little traffic. It would not be the first choice for new visitors to Scotland, however, since the scenery and sights are not the best that Scotland has to offer.

Bird-watching, golfing, swimming, fishing, boating and camping are major holiday activities here. Good golf courses – links in most cases – are plentiful and notable for being neither stuffy nor pricey. For the best beaches, head for the western end of the Solway Firth or the southern Ayrshire coast. The many lochs and bays offer good fly and coarse fishing as well as sea-angling, and the season, unlike that in England, is open. The few mountains are not spectacular and they are surrounded by forestry plantations, but there is greater scenic variety in the coastal regions. The narrow Rinns of Galloway has miles of remote coastline. Offshore islands, such as Arran and Cumbrae, are compact and satisfying for the island-hungry visitor who does not wish to venture to the more remote islands to the north. On Arran, there is golfing, water-skiing, sea-angling, yachting, bicycling and pony-trekking.

Gardens thrive in the acid soil and the warm and moist air brought by the Gulf Stream, and the region's public gardens, Threave and Kennedy, for instance, are known throughout Britain for their variety of flora, including many tropical species.

Sights associated with Robert Burns, concentrated around Dumfries and Ayr, are plentiful, and illuminate both his life and times. Amongst the best are his house in Dumfries, now a small museum; his farm (Ellisland), just north of Dumfries; the thirteenth-century bridge, Brig o' Doon, near Ayr, which features in his poem, Tam O'Shanter; and the Bachelors' Club in Mauchline, a fascinating museum of Burns memorabilia.

The Tourist Board's *Burns Heritage Trail* leaflet describes all the major and minor Burns sights.

The South-West has plenty of good caravan parks, many in out-of-the-way, seaside settings. Hotels, guesthouses and bed and breakfast accommodation are concentrated in and around towns or near tourist spots around the coast.

Good bases

● **Dumfries** An obvious stop-over en route to Ireland or the Ayrshire coast and a convenient base for touring eastern Dumfries and Galloway, Dumfries is an upbeat sort of place. It has a busy centre, wide winding river and solid, ruddy Victorian architecture, and is well stocked with hotels, bed and breakfasts and restaurants. In and around it, there is no shortage of things to do and see. Fans of Robert Burns can pass several days without leaving town. The new by-pass has improved life for visitors and residents alike.

● **Kirkcudbright** Old but spry, the capital of the district of Stewartry has many virtues: riverside setting, quirky architecture, handsome broad streets, plenty of craft and antique shops and good sightseeing. It manages to feel intimate yet is large enough to cater to fussy tourists, and is not commercialised. Its position along the Solway Firth is handy for water-minded visitors.

● **New Galloway** The smallest royal burgh in Scotland sits on the River Ken with Loch Ken to the south. It would be an obvious base for anglers using these waters, but the Galloway Forest Park is also nearby. There is only one main street so you could soon exhaust its facilities, but it is a cheerful town.

● **Portpatrick** Situated on the stormy western side of the Rinns of Galloway, this fetching little harbour town fills up with tourists in summer. There is lots of self-catering hereabouts, as well as a large hotel and harbour-side pub.

● **Ayr** A good departure point for visiting the Ayrshire coast, with fast roads up and down, and resort facilities right in town. Ayr's race course is one of Scotland's best. The town's fame is based on its close links with Robert Burns, and there are plenty of associated sights. Shops and restaurants are sophisticated, and accommodation ample.

worth visiting for the small dining-room with its period furniture and the poet's favourite chair.

The family rooms and study of **Burns House** in cobbled Burns Street (open all year, Mon to Sat 10 to 1, 2 to 5, Sun 2 to 5; Oct to Mar, closed Sun, Mon) now constitute a small museum, furnished in the style of the poet's day and displaying a good cross-section of letters and personal ephemera (snuff mills, sword stick and gun, for example). The original box bed is the one in which he died. Look for his name on a window pane in the tiny study where he wrote over a hundred poems and songs; though he may have scratched it in frustration over a temperamental muse, he seemed to fancy this form of calling card — look for his autograph in the glass at the Globe Inn, too. Burns spent the last three years of his life in this house and was buried a few hundred yards away, in **St Michael's Churchyard**. First

ROBERT THE BRUCE (1274–1329)

'The Bruce' remains a revered half-legendary figure to many Scots, perhaps because of the fact that his ambition and persistence culminated in success against the odds, but more importantly because his reign marks the emergence of a distinctly Scottish patriotism from among the welter of Anglo-Norman and Celtic loyalties.

Robert the Bruce was grandson of that Robert Bruce whose claim to the Scottish throne Edward I of England had rejected. His behaviour during Edward's invasion of Scotland in 1296 had been ambiguous and indeed his name appears on the 'Ragmans Roll' of Scots who had sworn allegiance to Edward at Berwick. But in 1306 Robert Bruce killed his rival John Comyn in the church of Greyfriars at Dumfries, laying himself open to charges of murder, treachery and sacrilege. His reaction was to make a bid for power, and he had himself crowned King of Scots at Scone.

His revolt against Edward seemed doomed. He was defeated almost at once by the Earl of Pembroke near Methven; within a year three of his brothers were captured and executed, and his wife and daughter imprisoned. Bruce fled, possibly to Arran, spending the winter as an excommunicated outlaw. The spring of 1307 saw him back in Scotland, in Galloway. He won a skirmish with the English

interred in 1796 in one of the closely packed graves (several of which are those of Covenanters), his body was transferred 21 years later to a more imposing, if inappropriate, Grecian-style domed and pillared mausoleum.

The **Robert Burns Centre**, in a converted grain mill on the riverbank opposite Whitesands, is a modern, well-organised display with a 20-minute audio-visual show to take you through the poet's life and works (open Apr to end Sept, Mon to Sat 10 to 8, Sun 2 to 5; Oct to Mar, Tue to Sat 10 to 1, 2 to 5). There is a café, and from the riverside picnic tables you get a fine view of the weir (or caul) and most of the town. The little **Old Bridge House Museum** (open Apr to late Sept, Mon to Sat 10 to 1, 2 to 5, Sun 2 to 5) is packed with furniture and everyday articles (as well as some chilling dental instruments), covering the Edwardian and Victorian as well as Burnsian periods.

who were pinning him in Glen Trool, and beat them more thoroughly at Ayr. But his real salvation in July of that year was the death of Edward I, who was already in Cumberland on his way north to flatten Bruce for once and for all. Edward II had no stomach for the Scottish campaign, and Bruce was left to himself.

He still had plenty of enemies within Scotland, but his greatest, the Comyns, were beaten at Inverurie and their lands of Buchan mercilessly harried. He then turned on the MacDougalls of the west while his supporters cleared south-west Scotland. The French King secretly recognised him and the clergy, despite his excommunication, gave him support. English-occupied castles fell one by one, and Bruce instigated the sensible policy of dismantling many of them so that they could not again be used against him.

With the Battle of Bannockburn in 1314 (see page 272), Bruce set the seal on his military success. Political success followed only some years later with a thirteen years' truce with England in 1323, the absolution of Bruce by the Pope in 1328 and the recognition by England of Scottish independence in the same year.

Bruce, increasingly ailing, was unable to go on crusade as he had vowed. Sir James Douglas, one of his companions from the start, promised to take his heart to the Holy Land (he was killed fighting Saracens in Spain and the heart was supposedly brought home to Melrose Abbey). Bruce died, possibly of leprosy, in 1329, and was buried at Dunfermline.

SOUTH-EAST FROM DUMFRIES

Caerlaverock Castle

(HS, standard times)
Some seven miles south of Dumfries, this is one of the most striking castles in Scotland, thanks to its unique triangular shape, double-towered gatehouse, water-filled moat and earthen rampart. On flat land by the shore, it may have been built on the site of an old Roman harbour. This stronghold of the powerful Maxwell family was probably built around 1290 and suffered its first siege in 1300 when Edward I of England captured it. His chronicler left an account of the ruthless efficiency with which the siege was conducted. Restored during the fifteenth and sixteenth centuries, the castle fell to the Covenanters in 1640, when it was partially demolished. What remains is very much a mix of styles, from the massive defensive walls of the fourteenth- and fifteenth-centuries to the Renaissance elegance of Lord Nithsdale's Building (1634), which stands within the walls. In complete contrast to the fortified exterior, this is a stately, three-storeyed dwelling built during the relatively tranquil reign of James VI. Much of it still stands.

Caerlaverock Wildfowl and Wetlands Centre

The flat, grassy moorland and endless mudflats of this coast attract birds in their millions, and at any time of year you can wander around and enjoy the wildlife. Amongst the many birds that live or come to feed and rest after their long migrations at the Caerlaverock Wildfowl and Wetlands Centre (open daily 10 to 5) are Bewick's swan, the white-fronted goose and at least nine species of duck. Towers and hides are well arranged by several ponds for close-up views. If you hit the right day in late September you will see the sky darken as the entire Spitzbergen flock of barnacle geese (around 10,500) arrive to winter here. Caerlaverock also has the northernmost colony in Britain of the rare natterjack toad.

Ruthwell

The small town of Ruthwell is home to the world's first savings bank (now a small museum), founded in 1810. The most important sight here is the early eighth-century **Ruthwell Cross** (HS, access from keyholder at all reasonable times; details at site) in the parish church. Eighteen feet tall, rising majestically from a sunken pit, the grey stone cross is Northumbrian rather than Pictish work. Runes spell out parts of the earliest-known Anglo-Saxon poem, *The Dream of the Rood*. The thin sides are carved with more runes and decorative birds and beasts entwined. The cross-piece is modern, but hard to distinguish from the original shaft.

NORTH AND WEST OF DUMFRIES

Nithsdale

Nithsdale runs along the fertile Nith valley from Dumfries north to Sanquhar. The A76, the old stage-coach route from Dumfries to Glasgow, stays fairly close to the river, threading its way through pastures, pine trees and moorland.

Six miles north of Dumfries, the road passes the single-storeyed **Ellisland Farm** (open at all reasonable times), which Burns leased with the proceeds of the Kilmarnock edition of his poems. It is still a working farm and, though a popular tourist attraction, is refreshingly low-key, although it has recently been refurbished and an audio-visual added. Burns memorabilia and period furniture are displayed in several rooms warmed by real coal fires. (One is in a kitchen range which Burns himself installed.) Old farming machinery and methods are displayed and explained in the granary. Burns made his last futile stab at experimental farming at Ellisland during 1788. Poetry came easier: he wrote *Tam O'Shanter* during his stay here.

Drumlanrig Castle

(Castle and park open late Apr to late Aug, daily 11 to 5) This theatrical, turreted quasi-palace surrounded by lawns and peacocks is now owned by the Duke of Buccleuch, although it was built in the seventeenth century for William Douglas, the first Duke of Queensberry. Inside, the collection of paintings rivals that of the other great Buccleuch house at Bowhill and includes the last oil painting by Leonardo da Vinci to remain in private hands – the *Madonna with the Yarnwinder* – and Rembrandt's marvellous *Old Woman Reading*. There is much of Scottish interest, too, including memorabilia of Mary Queen of Scots and of Prince Charles Edward Stuart, who spent a night here on his long retreat from Derby.

Wanlockhead

On the B797, at 1,409 feet above sea level in a dip in the Lowther Hills, Wanlockhead is Scotland's highest village and a correspondingly bleak place. From the Middle Ages until 1928 it was the centre of Scottish metal mining: gold and silver have both been found here, but lead was always the mainstay of the industry. At the **Museum of Scottish Lead Mining** (open Easter to Oct, daily 11 to 4.30; Nov to Mar weekends by appointment, call 01659 74387) you can visit a slightly claustrophobic mine with tool marks on the walls and abandoned machinery, and admire the carefully restored water-powered beam engine.

Not far away, **Sanquhar** (on the A76) boasts the world's oldest working post office and a museum of Nithsdale life in the restored Tolbooth.

Glenkiln Reservoir

This clear blue lake off the A75 west of Dumfries has become a tourist attraction because of the sculptures poised around it. The most famous, Henry Moore's *King* and *Queen*, have been removed after a vandal decapitated the king, but others, including works by Rodin and Epstein, remain.

SOUTH OF DUMFRIES

There are enough things to see on the 35-mile circular route from Dumfries via the A710 and the A711 to take up a day. The village of New Abbey is not a peaceful place because the main road bisects it, and parking, other than in the abbey car park, is almost impossible. However the thirteenth-century **Sweetheart Abbey** (HS, standard times; closed Thur pm and Fri in winter) must be seen. This was the last of Galloway's three Cistercian monasteries to be founded. It is big, red, remarkably complete, and has a romantic history to go with its lovely setting. The abbey was founded in 1273 by Dervorguilla de Balliol (mother of the luckless 'Toom Tabard', whom Edward I chose to be puppet king of Scotland) in memory of her husband with whom she founded Balliol College at Oxford. Devastated by his death in 1268, she carried his embalmed heart in a casket around with her during the 22 years she outlived him, and was buried with it. Little remains of the monastic buildings apart from the abbey church itself. Though the church is roofless, the wheel and lancet windows on the west wall and the arches of the nave are in amazingly good shape.

Arbigland is the birthplace of John Paul Jones (1747–92), father of the American Navy. His cottage can be seen in the grounds of the private stately home, but most people come for the gardens and beach (open May to Sept, daily 2 to 6; closed Mon exc public holidays). Huge pine trees, fine lawns, a handsome rose garden and a water garden are formally arranged but there are no 'keep off the grass' signs. A broad tree-lined avenue leads to a wide, often empty beach, with the Cumbrian mountains visible across the Solway Firth. You can picnic as well as swim here, and there is a tea-room.

Sandyhills Bay, near the junction with the B793, is wide and curved, with fine sand and craggy rocks. It is never crowded, unlike the popular beaches at Southerness Point to the east, perhaps because it is one of the few places in the whole region where you have to pay to park. **Kippford** and **Rockcliffe**, yachting and fishing villages with a population of just over 100, are reached via a short detour at Colvend.

The sixteenth-century, L-shaped **Drumcoltran Tower** (always open) is north of the A711. Severe, square and built to last, it stands amongst trees next to several eighteenth-century farm buildings. High above the door a Latin inscription exhorts: 'Keep hidden what is secret; speak little; be truthful; avoid wine; remember death; have pity.' There was some concession to creature comforts indoors, with heated bedrooms and vented latrines. The view from the parapet over gentle hills takes some beating.

Dalbeattie to Castle Douglas

Dalbeattie can claim some fame for having supplied granite to build London's Embankment and the Bank of England. Most of the town's buildings are also granite, and there is an old-fashioned feel to the place. A pleasant riverside park has a good play area.

Two miles north of the town, just off the B794, is one of Scotland's largest twelfth-century motte and bailey castles, the **Motte of Urr** (always open). This is one of the best examples of the type of defensive structures built by the earliest Norman settlers in Scotland. The motte, a tall, pudding-shaped mound surrounded by a ditch, sits inside and at one end of an oblong outer ditch, 164 yards long. You will need an Ordnance Survey map to locate it as there are no signposts.

Castle Douglas, the site of an ancient settlement, is now an orderly market town laid out on a grid. The 100-acre Carlingwark Loch, on the town's southern border, has two crannogs (artificial islands created from logs driven into the bottom) that served as protection for Bronze Age homesteads.

Threave Garden

(NTS, garden open all year, daily 9.30 to sunset, walled garden and glasshouses 9.30 to 5; visitor centre open Apr to end Oct, daily 9.30 to 5.30) Threave Garden, a training centre for gardeners, is one of the wonders of Scotland's South-West, although it suffered badly in the winter of 1995. The range of plants and flowers is impressive, especially of heather, and it is colourful even on wintry days. However, it is the composition and design, by students and staff from the horticultural school, that make Threave exceptional. In all directions are delicate patterns, shapely bushes and, beyond, pastures that seem to have been designed to match.

Threave Castle

An expedition to the fourteenth-century Douglas or Threave Castle (HS, standard times; closed in winter; charge includes ferry trip), which begins with a ten-minute walk and a two-minute ferry ride, is great fun. The tall rectangular tower is in fine shape, despite being taken by the Covenanters in 1640, and its stark outline and remote site on a small, flat, grassy island on the River Dee give it added appeal, the more so in grey weather. A fittingly large stronghold of the Black Douglases, and the last of their castles to surrender to James II during his campaign to bring the over-mighty family to heel, Threave later became a Maxwell seat. The five-storey tower, with a room on each floor, connected by a spiral stair, follows the conventional pattern for fourteenth-century towers, if on a rather larger scale than usual. The scramble to the top is rewarded by timeless views from all levels · and in all directions. Archaeological excavations conducted this century have uncovered Scotland's most complete medieval riverside harbour, a small but remarkably well-preserved walled inlet.

Dalbeattie to Kirkcudbright

Four miles south of Dalbeattie, well off the A711 in remote farmland, sits the fifteenth-century **Orchardton Tower** (HS, access from keykeeper at all reasonable times; details at site), as solid and austere as other self-respecting castles, but unique in Scotland for its cylindrical shape, a pattern common in Ireland. It is in good condition, but do not go too near the low parapet if you dislike heights.

Further along, beside the A711, stand the pinkish-grey ruins of the once formidable **Dundrennan Abbey** (HS, standard times, closed Thur pm and Fri; closed in winter), probably founded by King David in 1142 to become one of Galloway's three Cistercian abbeys (the others are Glenluce and Sweetheart). On 15 May 1568, Mary Queen of Scots stopped here on the last day of her flight after the Battle of Langside. The next day she sailed across the Solway Firth to Workington and to her final exile. The abbey passed into secular use at the Reformation and by the seventeenth-century had been substantially dismantled to provide building stones for the town. The north and south transepts and chapter house are in reasonable condition; the carving throughout is exceptional. The transition from Romanesque to Gothic can be seen in the pointed and semi-rounded arches, and while the nave is missing, a row of column bases and wall foundations mark the aisle.

KIRKCUDBRIGHT

At the mouth of the Dee halfway along the Solway coast, Kirkcudbright is arguably the most delightful town in the whole of the South-West (especially when the tide is in). It is thus a popular tourist haunt, but neither commercialised nor self-consciously gentrified. The likely origin of the name is the Kirk of St Cuthbert; his bones are said to have spent some time in the ancient church. Colourful houses flank the L-shaped High Street, the west side of which is the most ancient part of town. Several of them have dormer windows on sloping roofs and a few are Georgian. Despite the sprawling car park in Harbour Square it is not hard to appreciate how the seventeenth-century town might have looked, with the houses splayed out behind the castle and harbour. With its quaint houses and bobbing boats in the harbour, Kirkcudbright is an artists' colony. Dorothy L. Sayers often visited the town, and set her novel *Five Red Herrings* here.

In and near Kirkcudbright

• **MacLellan's Castle** (HS, standard times; weekends only in winter), the town's most easily spotted attraction, stands overlooking the harbour at the junction of High, Castle and St Cuthbert Streets. A grand tower-house sitting in the middle of a small green, it was built by Thomas MacLellan of Bombie, provost of Kirkcudbright, at the end of the sixteenth century. The fortified exterior of turrets and gun-loops is deceptive: the interior was conceived as a well-organised dwelling. More than a dozen rooms were heated, and there were large windows and enclosed water-closets. A huge fireplace dominates the great hall, and within it is a spy-hole or 'laird's lug', used for keeping tabs on guests and staff. MacLellan's heirs were ruined following their support of the royalist cause, and it is unlikely that anyone lived in the castle after the end of the seventeenth century. MacLellan's elaborate monument, showing him in a full suit of armour, is in nearby Greyfriar's Church.

● **Tolbooth** (same opening times as Stewartry Museum below.) Where the High Street turns a corner, the large Tolbooth looks rather like a church. It is half a century younger than the castle, and an endearing jumble of different stones and styles. Both ends, including the spired tower, were added on to the original building. On the forestair is a corroded stone mercat cross and iron 'jougs', used to shackle offenders for public ridicule. At the base is a well.

● The **Stewartry Museum** in St Mary Street is sure to entertain (open Mar, Apr and Oct, Mon to Sat 11 to 4; May, Mon to Sat 11 to 5; June, Sept, Mon to Sat 11 to 5, Sun 2 to 5; Jul, Aug, Mon to Sat 10 to 6, Sun 2 to 5; Oct, Mon to Sat 11 to 4; Nov to late Mar, Sat only 11 to 4). In the galleried main room is a first-rate collection of archaeological finds and bizarre objects including curling and quoiting gear, a crystal radio set, a witness box on castors, snuff-boxes and spinning materials. A small room is devoted to shipping, and in the upstairs gallery stuffed animals and birds occupy glass cases.

● **Broughton House** (open Apr to late Oct, daily 1 to 5.30), a specimen of Georgian architecture at its most dignified was bequeathed to the town by the painter E. A. Hornel, one of the 'Glasgow Boys' and a leader of the local artists' colony. The library is handsomely panelled. There are paintings, many by Hornel himself (Pre-Raphaelite meets Arthur Rackham), and a Japanese-style garden behind.

● **Tongland Power Station** (open May to early Sept, call 01557 330114 for details) This enormous hydro-electric power station mounts well-organised tours that collect you in Kirkcudbright and carry you off to the bold Art Deco headquarters two miles to the north. The one-and-a-half hour tour begins with a 15-minute video and a visit to the turbine hall. A mile's drive then takes you to the giant curved dam, which you can walk along.

THE COAST TO NEWTON STEWART

Gatehouse of Fleet and around

Sitting amongst green hills at the head of the Fleet estuary, Gatehouse of Fleet is a pretty, colourful town. In the eighteenth-century, the Murrays of Broughton built up a thriving cotton-spinning and weaving business here, along with tanning and brewing. Leave the town by the southern road and follow signs for Cally House Hotel to find the **Murray Forest Information Centre** and two-mile **Fleet Oakwoods Interpretive Trail**, which takes in the natural (broad-leaved trees, wetland flora, pheasants, woodpeckers, deer, foxes) and the man-made (twelfth-century Anglo-Norman motte and ditch), with explanation boards and demonstrations of tree maintenance along the way.

The fifteenth-century **Cardoness Castle** (HS, standard times; weekends only in winter), on top of a small neat hill just south of town, is set off by perfect lawns and especially pretty flower beds. Its four-storeyed, well-preserved mass is an object lesson in medieval castle building, with impressive defences (including inverted keyhole gunloops), well-organised accommodation (plenty of vented latrines, window benches, intramural vents) and more than a nod towards aesthetics (moulded fireplace surrounds). Note the 'murder hole' above the gateway, used for pouring boiling liquids on uninvited guests. The view from the top, which takes in the Water of Fleet, is magnificent. There are informative and readable signs everywhere. Look for the copperplate signature of John Bell, a frequently encountered early nineteenth-century graffiti enthusiast, on the outside wall by the entrance.

NEWTON STEWART

Newton Stewart lies on the banks of the Cree in a wooded valley. It is hard by the main A75 Carlisle to Stranraer route and is served by several major north–south roads, too. Like most of the towns of the South-West it is untouristy but not lacking in good tourist facilities. The **Newton Stewart**

Museum (open Apr to late Sept, Mon to Sat 2 to 5; Jul, Aug, Mon to Fri 10 to 12.30, 2 to 5; Jul to Sept, Sun 2 to 5), formerly St John's Church, on York Road above Victoria Street, has a fairly new collection and documentation of local and regional daily life. **Minnigaff**, across the bridge, is older and quainter than Newton Stewart. On working days you can watch mohair being woven at the **Creebridge Mill** (and visit the shop). Of Minnigaff's numerous prehistoric cairns, standing stones and circles, the best known are the **Thieves** standing stones beyond Cumloden, around five miles to the north of Minnigaff.

THE GLENKENS

The A713 from Castle Douglas to Ayr follows Galloway's largest glen through an area known as the Glenkens. The farmland, forest and moorland crisscrossed by rivers and lochs are typical of Galloway, but walks are well signposted and are less frequented than those in Galloway Forest Park just to the west. The mountains known as the Rinns of Kells rise to 2,600 feet above the forests lining the west of the A713 and form the boundary with Galloway Forest Park; a path runs along their ridge. The Glenkens are a good spot for fishing. The narrow **Loch Ken**, which meanders past flanks of pine trees, is home to roach, perch and pike. Sailing boats are found here, too (contact Galloway Sailing Centre 01644 420626), as are water-skiers. The River Ken, to the north of Dalry in an isolated valley, is autumn salmon-fishing territory.

GALLOWAY FOREST PARK

Covering 250 square miles of conifer plantation and open spaces in the middle of Scotland's south-west, Galloway Forest Park has a few sights and dozens of lochs and lochans. Merrick, at 2,776 feet, is its highest point. Most of the forest is traversed by well-marked trails, and the 200-mile Southern Upland Way passes through some of the South-West's most dramatic inland scenery.

The A712 between New Galloway and Newton Stewart is known as the Queen's Way. Along it you will find a wild goat enclosure and a red deer range, the large, artificial **Clatteringshaws Loch** (good views from outdoor picnic tables near the Wildlife Centre) and a boulder in a clearing against which Robert the Bruce supposedly leaned after winning the Battle of Rapploch Moss (1307). Named after the novel *The Raiders*, by S. R. Crocket, the unpaved, single-track Raiders Road off the main road (speed limit 20mph) follows the River Dee. You can see most of its ten-mile length from the Bennan Viewpoint. (The turn-off is signposted near Bennan just north of the eastern entrance of Raiders Road.)

Four miles of lovely road through Glentrool Forest wind, dip and climb, ending at the car park high above Loch Trool. The view over the loch, which takes in miles of lovely wilderness, must be the area's best. A plaque on Bruce's Stone just above the car park commemorates the Battle of Glentrool (1307). Park here if you are mounting an assault on Merrick.

Stroan Bridge, between Glentrool Village and Loch Trool, is good for less ambitious walking. Better still are the four marked trails in **Kirroughtree Forest**, just south of Glentrool, which take in a forest garden, lochs, long-distant views and disused lead mines.

The small town of **New Galloway** is a major lifeline for the Galloway Forest Park, and the region's smallest royal burgh. Along the one main street can be found all that any walker can ask for: sports shops, restaurants, and a reasonable choice of hotels and guesthouses, as well as the licensed Smithy tea-room.

THE MACHARS

This wide, triangular headland that points south between Wigtown and Luce Bays is fine touring country, well served by small roads that meander past whitewashed cottages and through the central farmlands patched with heather and gorse.

Wigtown is a sleepy burgh with one very wide street and a little museum. The **Martyrs' Monument** (also known as Windyhill Monument) stands on a hill above town. It is dedicated to two Covenanters, Margaret McLachlan and Margaret Wilson, who were tied to a stake and allowed to drown in the rising tide.

Nineteen knee-to-waist-high granite boulders make up the Bronze Age **Torhouse Stone Circle**, which overlooks a hilly, windswept plain a few miles west of Wigtown. Three larger stones, the purpose of which defies arch-aeologists, stand in the middle.

A mile south of Wigtown at **Bladnoch** is the south-west's only distillery (open Easter to late Oct, Mon to Fri 10 to 4.30, Sat 12 to 4).

Further south, **Whithorn** is the birthplace of Scottish Christianity, a part seventeenth-century town with brightly painted houses and a handsome broad avenue dotted with statues and trees. The name comes from the old English, 'hwit erne', meaning white house. The Latin equivalent, 'candida casa', was the name given to the church founded by St Ninian, Scotland's first saint. Its location is unknown, though Isle of Whithorn and Whithorn both lay claim. The **Whithorn, Cradle of Christianity Centre** (open Apr to late Oct, daily 10.30 to 5) combines exhibitions and information with a visit to the Whithorn dig, where the first known Christian church in Britain was discovered, as were numerous graves of early Christian settlers. You are likely to see archaeologists gingerly scraping away at the earth. Close by is a wattle and timber Viking house, reconstructed using evidence from the site. A small exhibition and audio-visual slide show tell of St Ninian's mission to convert the Picts.

You should also visit the **Priory** (open Apr to end Oct, daily 10.30 to 5) next to the excavations, where Mary Queen of Scots once stayed. It has a finely carved Romanesque south doorway and the vaulted crypt dates from the mid-fifteenth century. In the small museum next door (open Apr to end Oct, daily 10.30 to 5), are early Christian carved crosses and headstones, including the Latinus Stone, a crudely incised pillar stone which is Scotland's earliest known Christian artefact.

Rispain Camp, high up and overlooking valleys in all directions, is off the A746 just over half a mile south-west of Whithorn. Park in the farmyard and walk 100 yards or so up the hill. The large, rectangular earthwork, surrounded by a deep ditch with one entrance 'bridge', is well defined by its covering of mown grass. Radio-carbon-dating has established it at around 60 BC.

Isle of Whithorn is not an island but a pretty town built around a harbour. A walk along the wild bluff that overlooks the bay will probably be remembered longer than a visit to the thirteenth-century St Ninian's Chapel, or St Ninian's Cave, on the beach along the south-west point.

The Luce Bay coast between Monreith and Glenluce is one of the South-West's most beautiful. The road curves past sandy or rocky bays and steep headlands, sometimes rising high, then sweeping down. To reach **Monreith Bay**, follow signs to St Medan's golf course; you will pass an otter sculpture, memorial to Gavin Maxwell, author of *Ring of Bright Water*, on the right of the road, which ends in a peaceful sandy bay. A little further north along the main A747 at **Barsalloch Point** is the grass-covered Barsalloch Fort, dating from the end of the first millennium BC. The view from the top is more impressive than the fort itself. Thereafter the road hovers high over the rocky beaches of Luce Bay, then, in one dramatic sweep downwards, joins the shore just before the rather dour town of Port William.

GLENLUCE TO STRANRAER

Glenluce Abbey (HS, standard times; weekends only in winter) stands in a fertile valley near the Water of Luce, a mile north of the village of Glenluce. One of Galloway's three Cistercian monasteries, it was founded by Roland, Lord of Galloway, around 1191 as daughter-house of Dundrennan. Not much is left of the abbey church, but the chapter house, rebuilt in the fifteenth century, is an elegant, centrally pillared and vaulted room. Of particular interest is the sophisticated water-supply system consisting of inter-linking clay pipes and lidded junction boxes. Well-preserved remnants are displayed in the small museum, as are other finds such as cooking pots and coins.

Stranraer is a market town and Scotland's main port for ferries to Larne in Northern Ireland. It is also a holiday town, with a walled marine lake and leisure centre. The sixteenth-century **Castle** (the Old Castle of St John), on a square surrounded by shops, was a prison for Covenanters.

Just outside Stranraer, **Castle Kennedy Gardens** are amongst Scotland's finest. A tree-lined drive skirts the broad White Loch before arriving at the garden centre and tea-shop entrance to the monumental and formal gardens (open Easter to late Sept, daily 10 to 5), set on an isthmus between Black and White Lochs. The castle was home to the Stair family in the seventeenth century; it was ravaged by fire in 1716 and never rebuilt. The ruin is now almost entirely covered in ivy, and rises out of a seemingly endless velvety lawn. The gardens were almost as overgrown 150 years ago, and it was only luck that turned up the original plans to which they have since been tailored. Great expanses of lawn are bounded by tall trees and flowering shrubs, in particular rhododendrons, of which there are around 35 varieties. A broad grass avenue is lined with 100-year-old, 70-foot-tall monkey puzzle trees. Special to Castle Kennedy Gardens are the wide views of flower-edged lawn or lochs. If you go as far as Stair family's current home, the Victorian Lochinch Castle (recommended for its pretty sunken garden), you will see both lochs at once.

Meadowsweet Herb Garden (open May to late Aug, daily 12 to 5; closed Wed), on a promontory into Soulseat Loch, is only a little way south of Castle Kennedy but seems a world apart. A caravan acts as ticket booth, gift shop, even herbal tea bar. More than 100 herbs, organically grown, are compactly arranged. You are encouraged to rub the leaves and needles, so bring tissues to clean your fingers and keep scents distinct.

THE RINNS OF GALLOWAY

The narrow hammer-head protrusion off Scotland's extreme south-west corner is known as the Rinns of Galloway. As well as natural beauty, often turbulent seascapes and rocky, treeless headlands, the peninsula has several charming fishing villages and an excellent sub-tropical garden, yet is surprisingly uncommercialised.

Portpatrick

A likeable little harbour town, Portpatrick weathers its popularity well. Once a major port for importing Irish cattle (Northern Ireland is only 22 miles away), it lost out to Stranraer's larger and calmer waters in 1868. Fishing boats hide among the ranks of colourful craft. There are good boat trips, two golf courses, and the long-distance Southern Upland Way starts (or ends) here.

The Southern Rinns

The southern half of the Rinns is bleaker than the north, but there is more to see. All the sights are within easy reach of the A716, which winds past small coves on the east coast. The turn-off to the **Kirkmadrine Stones** is signposted south of Sandhead. A dirt track leads to a late nineteenth-century burial chapel. The earliest known Christian monuments after those at Whithorn – several pillar stones incised with crosses and Latin inscriptions – were found near where it stands and are now on display in its glassed-in porch.

Ardwell Gardens (open Apr to late Sept, daily 10 to 5) hold an impressive assortment of trees (including palms), a good rock garden, and, in spring, daffodils by the thousands. Better, however, is **Logan Botanic Garden** (open mid-Mar to late Oct, daily 10 to 6), an annexe of the Royal Botanic Gardens in Edinburgh and study centre for the Department of Agriculture and Fisheries for Scotland. There is a woodland and a walled garden; both are large and beautifully arranged. Proximity to two coasts makes for a subtropical microclimate ideal for exotic flora; what started a hundred years ago as a kitchen garden today boasts an enormous number of rare plants. Giant-leaved cabbage palms (actually of the lily family), tree ferns (palm tree shape, fern leaves) and Chusan palms with vast yellow flowers make a lovely jungle. Also commendable are the large salad bar/tearoom, and the low entrance fee.

Port Logan, like Portpatrick, is a small fishing village on the west coast, and was also a port for traffic from Ireland – witness the imposing jetty. At the natural but almost perfectly round fish pond, you can watch lunch being hand-fed to cod, pollack and plaice.

The **Mull of Galloway** is a narrow windswept headland with a car park and, at the edge of a 200-foot-high cliff, a lighthouse. Ireland and the Isle of Man are often visible.

The Northern Rinns

The northern part of the Rinns is largely pastureland, with more cows than trees. You can see Ireland and Ailsa Craig from its rocky shore on most days. Seabirds circle continuously, and the drive north from Stranraer along the western side of Loch Ryan is especially rewarding for birdwatching. The **Wig**, a wide, swooping bay, is a good viewing place, while **Lady Bay** a little further along is, by contrast, small and well protected, features that appealed to smugglers of the eighteenth century.

THE AYRSHIRE COAST

North of Stranraer

A favourite holiday destination for car-less Glaswegians once upon a time, this stretch of coast is now a weekenders' haunt. The A77 is also a major route linking the ferry ports of Stranraer and Cairnryan to Ayr and Glasgow. Consequently during the summer you can expect to be sandwiched between lorries as well as caravans.

The volcanic rock of **Ailsa Craig**, which lies ten miles off the coast, comes into view soon after you pass the ferry terminal at Cairnryan. It is also known as Paddy's Milestone because it lies midway between Glasgow and Belfast, and its strategic position at the mouth of the Firth of Clyde made it a convenient tolbooth for foreign sea traffic in past centuries. Now it is a bird sanctuary and source of fine red granite for curling stones. It can be reached on boat trips from Girvan (early Apr to late Oct, phone 01465 713219 for details).

The Victorian town of **Girvan** was once a major landing site for herring, but nowadays fishing boats are outnumbered by pleasure craft. This is one of Ayrshire's most popular resorts, thanks to its long beach, golf courses and amusement arcades. Inland in a high valley is **Barr**, the area's most picturesque village. The narrow River Stinchar runs right through the middle and small, whitewashed cottages line its banks.

Culzean Castle

(NTS, castle and visitor centre open Apr to late Oct, daily 10.30 to 5.30; other times by appointment, call 01655 760274; country park open all year, daily 9.30 to sunset)

From **Turnberry**, five miles north of Girvan and home to one of Ayrshire's top two golf courses (the other is at Troon), take the coastal A719 to reach Culzean Castle. The Robert Adam castle, the sensational clifftop setting above three miles of coastline, the woodland park and acres of gardens add up to a superb half-day visit. Start beside the car park at the Home Farm (now the information centre, exhibition, gift shop and restaurant complex), which is also by Adam and faithfully restored to his original design. The huge crenellated castle was built between 1772 and 1792 around a fortified medieval house. The size and the detail of the exterior are typically Scottish baronial but proportions have a graceful Georgian quality. The interior is opulently furnished, but with taste rather than ostentation. Shapes and dimensions are pleasing, especially in the oval staircase with its Greek columns; bright rooms look over the Firth of Clyde with views of sea and islands that almost upstage the interior. Adam's intricate plaster ceilings have been restored to the cool and subtle tones he intended.

The country park by the castle includes woodland, successfully designed to give shelter from sea gales, and a huge walled garden filled with herbaceous borders. At the large swan pond, also colonised by seagulls and ducks, there is a snack bar and aviary. A deer park and adventure playground are additional treats.

Crossraguel Abbey

(HS, standard times, closed Thur pm and Fri; closed in winter) A zigzag east from Culzean brings you to the noble ruins of Crossraguel Abbey. Founded in the early thirteenth century by Duncan, first Earl of Carrick, as a Cluniac monastery, it was plundered during the Wars of Independence and rebuilt in the fifteenth century. Its rich lands, a major prize during the Reformation, earned it more fame than its religious influence: probably no more than ten monks lived here in the fifteenth century. Little of the abbey still stands, but the chapter house, tower-house and dovecote are in fair shape.

Dunure

On the coast to the north is Dunure, a comely village with a miniature harbour and, near a cliff, the dilapidated **Dunure Castle**, one of the Kennedy family's residences. Mary Queen of Scots stopped here but the lay abbot of Crossraguel Abbey was a more noteworthy visitor, having been gently roasted on a spit by his host, the Earl of Cassillis, in 1570 to persuade him to hand over the abbey lands. (The coercion technique is said to have worked.)

On the A719 between Culzean Castle and Dunure, look for the sign marking the **Electric Brae**, an optical illusion best experienced travelling south: the road seems to slope downhill when in fact it climbs – an entertainingly jarring sensation.

Ayr and around

Ayr grew up around a castle which was destroyed by Robert the Bruce in 1298 to keep it from English hands. Today the town is important for commerce and tourism alike; a busy harbour, three golf courses and Scotland's foremost racecourse guarantee an unflagging pace of life. Three colourful parks are havens of peace and there are more than two miles of beach, looking out to Ailsa Craig and Arran. (Hope for clear weather: the sunsets are one of the town's unmissable sights.) However, modern Ayr has not made much of its sea and riverside setting. It might also frustrate Burns followers who come expecting the sights to match those in Dumfries. Robert Burns sights and memorabilia are neither as plentiful nor as rewarding, even if you include next-door Alloway; better are Mauchline and Tarbolton, not far inland. Nevertheless, souvenirs emblazoned with Burns' poems and portraits are everywhere. There is a good choice of places to stay, from cheap to expensive, a reasonable variety of restaurants, and plenty of craft and clothing shops.

On the south side of town is an accomplished statue of Burns by George Lawson, in pensive stance but with a whimsical expression; but its current setting is a disarray of modern buildings and noisy streets. In the centre of town, the Auld Kirk (parish church), at the end of Kirk Pont, is where the poet was baptised. Within the mellow stone archway at the entrance to the churchyard hang two huge iron mortsafes, once placed over coffins to thwart body snatchers. The cross-shaped church, built in 1653, was partly funded by Cromwell who dismantled its predecessor to build the armoury of his now mostly vanished fort. The churchyard, filled with several unusual sculpted bas-relief headstones, is wedged between the High Street and the river front, from where you can see all four bridges, including the thirteenth-century Auld Brig.

Loudoun Hall, in Boat Vennel near New Bridge, is one of Scotland's oldest houses, built by a wealthy merchant in 1503. It is one of the best examples of semi-fortified domestic architecture, and is nicely preserved. The balconies served for efficient slop hurling. Cromwell's fort is no longer, but a remnant of wall and turret stands at the corner of South Beach Road and South Harbour Street, giving an idea of its huge scale. Behind the Tourist Information Office, on Sandgate, is the compact **Queen's Court** shopping arcade, an ingenious restoration of Georgian and Victorian houses with old paving stones, lamp fittings and café tables.

On the northern side of Ayr, and merging with it, is **Prestwick**, as well known for its nearby airport as its resort facilities. **Troon**, not far beyond, is a much more appealing town. Off the main road, it has fine Edwardian and Victorian houses, quiet beaches and five 18-hole golf courses, including the Royal Troon, started in 1878.

Alloway

This small village, which blends into Ayr's leafy southern outskirts, is strictly for Robert Burns fans. The poet was born here and it was here that he set his epic poem, *Tam O'Shanter*. **Burns Cottage** makes a fitting first port of call (open Apr to end Sept, daily 9 to 6; end Sept to end Mar, Mon to Sat 10 to 4, Sun 12 to 4). William Burnes, the poet's father (his children dropped the 'e'), built the cottage and byre, now whitewashed and thatched, where Robert spent the first seven years of his life. The side-by-side rooms are as spartan today as they must have been then, unlike the gardens (dominated by four 100-year-old Irish yews) which have a pampered look. The first-rate small museum of manuscripts and ephemera accompanied by clear biographical panels has an original copy of the Kilmarnock edition of poems. The gift shop and tea-room are small but sufficient. The **Tam O'Shanter Experience** (open daily, 9 to 6) turns Burns' most famous poem into a multi-media event. Whether the poem actually benefits from being given this treatment is an open question. A gift shop and restaurant pad out the experience.

The **Auld Kirk** is a small and roofless chapel in a simple graveyard, hardly a mystical setting, but the spot where Tam witnessed 'warlocks and witches in a dance'. Just above it is the nineteenth-century **Burns Monument** (opening times as for Burns Cottage, above), a neo-classical, Corinthian-columned temple. Inside are a few oddments including a Bible owned by Burns' one-time fiancée, Highland Mary, and the wedding ring of his wife, Jean Armour. Come for a wander around the small garden packed with rare shrubs and lovely herbaceous borders, and for the view (best from the top of the Monument), which takes in the **Brig O'Doon**, the most picturesque of all stops on the Burns Heritage Trail. The small hump-backed bridge, which together with its reflection forms a neat O, spans a narrow river with lush banks and a backdrop of trees and fields. The bridge was Tam's means of escape, since witches, according to Burns' note to his poem, 'have no power to follow a poor wight any farther than the middle of the next running stream'.

INLAND FROM AYR

Robert Burns lived in and around **Mauchline** from when he was 18 until he was almost 30, and there is a plethora of sights – some with only vague associations – connected with him. Burns' parents had several farms around Mauchline and he married Jean Armour in the town. Their cottage is now

ROBERT BURNS (1759–1796)

Scotland's most famous poet was born in Alloway, a village just south of Ayr, on 25 January 1759. Hailed in his lifetime as 'ploughman-poet', Burns' agricultural antecedents appealed to the eighteenth-century idea that the well-springs of genius were the more intriguing for being found in a man of humble background.

In fact, Robert Burns, thanks to an intelligent and determined father, was an educated and well-read man. He read Ramsay, the Scottish poet, as well as Pope, Locke and Shakespeare. By the time he was 22, he had already worked in several agricultural jobs, without much success. Emigration to Jamaica seemed to be the solution to his problems. Though he had circulated manuscripts of his poems, none of his work was published until he was 27, but *Poems, Chiefly in the Scottish Dialect*, published in Kilmarnock in 1786, was an instant success.

He exchanged a pledge of marriage with Mary Campbell (Highland Mary), but in fact remained loyal (though far from faithful) to Jean Armour, whom he first declared his common-law wife at the age of 26. His womanising got him into trouble with the Presbyterian Kirk – a constant theme of Burns' best poetry is one of protest against the restrictions placed on mankind's freedom by artificial distinctions of birth, morals or custom.

He next published in Edinburgh, where he stayed and was fêted as literary hero for two winters, thereafter flinging himself into collecting, editing and writing the *Scottish Songs* which form such a large part of his work. In 1788, he moved, with his family, to Ellisland Farm north of Dumfries. A year later, after another failed attempt at agriculture, he moved to Dumfries and became a customs officer.

Burns hated hypocrisy and pomposity in all their forms, and there is little doubt that his most successful poems are the biting satirical pieces in Scots, such as *Holy Willie's Prayer*, though it is by such classic songs as *Auld Lang Syne* and the sanitised version of *Comin' Thro' the Rye* that he is often remembered. The cult of Burns – marked by Burns suppers held in his honour in Caledonian societies throughout the world – is often mawkish and sentimental. In fact, he was a tough, no-nonsense poet who loved sensual pleasures in the best tradition of his predecessors Ramsay and Fergusson.

He died at Dumfries in 1796 at the age of 37.

the **Burns Museum** (open Easter to end Sept, daily 9 to 6; end Sept to late Mar, Mon to Sat 10 to 4, Sun 12 to 4), notable more for displays of curling stones and local boxware than Burns memorabilia. Around the corner is **Poosie Nansie's Tavern** used as a setting in *The Jolly Beggars* and still serving good ale. The small but almost Disneyesque **Burns Memorial Tower** (open all year, Mon to Sat 9 to 5), to the north of the town, has had a facelift, and the poet's life and times are detailed on three floors.

A few miles west, in the centre of Tarbolton, the **Bachelors' Club** (NTS, open Apr to late Sept, daily 1.30 to 5.30; Oct, weekends 1.30 to 5.30; other times by appointment, call 01292 541940) is almost certain to intrigue. The top floor of this former inn was the meeting place for the debat-ing society started by Burns in 1780. The first debate concerned the relative merits of a woman with fortune but neither looks nor personality, and a poor woman with both attributes. The guided tour is detailed and erudite but also entertaining, with plenty of anecdotes to fire the imagination and bring to life the décor, manuscripts and paintings.

Dean Castle

Burns' first major collection of poems was published in 1786 in **Kilmarnock**, a town 13 miles north-east of Ayr. However, the main sight here has no association with the poet. Dean Castle (open daily 12 to 5, park dawn to dusk), the Boyd family's ancient home, stands on the northern outskirts of the town and, thanks to its variety, intimacy and informality, has high entertainment value for families. The compact fifteenth-century castle and fourteenth-century fortified keep are bursting both with fun and with worthy collections of musical instruments (lutes and small keyboards, in particular), medieval armour and tapestries. Children and brave adults will want to try out the *oubliette*, a cell just big enough to lie in, where prisoners were left and forgotten – try it in the dark if you dare. The guides, some of whom will even sing to demonstrate the acoustics of the minstrels' gallery, give an amusing and stimulating tour. The 200-acre country park, open year-round and free, has picnic areas, a duck pond, an adventure playground, nature trails, a riding centre and a small rare breeds farm.

THE NORTH AYRSHIRE COAST

The northern chunk of Ayrshire (called Cunninghame) suffers from its proximity to Glasgow, and industry tends to encroach on the holiday scene here. However, the views of offshore islands and landmasses are spectacular: Arran, Great Cumbrae, Bute and the tip of Kintyre. A couple of sights are worth seeking out around here, too, before you make for the ferries of Ardrossan (for Arran) or Largs (for Great Cumbrae).

Irvine

The horizon around Irvine is especially cluttered by factory smokestacks, and the town itself is a confusion of modern and old. **Glasgow Vennel**, near the intersection of the High Street and Townhead, is now a smart, renovated and pedestrianised street of stone and rendered cottages. It is home to the longest surviving **Burns Club**, as well as the thatched **Heckling Shop**, where Burns learned to dress flax. You can visit these year-round. There is also the **Scottish Maritime Museum** (open Apr to Oct, 10 to 5), where, among the vessels on display, is an old puffer – one of the small steamboats which once carried cargo to every tiny port on the west coast.

A short drive north, half-way between Kilwinning and Dalry, is the handsome stone **Dalgarven Mill** (open Easter to end Oct, Mon to Sat 10 to 5, Sun 12 to 5). This wholesome renovation of a sixteenth-century corn mill is enthusiastically run by the great-grandson of the miller who rebuilt it in the last century, and houses a museum of country life and a first-rate costume gallery. In the milling area, the water wheel creaks and clatters and the millstones grind. Home-made snacks and baked goods are on sale in the coffee room.

Largs

As well as being the ferry terminal for the island of Great Cumbrae, Largs is a stop-off point for the world's last sea-going paddle steamer, the *Waverley*, which cruises the Firth of Clyde. The town is home to the huge Art Deco **Nardini's**, an ice-cream emporium, cafeteria and restaurant, originally founded in 1890. Capitalising on Largs' one claim to historical fame, the battle of 1263 which was the climax of the long struggle between Scotland and Norway, **Vikingar** (open daily Oct to Mar, 10 to 4; Apr to Sept, 9 to 6) tells the story of the Vikings in Scotland – mostly through the medium of an imaginative film.

Just south of Largs is the **Kelburn Country Centre**. The thirteenth-century castle, open during late April to May only, has been home to the Earls of Glasgow for nearly three centuries. The grounds, complete with babbling burn, overlook the Firth of Clyde and Great Cumbrae. The artfully reconstructed Home Farm (*c*. 1700), arranged around a courtyard, now houses an information office, café, restaurant and gift shop. Around it are garden walks and steepish trails up the glen. In a three-sided grotto, just beyond the castle, two waterfalls tumble over vertical cliffs into black pools.

ARRAN

Arran is one of the four Clyde islands (the others being Great Cumbrae, Little Cumbrae and Bute). Within its 20-mile length are several mountains of 2,500 feet or more, glens, rivers, lochs, rocky coast, moorland, pine trees and colourful villages. Few islands with such variety are as easy and as inexpensive to reach: it takes only an hour by ferry from Ardrossan or half an hour from Claonaig on the Kintyre peninsula (seasonal sailings). Consequently, Arran has been a popular holiday retreat since the nineteenth-century. It is not the place to come for peace and quiet, particularly in high season.

The main road circles the coast, hugging the rocky shore much of the way with uninterrupted sea views. Forestry plantations dominate the south-eastern side and mountains and foothills fill most of the north-eastern end; here is Goat Fell, the island's main destination for hill-walkers. Two roads cut through the middle of the island; prehistoric cairns are to be seen scattered near the lower road. From the coast road several short walks, with sea views as well as prehistoric sites, are signposted, though parking can be a problem. You may spot rare wildlife, including red squirrels and, increasingly, basking sharks, a large variety that comes close to land in warm weather. There are also red deer and seals.

Brodick Castle

Look to your right as you approach the pier at Brodick and you will see the bold, reddish form of Brodick Castle on a cliff against a backdrop of peaked mountains (NTS, castle open Easter to late Sept, daily 11.30 to 5; Oct, weekends 11.30 to 5; grounds all year, daily 9.30 to sunset). To reach it, turn north past the hotels, guesthouses and gift shops that make up the town. Built in the thirteenth century on the site of a Viking fort, the castle has been home to the Hamiltons since 1503, when the earldom of Arran passed to the second Lord Hamilton. Restoration and extensions were carried out over the centuries (by Cromwell's men amongst others), and from most angles it now looks like a typical example of Victorian baronial architecture, incorporating Italian Renaissance elegance into defence structures such as turrets and corner towers. The interior is richly decorated and furnished, the porcelain and silver collections being particularly fine. In most of the rooms, dukes through the ages stare out of elaborate gilt frames; here also are landscape sketches by Gainsborough and paintings by Watteau. Do not miss the water-driven roasting spit in the huge, fully equipped kitchen. There are masses of rhododendrons in the surrounding woodland, and the early eighteenth-century walled garden is handsome, too.

Occupying several buildings of an eighteenth-century croft, the **Isle of Arran Heritage Museum** (open Apr to end Oct, Mon to Sat 10 to 5), between Brodick Castle and the town, gives a rounded if uninspired glimpse into daily life of the past through period furnishings and old tools. The island's geology and archaeology are also explained and worth studying; you should bone up on the latter if you are planning to track down Arran's prehistoric monuments. The tea-room and picnic area are pleasant and the cakes home-made.

The coast road

Travelling clockwise saves the dramatic mountain scenery for last. The road south from Brodick leaves the coast for several miles before rejoining it at **Lamlash Bay**, with the green-peaked Holy Island guarding the harbour. At the southern end, at **Torrylin**, an 800-yard path leads to a chambered cairn of the fourth to third millennium BC. No more than half a dozen slabs are stuck into the side of a small grassy mound, but the walk through woodland and fields and the panoramic view of the sea and pastures from the site make the trip worthwhile. Park at the shop.

The Kintyre peninsula, running parallel to the western coast, is in places only three or four miles across the Kilbrannan Sound, giving constant fine views. By the time you reach **Blackwaterfoot**, at the junction with the northern cross-island road (called 'the String'), the trees have given way to heather and bracken. Two miles north of Blackwaterfoot, by the golf course, a two-mile path leads along the shore to **King's Cave** where King Robert the Bruce supposedly watched the spider whose tenacious behaviour gave him courage for future battles against the English. The road rejoins the coast after a short stretch inland at **Machrie Moor**, a desolate and beautiful moor of heather and peat, framed by Goat Fell and its neighbouring mountains in the distance. Here is a rich and most remarkable collection of Neolithic and Bronze Age monuments. The mile-and-a-half-long track in from the road dips then climbs slightly as it meanders through sheep pastures, by the abandoned Moss Farm, and past stone circle after stone circle. Short cyst burials and food vessels have been found in several sites and occasional signs offer explanations of the discoveries. Boulders are scattered everywhere. Then, suddenly, as you reach the summit of a small hill, an enormous moor rimmed by hills comes into view; standing in the middle are three widely spaced and stately rust-coloured stones over 15 feet tall. The full circle must have been awesome.

Lochranza

From Machrie Moor until Lochranza the road stays close by a narrow strip of rocky and pebbly beach. The **Twelve Apostles**, a string of colourful cottages, appears on your right just before you reach Lochranza. What was once a prosperous herring fishing village is now used for holiday cottages, but it is unaffected and tranquil; you may well encounter sheep wandering the town's streets. The (seasonal) car ferry to the Kintyre peninsula that leaves from outside town hardly disrupts the peace.

Lochranza's striking harbour and views out to sea are its main selling points. Small painted houses and cottages sit in a rather jumbled fashion around a deeply inset sea loch with the impregnable-looking **Lochranza Castle** on a gravel spit right in the middle of the harbour (ask at the post office opposite for the key). Before recent renovations it was reckoned to be a typical sixteenth-century tower-house, but has now been discovered to incorporate a medieval hall-house. These comparatively modest dwellings were precursors of tower-houses and consisted of two storeys only, with storage below and the lord's hall above.

On bright mornings, a stroll to the far end of the harbour may well repay you with a close-up view of seals sunning themselves on barely submerged rocks.

From Lochranza to Brodick

Shortly after heading inland from Lochranza the road begins winding up through bracken-covered moorland. The craggy summit of Goat Fell becomes an increasingly overwhelming presence; a good starting point for its ascent is by a two-mile path that starts at the sawmill, a few miles north of Brodick. This is fine walking country, with wide, reasonably gentle swathes of hillside. **Sannox Bay**, at the end of a short track near the point where the main road returns to the shore, is

---

USEFUL DIRECTORY

Main tourist offices
Ayrshire & Arran Tourist Board
Burns House
Burns Statue Square
Ayr KA7 1UT
(01292) 288688

Dumfries and Galloway Tourist Board
Campbell House, Bankend Road
Dumfries DG1 4TH
(01387) 250434

Tourist Board publications Useful: annual guides listing accommodation and main attractions (Dumfries and Galloway, Ayrshire and Isle of Arran). Also *Exploring Dumfries and Galloway* – lists all attractions and activities with opening times. Special interest leaflets include golf and an outdoor activity guide.

Local tourist information centres
Brodick (01770) 302140/302401
Castle Douglas (01556) 502611 (Easter to Oct)
Culzean Castle (01655) 760293 (Apr to Sept)
Dalbeattie (01556) 610117 (Easter to early Oct)
Dumfries (01387) 253862
Gatehouse of Fleet (01557) 814212 (Easter to Oct)

---

a very secluded and sheltered cove – a fine place for a picnic.

Rust-coloured, striated rocks slant into the sea around **Corrie**; the pastel-coloured cottages that line the road make it Arran's most photogenic village.

GREAT CUMBRAE

The Clyde island of Great Cumbrae is less than four miles from top to toe and only ten minutes from the mainland (by ferry from Largs). Its size makes bicycles and walking a sensible way of getting around, and the coast road offers wonderful seascapes of Arran, Bute and the Ayrshire coast

Girvan (01465) 714950 (Apr to Oct)
Kilmarnock (01563) 539090
Kirkcudbright (01557) 330494 (Easter to Oct)
Largs (01475) 673765
Lochranza (01770) 830320 (May to mid-Oct)
Mauchline (01290) 551916
Millport (01475) 530753 (Easter to Oct)
Newton Stewart (01671) 402431 (Easter to Oct)
Sanquhar (01659) 50185 (Easter to early Oct)
Stranraer (01776) 702595 (Easter to Oct)
Troon (01292) 317696 (Easter to Oct)

Local transport
For Dumfries, Stranraer and Ayr rail services (0345) 212282
Western Scottish Omnibus (01387) 253496
Caledonian MacBrayne Ferries (crossings all year from Ardrossan to Arran, Largs to Great Cumbrae, also seasonal service from Lochranza to Claonaig on the Mull of Kintyre) (01475) 650100
Sealink Stena Ferries (Stranraer to Belfast, around eight crossings daily) (01776) 702262
P&O European Ferries (Cairnryan to Larne, up to six crossings daily) (01581) 200276

Recreation
Galloway Forest Park (01671) 402420
Waverley paddle steamer cruises from Ayr and Firth of Clyde resorts 0141-221 8152
Boat trips from Girvan to Ailsa Craig (01465) 713219

along its ten miles or so. Cumbrae's longstanding popularity with day-trippers, weekenders and holidaying families means that you are unlikely to be alone on its beaches or trails. **Millport**, the island's only town, is a pleasing array of houses lining the gently curving harbour and long, sandy beach; the waters are fine for boating and sub-aqua diving. There are not many trees on Cumbrae, and from the Glaid Stone, marking the highest point, you have 360-degree views of the mountains and indented shores of the surrounding land masses and islands.

WHERE TO STAY

£ – under £70 per room per night, incl. VAT

££ – £70 to £110 per room per night, incl. VAT

£££ – over £110 per room per night, incl. VAT

AUCHENCAIRN
Balcary Bay Hotel
Auchencairn, Castle Douglas DG7 1QZ
TEL (01556) 640217
FAX (01556) 640272
The cellars of this seafront hotel once hid smuggled contraband. Now the sun shines brightly through the conservatory windows and guests sit at ease in the bar or the elegant lounge. Good food can be enjoyed in the light blue dining-room. Cheerful bedrooms with co-ordinating fabrics, some with sea views.
££ Closed mid-Nov to Feb; 17 rooms; games room; drying-room

Collin House
Auchencairn, Castle Douglas DG7 1QN
TEL (01556) 640292
FAX (01556) 640276
Racing nostalgia pervades this lavishly furnished country house. Equine prints decorate the light and airy drawing-room and antique tables gleam in the russet dining-room. Adventurous, go-ahead cooking; excellent local cheeses.

Creature comforts provided in the individually furnished bedrooms.
££ Closed Jan to Mar; 6 rooms; drying-room (See Where to Eat)

AYR
Windsor Hotel
6 Alloway Place, Ayr KA7 2AA
TEL (01292) 264689
Traditional hotel near the beach, a few minutes' walk from the centre of the town. The dining-room has a beautiful ceiling and original fireplace. In the upstairs lounge, guests are treated to sea-views. Full Scottish breakfast is served and dinner is home-cooked. Comfortable bedrooms.
£ All year exc Chr and New Year; 10 rooms

BRODICK
Gowanlea
Sannox, Brodick, Isle of Arran KA27 8JD
TEL (01770) 810253
Charming small seafront house between Lochranza and Brodick with beautiful views over the Firth of Clyde. Cosy public rooms and good, home-cooked evening meals. Pretty bedrooms, shared bathroom and toilet.
£ All year exc Chr; 3 rooms; credit cards not accepted

DALBEATTIE
Briardale House
17 Haugh Road, Dalbeattie DG5 4AR
TEL (01556) 611468
Granite Victorian house on the
edge of town, with original
decorative work in all rooms
beautifully intact. Dinner is by
arrangement and packed lunches are
available. Spacious bedrooms, well
equipped with personal extras.
Bicycles loaned free of charge.
£ *Jan to end Oct; 3 rooms; credit
cards not accepted*

GIRVAN
Glen Tachur Hotel
Barhill, Ayrshire KA26 0PZ
TEL (01465) 821223
FAX (01465) 821466
Family-run white-harled hotel in a
largely unexplored part of Ayrshire.
Traditional decor predominates in
the sitting-room with its comfy
sofas; fresh flowers brighten the
panelled dining-room. Good,
straightforward food. Comfortable
bedrooms with neat bathrooms.
£ *All year exc Jan; 9 rooms; drying-
room*

KIRKCUDBRIGHT
Gladstone House
48 High Street, Kirkcudbright
DG6 4JX
TEL/FAX (01557) 331734
A bright and welcoming bed and
breakfast in a smart town house.
Tartan and rich burgundy drapes
form a backdrop for antiques in the
upstairs lounge. Luxury Scottish
breakfasts. Stylish bedrooms,
furnished in pine and plaid.
£ *All year; 3 rooms*

LARGS
Brisbane House Hotel
14 Greenock Road, Esplanade, Largs
KA30 9EP
TEL (01475) 687200
FAX (01475) 676295

Bright and stylish seaside hotel in a
popular resort. Photographs of Largs
in bygone days line the bar, which
boasts views over the water. Food is
served in the bar, the conservatory
and the light-blue formal restaurant.
Menus are varied and traditional,
with seafood a speciality. Attractive
bedrooms contain custom-made
rosewood furniture; bathrooms
decidedly smart and well equipped.
£-££ *All year; 21 rooms*

LOCHRANZA
Apple Lodge
Lochranza, Isle of Arran KA27 8HJ
TEL/FAX (01770) 830229
Originally the village manse, Apple
Lodge is now an elegant and
comfortable guest house. Polished
antique furniture shines in the
sitting-room and dining-room;
evening meals make use of local
produce and home-grown herbs.
Spacious and attractive bedrooms.
£ *All year exc Chr; 4 rooms; credit
cards not accepted*

Butt Lodge Hotel
Lochranza, Isle of Arran KA27 8JF
TEL (01770) 830240
A former shooting lodge in two
acres of gardens outside the village,
close to the Kintyre ferry. The
atmosphere is welcoming and
friendly. An open fire warms the
sitting-room and home-cooked
meals are served in the dining-
room. Bedrooms are fresh and
bright. There is a golf course next
to the hotel.
£ *Apr to end Oct; 6 rooms*

MINNIGAFF
Auchenleck Farm
Minnigaff DG8 7AA
TEL (01671) 402035
Farmland and forest surround this
stone-built house about five miles
from Newton Stewart. A turreted

tower bears testimony to the building's former incarnation as a shooting lodge, though the present working farm is comfortable and friendly. Breakfast only is served in the dining-room; packed lunches are available. Fresh and neat bedrooms.

£ Easter to end Oct; 3 rooms; credit cards not accepted

OLD DAILLY
Hawkhill Farm

Old Dailly, nr Girvan KA26 9RD
TEL (01465) 871232

Working farm with comfortable and spacious rooms, filled with fresh flowers. An open fire greets guests in the sitting-room and the bedrooms are pretty. There is a croquet lawn.

£ Mar to Oct; 3 rooms; credit cards not accepted

PORTPATRICK
Carlton House

21 South Crescent, Portpatrick DG9 8JR
TEL (01776) 810253

Fresh and welcoming terraced house on the seafront in the centre of town. Large windows in the lounge offer views over the bay and harbour. Meals, including cream teas, are served in the pretty dining-room. Comfortable bedrooms.

£ All year; 7 rooms; credit cards not accepted

Knockinaam Lodge

Portpatrick DG9 9AD
TEL (01776) 810471
FAX (01776) 810435

Wonderfully located classical country house, recently taken over by dynamic new owners. Light and sunshine seem to fill the sumptuous, glamorous interior. French-style food is given an imaginative, modern twist. Extremely comfortable bedrooms; splendid bathrooms.

££-£££ All year; 10 rooms; drying-room; shooting (See Where to Eat)

Melvin Lodge

Dunskey Street, South Crescent, Portpatrick DG9 8LE
TEL (01776) 810238

A welcoming house at the end of a small harbour with fine views over the town and the sea. Breakfast only is served in the dining-room. Packed lunches are available. Pretty, small bedrooms, most with sea views.

£ All year exc Chr week; 10 rooms; credit cards not accepted

STEWARTON
Chapeltoun House

Irvine Road, nr Stewarton KA3 3ED
TEL (01560) 482696
FAX (01560) 485100

Welcoming country-house hotel a few miles outside Irvine. Thistle and rose plasterwork in the hall embodies the romantic gesture of a Scottish coal magnate who built the house for his English bride at the turn of the century. Accomplished and delicious meals are served in the baronial restaurant. The spacious bedrooms have a sprinkling of antiques. Sherry in the rooms is one of a number of thoughtful gestures.

££-£££ All year; 8 rooms; fishing (See Where to Eat)

STRANRAER
Kildrochet House

Kildrochet, Stranraer DG9 9BB
TEL (01776) 820216

A former dower house built in 1723 with spacious and elegant public rooms and a warm, welcoming atmosphere. Dinner is by arrangement and breakfast is served in the pleasant dining-room. Comfortable, attractive bedrooms.

£ All year; 3 rooms; games room; croquet

TURNBERRY
Turnberry Hotel
Turnberry KA26 9LT
TEL (01655) 331000
FAX (01655) 331706
Stately Edwardian hotel with a
welcoming ambience and excellent
service, situated above the famous
golf course. Elaborate decoration,
fine art prints and lovely views of
Ailsa Craig lift the hotel out of the
ordinary. Various dining options
from the traditional to modern
available. Comfortable bedrooms
with antiques and personal touches.
*£££ All year; 132 rooms; drying-
room; games room; golf; tennis;
solarium; sauna; indoor heated
swimming-pool; gym; health spa (See
Where to Eat)*

WHERE TO EAT

Key: A * marks a place that is
particularly good value for money

AUCHENCAIRN
Collin House
Auchencairn, Castle Douglas DG7 1QN
TEL (01556) 640292
FAX (01556) 640276
Simple, stylish cooking and top
quality fresh produce at this peaceful
country house, where inventive
five-course dinners and noteworthy
puddings feature. Good variety of
fairly priced bottles on the
interesting wine list.
*All week 7.30 for 8; closed Jan to
Mar (See Where to Stay)*

AYR
Fouters
2a Academy Street, Ayr DA7 1HS
TEL (01292) 261391
An old bank's vaulted basement,
now the venue for good value bistro
food and fish/seafood specialities. A
local merchant supplies the good
wine list. Lively atmosphere.
*Tue to Sun 12 to 2, 6.30 to 10,
Sun 6.30 to 10; closed Mon, 25-26
Dec, 1-2 Jan*

MINNIGAFF *
Creebridge House Hotel
Minnigaff, Newton Stewart DG8 6NP
TEL (01671) 402121
Well prepared dishes with an
international flavour found in the
Bridges Bar at this elegant Scottish
manor; grander evening meals in the
restaurant. Great value Sunday lunch
carvery. Fine wine list from a local
cellar; first-rate real ales.
*Open for food Mon to Sat 12 to 2,
all week 6 to 9; restaurant Sun 12.30
to 2, all week 7 to 9*

NEWTON STEWART
Kirroughtree Hotel
Newton Stewart DG9 6AN
TEL (01671) 402141
FAX (01671) 402425
Elaborate modern hotel cooking.
Seafood makes a splash and luxury
ingredients contribute to some
outstanding sauces. Excellent
Scottish cheeseboard.
*All week 12 to 1.30, 7 to 9.30;
closed 6 weeks from 3 Jan to mid-Feb*

PORTPATRICK
The Crown *
North Crescent, Portpatrick DG9 8SX
TEL (01776) 810261
FAX (01776) 810551
Lively Georgian inn on the

waterfront serving good traditional food in its old-fashioned bar, elegant dining-room and conservatory. Local seafood and rich meaty dishes are popular menu choices. Decent wine list and excellent selection of malt whiskies.
Open for food 12 to 2, 6 to 10

Knockinaam Lodge

Portpatrick DG9 9AD
TEL (01776) 810471
FAX (01776) 810435
French-style cooking with modern touches. The wide-ranging menu embraces simple dishes and more complex concoctions, and offers a decent cheese selection. The wine list is extensive, the malt selection impressive.
All week 12 to 2, 7 to 9.30 (See Where to Stay)

STEWARTON
Chapeltoun House

Irvine Road, nr Stewarton KA3 3ED
TEL (01560) 482696
FAX (01560) 485100
Grand setting for good cooking and relaxed eating. Tip-top local produce including fish, game and cheese used in mostly simple dishes, with some more high-flown creations. Quality wine list with good value house recommendations.
All week 12 to 2, 7 to 9.15; closed first 2 weeks Jan (See Where to Stay)

TROON
Lochgreen House

Monktonhill Road, Southwood, Troon KA10 7EN
TEL (01292) 313343
FAX (01292) 318661
Accomplished, inventive cooking at Lochgreen House, a restaurant which makes its own pasta and rich sauces. Modern style and crisp details impress and puddings excel. Robust French classics on the wine list and a sprinkling of bottles from further afield.
All week 12 to 2, 7 to 9

TURNBERRY
Turnberry Hotel

Turnberry KA26 9LT
TEL (01655) 331000
FAX (01655) 331706
This grand hotel next to two championship golf courses offers a variety of eating options and impressive service. Among its three restaurants the Clubhouse serves salads, roasts and sandwiches, the Bay fish, pasta and light meals, while the Turnberry has the reputation of culinary showcase. Both old and new techniques combine in the manufacture of simple, rich dishes; puddings are fabulous. Lengthy, expensive wine list.
Sun 1 to 2.30, all week 7.30 to 10, lunches in Bay and Clubhouse restaurants Mon to Sat (See Where to Stay)

EDINBURGH

- A city in an outstanding natural setting, one of the most beautiful in Europe
- The best Georgian town-planning in Britain
- A wide variety of sights within a compact area
- The Edinburgh Festival

Houses in Charlotte Square

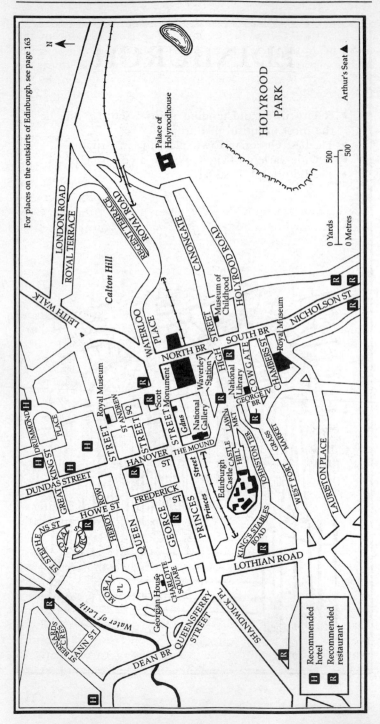

N

For places on the outskirts of Edinburgh, see page 163

HOLYROOD PARK

Arthur's Seat ▲

Palace of Holyroodhouse

500
500
0 Yards
0 Metres

Calton Hill

LEITH WALK
LONDON ROAD
ROYAL TERRACE
REGENT TERRACE
ROYAL TERRACE
WATERLOO PLACE

CANONGATE
HOLYROOD ROAD
Museum of Childhood
STREET
HIGH
SOUTH BR
NORTH BR
Waverley Station
National Library
COWGATE
Royal Museum
NICHOLSON ST
CHAMBERS ST
George IV BR

Royal Museum
Scott Monument
ST ANDREW SQ
Gdns
National Gallery
LAWN MKT
Edinburgh Castle
CASTLE HILL
JOHNSTON TER
GRASS MARKET
WEST PORT
LAURISTON PLACE

DRUMMOND
KING ST
ST ANDREW STREET
DUNDAS STREET
HANOVER ST
FREDERICK ST
HOWE ST
GREAT KING ST
HERIOT ROW
QUEEN STREET
GEORGE ST
PRINCES Street
Princes Street
THE MOUND
KING'S STABLES ROAD
LOTHIAN ROAD

ST STEPHENS ST
ROYAL CIRCUS
MORAY PL
Georgian House
CHARLOTTE SQUARE
Water of Leith
ST BERNARDS CRES
ANN ST
DEAN BR
QUEENSFERRY STREET
SHANDWICK PL

H Recommended hotel
R Recommended restaurant

EDINBURGH is the capital of Scotland and one of the most beautiful cities in Europe. Any catalogue of its virtues will include the lucky combination of crags and ridges on which it is built, the backdrop of the Firth of Forth, the hidden valley of the Water of Leith, the dominating castle and the contrast between the seventeenth-century warrens of the Old Town and the spacious neo-classical architecture of the New. However, this list cannot begin to convey the experience of emerging from Waverley Station into the city centre for the first time. Princes Street, bounded by gardens all along one side, marks the beginning of the New Town, while the castle on its precipitous crag looms over the middle distance with the spires and jumbled roofscapes of the Old Town tumbling down from it. Few cities make such a strong first impression on the visitor.

Edinburgh is a city where there is almost always a view. In one direction there are the hills of Fife rising beyond the blue estuary of the Forth. In others there are the monuments on Calton Hill, or the great bulk of Arthur's Seat, or the castle. From Edinburgh's many high points – the Castle Esplanade, Calton Hill, the Scott Monument, or, further out, Arthur's Seat, the Braid Hills, Blackford Hill or Craiglockhart – there are panoramas to be had of the complete city, sprawling between the sea and the Pentland Hills.

It is a city that is compact enough to repay casual wandering – though you have to work at it, for the hills are many and steep. To explore the wynds and closes of the Old Town or the architectural details of the squares, streets and terraces of the New Town is to make constant discoveries, and there is a sufficient sprinkling of pubs, cafés and interesting shops to provide suitable breaks. Edinburgh is also a place for breaking away from the more obvious itineraries – exploring the half-hidden valley of the Water of Leith or the old harbour villages on the edge of the Forth, for example.

There are disadvantages. The wind is one, for every bitter breeze from the north or east is funnelled through the streets. Edinburgh citizens, despite their overcoats and furry hats, have a raw, stoical look to them from facing up to a lifetime of wind-chill. Fog is another hazard – cold easterly haars (sea mists) can blanket Edinburgh while the country to the west is in bright sunshine. There is also Edinburgh's reputation for spending six months going to bed early to recover from its Festival, and the following five going to bed early to prepare for the next one. It is not quite justified, but the nightlife is inclined to be on the quiet side of respectable.

The New and the Old

The gunfire from the castle ramparts which shatters the peace of Edinburgh at one o'clock each day and leaves visitors in danger of heart failure does not herald the start of an invasion – it is merely a traditional time signal to shipping in the Forth. However, Edinburgh is close enough to the

---

Practical suggestions

The most important decision to make is whether or not to visit Edinburgh during the Festival. You should really visit twice, for the blanket of frenetic glamour which descends on the city during the weeks of the Festival turns it into a completely different place. Edinburgh is probably at its most beautiful and its most peaceful during autumn, when the slanting light of the evenings softens the stonework.

Arriving by train, or coming by car from east or south, gives you the best first impression of the city. However, if you fly, and are lucky enough to land at the airport from the east on a clear day (sit on the left-hand side of the aircraft), the view of Edinburgh is also superb. Buses run to the city centre half-hourly from the airport, which is around ten miles to the west.

While it is convenient to be based right in the middle of the city, Edinburgh's most central hotels are apt to be either pricey or in need of refurbishment. However, off-season or weekend breaks may be worth pursuing at the Sheraton, the Caledonian, the Balmoral or the Scandic Crown or in some of the smaller hotels in Princes Street, the Bridges or the New Town. There are few good guesthouses right in the centre, but large clusters exist among the Georgian terraces round Calton Hill, at Haymarket (west of the city centre but with frequent train connections to Waverley) and in the Victorian fringes to the north round Comely Bank and to the south, especially around Minto Street. There are good bus services from both.

English border to have been on invasion routes many times.

Until the end of the eighteenth century the citizens remained huddled behind the walls of what is now the Old Town, a city whose buildings grew taller and more crowded as the population increased. Eighteenth-century visitors marvelled at the height of the tenements in much the same way as we now admire the skyscrapers of Manhattan, but at the same time had to suffer the insanitary conditions that went with them. The cry of 'gardy loo' warned passers-by that waste water (and worse) was about to descend from above, while Dr Johnson muttered to Boswell, 'I can smell you in the dark'. The old town of Edinburgh was a seething

---

Getting around Edinburgh is easiest by using your feet to go downhill and buses (or taxis) to come back up again. Having your own car can be an advantage for visiting outlying areas, but parking in the city centre is very expensive and space is in short supply. Bus tours run from Waverley Bridge, just beside the station, and there are a number to choose from, complete city tours being especially good.

Edinburgh is well supplied with interesting shops, though Princes Street, the main shopping area, is largely given over to chain stores. For independent booksellers, try Thins (South Bridge), Bauermeisters (George IV Bridge) and Macnaughtan's (at the top of Leith Walk) for old books. Kinloch Anderson (Commercial Street, Leith) is a long-established kilt-maker. Jenners (Princes Street) is a stylish Victorian emporium, with the atmosphere of grander days. Dundas Street and the streets round the Grassmarket are the places to look for antiques, while Rose Street is stuffed with boutiques selling knick-knacks, clothes and crafts. Valvona and Crolla (Elm Row) is an Italian delicatessen with style, a shrine for Edinburgh gourmets and wine lovers. For haggis, make the trip to Macsweens in Bruntsfield Place – they also send them by post – and don't leave Edinburgh without trying some of the stickily sweet confectionery called Edinburgh Rock. Last-minute gifts can be found in the Waverley Market, a pleasant indoor mall by the station.

Edinburgh's Tourist Office is on top of Waverley Market, and has an excellent computer which can track down restaurants or hotels for you in the blink of an eye (though you may have to queue).

mix of people, with aristocrats, tradesmen and prostitutes living on different floors of the same buildings. Deacon Brodie, one of Edinburgh's folk heroes, could happily be a city councillor by day and a criminal by night, for his contacts in both worlds probably drank in the same taverns or 'howffs'. Throughout the constant crises of Mary Queen of Scots' reign, and throughout the religious and dynastic upheavals of the seventeenth-century, the Edinburgh mob, boiling out of closes and wynds, could be relied on to take a hand in affairs, rioting at the attempted introduction of a new prayer book, stoning the coach of a commissioner, or lynching the unpopular captain of the town guard.

There could hardly be a greater contrast between this jostling muddle of a city and Edinburgh's New Town, started at the end of the eighteenth century. Beneath the castle, across the valley once filled by the swampy Nor' Loch, a Georgian town rose to a precise plan, with every

THE EDINBURGH FESTIVAL

For three weeks every August/September the character of Edinburgh changes radically as performers and audiences pour into the city. The first Edinburgh Festival was held in 1947 and it has never looked back, although there are usually grumbles about funding and sometimes grumbles about quality. At a time when there is scarcely a large city without its International Arts Festival, Edinburgh manages to hang on to its premier position.

The Edinburgh Festival is broadly divided in two. There are the 'official' events, with invited companies or performers, and the famous 'Fringe', where teeming hordes of amateur and professional performers compete frantically for audiences in about 180 different venues ranging from graveyards to galleries. In addition there are separate film and jazz festivals, and a book fair every two years. There is now also a children's festival which is held at Easter. Then there is that perennial favourite, the Tattoo on the Castle Esplanade.

During the Festival, Edinburgh's normal respectability vanishes under a sea of leaflets. Weirdly be-costumed performers tout their events, grassy spaces fill with floodlights, student groups bed down in any spare space they can find. The Fringe has its own legends; the overnight discovery that is wafted like magic to London's West End is a less common phenomenon than the traditional performance

street standing for order, harmony and reason. The great upsurge of intellectual and literary life at the end of the eighteenth-century, which is now called the Scottish Enlightenment, started in the warren of the Old Town but ended up here, in the elegant drawing-rooms and round the dinner tables of Princes Street, George Street and Charlotte Square. If the old Edinburgh was all squalor and fervency, the new Edinburgh was all self-confidence and reason.

If the Edinburgh of today seems less subject to change than any other Scottish city, it may be because it has never managed either to forget or to recapture these distinctive times. Comfortable in its much-parodied prosperous respectability, Edinburgh waits, a capital without a nation, for something to happen to bring it to centre-stage again. It is a city which is beautiful and enticing, but one which you know is unlikely to have changed when you next return.

to two old ladies and a tramp, but it has happened. Reviews in *The Scotsman* or the national papers are anxiously awaited.

For the first-time visitor, the Festival can be daunting. The best accommodation is booked months in advance, but if you arrive with no booking the Tourist Office can usually squeeze you in somewhere. Advance tickets for the big-name events of the official Festival, especially operas, sell out fast, and there will be a heavy demand for seats at any Fringe show that suddenly attracts attention. However, there is so much to choose from that it is unlikely you will be confined to an evening at home.

The energetic may visit exhibitions in the morning, take in one, or perhaps two, Fringe events in the afternoon, an official event in the evening, then as many more revues or late-night events as they have stamina for. A week at this pace and you will be suffering from severe culture shock, will have seen the inside of some very odd places and have sat through some very odd shows. You find out what is good and what is not by reading *The Scotsman* or the London press, watching the round-ups, previews and reviews on television, and, best of all, by talking to people on buses, in pubs or in your hotel.

If you are serious about Festival-visiting, it is best if you send off for programmes around March/April from the Festival addresses listed on page 153, and get your bookings (including accommodation) sent in plenty of time (postal bookings open from mid-April, telephone and counter bookings late in the month).

THE OLD TOWN

When big as burns the gutters rin
Gin ye hae catcht a droukit skin
To Luckie Middlemist's loup in
And sit fu' snug
O'er oysters and a dram o' gin,
Or haddock lug

(Robert Fergusson)

In the shelter of the plug of volcanic basalt which is now the Castle Rock a long tail of sloping land survived the scouring of the eastward-flowing glaciers of the last Ice Age. The two separate burghs which grew up around the castle at the top of this rocky spine and the abbey of Holyrood at the bottom eventually merged, but it was not until 1767 that Edinburgh expanded much beyond the confines of the ridge and the streets immediately to the south – confines marked by the remains of the old wall built after Flodden (1513). This area is now the Old Town, and it is here that you will get a flavour of what sixteenth- and seventeenth-century Edinburgh was like – a cramped, impossibly crowded area of tall buildings on either side of the mile of road between the Castle and Holyrood. Here, many of the dramas of the time took place. John Knox, the Protestant firebrand, preached in St Giles, Montrose was taken to the gallows, the National Covenant was signed, the Treaty of Union debated and Cromwell's troops and Bonnie Prince Charlie's Highlanders paced the streets. Citizens kept pigs under their entrance stairs, drank in 'howffs', patronised the stalls of the Grassmarket or the luckenbooths (lock-up shops) round St Giles and followed the goings-on of the Scottish parliament in its new home at Parliament House.

The Old Town of Edinburgh has lost much of its life. It had more or less become a slum by the 1860s, the prosperous having long since moved out to the New Town or the spacious Victorian suburbs. Slum clearance programmes have left their mark on much of it, and genuinely antique buildings rub shoulders with restored or rebuilt houses. The 'cadies' who could track down and deliver a message to anyone you cared to name in the taverns and coffee shops are long gone, as (probably) are the days when an English visitor could record standing by the Mercat Cross and taking, in a few minutes, fifty men of genius and learning by the hand. The Old Town is not quite a tourist enclave, for city administrators, bankers, booksellers and lawyers work here, but there are ancient pubs lurking between the tourist sights and the giftshops and any number of forbidding closes and wynds to explore.

Edinburgh Castle

(HS, open Apr to Sept, Mon to Sat 9.30 to 6, Oct to Mar, daily 9.30 to 5; guided tours as and when required)
This is neither the most beautiful nor the most interesting castle in Scotland, yet its age and the magnificence of its setting make a visit here virtually compulsory. The rock it stands on dominates the city, and the views from its walls are superb. The approach over the sloping esplanade towards the toy gatehouse with the grim semi-circle of the Half Moon battery rising behind it is an experience in theatre best appreciated at the annual military tattoo.

This is not a simple fortification: the complex of buildings on top of the sheer-sided rock is more like a small military town, with a number of different things to see inside it. From the Iron Age to the twentieth century, Edinburgh Castle has been extended, altered, demolished and rebuilt to such an extent that it is hard to puzzle out the historical sequence, even armed with the guidebook. For those who enjoy this sort of detective work it is a satisfying place.

Edinburgh Castle once doubled as a royal residence but Scottish monarchs grew to prefer the greater comfort and space of Holyrood, leaving the castle's chief function as a military strong-point and, later, as barracks and prison. In the centuries since Randolph Murray scaled the rock and took the castle from the English in 1313 there have been many sieges. Although it is no longer a barracks, Edinburgh Castle is still a military headquarters, and there are two military museums within its walls as well as the Scottish National War Memorial.

Touring the castle is a matter of puffing up and down steep slopes or steps between buildings and ramparts and pausing to look at the view. Guided tours are frequent in season and Historic Scotland's custodians have a good store of anecdotes. If you prefer to make your own way, the main points of interest are these:
● **St Margaret's Chapel** This tiny twelfth-century building is thought to have been built by David I in memory of

his mother, Queen Margaret, who died in the castle in 1093. It was rediscovered in 1845 after being used as a powder magazine, and restored. A pretty Norman chancel arch divides the miniature nave from the apse. You will need to slip in during a gap between two tour groups to have any chance of appreciating its peace.

• **Mons Meg** A huge siege gun or bombard, manufactured in Flanders and given to James II in 1457. It used to stand on the battlements exposed to the elements and the depredations of schoolchildren, but has now been taken down into the vaults beneath the Great Hall and given its own audio-visual display (with suitable bangs and flashes), together with lucid descriptions of how it was manufactured and transported over medieval Scotland's boggy roads. The gun burst while firing a birthday salute to the Duke of York in 1680 and spent some years in the Tower of London before being returned to Edinburgh in 1829, after a petition by Sir Walter Scott. It was in these same vaults that French prisoners were confined: their graffiti are still visible.

• **The Great Hall** Built for James IV, this is the last of a series of medieval halls. Its use was probably entirely ceremonial. An earlier hall saw the notorious 'Black Dinner', when two Douglas scions were invited to dinner and casually slaughtered in front of the eight-year-old James II. The Great Hall was ignominiously turned into a barracks in the eighteenth-century and only restored in the late nineteenth. The hammer-beam ceiling, despite being knocked about and restored, is outstanding; the rest of the restoration being rather gloomily Wagnerian. The Hall was the meeting place for the Scottish Parliament until 1639.

• **The Palace** The nineteenth-century clock-tower makes this building look more like a town hall than a royal residence. The two main points of interest are the room where Mary Queen of Scots gave birth to James VI and the small vaulted chamber where the crown jewels of Scotland are displayed. James was born in a chamber not much larger than a cupboard, and the event became the subject of speculation in 1830 when what was said to be the body of an infant wrapped in a cloth with the initial J was discovered behind a panel, suggesting a last-minute substitution for a stillborn heir. 'Probably the legend will persist as meet fodder for trivial minds despite any attempt to dislodge it,' commented the historian George Scott-Moncrieff, and he was right.

The regalia of Scotland are also the stuff of legend. The crown which is on display may have been used by Robert the Bruce (though James V made it more imposing). It survived the Cromwellian melt-down (which is more than the English crown did) due to the cunning with which it was smuggled out of the besieged Dunottar Castle. The sword and the sceptre were given to James IV by different popes.

In 1707, after the Act of Union had been passed by the Scottish Parliament, the regalia were placed in a chest and walled up in the room where they now lie. Sir Walter Scott, who led the search which resulted in their rediscovery in 1818, thought this was done because such potent symbols were dangerous at a time when 'men's minds were agitated by the supposed degradation of Scotland beneath her ancient enemy'.

A walk-through display of the events associated with the regalia uses models and commentary to fill in the background. Bronze replicas of the crown and sword allow you to sense the size and shape with your fingers.

- **The Scottish National War Memorial** Sir Robert Lorimer transformed an old barracks block into a shrine to Scotland's war dead after World War I. Opinions of his architecture vary from enthusiastic to scathing, but there is much that is sombre and moving about the place. Douglas Strachan's windows are mystical and beautiful.
- **The Scottish United Services Museum** A scholarly foundation rather than a tourist attraction, the museum none the less has extensive displays tracing aspects of Scottish military history. It is a fascinating place for military history buffs, and a good spot to retreat to if it is raining. There is also the Regimental Museum of the Royal Scots and Royal Scots Dragoon Guards within the castle.
- **Mills Mount Battery** One o'clock is the time to be here, for that is when the gun is fired. Small crowds of children and camera-toting Japanese vie for position as soldiers time the explosion to the second.

THE ROYAL MILE

Four streets (Castlehill, Lawnmarket, High Street and Canongate) make up the long descent from the Castle to the Palace of Holyroodhouse. Together they form the so-called Royal Mile.

On either side of the streets, grey seventeenth-century stone houses rise, their frontages pierced by the dark mouths of closes, wynds and courts. Some of these lead into dank courtyards, some to restored or rebuilt houses, while others take you by way of steep steps or precipitous slopes through to the streets which run parallel to the Royal Mile in the glacier-gouged valleys on either side.

It makes sense to start at the top by the castle and work downwards. At least a day is needed for a respectable sample of the sights, and more if you want to see everything there is. What follows is a brief listing to indicate the main points of interest.

● **Camera Obscura**, **Castlehill** (open Apr to Oct, Mon to Fri 9.30 to 6, Sat and Sun 10 to 6; Nov to Mar, daily 10 to 5) This is the home of one of Edinburgh's oldest attractions – a camera obscura built on the summit of a seventeenth-century house. A periscope projects an image of the city outside on to a white table, round which enthralled children cluster, watching buses run up their arms. It is laughably simple, enthrallingly voyeuristic and enthusiastically explained. Go on a clear day – the system needs plenty of light to function at its best.

● **The Scotch Whisky Heritage Centre**, **Castlehill** (open all year, daily 10 to 5.30; extended hours in summer) A better sight than its title suggests: if you are not likely to be going distillery-visiting, this is the next best thing. The process of distilling is well set out, and it is interesting to find explanations of the role of grain whisky, which is often ignored in tours of single malt distilleries, and of the art of blending. There is, inevitably, a short audio-visual ride in a whisky cask past various historical tableaux, and a shop to end up in, with a good selection of whiskies on sale and admirable descriptions of their various qualities.

● **Milne's Court** and **James Court** These two courtyards on the north side of Lawnmarket are seventeenth- and eighteenth-century constructions designed to carve space out of the crowded closes. Hume and Boswell both lived in James Court and it was here that Dr Johnson stayed at the start of his tour to the Hebrides. Some of the buildings are original, but much has gone.

● **Gladstone's Land (NTS), Lawnmarket** (open Apr to end Oct, Mon to Sat 10 to 5, Sun 2 to 5) The National Trust for Scotland has furnished this early seventeenth-century building to give a comprehensive idea of what life for a prosperous Edinburgh merchant might have been like in the closing decades of the seventeenth century. In the vocabulary of tenement life, a land means a house, while a house means a flat (see box, page 214). Thomas Gledstanes bought this land in 1617, added rooms to its street frontage and let out much of his property to various tenants. The house suffered the fate of many similar buildings in the Old Town, gradually degenerating into a slum as the better-off members of the population moved out to the New Town. It was rescued from demolition in 1934 and restored. There would have been stalls under the arcades at street level, and a pig might have been kept beneath the stairway. Inside the house a good collection of seventeenth-century furniture has been put together, and there is a beautiful painted ceiling.

● **The Writers' Museum, Lady Stair's House, Lawnmarket** (open June to Sept, Mon to Sat 10 to 6; Oct to May 10 to 5; also Suns in Festival 2 to 5) Another seventeenth-century building, which is now a museum to Sir Walter Scott, Robert Burns and Robert Louis Stevenson. It is a little old-fashioned but has some good portraits, some manuscripts and a few of the writers' personal possessions.

● **Brodie's Close, Lawnmarket** This was the home of the famous Deacon Brodie, respectable councillor by day and burglar by night, whose eventual execution in 1788 was watched by huge crowds. His daytime trade as carpenter allowed him into the houses of his victims (and also to take wax impressions of their keys), while at night he and his contacts conducted their robberies. He took flight for Holland after trying to rob the Excise Office but foolishly wrote to his mistress on his journey, and this led to his capture. Brodie is supposed to have become the model for Stevenson's tale of Dr Jekyll and Mr Hyde. There is a pub named after him opposite the close.

● **Parliament Square, High Street** This oasis of classical architecture in the middle of the Old Town's huddle is the result of early nineteenth-century rebuilding. A heart on the cobblestones marks the site of Edinburgh's Old Tolbooth, which was built in 1466 and served as council chamber, law court, meeting place for the General Assembly of the Reformed Kirk and as a prison. Montrose's head was displayed here after his execution. The ancient building was swept away in 1817, and Sir Walter Scott acquired the door (now built into Abbotsford). His description of the Old Tolbooth at the beginning of *The Heart of Midlothian* gives a good impression of what it may have been like.

It is worth going into **Parliament House** to see the Parliament Hall (open Mon to Fri 9 to 4), where the Scottish Parliament sat between 1639 and 1707. This splendidly roofed building dates from 1632 and is now the home of the Court of Session, Edinburgh's legal heart. In front of Parliament House, a statue of John Knox is a near neighbour to one of Charles II seated on a horse. Two more opposite temperaments can hardly be imagined.

Edinburgh's **Mercat Cross** stands close by with a few pieces of medieval stonework built into the nineteenth-century construction. The excuse for the demolition of the old cross in 1756 was that it held up the traffic, but there is a suspicion that it was destroyed because Bonnie Prince Charlie had his father proclaimed king here. The elegant Royal Exchange across the road was built to replace it as a bargaining spot for Edinburgh merchants, but it never appears to have caught on. The building is now the City Chambers. For a glimpse of the past far away from the tourist trail, try making an appointment at City Chambers to see the remains of Mary King's Close, preserved half-intact among the cellars of the newer building. Ring 0131-529 4193 for information, as far in advance as possible.

● **St Giles' Cathedral, High Street** The High Kirk of

THE UNION OF THE PARLIAMENTS, 1707

I had not been Long There but I heard a Great Noise and looking Out Saw a Terrible Multitude Come up the High Street with a drum at the head of them shouting and swearing and Cryeing Out all Scotland would stand together, No Union, No Union, English Dogs and the like. (Daniel Defoe 1660–1731)

It is ironic that the union of the Scottish and English parliaments came at a time when the two nations were closer to war than had been the case for almost half a century.

Under King William, in the period between 1689 and 1702, relations between Scotland and England had been uneasy, partly because of William's vendetta against France – Scotland's oldest ally – but mostly as a result of the Darien venture. Frustrated (by English interests) in setting up Scottish trading companies to the East Indies or to Africa, the Scots had turned their minds to establishing a colony of their own, on the Darien peninsula of Central America. It was an ill-starred venture from the first, but active English hostility was held by many to be accountable for the failure of the colony. Scotland was bankrupt, for everyone with money to spare had invested in the scheme. A series of confrontational Acts of Parliament in England and Scotland over who should succeed to the British

Edinburgh was only briefly a cathedral during the periods under Charles I and James VII when episcopacy was uneasily established, but its title has lingered on. John Knox was minister here in the time of Mary Queen of Scots, and this was the base from which he set out to confront the Queen in a series of stormy interviews at Holyrood. The old twelfth-century church was burnt by the English, and the present building dates from the fifteenth century. Before the rebuilding of Parliament Square, the church was virtually buried behind the Old and New Tolbooths and the luckenbooths and tiny stalls which traded in its shelter. The demolition of these revealed a much knocked-about church. Unfortunately, William Burn, who was commissioned to restore the fabric in 1826, drastically reshaped the exterior, so that it now looks antiseptic and bland. Only the tower, with its beautiful crown, survived the wholesale restoration.

Inside, various add-ons have turned the originally

Crown worsened the situation, and in 1705 the Scots hanged a blatantly innocent English captain for alleged piracy.

Yet, despite all this, active moves to create the Union were taking place. Under William's successor, Queen Anne, 31 commissioners from each country were appointed, and they managed to draft a treaty within nine weeks. In October 1706 the debate started in the Scottish Parliament to massive public hostility. There were riots in Glasgow and Dumfries, and the Lord High Commissioner's coach was stoned in Edinburgh. But the Scots had little choice: union offered freedom of trade and monetary compensation; independence meant probable bankruptcy and possible civil war. The treaty was approved by 110 votes to 69. The Scottish Parliament adjourned on 19 March 1707, and never met again.

The Act of Union preserved the Scottish church, the law, the judicial system, the rights of the Scottish nobles and the privileges of the Scottish burghs. It approved the Hanoverian succession and gave the English the security they needed in facing the French. The Scots were to receive £400,000 'Equivalent' to reimburse the Darien investors and to provide a boost for industry. Whether it was a fair settlement, whether Scottish parliamentarians were bribed, whether the English had broken the terms of the treaty, and whether Scotland could have survived as an independent nation are still matters for (often heated) debate.

cruciform church into something closer to a square. It is rather a gloomy place, but worth exploring to see Sir Robert Lorimer's **Chapel of the Thistle** (1911) with an angel playing the bagpipes carved on the entrance arch. The scattered pieces of Montrose's body were buried in St Giles after his rehabilitation at the Restoration. There is also a memorial to his enemy, the covenanting Marquess of Argyll, who lost his head at the same time.

• **Tron Kirk, High Street** At New Year, Hogmanay revellers gather outside the old church. The spire, though a nineteenth-century replacement for one that was destroyed by fire, acts as a fine counterbalance to the crown of St Giles. The disused kirk is currently a part-time information centre about the Old Town. More ambitious plans for it are occasionally aired.

• **Paisley Close, High Street** It was the collapse of a tenement here in 1861, killing 35 and injuring many more, that brought the appalling conditions of those living in the Victorian Old Town to public attention and led to the appointment of Edinburgh's first Medical Officer. Widely known as 'Heave Awa' House', it has a scroll on the entrance recalling the words of a boy buried in the rubble: 'Heave awa' chaps, I'm no deid yet'.

• **Museum of Childhood, High Street** (open June to Sept, Mon to Sat 10 to 6; Oct to May, 10 to 5; Suns in Festival 2 to 5) The first of its kind in the world, and one of the noisiest museums going (more on account of music than of children), this is actually a serious-minded establishment. It was founded in 1955 by a man who claimed to have 'a rooted conviction that children are only tolerable after their baths and on their way to bed' and tried to set up a memorial window to 'Good' King Herod. Joseph Murray's tongue-in-cheek humour is still to be found on many of the caption cards. Despite the supposed adult emphasis of the museum, the place fascinates children and parents alike. There are some splendid dolls' houses and unusual automata and slot-machines (including a gruesome execution), together with clothes, railways, dolls, board games, theatres, samplers, teddy bears and toy soldiers. The museum is housed in a steep and narrow old building, and it can sometimes be a bit of a squash.

• **John Knox House, High Street** (open all year, Mon to Sat 10 to 4.30) The oldest house on the Royal Mile (dating from 1490) looks suitably medieval as it juts out, slightly askew, into the High Street. The connection with Knox may be apocryphal, but it saved the house from demolition. The ground floor is a shop, but above it you will find a good painted ceiling and displays about the man who did more than anyone else to establish the Scottish Reformation.

The figure of Knox still provokes controversy. He had the bigot's inability to tolerate opposing views and the fanatic's zeal in propagating his own. Nor did he hesitate to blacken his opponents, Mary Queen of Scots in particular, whose tolerant religious policies were anathema to him. On the other hand he was courageous, inspiring to those who heard him, and he held a genuine vision of the spiritual regeneration of the country to which he belonged. Nevertheless, Knox turned the course of the Scottish Reformation towards that extremism which was eventually to plunge the country into a turmoil of suffering, truncate its artistic heritage and cut it off from its medieval roots.

● **Netherbow, High Street** A plaque marks the spot where the Netherbow gate stood until 1764, marking the eastern end of Edinburgh. The city fell to the Jacobites in 1745 when a raiding party under Cameron of Lochiel took advantage of the exit of a coach through this gate and stormed in – not that Edinburgh looked like organising much effective resistance anyway.

● **Morocco Land, Canongate** Look for the bust of a Moor outside the building (which itself is modern). It commemorates the pretty story of a persecuted Edinburgh student who fled abroad to Morocco, made his fortune and returned to exact his revenge on the city which had mistreated him. Instead he cured the Provost's daughter of the plague and married her, coming to live in the old building here.

● **The People's Story Museum, Canongate Tolbooth**, **Canongate** (open Oct to end May, Mon to Sat 10 to 5; June to Sept, 10 to 6; Suns in Festival 2 to 5) Canongate kept its tolbooth when the Edinburgh one was swept away. The building, with its curious Germanic tower and turrets, dates from 1591; the clock, which looks as if it had just sprung from the front wall, like a cuckoo, is from 1884. Inside, the main attraction is an audio-visual exhibition with added smells, called the People's Story. It describes the everyday lives of Edinburgh people in the eighteenth and nineteenth centuries and, while a bit thin on exhibits and rather too worthily educational, it is a good counterbalance to the historical glamour of the Castle and Holyrood.

● **Huntly House, Canongate** (open June to Sept, Mon to Sat 10 to 6; Oct to May, Mon to Sat 10 to 5; Suns in Festival

2 to 5) Three old sixteenth-century houses contain this museum of the city of Edinburgh. It is like a huge antique shop, easy to get lost in, and with embarrassingly squeaky floors if you wear rubber soles. Glass cases contain Roman remains from Cramond, medieval shards, pottery, glass, silver and plenty of civic memorabilia. There is an exhibition devoted to Field-Marshal Earl Haig, who was born in Charlotte Square, and a copy of the 1638 Covenant. It is a genial, old-fashioned kind of museum, concentrating on things rather than stories, and often undeservedly neglected by visitors in a hurry.

● **Site of Girth Cross and Holyrood Sanctuary** The circle of stones in the roadway is where Girth Cross stood at the foot of Canongate, marking the western boundary of the sanctuary of Holyrood Abbey. In a curious anachronism, this remained a sanctuary for debtors right up until 1880. Inside it they were safe from their creditors, and they were also allowed outside between Saturday and Sunday midnights. One of the most famous 'Abbey Lairds', as the debtors who sought shelter here were known, was Charles X of France, who abdicated in 1830, and was known in Edinburgh as 'Monsieur'. The Edinburgh historian E. F. Catford relates how he used to go snipe-shooting on the slopes of Arthur's Seat, with the Edinburgh children pursuing him, crying, 'Frenchy, Frenchy, dinna shoot the spruggies' (sparrows).

The Palace of Holyroodhouse

(Open Apr to end Oct, Mon to Sat 9.30 to 5.15, Sun 10.30 to 4.30; Nov to end Mar, daily 9.30 to 3.45; closed when the Queen is in residence)

The Queen's official Edinburgh residence, site of garden parties and other royal occasions, Holyrood (for short) is, like the castle, firmly on the list of 'necessary' sights for visitors to Edinburgh. If you have little time for Scottish history, however, you can safely leave it alone, for as palaces go it is rather disappointing – the formal rooms that visitors see are scarcely luxurious, and the long period between the reigns of James VI and Queen Victoria when it was more or less neglected by British monarchs has left the place still feeling curiously untenanted. Nevertheless, the tour is well worthwhile for those interested in architecture or Mary Queen of Scots, and for the sake of one or two notable curiosities.

The Scottish kings grew to prefer Holyrood Abbey

(whose remains are in the palace grounds) to Edinburgh Castle as a place to stay, and their lodgings gradually became a proper palace. James IV and James V were responsible for most of the earliest building, but their work, with the exception of one tower, was demolished when Holyrood was rebuilt for Charles II between 1671 and 1679. Sir William Bruce was the architect (see also Kinross House, page 281, and Hopetoun, page 178), and the elegantly classical façades of the central courtyard are considered to be one of his best achievements.

The tour, conducted by smartly uniformed guides with stentorian tones, leads you up the Great Stair, past a portrait of the Queen wearing the robes of the Order of the Thistle, through the royal dining-room, the throne room, the evening drawing-room and the morning drawing-room. The plaster-work of the ceilings is the best part of these. The private rooms designed for Charles and his Queen are more interesting because they are more intimate, though somehow the fact that Charles II never even saw them nor, indeed, any of Holyrood makes them rather sad places. The Great Gallery is much more cheerful; not only is it a splendid, bright corridor of a room, but it contains the palace's greatest folly – the series of paintings by Jacob de Wet. These, commissioned in 1684, show the complete line of Scottish kings. There were 111 paintings altogether (half of them of shadowy, half-legendary figures), of which 89 are still here. Poor de Wet finished the lot in two years, so it is hardly surprising that his imagination got a bit overstrained at times. Every portrait faithfully reproduces the prominent nose owned by Charles II – a quick way of proving the royal descent.

It is the two rooms in the old north-west tower where Mary Queen of Scots had her apartments that provide the climax of the tour. The outer chamber, with its marvellous ceiling (embellished for the brief homecoming of James VI), is where she argued over religion with John Knox, which left him impressed by her force of character, but unmoved in his opinions. This is also the scene of the murder of her secretary, Riccio, by a band of scheming nobles, her own husband Darnley among them. Riccio was left on the floor here with 56 dagger wounds in his body. In less scrupulous days not all that long ago visitors used to be shown an 'indelible bloodstain' on the floor, but this touch has been dropped, to the regret of many.

Of various exhibits in these rooms, the needlework by Mary and the Lennox jewel are particularly beautiful.

Holyrood Abbey

Only the nave of the abbey church remains, a small, black-ened fragment of what was once a beautiful building. David I founded it, but what you see is largely thirteenth-century. The west door and the arcading in the aisle show what a richly decorated place it once was. Burnt by the English during the fifteenth-century Rough Wooing, and suffering further after the Reformation, the abbey church was used for the wedding of Mary and Darnley and for the Scottish coronation of Charles I (though the church needed a lot of repair before then). James VII's attempts to make it into a Catholic place of worship led to a sacking (and desecration of the royal graves) by the Edinburgh mob in 1688. The roof collapsed in 1768. Various proposals to rebuild the nave have come to nothing.

South of the Royal Mile

The Flodden wall, which for so long contained the entire city of Edinburgh, ran steeply downhill from the south side of the castle and roughly along the line of the ridge opposite. It enclosed the open area immediately beneath the castle known as the Grassmarket, the street called the Cowgate, and what is now Chambers Street. Parts of the wall can still be seen.

Grassmarket

This open rectangle surrounded by old houses and some modern intrusions used to be the haunt of Edinburgh's dossers, as was the Cowgate, which runs darkly east-ward, parallel to the Royal Mile. Most of the area has been smartened up, but one or two mission houses remain as evidence of the way this old medieval marketplace degen-erated into a nineteenth-century slum. With the smartening-up came clothing and antique shops, and several cheerful eating places, but one or two fascinating old shops survive amongst their more fashionable successors in West Bow, Victoria Street and Candlemaker Row. Keep a special watch for the one in Victoria Street selling every conceivable variety of brush.

The Grassmarket is probably best known as Edinburgh's place of public execution until 1784. Although some of the better-connected victims, such as Montrose, were executed by the Mercat Cross, hundreds of criminals or those condemned for their religion died in the Grassmarket, especially the hapless Covenanters who held out for their faith during the 'Killing Time' after the Restoration. The ex-Captain of the Town Guard, John Porteous, was lynched by a mob and strung up here in 1736. The most notorious inhabitants of the Grassmarket were Burke and Hare, body-snatchers who turned to murder as a quick way of providing corpses for doctors to dissect. After Burke's execution, his skeleton was given to the Department of Anatomy at Edinburgh University, where it can still be seen.

The Russell Collection of Early Keyboard Instruments, St Cecilia's Hall (Cowgate)

(Open Wed and Sat 2 to 5; in Festival Mon to Sat 10.30 to 12.30; closed some public and local holidays; enquiries 0131-650 2805) Down at the brighter, eastern end of the Cowgate is an eighteenth-century music room (where concerts are occasionally held) which now contains the Russell Collection of early keyboard instruments, an unrivalled source of information for build-your-own harpsichord enthusiasts.

Greyfriars Kirk (George IV Bridge)

In 1638, the churchyard here was the scene of the signing of the National Covenant, an event which indirectly led to civil war in Scotland, England and Ireland (see the box on the Covenanters). Memorials to many of Edinburgh's worthies line the walls, but, sentiment being more interesting than history, most visitors make for the spot where Greyfriars Bobby, a Skye terrier, stood watch over his master's grave for 14 years. The church itself is rather uninteresting.

National Library of Scotland (George IV Bridge)

(Exhibition Room open Mon to Sat 10 to 5, Sun 2 to 5) An oppressive building houses one of the largest libraries in Britain. Exhibitions, especially at Festival time, are usually worth a visit for bibliophiles, particularly if there is a display of characteristic Scottish bindings.

Royal Museum of Scotland (Chambers Street)

(Open Mon to Sat 10 to 5, Sun 12 to 5) Dating from 1861, this magnificent building recalls the

THE COVENANTERS (1638–90)

The National Covenant, signed in Greyfriars churchyard in 1638, is the document which marks the start of a period in Scottish history which was triumphant, terrible and bitter. The Covenanting movement, which started as a proud, nationalistic and spiritual revolution, was to become an intolerant theocracy and eventually a pitiful remnant of stalwarts pursued and slaughtered by the forces of government. The events of these years are complicated, and intimately bound to the civil struggles going on in England, including the English Civil War.

1638 After riots in Edinburgh when King Charles I attempts to introduce an anglicised prayer book, the National Covenant is signed in Greyfriars. It makes no threats, merely rejects interference in the practice of the Reformed Kirk of Scotland. However, its appeal has to do with the symbolic nature of a covenant, drawn from the Old Testament; it is a bond between God and his chosen people. King Charles thinks it treason.

1638 In Glasgow, the Assembly of the Kirk becomes more radical. It abolishes bishops and disallows royal authority over the church. Charles attempts to raise an English army to curb this constitutional rebellion, but fails to invade. Subscription of the Covenant is made compulsory in Scotland.

1640 The Scots invade England to make Charles come to a settlement and force him, in 1641, to assent to the religious and constitutional changes. Splits now appear among the Covenanters, with some, Montrose in particular, unwilling to continue hostility to the King.

1643 Embroiled in a civil war they look like losing, the English Parliamentarians strike a deal whereby in return for Scottish military aid Presbyterianism will be established in England and Ireland. A Scottish army enters England.

1644–5 Montrose, now siding with the King, inflicts six defeats on the Covenanters in Scotland. Their confidence in their invincibility as God's chosen is severely dented.

1646–8 King Charles, defeated in war, surrenders himself to the Scottish Covenanting army, but refuses to sign the Covenant. The Scots, unable to take an unregenerate King back to Scotland, are forced to hand him over to the English. The Covenanters split further, and eventually the extreme 'Kirk' party takes power, purging all those whose religious fervour does not measure up.

1649 Execution of Charles I. All the Scottish factions are horrified and Charles II is immediately proclaimed King in Scotland, while the English abolish the monarchy entirely. The rift between the two countries is complete.

1650 Oliver Cromwell invades Scotland and defeats the Covenanters at Dunbar.

1651 A Scottish invasion of England is defeated at Worcester. Charles II flees, leaving Cromwell to conquer Scotland and establish the Commonwealth. Scotland is under occupation for nine years.

1660 Charles II is restored. Over the next few years, the Covenants and all the acts passed by Covenanting parliaments in Scotland are repudiated. Bishops are reintroduced and kirk ministers from the previous regime must seek episcopal approval. Many ministers refuse to comply and become 'outers'. Despite increasingly repressive measures, congregations follow them to 'conventicles' in the hills rather than conform to the law.

1666 Covenanters from the west rebel and march on Edinburgh. They are defeated at Rullion Green. Executions in the Grassmarket follow.

1679 A further Covenanter rebellion is defeated at Bothwell Brig.

1680–1688 Continued persecution of increasingly small, extreme, Covenanting minorities; the period known as the 'Killing Times'.

1685 The accession of Catholic James VII is such a threat to the established Scottish church that Presbyterianism becomes respectable again.

1688 James VII deposed in an essentially English revolution.

1690 A mild version of Presbyterianism is re-established under William in a compromise between church and state. The Covenanting dream of establishing Christ's kingdom in Scotland is relegated to history.

Crystal Palace. The dour, blackened exterior conceals a cathedral-like galleried main hall, which stretches skywards in a beautiful combination of iron and glass. A multitudinous collection of objects ranges from relics of ancient Egypt to a spruced-up evolution gallery. The most interesting section is the Hall of Power, which contains numerous scale models, many working, of various types of steam engine, plus the oldest locomotive and oldest glider in existence. The Hall of Victorian Engineering is almost as good. The Natural History section is notable for the huge skeleton of a blue whale which overhangs it. The museum is being extended to take in the archaeological collection currently in the Queen Street building – major changes may result when the project is completed in 1998.

Edinburgh University old buildings (South Bridge)

The university was founded in 1582 (making it younger than Aberdeen, Glasgow or St Andrews). The Old College stands on the spot where Mary Queen of Scots' second husband Darnley was murdered after his house at Kirk o' Fields had been blown up. It is a Robert Adam/William Playfair building, interesting only for those keen on architecture or wishing to visit the **Talbot Rice Art Centre**, where a small collection of paintings is quietly exhibited in a lovely gallery designed by Playfair (open Tue to Sat 10 to 5).

A short way to the south lies George Square. This was laid out in 1770 as one of the first residential schemes outside the Old Town. The University has still not been forgiven in many quarters for demolishing much of the square and replacing the Georgian houses with modern, functional buildings.

The Meadows, to the south again, is a welcome patch of greenery for university students and for medical staff toiling in the complex of hospitals round Edinburgh's famous **Royal Infirmary**, whose first building was started in 1738.

While you are in the area, glance at the **Edinburgh Festival Theatre** in Nicholson Street. This imaginative conversion of a run-down old building is the most recent addition to the city's entertainment facilities, and has put an end to long-running demands for an opera house.

THE NEW TOWN

Albert said he felt sure the Acropolis could not be finer.
(Queen Victoria)

The New Town of Edinburgh was the brainchild of George Drummond, six times Lord Provost, and not for nothing called Father of the City. His vision was of a new residential town rising on the fields beyond the Nor' Loch, and his energy eventually drove the town council to back it by getting an architectural competition under way. In 1767, a year after Drummond's death, the winning plan was chosen. It was by a virtually unknown architect, James Craig, and was simple but precise: two elegant squares linked by the three parallel streets now known as Princes Street, George Street and Queen Street.

No one seems to have wanted to be the first to move out of the familiar clutter of the Old Town. Incentives had to be offered before the initial house was built near St Andrew's Square in 1769, but the new development rapidly became fashionable. The unity of design (which can still be seen beneath the Victorian and modern intrusions) was imposed by the council, and reaches its climax in the perfection of Charlotte Square (1791) – Robert Adam's finest achievement. One of Edinburgh's best features, the open valley between Princes Street and the Old Town, was saved from being built on, but only after an extensive lawsuit. The streets of Craig's New Town today form the commercial and financial heart of Edinburgh.

It was not long before new development started on the hill sloping down to the Forth beyond Queen Street. A second New Town, planned very much on the same lines as the first but with more uniformity of frontage, sprang up between the grand enclosures of Royal Circus and Drummond Place. During the first few decades of the nineteenth century, building went on apace. On the Moray Estate, immediately to the north of Charlotte Square, the grid-plan gave way to a series of linked circuses with some of the grandest architecture yet. Splendid terraces, designed for the wealthiest of Edinburgh's citizens, girdled the lower slopes of Calton Hill, while further building went on to the west of Charlotte Square – the area now known as the West End.

The result of this frenzied, often speculative, building is an expanse of Georgian architecture unrivalled in Britain. The New Town is a treasure trove for lovers of architectural detail, for within the streets, terraces and squares there is endless variation of design and ornament. It is a pleasure to walk round even if you have little knowledge of the period, for much of the New Town remains residential, much has been well restored, and there are views, shops, pubs and constantly interesting corners to enjoy.

Exploring the New Town

Some of the best areas of the New Town to walk through are picked out here; there are plenty of others. The **New Town Conservation Centre** at 13a Dundas Street (open all year, Mon to Fri 9 to 1, 2 to 5, closed weekends; for information call 0131-557 5222) mounts exhibitions on the architecture of the area and also runs guided walks on request.

Princes Street

At the West End, where Lothian Road runs south towards the copper-roofed Usher Hall, scene of Edinburgh's large concerts, the restored red sandstone Caledonian Hotel is all that remains of the demolished Caledonian Station. It looks the length of Princes Street to its rival, the North British (now the Balmoral) above Waverley Station. Between these old competitors lies half a mile of shops on one side and Princes Street Gardens on the other. The gardens are the place to go statue-hunting, picnicking and strolling; in summer there are concerts at the bandstand in the centre. Slightly more than half-way down, the gardens are blocked by the Mound, up which a steeply curving road runs to link Old Town and New. The Mound was made from the earth scooped out from the excavations for the New Town, and started as a piece of private enterprise – a 'mud brig' across the marshy expanse beneath the Old Town where the waters of the Nor' Loch had been drained.

The two Greek temples lying at the foot of the hill (one Doric, the other Ionic) are both by William Playfair and date from the early nineteenth century; they house the Scottish National Gallery and the Royal Scottish Academy (see below). The impact of these temples on Princes Street is superb and, combined with the Calton Hill monuments, they go some way towards giving substance to Edinburgh's epithet, the Athens of the North. The Royal Scottish Academy, closest to Princes Street, has a statue of Queen Victoria lording it over the roof, easily mistaken for Athena.

The eastern end of Princes Street is dominated by the

spire of the Scott Monument (see below), but the most beautiful building in this area is Robert Adam's Register House, with the Duke of Wellington on horseback before it. Don't miss the Café Royal tucked away in the narrow streets behind it – this excellent oyster bar and restaurant has opulent late-Victorian tiling and stained glass. The splendours of Waterloo Place, the eastern extension to Princes Street, are marred by two bureaucratic blots: the 1930s St Andrew's House in Regent Road, once described by Charles McKean as having 'the brooding, authoritarian characteristics of the secure headquarters of an occupying power' and the universally derided St James Centre, a nasty bulwark housing a bus station and a shopping mall.

Calton Hill

This is the area where Edinburgh's obsession with Athens is most visible. The fragmentary Doric temple which you see from Princes Street is the **National Monument**, which was started in 1822 as a memorial to the dead of the Napoleonic Wars. It was intended to be a copy of the Parthenon in Athens, but funds ran out after only 12 columns. A more successful classical monument, by Playfair, is the little circular memorial to Dougald Stewart; among other striking buildings is the Nelson Monument (1807), a miniature battlemented tower in stark contrast to the classical work around it. Calton Hill provides one of the best panoramas of Edinburgh, but after dark it becomes inhabited by some pretty strange types and is probably best avoided.

Beneath the hill, beyond the magnificently processional exit from Princes Street through Waterloo Place, the Royal High School stands beside Regent Road. Built between 1825 and 1829, this is another Greek revival edifice of considerable ambition. Its modern history is a sad one, for it was totally converted internally between 1977 and 1980 in the hope that it would be used as the seat of the Scottish Assembly. The referendum of 1979 failed to produce the necessary majority to establish this. The building remains in mothballs until the next attempt to give Scotland some degree of devolution.

A little further on, on the opposite side of the road, the Burns Monument (1830) hardly competes with the Scott Monument, and is much less visited.

Round the eastern spur of Calton Hill stretch two of the New Town's most magnificent terraces, Regent Terrace and Royal Terrace. These huge houses were designed to attract the wealthy because of their wonderful views and the spacious greenery at their back. Many are now hotels, where utilitarian subdivision of the interior has rather spoiled the effect.

Charlotte Square

Widely held to be one of the finest squares in Britain, this is the New Town's showpiece. The northern side, where Victorian alterations have been carefully suppressed, is especially beautiful in its regularity. The dome of St George's Church (1811) is the focal point for westward views along George Street. The church now houses part of the Scottish Record Office, and there is an exhibition of documents. Charlotte Square is at its best in spring, when the central garden blazes with crocuses. Traffic and parked cars spoil the tranquillity somewhat.

George Street

This was designed as the principal street of the first New Town and, with its breadth and its long vistas from Charlotte Square to St Andrew's Square, remains an impressive thoroughfare despite the cars which clutter its centre and the occasional intrusion of a modern building. Statues stand at street intersections, providing a headache for traffic planners. Several good shops are to be found in George Street, including Aitken and Niven for tweeds and Hamilton and Inches for silver and jewellery.

Moray Place

Development here started around 1822. Gillespie Graham drew up the two circuses and crescent, which for many are the most impressive sections of the New Town. Every last detail, down to the railings, is part of the design; the overall harmony is remarkable, even if there is a hint of the bombastic. In the 12-sided Moray Place the buildings are at their grandest, with Tuscan porticos gazing on the central garden. The backs of many of the houses hang sheer above the Water of Leith, best appreciated by walking down the valley from the Dean Bridge (page 147).

Dundas Street

A walk down this steep hill and through some of the streets on either side takes you through the best of the second New Town, with the elegant frontages of **Heriot Row** (much favoured by lawyers) and **Great King Street** contrasting with humbler but equally fascinating streets such as Northumberland Street and Nelson Street. Quirky shops selling antiques, fine arts and books rub shoulders with sandwich bars. If you get sated with Georgian houses, catch a bus back up Dundas Street to the High Street and the seventeenth century again.

New Town sights

• **The Georgian House (NTS), Charlotte Square** (open Apr to end Oct, Mon to Sat 10 to 5, Sun 2 to 5; closed in winter) This is the National Trust for Scotland's figurehead property, and a recreation of gracious eighteenth-century living sufficiently infectious to make you long to have been born 200 years ago. The drawing-room, with chairs arranged round the sides and paintings adorning the walls, stands ready for a formal soirée, while in the comfortable and casual parlour the imaginative may catch a hint of snuff or hear long-vanished voices debating the latest scathing piece from the *Edinburgh Review*. The dining-room too gives some idea of what an Edinburgh dinner party during the Enlightenment would have been like, with gleaming silver and heavy fabrics. However, it is probably the kitchen and the adjacent china cupboard and wine cellar which are most fascinating. Here you can sense the hectic activity round the open range and imagine the huge numbers of copper utensils being clattered from table-top to scullery, while the bells in the passage jangled their summonses to attend on the drawing-room. The guides here are extremely knowledgeable, and there is a good, scene-setting audio-visual programme.

• **The National Gallery of Scotland** (open Mon to Sat 10 to 5, Sun 2 to 5; in Festival, Mon to Sat 10 to 6, Sun 11 to 6) The National Gallery has probably the finest collection of paintings outside London, and when the collection in the National Gallery of Modern Art (see page 148) is added in, there is scarcely a period or a movement left unrepresented. Internally, the National Gallery is arranged in a series of octagonal rooms, and their claret-and-green colour scheme is a copy of Playfair's original 1859 design. On the upper floor you will find the excellent collection of French Impressionists, and downstairs, in a modern extension, hangs the collection of Scottish painting. Lighting is somewhat on the dim side throughout the gallery, and the hanging – designed to be like a garden full of different views, architectural shapes and colour combinations – is fascinating, but may not please everyone.

Of the early paintings, the *Madonna and Child* by Verrocchio is the undoubted star. Five Titians compete for attention, the erotic *Diana and Actaeon* prominent among them. El Greco's *The Saviour of the World* gazes, icon-like, from the wall. Goya's *El Medico* in his vermilion cloak warms his hands over a brazier. Rubens' *Feast of Herod* shows John the Baptist's head being uncovered like a pork roast in front of a nauseated Herod, while all the guests scramble for a view. Gainsborough's *The Hon. Mrs Graham* is a lovely study of haughty beauty. Among the more modern works, Courbet's *Wave* is popular with visitors. Van Gogh is represented by his twisted olive trees, Monet by frosted haystacks, Cézanne by Mont St Victoire.

The Scottish collection, cramped in a room like an hotel foyer, has some fine portraits – many by Raeburn (including his well-known *Rev. Robert Walker Skating on Duddingston Loch*), and by Allan Ramsay. William McTaggart's impressionistic landscapes form a radical contrast with Noel

THE SCOTTISH ENLIGHTENMENT

Scots are capable of waxing fairly tedious about the disproportionate number of men of genius, especially inventors, that the nation has produced, but the period known as the Scottish Enlightenment, when Scotland led Europe in ideas, is widely recognised as extraordinary. What provoked the sudden upsurge in Scottish intellectual and artistic life between 1760 and 1790 is a matter for social historians, but the result was a gathering of minds in clubs, howffs and later at New Town dinner parties, where arguments could be thrashed out and discoveries communicated. The men of the Enlightenment were humane, moderate, curious, rational and above all enjoyed conversation and the society of others.

Chief among them was the philosopher David Hume, whose religious scepticism shocked many of his contemporaries, but whose ideas, particularly about causation, had, and have, enormous influence. Adam Smith, whose *Wealth of Nations* is the cornerstone of modern economics, was his friend. Then there was James Hutton, whose *Theory of the Earth* first proposed continuous erosion and

Paton's *The Quarrel of Oberon and Titania* – a biscuit-box fairy scene. David Wilkie's highly coloured scenes from Scottish rural life include *Distraining for Rent* – a real tearjerker.

● **The Scott Monument, Princes Street** Few, if any, other, writers have a memorial like this. A huge Gothic spire, pinnacled, buttressed and loaded with crockets, finials and statuettes, rises 200 feet and 6 inches above Princes Street Gardens, and acts as a canopy for a statue of Sir Walter Scott, seated with a book in his hand and his dog by his side. The monument, designed by a previously unknown draughtsman, George Kemp, and inaugurated in 1846, was funded by private subscription, most of it raised in Edinburgh.

The monument is said to draw much of its inspiration from Melrose Abbey, Scott's favourite Gothic building. Its niches are filled with statuettes of Scottish poets and characters from Scott's works. At the level of the first gallery there is a small museum. Climbing the 287 steps of the narrow spiral stair to the top is an exercise in persistence, rewarded by views of central Edinburgh which beat even those from the castle walls.

This 'florid cenotaph' reflects the feeling of Scott's

uplift as the mechanism by which the Earth's surface was under constant change, and Joseph Black who discovered carbon dioxide. The interests of Lord Kames and Lord Monboddo extended beyond the law into linguistics, philosophy and history. The Adam family, the most famous architects of their age, Allan Ramsay and Henry Raeburn among the portrait painters and Robert Fergusson, whose vernacular poetry marked a new interest in Scots as a language, all lived during this period.

The 'second wave' of the Enlightenment came after the Napoleonic Wars, when, with figures such as Scott, Hogg, Cockburn and Jeffrey, and periodicals such as the *Edinburgh Review*, Edinburgh became a literary town *par excellence*. This pre-eminence was to last into the start of the Victorian period, when Edinburgh literary life went into a decline, with only Robert Louis Stevenson's affectionate and frustrated voice to give life to the city. Not until the 'Scottish Renaissance' of the 1930s, when writers such as Hugh Macdiarmid, Norman McCaig, Sidney Goodsir Smith and Robert Garioch started to reinject Edinburgh with political and literary life, was the Enlightenment to have any echo.

contemporaries that he, almost alone, had put Scotland back on the map after years of neglect, culminating in the triumphant visit of George IV to the city in 1822 which Scott stage-managed. The monument is currently closed for restoration but it can still be viewed from the outside.

• **The Royal Museum of Scotland, Queen Street** From January 1996, Scotland's premier historical and archaeological museum will be closed until its amalgamation with its sister museum in Chambers Street in 1998. Temporary exhibitions are the best that visitors can hope for until then. The collection held by the museum contains some of the country's greatest treasures, including the Hilton of Cadboll Pictish stone, St Ninian's Treasure from Shetland and the Traprain Hoard of Roman silver. A new setting should much improve the display of these wonderful objects.

• **Scottish National Portrait Gallery**, **Queen Street** (open Mon to Sat 10 to 5, Sun 2 to 5; in Festival, Mon to Sat 10 to 6, Sun 11 to 6) When the archaeology collection moves out, the Portrait Gallery will take over the entirety of this red sandstone building on Queen Street, allowing room for more paintings. This is the place to come if you want to see the faces that have dominated Scottish history. A procession of mournful Stewart monarchs, nobles, churchmen and great thinkers and writers share the wall space. Here you will find Scott, Burns, Hogg, Boswell and Hume, along with Mary Queen of Scots, Montrose and Dundee. The collection moves well into the twentieth century, keeping up to date with the great and the good of Scottish life.

THE WATER OF LEITH

You cannot yet walk all the way from the suburbs to the sea by the Water of Leith, but if you have a car, or use buses creatively to follow the course of Edinburgh's own trout stream, you will be taken into some interesting and unfrequented parts of Edinburgh. This is something of a do-it-yourself adventure, and will take the better part of a day.

On the far south-western fringe of Edinburgh, where the 'lang whang' road from Lanark (A70) enters the city through the smart suburbs of Balerno (visit Malleny Gardens – page 177 – while you are here), Currie and Juniper Green, a walk-way of the *rus in urbe* variety runs by the river. Old mills and the remains of a railway show how important, even out here, the Water of Leith has been to Edinburgh's light industries, though it is now a semi-rural landscape, particularly beautiful

at Colinton Dell and Craiglockhart Dell. The unspoilt
village of Colinton lies tucked among some of Edinburgh's
most palatial villas. A little further on, a detour east brings
you to the whins and rocks of Craiglockhart hills (where the
views are good).

Unless you want to make a pilgrimage to the rugby
ground at Murrayfield, the best place to pick up the Water
of Leith again as it nears the city centre is at Belford Bridge,
west of Queensferry Street. The streets and crescents to the
south of the river show how the Georgian pattern of
the New Town was transformed into a Victorian version of
the same idea. At the western end of Melville Street, St
Mary's Cathedral (often unjustly ignored merely because it
is Victorian) towers over the West End.

Downstream of Belford Bridge, the Water of Leith enters
a steep gorge. If you come down Queensferry Street and
over Telford's Dean Bridge (1829), you will hardly be aware
of it. But just before the bridge plunge down Bell's Brae
and you will arrive at the tiny Dean Village, an old milling
centre now virtually lost among the cliff-like terraces of the
New Town. It has been heavily restored where not demolished, and has become rather deliberately charming, but it
remains a curious hidden enclave in the middle of the city.

Beneath the Dean Bridge, more greenery lines the banks
of the river, hiding the little neo–Classical temple housing
St Bernard's Well, whose sulphurous waters were once
much favoured by New Town gentry. On the heights of the
northern bank, and well worth seeking out, is Ann Street,
one of Georgian Edinburgh's prettiest spots with long front
gardens shielding the façades of the houses, and St Bernard's
Crescent, an exercise in Doric grandeur.

At Stockbridge, further downstream, you will find plenty
of curiosities in St Stephen Street and one of the least-
known but best of Edinburgh's Georgian squares in the
unfinished Saxe-Coburg Place. Further down the river you
come across the Colonies, a collection of neat little cottage-
lined streets designed as a workers' community, but now
much sought after for their position and charm.

Apart from the semi–secret hideaway of Warriston Cemetery,
there is now little to be said for the Water of Leith until you reach
its junction with the sea at the old town which gives it its name.
Leith was and is Edinburgh's port, and has seen almost as much
history as the city behind it. Mary Queen of Scots returned to her
kingdom here on a melancholy day of mist, and later George IV
landed to cheering crowds. Fiercely independent of Edinburgh

for years, Leith was eventually forced to capitulate for administrative convenience in 1920. The port has been much polished
up of late and many of its old buildings have been restored,
though heavy lorries still make strolling through it something of
a hazard. The area called the Shore, where the river makes its
final curve to the sea, is the most pleasantly nautical part, and
there are thriving lunchtime bars and bistros.

Water of Leith sights

• **The National Gallery of Modern Art, Belford Road**
(open Mon to Sat 10 to 5, Sun 2 to 5; in Festival, Mon to
Sat 10 to 6, Sun 11 to 6) A reclining figure by Henry Moore
takes its ease on the green lawns which front the long
neo-classical façade of John Watson's School, which now
houses the National Gallery's modern art collection.
Displays in the series of cool, sparse rooms inside frequently
change, but most of the main periods of twentieth-century
painting are represented, and there is an excellent bookshop
to back up the paintings (though there is disappointingly
little about the gallery's own collection). Although the
collection was started only in 1960, there is a good core
holding, with Picasso, Nash, a selection of Cubist paintings,
some Surrealists and works by Hockney, Leger, Mondrian
and others. The Scottish Colourists are well represented, but
you may have to look hard to find samples of Glaswegian
'New Wave' painting on permanent display.
• **The Royal Botanic Garden** (open daily, Nov to Feb 10
to 4; Mar to Apr 10 to 6; May to Aug 10 to 8; Sept to end
Oct 10 to 6; plant houses open all year) This is one of the
best Botanic Gardens anywhere, and a spot well worth
knowing about on a freezing day for its sequence of bright,
warm and modern plant houses. The collections of
ericaceous plants from the tropics are particularly unusual,
but, on a fine day, there is much more to enchant the plant
lover. The collection of rhododendrons and azaleas is
renowned, and there is a splendid arboretum, as well as the
first peat garden to be established in Britain. This is in no
sense a formal garden – it is a large, wooded area that it is
quite possible to get lost in.

FURTHER AFIELD

In its nineteenth- and twentieth-century expansions Edinburgh
has absorbed a number of villages, many of which have

retained their character in the middle of the surrounding streets. Those by the Forth make good lunching spots. If you are weary of the bustle of central Edinburgh, make for the following (the order is clockwise round the city, starting with Queensferry on the banks of the Forth).

Queensferry

The old village is now completely overshadowed by the two great Forth Bridges which sweep by it. Malcolm Canmore's queen, Margaret, used the crossing as early as 1070, but the first official ferry was not established until 1129. It ran for over 800 years before the opening of the Forth Road Bridge in 1964 made it obsolete. However, the village, with its lovely old terraced houses and small museum, is still worth wandering round, while readers of Robert Louis Stevenson's *Kidnapped* will want to visit the Hawes Inn, from where David Balfour was lured aboard the brig *Covenant*. Queensferry is also the best spot from which to admire the bridges, especially the Rail Bridge, which celebrated its centenary in 1990 and remains one of the finest cantilever structures in the world. Try the pedestrian walkway along the Road Bridge for splendid views over the Forth, though the swaying sensation as lorries rumble past can be alarming!

Boats run from Queensferry to the island of Inchcolm close to the Fife coast from Easter to the end of September (call 0131-331 4857 for details). The thirteenth-century abbey with its well-preserved monastic buildings and considerable restoration is the goal of this trip, made all the better for its isolated setting among the busy shipping lanes of the Forth.

Near Queensferry, the neat estate village of **Dalmeny** is a draw for church-lovers; the little Norman church here is one of the best-preserved in the country.

Dalmeny House

(Open May to Sept, Sun 1 to 5.30, Mon and Tue 12 to 5.30; groups by prior arrangement; call 0131-331 1888)
Home of the Earl of Rosebery, and the closest to Edinburgh of the sequence of stately homes along this bank of the Forth, this neo-Gothic house (1815) has splendid views over the Firth. The collection inside, including the library, owes much to the fifth Earl, who not only married the richest heiress in England but became Prime Minister in

1894 and had three Derby winners into the bargain. Many of the finest treasures from Mentmore, which the fifth Earl's wife inherited, are now at Dalmeny. There is much fine eighteenth-century French furniture and some very unusual tapestries designed by Goya. The fifth Earl was an expert on Napoleon, and his collection of relics of the Emperor is also here. Dalmeny is very much a family home, and all these treasures are offered for admiration in a setting which could hardly be less like a stuffy museum.

Cramond

Cramond, at the mouth of the River Almond, is where the Romans based themselves on this bank of the Forth (some of the finds in Huntly House and the Queen Street museum came from here). The remains of a fort are just visible. Romans apart, Cramond is a tranquil place, popular for weekend excursions from the city, and with small yachts and motor boats lying off the river mouth. Walk up the River Almond to see the seventeenth-century bridge at the spot where James V was rescued from footpads by the local miller. If beachside walks are more to your taste than leafy riverbanks, go across the small ferry to a fine stretch of shoreline leading westwards towards Queensferry or head back east along a rather tamer but breezy esplanade, trying to ignore the large storage silos which blot the shoreline.

Lauriston Castle (Cramond Road South)

(Open Apr to Oct, daily 11 to 1, 2 to 5, closed Fri; mid-June to mid-Sept, 11 to 5, closed Fri; Nov to Mar, Sat and Sun only 2 to 4; grounds open 9 to dusk all year)
An old tower-house with a mansion added to it in 1827, this is a curious place, well worth seeking out among the quiet housing estates near Cramond. It is the interior that fascinates. The castle was given to the city in 1926 by its last owners, the Reids, who stipulated that as few changes as possible should be made to its contents. Mr Reid owned a firm of cabinet-makers which did a lot of work fitting out railway carriages, while his wife's family were sanitary engineers. The result is some fine panelling and remarkable plumbing, but Lauriston is especially interesting for the extraordinary collection of objects that the Reids assembled. They seem to have collected what they liked without regard for value or antiquity – huge numbers of commodes, masses

of prints (some execrable), and a collection of 'wool mosaic' pictures, made by slicing longitudinally laid threads into a number of pictures, like a stick of rock. There is a sit-down weighing machine in Mrs Reid's bedroom, coconut shells in silver mounts, and a fine assembly of Derbyshire 'Blue John Ware'. The overall impression is of a homely clutter, full of things to gaze at.

Part of the charm of Lauriston lies in the enthusiasm of the guides, who genuinely love the house they look after and, this far away from the tourist trail, have time to spare.

Newhaven

The harbour here was where Edinburgh's fishing fleet once landed its catch. Part of the old fish market is now a museum (open all year, Mon to Sat 12 to 5) while fish is still sold in the remainder. A few old houses and a few fishing boats remain to remind you of the past.

Duddingston

Tucked under Arthur's Seat, Duddingston is the goal of countless walks across the expanse of Holyrood Park for lunch at what is thought to be the oldest pub in Scotland, the Sheep's Heid Inn. You can also get there by the lazier method of driving round the mountain-girdling road which runs under the columnar stratifications of Salisbury Crags and round the shoulder of the great volcanic plug which dominates the eastern side of Edinburgh. Arthur's Seat is easily climbed from Duddingston or from Dunsapie Loch (saving 300 feet of climbing) and the views of Edinburgh are worth the effort, though try to choose a day when the wind will allow you to enjoy them. Duddingston Loch is a bird sanctuary and enthusiasts with binoculars can be glimpsed among the reeds, while children throw bread to the more common species of duck and goose along the shore.

Craigmillar Castle (HS) (Craigmillar Castle Road)

(Open Apr to Sept, Mon to Sat 9.30 to 6.30, Sun 2 to 6.30; Oct to Mar, Mon to Wed and Sat 9.30 to 4.30, Sun 2 to 4.30; closed Thur pm and Fri; enquiries 0131-661-4445) Driving southwards from Duddingston you quickly realise that the surrounding housing estates cannot improve Craigmillar's outlook, but once you arrive you see that they fail to diminish the impact of this substantial ruin. Two successive curtain walls rise in front of a fourteenth-century tower house, with later ranges added to it. The massive fortress was the place where the murder of Mary Queen of Scots' husband Darnley was planned, and where Maitland, Bothwell, Argyll, Huntly and Balfour probably signed a bond agreeing to his removal (though the bond, hardly surprisingly, no longer exists). As a scene for the planning of an assassination, Craigmillar can hardly be bettered.

Blackford

A very fine viewpoint on Blackford Hill and the Royal Observatory, with an informative visitor centre, make a short expedition out to Blackford a pleasure, especially for astronomers. The pond is a famous toy boat-sailing spot.

Swanston

A favourite haunt of Robert Louis Stevenson and described in *St Ives*, Swanston's seventeenth-century cottages lie at the foot of the Pentland Hills, on the far side of the Edinburgh by-pass. Apart from the undisturbed old houses and the surrounding golf course there is nothing much to see, but paths lead into the Pentlands and across to the dry ski slope at Hillend. (See page 176 for description of the Pentlands.)

Corstorphine

Residents of Corstorphine are kept awake by the roar of lions, for Edinburgh Zoo (open Apr to Sept, daily 9 to 6; Oct to Mar, 9 to 4.30; all Suns from 9.30) lies on the bank of the hill. It is a steeply banked, fairly traditional zoo, good for a day out with children. The 'Penguin Parade' – a shuffle down the paths by the zoo's fine collection of the birds – is a high spot. If you are interested in agriculture, a short journey (follow signs to the airport) takes you to Ingliston and the **Scottish Agricultural Museum** (open Apr to end Sept, daily 10 to 5; Oct to Mar, Mon to Fri 10 to 5), where there is a large collection of implements from the past, reconstructed farm interiors and lots of photographs. Ingliston is also the scene of the Royal Highland Show in June each year, an agricultural show with distinctive Scottish tinges.

USEFUL DIRECTORY

Main tourist office
Edinburgh and Lothians Tourist Board
3 Princes Street
Waverley Market
EH2 2QP (0131-557 1700)

Tourist Board publications Very useful is the free *Welcome to Edinburgh* brochure (Landmark Press) which has a small city centre map with an outline of the city's history, and a list of tourist attractions and places to go. Also available is the *Essential Guide to Edinburgh*. Useful newspapers listing cinemas and places of interest are *The Scotsman* and the *Edinburgh Evening News*.

Local transport
Edinburgh Airport 0131-333 1000
Waverley Station (Scotrail) Passenger Information Department
0131-556 2451
National Rail Enquiries (0345) 212282
St Andrews Square Bus Station (Green Buses) 0131-558 1616
Regional transport and city tours information 0131-555 6363
Scottish Citylink (bus) (0990) 505050

City guides
Robin Sinton 0131-661 0125
Scotline Bus Tours 0131-557 0162

Entertainment
Edinburgh Festival Theatre 0131-529 6000
Edinburgh Filmhouse (enquiries) 0131-228 6382 (bookings after
12) 0131-228 2688
Kings Theatre (enquiries) 0131-228 5955 (bookings) 0131-220 4349
Playhouse Theatre 0131-557 2590
Royal Lyceum Theatre 0131-229 9697
Usher Hall 0131-228 1155

The Edinburgh Festival
Festival Offices: 21 Market Street 0131-226 4001
Fringe Office: 180 High Street 0131-226 5257
Tattoo Office: 32 Market Street 0131 225 1188

Miscellaneous
Heart of Midlothian Football Club: 10 Castle Park 0131-337 6132
Meadowbank Sports Centre: 139 London Road 0131-661 5351
The Royal Commonwealth Pool: 21 Dalkeith Road 0131-667 7211

WHERE TO STAY

£ – under £70 per room per night, incl. VAT

££ – £70 to £110 per room per night, incl. VAT

£££ – over £110 per room per night, incl. VAT

17 Abercromby Place
17 Abercromby Place, Edinburgh
EH3 6LB
TEL 0131-557 8036
FAX 0131-558 3453
An upmarket and centrally based bed and breakfast, smartly furnished with antiques and white wicker furniture. Breakfast is served in the high-ceilinged green dining-room at a long mahogany table. Choose from fruit, cereals and yoghurt or a cooked breakfast; good coffee. Bedrooms are on the lower ground floor or in the converted stable block across from the car park.
£ All year exc Chr; 5 rooms

Balmoral Guest House
32 Pilrig Street, Edinburgh EH6 5AL
TEL 0131-554 1857
Small and friendly terraced guesthouse with basic amenities and simple furnishings. Breakfast is served in the tartan-carpeted dining-room. Immaculate bedrooms. Unrestricted street parking available nearby.
£ All year; 7 rooms all with wash-basin; credit cards not accepted

Bonnington Guest House
202 Ferry Road, Edinburgh EH6 4NW
TEL 0131-554 7610
A Victorian house on the north side of town, set a little back from the main road and not far from the docks; city centre ten minutes by bus. Breakfast only, packed lunches available on request. Neat bedrooms.
£ All year exc Chr; 6 rooms; credit cards not accepted

Channings
South Learmouth Gardens, Edinburgh
EH4 1EZ
TEL 0131-315 2226
FAX 0131-332 9631
A conversion of five Edwardian terraced houses in quiet surroundings, a short drive from Princes Street. Three ground-floor lounges and a dashing basement brasserie, red and green with gold-starred wallpaper. The menu has a selection of Scottish dishes; bar lunches in the lounge. Bedrooms are smallish, bathrooms neat and bright.
£££ All year exc 24-28 Dec; 48 rooms

Classic Guest House
50 Mayfield Road, Edinburgh EH9 2NH
TEL 0131-667 5847
FAX 0131-662 1016
Small, terraced Victorian house on a main route to the city centre. Attractive breakfast room; dinner and packed lunches provided on request. Pretty bedrooms furnished in modern style.
£ All year; 6 rooms

Drummond House
17 Drummond Place, Edinburgh
EH3 6PL
TEL/FAX 0131-557 9189
Restored Georgian house a short walk from Princes Street. Extravagant breakfasts include smoked salmon, scrambled eggs and home-made preserves. Bedrooms have bold colour schemes and fine antique furnishings. A yellow sitting-room contains the only TV.
££ All year exc Chr; 3 rooms

Hopetoun Guest House
15 Mayfield Road, Edinburgh
EH9 2NG
TEL 0131-677 7691
A small, terraced Victorian house situated in a pleasant residential area

on a main road and bus route, with easy access to the city centre. There is a breakfast room at the rear; bedrooms are spacious and comfortable and share two bathrooms.

£ All year exc Chr; 3 rooms; credit cards not accepted

Malmaison

1 Tower Place, Leith, Edinburgh
EH6 7DB
TEL 0131-555 6868
FAX 0131-555 6999

Beautifully refurbished turreted building in water-front position at Leith docks with striking modern decor and friendly young staff. Enjoyable food, simple bedrooms with definite contemporary style and many thoughtful extras. Breezy service.

££ All year; 25 rooms

Ravensneuk

11 Blacket Avenue, Edinburgh
EH9 1RR
TEL 0131-667 5347

Restrained and formal guest house in a leafy city conservation area. The sitting-room complete with lamps, gilt-framed pictures, china and books is reminiscent of an old-fashioned parlour. The fresh bedrooms display pretty decorative touches.

£ All year; 7 rooms, 2 with bath/shower

Sibbet House

26 Northumberland Street, Edinburgh
EH3 6LS
TEL 0131-556 1078
FAX 0131-557 9445

A lovely, spacious Georgian house. The large first-floor drawing room is filled with antiques and the light from three floor-to-ceiling windows. The red dining-room doubles as a library. Silver and china on the table complement freshly cooked breakfasts, fruit salad,

yoghurt and cereals. Bedrooms are ample, comfortable and well furnished.

£ All year; 3 bedrooms

Sonas Guest House

3 East Mayfield, Edinburgh EH9 1SD
TEL 0131-667 2781
FAX 0131-667 0454

Built in 1876 for a railway director, this guesthouse is located in a quiet residential street about a mile south of the city centre. A small car park exists for guests' use. The breakfast/sitting-room is on the ground floor; bedrooms are small, bright and well equipped.

£ All year exc Chr; 8 rooms; credit cards not accepted

Turret Guest House

8 Kilmaurs Terrace, Edinburgh
EH16 5DR
TEL 0131-667 6704
FAX 0131-668 1368

A homely guesthouse in a quiet road on a bus route with easy access to the city centre. The bay-windowed sitting-room is a pleasant spot furnished with squashy sofas. Excellent breakfasts include haggis and clootie dumplin'. Bedrooms are prettily decorated and full of knick-knacks.

£ All year exc Chr; 6 rooms

Twenty London Street

20 London Street, Edinburgh
EH3 6NA
TEL 0131-557 0216
FAX 0131-556 6445

Recently renovated Georgian townhouse in the New Town district, within easy reach of Princes Street. Guests have the use of a large sitting-room where breakfast is also served. The well-equipped bedrooms look over the back garden; bathrooms are small.

£ All year exc Chr; 3 rooms

WHERE TO EAT

Key: A ★ marks a place that is particularly good value for money

Ann Purna
45 St Patrick's Square, Edinburgh
EH8 9ET
TEL 0131-662 1807
Family-run vegetarian restaurant with excellent value South Indian and Gujarati food. Good rice beer and genuine service.
Mon to Fri 12 to 2, all week 5.30 to 11; closed 25-26 Dec, 1 Jan

Atrium
10 Cambridge Street, Edinburgh
EH1 2ED
TEL 0131-228 8882
Bold decor featuring a glass lift, visible ventilation ducts, tables made from railway sleepers and candle lighting. The short menus offer a light and lively version of brasserie food, and vegetarians can dine seriously well here. The wine list is modern, akin to the food.
Mon to Fri 12 to 2.30, Mon to Sat 6 to 10.30 (11 during Festival); closed 1 week Chr

Café Florentin
8 St Giles Street, Edinburgh EH1 1PT
TEL 0131-225 6267
Trendy pâtisserie serving fruit tarts and coffee.
Sun to Thur 7 to midnight, Fri and Sat 7 to 2am; closed 25 Dec; credit cards not accepted

Crannog ★
14 South St Andrew Street, Edinburgh
EH2 2AZ
TEL 0131-557 5589
FAX 0131-558 3067
Third restaurant of a chain also based Glasgow and Fort William. West Coast fish and shellfish lead the way; fresh hot langoustines with

garlic butter make a winning combination. Salad, new potatoes and chunky bread served as standard. Well-tailored wine list.
All week 12 to 2.30, 6 to 10.30 (later during Festival); closed Sun and Mon in winter

Denzler's 121 ★
121 Constitution Street, Leith, Edinburgh EH6 7AE
TEL 0131-554 3268
FAX 0131-467 7239
Eat food direct from the Swiss Alps in marble-fronted vaults lined by contemporary Scottish art. Try air-dried beef and ham, and a choice of many New World wines.
Tue to Fri 12 to 2, Tue to Sat 6.30 to 10; exc Chr and 1 week Jan, 2 weeks end July

Gran Via
3 South St Andrew Street, Edinburgh
EH2 2AU
TEL 0131-556 1020
Tapas bar with views over Princes Street.
All week 12 to 11; closed 25 Dec, 1 Jan

Indian Cavalry Club ★
3 Atholl Place, Edinburgh EH3 8HP
TEL 0131-228 3282/2974
FAX 0131-225 1911
A wide range of dishes with subtle flavours and fragrant, spicy tastes. Exciting fish choice, vegetarian dishes worthy of starring roles and good Indian drinks.
All week 12 to 2, 5.30 to 11.30

Kalpna ★
2-3 St Patrick Square, Edinburgh
EH8 9EZ
TEL 0131-667 9890
Distinctive South Indian vegetarian cooking with impressive thalis and great value lunchtime buffets. Intriguing wine list.

*Mon to Fri 12 to 2, Mon to Sat
5.30 to 11; closed 25-26 Dec, 1 Jan*

Kelly's
46 West Richmond Street, Edinburgh
EH8 9DZ
TEL 0131-668 3847
Small and quietly civilised
restaurant with modern cooking
and excellent soups. A lively and
fair-priced wine list.
*Wed to Sat 6 to 10.30; closed Oct,
first week Jan*

The Laigh Kitchen
117a Hanover Street, Edinburgh
EH2 1DJ
TEL 0131-225 1552
Excellent home baking, scones and
tea in atmospheric flagstoned coffee
shop.
*Mon to Sat 8 to 4 (later during
Festival); closed Suns, 25-26 Dec,
1-2 Jan and some local hols; credit
cards not accepted*

The Lower Aisle
High Street, Edinburgh EH1 1RE
TEL 0131-225 5147
Good value light lunches in
advocates' haunt below St Giles
Cathedral; salads, coffee.
*Mon to Fri 8.30 to 4.30, Sun
10.30 to 2; closed Sat (exc during
Festival), 2 weeks Chr; credit cards
not accepted*

Le Marché Noir
2-4 Eyre Place, Edinburgh EH3 5EP
TEL 0131-558 1608
FAX 0131-556 0798
French-style dining in a welcoming
and friendly atmosphere. The
predominantly Gallic wine list
offers brilliant value.
*Mon to Fri 12 to 2.30, Sun to Thurs
7 to 10, Fri and Sat 7 to 10.30*

Martin's
70 Rose Street, North Lane, Edinburgh
EH2 3DX
TEL 0131-225 3106
By contrast with the unpromising
location, the air of welcome and
food inside are superb. A daily-
changing, inventive menu
engenders high praise. So too does
the serious cheeseboard. Seek out
gems on the shrewd wine list.
*Tue to Fri 12 to 2, Tue to Sat 7 to
10; closed 24 Dec-24 Jan, 1 week
Jun, 1 week Sept/Oct*

Montpeliers
159-161 Bruntsfield Place, Edinburgh
EH10 4DG
TEL 0131-229 3115
A buzzy atmosphere, with everything
from bacon butties to guinea-fowl
and good puddings served up
accompanied by loud music.
All week 9am to midnight

Pierre Victoire ★
38 Grassmarket, Edinburgh EH1 2HG
TEL 0131-225 6267
Informal, superb value French
restaurant with other branches at 10
Victoria Street and 8 Union Street.
*Mon to Sat 12 to 3, 6 to 11, closed
Sun*

La Rusticana
90 Hanover Street, Edinburgh
EH2 1EL
TEL 0131-225 2227
Classic Italian basement restaurant
with red-checked tablecloths.
Excellent pizzas and decent wines.
*Mon to Sat 12 to 2.30, 5 to 11;
closed Sun, 25 Dec, 2 Jan*

Rendezvous ★
24 Deanhaugh Street, Stockbridge,
Edinburgh EH4 1LY
TEL 0131-332 4476
Tiny restaurant with short but
sweet lunchtime menu. A more
ambitious evening repertoire is on

offer amid the ornithological art.
Beware dreadful lunchtime parking.
*Wed to Sun 12 to 2.30, Tue to Sun
6.30 to 10.30*

Shore *

3-4 Shore, Leith, Edinburgh
EH6 6QW
TEL 0131-553 5080
Emphasises modern fish cookery;
traditional observances enhanced by
Mediterranean/oriental style.
*Mon to Sat 12 to 2.30, Sun 12.30
to 3, all week 6.30 to 10.15; closed
25-26 Dec, 1-2 Jan*

Siam Erawan

48 Howe Street, Edinburgh EH3 6TH
TEL 0131-226 3675
Simple and tasteful basement
restaurant, the best of the city's
Thai specialists. Prime ingredients
and fresh local seafood.
*All week 12 to 2, 6 to 10.45; closed
25-26 Dec, 1-2 Jan*

Spices *

110 West Bow, Grassmarket, Edinburgh
EH1 2HH
TEL 0131-225 5028
Mackintosh furniture meets Indian
art, the perfect setting for princely
cuisine. Meat-eaters catered for,
vegetarians best off.
Mon to Sat 12 to 2, 6 to 11

Vintners Rooms *

The Vaults, 87 Giles Street, Leith,
Edinburgh EH6 6BZ
TEL 0131-554 6767
FAX 0131-467 7130
Celebrated dockland restaurant with
exotic decor. Inventive and
successful cooking, great attention
to detail. Wine bar set-price
lunches of commendable value.
*Mon to Sat 12 to 2.30, 7 to 10.30;
closed 2 weeks Chr*

Waterfront Wine Bar

1c Dock Place, Leith, Edinburgh
EH6 6LU
TEL 0131-554 7427
A blackboard menu of fish, ribs and
salads at the best tables in the
conservatory. Good wine list at
affordable prices.
*Sun to Thur 12 to 2.30, Sun 6 to
9, Mon to Thur 6 to 9.30; Fri and
Sat 12 to 3, 6 to 10*

EAST LOTHIAN AND THE CENTRAL BELT

- A region of industrial relics, stately homes, interesting coastline and gentle hills
- Fine pastoral scenery in East Lothian and some excellent castles
- Plenty of history in the Clyde Valley and along the Forth coast

Chatelherault

TWO revolutions have left their mark on this swathe of country – the Agrarian and the Industrial. The fertile strip of East Lothian between the Lammermuir Hills and the beaches of North Berwick and Gullane became the proving ground for the late eighteenth-century transformation of Scottish agriculture from a virtually feudal system of strip-farming and common land into a productive and stable industry. Long leases were granted to tenant farmers and new crop varieties were bred; the threshing mill was invented and farming turned from a haphazard activity into something approaching a science. The neat villages, the enclosed fields, the solid farm-steadings, the woods and the pastureland which in many ways make East Lothian the most English of all the Scottish counties are the products of this revolution.

While the model for the Scottish Agrarian Revolution was largely taken from south of the Border, it may be argued that the Industrial Revolution really started in Scotland. For it was in Scotland that James Watt, by his invention of the separate condenser and the governor, turned the steam engine from an inefficient machine into an economical source of power for everything from pumps to locomotives.

Scotland's coalfields lie scattered in an arc around the Central Lowlands; her iron and steel industries were concentrated in the lower Clyde Valley, her spinning and weaving round Glasgow. It was in the Central Lowlands, too, that the petroleum industry was pioneered, at Bathgate and in Broxburn where paraffin and lubricating oils were distilled from coal and shale for the first time by 'Paraffin' Young, whose 1850 patent marks the start of commercial oil refining.

Today, the shale mines, the coal mines and the iron and steel works are extinct or moribund, and only their effects on the landscape remain. Even these are disappearing as the pink jelly-shaped 'bings' (slag-heaps) of waste shale are flattened and the old coal tips landscaped and planted under environmental improvement schemes. Even the sour old mining villages are slowly being given new leases of life as their housing is upgraded and commuters to Edinburgh or Glasgow settle in new estates on their fringes. Light industries are replacing the 'heavies' across the region, and there is a breath of regeneration which was non-existent 20 years ago.

Kings and Covenanters

Beneath the industrial debris lies a much older layer of Scotland. Stirling, Linlithgow and Edinburgh were the pivotal towns of the Scottish Court and it is hardly surprising that the country around them witnessed many of the power struggles that dogged medieval Scotland. The Central Lowlands were also the first stop for any invading army: the burghs of East Lothian at the end of the easiest route from the south were burnt almost as often as the Border towns. Everywhere in the region there are memories of the past – Sir James Douglas setting fire to his castle, the corpses of his enemies, his food, his wine and his horses to deny them to the English; James IV being warned of his death at Flodden by an apparition in Linlithgow church; Mary Queen of Scots surrendering to her enemies at Carberry Hill; George IV supping turtle soup at Hopetoun . . .

This region, together with neighbouring Dumfriesshire, has a tragic history for it was the battleground for the final struggle of the Covenanters against the doctrinal impositions of the restored Stewart kings. For almost 30 years, sustained by little more than faith, men and women deserted the churches where the law decreed they must worship and followed their outlawed ministers to the hills and bare moors to attend services known as conventicles. Every means of coercion was used against them and torture, on-the-spot execution, imprisonment or transportation to the colonies was often their fate. Yet they persisted.

EAST LOTHIAN

If you drive up the A1 from the south you will see the coast begin to flatten out as the Lammermuirs recede further from the sea. The huge bulk of the Torness nuclear power plant and the Dunbar cement works beyond it are not a propitious beginning to East Lothian's pleasures, but if you have time a detour to the sea at Barn's Ness is worthwhile, especially for geologists – lumps of coal and fossil coral beds are two of the pleasures. Equally, a journey round the back roads past the villages of Oldhamstocks and Spott is more enjoyable than sticking to the main road. Two crucial battles were fought near Dunbar. The first, in 1296, marked the beginning of Edward I's ruthless conquest (he had already sacked Berwick), while the second, in 1650, was the turning point

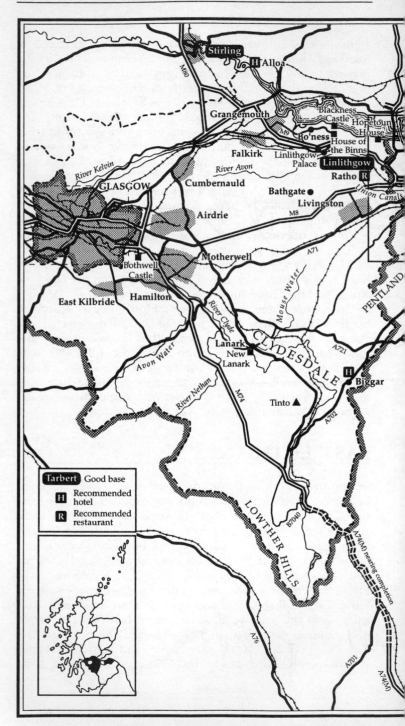

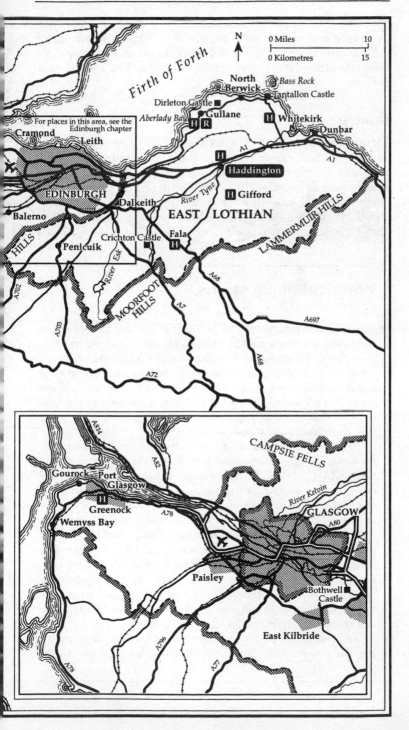

of Cromwell's invasion of Scotland. 'The Lord has delivered them into our hands,' he is supposed to have said, watching the Covenanters leaving the high ground in the mistaken belief that they could overwhelm his army. The reverse was the case.

Dunbar

The decay of some of Dunbar's huge resort hotels suggests that as a seaside resort it is no longer as popular as it once was, and the town now seems to be realigning its image more towards heritage than sand. Interesting attempts are being made to slot modern housing into the vernacular tradition, continuing the work done by the architect Basil Spence, while some of the town's older buildings have been

---

Practical suggestions

This urbanised region is not the first part of Scotland that springs to mind when planning a holiday. Most people take in a few of its sights on a visit to Edinburgh or Glasgow, and this is probably the most sensible way of doing things. However, if you have a day or two spare and the weather forecast is too bad to venture further north, if you are tacking a weekend on to a business trip, if you want to play golf or build sandcastles, or if you want to do some walking on gentle hills, then this region is ideal.

The Forth coast and the Clyde Valley are the two most self-contained areas for touring, and both have some good scenery and sights. There is a lot to be said in favour of basing yourself for a day or two in East Lothian, where you can swing between seaside, golf course and moorland at whim, and where the towns and villages are interesting and attractive. The Pentland Hills provide some fine walks and are in easy reach of Edinburgh. Those who like industrial archaeology will find plenty of interest in the relics of the mines, canals, and industries of Mid and West Lothian which have been preserved and opened up to visitors, while the old ship-building towns on the bank of the Clyde west of Glasgow still have some atmosphere. No one should miss the old mills at New Lanark, scene of a remarkable experiment in social engineering.

Accommodation can be a problem, largely because Edinburgh and Glasgow are so close and tend to attract all the trade. In the

spruced up. The place to start (and maybe finish) exploring is down at the **Victoria Harbour**, where the general picturesqueness of small fishing boats in a rocky enclave is enhanced by the red sandstone pillar which is all that remains of Dunbar Castle. The cacophony of the resident colony of kittiwakes adds to the nautical flavour. It is hard to imagine now, but Dunbar was once a major whaling and smuggling port.

Dunbar Castle, once one of the strongest fortresses on the coast, has had its moments. The castle's most famous piece of history occurred when Black Agnes, daughter of Robert the Bruce's companion Randolph, held out here against the English for five months in 1338, being relieved from the sea just when all hope seemed to be lost and promptly sending bread and wine to her besiegers to show

---

country around both cities there are several plush hotels (often in venerable castles), and while these are used largely by business or sporting people and have correspondingly fat tariffs, you might find it worth ringing them on spec at weekends or off-season to see if you can pick up a bargain. East Lothian has a number of old inns in its towns and villages, and substantial numbers of seaside guesthouses and hotels in its coastal resorts. Elsewhere you are likely to find the scattered bed and breakfasts the best value – the biggest clutches are round Linlithgow and Lanark.

Good bases
● **Haddington** This old burgh makes an ideal base for exploring East Lothian. It is a small but lively town, the centre-piece for the prosperous farming countryside. Streets lined by elegant eighteenth-century houses run from its old triangular marketplace down to the River Tyne.
● **Linlithgow** The ruins of the royal palace and the loch behind its High Street dominate this old town, the most attractive in West Lothian. It has managed to retain a little of its market-town tranquillity despite the coming of the canal, the railway and the M9 motorway. It is well placed for exploration of the southern coast of the Firth of Forth, and also for picking through the industrial archaeology of the area.
● **Stirling** (page 266) also makes a good base for the north-western part of the area.

that her supplies were better than theirs. The prophet True Thomas was here too, telling the Earl of Dunbar in 1286 that the following noon would bring a storm the like of which had never descended upon Scotland. A messenger arrived the next day bringing news of the death of Alexander III, the event which marked the beginning of the long agony of the Wars of Independence – a storm indeed.

The stump of the castle is all that remains of a building that appears once to have bridged several sea stacks outside what is now the harbour entrance: much was demolished in 1567 and yet more fell to Cromwell.

Elsewhere in Dunbar, the **Tolbooth** is early seventeenth-century and rather fine, while the imposing **Lauderdale House**, which stands at one end of the High Street, owes its current appearance to Robert Adam. The old promenade which fringes the cliffs between Dunbar and Belhaven Bay to the west makes a good walk. The **John Muir House** (open late May to end Aug, Mon to Sat 11 to 1 and 2 to 5.30, Sun 2 to 5.30; closed Wed exc Aug) contains, among other pieces of domestic Victoriana, 'a midwifery potty for post-natal comfort'. The house and the nearby John Muir Country Park are memorials to the American pioneer of conservation, who was born here (though he moved next door when he was one and emigrated when he was ten). 'Country Park', with its suggestion of neatly ordered recreational landscape, is an unfortunate term for the wild sweep of Belhaven Bay, backed by dunes and a labyrinth of ancient tank-traps, with the saltmarshes and rocky outcrops of Tyninghame beyond. There are few better stretches of seashore south of Fife.

Dunbar to Gifford

This back route to Edinburgh (B6370) takes you along the fringe of the Lammermuir Hills and through some of East Lothian's prettiest villages. All over the countryside you will see the stone farm-steadings and rows of pantiled cottages which are reminders that East Lothian was in the forefront of the agricultural improvements of the late eighteenth century. The threshing machine was invented by an East Lothian man; new strains of wheat and oats were bred here and the editor of the first farming journal in Scotland came from East Linton.

Stenton is an extremely photogenic village, with its pantiled houses, its green, its medieval well and the remains of its old church. It once had a reputation for being in the forefront of the witch-burning craze. Now it has become rather gentrified, to the extent of having a small art gallery. Close to Stenton is the hidden valley of Pressmennan, where the nineteenth-century artificial Lake of Pressmennan lies concealed among the trees, now the setting for a secluded nature trail.

Further west, and a short way off the B6370, **Garvald** is a tiny place tucked into the shadow of the Lammermuirs with some lovely old cottages and a church going back to the twelfth century. Above the village on the edge of the moors is the modern **Nunraw Abbey**. The Cistercian community here has long links with the area, for Nunraw was originally a house belonging to the twelfth-century convent at Haddington, which was bought back by the Cistercians in 1946. It is possible to visit the chapel of the modern abbey, and you are quite likely to meet a white-habited monk on a tractor. The old tower-house is now a guesthouse. The narrow road winds up into the hills above Nunraw and eventually over into the valley of the Whiteadder. Back on the B6370, **Gifford** – another planned village from the eighteenth-century, with a particularly harmonious church of Dutch appearance – makes a good centre for walks into the Lammermuirs and is a pleasant place to stop for lunch. Avoid weekends, though, when half of Edinburgh may join you.

Dunbar to Haddington

Neatly bypassed by the A1, **East Linton** is quiet and attractive, the sort of village where there is plenty of time for a gossip in the grocer's shop. The River Tyne pours through the centre in a rocky gorge, inhabited by fishermen optimistically loitering by dark pools and crossed by a fine old bridge – you will have to take to your feet to see it properly. A short distance downstream is the renowned **Preston Mill** (NTS, open May to end Sept, Mon to Sat 11 to 1, 2 to 5.30, Sun 1.30 to 5.30; Oct weekends only, 1.30 to 4). This red-tiled seventeenth-century watermill with its conical-roofed kiln is surrounded by the sort of ducks-and-placid-water scenery which has made it the subject of countless paintings and photographs from the nineteenth century onwards. The working machinery inside is not, in this age of restored watermills, as rare a sight as it once was, but the age of the place and the excellent explanatory notices still make it essential visiting. **Phantassie Doocot**

167

(NTS, times as Preston Mill) close by is perhaps not quite so deserving of notice but is nevertheless worth a look, especially if you have already remarked how well-sprinkled Lowland Scotland is with ancient *pigeonniers* (perhaps a lasting memento of the Auld Alliance with France). The dovecote at Phantassie has more than 500 pigeon nests and a revolving ladder to reach them by, plus a string course in the wall to stop the rats getting up.

Sticking up from the surrounding countryside south of East Linton, the rounded hill of **Traprain Law** is the plug of an ancient volcano. Traprain, despite being half quarried away, is an important archaeological site. It seems to have been the capital for local tribes from the Stone Age until the end of the Dark Ages and it was here that the famous Traprain Hoard of Roman silverware was found. Views from the summit are hard to beat.

In the valley of the Tyne below Traprain Law stands **Hailes Castle** (HS, standard times). Its position may seem odd until you realise how completely it blocks the strategic route of the Tyne and preys upon the road leading towards Edinburgh. For a castle on the main invasion route from England a lot remains, and some of it dates from before the Wars of Independence. The square *donjon*, the curtain walls and the remains of a sixteenth-century range are perhaps less memorable than the extremely unpleasant pit prisons and the peaceful setting on the banks of the river.

The old airfield at **East Fortune** is now the home of the Museum of Flight, an outstation of the Royal Museum of Scotland (open Apr to end Sept, daily 10.30 to 5). Its old hangar is crammed with aircraft ranging from the airship which made the first double crossing of the Atlantic to a Vulcan bomber. If you are in the area at the right time and are fond of aeroplanes, give it a try.

Haddington

Although most of its best buildings date from the seventeenth or eighteenth centuries, Haddington is a very old town, having been made a royal burgh in the twelfth-century. Its position made it an obvious target for a spot of burning during the various English invasions of medieval times, and there was a period between 1548 and 1549 when the English actually occupied the town and defended it from the French troops sent against them by Mary of Guise. It was during this siege that the stone crown on the tower of

St Mary's church was destroyed. John Knox the preacher was born here in 1505.

Haddington is a busy small town, acting as local shopping centre for much of prosperous East Lothian, so its central streets – where there was once a large, triangular market-place – are studded with parked Range Rovers and farmers stocking up on supplies. But there is more to the town than this, for the energy and enthusiasm of its inhabitants have brought about a careful programme of restoration and conservation, and there are many splendid old houses to gaze at while walking round the streets, following the *Walk around Haddington* leaflet, available locally. Behind all the elegant eighteenth-century buildings, which culminate in William Adam's Town House, lies the street plan of the older burgh, and you can find fragments of the old town wall. If architecture palls, wander down to the banks of the River Tyne to look at the old bridges, photograph the occasional swan, or to take a stroll round **St Mary's Pleasance**, a beautifully restored garden.

Haddington is an ideal base from which to explore East Lothian, and is perfectly acceptable for day trips to Edinburgh too. There is often some cultural event or other going on, mounted by the Lamp of Lothian Collegiate Centre (01620 823738), the body responsible for so much of Haddington's conservation. The town-centre hotels lean more towards country trade than towards tourism, and are acceptable if uninspiring. The alternative is to stay in one of the guesthouses in or near the town – probably the best option.

In and near Haddington

• **St Mary's Collegiate Church** (open Apr to end Sept, Mon to Sat 10 to 4, Sun 1 to 4), down by the river, was built in the fourteenth century. A massive restoration programme, completed in 1973, re-roofed the chancel and transepts (which had been abandoned after the Reformation) and rebuilt much of the stonework of the eastern end of the church. The result, as at Dunblane Cathedral, is an inspiration, particularly when you look at the photographs of the work being carried out and realise what a mammoth task it was and how authentically it has been executed. Concerts are sometimes held in the old church – ask inside.

• **Lennoxlove House** (open Easter weekend 2 to[ ] to Sept, Wed, Sat and Sun 2 to 5), a mile

Haddington on the B6369, is worth making an effort to see (despite its limited opening hours) either if you are a Mary Queen of Scots follower or if you simply like stately homes. The seat of the Duke of Hamilton, the old extended and revamped tower–house, now contains much of the coll- ection of portraits and chinaware which was removed from the huge Hamilton Palace before its demolition. The Hamiltons were the chief supporters of Mary Queen of Scots after her escape from Loch Leven and during the battle of Langside that followed. Mary's death mask is at Lennoxlove, as is the silver casket which once contained the series of letters purporting to prove Mary's obsession with Bothwell and her part in the conspiracy to murder Darnley. They are likely to have been forged (Mary herself was never allowed to see them) but served their purpose in helping to keep her exiled in England.

North Berwick and the Forth coast

The semi-circle of land which juts northwards into the Forth contains East Lothian's best seaside and nature reserves, greatest number of golf courses and the remarkable Tantallon castle. It has long been the stamping-ground for inhabitants of Edinburgh on fine weekends, but there is usually room to spare for everyone.

As you drive along the eastern coast towards Tantallon, keep an eye open for the sixteenth-century tithe barn at Whitekirk, which has survived more intact than Holyrood Abbey, whose monks used to store grain here.

Tantallon Castle

(HS, standard times, closed Thur pm and Fri in winter)
The great red walls of Tantallon rise from red cliffs against which the sea lashes. 'Three sides of wall-like rock, and one side of rock-like wall' give the castle its superb defensive capabilities. A curtain wall with central keep/gatehouse and two flanking towers cuts the neck of a peninsula, which drops sheer to the sea on the other three sides. Although time and the guns of Cromwell's general, Monk, have done their best to destroy it, Tantallon still overawes the visitor by its scale and setting. This was a Douglas stronghold, pro- bably started in the late fourteenth century, and both a bar- gaining counter and a place of refuge for that powerful family when they were out of royal favour.

One and a half miles offshore, the **Bass Rock** floats in similar impregnability, streaked with white by its innumerable seabirds. Whatever the weather or time of day, the setting of castle, sea and cliff is one of the finest in the whole of lowland Scotland.

North Berwick

A popular seaside resort in Victorian and Edwardian times, North Berwick is still very much a going concern, with the necessary ingredients of golf courses, a pretty harbour and nearby sandy beaches. Just outside the town, a path leads to the top of **North Berwick Law**. It is well worth the short but steep climb to the top on a clear day – the views are magnificent. The curious arch on top turns out to be made from a pair of whale jawbones.

It was in North Berwick in 1591 that a well-known coven of witches were believed to have nearly caused the death of James VI by a storm. Their subsequent torture, trial and execution was a subject of much interest to the King, who not only wrote a book about witchcraft but may have let it be known to Shakespeare that *Macbeth* would be all the better received for having a touch of the occult in it. More prosaic grounds for the King's interest may have been the opportunity the North Berwick witches presented to discredit Francis, Earl of Bothwell, who was cited as the coven's devil. The Auld Kirk is the scene of the witches' arrest.

North Berwick is the place to look for a boat trip around the Bass Rock (see above), or perhaps to the other small islands of Fidra and Craigleith, which lie just offshore. A trip around the Bass, especially when the gannet colony is breeding, can be a deafening experience, but not one that you are likely to forget.

Dirleton

A few miles west of North Berwick, Dirleton is held by many to be the prettiest village in Scotland, but since English-style villages with houses clustered around a green are rare in Scotland, and pretty ones even rarer, there are none too many candidates. Certainly, for experts in domestic architecture, the cottages and houses clustered around the large green compose a remarkable collection of seventeenth- and eighteenth-century buildings.
untutored eye, they are quaint or photogenic by tu

However, Dirleton is so dwarfed by its castle that you are likely to be drawn to that massive building after no more than a cursory glance at the village. **Dirleton Castle** (HS, open Apr to Sept, Mon to Sat 9.30 to 6.30, Sun 2 to 6.30; Oct to Mar, Mon to Sat 9.30 to 4.30, Sun 2 to 4.30) is older than Tantallon, and almost as colossal, even if its setting is not quite so fine. The gatehouse, where a modern wooden bridge replaces the old drawbridge, is just as imposing. As you walk up the long slope of the bridge, a round tower to your left is what remains of the thirteenth-century fortifications, and you need only compare the neat lines of ashlar masonry with the rubble-work of much of the later building to see that the castle was at its most formidable when it was first built. The interior of this tower, with its domed Lord's Chamber, is the most impressive part of the ruin. On the whole, you get a better feel for the place by walking round the outside under the looming walls. The interior is a bit of a muddle, the passages and chambers of the various periods of rebuilding all seeming to run together. Do not omit the beehive-shaped dovecote from your visit, and do not hurry through the garden either.

Gullane and Aberlady

Gullane has always been considered the posh resort of the peninsula, and a glance at the size of the villas on its fringes will go some way to proving the point. More importantly, it is probably second only to St Andrews in its reputation for golf. **Muirfield** is one of the best-known Scotland championship courses, and half the business deals of Edinburgh are said to be struck on its greens. Even if you cannot pull the strings which will get you on to the fairways here, Gullane has four other courses in the immediate vicinity.

For non-golfers, Gullane has sand in abundance – indeed, too much of it, for drifting sand was the original settlement's ruin. The last incumbent of the ruined twelfth-century church was dismissed from his post by James VI for smoking: the King was as intolerant of smokers as he was of witches.

The next bay down the coast is **Aberlady**, now a nature reserve of the mudflat and saltmarsh variety, good for migrant birds. The village here used to be the port for Haddington, but the silt that is good for birds was not so good for ships. The **Myreton Motor Museum** (open all year, daily 9 to 5 summer, 10 to 4 winter), a short way inland, is an idiosyncratic collection of motoring memorabilia, going beyond vehicles to include posters, signs and general paraphernalia. West of Aberlady, church-lovers should visit **Seton Collegiate Church**, largely fifteenth-century, but dating further back than that. Seton was one of the favourite haunts of Mary Queen of Scots.

Prestonpans

The ground between this ancient salt-panning centre and the ridge-top mining village of Tranent was the scene of the Jacobite victory of 1745 when the Hanoverian army under Sir John Cope was cut to pieces by Bonnie Prince Charlie's Highlanders in under ten minutes. The victory put all of Scotland, apart from a few castles, into Jacobite hands, and came as a terrible shock to the Westminster government. It may also have instilled the fatal belief of invincibility into Prince Charles. It is difficult to see the shape of the battlefield under the modern development, and a good guide will be necessary if you want to pick out the course of events.

If you are exploring the area, the group of old houses in the centre of **Preston** is worth finding, as is the unspoilt and splendid mercat cross. On the edge of the sea, **Preston Grange Industrial Heritage Museum** (open Apr to Oct, daily 11 to 4) is the bleak site of a former colliery with relics for industrial archaeology enthusiasts, notably a Cornish beam engine and a number of viciously toothed coal-cutting machines from different periods. A neat visitor centre, helpful custodians and a small collection of railway locomotives and cranes add interest.

Musselburgh

The Edinburgh bypass has removed the traffic which used to plague this old town at the mouth of the River Esk. The bridge which crosses the river is sixteenth-century, as is the tolbooth. Both are attractive. The extensive buildings of Loretto school stand on the grounds of an old pilgrim chapel. Pinkie House, part of the school, and open to the public on Tuesdays (2.30 to 4.30) during term-time (by arrangement only 0131-665 2059), has fine plaster ceilings from the seventeenth century. South of the town, on the low Carberry Hill, Mary Queen of Scots and Bothwell drew up an army against the lords who had taken arms against her. Her troops melting away, Mary put herself into the hands of her opponents, who promptly whipped her off to Loch Leven and forced her to abdicate. The leaflet *A walk around historic Musselburgh* will guide you to the best buildings.

SOUTH OF EDINBURGH

For the visitor, the district of Midlothian is best described as good in parts. There is a lot of urban sprawl left from the days when the Midlothian coalfield was thriving. Now, places like Newtongrange and Penicuik have become dormitory towns for Edinburgh. However, hidden away in the valley between the Pentland Hills and the Moorfoot Hills, at the headwaters of the North Esk, South Esk and Tyne Rivers, there are stretches of attractive country, old houses and castles, and a few sights it would be a shame to miss.

On the A7 Galashiels road, **Newtongrange** is home to the Lady Victoria Colliery, once the showpiece pit of the area and now part of the **Scottish Mining Museum** (open Mar to end Oct, daily 10 to 4). Only some of the actual colliery buildings are accessible although there is a simulated coalface to see, but the museum is worth finding, for it contains probably the best steam-engine in Scotland – an enormous winding engine, gaily painted and still in full working order. There is also a very well-put together display about the conditions of a miner's life, using voice-overs and models.

To the west, best reached from the A6094 or A703, is **Rosslyn Chapel** (open Easter to end Oct, Mon to Sat 10 to 5, Sun 12 to 4.45). Confusingly, the village is spelt Roslin. The chapel lies down a small track below it, and, for such a famous building, looks curiously neglected and ordinary from the outside. This impression is rapidly dispelled inside, for nowhere else in the country will you be confronted with such a superabundance of stone carving. Every surface which has lent itself to ornamentation has been covered in foliage, flowers, human figures and animals. Reactions vary, and many people find the chapel too over-decorated to be beautiful. The star piece of carving is the Apprentice Pillar, an even more elaborately encrusted piece of work than the rest, with its own (probably apocryphal) legend of the apprentice who carved it being murdered by the jealous master mason.

The chapel is fifteenth-century, though its style is early Gothic, and the aisle vaulting is very peculiar. It was the creation of William St Clair, who lived in Rosslyn Castle and seemingly felt that founding a luxurious collegiate church was a suitable spiritual compensation for his sumptuous baronial life. After his death the project fell into abeyance, with only the choir complete.

It is well worth the hundred yards' stroll from the chapel to have a peek at **Rosslyn Castle**. The building itself is private, but the castle is surrounded by a country park, so you can gaze at its exterior. Its ruins are poised on a crag by the brink of Roslin Glen, where the ground drops sheer to the River Esk beneath. The crag can be reached only across a bridge; the ruins of the keep stand beyond, as does the intact sixteenth-century north range.

If you have come across Edinburgh Crystal glassware in the shops, the town of **Penicuik**, just south-west of Roslin, is the place to see it being manufactured. Guided tours run regularly between 9.15 and 3.30 (Mon to Fri) from the visitor centre just off the A701 (children are discouraged for safety reasons). A walkway on the track of an old railway runs all the way from Penicuik to Bonnyrigg, passing through the remains of old industries and with some good woodland scenery along the way.

Crichton Castle

(HS, standard times; closed Oct to Mar)
This castle is a surprise. It is not until you actually arrive underneath its walls after walking along a short track that you realise that not a trace of modern development is visible. The ruin sits on a sharp promontory above a haugh (flat piece of land beside a river) where the River Tyne meanders between trees – a landscape which is easy to imagine unchanged for centuries. It inspired both Turner and Scott (in *Marmion*), and it was largely thanks to the interest they stimulated that the castle was preserved.

From the outside, the castle appears at first glance to be another of those uncompromising and probably uncomfortable Scottish fortresses, riddled with gun-loops. However, once in the courtyard, you are confronted with a façade which seems to have come straight from the Italian Renaissance. An arcade is crowned by a wall studded with diamond facets, looking like nothing so much as a huge bar of pale chocolate, while at one end there was once a balcony, worthy of Romeo and Juliet, overhanging the courtyard. A proper Renaissance staircase, with treads, risers and the remains of carved embellishments, leads upwards to what were once grand rooms lit by large windows.

This is the work of Francis Stuart, fifth Earl of Bothwell (nephew to Mary Queen of Scots' second husband), who spent much of his life in Spain and Italy. Although he had his King to dinner in March 1586, he was too unstable a character to last long under the canny James VI – there was the affair of the North Berwick witches for a start (page 171). Eventually he fled abroad and never came back.

A path runs between Crichton and **Borthwick Castle**, two miles distant. Borthwick is a very tall (eight floors) fifteenth-century tower, with twin keeps, and is one of the best-preserved medieval castles in Scotland. It was to Borthwick that Mary Queen of Scots and Bothwell came shortly after their marriage. Now it is an hotel, but even if it is beyond your pocket to stay here the exterior is still well worth seeing.

THE PENTLAND HILLS

No peak in the Pentlands reaches 2,000 feet, yet this small range of hills stretching away south-west of Edinburgh has some good wild country in an area which is in dire need of it. For the visitor, the Pentlands are hills where it is possible to walk to the heart's content without having to worry too much about precipices or getting lost on a trackless plateau. The hills are, however, wet and steep in places, so it is as well to be prepared for adverse conditions. The closer to the Edinburgh end of the Pentlands you are the more fellow-humans you are likely to find, especially at weekends, but this north-eastern end of the range also has the most shapely hills and the most scenic stretches of water. Some possible expeditions are described below.

Reached from the A702

- **Hillend Ski Centre** (open Mon to Sat 9.30 to 9, Sun 9.30 to 7) This used to be Britain's longest dry ski-slope. If you enjoy skiing on upturned toothbrushes, the extensive network provides everything you need. Alternatively you could wait until winter and head for Aviemore. Non-skiers may find the chair-lift here a useful way of getting up into the Pentlands without effort.
- **Glencorse Reservoir** lies in a dog-legged valley under Turnhouse Hill, and the track up to it and beyond up the

Logan Burn is probably the most popular walk in the area. This part of the Pentlands has been designated a Regional Park. It was on the southern slope of Turnhouse Hill that the battle of Rullion Green was fought in 1666. A pathetic army of probably fewer than a thousand Covenanters, mostly from the south-west, was defeated by General Tam Dalyell. Most of the prisoners were either executed or transported to the plantations of the West Indies (a favourite method of getting rid of stubborn religious dissenters).

Reached from the A70

• **Malleny Gardens, Balerno** (open daily, 9.30 to sunset) Where the posh Edinburgh suburb of Balerno laps against the end of the Pentland Hills, these gardens surrounding a private seventeenth-century house hold an admirable collection of shrub roses. The garden is quite formally laid out, though there is a short woodland walk, and is well worth visiting if you are a rose enthusiast.
• **Threipmuir Reservoir** An extensive reservoir with plenty of bird-life in its thick reed-beds. Up the hill behind, paths lead in towards the waterfalls at the head of Logan Burn.
• **Cauld Stane Slap** The old drove road across the hills from the Harperrig Reservoir passes between the East and West Cairn Hills, through the slap (break in hills) to West Linton. This makes an excellent half-day's walk, though coordinating transport to and from either end can be difficult. Robert Louis Stevenson's *Weir of Hermiston* is the novel to take with you.

THE CENTRAL BELT

Between Edinburgh and Glasgow stretches a great Lowland valley of sour land, scarred by pit workings and dotted with mining towns and villages. Nor do the area's new towns – Cumbernauld and Livingston – contribute much joy. Neither of them has a single modern building worth a detour to see, although if you want to know more about the shale industry, the **Almond Valley Heritage Centre** (open daily 10 to 5) in Livingston has some respectable displays.

Yet this is not the whole picture. There was life here before the Industrial Revolution – great houses by the Forth, prehistoric sites in the depth of the Bathgate Hills, the royal palace at Linlithgow and the cattle trysts of Falkirk. There are patches of fine country on the edge of the bleak

177

mosses, or in the Bathgate Hills, which are all the more beautiful for being so unexpected. Finally, there are heartening signs of life, perhaps stimulated by the energetic resurgence of Glasgow, where communities have seized upon their past as an incentive to look forward, and are busy creating museums, dredging canals, bringing mines or railways back to life or constructing country parks.

Hopetoun House

(Open Easter to Sept, Mon to Sat 10 to 5.30)
This huge stately home is an amalgam of the work of Scotland's greatest architects. It was begun by William Bruce in 1699, extended and altered by William Adam in 1721, and finished off by his sons, the whole edifice not being completed until 1767. Bruce's interior work remains intact in several rooms, and it is interesting to compare his warm, homely style with the magnificent formality of the Adam state rooms. The most striking feature of Hopetoun is the pine-panelled front staircase, with intricate carvings, modern mural paintings (though you would never guess) and the recently uncovered and restored painted cupola where anxious cherubs support a cracked globe – *At spes non fracta* is the Hope motto.

The Adam state apartments are on the stiff side, with an abundance of gilded stucco and rococo furniture, making an interesting comparison with some of the family's more relaxed interiors such as those at Mellerstain (page 62). Paintings abound, notably a specially commissioned series by Tideman, and there are portraits by Raeburn, Ramsay and Gainsborough.

Hopetoun's carefully landscaped grounds overlook the Forth Bridges, and are seen at their extensive best from the rooftop viewing platform of the house. Events at Hopetoun range from balls to antique fairs, but nothing is likely to come up to the splendour of George IV's visit here in 1822, when the portly monarch lunched on turtle soup and three glasses of wine. Four-horned St Kilda sheep inhabit the grounds along with red and fallow deer.

House of the Binns

(NTS, open May to end Sept, Sat to Thur 1.30 to 5.30; parkland Apr to end Oct, daily 9.30 to 7; Nov to end Mar, daily 9.30 to 4)
This is the next stately home westward along the banks of

the Forth, and the contrast with Hopetoun could hardly be greater. The house is early seventeenth-century, and has gone firmly down the neo-Gothic road, helped by nineteenth-century embellishments. The guided tour is inclined to be slow but is worth enduring for the sake of the plasterwork in particular, and for the tall tales of General Tam Dalyell, the house's most notorious owner.

General Tam, nicknamed 'The Bluidy Muscovite', entered Covenanting demonology as one of their most dedicated enemies. A committed royalist who had fought with Charles II at Worcester, escaped from the Tower of London and served the Tsar in Russia, he was recalled at the Restoration and was instrumental in the defeat of the Covenanting army at Rullion Green (1666) in the Pentland Hills. The General's prowess against the godly was logically attributed to his alliance with satanic power, and in the entrance hall of the Binns you can see the magnificent table which the Devil hurled into a nearby pond after losing to Tam at cards. It remained there for 200 years. You leave the Binns with tales of flagellation parties and of Tam's waist-length beard (he refused to shave in protest at the execution of Charles I). He also raised that most famous of Scottish Cavalry regiments, the Scots Greys.

Blackness Castle

(HS, standard times; closed Thur pm and Fri in winter)
From a distance Blackness looks just like a small coaster stranded on the rocks, and this impression is heightened when you walk round the parapet to the sharpened 'prow' of the walls, with the halyards of the flagstaff flapping in the wind, the waves crashing on the shore directly beneath, and the Firth of Forth stretching away in both directions.

The shape of Blackness was determined by the rocky spit on which it was built in the fifteenth century. It started by acting as guardian for the harbour which served as Linlithgow's outlet to the sea, became a state prison for those out of favour with the king, and ended as an ammunition store. A secret passage is said to have linked it to the House of the Binns (see above).

From the point of view of military history, Blackness is a fascinating example of a fortification where the response to the invention of siege artillery was simply to thicken the walls and to go on thickening them until in places they became a solid mass of stonework pierced by chambers for gunners. The transformation of Blackness into this bulwark took place between 1532 and 1567. In any event, the castle's fortifications did not prove strong enough to resist Cromwell, whose siege of 1650 did much damage (now repaired).

Bo'ness

Bo'ness is an old port on the shores of the Forth which has seen better days but is now determinedly capitalising on its past. A reawakened steam railway with accompanying exhibition centre is the most prominent example. More unusual is the nearby **Birkhill Clay Mine** in the gorge of the Avon. You can travel direct on the railway, reaching a tiny brown and white station beneath the old mine buildings (trains at 11.30, 1, 2.15 and 3.30; early Apr to early Jul weekends only; Jul to mid-Aug daily; mid-Aug to end Oct weekends only). These are still derelict, but the mine has now been made safe enough for you to walk through the old caverns where fire-clay was dug from the side of the hill (it is a long stairway down to the mine entrance). The firebricks produced from the mine were used as linings for the locomotives and furnaces of the Industrial Revolution.

Nearby **Kinneil House** (HS, open Apr to Sept, daily 10 to 12.30, 1.30 to 5 exc Mon, Fri and Sat 10 to 5; May to Aug, Sun also 10 to 5; Oct to Mar, Sat only 10 to 5) has some ancient painted ceilings, but its main claim to fame is that it was in an outhouse in the grounds here that James Watt worked on his inventions.

A short way upstream from Bo'ness lies Grangemouth, Scotland's petro-chemical city, a mass of pipes, tanks and flares. From a distance its flames can create astonishing effects against the clouded Ochil Hills on the far side of the river.

Linlithgow

For a town which once ranked alongside Edinburgh and Stirling as the setting for a royal palace, time has not treated Linlithgow well. This is mostly the fault of the planners – of the Victorian era and of more modern times as well. Indeed, it would be hard to find a more crass ruination of an ancient burgh than that thrust upon Linlithgow in the late 1960s. The sawn-off, out-of-proportion monstrosities that break up the line of the old High Street can only make visitors shake their heads in baffled despair.

For all that, if you need a base in this area of the country, Linlithgow is the place to choose. It is free from the worst industrial scars and has managed to retain much of its gentle county-town atmosphere. The palace and St Michael's church on their mound above the town centre, the perfect loch-side setting (alas, the M9 motorway is too close to allow it to be called peaceful) and the remaining houses of the ancient royal burgh combine to make it an interesting town to explore, or even to relax in for a day or two. Bed and breakfasts provide the greatest choice of accommodation, and there are several in the pretty country round the River Avon outside town.

In and near Linlithgow

● **Linlithgow Palace** (HS, standard times) Windowless, roofless and weathering, the palace is still an outstanding *tour de force* of Scottish architecture over 200 years. Started by James I around 1425 and finished by James VI in 1624, the building silently demonstrates the level of luxury and functional magnificence which the Scottish kings expected of their palaces.

Standing in the central courtyard, in front of the elaborate fountain − said to be a wedding present from James V to Marie of Guise − you have James VI's plain and harmonious Renaissance façade in front of you, with James I's massive medieval hall in the range to your right, the state apartments of James IV to your left, and the English-style gallery of James V behind you. The cascades of reddish stone which make up the four frontages are vigorous and harmonious. Everything else inside the burnt-out shell, even the Great Hall, or the vaulting at the head of the stair to the royal apartments, is something of an anti-climax after the courtyard.

● **St Michael's Church** The curious spire which crowns the tower is not fifteenth-century like the rest of the church − it was lowered into position by helicopter in 1964. It is undeniably adventurous, but whether it is appropriate, or even elegant, is another matter. The window tracery − high Gothic, elaborate and yet simple − is the feature to admire inside the church, though some of the modern stained glass is worth a glance too. Spare a thought for James IV, who saw an apparition in the south transept which warned him of his doom at Flodden. Since he was too much the Renaissance man to pay heed, he went to war and died, leaving his Queen to wait in vain for his return in the top-most room of Linlithgow Palace (still known as Queen Margaret's bower).

● **Canal Museum** (open Easter to Sept, Sat and Sun 2 to 5) For canal enthusiasts, the museum has a good, if small, collection of memorabilia of the Union Canal. There are boat trips too along a reopened stretch of what was in 1822 the most comfortable means of travel between Edinburgh and Glasgow. Unfortunately the railway (1842) was just as comfortable, charged the same, and took two and a quarter hours instead of fourteen. Hence the museum.

● **Cairnpapple Hill** (HS, now open only for groups by arrangement) You hardly expect the low-slung Bathgate hills behind Linlithgow to produce the spectacular views they do. From this Bronze Age burial cairn you can gaze out over huge chunks of Lowland Scotland, bounded by the Ochil Hills and the Pentlands to north and south. Cairnpapple started as a Neolithic site and at one stage had a stone henge, but what is most visible today is the Bronze Age cairn (with modern roof). Descending a ladder out of the wind, you are confronted with the stones of the grave. The sepulchral voice from the shadowy corner turns out only to be Historic Scotland's tape-recorded commentary.

● **Torphichen Preceptory** (HS, weekends only in summer) The tall grey building rising above the houses of the small village on the B792 a few miles south of Linlithgow was once the headquarters in Scotland of the great monastic-military order, the Knights Hospitallers of the Order of St John of Jerusalem. What remains are the tower and two transepts of their church. Parts of it date from the twelfth-century, but most is fourteenth- or fifteenth-century. The vaulting of the crossing and transepts is monumental, and you can climb into the bell chamber above and look down on to the floor of the crossing. The rooms up here are used to tell you the history of the Order of St John, from its earliest beginnings down to its current role as the St John Ambulance Brigade (which is known in Scotland as St Andrew's Ambulance Association).

Falkirk

Although it looks like just another small industrial town, Falkirk is a very ancient place. The **Falkirk Museum** (open all year, Mon to Fri 10 to 5; Apr to Sept, Sun 2 to 5) traces the town's history from Roman times to the days of the

Carron ironworks (from which comes the word carronade), and makes a good starting-point for exploration.

Falkirk was the site of two major battles – first in 1298 when Wallace ran up against the English archers and lost, and later when Charles Edward Stuart's Highlanders attacked the Hanoverians and won. However, it is the Roman remains that most people visit Falkirk to explore, for the town stands on the line of the Antonine Wall which ran between the Forth and the Clyde, and the most substantial remains of that fortification are in the area. It was built around AD 140, as a result of a decision to move the chief frontier defences forward from Hadrian's Wall. Unlike Hadrian's Wall, the Antonine Wall was constructed largely of turf, so there is a lot less of it left today. Nevertheless, at **Rough Castle** (HS, standard times), signposted from Bonnybridge, west of Falkirk, there are the earthworks of a large fort and the remains of ditch and rampart in pleasantly wooded surroundings, while at **Callander Park** and at **Watling Lodge**, both in Falkirk, the old defensive ditch can be seen. Bits and pieces of the wall can be found all the way along its line as far as Bearsden near Glasgow, and trying to trace it among the clutter of modern development can provide an intriguing day's work.

Less easily traced are the remains of Falkirk's great days as a cattle fair for beasts from all over the Highlands. The driving of the black cattle south from the glens to the great Lowland trysts, where they were bought by dealers before continuing the journey towards England, is one of the little-known stories of Scotland. The practice began almost as soon as the frontier disappeared after the Union and continued for as long as cattle rather than sheep were raised in the hills. The drovers are gone, but their tracks across the hills remain, often used now by walkers.

Falkirk is the starting point for drives and walks into the Campsie Fells (page 273), and it is only a few minutes' drive from Stirling (page 266).

The Pineapple

(NTS', grounds open all year, 9.30 to sunset)
This is Scotland's most eccentric folly. It is a mile north-west of Airth on the A905. The Pineapple was in fact once a garden retreat on the Dunmore estate – a retreat in the shape of a 45-foot-tall stone pineapple, with a little domed room right at the top of the fruit, under the leaves. Each leaf is composed of cantilevered blocks of masonry which spring

away from the dome with a realistic degree of spikiness. Built in 1761 by an unknown architect, the Pineapple is a reminder of the fact that eighteenth-century gentry expected exotic fruit along with their cabbages.

If you fancy a holiday inside the fruit, contact the Landmark Trust (01628 825925), which leases the building from the National Trust for Scotland – but be prepared to book two years in advance.

THE CLYDE VALLEY

The Clyde is probably the most celebrated of Scotland's rivers, though its popular image as a waterway surrounded by a hubbub of heavy industry is now long out of date. The industries are dead or dying and though weekend excursions for Glaswegians 'doon the watter' to the resorts of the Clyde estuary still linger, they are not what they used to be. Increasingly, the Clyde in its lower reaches is becoming a recreational asset: walkways or country parks line its banks, and all is (nearly) tranquillity where once the night sky was lit by the glow of blast furnaces. The Clyde, especially in its upper reaches above Hamilton, is a beautiful river, and well worth a leisurely day's journey through its various sights.

If you have reason to go straight to Glasgow from Carlisle, the A74/M74 heads straight across the moors, past **Douglas**, the stronghold of the 'Black' branch of that remarkable family from the time of Robert the Bruce, but without much to see now except for **St Bride's Church**, where the tombs and effigies of such characters as 'Good Sir James' (who was chosen to carry Bruce's heart to the Holy Land) and Archibald 'Bell-the-Cat' (who hanged the favourites of James III from a bridge in Lauder (page 59) are laid out as a kind of exhibition of the great and the grim.

Douglas Castle itself was a victim of a common form of destruction in this area – the opening up of a coal seam beneath ancient buildings and their consequent subsidence.

If you are in no hurry to reach Glasgow, take the A702 at Abington and follow the Clyde.

Biggar

This used to be a quiet agricultural town with a wide, tree-lined high street but without any great claim to fame, except that William Wallace (page 271) once crossed Cadger's Brig here while in disguise. In recent years, however, Biggar seems to have suffered a rush of blood to the head and has started spawning museums and a whole industry of leaflets, commemorative pencils and T-shirts to go with them (you can even find Biggar's motto – *London's London but Biggar's Biggar* – translated into Latin on the latter). They are exceptionally fine small museums, too, especially good for curious children but worth a day of anyone's time. Between them they will send you away thinking that Biggar is one of the most interesting places in Scotland (a huge compliment to the Biggar Museum Trust which runs three of them, plus the John Buchan Centre in nearby Broughton – page 49).

Gladstone Court (open Apr to end Oct, Mon to Sat 10 to 12.30, 2 to 5, Sun 2 to 5), the oldest of the museums, is the result of one man's inability to leave anything from a de-molished building unsalvaged. Here you can find Biggar's old manual telephone exchange with rows of jack plugs on wires and the nineteenth-century bank with its high wooden counter and air of Scottish financial integrity, to-gether with the lovingly reconstructed interiors of many other shops and offices.

Moat Park Heritage Centre (open Easter to end Oct, Mon to Sat 10 to 5, Sun 2 to 5; off-season call at rear office), in an old church a few minutes away from Gladstone Court, is one of the best local museums in Scotland, with plenty of scale models and highly literate explanations. Imaginative touches abound – the geological section is fronted by poems from Hugh McDiarmid, while the Roman legionary in his glass case is far from being a sanitised model: he is covered in blood and carries the gory head of a vanquished tribesman.

Greenhill (open Apr to mid-Oct daily 2 to 5), in a small green dell below the town (near a good playground), is a rebuilt seventeenth-century farmhouse from the nearby countryside, turned into a Covenanting Museum. Relics are few, but the explanations of the conventicles and the per-secutions of the Killing Time are as good as is possible with such a confusing period. Among the furniture, there is a fine old press bed (a bed in a cupboard).

Finally, there is **Biggar Gas Works** (open June to end Sept, daily 2 to 5) – a completely contrasting piece of history, dating from the time when many small towns like Biggar had their own local gas plant. Sheds contain various ovens and retorts, together with the machinery to ensure a good supply of light and heat to the town. All that is missing is the smell.

To complete the town's effervescent self-confidence,

185

there is a small puppet theatre of renown which you can look round (Mon to Sat 10 to 5, Sun 2 to 5) even if there is no show on.

West of Biggar, the isolated bulk of Tinto Hill rises above the Clyde. Climbing it is easy, and the views from the top take in much of southern Scotland.

Lanark and New Lanark

This market town perched above the Clyde is a great deal older than it looks — it was made a royal burgh as early as 1140. It is famous as the place where Wallace first committed himself to open rebellion against the English by attacking the local garrison. The statue of the great man at the end of the High Street must be Scotland's most idiosyncratic: Wallace is adorned with a great woolly beard, which makes him look more like a genial pantomime character than a resistance hero. A few arches remain of the church where Wallace may have been married, but otherwise there is not much left of Lanark's past.

On the very banks of the Clyde at the bottom of a steep gorge behind Lanark lies **New Lanark** (open daily 11 to 5; closed Chr and New Year), Scotland's most important memorial to the Industrial Revolution. It is nominated as a World Heritage Site and attracts more than 400,000 visitors a year, making it difficult to believe that the elegant eighteenth-century spinning mills and the village surrounding them were almost lost for good — only last-minute efforts in 1975 saved the virtually derelict buildings from the bulldozers.

New Lanark holds a unique place in social history, for this is the spot where Robert Owen, the son-in-law of the founder of the cotton mills, David Dale, put into action the unfashionable principle that the welfare of an industrial workforce was of fundamental importance to commercial success. Between 1814 and 1824 New Lanark became the scene of a pioneering social experiment. Education lay at the heart of this: no child under 10 was allowed to work in the mills (a revolutionary forgoing of labour), while in the company's school both punishment and reward were banned, and singing and dancing were taught to all. A sick fund, a co-operative village shop and the introduction of adult education classes were also part of 'Owenism'. Robert Owen's ideas were of great influence, not only on what we might now call benevolent capitalism, but on co-operative movements and on trade unionism.

New Lanark is also worth seeing for the beauty of its setting and for the fascination of its architecture. The Clyde, which flows under the walls of the grey stone mills, was the only river in central Scotland powerful enough to turn the water-wheels from which thousands of cotton bobbins were powered. The three mills that remain were built between 1789 and 1826 with strong Palladian overtones, forcefully proving the point that industrial architecture does not have to be ugly. Around them cluster the other buildings of the community – the workers' housing mostly built by David Dale in the last years of the eighteenth century, Robert Owen's rounded Counting House, the classical-style Institute for the Formation of Character, and the impressively large School for Children. Most of the housing has been fully restored and is now privately owned or rented out by the New Lanark Conservation Trust, but you can look round a tenement which has been restored to reflect life in the 1930s as well as the Institute, the industrial buildings and Robert Owen's house.

New Lanark plays host to a variety of enterprises. There is more than enough space for them in the old mills. Industrial relics include a steam-engine and a spinning mule (which you can see in operation), while a theme-park style ride carries you through New Lanark's history, guided by the spirit of one of the children who worked there in the 1820s. There is also a collection of classic cars, a model railway, several shops, a 'period store' in 1920s style and a variety of craft workshops. More than enough for a good family day out.

Falls of Clyde

Immediately above New Lanark, the Falls of Clyde Nature Reserve stretches along the bank. After about half a mile's slightly muddy walk upstream, you reach **Corra Linn**, the most famous and the best of the three falls where the Clyde plunges into its gorge. Corra Linn has lost much of its muscle to hydro-electricity since the days when it was a port of call for every landscape-lover in the district, but the situation, where the river tumbles into a huge rock cauldron, is still impressive enough to be worth the walk. If you are there during a spate, or on one of the days when the flow of water is fully restored (call Scottish Power on 0141-637 7177), the waterfall is magnificent.

187

Lanark to Hamilton

Below Lanark, almost as far as Glasgow, the Clyde is sunk in a deep valley, well sheltered from the winds that blast the barren moors above it. As you descend from the bogs round Forth or Carluke into the micro-climate of the valley, trees grow without being wind-shorn, fruit is on sale at the road-side, and rows of glasshouses grow chrysanthemums, pot plants and bedding plants to be sold in the many garden centres. The Clyde's tributaries here are also pretty – the Nethan is good for aimless pottering, while more strenuous efforts need to be made to trace the Mouse Water through its narrow gorge. The valley of the Avon is the most access-ible, running as it does through Chatelherault Country Park.

Craignethan Castle

(HS, standard times; Mar to end Oct, closed Thur pm and Fri)
Two miles west of Crossford, this fifteenth-century castle is well preserved and under-visited. The approach road across a desolate, scrub-covered land suddenly reveals the ruins on their high spur above the Nethan. Enthusiasts of military architecture go to see its *caponier* – a dank, vaulted chamber built across the moat to help defend the place against artillery – but the ruins are worth a stop if you are at all fond of castles, or of Walter Scott, for Craignethan features in *Old Mortality* in the guise of Tillietudlem.

Chatelherault Country Park

(Open daily to sunset; visitor centre all year, Mon to Sat 10 to 5, Sun 12 to 5)
This French-style name in the middle of the Clyde land-scape goes back to the time of Mary Queen of Scots' childhood, when the French title of Duke of Chatelherault was given to James Hamilton, second Earl of Arran, partly to make up for losing the regency to Mary of Guise, the young Queen's mother. The Hamiltons were heavily invol-ved in the confused civil struggle following Mary's flight to England, and were eventually defeated. In a later century, the exploitation of the rich coal seams of this area brought huge prosperity to the Dukes of Hamilton, though the effect on the landscape was less pleasing.

The **Chatelherault Hunting Lodge** (open same times as visitor centre), which stands in the middle of what is now the country park, is a William Adam building dating from 1740. Two pavilions flank an expanse of curtain wall in Adam's usual harmonious symmetry. Its restoration from a state of near-total dereliction has been a remarkable success; only the curious lean of the building remains to show the dire effect that coal extraction had on the structure. The lodge is not large, but the magnificence of the various rooms leaves you in no doubt that splendour is more important than size. Much of the plasterwork that adorns walls and ceilings has had to be re-created from photographs and the few fragments left by vandals, fire and weather, while the urns and finials on the roof are also modern copies of the missing originals. Even the formal garden behind one of the pavilions has been lovingly put back. A visitor centre built in the kennel yard, where the dukes' hounds once jostled, gives you some idea of how the lodge was built and how it was restored.

Elsewhere in the park, you come across the remains of old Cadzow Castle, the Cadzow herd of wild white cattle, and the memorial monument to the eleventh Duke. A fitting climax to the tour of the remnants of Hamilton grandeur is a visit to the nearby mausoleum (tours enquiries call 01698 283981). Its curious acoustics have given it the longest echo in Europe, and so have prevented it from ever being used as a chapel.

Hamilton to Bothwell

Near Hamilton the landscape changes abruptly from rural to urban as the Clyde passes beside the towns which were once the centre of Scotland's coal, iron and steel industry. The sprawl of towns like Motherwell and Wishaw may not look very inviting, but there are one or two places worth knowing about — notably, for a wet day, the modern Aquatec Leisure Centre (01698 276464) at **Motherwell** with its tropical swimming-pool and adjacent ice-rink. At **Blantyre**, the David Livingstone Centre (open early Mar to end Oct, daily 10 to 5; times vary in winter, call 01698 823140) is worth visiting not only for an insight into the explorer's life but also for a look at the cramped tenement where he was brought up. Through imaginative use of pictures and exhibits, the African Pavilion takes you into the continent which Livingstone explored.

Where the A74 crosses the Clyde below Hamilton is the site of the battle at Bothwell Brig, where the Covenanters were routed by the Duke of Monmouth in 1679. This was more or less the final convulsion of the Covenanting movement — an unequal battle between a government determined to impose at least some kind of order on religious affairs in Scotland and an army whose fervency was almost their only weapon, but which was fatally riven by sectarian debate. Walter Scott gives a clear, if cynical, picture of the battle in *Old Mortality*.

Bothwell Castle

(HS, standard times; closed Thur pm and Fri in winter)
This red sandstone ruin in its pleasant park above the Clyde was once one of the most strategically important strongholds in Scotland, and a crucial point in the Wars of Independence. Its most notable feature is the ruined *donjon*, a great circular tower of enormous strength, which may have been almost all that existed of the castle in the

USEFUL DIRECTORY

Main tourist offices
Edinburgh and Lothians Tourist Board
Edinburgh and Scotland Information Centre
3 Princes Street, Waverley Market
Edinburgh EH2 2QP
0131-557 1700

Greater Glasgow and Clyde Valley Tourist Board
39 St Vincent Place
Glasgow G1 2ER
(moving end of summer 1996)
0141-204 4400

Tourist board publications The newly formed tourist boards are planning to change their publications list. Contact them at the above addresses for information on the latest practical listings and other leaflets.

Local tourist information centres
Abington (01864) 502436
Biggar (01899) 21066 (Apr to Oct)
Bo'ness (01506) 826626 (May to Sept)

thirteenth-century. Held at first by the English after the ill-fated resurgence of courage on the part of 'Toom Tabard' (John Balliol), then taken by the Scots in 1290, the castle became the object of an expert piece of siege warfare when Edward I of England came hastening to take his revenge in 1301. He commissioned an enormous siege tower as high as the parapet and this monstrous machine forced the surrender of the castle in less than a month.

After changing hands several more times until 1377 the castle had a relatively peaceful existence before being largely cannibalised for a new mansion, demolished (subsidence again) in 1926. Not surprisingly, the ruins are complicated to sort out, but the remains of the massive *donjon* with its first-class masonry are unbeatable. A small heap of round stones – precursors of cannon balls – salvaged during excavation bear witness to the various sieges in the castle's history.

Dalkeith 0131-663 2083/660 6818
Dunbar (01368) 863353
Falkirk (01324) 620244
Hamilton (01698) 285590
Lanark (01555) 661661
Linlithgow (01506) 844600
Motherwell (01698) 373989
North Berwick (01620) 892197
Old Craig Hall, nr Musselburgh 0131-653 6172
Penicuik (01968) 673846

Local transport
Edinburgh Airport Information 0131–344 3212
Glasgow Airport Information 0141-887 1111
National rail enquiries (0345) 212282
A large number of bus companies serve this area; route information and timetables are available from all the tourist offices listed above.

Ferries
Gourock–Dunoon (Caledonian MacBrayne) 01475 650100; (Western Ferries) 0141-332 9766
Gourock–Kilchreggan–Helensburgh (Clyde Marine Motoring Co Ltd) 01475 721281
Wemyss Bay–Rothesay (Caledonian MacBrayne) 01475 650100

PAISLEY/THE CLYDESIDE TOWNS

Paisley

For many people, Paisley means the curious swollen comma shape used to decorate shawls, dressing-gowns and now duvet covers. The pattern in fact came from Kashmir, but Paisley rapidly gained a monopoly of it. The place to learn everything there is to know about it is the **Paisley Museum and Art Gallery** (open Mon to Sat 10 to 5), where there is an exhibition of about 500 different shawls. You should also come to Paisley for the sake of its abbey, a twelfth-century foundation, rebuilt in the fourteenth and fifteenth centuries and subjected to the usual neglect at the time of the Reformation. Restoration was begun in 1897, and, thanks to Sir Robert Lorimer, has resulted in a very beautiful church (do not be put off by the bland exterior). Keep an eye open for the very rare twelfth-century panels showing scenes from the life of St Mirren.

Paisley seems to be almost swamped with churches, for the town's weavers participated enthusiastically in all the various secessions and schisms of the Scottish Kirk. Many are now vacant or put to other uses, but a quick count will prove the depth of religious feeling that once existed here. Now Paisley is a pleasing industrial town, once important in the manufacture of cotton thread. The weaving industry, which thread-making replaced, is recalled at the small Weaver's Cottage at **Kilbarchan**, west of Paisley, where there are relics, a loom and weaving demonstrations (NTS, open Easter, May to end Sept, daily 1.30 to 5.30; Oct, Sat and Sun 1.30 to 5.30).

The Clyde coast

West of Glasgow, on the southern bank of the Clyde, a succession of bleak industrial towns lie squeezed between the river and the steepening moorland behind them (much of this is now a Regional Park, with visitor centres, nature reserves, views and walks). The things to see here are limited in number but provide a happy variety, and a trip down here will be worth the effort.

At **Finlaystone House** (grounds open all year, daily 10.30 to 5; house Apr to end Aug, Sun 2.30 to 4.30; Victorian kitchen Apr to end Aug, Sat 2.30 to 4.30), west of Langbank, the garden should please most visitors with its imaginative design and its series of garden 'rooms'. The house (when open) is worth visiting to see the collection of dolls. John Knox may well have held the first reformed communion in Scotland in the grounds, and a yew tree commemorates him. There is also a Burns signature – scratched on a window, as usual. At **Port Glasgow**, an otherwise unlovely town, the sixteenth-century Newark Castle (HS, standard times; closed in winter) is an elegant building, fairly intact, though its setting is now ugly. **Greenock** is the birthplace of James Watt, and you can find some relics in the McLean Museum and Art Gallery (open Mon to Sat 10 to 12, 1 to 5) as well as a small collection of paintings by James Guthrie and others. The history of the Customs and Excise service is lovingly explained in the **Greenock Custom House Museum** (open Mon to Fri 10 to 12.30, 1.30 to 4.30). Adam Smith and Robert Burns were both customs officers at one time in their lives. On a hill behind Greenock stands a memorial to the Free French of World War II from which the views are wonderful. **Gourock** is a resort rather than an industrial town, and the place to catch ferries heading across the Clyde for Dunoon on the Cowal Peninsula, Kilchreggan and Helensburgh. Round the corner of the coast, and heading south, you will come to **Wemyss Bay**, the ferry port for Bute, and the site of a beautiful station.

WHERE TO STAY

£ – under £70 per room per night, incl. VAT
££ – £70 to £110 per room per night, incl. VAT
£££ – over £110 per room per night, incl. VAT

ALLOA
Gean House
Gean Park, Tullibody Road, Alloa
FK10 2HS
TEL (01259) 219275
FAX (01259) 213827
Creeper-clad vernacular-style house with leaded windows and tall chimneys, set in twenty acres of parkland. An impressive staircase leads from the panelled Grand Hall. The dining-room overlooks the gardens and the light drawing-room has gold, garlanded wallpaper and an ornate plaster ceiling. The avowedly Scottish menu makes use of fresh local produce. Bedrooms are smartly and boldly decorated.
£££ All year; 7 rooms; drying-room; ballroom

FALA
Fala Hall Farmhouse
Fala, nr Pathhead EH37 5SZ
TEL (01875) 833249
Fala Hall lies half a mile down a rough track from the hamlet of the

same name. This sixteenth-century stone house is part of a 285-acre farm. Guests may use the pretty garden. Breakfast only served; packed lunches are available. Spacious, ample bedrooms.

£ All year exc Chr; 2 rooms, sharing a bathroom; credit cards not accepted

GIFFORD
Eaglescairnie Mains
Gifford, nr Haddington EH41 4HN
TEL/FAX (01620) 810491
White eighteenth-century farmhouse in the countryside a mile from Gifford. Breakfast is served in the conservatory and there is a large drawing-room. Pretty, spacious bedrooms.

£ All year exc Chr and New Year; 3 rooms; tennis; credit cards not accepted

Forbes Lodge
Gifford, Haddington EH41 4JE
TEL (01620) 810212
The splendid gardens of this substantial eighteenth-century house supply fruit and vegetables, put to good use in the kitchen. Elegant and lived-in, the building contains an inviting library, a comfortable drawing-room and a range of family portraits on the walls. Straightforward food. Large, well-furnished bedrooms.

££ All year; 5 rooms, 2 with bathroom/wc

GREENOCK
Lindores Guest House
61 Newark Street, Greenock PA16 7TE
TEL (01475) 783075
Stone-built Victorian house in a residential street above Greenock. A tiled floor occupies the ornate, pillared hall; guests eat in a wood-panelled breakfast-room. Very large bedrooms with lovely views over the Clyde.

£ All year; 3 rooms

GULLANE
Greywalls
Muirfield, Gullane EH31 2EG
TEL (01620) 842144
FAX (01620) 842241
This first-division country-house hotel sits amid the gardens of Gertrude Jekyll, hard against Muirfield Championship Golf Course. Designed by Lutyens in honey-coloured stone, Greywalls is graceful and stylish within and without. Relax by the fire in the panelled library or in the small bar. Ambitious food can be sampled in the restaurant. Bedrooms in the new wing have views of the links.

£££ Closed Nov to Mar; 22 rooms; drying-room; tennis; croquet (See Where to Eat)

HADDINGTON
Brown's Hotel
1 West Road, Haddington EH41 3RD
TEL/FAX (01620) 822254
The formal symmetry of this neo-classical mansion hides an extravagant interior with airy cupola and elegant staircase. Golden walls and an elaborate fireplace enhance the bright, light drawing-room. A collection of contemporary Scottish art lines the walls of the mint-green dining-room. Original, accomplished food. Pleasant bedrooms, not quite as stylish as the public rooms.

££ All year; 5 rooms; drying-room

QUOTHQUAN
Shieldhill Hotel
Quothquan, Biggar ML12 6NA
TEL (01899) 220035
FAX (01899) 221092
Historically interesting hotel with a ghostly legend to enthrall guests. Modern country-house interiors and inventive, up-to-date cooking make this old building an extremely

comfortable place to stay. Spacious and attractive bedrooms.

££-£££ All year; 11 rooms

WHITEKIRK
Whitekirk Mains
Whitekirk EH42 1SX
TEL (01620) 870245
FAX (01620) 870330
Old farmhouse with creeper-clad

Georgian frontage located in the centre of the small village, near the church. Guests use a comfortable sitting-room. Breakfast only is served; dinner can be had at the golf course restaurant next door. Delightful, well-equipped bedrooms.

£ Mar to end Oct; 3 rooms

WHERE TO EAT

Key: A * marks a place that is particularly good value for money

GULLANE
Greywalls
Muirfield, Gullane EH31 2EG
TEL (01620) 842144
FAX (01620) 842241
Plush, comfortable restaurant overlooking Muirhead's famous golf holes. Daily-changing four-course menu, inclined towards seafood; showy and accomplished modern cookery. Classic French wine list with limited selections from Europe and the New World.

All week 12.30 to 2, 7 to 9.15, closed Nov to Mar (See Where to Stay)

La Potinière
Main Street, Gullane EH31 2AA
TEL (01620) 843214
A pleasurable way to experience

outstanding innovative cooking with personal touches in quietly French dining style. Good preparation of high quality ingredients for superior flavour. Decent value bottles on the fine wine list.

Mon, Tue, Thur and Sun 1pm, one sitting; Fri and Sat 8, one sitting; closed Oct, 25 Dec, 1 Jan, 1 week Jun

RATHO
Bridge Inn *
27 Baird Road, Ratho EH28 8RA
TEL 0131-333 1320/1251
Busy inn opposite the Edinburgh Canal Centre with decidedly good food and excellent facilities for families.

Open for food Mon to Sat 12 to 9, Sun 12.30 to 8; restaurant 12 to 2, 7 to 9

GLASGOW

- Scotland's largest city, famous for its industrial past and for its resurrection as a modern cultural capital
- The home town of architect Charles Rennie Mackintosh, and the site of some magnificent nineteenth-century architecture too
- A city with some of the best museums and galleries in Britain

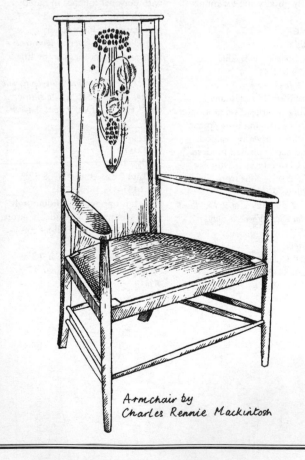

Armchair by
Charles Rennie Mackintosh

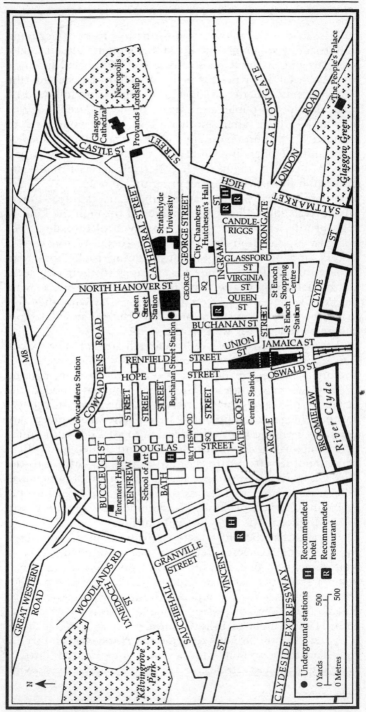

THE story of Glasgow's transformation from a moribund industrial city which no one loved to a vibrant cultural capital ready to sing its own praises to anyone who will listen, is by now well known. A touch of genius lay behind the 'Glasgow's miles better' campaign of 1983, soon followed by huge amounts of public and private money poured into one ambitious project after another. The city's willingness to compete across Europe for any cultural award going, allied to its seemingly unending ability to create new festivals and make a success of them, has left its rivals across Britain, and Edinburgh in particular, scampering to catch up.

It is somewhat ironic that this most successful of inner-city revivals should have been achieved through the kind of high-profile, big money projects beloved of capitalists. For Glasgow is, traditionally, a fervently socialist city, with a history of working-class radicalism going back more than two centuries. The bewildering changes to their city seem to have left many Glaswegians torn between a pride at what has been achieved and a certain ruefulness at what they feel may have been a betrayal of principle. But the new Glasgow is here to stay, and is well worth seeing.

The signs of Glasgow's rebirth are all around. The extensive stone-cleaning programme has freed whole streets of Victorian buildings from black grime and left them basking in their warm sandstone. The rebuilding has studded the skyline with cranes, while street hoardings announce yet another mega-development. Urban renewal projects are gradually bringing life to the decaying East End, with buildings being dusted down or renovated and turned into offices or yet another arts centre. For an immediate entry into the new Glasgow, make straight for St Enoch shopping centre, where, under the largest glass roof in the whole of Europe, you can wander for hours, surrounded by greenery and Muzak, ignoring the grey drizzle outside.

Worries that the old Glasgow spirit has been smothered by glass and concrete seem to be unfounded. Take a 'refreshment' in one of the legion of pubs, go to the fitba', wander about the Barras or Paddy's Market and you will not have to look far for the raucous, humorous, argumentative and slightly inebriated Glasgow made famous by its comics from Harry Lauder to Billy Connolly.

Apart from the fun of exploring the city centre and trying to calculate how much money is being poured into it, Glasgow's greatest attractions are its capacity to provide entertainment and its nineteenth-century architecture. The galleries and museums are superb. The city is home to the Scottish Opera, the Scottish Ballet and the Royal Scottish Orchestra, not to mention the renowned Citizens' Theatre and the BBC Scottish Symphony Orchestra, so opportunities for highbrow culture abound. However, you only have to be in Glasgow for the Mayfest – the trade-union-inspired festival which is now Britain's second biggest arts festival – to realise that it does not stop there. June/July sees a mammoth jazz festival; there's a folk festival in August, the world pipe band competitions in the same month, and the 'Celtic Connections' pan-Celtic festival of music in January. Glasgow's long love affair with popular theatre is far from dead – the Christmas pantomimes are a sell-out, and appearances by hypnotists, variety acts and comedians hugely popular. Try being among a Friday night audience for atmosphere. Even away from the theatres and concert halls, there is always something going on, right down to the round of folk evenings in the pubs, the flourishing nightclubs, or the pavement artists at work in Buchanan Street. The city bounces with energy – the reason why New Yorkers claim to feel more at home here than anywhere else in Britain.

As for Glaswegian architecture, it is the work of Charles Rennie Mackintosh (1868–1928) that people most want to see; his most accessible buildings are the School of Art, the Willow Tea Rooms and nearby Hill House. The other great Glasgow architect, Alexander 'Greek' Thomson (1817–75), is less well known outside the city, but is being enthusiastically promoted.

Throughout the streets of the Merchant City, and westward from it, impressive, sometimes self-important, nineteenth-century warehouses and offices rear above the streets. Almost every style, from Palladian through Venetian to Egyptian, can be found, sometimes cleaned up and pristine, sometimes still covered in industrial grime.

Not everything about Glasgow is appealing. It is a big, sprawling, superficially ugly city, with great gaps in its centre where motorways, railways and slum clearance programmes have torn out chunks of the old town. It has suffered, especially in its outlying housing estates, from some of the worst planning mistakes of the 1960s, and is virtually split in half by expressways. The contrast with elegant, compact Edinburgh could hardly be greater. That contrast extends to the character of the two cities, and it is hardly surprising that each of them is subject to outrageous stereotyping – often propagated by the inhabitants of the other. Part of the enjoyment of visiting

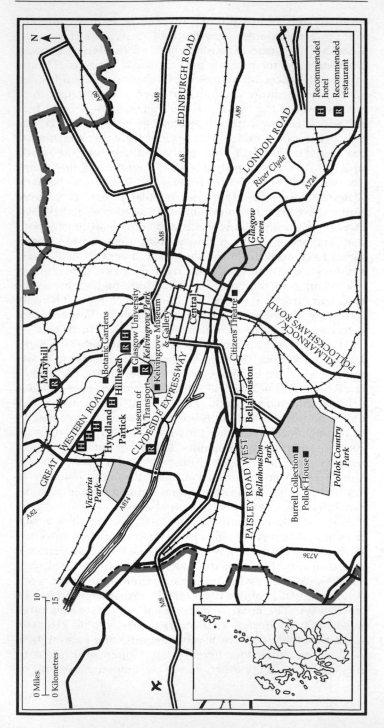

Glasgow and Edinburgh in sequence is to test whether their citizens really are warm-hearted, humorous, drunk and violent on the one hand or dignified, clean-living, stuck-up and offhand on the other.

Second City of Empire

This was the name Glasgow adopted for itself in its manufacturing heyday. Since the union with England first opened up the opportunity to trade with America, Glasgow has been a city of merchants and industrialists. Tobacco brought the first wave of prosperity, followed by cotton, followed by engineering. Ship-building is probably Glasgow's most famous industry, but building locomotives for half the railways of the British Empire came only a short way behind. Heavy industry of every kind made Glasgow into a nineteenth-century boom town, and made it desperately vulnerable in the lean years of the twentieth.

The population in 1800 was around 50,000; by 1870 it was half a million. Refugees from the Highland Clearances and from the Irish potato famines of the 1840s poured into the town. In their wake came the urban poverty and disease which were to dog Glasgow for the better part of a century. The infant mortality rate was appalling. This was the reverse side of the civic pomp and commercial rivalry which stocked Glasgow with so many fine buildings and endowed its galleries and museums.

The slump which followed World War I was bad everywhere but especially so in Glasgow, with its dependence on ships and heavy engineering. It was around this time that the 'Red Clydeside' epithet was coined, confirming Glasgow's working-class radicalism, which started as early as 1787 when the hand-loom weavers went on strike rather than suffer a 25 per cent pay cut, resulting in the death of three of them. In 1848, the year of the Communist Manifesto, six more people died in riots. Ten members of the Independent Labour Party were elected from Glasgow in 1922, and in 1972 the famous sit-in took place in defence of the threatened yards of Upper Clyde Shipbuilders. This long tradition of political awareness and action is still an inspiration to many of Glasgow's writers and artists, even now that so many of the old industries have gone painfully to the wall and are rapidly being superseded by the bright offices of computer software specialists and graphic designers.

THE EAST END

This was the medieval part of the city, though nothing much of that period remains now. The High Street, once at its centre, is now on the eastern fringe of all the activity, and is a fairly dismal place, with old railway yards at its top and crumbling shops and houses where the Gallowgate and London Road meet at Glasgow Cross. However, the urban renewal project here has saved several of the best buildings and there are several good things to see within walking distance of Glasgow Cross.

Practical suggestions

In some respects, Glasgow has yet to catch up with itself in terms of providing infrastructure for visitors. The city is too big to see on foot, and the routes of the colourful horde of buses and the extensive suburban railway network can seem baffling at first. The circular subway – dubbed the Clockwork Orange because of the colour of its carriages – trundles round the periphery of the city centre, and is useful for sights on the western side of the city (but not the eastern). You can get a one-day unlimited-travel ticket called a Heritage Trail which comes with a booklet listing places of interest at each stop. City-centre parking is expensive and the traffic lights on the grid of streets are reputed to have the slowest changes in Europe. Travelling by taxi is certainly the quickest and liveliest way of getting around (Glaswegian taxi drivers are the chattiest, wittiest, kindest and perhaps the least comprehensible in Britain), but costs mount up. To solve travel problems, start at the **St Enoch Square Travel Centre** (open Mon to Sat 9.30 to 5.30). Inner city transport guides do exist but it is advisable to check details first as bus routes are constantly changing. Much the best way of orientating yourself in Glasgow is to take a city bus tour, a mammoth and comprehensive round trip from George Square (running every day between the end of April and the end of September).

The two obvious areas to base yourself in are the city centre with its numerous chain hotels (some of which offer short break or weekend bargains) or the area round the University of Glasgow at Hillhead and Hyndland on the western side of the city. Here

Medieval Glasgow

Glasgow's origins are lost in the legends surrounding St Kentigern (or Mungo as he came to be known), who came to Glasgow on a cart yoked to two wild bulls somewhere towards the end of the seventh century, and founded his monastery on the banks of the Molendinar burn. To him, Glasgow owes its motto, 'Let Glasgow flourish by preaching of the word' (the last five words have been dropped by a more secular age).

Glasgow Cathedral, started in 1136, is the best relic of the

---

the hotels have more character and are supplemented by guesthouses, but the city centre is not within walking distance.

There is about three days' worth of solid sightseeing before you exhaust Glasgow's attractions, and much more if you are interested in architecture, or want to explore some of the less obvious corners, or share the city's shop-until-you-drop mentality. Many of the best museums are free – a great incentive. Another of Glasgow's advantages is an enviable location within range of splendid countryside – from the popular attractions of Loch Lomond to the gentler Campsie Fells. For entertainment listings, consult *The Herald* or the *Evening Times* or arm yourself with *The List*, published every fortnight and available from newsagents, bookshops and the Tourist Information Centre. The Ticket Centre in City Hall (Candleriggs) sells tickets for most of the theatres in Glasgow.

The chief shopping streets are Argyle Street, Buchanan Street and Sauchiehall Street. Most chain stores have branches here. Among the specialist shops, try: Cooper Hay Rare Books (Bath Street) for antiquarian books and prints; the Victorian Village (West Regent Street) for a series of antique stalls; the Whisky Shop (Princes Square) for whisky; James Begg (Renfield Street) for bagpipes; the Glasgow Style Gallery (487 Great Western Road) for Mackintosh, Art Deco, Art Nouveau and Glasgow-style furniture.

To get to grips with the Glasgow dialect, you can do no better than to buy *The Patter* by Michael Munro (Glasgow District Libraries, 1985), which gives a glossary of most local expressions, including the vulgar ones.

medieval city. It is the only cathedral in Scotland to have survived the Reformation virtually intact, being saved from the mob by local craftsmen, and is a first-class, if rather gloomy, example of mid-thirteenth-century Gothic. As Scott's character Andrew Fairservice describes it, it has 'nane o' yere whigmaleeries and curliewurlies and opensteek hems about it', and the exterior is very plain. The interior, though, is fascinating – especially in the choir, where the outgrowth of mouldings create a waterfall of stone pouring downwards from the clerestory to the forceful chutes of the aisle columns. The vaulted lower church made necessary because of the fall of the land underneath the choir is more forest-like, its massive piers sprouting springers in all directions. Here is to be found the tomb of St Kentigern. Other good parts of the cathedral are the Lady Chapel, with magnificent vaulting, and the unique rood screen. The last archbishop, James Beaton, brother of the more famous cardinal who was murdered at St Andrews, fled to France at the Reformation, taking the cathedral's relics and many of its treasures with him.

East of the cathedral, the **Necropolis** is a magnificent graveyard on a hill, covered with the elaborate tombs of rich industrialists and merchants. The figure of John Knox stands on top of a huge pillar, glowering down on the city and the cathedral below. Views of the city are very good.

Opposite the cathedral, across Castle Street, you will find **Provand's Lordship** (open Mon to Sat 10 to 5, Sun 11 to 5), which is Glasgow's oldest house, dating from 1471. It was once the home of the Canon of Barlanark, and later became a sweet-shop, a pub and a furniture-maker's workshop. Now it is a museum, with mementoes of its later roles (the sweeties are especially welcome), but particularly interesting for the reconstruction of a pre-Reformation room, with appropriately uncomfortable furniture.

Opposite Provand's Lordship, the **St Mungo Museum of Religious Life and Art** is housed in a building which fits in well with its medieval surroundings. The star exhibit here is Salvador Dali's *Christ of St John of the Cross*; nothing else in the building approaches the numinous power of this painting, and its presence alone should be sufficient reason for making your way to this museum.

The **Royal Infirmary** overshadows the cathedral and stands on the site of the Bishop's Palace. Here Joseph Lister introduced the concept of an antiseptic surgical environment. Many of the other buildings a little to the west are part of Glasgow's second university, the University of Strathclyde. They occupy some of the site of the original Glasgow University, founded in 1451 and Scotland's second oldest. Don't miss the equestrian statue of King William at the edge of the High Street below the cathedral. As tour guides will happily relate, many a Glaswegian has questioned his own sobriety on seeing the horse's tail move. But it does – it is jointed on.

Around Glasgow Cross

The mercat cross is a replica of the original, but the **Tolbooth Tower**, all that is left of the original building, is seventeenth-century, and dominates the area which was once Glasgow's heart, especially in the days of the tobacco merchants who gathered nearby. The other tower in view is the **Tron Steeple**, once part of a church but now the home of the Tron Theatre, scene of many locally written productions and with a popular bar. Trongate merges into Argyle Street, Glasgow's most populous shopping street, crammed with buses for most of its length, but with a curiously isolated pedestrian area at the Trongate end.

East of Glasgow Cross, between Gallowgate and London Road, is the market universally known as the **Barras**. Everything from junk to fresh fruit can be found here, but it is not so much what is sold as the way it is sold that draws visitors. This is the place to hear the inimitable Glasgow patter – a flow of earthy wit and shameless come-on lines – with which the traders assail and entertain their customers. Weekends are the time to go; the market opens between 9 and 5 and is always busy.

Saltmarket running south towards the Clyde, was once an appalling warren of slums (an estimated 200 brothels lined it), and is still fairly tatty. To the east of it lies the beautiful eighteenth-century **St Andrews Parish Church**, with a portico like a Greek temple, rescued in the nick of time from decay. Another interesting eighteenth-century church, just to the south, is **St Andrews-by-the-Green** a Georgian building, now the headquarters of a housing association.

If you explore round the railway arches to the west of the **Briggait**, which was once a fish-market and more recently a shopping centre, you will find **Paddy's Market**, where the goods are extremely second-hand. It makes a contrast to the glamour of the New Glasgow, and there seems to be a creeping conspiracy to get rid of it – something strongly resisted by those who see it as a popular Glasgow institution.

Glasgow Green

Officially adopted as a public park in the seventeenth-century, this large, open patch of greenery by the Clyde has long been the focus of all kinds of open-air activity, from football to political meetings. Freemen of Glasgow still have the right to graze a flock of sheep here. Nelson stands on a column at the western side, and a ceramic version of Queen Victoria is nearby. Glasgow Green is where James Watt hit on the idea of a separate condensing cylinder for the steam engine, thus sparking off the Industrial Revolution. A boulder marks the site where he had his brain-wave.

The **People's Palace** (open Mon to Sat 10 to 5, Sun 11 to 5), on the north-east edge of the Green, started as a late-Victorian piece of cultural do-goodery for the people of East Glasgow. Now it is a splendid and idiosyncratic museum of the city, one of the most fascinating places in Glasgow. It is a popular and populist place, full of schoolchildren and family groups gazing at the ephemera of Glasgow of old, gathered in a warren of glass cases, reconstructed shops and tableaux. There are salvaged bits from old houses and churches, fragments of the medieval city dug out of holes, newspaper cuttings about the blitz, football memorabilia, weapons confiscated from suffragettes, and much more. The People's Palace was busy salvaging what it could of Glasgow long before the first yuppies arrived on the scene, and it has plenty of stories to tell. Do not leave without having a cup of tea in the Winter Gardens at the rear, where the glass roof covers neat arrays of flowers, and do not miss the murals by Ken Currie (one of Glasgow's latest generation of excellent painters), which adorn the ceilings of the top floor and are peopled by idealised muscular figures from Glasgow's working-class history.

Almost opposite the People's Palace, the **Templeton Business Centre** is an extraordinary orange (in some lights) replica of the Doges' Palace in Venice, built as a carpet factory in 1889. The story goes that the architect was asked to name his favourite building – this was the result.

THE CLYDE

The famous 'Song of the Clyde' would be different if it were written today. Sanitised, smartened and with barely a boat to be seen on it, the Clyde, where it flows through

Glasgow, now looks more like a municipal pond than a great waterway. The docks and the warehouses on its banks have gone. So has the great fleet of paddle-steamers which used to throng Broomielaw long ago, ready to take passengers 'doon the watter' to the resorts of the Firth of Clyde.

Now the **Clyde Walkway** runs beside the river from the bottom of Saltmarket as far as the Scottish Exhibition Centre two miles away. It can be a windy walk, and an interesting one in places. Look out for the statue of 'La Pasionaria' close to Glasgow Bridge on the north side of the Clyde, set up to commemorate those Glaswegians who joined the International Brigade in the Spanish Civil War, and for the two rotundas of the old **Clyde Tunnel**, one now a complex of restaurants and the other soon to become a part of yet another large-scale development on the south bank of the river. The **Finnieston Crane** once the largest in Europe, forms a distant landmark. It was used for loading locomotives on to ships, and in 1988 a locomotive made entirely from straw was hung from it – a good example of Glasgow sculptors' love of large-scale humour.

The *Waverley* down by Anderson Quay is the last ocean-going paddle-steamer in the world, and makes regular excursions down to the Clyde coast in summer, if her boilers are in order (call 0141-221 8152 for details).

CENTRAL GLASGOW

The Merchant City

After the Union of Parliaments in 1707 the Scots were suddenly free to trade with America, and Glasgow was ideally positioned to take advantage of this. The merchants who traded in the tobacco, sugar and cotton of the New World built their houses and warehouses to the west of the High Street, in the area roughly bounded by George Street to the north and Buchanan Street to the west, the area now known as the Merchant City. After falling on lean times, like much of the centre of Glasgow, the Merchant City has now filled with the wine-bar and bistro culture of the New Glasgow, and is being much touted as a place for the visitor to explore.

It is certainly worth doing this, for the sake of the buildings (though few remain from the eighteenth century). This is an area to wander through or to eat in rather than to shop in. Worth looking out for are:

- **Hutchesons' Hall, Ingram Street** (NTS, generally open Mon to Fri 9 to 5, Sat 10 to 4; shop open Mon to Sat 10 to 4) This was the site of a hospital founded in the seventeenth century. The statues of its founders, made in 1649, now occupy niches in the pretty early nineteenth-century building, with its neat white clock tower and spire. The hall on the first floor is open, and well worth seeing for its rich decoration.
- **Trades Hall, Glassford Street** A Robert Adam building from 1794, still fulfilling its original function as a home for Glasgow's 14 guilds. Go in here to see the banqueting hall and the saloon.
- **Virginia Galleries, 33 Virginia Street** This is where Glasgow merchants once haggled over cargoes of tobacco or sugar. Now it is more likely to be Glasgow shoppers bargaining for antiques.
- **Royal Exchange (Stirling Library), Royal Exchange Square** The mansion hidden at the heart of this porticoed building once belonged to a tobacco merchant. It is now the oldest and largest lending library in Glasgow, having also been the Royal Exchange, where dealings in sugar, rum, cotton and other commodities went on. The old hall – a massive Byzantine construction with a lovely roof – is full of neat shelves of books.
- **Royal Bank of Scotland, Royal Exchange Square** This is a wonderfully positioned building, flanked by arches and columns and with an elegant Ionic portico. The interior is worth a look, too, even if you do not want to cash a cheque. The well-known **Rogano** seafood restaurant is just round the corner, with exuberant Art Deco design.

George Square and Buchanan Street

This was the heart of Victorian Glasgow, and is the heart of the New Glasgow too. You will step straight into it if you have just arrived by train at Queen Street Station. George Square is a welcome open space in the grid of streets, with small areas of green and a liberal sprinkling of statues. Sir Walter Scott is at the centre of things, on top of a Doric column. George III, after whom the square is named, has no statue – his failure to preserve the American colonies, and hence Glasgow's tobacco trade, saw to that. However, Queen Victoria, Robert Burns and James Watt are all there, flanked by Glaswegians of varying degrees of fame.

The square is dominated by the lavishly ostentatious **City**

Chambers erected in 1888 in best Italian Renaissance style. No building says more about Glasgow's self-confidence and civic pride in its Victorian heyday, particularly if you take a tour of its magnificently (if sometimes excessively) decorated interior. (Tours normally run Mon to Fri at 10.30 and 2.30, and last about 45 mins. It is best to call first on 0141-227 4017.) Granite columns, marble capitals, mosaic upon mosaic, a massive staircase adorned with arches, more pillars and more purple and red marble culminate in a cupola of tinted glass. The council hall has carved mahogany in abundance, while the banqueting hall, with murals and arched ceilings, just stuns. The guides who take you round are out-and-out enthusiasts for this extraordinary piece of wedding-cakery.

At the corner of West George Street, **Merchant's House** (open Mon to Fri 2 to 4, subject to alteration) is a further lavish memorial to Glasgow's trade. Amazons support the windows and a sailing ship tops the dome. The banqueting hall is yet another *pièce de résistance*.

A block to the west of George Square, Buchanan Street is the city's smartest shopping area. Towards the bottom of it, Argyle Arcade houses jewellers by the score. Further up, the Princes Square shopping mall is a piece of 1980s chic, where whispering escalators carry you up from a central courtyard to an array of eating places and fashionable shops. This is the place for conspicuous consumption. Where Buchanan Street crosses St Vincent Street, the Clydesdale Bank is almost as conspicuous. Roman emperors line an astonishing black and gold hall. Victorian Venetian architecture breaks out again at the Stock Exchange and the Royal Faculty of Procurators.

At the very top, without warning, Buchanan Street suddenly starts to go seedy. Just where it begins to peter out to the desolate expanse of the Buchanan Street Bus Station stands the 1990 **Glasgow Royal Concert Hall**, a squat sandy building, about which many rude things have been said. If you cannot go to a concert here (few people are rude about the acoustics), there are guided tours. (Tours run Mon to Fri at 2; call 0141-332 6633 for details.)

Queen Street, which runs south from George Square, is the setting for the most recent of Glasgow's galleries, the **Gallery of Modern Art**. It opened at Easter 1996, too late for us to be able to give useful comment. But we are promised interactive exhibits and mechanical sculpture – both less important perhaps than the space to be given to

Glasgow's latest generation of painters: Davie, Howson and Bellany (currently often honoured more in the galleries of New York than in their home country). It should be a place well worth visiting.

The City Centre

The grid of streets lying between Buchanan Street and the M8 to the west makes up the heart of Glasgow's shopping and office districts, with residential streets on the edges. It is, in best American style, a separate downtown area, and feels, after a hard day's footslogging, about as big as Manhattan.

In pauses between the shops (Sauchiehall Street, partly pedestrianised, is the chief shopping street here), look out for:
- **Gardner's Building, Jamaica Street** The first building in Europe built of cast iron and glass, and a very elegant one.
- **Ca'd'oro, Union Street** Another cast-iron and glass building in lavish Venetian style, recently restored after a fire.
- **St Vincent Church, St Vincent Street** An extraordinary building by Alexander 'Greek' Thomson – a mixture of ancient Egypt, ancient Greece and smatterings of India.
- **Blythswood Square** A beautiful neo-Classical square – the nearest Glasgow comes to approaching the elegance of Edinburgh's Charlotte Square.
- **Willow Tea Rooms, Sauchiehall Street** Reconstruction though it is, this is a must for all fans of Charles Rennie Mackintosh. It is one of four tearooms he was commissioned to design, and is to be found above a jeweller's shop. Typical Mackintosh high-backed chairs pierced with little squares are grouped round the tables; mirrors and painted glass decorate the walls. The effect Mackintosh had on ordinary Glaswegians is caught by Neil Munro: '. . . the chairs is no' like ony ither chairs ever I clapped eyes on, but you could easy guess they were chairs; and a' roond the place there's a lump of lookin'-gless wi' purple leeks pented onit every noo and then . . .' You may have to queue for some time.
- **The McLellan Galleries, Sauchiehall Street** (exhibition times variable, call 0141-331 1854) Refurbished and reopened in 1990, the Galleries now contain the largest temporary exhibition space in the country outside London, hosting half a dozen major exhibitions a year.
- **The Glasgow School of Art, Renfrew Street** This, the most famous of Mackintosh's buildings, was built in two

stages between 1897 and 1909, and shows the architect at his most adventurous. Each façade is different, and enthusiasts will be able to trace Mackintosh's influences, from Elizabethan mansion to Scottish baronial. The oriel windows, stretching over several floors, are the most eye-catching part of the exterior. Tours of the interior are usually run Mon to Fri 11 to 2, Sat 10.30, but it's best to call first to check details (0141-353 4526). The interior of the building is even more fantastical than the outside. The two-storey library has lamps like miniature ziggurats, and wood carved into endless fascinating shapes, while the top-floor gallery contains many splendid examples of Mackintosh furniture. The Glasgow School of Art has had, and still has, an inestimable influence on the success of generation upon generation of Glasgow painters.

• **The Tenement House, Buccleuch Street** (NTS, open Mar to end Oct, daily 2 to 5, groups should book in advance; call 0141-333 0183 for details) This museum is a time-capsule, where the way of life of a previous generation has been preserved intact. The Glasgow tenement (see box) is still the city centre's most typical form of housing, and this is your chance to see what life used to be like for the inhabitants. The flat ('house' in tenement terminology) belonged to Miss Agnes Toward, who moved here in 1911 and died in hospital in 1975. Apparently unimpressed by modernity, this ordinary Glasgow woman lived in a way almost unchanged from Edwardian times, rarely disposing of anything. Now you see her hall, parlour, bedroom, bathroom and kitchen with everything in place, from the box beds carefully tucked away in the walls to the great black kitchen range. Pots of jam stand in the cupboard and the mangle and washboard remain by the sink.

THE UNIVERSITY AND THE WEST END

At one time the M8 and the Clydeside Expressway were not going to be alone in carving through Glasgow – the whole of the Great Western Road was also going to be remodelled in favour of the car. Luckily, motorway developments came to a halt, but only after the 'bridge to nowhere' over the M8 had been built (you can see it standing forlornly near the end of Waterloo Street). The change of plan has left central

A MACKINTOSH CHECKLIST

Born in Glasgow in 1868, and hailed in Europe in his own day, Charles Rennie Mackintosh was largely ignored at home except by the few visionaries, such as Kate Cranston, who loved his work and were prepared to put up with his unpredictable temper. Despairing of success, Mackintosh left Glasgow in 1913. He died in 1928. Today, his sparse but distinctive style has become something of a cult, and you will find postcards, posters or reproductions of his designs throughout Glasgow and the world.

- **Queen's Cross** Mackintosh's only church. Now headquarters of the Charles Rennie Mackintosh Society. Information centre and an exhibition. Open Sun 2.30 to 5.

- **Glasgow School of Art, Renfrew Street** His best-known building. The interior is remarkable. For information on tours, see page 211.

- **Willow Tea Rooms, Sauchiehall Street** Exact reconstruction of one of the four tearooms built for Kate Cranston.

- **Ruchill Church Hall, Ruchill Street** The Church Hall was designed by Mackintosh in 1898.

- **Hunterian Art Gallery, University Avenue** Has a reconstruction of three floors of the Mackintoshs' own home (open Mon to Sat 9.30 to 5).

- **House for the Art Lover, Bellahouston Park** Built from Mackintosh's entry for an architecture competition.

- **Scotland Street School, Scotland Street** Now a museum of education.

- **Martyrs' Public School, Parson Street** Difficult to reach because of motorways and generally not open to the public.

- **Former Daily Record Building, Renfield Lane**

- **Former Glasgow Herald Building, Mitchell Street**

- **Craigie Hall, Drumbreck Avenue** Mackintosh helped to extend the house in 1893. It contains furniture and decorative fittings completed for the interior of the House for the Art Lover. (Craigie Hall is currently closed to visitors – for information call 0141-427 6884.)

- **The Hill House, Helensburgh** Reached by train from Glasgow Queen Street. Mackintosh built this house for the publisher William Blackie. Now run by the NTS (see Argyll chapter).

Glasgow linked to the West End by only the most tenuous of threads across the gulf of the motorway. You will rapidly discover just how tenuous it is if you attempt to drive from the centre to the university area without consulting a street map first: you may find yourself swept out to the airport before you know it.

Kelvingrove

The **Mitchell Library** (open Mon to Fri 9 to 9, Sat 9 to 5), on the edge of the motorway and reached from Granville Street, is best seen at night, when the domed building is lit up by floodlights. It is the biggest reference library in Europe, and has collections devoted to Glasgow and to Burns.

North of the library, make for Woodlands Road and Lynedoch Street, for this is the way to reach the **Park Conservation Area**. This cloistered little enclave of houses and towers draws superlatives, such as 'the most perfect piece of mid-nineteenth-century planning'. It has also been likened to an Italian hilltop town, and when you see the towers of Trinity College rising over the curving crescents of sandstone houses you can see why. However, the genius of the planners ran out when it came to naming the streets: Park Circus, Park Gate, Park Gardens, Park Quadrant, Park Street and Park Terrace. Even if you are not an architecture fan, it is worth finding your way here for the views of Kelvingrove Park and of the city.

Museum of Transport

(Open Mon to Sat 10 to 5, Sun 11 to 5)
Sited in part of the immense interior of **Kelvin Hall**, this is a transport museum to beat all others in the size and range of its collection. Fleets of bicycles and motor-bikes, early cars – especially from the Scottish builders – and, of course, the famous Glasgow trams make up a large part of the display. There are also steam locomotives to remind you that Springburn was once the largest locomotive building centre in the world. Yet it is the Clyde Room, with its display of model ships, which probably draws most people. The majority of models are of ships built on the Clyde, the *Queen Mary* and the *Queen Elizabeth* among them. This museum is a good place for children for there is almost bound to be something that will catch their eyes and,

though most of the exhibits are out of bounds as far as climbing over them is concerned, it is a cheerful and friendly place.

Kelvingrove Art Gallery and Museum

(Open Mon to Sat 10 to 5, Sun 11 to 5)
Opposite the Kelvin Hall, on the edge of Kelvingrove Park, this turn-of-the-century spiked and turreted building seems to have its rear facing the road. The story goes that the architect built it the wrong way round and was so mortified that he leapt to his death from the topmost floor when it was complete. Alas, road alterations provide the more prosaic explanation. Inside, it is easy to be waylaid by the museum on the ground floor, which has a superb collection of arms and armour, but most visitors come to see the paintings.

Although Kelvingrove has lost Dali's *Christ of St John of the Cross* to St Mungo's Museum (page 204), and may lose more to the new Gallery of Modern Art, what remains is still one of the best small collections in Britain. Rembrandt's *Man in Armour* and Whistler's *Portrait of Thomas Carlyle* probably draw most onlookers, but there is plenty more to see among the Dutch and French works in particular. Prints, sculpture and the decorative arts round off

THE TENEMENT

Long before Glasgow's nineteenth-century expansion, tenements were a common form of Scottish urban existence, especially in Edinburgh. However, the best nineteenth-century examples are to be found in Glasgow. Tenements are essentially blocks of flats joined together to form a unified frontage which is pierced at intervals by narrow passageways, called closes, leading to the back of the building. The flats (called houses) open on to a single staircase which leads up from the close. In Edinburgh's old seventeenth-century tenements, there would have been a social mix within one building, the gentry occupying the first floor, and increasingly poorer families in the flats and rooms higher up. Today, tenements are becoming the province of the refurbishing middle classes. At their best, they are magnificent dwellings, and some of Glasgow's splendid red

the collection.

If you are in need of a refreshment afterwards, try the Exchequer Bar at 59 Dumbarton Road – a big, interesting pub full of paintings.

Kelvingrove Park

This park, between the Kelvingrove Art Gallery and Museum and the University of Glasgow, is the most pleasant open space in the city – well worth strolling through. It is dominated by the long Victorian Gothic frontage of the university at the top of the hill. You can easily get diverted up the Kelvin walkway beside the river of that name, which will lead you up through Kelvinside towards the Forth and Clyde canal. The massive fountain standing in the park commemorates the Lord Provost under whom the waters of Loch Katrine were piped into Glasgow to form the water supply. This enlightened piece of civil engineering did much to reduce the awful statistics of death from cholera and typhus in Glasgow's Victorian slums.

The University of Glasgow

Founded in 1451, the university moved to this site in 1870, away from its old position on the High Street. It now

---

sandstone terraces contain flats with five or six high-ceilinged rooms, many with elaborate plasterwork and spacious halls, putting the housing estates of most English towns firmly in the shade.

Yet the tenement could also become a slum. The 'single-ends' or one-room flats of the Gorbals, where sometimes a dozen people would live with no plumbing and lavatories shared between the whole building, were awful. It was the massive overcrowding of the inner-city tenements – even though the buildings themselves were often substantial – that gave rise to Glasgow's terrible nineteenth- and twentieth-century housing problems. The wholesale demolition of the worst tenements and the rehousing of their inhabitants in high-rise blocks within the city or on satellite estates nearby is now acknowledged to have been an inadequate solution to the problems of urban deprivation. These days, Glasgow's tenements are preserved wherever possible.

forms a complex of buildings around its Victorian Gothic centrepiece, with the quiet streets of Hillhead behind it, and the lively shops and eateries of Byres Road immediately to the west. Once through the 1951 memorial gates, you will find the visitor centre. If you do not have time or inclination to tour everything, try to see the splendidly Gothic **Bute Hall** and the **Hunterian Museum** with its geological, numismatic and archaeological collections. On no account miss the **Hunterian Art Gallery** (open Mon to Sat 9.30 to 5).

The doors, by Eduardo Paolozzi, are the first indication of the gallery's style. They are cast-aluminium, and burnished like some precision piece of aerospace engineering. Inside, the impression is of brightness and space – the paintings are hung to splendid effect. The collection is small but surprisingly comprehensive, and, for followers of Whistler, unrivalled outside Washington. There are further examples of Glasgow painters and a superb collection of prints, including some by Hockney, Picasso and Dürer.

At one end of the gallery is a reconstruction of Mackintosh's home. There are three floors' worth of his fascinating furniture, and plenty of ideas for budding cabinet-makers and interior designers alike. One of the peculiarities of the reconstruction, which you can see from the outside, is the entrance door built several feet off the ground.

In close proximity to the University is the Halt Bar (Woodlands Road). The décor is minimal but the atmosphere more than makes up for that – you may even be treated to an impromptu folk song.

Great Western Road

A drive or a bus ride down this long ruler-straight avenue reveals more of Glasgow's best planning. The terraces and crescents along the road were laid out in the 1830s, and some are superb. Keep your eye open for Grosvenor Terrace, with its massively long uniform frontage, and for Great Western Terrace, by Alexander 'Greek' Thomson. On the opposite side of the road from Grosvenor Terrace lie the **Botanic Gardens**. The gardens themselves, lovely though they are, are rather put in the shade by the huge glasshouse of **Kibble Palace**, brought here on a boat from Loch Long in the late nineteenth century and now filled with ferns to provide a warm green atmosphere. Elsewhere there is a rock garden and a herb garden and plenty of space to sit. By following the walkway up the River Kelvin or by driving up

Maryhill Road, you reach the **Forth and Clyde Canal**. For canal-lovers, the Kelvin Aqueduct (1790) and the Maryhill Locks are the things to see.

SOUTH OF THE CLYDE

To explore down here you will need a car, or else to have grown accustomed to the buses, for the sights are scattered and few are within walking distance of the city centre. The Clockwork Orange subway helps for some. The district of the **Gorbals** lies south of the river from the High Street. The name's association with slum living and razor-wielding gangs is largely the responsibility of Alexander MacArthur, who wrote the novel called *No Mean City* (published by Corgi). The days of the slums are only to be seen in old photographs now, for the Gorbals has been cleared in favour of tower blocks. These days you go through the Gorbals to visit the Citizens' Theatre or the Tramway Theatre, with its huge space for epic productions, or to admire the lines of the modern Glasgow Central Mosque. Mackintosh fans make for the Scotland Street School, now a museum of education.

At **Ibrox**, with its own subway station, is the stadium which is home to Glasgow Rangers, and a shrine for football-lovers, while in **Bellahouston Park**, the House for the Art Lover is due to open, at last, in 1996. It has been constructed from the plans submitted by Mackintosh for a German competition, and will serve as part of Glasgow School of Art. But for visitors there will be a suite of Mackintosh-designed rooms, complete with fittings, brought into being for the first time almost seventy years after the architect's death.

Pollok Country Park and House

The estate of Pollok was held by the Maxwell family from 1269 to 1966, when it was donated to Glasgow. It has now been turned into a country park in the middle of the city, and a most tranquil place it is, with a herd of Highland cattle mournfully surveying the strollers and the golfers.

At the centre of the park lies **Pollok House** (open Mon to Sat 10 to 5, Sun 2 to 5). This is an excellent counterpoint to the Burrell Collection, for here, in contrast to the purpose-built modernity of the Burrell building, is a neo-classical house whose homely interior acts as the setting for a superb collection of Spanish, Dutch and British paintings. In particular, there are fine works by William Blake, Hogarth, Goya, El Greco and Murillo. There are also many portraits – often of the Maxwell family. The setting of these paintings among the furniture and plasterwork of the airy rooms is part of the charm. It is foolish to traipse hotfoot to the Burrell and neglect Pollok, though all too many do. Apart from anything else, the formal gardens round the house are beautiful.

The Burrell Collection

(Open Mon to Sat 10 to 5, Sun 11 to 5)
More than a decade since the Burrell Collection opened to

USEFUL DIRECTORY

Main tourist office
Greater Glasgow and Clyde Valley Tourist Board
39 St Vincent Place
Glasgow G1 2ER
0141-204 4400

Tourist Board publications Useful brochures, all available free from the Tourist Board, are *Greater Glasgow Quick Guide, Where to Stay in Greater Glasgow* and *Greater Glasgow Short Breaks.*

Local transport
Glasgow Airport 0141-887 1111
Prestwick Airport (01292) 479822
Glasgow Central Station (for trains to/from the south) and
Glasgow Queen Street (for fast trains to Edinburgh, and trains north) 0141-204 2844 or (0345) 212282
National Express and Citylink bus services (0990) 505050
Strathclyde Transport and Buchanan Bus Station
(cross border services and in and around Glasgow) 0141-332 7133
Travel Centre (St Enoch Square) 0141-226 4826
Discovering Glasgow Tours (bus) 0141-204 0444
Helicopter trips (Clyde Helicopters) 0141-226 4261

City walks
For details of City Walks contact Iris Sommerville 0141-942 7929
(fax 0141-943 0810)

the public, it is still difficult to divorce its symbolic value from its actual worth as a collection to visit and admire – for some would say that it was the opening of the Burrell in 1983 and the 'Glasgow's Miles Better' campaign of the same year that together succeeded in putting the city back in the minds of the art, media and subsequently business worlds.

The story of the Burrell Collection is also, in its way, symbolic. It is the collection of one man, a Glasgow ship-owner, who bought throughout his long life (he died in 1958 at the age of 97), using the fortune amassed from the shrewd timing of the sale of his fleet. He donated the collection to Glasgow in 1944, but surrounded the gift with restrictions, notably that the collection should be exhibited

Entertainment
Academy box office also for: Chandler Studio Theatre, Guinness Room, New Athenaeum Theatre and Stevenson Hall 0141-332 5057

Ticket centre for: City Hall, Glasgow Royal Concert Hall, King's Theatre, Mitchell Theatre and Tramway Theatre 0141-287 5511

Citizens' Theatre 0141-429 0022
Glasgow Film Theatre 0141-332 8128
Henry Wood Hall (Royal Scottish Orchestra) 0141-226 3868
Old Athenaeum Theatre 0141-332 2333
Pavilion Theatre 0141-332 1846
Scottish Opera 0141-248 4567
Scottish Youth Theatre 0141-332 5127
Theatre Royal (Scottish Opera) 0141-332 9000
Tron Theatre 0141-552 4267
Year-round Mayfest 0141-552 8000

Football
Glasgow Rangers FC 0141-427 8500 (ticket centre) 0141-427 8800
Glasgow Celtic FC 0141-556 2611

Miscellaneous
Trips on the Clyde, July and August (Waverley Excursions) 0141-221 8152
Headquarters of Charles Rennie Mackintosh Society 0141-946 6600

in a purpose-built gallery, and that it should be in a rural setting removed from Glasgow's pollution. It took almost 40 years before Glasgow was able to comply, first finding a site in the Pollok estate (donated in 1966) and then running an architectural competition to come up with a building that could best display the diversity of the collection.

The result is something of a triumph, for the building is remarkable, its glass walls in one place allowing the shady woodland against which it is built to merge with the objects inside, and in another acting as the setting for medieval stained glass. Medieval ceilings and gateways are built into it, and the Hutton Rooms – from Burrell's castle near Berwick – form a kind of medieval house within a house.

The collection's strongest point is the medieval European collection of furnishings, tapestry, woodcarving and stained glass, but the range of objects from the ancient Mesopotamian and Egyptian civilisations and the Chinese ceramics, bronzes and jades are also remarkable. Then there is the glass, the silver and the needlework, and finally of course the paintings. These are chiefly nineteenth-century French, and include some fine examples of Degas and Cézanne. Works of the Hague School were also among Burrell's favourites.

Burrell's taste, especially in paintings, is seen by some as ultra-conservative. This is perhaps a little unfair. If the collection as a whole can give an insight into his pre-ferences, it would seem that he avoided the florid and enjoyed simplicity of line. This is best seen in the collection of silver and glassware, but is also reflected in the German woodcarving and the objects from the ancient civilisations.

WHERE TO STAY

£ – under £70 per room per night, incl. VAT
££ – £70 to £110 per room per night, incl. VAT
£££ – over £110 per room per night, incl. VAT

Babbity Bowster
16-18 Blackfriars Street, Glasgow
G1 1PE
TEL 0141-552 5055
FAX 0141-552 5215/7774

Popular café/bar/restaurant in restored Adam town house, Merchant City area. The bar blackboard menu includes seafood and savoury staples; upstairs is a quiet, simple and stylish restaurant. Extremely plain bedrooms with pine furniture and functional shower rooms; not much hope of sleep before midnight.
££ All year; restaurant closed Sun eve; 6 rooms with shower/wc

The Devonshire
5 Devonshire Gardens, Glasgow
G12 0UX
TEL 0141-339 7878
FAX 0141-339 3980
A smart, top-of-the-range West
End town house. Light and airy
pastel florals and modern pine
furniture blend well with original
stained glass. The sea green dining-
room feels small and private.
Modern and stylish bedrooms.
££ All year; 14 rooms

Glasgow Hilton
1 William Street, Glasgow G3 8HT
TEL 0141-204 5555
FAX 0141-204 5004
Smart hi-tech tower-block hotel
offering comprehensive leisure
facilities, based in an unregenerated
part of the city. Themed bars and
restaurants lead off from the
atrium-style open-plan reception;
chic and spacious bedrooms.
*£££ All year; 319 rooms; ballroom;
swimming-pool; solarium, sauna, gym*

Kirklee Hotel
11 Kensington Gate, Glasgow G12 9LG
TEL 0141-334 5555
FAX 0141-339 3828
Close to the city centre in a
conservation area, the Kirklee was
built in 1904 for a shipping
magnate. Many original
architectural features remain
including the wood-panelled hall
and drawing-room. Breakfast served
in bedrooms equipped with tables
and chairs. Good facilities and
unrestricted on-street parking.
£ All year; 9 rooms

Malmaison
278 West George Street, Glasgow G2 4LL
TEL 0141-221 6400
FAX 0141-221 6411
Aesthetic new city centre hotel
formerly St Jude's Church, a neo-
Grecian temple and fashionable

place of worship. The building, the
work of Ken McCulloch (also behind
One Devonshire Gardens, see entry)
remains the place to be with dazzling
interior design and a brasserie
emblazoned with Rennie
Mackintosh-style motifs. Food is
standard French; the bedrooms starkly
modern with CD players hidden
inside commissioned furniture.
££ All year exc Chr, 1 Jan; 21 rooms

One Devonshire Gardens
1 Devonshire Gardens, Glasgow
G12 0UX
TEL 0141-339 2001
FAX 0141-337 1663
Splendidly flamboyant West End
terrace hotel with dramatic rooms
and magnificent stained glass. Past
the lavish entrance hall are a refined
dining-room and bright, harmonious
drawing-rooms. The panelled
restaurant serves memorable,
inventive food. Desirable, stylish
bedrooms feature opulent fabrics and
antique furniture; highly glamorous
marble bathrooms.
*£££ All year; 27 rooms (See
Where to Eat)*

Scotts Guest House
417 North Woodside Road, Glasgow
G20 6NN
TEL 0141-339 3750
Located in a quiet cul-de-sac
overlooking Kelvin Park, just off the
Great Western Road. Breakfast is
served in the recently refurbished first
floor dining-room with views over
the park; comfortable bedrooms.
*£ All year; 8 rooms, 4 with
bath/shower*

The Town House
4 Hughenden Terrace, Glasgow G12 9XR
TEL 0141-357 0862
FAX 0141-339 9605
An elegant Victorian house offering
real value in a very desirable West

End location. Part of an impressive sandstone terrace, the house retains attractive original architectural features. The spacious sitting-room is warm and inviting with a well-stocked library; home-cooked dinners are served in the dining-room. High-ceilinged stylish bedrooms, generously equipped.
£ *All year; 10 rooms*

WHERE TO EAT

Key: A * marks a place that is particularly good value for money

Buttery
652 Argyle Street, Glasgow G3 8UF
TEL 0141-221 8188
FAX 0141-204 4639
A pleasurable restaurant which goes in for challenging cooking; over-complex combinations more than balanced by successful modern dishes.
Mon to Fri 12 to 2.30, Mon to Sat 7 to 10.30; closed Sun, public and local hols

Cabin
996 Dumbarton Road, Whiteinch, Glasgow G14 9RR
TEL 0141-569 1036
A lively mix of serious cooking and dancing on the tables. Menus change daily; fish wins particular praise.
All week 12 to 2.30, 7.30 to 9

Café Gandolfi
64 Albion Street, Glasgow G1 1NY
TEL 0141-552 6813
Sophisticated, European-style cafe popular with enthusiastic, youngish crowd. Good brasserie food served from breakfast onwards in candlelit setting of stylish stained glass.
All week 9 to 11.30, Sun 12 to 11.30; closed 25-26 Dec, Easter Sun, bank hol Mons

Crannog *
28 Cheapside Street, Glasgow G3 8BH
TEL 0141-221 1727
Virtually self-sufficient offering langoustines and prawns from its own boats and salmon, mussels and trout from its smokery, Crannog has hot and successful daily specials and belongs to a small chain of fish restaurants.
Tue to Sat 12 to 2.30, 6 to 9.30, Fri and Sat 6 to 10.30; closed Chr and New Year

Fire Station
33 Ingram Street, Glasgow G1 1HA
TEL 0141-552 2929
Marble-walled former fire station now on duty as a cheerful eating-place manned by amazingly helpful young staff. Pizza/pasta/burger menu with very drinkable wines.
Weekdays 12 to 2.30, Mon and Tues 5 to 9.30, Wed and Thur 5 to 10, Fri 5 to 10.30; Sat, Sun 12 to 10.30; closed 25 Dec, 1 Jan

Killermont Polo Club *
2022 Maryhill Road, near Bearsden, Glasgow G20 0AB
TEL 0141-946 5412
A converted manse doubling as a themed restaurant/polo club linking sport and Raj nostalgia. Specialist Indian cooking intermingles with traditional British fare; set-price deals are lunch and the start-of-the week evening buffet.
Mon to Sat 12 to 2, all week 5 to 10.30; closed 25 Dec, 1 Jan

Mitchells West End
31-35 Ashton Lane, off Byres Road, Glasgow G12 8SJ
TEL 0141-339 2220

FAX 0141-204 1818

Brisk bistro cooking in a light and bright room. Mitchells looks Mediterranean but serves international style food using prime Scottish ingredients. Licensed, but still operating bring your own policy.
Mon to Sat 5.15 to 10.30

One Devonshire Gardens

1 Devonshire Gardens, Glasgow G12 0UX
TEL 0141-339 2001
FAX 0141-337 1663

Serene, refined surroundings in which to enjoy polished cooking. The light, unlaboured main dishes are delightful while puddings are sharp and exciting. Set price lunch and dinner, and an extensive wine list.
All week exc Sat lunch 12.30 to 2, 7.15 to 10.15 (See Where to Stay)

La Parmigiana *

447 Great Western Road, Glasgow G12 8HH
TEL 0141-334 0686
FAX 0141-332 3800

Bright restaurant both cool and relaxing, hectic and lively. Excellent renditions of familiar Italian cooking; praiseworthy pesto, seafood and puddings. The decently priced wine list consists mostly of Italian bottles.
Mon to Sat 12 to 2.30, 6 to 11; closed 25-26 Dec, 1-2 Jan and bank hol Mons

Puppet Theatre

11 Ruthven Lane, Glasgow G12 9BG
TEL 0141-339 8444
FAX 0141-339 7666

A series of themed rooms, the highlight a Gaudi-esque conservatory. Modern cooking with lively flavours, traditional dishes and trendy salads; fruit-dominated puddings and excellent coffee. Inspired presentation.
Sun to Fri 12 to 2.30, Tue to Sun 7 to 10.30; closed 25-26 Dec, 1-2 Jan

Rogano

11 Exchange Place, Glasgow G1 3AN
TEL 0141-248 4055
FAX 0141-248 2608

Amazing period piece unaffected by latest fashion; continues to serve an enjoyable menu in which fish and seafood major. Impressive puddings and plenty of half-bottles on the reasonably priced wine list. Café Rogano in the basement has a cheaper 'mixed bag' menu.
All week 12 to 2.30, 6.30 to 10.30, Sun 6.30 to 10; closed 25-26 Dec, 1-2 Jan

Ubiquitous Chip

12 Ashton Lane, Glasgow G12 8SJ
TEL 0141-334 5007
FAX 0141-337 1302

Something of a city institution, its cooking remains refreshingly unpompous and gutsy. Satisfying dishes and delicious puddings outshone by a dazzling wine list studded with real gems. Downstairs dining more expensive.
All week 12 to 2.30, 5.30 to 11, Sun 6.30 to 11; closed 25 and 31 Dec, 1 Jan

ARGYLL AND AROUND

- A ragged coastline hiding unruffled sea lochs
- St Columba's sacred island of Iona
- Islands to suit all tastes from tiny Gigha to the wilds of Mull

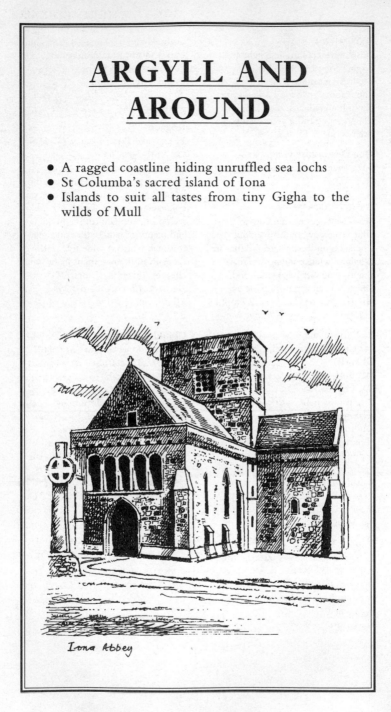

Iona Abbey

Deeply indented coastlines and a web of offshore islands make Argyll at once distinct and enticing. The view across lochs and firths is almost always decorated by close or distant land masses of overlapping hills or mountains, misty or sharp contours and shapes that are forever changing as you drive along. Long and low-lying Kintyre, for instance, is more memorable for views across water than for inland scenery. Reflections of hills or mountains, castles or sheep-dotted slopes are true and sharp in this land of narrow and mirror-smooth bands of water.

Most sights in Argyll are minor, but there is a fair variety. Popular spots include Inverary, home to one of Scotland's most famous castles, and Oban, busy fishing port and tourist centre. Close to Glasgow is Charles Rennie Mackintosh's Hill House – not to be missed. The hill fort of Dunadd, the capital of the ancient kingdom of Dalriada, gets its fair share of visitors; it is surrounded by one of the highest concentrations of prehistoric monuments anywhere in Scotland. Amongst the castles, many of which are in advanced stages of ruin, are Kilchurn on Loch Awe, and Castle Stalker – both with atmospheric settings. Other sights include an underground power station, a couple of wildlife centres, a clutch of woodland gardens, and a reconstructed old Highland township. Finally, there is Iona, the sacred heart of old Scotland and still the centre of popular pilgrimage.

The Inner Hebridean islands included in the chapter – Mull, Colonsay, Islay, Jura, Coll and Tiree among them – vary from very small to very large, and from flat and fertile to mountainous and desolate. In many cases the smaller they are, the more interesting: consider the religiously important Iona, the freakish geology of Staffa, or the lush and untrampled Colonsay. But if you are after total seclusion, look further north. Above all, be warned that the loch-pierced mainland and erratic ferry schedules are not designed for time-conscious travellers; do not assume that you can slip in a quick island tour to top up your Scottish experience. Yet you should not exclude the islands from your itinerary if you do have time. The rich endowment of hill forts, burial cairns and Celtic remains are rewarding even if you have only the faintest knowledge of pre- or ancient history.

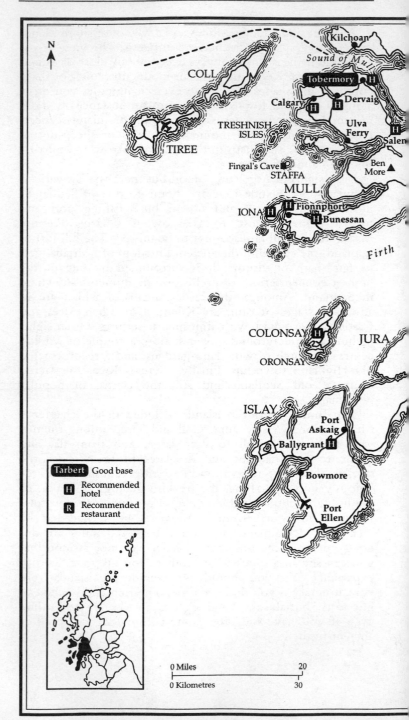

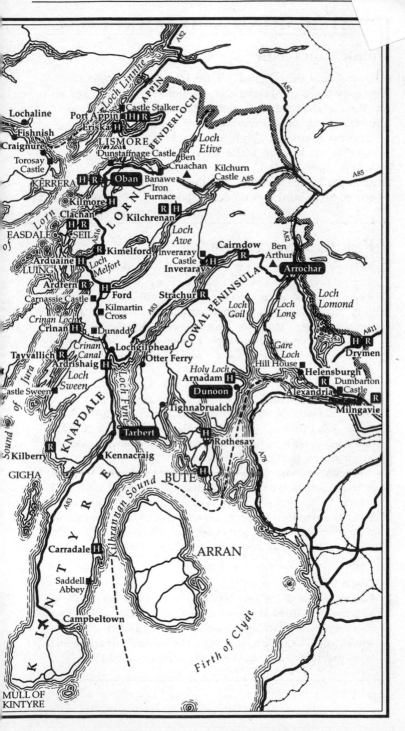

LOCH LOMOND AND LOCH LONG

Dumbarton Castle

(HS, standard times; closed Thur pm and Fri in winter)
The grey town of Dumbarton, capital of the old kingdom of Strathclyde before Norse raiders seized it in AD 877, appears almost as soon as you have crossed the Erskine Bridge.

The castle sits on a high, steep-sided rock near where the River Leven flows into the Clyde. There is an eighteenth-century, box-shaped, windowless magazine, but apart from some ramparts and a few gun batteries little else is left of the fortress which once defended all of western Scotland.

Practical suggestions

Although this part of the country boasts virtually as much geographical variety as can be found in the whole of Scotland, you should not assume that a holiday in Argyll will provide the complete Scottish experience. For a start, main roads (though improved) are few and narrow lanes the norm. Popping over to the islands is not necessarily a simple business either, unless you are happy to stick to Gigha and Mull: ferries go far less frequently to Jura, and only a few times a week to Coll, Tiree and Colonsay. You cannot just arrive and expect to find a bed for the night, either – Colonsay has just one hotel, for instance.

Prime tourist spots such as Oban, Inverary Castle, Loch Lomond and Bute can get unpleasantly touristy, but since much of the area is often passed through rather than visited, in much of Argyll you are unlikely to feel crowded.

Common holiday activities include fishing and walking, as well as boating, which is ideal in the protected water round the myriad islands. From Oban south to Kintyre, marinas swell with yachts. You don't need to bring your own boat or spend all your time on water, of course. Charter and cruise boats line the quays of lochs and harbours such as Loch Fyne and Loch Lomond, as well as Oban itself.

Good bases
● **Arrochar** Small but stretching over more than a mile of shore, with many B&Bs looking out across Loch Long to uninhabited mountains. Good facilities, especially at the cheaper end. Fine boating and walking area and central for the high moorland and mountains north and the Dunoon peninsula to the south.

During the Wars of Independence, the governor of Dumbarton, Sir John Monteith, turned traitor against William Wallace (see page 271) and imprisoned him here before sending him to his gruesome execution in London.

If you climb the long staircase up the White Tower rock you will be rewarded with an intriguing panorama over the industrial lower Clyde. Long views of moors and mountains to the north are also revealed.

Loch Lomond

Twenty-three miles long and five miles across at the widest point, Loch Lomond's 18,000 acres cover the largest area of

---

- **Dunoon** The best place to stay if you are visiting the Cowal peninsula, especially if you arrive there on the ferry from Gourock. A good town for strolling in, with four miles of promenade and a large harbourside park complete with castle ruin. Plenty of B&Bs in Kirn, a suburb a little to the north. You are unlikely to find accommodation on the last Friday and Saturday in August, when the Cowal Highland Gathering takes over the town.

- **Tarbert** Halfway along the Kintyre peninsula and handy for catching ferries: Claonaig to Arran (during the summer), Tayinloan to Gigha, Kennacraig to Islay and Jura. Small, with no sights to speak of, but pleasant and not often inundated by tourists. The main part of town, facing west, curves round a very deep harbour. Average restaurants and accommodation.

- **Oban** Oban is easy to like for the quick pace of life as well as its broad and handsome harbour. It is perfectly placed for day trips up and down the coast, and a primary port that links the mainland with Mull, Coll and Tiree. Smaller ferries to many of the little islands in and around its harbour leave from landings just outside town. A wide choice of sights in and around town, and a plethora of small, carless islands to explore means that you are unlikely to get bored. No shortage of accommodation, and the best range of restaurants and shops for miles around.

- **Tobermory** Mull's capital, near the north-east tip, can be reached via ferry from Oban. The town consists of one great swoop of harbour street, with some houses raked up the hill behind: colourful and unassuming guesthouses are scattered around outside of town, but there are a few mid-range hotels on the harbour.

---

any lake in Britain. Although it sits right at Glasgow's door-step, it is remarkably clean and very much less spoilt than you might expect. Its tree-lined shores and mountainous backdrop are not seen at their best from a car – you must get out and walk down to the shore.

Open farmlands and wooded islands mark the southern end. There are good facilities, especially for boating: the **Duck Bay Marina**, near the south-western tip, is a pleasant, if touristy, spot with a sizeable stretch of beach and a playground as well as a marina and hotel.

As the lake starts to narrow halfway up, so trees close in on you and Ben Lomond comes into view; by the time you reach Tarbet, the road is almost lost between a bank of thick pines and the water's edge. Stop at the observation site at the northern tip for a splendid view that extends far down the loch.

The problem with this side of Loch Lomond is Highland-bound traffic; Loch Lomond's western shore is never entirely peaceful and is often exasperatingly crowded, particularly at weekends. If you want to escape the A82, the B831 to Glen Fruin makes a good trip, the narrow road rising through a broad, gentle valley to high moorland and an eventual view of Gare Loch. But the best way to appreciate the virtues of Loch Lomond is by boat – hire your own or take a cruise.

Helensburgh

The less direct route to Arrochar along the A814 leads you to this sedate but stylish seaside resort. Victorian houses flank wide avenues that are tidily arranged on a grid. As you move up the hillside, views of the Firth of Clyde and Gare Loch get bigger and better and so do the properties. Helensburgh is both a popular spot for day-tripping Glaswegians and a desirable residence. John Logie Baird, inventor of the television, lived here, but most people associate Helensburgh with Charles Rennie Mackintosh. **Hill House** (NTS, open Apr to late Dec, daily 1.30 to 5.30), which he built in 1902 for publisher Walter Blackie, is a delight. Outside the gates are six large street lamps, con-structed from recently discovered Mackintosh sketches; inside the house, bold, angular shapes are mixed with jub-ilant, decorative patterns of sinuous, swirling lines. The colour scheme of black, pinks and purples is equally self-confident. Restrained by cost and by Blackie's taste, Mackintosh had to forgo designing every bit of furniture and decoration, but you have to look hard to find a single hinge or nail at odds with his grand scheme. The dining-room shows how clever he was at integrating Blackie's old furniture with Art Nouveau. The house is essential visiting for Mackintosh fans, and nearly everyone will find pleasure in the harmonious design. You can stock up on Mackintosh motif tea towels, mugs and books at the gift shop, and there is now a tea-room. Hill House has been suffering from excessive numbers of visitors; if you turn up at peak times you may be asked to wait before being allowed in.

As you leave Helensburgh and travel north you drive along the shore of **Gare Loch**, a Combined Operations base during World War II.

Then the road takes you up the eastern shore of **Loch Long**, a narrow, deep and sheltered sea loch. Its name comes not from its shape but from the Gaelic 'loch of the ships', harking back to Viking times when longships were dragged across the narrow strip between Arrochar and Tarbet to Loch Lomond. Tankers are often moored along its southern shores, but recreational sailing takes over in the north.

Arrochar

A popular tourist centre and stepping-off point for the nearby mountains, the so-called 'Arrochar Alps', Arrochar makes the most of its position at the head of Loch Long. The town spreads along more than a mile of the eastern shore with its houses and hotels looking over the water to the much-climbed Ben Arthur, known as 'the Cobbler'.

From Arrochar the A83 heads west past the Argyll Forest Park and up Glen Croe. The Cobbler remains in view for the first few miles and is then replaced by craggy Beinn Ime and Beinn an Lochain, which soar upwards from a valley choked with bracken and populated by sheep and trees. The **Rest and Be Thankful** pass at the watershed between Lochs Long and Fyne is a good place to breathe the air and gaze at mountains. The narrow road (B828) that runs along the west side of Loch Goil eventually reaches **Carrick Castle**, a privately owned, unblemished ruin from the fifteenth-century.

COWAL AND BUTE

The deeply indented, lobster-claw-shaped Cowal Peninsula is easy to reach from Glasgow (by ferry from Gourock), and in summer, walkers and boating types, fond of its gentle hills and calm inlets, come here in droves. However, there is plenty of undeveloped wilderness and many miles of lightly populated coast. The **Argyll Forest Park** covers much of north-east Cowal, but not all of it is plantation, and there is a reasonable variety of vegetation. It is criss-crossed by woodland and hill trails and forest roads, popular with walkers but hardly overrun.

Dunoon

The regular car ferry from Gourock to Dunoon connects with the train from Glasgow, while cruises on the Clyde also stop here. So the place really buzzes in the summer, especially on the last Friday and Saturday in August, when the Cowal Highland Gathering overtakes the town.

Dunoon is the largest town on the peninsula, with many fine houses remaining from Victorian and Edwardian days when wealthy Glaswegians came on holiday. The four miles of promenade are as popular for evening strolls now as they were then. **Castle Hill**, a spacious green park above the pier, rises steeply to the few remaining fragments of a thirteenth-century castle from where you can see many miles of shore and sea. A statue of Highland Mary, whom Burns almost married, stands just below.

The waters have not always been entirely the province of pleasure craft. **Holy Loch**, an inlet on Dunoon's northern side, was a base for American nuclear submarines from the early 1960s to late in 1991. For the best loch views, travel north up the A880 to the little holiday village of Ardentinny.

Younger Botanic Garden

(Open mid-Mar to Oct, daily 10 to 6)
The entrance to these wonderful gardens is just north of Ardbeg on the A815. They were planted by James Duncan between 1870 and 1880, later owned by Younger (of brewery fame) and in 1928 were handed over to the nation. They are naturally laid out and sheltered by tall trees. A striking grass avenue, planted with Californian redwoods, channels you into undulating parkland, dotted with flowering shrubs (some say Younger has the best collection of rhododendrons in the world), enormous Scots pines, little ponds and occasional formal flower beds. You can also climb into the wooded hillside.

South-west Cowal

This is the most peaceful part of Cowal. The A886, the Strachur–Tighnabruaich road, runs through green fields; the B8000 hugs the shores of Loch Fyne. At Otter Ferry (from the Gaelic 'oiter' for sandbank) a single-track road connects the two, crossing a high, craggy moor from which you have several good vantage points.

South of Otter Ferry the road veers inland through quiet farmland. **Kilfinan** consists of a few buildings, one of which is an excellent inn, and a good beach. The small Victorian village and yachting centre of **Tighnabruaich** lies on the shore of the Kyles of Bute and makes a good goal for a trip, with fine views from the A8003 north.

Bute

Fifteen miles long and no more than five across, Bute has long been a popular holiday island. Previous generations stuck to Rothesay, but now that more people bring cars, the island's remoter shores have sprouted camping and riding centres, and there are three golf courses. Much of Bute is pasture and farmland, tame and undemanding but memorable when seen against the far-off, stark mountain ranges of Arran. The north-western side offers uncrowded, sandy and rocky bays.

Rothesay

The old resort has an endearingly buoyant air during the summer months, and has recently had a face-lift: the cast-iron Winter Garden Pavilion has been returned to its former exuberant glory and yachts, sea birds and bathers populate the wide harbour.

● **Rothesay Castle** (open Apr to Oct, daily 9.30 to 6, Sun 2 to 6; late Oct to late Mar, Sun to Wed 9.30 to 4, Thur 9.30 to 1), one of the best-preserved early castles in Scotland, is in itself a justification for joining the ferry queues. It was probably first built in the late twelfth century, though the earliest confirmed date is 1230, when Norsemen stormed it. There are no other circular core castles in Britain, and Rothesay's round silhouette is startling. Its solid, ivy-covered walls are more than 130 feet in diameter. Of the four great drum towers, one is still standing. Cottages once filled the middle, as demonstrated by a small but illuminating model in the Great Hall, with its large window seats and high arched fireplace. A reconstructed wooden ceiling hung with Gothic-style wheel lamps shows how the principal chamber might once have looked.

● **Bute Museum** (open Easter to late Oct, daily 10 to 5, Sun 10 to 4; late Oct to late Mar, Tue to Sat 2 to 4), behind the castle on Stuart Street, has two small but well-arranged skylit rooms devoted to geology, archaeology, old Clyde steamer models and photographs of old Rothesay.

● **Ardencraig Gardens** (open May to late Sept, Mon to Fri 9.30 to 5, Sat and Sun 1 to 5), on the southern outskirts of town, has a stunning show garden and several spectacular fuchsia greenhouses. It also does a fair line in cactuses and has a tea-room, too.

St Mary's Chapel

Also known as Lady Kirk, the chapel is possibly 800 years old. It stands about half a mile south of Rothesay next to the parish church. It is small and roofless but two recessed canopy tombs and the effigy of a man in armour have survived remarkably well. The tomb on the north wall, possibly that of Alice, stepmother of Robert II, consists of a flat, nearly formless figure and baby, and, carved on its base, a row of female figures in heavily pleated robes.

St Blane's Chapel

This chapel is older and more handsome than St Mary's, but its setting, a fertile dip near the southern windswept tip of the island that gets the best view of Arran's blue-grey mountains, is its most memorable attribute. St Blane was born on Bute in the sixth century and a monastery dedicated to him was built here. The narrow, roofless chapel is worth seeing for the delicately carved columned Romanesque arch of the chancel.

LORN AND OBAN

Inveraray

In the heart of Campbell country, the Georgian town of Inveraray sits near the northern tip of Loch Fyne. The town is debonair and well kept, but it can sometimes feel like an open-air gift emporium for Inveraray Castle: the handsome façades of the houses lining Main Street East are hard to appreciate amongst the array of tartans flowing from gift-shop doorways. A stroll around is unlikely to be boring even so, for the town is photogenic, especially down by the harbour. It is here, within a wall right by the water's edge, that you will find **Inveraray Jail** (open Easter to Oct, daily 9.30 to 6, extended hours Jul, Aug; Nov to Easter 10 to 5), a clever reconstruction of prison buildings that have life-sized models of inmates sleeping, making herring nets or, in one case, nursing a baby. Try out the hammocks (or the bare wood floor) and crank the hard labour machine as you listen to grim tales of prisoners' fates. The courtroom (1920) is always in session, and you can sit amongst the grey-clad models and listen to the trial of a farmer accused of an insurance fraud. The Crime and Punishment exhibition, relating cases of benighted suspects and evil criminals, rounds out the visit.

Walk directly inland from the jail to find the **Episcopal Church of All Saints**, from the bell tower of which you get an especially good all-round survey of town, castle, mountains and loch, as well as a close-up glimpse of the ten bells which together weigh eight tons.

Inveraray Castle

(Open Apr to June and Sept, 10 to 1, 2 to 5.45, Sun 1 to 5.45, closed Fri; Jul, Aug, 10 to 5.45, Sun 1 to 5.45, closed Fri)
This, the seat of the Duke of Argyll, is one of Scotland's grandest stately homes. It was planned in 1745 by the third Duke, who wanted to build it on the elevated site then occupied by the town, so the town was rebuilt in its present position. The solid, square bulk of the Gothic-revival castle has crenellated turrets at each corner; witch-hat tops were added in 1877. Inside, hardly a surface remains ungilded. The state dining-room is a French *tour de force*, with delicate flower garlands painted within panels defined by gilt mouldings. Much of the fine period furniture is also French. The spectacular arms room and large, stone-floored kitchen are other highlights. Portraits of Campbells hang throughout the building, and their lives are documented in exhaustive detail. In the grounds, a Combined Operations Museum commemorates through photographs, models and posters Inveraray's role as a training centre during World War II.

Loch Fyne

Argyll Wildlife Park (open Apr to late Oct, daily 10 to 5; Nov to Mar, daylight hours) shows off pens and cages filled with wildcats, badgers, rare birds of prey, foxes and wild boar. Tame roe deer, goats, sheep and ducks of every description follow you along the paths, especially if you are carrying a bag of feed.

Auchindrain Old West Highland Township (open Apr to late Sept, daily 10 to 5; closed Sat in Apr), three-and-a-half miles south of Argyll Wildlife Park, was a working farm until the middle of this century, and the last to be run on communal-tenancy terms. Twelve tenants paid a single rent to the Duke of Argyll and worked plots of land, annually reallocated (by lot) to give every farmer a turn at the best. Houses and barns, a few thatched but most with red corrugated roofs, are spread out beside a narrow burn. A few are ruined shells; the rest are furnished in different period styles, with the minutiae of daily life on display.

Crarae Garden (open all year, daily 9 to 6) has been described as the closest Scotland comes to a Himalayan gorge. Azaleas and rhododendrons grow from niches in the rocks which fringe a steep torrent, and drop flame-coloured petals into the peaty water. Huge specimen conifers tower above the rapids and there are groves of acer and eucalyptus. Three colour-coded walks, lasting from half an hour to two hours, criss-cross their way up the glen, leading you through a landscape which intrigues in its combination of inspired planting and natural grandeur. The plant sales area is expertly run.

Lochgilphead, curving around the head of Loch Gilp, has pleasant wide streets and plenty of guesthouses. At the beginning of the nineteenth century, a developer tried to attract people and industry; the town mustered a few mills and a gasworks, but they had closed by the end of the century. That left fishing, but the herring in Loch Fyne vanished suddenly before World War I. Nowadays, Lochgilphead is a market town and tourist centre.

Loch Awe

Loch Awe is a 23-mile sliver of prime trout-fishing water running parallel with the upper reaches of Loch Fyne.

Its most dramatic scenery and its best sights are at its northern end, but a long round trip on the minor roads beside the loch is also rewarding. The ruined but still substantial and renovated **Kilchurn Castle**, on a shingle tongue at the northern tip, has an especially magnificent approach. As you walk the 500 yards from the road, the hills and mountains give way to a view of the loch with the silhouette of the castle looming centre stage. The original tower was built by Colin Campbell, first Earl of Argyll, in 1440, and was a crucial stronghold of the Campbells of Glenorchy. At the end of the seventeenth century, barracks that included the two round corner towers were added, turning it into a formidable castle. It was never conquered; the enormous fallen turret that dominates the courtyard was the victim of a gale. An information board at the top of the five-storeyed tower identifies the glorious range of mountains to the north. Boat trips on the loch leave from a pier beside Loch Awe Hotel.

Ben Cruachan, rising steeply above the **Pass of Brander**, bars the passage westward, apart from the narrow channel forced by the river. Here Robert the Bruce won a battle against the MacDougalls before taking Dunstaffnage Castle. Under the mountain is a hydro-electric plant with a difference, for it is buried in the guts of the mountain (open end Mar to late Oct, daily 9 to 4.30). A half-mile ride under the mountain delivers you to the turbine hall, where the guides explain the pumped storage system.

On the shore of Loch Etive is **Bonawe** (HS, standard times; closed in winter), Britain's most complete charcoal-fuelled, iron ore smelting furnace. It was founded in 1753 and worked for just under a century, cannon-balls being one of its main products. The Cumbrian ironmasters who built Bonawe have been accused of exploiting the region, denuding it of nearly all its original forests, but it is hard not to admire the handsome, solid stone furnace building and storage rooms. Maps suggest a route and plaques describe the buildings. A little of the oak forest that fuelled Bonawe remains in the **Glen Nant Nature Reserve**, two miles south of Taynuilt.

Turn on to the B845 at the foot of the pass to visit **Ardanaiseig Gardens** (open all year, 9.30 to sunset), which are at their best during the spring and summer when the rhododendrons, azaleas and wild flowers are out.

Crinan Canal

By driving down Loch Awe to the sea-coast of Lorn, you reach an area of low hills, jagged rocks, heavily indented shoreline and offshore islets. The canal cuts across the peninsula between Loch Fyne and Crinan Loch, the short-cut saving boats the long and dangerous journey around the Mull of Kintyre. The Crinan Canal, opened in 1801, is nine miles long and has 15 locks. Its engineer was Sir John Rennie, but Thomas Telford was called in to sort out early snags and often gets all the credit.

You need not come in a boat to enjoy the Crinan Canal – a walk along the towpath watching boats of all shapes and sizes jockeying for position and negotiating the locks has plenty to recommend it.

Dunadd and Kilmartin

The strange flat basin of land fringing the Crinan Canal to the north has a dense collection of ancient settlements. The Iron Age hill fort of **Dunadd** is recognised as the capital of the ancient kingdom of Dalriada and the site of its monarchs' investiture. Unfortunately, knowing its historical significance ahead of time can spoil your visit, because there is not much left to see on the steep-sided hill rising abruptly from the great Moss of Crinan. Just below the grassy peak is a footprint, and a shallow dip in a rock – from which collected rainwater may have been used to bless newly-crowned monarchs. You have to use a lot of imagination to visualise the scene – not easy in high season, because Dunadd is very popular.

Older fragments of the past litter the valley just to the north and many are more satisfying than Dunadd with more to see and fewer people to get in the way. **Dunchraigaig Cairn** dates from the second millennium BC, and consists of sea-worn boulders piled above several stone coffins (cists). It is typical of several other burial cairns, though with a diameter of 98 feet it is larger than most. Tongue-and-groove carving on the slabs at **Ri Cruin** cairn suggests good woodworking skills. Grave robbers were active in these parts, but **Nether Largie** was left intact. **Nether Largie South** is the most remarkable cairn in the district; chambered, large enough to enter, and left in its natural state. Across the road the upright stones of **Templewood Circle** form an incomplete circle around a burial cairn. Look for the double spiral carving on an orange-coloured stone, thought to have been connected with sun worship. **Kilmartin** itself has a castle of little interest, but in the church the Celtic **Kilmartin Cross** has what is thought to be one of the oldest images of Christ in Britain and the pretty churchyard has a wealth of medieval crosses and gravestones, with informative signs to help you appreciate the carvings.

Kilmartin to Oban

Carnasserie Castle (open at all reasonable times) is an imposing and strategically sited tower-house built in the sixteenth century by John Carswell, who translated the first book to be printed in Gaelic, *The Book of Common Order* (1567). The five-storeyed castle is in fair shape, and important because it was transitional between castle and mansion house. Given that the fireplace on the first floor is made of hard schist, its detail is remarkable. Carnasserie sits well above the A816, two miles north of Kilmartin, but a track brings you quite close.

From Carnasserie Castle to Oban you are in the thick of boating and riding country. **Ardfern** is a good place to watch yachts and powerboats, or you could drop into **Craobh Haven** on the Craignish peninsula's northern coast to see a wonderfully sited eighteenth-century Scottish fishing village which turns out, on closer inspection, to be reproduction, its modest size making it all the more realistic.

A short distance to the north of Craobh Haven, **Arduaine Garden** (NTS, open daily 9.30 to sunset) is another woodland lochside garden which benefits from the mildness of the climate. Views here are especially fine, and the place is paradise for rhododendron enthusiasts.

The B844, which leaves the main road halfway between Loch Melfort and Oban, leads to the islands of **Seil** and **Luing**. Seil is connected to the mainland by the splendid humpbacked **Clachan Bridge** (1791), referred to as the Bridge over the Atlantic. Where the road ends you look across to Easdale, a little island off Seil's western coast, which gives a vivid glimpse into a slice of Scotland's heritage. This is slate-quarrying land, and the life and times of the once large population of Easdale is displayed at the **Easdale Island Folk Museum** (open Apr to Sept, Mon to Sat 10.30 to 5.30, Sun 10.30 to 4.30). Nearby abandoned quarries serve as an outdoor exhibition. A little ferry goes from Seil to the pier of the touristy hamlet of Easdale. Luing, whose slate was used on the roof of Iona's Abbey, can be reached by car ferry from Seil.

Oban

The tourist centre and ferry port of Oban is a likeable place, its energy generated by townsfolk, fishing boats, visitors and pleasure craft alike. The broad harbour, lined by shops, restaurants and large, old-fashioned hotels, is nearly cut off from the sea by the island of Kerrera, and houses are closely packed on the hillside.

Oban offers a standard diet of tourist sights and events, but if you have only a few hours here, forget them all and just savour the town, the harbour and perhaps a woollen shop or two. Pick up a smoked salmon sandwich or a dish of cockles at any of the seafood snack bars near the terminal on Railway Quay and watch ferries arriving and departing. Climb up to **McCaig's Folly**, a nineteenth-century coliseum crowning Oban's hillside. The view of town, harbour and islands from its park is superb, even if the folly itself falls short of expectations. McCaig was a local banker, but his attempt to immortalise himself while providing employment for hard-up townsfolk bankrupted him.

Of the more conventional things to see, the **World in Miniature** (open Easter to Oct, Mon to Sat 10 to 5, Sun 2 to 5), on one arm of the harbour, is more British than universal; its 50 miniature rooms and dioramas are intricately worked, but if it is crowded you cannot appreciate it fully. This and a tour of **Oban Distillery** (open Mon to Fri, 9.30 to 5, also Sat Easter to Oct, last tour 4) are the town's best rainy day activities.

Oban Rare Breeds Farm Park (open late Mar to late Oct, daily 10 to 5.30; late Jun to mid-Aug, daily 10 to 7.30), a few miles north of the town, is blessed with a lovely hilltop location. It is good fun, too, and well organised, with farm animals, common and uncommon, enclosed in pens (which you may enter) or roaming free.

A bewildering collection of islands lies in the Firth of Lorn and Loch Linnhe near Oban, many little more than rocks poking out of the sea. Ferries go to **Lismore** and **Kerrera**, the most popular destinations for walking. Lismore is nine miles long, very green, with the occasional farm-steading and with excellent shore walks. Kerrera, opposite Oban and reached from a jetty at Gallanach, south of the town, is slightly hillier. Two circular walks begin at the jetty. The northern loop is longer but defined by a track; go south and you walk over grass and along the rocky shore. Views from **Gylen Castle**, built in 1587 by the MacDougalls, justify the trek.

BENDERLOCH AND APPIN

The imposing **Dunstaffnage Castle** (HS, standard times, closed winter), three-and-a-half miles north of Oban, grows from a rock foundation at the entrance to Loch Etive. The MacDougalls founded the castle in the thirteenth century, since when it has changed little. Robert the Bruce took the castle from the MacDougalls in 1309, and by the late fifteenth century it was in Campbell hands (the Duke of Argyll owns it today). Flora Macdonald was imprisoned here in 1746 on her way to brief confinement in London. A seventeenth-century tower-house and three towers are integrated with the curtain wall, within which stands an early eighteenth-century dwelling. The chapel, a short distance away in a wood, is also thirteenth century and is most notable for the dog-tooth carving on its Gothic windows.

At the mouth of **Loch Etive**, which plunges deep into the hills, the **Falls of Lora** are a fierce tide-race created by this sea-loch's narrow mouth and the broad reef that spans more than half of it. Water flow is so restricted that the loch cannot empty and fill at the same rate as the tide comes and goes. The result is a rushing and swirling of angry water. Stand in the middle of the long, cantilevered Connel Bridge to get a bird's-eye view or walk down to the shore in the village of Connel.

Five miles east of Connel Bridge, on the north shore of the loch, **Ardchattan Gardens** surround a mansion by the ruins of a priory built in 1230 (open Apr to early Nov, daily 9 to dusk). Robert the Bruce convened a parliament here in 1308. The gardens, specialising in shrub roses, potentillas and herbaceous borders, were planted to be at their best between July and September, but the spring flowers can be just as gratifying. The ruins are worth exploring too: medieval tombstones with carvings of skeletons, skulls and cross-bones abound.

Port Appin

From Connel Bridge, the A828 runs north through peaceful countryside. A turn south after doubling round the Loch Creran brings you to a flat, half-hidden peninsula, a country of marshy fields, oak and rocky shore. Port Appin is the place to stop for a walk, or to cross to Lismore, or to watch the yachts.

241

After leaving Loch Creran, look out for **Castle Stalker** rising out of the sea. Almost as much a favourite for photographers as Eilean Donan Castle on Loch Duich, this grey keep, lapped by the sea and with a background of islands and hills, makes a magical image of Scotland – the more so since the castle is usually inaccessible to the public.

KNAPDALE AND KINTYRE

Knapdale, south of the Crinan Canal, is a forested, hilly area with many walking trails, few inland roads and some exciting coastal drives. The western side has the most sights and views over to the mountains of Jura – unforgettable with a sunset behind them.

Both shores of **Loch Sween** are worth touring, the roads winding through bracken and trees, with the opposite shore reflected in the water. A few small islands sit at the mouth, but beyond is nothing but the Sound of Jura. **Castle Sween** (always open) is on the eastern arm and your first glimpse of its setting is bound to make an impact, whether to exclaim at the beautiful loch and its surrounding landscape, or to groan at the caravan park by the ruin. The castle dates from the middle of the twelfth century, with towers added in the thirteenth. Robert the Bruce attacked it twice during his western campaigns. Things to note are the shallow buttresses, the 7-foot thick, 40-foot high curtain walls, and the round tower at the north-west angle which had a prison and sophisticated plumbing.

Three miles south is the ruined thirteenth–century **Kilmory Knap Chapel**, as gaunt as its scrubland surroundings. Its roof is now glass, to protect the carved stones within. Most notable is the tall, fifteenth-century MacMillan's Cross which has a crucifix on one side and a hunting scene on the other.

The land now narrows into the **Kintyre** peninsula. Were it not for a one-mile strip of land at **Tarbert**, Kintyre would be an island. The town is a cluster of Victorian houses surrounding the tip of the deep West Loch Tarbert. Fishing boats and yachts vie for space along the harbour piers; above them stands the small, ivy-cloaked ruin of Bruce's Castle (renovated rather than built by Bruce). Kennacraig, the main ferry port for Islay and Jura, is six miles to the south.

Gigha

Gigha, connected by ferry from Tayinloan, lies just three miles off the west coast of Kintyre. It is a tiny island, criss-crossed with dry stone dykes and with everything in miniature, from the trout loch to the golf course. Gigha has one road so a bicycle is the best transport (especially since space for cars on the ferry is limited). You can hire a bike at the post office. Head for the lush **Achamore House Gardens** (open dawn to dusk) created by Sir James Horlick (of hot drink fame) who owned the island, they make the most of Gigha's mild climate and acid soil. Azaleas, rhododendrons, camellias, palms and palm lilies all thrive in the almost frost-free conditions.

Campbeltown and south

In the nineteenth century, Kintyre's main town boasted a large herring fishing fleet and over 30 distilleries. It now survives on tourism, local commerce and just two distilleries. Despite an attractive harbour, the town is neither quaint nor beautiful. The late fourteenth-century, disc-headed **Campbeltown Cross** is unfortunately placed in the centre of a roundabout, but it is superb, both in its design and the delicacy of carving, including a mermaid and a sea monster. **Campbeltown Museum** (open all year, Mon 2 to 7.30, Tue, Thur 9.30 to 7.30, Wed, Fri, Sat 9.30 to 1, 2 to 5), on Hall Street, has many archaeological specimens, and the eighteenth-century **Town House** on Main Street has a surprising but stylish octagonal steeple. **Davaar Island**, at the mouth of Campbeltown Loch, can be reached on foot at low tide, via a long shingle causeway. In 1887, Archibald MacKinnon painted a crucifixion scene on the wall of a large cave on the island's south side. It is sometimes hard to see, as the only light comes from a hole in the rock, but it is a novel sightseeing experience all the same.

As you head south towards Keil Point, an overgrown medieval chapel, possibly the successor to the original chapel of St Columba, is easily mistaken for a large hedge. **St Columba's Footprints**, at the top of a grassy knoll just beyond the chapel, are the supposed proof that the saint first entered Scotland through southern Kintyre.

The **Mull of Kintyre** is the southernmost point of the peninsula. A narrow road snakes from Southend through rich farmland, and delivers you to a scraggy headland. The road ends by a lighthouse, only 12 miles from Ireland.

The east coast of Kintyre

The B842 which runs down the east side of Kintyre gives you superb views of Arran across the Kilbrannan Sound. **Saddell Abbey** sits by a burn in a tranquil glen shielded from the road by a thick copse. A Cistercian abbey was founded here in the late twelfth century either by Somerled or his son, Reginald. Today it is a tumbledown ruin, with gravestones dating from the fourteenth to sixteenth centuries, protected under a shelter. Their artistic merit is admirable and their condition variable. Among the carvings, look for the galleon, the priest holding a chalice and the deer hunt.

Carradale, at the foot of a steep, hairpin-bend road, is a holiday village with a tiny, working fishing harbour – unpretentious, pleasantly isolated and with a sandy beach and caravan park. **Grogport Tannery** sells sheepskins and the process is explained in the small adjoining workshop.

Skipness Castle (always open), the Campbells' southernmost stronghold, is two-and-a-half miles north of Claonaig (ferries to Arran) on a dead-end road. A short walk through a wood brings you to a huge fortress built around a thirteenth-century hall and sixteenth-century tower-house.

ISLE OF MULL

Of the Scottish islands, Mull comes closest to Skye in popularity, though many visitors are really bound for Iona. Mull is large and bleak, with mountains of respectable size at the southern end but elsewhere largely covered by moorland or plantations. The real draw is Mull's wild coast, much of it accessible only on foot. Walking is the way to get the most out of the island; see Olive Brown and Jean Whittaker's *Walking in North Mull* and its companion, covering South Mull and Iona, for a wide choice of routes.

Getting to Mull is easy. Car ferries run from Oban to Craignure and Tobermory, from Lochaline to Fishnish and, in season, from Kilchoan on Ardnamurchan to Tobermory. If you take a car, arrive with a full tank and keep topping up: petrol stations are few and far between.

Torosay and Duart Castles

Close to the ferry port of Craignure are two distinctly different castles, each within sight of the other. The A849 south from Craignure terminal brings you first to **Torosay Castle** (open Easter to mid-Oct, daily 10.30 to 5.30; gardens open daylight hours in winter, 9 to 7 in summer), a nineteenth-century baronial stately home. Inside, there are fine Edwardian furnishings, but everything is informal and approachable. There are no 'do not touch' signs, and you are encouraged to look through giant scrap-books full of clippings and photos of the family's ventures. Among the paintings and drawings are works by Landseer and Sargent. The formal gardens are especially fine, with a walk bordered by eighteenth-century Italian statuary. In converted stone barns you can watch Isle of Mull weavers in full production. An anecdotal, informative and refreshingly modest guide book is a further plus point. You can walk to Torosay along a forest path starting just south of Craignure, or take the narrow-gauge **Mull and West Highland Railway**, which chugs along sedately for 20 minutes (under steam and diesel) through gorse and woodland.

Duart Castle (open May to mid-Oct, daily 10.30 to 6), perched at the end of a promontory overlooking Loch Linnhe and the Sound of Mull, has the best view on Mull. The castle, seat of Maclean chiefs, goes back to 1250, but most of the present building is a reconstruction, the achievement of Sir Fitzroy Maclean in 1912. Several rooms display sea, war and scouting memorabilia.

North Mull

The north-east coast is Mull's tamest and smoothest and is separated from the mainland by the narrow Sound of Mull. **Pennygown Chapel**, nine miles north of Craignure, is a good example of a pre-Reformation chapel, more than a dozen of which were built on Mull by missionaries from Iona. Note the thick walls and carved gravestones.

Tobermory is Mull's small capital, and lies tucked into the shore at the island's sparsely populated northern end. Its sheltered harbour is lined by smart Georgian houses painted in bold colours; shop windows display fishing tackle and walking gear more prominently than souvenirs. **Mull Museum** (open Easter to mid-Oct, Mon to Fri 10.30 to 4.30, Sat 10.30 to 1.30), in an old baker's shop on the harbour front, is small and old-fashioned, a good place to learn about Mull's history and to read about the galleon from the Spanish Armada (the *San Juan de Sicilia* or *Florencia*), which sank in mysterious circumstances in

Tobermory harbour. Its treasure of doubloons, now well buried in silt, has eluded salvage crews ever since.

West of Tobermory, **Dervaig**, a little hamlet with paired whitewashed cottages and a pencil-spired church, sits at the head of Loch Cuin. Stop at **Coffee & Books** for old and new books, wines and spirits, cheeses and vegetables as well as information, local lore and first-rate coffee.

Two sights are within a few miles of town. The **Old Byre Heritage Centre**, on the hill road to Torloisk, has an audio-visual show above the gift shop and licensed tea-room, but the stone buildings are the best feature. Once the smallest professional theatre in the world, the **Little Theatre of Mull**, on the Salen Road, has expanded to 43 seats. Plays written or adapted for a cast of two are performed through the summer and seats should be booked in advance at Cottage Crafts or Druimard Country House Hotel in Dervaig (see page 256), or by phone (01688) 400245.

A major Canadian city took its name from the small fishing village of **Calgary**, whose grand sandy beach, ringed by old trees and cliffs, is the island's most alluring. **Kilninian Church** deserves a look for its imposing medieval gravestones where Maclean, Chief of Torloisk, is shown with pointed helmet, kilt and broadsword, his elaborately carved wife at his side. Tours to the terraced **Treshnish Isles** off the north-west coast of Mull, sanctuary to birds and grey seals, run from Ulva Ferry and Dervaig in calm conditions.

Ben More and Ardmeanach

Ben More, at 3,267 feet, is one of the highest mountains in the Hebrides, yet the ascent is gentle. Start at Dishaig, four miles past Knock on the B8035.

MacKinnon's Cave on the coast west of the point where the B8035 turns south towards Loch Scridain, is one of Mull's best-known sights, but accessible only on foot. The track to Balmeanach Farm takes you to a path leading to a magnificent clifftop and then steeply down to a beach of large boulders. Various theories, one concerning an abbot, another a piper, explain the cave's name. It is huge and very deep, with a wide interior chamber. Keep to the path, make sure to arrive at half tide on a falling tide, and take a torch.

The Ardmeanach peninsula has another famous destination, more out-of-the-way but more unusual than

MacKinnon's Cave. **MacCulloch's Fossil Tree** has suffered more damage since the famous geologist discovered it
in 1819 than during the previous 50 million years, but it is
now protected from souvenir hunters and geology students.
The cast of the large pine tree, 40-feet tall, 5-feet across, and
hollow, is still a fascinating sight. You can walk the 10-mile
round trip of the peninsula, but plan to reach the tree on a
falling tide.

South Mull

Pilgrims en route to Iona once trudged along a narrow track
from Glen More to Fionnphort, the route now followed by
the A8490, and south Mull is still a country for energetic
walkers. There are basalt arches, a stone circle and several
deserted lochs to see, but they are all well away from the
road. **Bunessan**, the largest village for miles around, is now
a base for holidaying families rather than a fishing village,
though lobster boats still operate. At **Fionnphort**, less a
town than a car park, the road ends. Iona lies offshore and
regular passenger ferries connect the two islands.

IONA

'The morning star of Scotland's faith' is small (three miles by
one-and-a-half) and mostly flat and windswept, but its
importance to Christianity is great. Christian roots go back
before St Ninian, but Columba usually gets the credit for
sanctifying this ancient isle. The missionary-saint arrived
from Ireland in AD 563 with 12 companions, founded a
monastery (now destroyed), and began his long journeys
to convert the pagan Picts. Scottish kings (48 in all)
were buried here until the eleventh century. Reginald, son
of Somerled, founded a Benedictine monastery and
Augustinian nunnery at the beginning of the thirteenth
century, but both were vandalised during the Reformation.
The Iona Cathedral Trust now owns the sacred precincts;
the rest of the island belongs mostly to the National Trust
for Scotland.

The small medieval **nunnery** is a well-maintained ruin;
the church and chapter house are original, while the cloister
and refectory were built around 1500. **MacLean's Cross** is
one of Iona's best medieval religious carvings, decorated
with Celtic motifs. The **Abbey**, near the site of the original

monastery and stark and severe against the flat expanse of green, has been massively restored, but the north transept and arcade of the north wall of the choir, along with some elaborate carvings, are original. The **Abbey Museum** has a rich collection of cross-marked gravestones. The eighth-century **St Martin's Cross** is remarkably complete, with serpent-and-boss ornament on the east face and holy figures on the other. The restored twelfth-century **St Oran's Chapel** is the island's oldest building, and arguably the most handsome. Of pinky-grey stone, it is unadorned save for its one splendid Norman doorway with bold chevron and beak-head decoration on three round arches. To take in the abbey, cross, chapel and graveyard, with the sea and Mull beyond, stand on the small knoll directly opposite the entrance. This is **Torr an Aba**, where Columba's cell is said to have been.

Few will remain unmoved by Iona's spiritual peace. Despite throngs of day-trippers in and around the main sights, finding tranquil spots is easy. Beaches of white sand or colourful pebbles distinguish the coast. At the **Bay at the Back of the Ocean** on the western coast, there is a golf course, tended by sheep, and a spouting cave. The **marble quarry**, last active around 1915, has a rock-cut reservoir, and crude, rusted remains of the cutting frame. It is near the southern tip of the island and just around the corner from **St Columba's Bay**, yet another fine sandy beach, and the saint's supposed landing site.

Staffa

Staffa is one of the most popular excursions from Mull and Iona. Its covering of grass and orchids over a shiny black base of hexagonal basaltic pillars gives it the look of a not altogether successful soufflé rising above a misshapen fluted dish. **Fingal's Cave**, or, as locals often refer to it, 'Musical Cave', inspired Mendelssohn's overture and John Keats' remark: 'For solemnity and grandeur it far surpasses the finest cathedral.' Individuals run trips to Staffa from Dervaig, Ulva and Iona. A new pier now makes landing easier, but the Atlantic swell is often fierce around Staffa unless conditions are good.

THE OTHER ISLANDS

Islay

Islay is among the most populous and fertile of the Hebrides. The trim towns have simple, unadorned houses and the landscape is often spartan, though peat bogs, fertile farmland, low heather-clad hills and stone outcroppings provide variety. Some visitors come just for the golf, others for the wildlife, the monuments or the whisky.

From the ferry at Port Ellen it is a short walk (past three distilleries) to the island's most highly prized artefact, the **Kildalton Cross**, carved (probably by a sculptor from Iona) 1,200 years ago. The blue-grey stone cross is impressively large and neatly decorated with Celtic motifs and stylised figures. It seems odd that, although it has survived the elements well enough so far, it is still left outside. The fierceness of the elements on Islay is easy to appreciate on the **Oa**, a little rounded peninsula of hillocks, machair, cow and sheep pastures to the west of Port Ellen. On the **Mull of Oa** stands a bulbous, rocket-shaped monument to the Americans lost when the *Tuscania*, bound for France during World War I, rammed the rocks. It is a short walk from the end of the paved road.

Bowmore is reached from Port Ellen on a ruler-straight road originally designed to take a railway. On either side stretch miles of peat bog scarred by angular cuts and grooves where it has been harvested to fuel home and distillery fires. Bowmore has an intriguing round church designed to ward off evil spirits, who can hide only in corners. The town also has the island's most tourist-friendly distillery (founded in 1779), should you fancy a tour and a nip.

On the **Rinns of Islay**, a hammer-head protrusion in the west of the island, stone walls and a few abandoned homesteads decorate a desolate land. Surf booms along the whole of the western shore. The cliffs at **Sanaigmore** offer prime viewing. A track off the B8018 leads to the calmer waters of **Loch Gorm**, seasonal home to over 20,000 barnacle geese. The town of **Port Charlotte**, stretched along a wide bay, is known for its cheeses, and its beaches (good for shell-hunting and bathing) as well as the **Islay Field Centre** (for serious or occasional naturalists), and the compact **Museum of Islay Life**. **Portnahaven**, at the southern tip of the Rinns, is a pretty, steeply raked town with a deeply indented, angular harbour which provides a sanctuary for seals and a mooring for fishing boats.

The A846 Bridgend to Port Askaig road cuts through the island's least populous, more forested eastern side. The **Islay Woollen Mill**, a mile and a half beyond Bridgend, has a well-stocked gift and clothing shop. The mill was established in 1883 on the site of an earlier seventeenth-century enterprise. You are free to walk around the antiquated and dusty workshop and inspect the rare Spinning Jenny and Slubbing Billy (for twisting and knobbling yarn). The clatter and rumble now emanates from modern warping and power weaving machines. **Finlaggan**, a few miles short of Port Askaig, has a loch, castle ruins and a helpful new visitor centre which displays archaeological remains. **Port Askaig**, huddling at the base of a steep, wooded hillside, is little more than dock and car park.

Jura

Jura's cone-shaped peaks, the **Paps of Jura**, have been landmarks for passing ships down the ages. Nothing else on Jura can hold a candle to their beauty, although they are less easy to appreciate from the island itself than from the Kintyre peninsula. Wildlife, remote moor and timeless seascapes are Jura's finest assets. Red deer graze nonchalantly beside Highland cattle. Wild goats are commonplace. Views out to sea from the island's one road are especially rewarding because of the height from which you look over the water. Jura has only one true village (Craighouse), which would almost fit into the shadow of its distillery. Otherwise, crofts, some abandoned, are the only sign of habitation. **Barnhill**, a rambling stone house where George Orwell wrote *Nineteen Eighty Four*, stands in forlorn isolation at the end of a bumpy track that continues where the main road stops. From here a path winds north along the shore to reach the **Gulf of Corryvreckan**, which divides Jura from Scarba. Arrive one hour after low tide to see and hear the whirlpool, notoriously hard to navigate but wonderful to behold, at its best. Corryvreckan, whose roar can be heard long before you reach it, is the most dangerous tide race in Scotland. It is named after the legendary Breacan who anchored his boat here by a rope of maidens' hair. One maiden had been untrue so the rope parted and Breacan was drowned.

Jura is large enough to accommodate the most reclusive walker, but pause for thought before taking a car over. The island is a popular excursion from Islay, so its narrow road sometimes chokes with day trippers. The uninhabited west coast is hard to reach, but raised beaches of smooth pebbles and a series of huge caves are incentive enough for trekkers.

Colonsay and Oronsay

Colonsay lies 25 miles from the mainland and, with Oronsay, is only 10 miles long from tip to toe. It has several historical and archaeological sites, but you will probably remember it best for its tranquillity. Quiet, undemanding, with only three ferries per week, it is the perfect retreat, though in danger of becoming an island with more holiday homes than permanent residents. Apart from one hotel and a couple of bed and breakfasts, all accommodation is self-catering.

Colonsay is an island of green pastures, fine beaches, cliffs, rocky coves, woodlands, moors, and lochans covered in water-lilies. Five hundred varieties of local flora and 150 species of birds have been recorded. **Colonsay House Garden**, a small but concentrated woodland of rhododendrons, giant palms, and exotic shrubs, is worth a stroll. The curved **Kiloran Bay**, not far to the north, has a magnificent half-mile-long beach of honey-gold sands, just right for surfing after strong Atlantic winds. Of the island's various standing stones, those at Kilchattan, **Fingal's Limpet Hammers**, are most imposing but you cannot get very close because they are enclosed in a fenced-off field. Near Kilchattan is **Port Mor**, a pebbly beach with large rocks, chattering seabirds and good surf. Bronze Age forts or duns are plentiful on Colonsay; **Dun Eibhinn**, a dramatic hump next to the hotel, is an easy climb.

Some say the name of **Oronsay** comes from the Norse for ebb-tide island, which is a just description of Colonsay's near-appendage. At low tide the Strand is easy to cross on foot. St Columba first set foot in Scotland on Oronsay but did not settle because he could still see his native Ireland. The present, fourteenth-century **Priory**, sitting within sight of the sea in surprisingly lush pasture, supposedly occupies the site of his original monastery. Oronsay's owner has tidied up the mellow stone ruins and created a museum of ancient carved gravestones within the old **Prior's House**. For many people, the two-and-a-half-mile walk from the car park, almost half of which takes you over wet sand scattered with seaweed and crab shells, remains the high point of a visit to the island.

USEFUL DIRECTORY

Main tourist office
Argyll, the Isles, Loch Lomond, Stirling &
Trossachs Tourist Board
41 Dumbarton Road
Stirling FK8 2QQ
(01786) 475019

Tourist Board publications Annual visitors' guides listing main
sights and accommodation. Special interest: forest and hill walks,
Islay and Jura Whisky Tour, *What to do in a Day/Afternoon*,
birdwatching, plus leaflets on fishing, walks. Order by post or phone
from above address.

Local tourist information centres
Balloch (01389) 753533 (Mar to Nov)
Bowmore (01496) 810254
Campbeltown (01586) 552056
Craignure (01680) 812377 (Apr to Oct)
Dumbarton (01389) 742306
Dunoon (01369) 703785
Helensburgh (01436) 672642 (Apr to Oct)
Inverary (01499) 302063
Lochgilphead (01546) 602344 (Apr to Oct)
Oban (01631) 563122
Rothesay (01700) 502151
Tarbert (01880) 820429 (Apr to Oct)
Tobermory (01688) 302182

Local Transport
British Airways (direct air services from Glasgow to Islay,
Campbeltown and Tiree) (0345) 222111
West Coast Motors/Scottish City Link (runs bus service from
Glasgow to Lochgilphead and Campbeltown) (01586) 552319 or
(0990) 505050

Ferries
All run by Caledonian MacBrayne (01475) 650100 except where
other numbers are given.

Car ferries
Claonaig-Lochranza, Arran (mid-Apr to mid-Oct, up to ten sailings
daily; winter Tue, Wed twice a day)
Colintrive-Rhubodach, Bute (frequent sailings daily)

Kennacraig-Port Askaig, Islay (one or two sailings daily Mon to Sat, also Sun Apr to Oct)

Kennacraig-Port Ellen, Islay (one to three sailings daily)

Kilchoan-Tobermory, Mull (Mon to Sat mid-Apr to mid-Oct, up to seven sailings daily; Jul, Aug also   Sun, five sailings; winter sailings Tue, Thur, Sat)

Lochaline-Fishnish, Mull (frequent daily service Mon to Sat, also Sun early Apr to Aug)

Oban–Castlebay–Lochboisdale (three to five sailings a week)

Oban–Colonsay (three sailings a week)

Oban–Craignure, Mull (up to six sailings daily)

Oban–Lismore (Mon to Sat, up to four sailings daily)

Oban–Tobermory–Coll–Tiree (three to five sailings a week)

Seil–Luing (frequent daily sailings, passenger only Sun) (01852) 300252

Tayinloan–Gigha (up to nine sailings daily Mon to Sat, also Sun from Mar to mid-Oct)

Wemyss Bay–Rothesay, Bute (up to 20 sailings daily)

Passenger ferries

Fionnphort-Iona (frequent sailings every day, reduced service Sun out of season) (01475) 650100

Gallanach, Oban-Kerrera (several sailings daily, reduced service Sun) (01631) 563668

Port Appin-Lismore (several sailings daily) (0131) 730217

Seil-Easdale (frequent sailings daily, reduced service Sun) (01852) 300370

Boat trips

Loch Etive cruises from Taynuilt (01866) 822430

Loch Lomond cruises from Balloch (01389) 752376/751610; (01389) 751481; and from Tarbert by Arrochar (01301) 702356

Trips from Iona and Fionnphort to Staffa (01475) 650100

Trips from Ulva Ferry on Mull to Staffa, the Treshnish Isles and Iona (01688) 400242

Trips out of Rothesay, Bute 0141-221 8152; (01475) 650100; (01475) 721281

Whale-watching trips from Dervaig to Staffa, the Treshnish Isles and Coll (01688) 400223

Other

Information and tickets for the Little Theatre, Mull (Apr to Sept) (01688) 400245

Bus trips from Oban to Mull and Iona (01680) 812313 or (01631) 562133

For cruises on the Clyde, see under Glasgow

Coll and Tiree

Coll and Tiree are both quiet, gentle islands, whose attractions for visitors are undisturbed peace, bird-life, views, coastal scenery and gentle walking. They lie to the west of Mull and can be reached by ferry from Oban, or, in the case of Tiree, by plane from Glasgow.

Both islands are flat, but where Tiree is fertile and sprinkled with crofts, Coll is more conventionally Highland, with hard rock and peat hags, and has a much smaller population. Both islands have magnificent, deserted beaches – those on Tiree are likely to be populated by surfers, for the island's waves are reputed to be excellent. Sunshine is common out here away from the rain-attracting hills, but so too are strong Atlantic winds.

There is little point in using a car – hiring a bicycle is cheaper and a more sensible way of getting around. There are a number of small sights – prehistoric remains and a ruined castle or two. There are guesthouses and self-catering accommodation on both islands. You should be able to buy enough for picnics locally, but do not expect anything sophisticated in the islands' shops.

WHERE TO STAY

£ – under £70 per room per night, incl. VAT

££ – £70 to £110 per room per night, incl. VAT

£££ – over £110 per room per night, incl. VAT

ARDNADAM
Lochside
Fir Brae, Ardnadam, Sandbank
PA23 8QD
TEL (01369) 706327
Whitewashed Edwardian villa with views over Holy Loch. Breakfast is served in the pretty dining-room. Cheerful bedrooms.
£ Jan to Nov; 3 rooms with wash-basin; credit cards not accepted

ARDRISHAIG
Fascadale House
Tarbert Road, Ardrishaig, by

Lochgilphead PA30 8EP
TEL (01546) 603845
Scottish-style house built as a summer retreat for a Clyde shipping merchant, now a civilised bed and breakfast. The large drawing-room is light and bright with beautiful plasterwork and country-house style furnishings. Excellent breakfasts. Bedrooms are individually furnished to a high standard.
£ Closed Nov to Feb; 3 rooms; drying-room; fishing; credit cards not accepted

ARDUAINE
Loch Melfort Hotel
Arduaine, by Oban PA34 4XG
TEL (01852) 200233
FAX (01852) 200214
Superb views from this lochside hotel. Inside, the Chartwell Bar is

warm and welcoming and the wood-panelled library makes an inviting retreat. Modern-style food in the restaurant, where fish and seafood shine. Pleasant bedrooms.
££ *Closed mid-Jan to mid-Feb; 27 rooms; drying-room (See Where to Eat)*

BALLYGRANT
Kilmeny Farmhouse
Ballygrant, Isle of Islay PA45 7QW
TEL (01496) 840668
A welcoming working farm with wonderful valley views. Dinner is served in the elegant dining-room and meals are imaginative, based on fresh produce. Warm, comfortable bedrooms.
£ *All year exc Chr and New Year; 3 rooms; credit cards not accepted*

BUNESSAN
Ardfenaig House
by Bunessan, Isle of Mull PA67 6DX
TEL/FAX (01681) 700210
Lochside country-house hotel and former shooting lodge, on the south side of the island. Its homely and inviting drawing-room has a log fire and comfortable sofas. Good Scottish food is served in the dining-room at pine tables. The bright, airy bedrooms have floral soft furnishings. Mountain bikes are available for hire and the owner has a boat on the loch for fishing. Rates include dinner.
£££ *Closed Nov to Mar; 5 rooms; drying-room; fishing*

CALGARY
Calgary Farmhouse Hotel
Calgary, nr Tobermory, Isle of Mull PA75 6QW
TEL/FAX (01688) 400256
Conversion of old stone farm buildings above one of the island's finest beaches. A gallery displays the work of local artists. The old

dovecote is now a charming restaurant. There is a cosy lounge for residents. Bedrooms are comfortable.
£ *Apr to Nov; 12 rooms*

CARRADALE
Dunvalanree Guest House
Port Righ Bay, Carradale PA28 6SE
TEL (01583) 431226
FAX (01583) 431339
In a lovely position overlooking the isle of Arran, this guesthouse has welcoming hosts and a comfortable lounge with a warm open fire. Evening meals are by arrangement. Most bedrooms have a sea view.
£ *End Mar to mid-Oct; 12 rooms with wash-basin; credit cards not accepted*

CLACHAN
Clachan Beag
Clachan Bridge, nr Kilninver, Oban PA34 4RH
TEL/FAX (01852) 300381
Comfortable family home set in a lovely garden. Inside, the house is attractively decorated with two sitting-rooms. Evening meals by arrangement are served in the licensed dining-room; local seafood is a speciality. Pretty bedrooms.
£ *All year exc Chr and New Year; 3 rooms*

COLONSAY
Colonsay Hotel
Isle of Colonsay PA61 7YP
TEL (01951) 200316
FAX (01951) 200353
Good food and genuine Scottish hospitality at this remote listed nineteenth-century house. Public rooms are welcoming; high tea is available early for children if requested. Bright, warm bedrooms.
££ *1 Mar-5 Nov and at New Year; 11 rooms; drying-room; fishing; golf; bicycles (See Where to Eat)*

CRINAN
Crinan Hotel
Crinan, by Lochgilphead PA31 8SR
TEL (01546) 830261
FAX (01546) 830292
Enthusiastically run hotel with modern decor and outstanding food, where Loch Fyne meets the Atlantic via the Crinan Canal. A large yachting clientele follow the shipping forecasts in a buzzing atmosphere. Bold decorating schemes enliven the public rooms. Food is modern and inventive with fish and seafood in starring roles. Rates include dinner.
£££ *Closed one week at Chr; 20 rooms; water sports; boat trips (See Where to Eat)*

DERVAIG
Druimnacroish
Druimnacroish, Dervaig, Isle of Mull PA75 6QW
TEL (01688) 400274
FAX (01688) 400311
Friendly house, once a watermill, in a lonely glen. Comfortable lounges are brightened by books, maps and fresh flowers. Dinners are traditional. Spacious, well-equipped bedrooms decorated in autumn hues.
£££ *Closed Nov to Apr; 6 rooms*

Druimard Country House
Dervaig, Isle of Mull PA75 6QW
TEL/FAX (01688) 400345
Restful country-house hotel with a relaxing air. Decoration in the public rooms follows a theatrical theme and the conservatory bar is light and bright. Delightful dinners with fresh produce are rounded off with an excellent Scottish cheeseboard. Spacious bedrooms with good, old furniture.
£-££ *Closed Nov to end Mar; 6 rooms (See Where to Eat)*

DRYMEN
Dunleen
Milton of Buchanan, Drymen G63 0JE
TEL (01360) 870274
See full description in Stirling and Perth chapter.
£ *May to Oct; 2 rooms with wash-basin; credit cards not accepted*

ERISKA
Isle of Eriska
Ledaig, Oban PA37 1SD
TEL (01631) 720371
FAX (01631) 720531
Solid baronial mansion with an imposing façade and classic, graceful public rooms. Excellent sporting facilities. Spacious, tastefully decorated bedrooms.
£££ *Closed Jan and Feb; 17 rooms; games room; fishing; golf; tennis; horse-riding; water sports; solarium; sauna; gym; clay pigeon shooting; croquet (See Where to Eat)*

FIONNPHORT
Achaban House
Fionnphort PA66 6BL
TEL (01681) 700205
This spacious guesthouse close to the Iona ferry was once a manse. Breakfast and dinner are served at large wooden tables in what was the original kitchen. The simple bedrooms have pine furniture.
£ *All year exc Chr; 7 rooms, most with wash-basin; credit cards not accepted*

FORD
Tigh an Lodan
Ford, nr Lochgilphead PA31 8RH
TEL (01546) 810287
Wooden chalet-style bungalow at the foot of Loch Awe, plainly furnished. The sitting-room has views out over the loch. Evening meals by arrangement feature local produce and vegetarian dishes are always available with notice.

£ Apr to end Oct; 3 rooms; credit cards not accepted

INVERARAY
Creagh Dhubh
Inveraray PA32 8XT
TEL (01499) 302430
Old stone-built house set in a large garden. Accommodation is simple and comfortable; breakfast only is served. Front bedrooms look out over the loch.
£ Mar to Nov; 4 rooms, 1 with bath/shower; credit cards not accepted

IONA
Argyll Hotel
Isle of Iona PA76 6SJ
TEL (01681) 700334
FAX (01681) 700510
Welcoming waterfront inn with cosy lounges and glorious views from the sun room. Food in the attractive dining-room is good with a vegetarian dish always available. Modest bedrooms.
££ Closed 7 Oct-4 Apr; 17 rooms; drying-room

KILCHRENAN
Ardanaiseig Hotel
Kilchrenan, by Taynuilt PA35 1HE
TEL (01866) 833333
FAX (01866) 833222
Inspiring views and delightful gardens at this Scottish baronial mansion on a promontory beside Loch Awe. Relaxing public rooms; pleasantly decorated bedrooms.
££-£££ All year; 14 rooms; drying-room; billiard room; boating; fishing; clay pigeon shooting; tennis; croquet

KILMORE
Glenfeochan House
Kilmore, by Oban PA34 4QR
TEL (01631) 770273
FAX (01631) 770624
Carefully-restored splendid baronial house with a peaceful air. The luxurious interior and public rooms are distinctive. Fresh ingredients are used in cooking and home-made oatcakes complement the Scottish cheeseboard. Bedrooms are a delightful blend of antiques and good fabrics.
£££ Closed Nov to Mar; 3 rooms; drying-room; fishing; clay pigeon shooting

LOCHDONHEAD
Old Mill Cottage
Lochdonhead, Craignure, Isle of Mull PA64 6AP
TEL (01680) 812442
Simple, whitewashed cottage with a good reputation for home cooking. The restaurant serves delightful food. Plain, neat bedrooms.
£ All year; 2 rooms

OBAN
Dungrainach
Pulpit Hill, Oban PA34 4LX
TEL (01631) 562840
Old house in a beautiful large garden on a hill above the town, with views out to sea. The lounge is bright and attractively decorated. Breakfast only is served. Pretty, neat bedrooms.
£ Easter to Oct; 3 rooms; credit cards not accepted

The Manor House
Gallanach Road, Oban PA34 4LS
TEL (01631) 562087
FAX (01631) 563053
Excellent service and good cooking at this stylish seaside resort hotel. An imposing staircase and Minton tiles in the reception area set an elegant tone; the cocktail bar has beautiful views over the harbour. Cheerful and cosy bedrooms with personal extras.
££-£££ All year exc Jan; 11 rooms

PORT APPIN
Airds Hotel
Port Appin, Appin PA38 4DF
TEL (01631) 730236
FAX (01631) 730535
Welcoming inn on the shores of
Loch Linnhe with an atmospheric
setting and interior. This
comfortable and relaxing retreat
attracts a lot of return visitors. The
menu is a happy blend of traditional
and modern styles. Bright bedrooms
with luxurious touches.
*£££ All year; 12 rooms; drying-
room; stalking and wildlife trips (See
Where to Eat)*

ROTHESAY
Alamein House Hotel
28 Battery Place, Rothesay, Isle of Bute
PA20 9DU
TEL (01700) 502395
Whitewashed Victorian house on
the seafront with wonderful views.
Delightful meals are served in the
dining-room. Bedrooms are prettily
furnished. Aromatherapy and
calligraphy breaks are offered.
*£ All year exc 3 weeks Nov, Chr
and New Year; 7 rooms; credit cards
not accepted*

SALEN
Glenforsa Hotel
Salen, by Aros, Isle of Mull PA72 6JW
TEL (01680) 300377
FAX (01680) 300535
Family-oriented log cabin-style
hotel overlooking the Sound of
Mull. There are views out over the
water from the lounge. The bar is
cheerful; food is hearty. Bedrooms
are basic but cosy.
*££ All year; 13 rooms; snooker;
clay pigeon shooting; stalking*

TOBERMORY
Failte Guest House
Main Street, Tobermory, Isle of Mull
PA75 6NU
TEL (01688) 302495
Attractive terraced house
overlooking the harbour. Breakfast
only is served in the dining-room;
packed lunches are available. Neat,
smartly decorated bedrooms.
*£ Mar to Oct; 7 rooms; credit cards
not accepted*

WHERE TO EAT

Key: A * marks a place that is
particularly good value for money

ALEXANDRIA
Cameron House Hotel, Georgian Room
Loch Lomond, Alexandria G83 8QZ
TEL (01389) 755565
FAX (01389) 759522
Lovely loch-side hotel with an
ambitious repertoire of confident
cooking. Enjoyable creations
embody inventiveness and flair;
artistic puddings follow. Some very
fine bottles on the conservative
wine list if money is no object.

*Mon to Fri 12.30 to 2, all week 7
to 10*

ARDFERN
Galley of Lorne Inn *
Ardfern PA31 8QN
TEL (01852) 500284
Loch-side inn where the local catch
features on the daily-changing
blackboard menu. Pub fare is also
found in the bar; steak and seafood are
mainstays of the separate restaurant.
Wide choice of malt whiskies.
*Open for food: 12 to 2, 6 to 9 (8 in
winter); restaurant closed Nov to Mar
exc New Year and Easter; credit cards
not accepted*

ARDUAINE
Loch Melfort Hotel ★

Arduaine, by Oban PA34 4XG
TEL (01852) 200233
FAX (01852) 200214

Blackboard menu featuring enterprising dishes in the Chartroom Bar of this imposing hotel, served amid nautical paraphernalia. The printed menu is rather more straightforward. Morning coffee and afternoon tea are also served.
Open for food: 12 to 2.30, 6 to 9; restaurant all week 7 to 9 (See Where to Stay)

CAIRNDOW
Loch Fyne Oyster Bar ★

Clachan Farm, Cairndow PA26 8BH
TEL (01499) 600236
FAX (01499) 600234

Simple conversion of an old cow byre with tables and alcoves made from home-grown larch and pine. Plain, confident cooking brings out the flavour and texture of fresh ingredients. Flexible eating arrangements – all menu options are available any time of day. Reasonably priced wine list.
All week 9 to 9; 1 Oct to end Mar, Mon to Thur 9 to 6; closed 25 Dec and 1 Jan

CLACHAN
Tigh an Truish Hotel ★

Clachan Bridge, Isle of Seil PA34 4QZ
TEL (01852) 300242

The menu here is seasonal, but seafood is treated kindly whatever the time of year. In the depths of winter variety dwindles to soup and simple snacks at lunchtime.
Open for food 12 to 2.15, 6 to 8.30; snacks only 12 to 2 in winter; credit cards not accepted

COLONSAY
Colonsay Hotel

Isle of Colonsay PA61 7YP
TEL (01951) 200316
FAX (01951) 200353

This hotel has the only bar on the island and serves simple lunches and delicious suppers. You need to book for fixed-price dinners in the restaurant. Good wine list.
Open for food Mar to mid-Oct 12.30 to 1.30, 7 to 8.30; restaurant New Year and Mar to Nov 7.30, booking essential (See Where to Stay)

CRINAN
Crinan Hotel

Crinan PA31 8SR
TEL (01546) 830261
FAX (01546) 830292

Shellfish are landed near the hotel shortly before dinner, when culinary skills perform the necessary transformation. Five-course meals in the Lock 16 restaurant incorporate a pleasant variety of seafood. The Westward restaurant has a four-course menu including steak and roasts. Quality wine list with scope for those on a more modest budget.
Lock 16 Tue to Sat 8, one sitting, closed Oct to May; Westward all week 7 to 9, closed 1 week Chr (See Where to Stay)

DERVAIG
Druimard Country House

Dervaig, Isle of Mull PA75 6QW
TEL/FAX (01688) 400345

The smallest professional theatre in the world stands in the grounds of this country house and during the season pre-theatre dinners are popular. Local seafood and game feature and vegetables fare well. Sauces are liberally splashed with alcohol and cream. Puddings are delicious and the cheeseboard first-rate. Reasonably priced wine list.

259

Mon to Sat 6 to 8.30, Sun residents only; closed end Oct to 1 Apr (See Where to Stay)

DRYMEN
Clachan Inn ★
2 Main Street, Drymen G63 0BG
TEL (01360) 660824
See full description in Stirling and Perth chapter.
All week 12 to 4, 6 to 10, Sun 5 to 10

ERISKA
Isle of Eriska
Ledaig, Eriska PA37 1SD
TEL (01631) 720371
FAX (01631) 720531
Substantial, daily-changing fixed-price dinners not for the faint-hearted. Seafood and game are both given royal treatment and accompanying service is delightful. Simple puddings; coffee is served with miniature pastries. The wine list contains entrants from most of the world's wine regions.
All week 8 to 9; closed Jan to end Feb (See Where to Stay)

KILBERRY
Kilberry Inn
Kilberry, by Tarbert PA29 6YD
TEL (01880) 770223
A 16-mile single-track road leads to this crofter's cottage. Home-baking, preserves and pies are fine examples of the best of country Scottish cooking. Generous portions of vegetables cooked to order; puddings are excellent. To finish there are bottled brews, malt whiskies and a creditable wine list.
Open for food Mon to Sat 12.15 to 1.45, 6.30 to 8.45

KILCHRENAN
Taychreggan
Kilchrenan, by Taynuilt PA35 1HQ
TEL (01866) 833211/833366
FAX (01866) 833244

Highly rated country hotel with friendly service and good home baking. The five-course set-price dinners are skilfully prepared and ambitious. Inventive puddings precede a fine cheeseboard. Plenty of choice on the wine list.
All week 12.30 to 2, 7.30 to 8.45

KILMELFORD
Cuilfail Hotel
Kilmelford PA34 4XA
TEL (01852) 200274
Popular home-made dishes and nicely prepared vegetables at this simple, stone-built inn with wholesome daily specials. Choose from over 80 malt whiskies and a reasonable selection of wines.
Open for food 12.30 to 2.30, 6.30 to 9.30

MILNGAVIE
Gingerhill ★
1 Hillhead Street, Milngavie G62 8AF
TEL 0141-956 6515
Predominantly fish-based menu in this little room overlooking the town's shopping centre. Fine eating with good fresh seafood and rich sauces. Straightforward puddings, good bread and coffee. No corkage for bringing your own bottle.
Mon to Sat 11 to 3, Thur to Sat 7.30, one sitting

OBAN
Heatherfield House
Albert Road, Oban PA34 5EJ
TEL/FAX (01631) 562681
This small, family-run restaurant-with-rooms serves good home-cured meat and preserves and grows its own herbs, fruit and salad. Beautiful fish and flavoursome dishes cooked with flair; good bread. Wide-ranging wine list.
Apr to Oct all week 12.30 to 2.30, 7 to 10; Nov to Mar, Wed to Sat, dinner bookings only; closed 2 weeks Jan

Knipoch Hotel
Knipoch, by Oban PA34 4QT
TEL (01852) 316251
FAX (01852) 316249
Plain hotel with outstanding views
and a fixed-price, no-choice menu.
Good soups, tasty main dishes and
excellent puddings are the order of
the day. The set dinner is fairly
pricy but the reasonable wine list
offers something for everyone.
*All week 7.30 to 9, lunch by
arrangement; closed mid-Nov to
mid-Feb*

PORT APPIN
Airds Hotel
Port Appin PA38 4DF
TEL (01631) 730236
FAX (01631) 730535
Consistently excellent cooking on
the shore of Loch Linnhe.
Traditional and modern dishes
feature. From light lunches to four-
course dinners, food is fresh and full
of flavour. Puddings are
memorable, service faultless. Super
wine list with plenty of half-bottles,
suited to every taste and pocket.
*All week 8, one sitting; light lunches
available (See Where to Stay)*

Pierhouse
Port Appin PA38 4DE
TEL (01631) 730302
FAX (01631) 730309
Seafood served at this family-run
restaurant by the edge of Loch
Linnhe has been landed yards from
the kitchen. Simple treatment of

the fresh catch allows flavours to
shine. Good wine list, reasonably
priced.
All week 12 to 3, 6.30 to 9.30

STRACHUR
Creggans Inn ★
Strachur PA27 8BX
TEL (01369) 860279
A remote white farmhouse on the
shores of Loch Fyne offering good
traditional food and game from the
estate of Sir Fitzroy Maclean. More
formal meals are served in the
restaurant and there is also a coffee
shop. Extensive wine list.
Open for food 12 to 2.30, 5.30 to 9

TAYVALLICH
Tayvallich Inn
Tayvallich PA31 8PR
TEL (01546) 870282
At the end of the road running
alongside Loch Sween, this peaceful
inn enjoys views over a bay full of
boats. The pub has a definite bistro
air; cooking is fresh, simple and
seafood-based. Other fare is
imaginative with interesting
vegetarian dishes. Good selection of
local Islay malt whiskies.
*Open for food 12 to 2, 6 to 9; exc
Mon Nov to Mar*

STIRLING AND PERTH

- Boundary country between Lowlands and Highlands, with landscapes from raspberry fields to mountains
- Outstandingly beautiful rivers
- Historic towns in Perth and Stirling, shapely mountains such as Schiehallion and Ben Lawers, and the lovely Glen Lyon
- Heather, good castles, skiing, Picts, Pontius Pilate and Mary Queen of Scots

Caledonian pine

THIS large area of central Scotland has enough variety for several holidays. The geological boundary separating the Lowlands from the Highlands runs diagonally across it from the south-west, so wherever you go you are in easy reach of both mountain scenery and the attractions of the Lowland valleys. Historically, it is one of the most intriguing parts of the country. The Picts and the Romans both left traces here, while many of the most critical moments in Scotland's history were witnessed by the old towns and castles of the area.

Although the cities of Edinburgh and Glasgow have moved Scotland's centre of gravity south of the River Forth, it was the fertile lands beyond that natural river barrier which were the strategic heartland of the kingdom in medieval times. The chief battles of the Wars of Independence – Stirling Bridge (1297), Falkirk (1298) and Bannockburn (1314) – were fought here, while it was to the quiet priory of Inchmahome that Mary Queen of Scots was taken in 1547 to keep her out of English clutches. Crossing the River Forth northwards can still feel like entering a sanctuary. Southern Scotland is left behind.

However, while the River Forth formed a barrier to invaders from the south, trouble has not always come from that direction. It was from the northern mountains that the royalist forces of Montrose emerged to inflict two terrible defeats on the Covenanters at Tippermuir (1644) and Kilsyth (1645), and it was from the same direction that Dundee led his Highlanders to the Jacobite victory at Killiecrankie in 1689. Half a century later, the troops of Prince Charles Edward Stuart descended from the mountains to take Perth at the start of the last of the Jacobite uprisings – that of 1745.

So there is an ambiguity about the fertile countryside round Perth and Stirling, with its magnificent, spate-heavy rivers, its sunny fields and its chains of low hills: it is at once the centre of old Scotland and its vulnerable edge.

Beyond the Highland line

Like many another vanishing tribal society, the Highlanders of Scotland started to become the subjects of romantic legend the moment they ceased to be a threat. This happened early in the nineteenth century, and nearly two centuries-worth of tartanry, bagpipes, clan gatherings and other images carefully fostered to this day by the tourist industry have totally obscured the suspicion or fear with which the Highlands were once

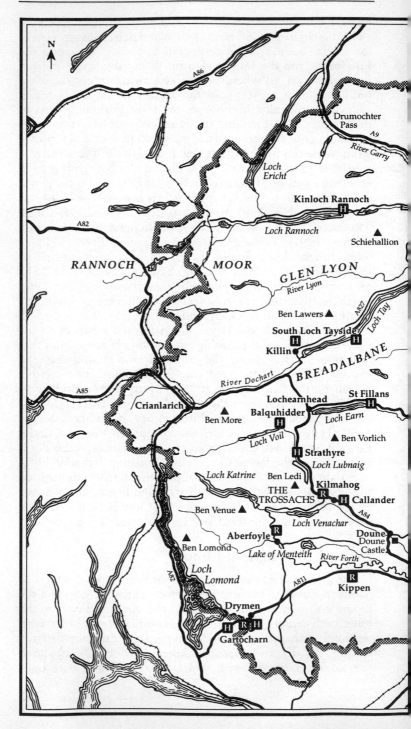

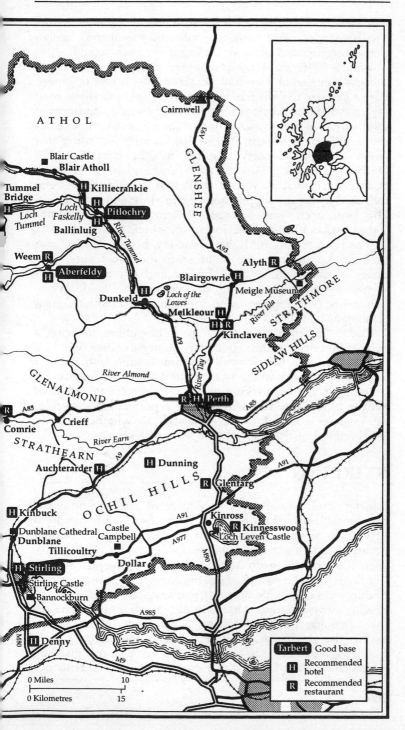

ATHOL

Cairnwell

Blair Castle
Blair Atholl

Tummel
Bridge
H **Killiecrankie** H

H **Pitlochry**

Loch
Faskelly

Loch
Tummel **Ballinluig**

River Tummel

GLENSHEE

A93

A93

Weem R

H **Aberfeldy**

Alyth R

Blairgowrie H

Dunkeld H

Loch of the
Lowes

Meigle Museum

Meikleour H

H R
Kinclaven

STRATHMORE

River Isla

SIDLAW HILLS

River Almond

GLENALMOND

A9

River Tay

R H **Perth**

A85

R A85

Comrie

Crieff

River Earn

STRATHEARN

A9

Auchterarder H

H **Dunning**

A91

R **Glenfarg**

H **Kinbuck**

OCHIL HILLS

A91

Kinross

R **Kinnesswood**
Loch Leven Castle

Dunblane Cathedral
Dunblane

Castle
Campbell

Tillicoultry

A977

M90

H **Stirling**

Dollar

Stirling Castle
Bannockburn

A985

M80

H **Denny**

M9

0 Miles   10

0 Kilometres   15

Tarbert Good base

H Recommended
hotel

R Recommended
restaurant

regarded – as late as 1773, Dr Johnson provided himself with a pair of pistols before venturing into the mountains, though Boswell managed to persuade him to leave them behind.

Before 1746, the Highlands posed a degree of threat to the government of Lowland Scotland which was the more feared because the allegiances, the language, and the way of life of the Highland clans bore little relationship to those of their Lowland compatriots. In the age of classicism, coffee-shops and taffeta gowns, it is perhaps hardly surprising that when a Highland army erupted into England, reaching Derby and causing George II to make plans to flee the country, its final defeat at Culloden should have been followed by savage suppression of the Highland way of life. Highland dress was banned, the carrying of weapons forbidden, and the jurisdiction of the chiefs removed.

The breaking up of Highland society, begun in 1746, was to continue through the eighteenth and nineteenth centuries. Poverty, emigration, famine and eviction were to break the clan system and depopulate the land. When you enjoy the emptiness and solitude of a Highland glen, remember that it was not always so.

Today, information technology is beginning to bring a new prosperity to the Highlands. Long-distance working now enables a crofter to work part-time dealing with data for an employer many miles away. Four London boroughs, for example, have their parking tickets processed in the north of Scotland. Whether this will provide a permanent answer to the long-term decline of the Highlands, or whether it is just another kind of exploitation, has yet to be seen.

STIRLING

Stirling stands on about the only piece of firm ground in the marshy flatlands round the tidal River Forth. For hundreds of years it was the lowest point at which the Forth could be bridged, so the town commanded all routes northwards. That it overlooks seven battlefields is hardly surprising.

Like Edinburgh, which it uncannily resembles in miniature, Stirling has a grey castle on a crag and a warren of old buildings ranging down the steep slope to its east. It is a friendly, carefree town, less dignified than Edinburgh, but ready to remind you that its place in Scotland's history is just as important.

Stirling was not just a stronghold to prevent invading armies crossing the Forth; it was also a favoured royal residence

– and there are plenty of stories connected with it, from the stabbing of the Black Douglas to the crowning of Mary Queen of Scots. The town has some fine buildings, especially the **Guildhall** (1634), the **Church of the Holy Rude** (1415) and the eroded façade of **Mar's Wark**, a Renaissance-style demonstration of wealth, set off by the plain competence of the seventeenth-century **Argyll's Lodging** opposite. Extensive restoration based on an ancient inventory of furnishings promises to turn this building into a good reconstruction of an old town house. Joint tickets with the castle should be available. Best of all, perhaps, is the low, multi-arched **Old Bridge** (1400) across the Forth, still in use as a footbridge.

Stirling lies close to the industrial belt round Falkirk and Grangemouth, but is barely affected by it. It has its modern side (notably the Thistle Centre Shopping Mall) but the atmosphere of the town is more Victorian with medieval and Renaissance overtones – a pleasant combination. The streets leading up to the castle are sprinkled with cafés and pubs, of which Whistlebinkies in St Mary's Wynd is one of the most atmospheric. Nearby Stirling University has the MacRobert

Practical suggestions

In this part of Scotland it is better to get to know one area well rather than for going on great tours through the scenery (though that is possible too). **The Trossachs**, sometimes called the Highlands in miniature, is the most popular small area – perhaps too popular in high season – full of small lochs, medium-sized mountains and a network of walks. The **Ochil Hills** are much less frequented, and there is a scatter of interesting sights along their fringes. The Lowlands of **Strathearn** and **Strathmore** are for those who like their scenery constantly interesting but not necessarily spectacular. The glens leading westward from the A9 north of Perth are each blessed with more history, legend and fine scenery than this book can cover. **Glen Lyon** is the prettiest, with **Loch Rannoch** running it a close second. Everyone should spend a day or two in **Stirling** and have a look at **Perth**, in both of which it is possible to have a happy Scottish holiday without once getting your feet wet or being bitten by a midge. Accommodation is plentiful in Perth and Stirling and in the resorts of Callander and Pitlochry. Outside these places there is a sprinkling of good hotels and plenty of guesthouses and bed-and-breakfasts.

Arts Centre, with a variety of exhibitions and performances. Stirling's forte, so far as the visitor is concerned, is live performance. In summer, the town is alive with actors, dancers and fiddlers, and there are set-piece displays such as a medieval market, Beating the Retreat (with fireworks), and a tartan festival. You are likely to be assailed by a gruff James IV or a forceful Mary Queen of Scots on a street corner, or else urged to go on a ghost walk, take part in a ceilidh or watch Highland dancing. Stirling has also unilaterally shifted Burns Night (normally 25 January) to the height of summer. All this could easily have turned the town into a theme-park of Scottish kitsch, but the effect (so far) is to inject energy into a place that might otherwise be too comfortably normal.

Good bases

● **Stirling** If you want to meet James IV wandering the streets or join in some Scottish dancing, this is the place to do both: there is a constant round of live performances and street activities in summer. Stirling is a fine and important town, its castle alone being worth the better part of a day's exploration. There is no difficulty in finding somewhere to stay, and the town is in the best possible position for exploring the Trossachs and the Ochils.

● **Perth** The town does not have much left by way of old buildings, but there are a few curiosities and some fine green spaces. Perth is large, bustling and not at all touristy, with good shopping and a fair range of places to stay. Getting there by road or rail is easy, and the town makes an excellent touring base for Strathearn, the Angus glens and the Highlands.

● **Pitlochry** This has been the tourist resort for the southern Highlands since the coming of the railway in 1863, and it retains something of the atmosphere of a Victorian holiday spot. It is extremely busy in season but manages to remain unspoilt. There is a superabundance of places to stay, and it is worth having a good look round before deciding. Pitlochry's strong point is the large number of gentle walks in the area, and it is also a good place from which to explore the valleys of the Tay and the Tummel.

● **Aberfeldy** Smaller and quieter than Pitlochry, Aberfeldy is an attractive town where it is possible to feel part of the local life even in high season. While it lacks a huge choice of places to stay it is well situated on the banks of the Tay, right in the centre of the best mountain country in the region.

Stirling's further advantage is its position for touring. The Trossachs are half an hour distant; there are good day trips to the Campsie Fells, Crieff, Aberfeldy and Loch Tay or to Kinross and Perth, and it is easy to reach the sights south of the Forth, such as Linlithgow Palace or Cairnpapple Hill.

In and near Stirling

Stirling Castle

(HS, summer: Mon to Sat 9.30 to 6; winter: Mon to Sat 9.30 to 5)

Whisper it who dares, this is a more interesting castle to visit than Edinburgh. It takes some getting into, for you must first escape from the National Trust Visitor Centre (open daily, closed Jan) by the Esplanade and then penetrate the grossly thick Outer Defences (built against artillery in fear of a Jacobite uprising) and the further wall of the Forework (built by James IV but much chopped about later). A sunny former bowling-green with a good view over the parapet delays you further. Below the cliff, the grass-covered earth-works are the remains of what was once a formal garden where kings and courtiers would wander.

Eventually you arrive at the two buildings at the heart of the castle, the Palace and the Great Hall. Start with the Great Hall and do not be put off by the fact that it seems to be a building site, for this is one of the most stimulating restoration pro-grammes in Scotland. The hall (probably built around 1500) was divided and sub-divided when it was later used as barracks, and all the windows were altered. Now the original room, complete with massive fireplaces, is re-emerging, with new mouldings being dovetailed into the medieval stonework. The medieval kitchens have recently been re-opened and a start is being made on the rebuilding of the hammer-beam roof. Meanwhile, a corner of the hall has been turned into a medieval building site with rope scaffolding and model labourers in amongst the real craftsmen, so that for a second you are caught in a time-warp. The project is due to finish in 1999.

The Palace next door has one of the earliest classical façades in Britain. The niches, statues, gargoyles, string courses and pediments are French in inspiration, Scottish in craftsmanship, and were instituted by James V. Inside, the royal apartments are now bare except for the grand fireplaces, and are used for dis-playing the Stirling Heads, a series of beautifully carved wooden bosses which once adorned the ceilings. The figures are emblematic, from a king to a cook, from Venus to Lust, but carved with such verve that they are more like character-portraits.

The King's Old Buildings now house the regimental museum of the Argyll and Sutherland Highlanders, with medals, paintings, uniforms and silver. In 1542, James II stabbed the Earl of Douglas here, whom he suspected of treachery, and threw him out of the window. A skeleton was conveniently found underneath the window in 1797 to prove it.

There is more, though these are the best parts. The view from the walls westwards to the peak of Ben Lomond and north-east to the Ochils rising vertically out of the plain is marvellous.

The Old Town Jail

(Open Apr to Sept, daily 9 to 6; Oct to Dec, Feb to Mar, daily 9.30 to 4; closed Jan)
The jail in St John's Street, which replaced the town prison in the Tolbooth, held prisoners between 1847 and 1935. Now the summer months see actors taking their places to give visitors an impression of Victorian prison life. In winter, hand-held audio guides do the same job. The visit takes in the jail's roof for extensive views of the town and suitable information about what you see and what it used to be like.

Cambuskenneth Abbey

(HS, open in summer; call 0131-668 8800 to arrange a visit)
This was once an important Augustinian foundation, but there is little left of it today, for the builders of the seventeenth-century houses in Stirling had scant respect for their old abbey and used it as a stone quarry. From the top of the twelfth-century bell-tower you can see the foundations of the abbey church and enjoy a peaceful view of the custodian's immaculate lawn and of Stirling beyond.

The Wallace Monument

(Open Feb and Nov, Sat and Sun 10 to 4; Nov to May and Oct, daily 10 to 5; June and Sept, daily 10 to 6; Jul and Aug, daily 9.30 to 6.30; closed Dec and Jan)
Sticking up like a kind of Gothic candle from Abbey Craig to the north of Stirling, and almost as prominent in the landscape as Stirling Castle, the Wallace Monument is a Victorian folly. The view from the top is not as good as from Stirling Castle, but you have the compensation of standing where Wallace

once stood watching the English army winding its way over the Forth before the battle of Stirling Brig in 1297.

Wallace's massive sword awaits you inside the Monument, as does an account of his trial and execution. An audio-visual display does its best to bring to life the Hall of Heroes, an unpleasantly Teutonic collection of white marble busts of famous Scots, including a sour Argyll, a bristly John Knox, Adam Smith and David Livingston.

Bannockburn Heritage Centre

(NTS, open Mar, mid–Nov to end Dec, daily 11 to 3; Apr to end Oct, daily 10 to 5.30)

WILLIAM WALLACE

By the end of 1296 Edward I of England had thoroughly conquered Scotland, deposing John Balliol (known as 'Toom Tabard' – empty coat) and turning the country into an occupied province. Yet, by the very next year, Scotland was stirring with revolt against English rule. This movement was less inspired by the Scottish nobility (many of whom had lands in England which they stood to lose) than by the small landowners, among whom was William Wallace, the son of a Renfrewshire knight.

Wallace, despite the many statues of him up and down the country, is a shadowy figure but his achievement in crystallising the resistance to English occupation was extraordinary. The nobles, including Robert the Bruce, were fickle or timorous by turns, and more inclined to put store by rank than ability. Nevertheless, Wallace succeeded in conducting successful guerrilla warfare against the English and, together with Andrew de Moray, inflicted a major defeat on an English army at Stirling Brig in 1297. After this, he was knighted and elected Guardian of Scotland in the name of the exiled King John.

However, guerrilla tactics did not save the Scots at Falkirk in 1298, when Edward appeared on the scene with another army. The Scottish pikes were no match for the English archers, and the battle became a rout. Wallace was forced to flee and shortly after resigned the Guardianship. He was eventually captured – perhaps betrayed – in 1305, and executed in London with the barbarity reserved for traitors, on the command of a king whose sovereignty he never acknowledged.

Don't look for this in the village of Bannockburn (though there is a short town trail for battlefield seekers gone astray – leaflet from Stirling Information Office). The Heritage Centre is actually a mile to the west, separately signposted from the M80.

Robert the Bruce's victory over the English at Bannockburn carries so much symbolism in Scotland that a Heritage Centre was probably unavoidable, although the correspondingly devastating English victory at Flodden is marked only by a simple and sad memorial. Even so, the National Trust's strictly neutral presentation may seem timid to fervent Scottish patriots, while outsiders may wonder why there is so much fuss about a battle fought in 1314.

No one seems to be certain precisely where the action took place and housing estates cover the area anyway, so this is not the most interesting of battlefields. The audio-visual display in the Heritage Centre goes a long way to make up for this, and there is a statue of Robert the Bruce and the remains of the stone where he may have grounded his standard. Nevertheless, it is a difficult place in which to be overcome by elation or despair.

THE BATTLE OF BANNOCKBURN

The eight-year campaign fought by Robert the Bruce not only to drive the English from Scotland but also to have himself recognised as king inside his own country reached its climax at Bannockburn in June 1314. For a leader who understood the virtues of guerrilla warfare and recognised the danger of confronting the English in pitched battle, the prospect of fighting the enormous force brought to Scotland by Edward II must have been a dreadful one. He was forced into it by the rash bargain made between his brother, Edward, and the English garrison of Stirling Castle: if the castle were not relieved by mid-summer it would surrender. The English rose to the challenge, and Bruce had to confront them to retain any credibility.

The dispositions made by Bruce, including skilful choice of ground and the digging of pits, would have been unlikely to have saved the Scots but for a terrible tactical mistake on the part of the English. Following preliminary skirmishing in the evening of 23 June, during which Bruce killed the heavily armed De Bohun with

The Campsie Fells and East Loch Lomond

To the south-west of Stirling, the Campsie Fells conveniently separate the industrial unpleasantness of the western Central Belt from the upper Forth Valley. Unless you climb to the top of the range, you may not suspect that the suburbs of Glasgow lie on the far side. The hills provide a breath of fresh air and some rural peace and quiet for many people, and the A818 road which runs beside the River Carron through the pretty village of Fintry and on to the equally attractive Drymen is unspoilt and makes a gentle outing.

East Loch Lomond is much prettier. This is the quiet shore of the loch, for the road running along it ends at Rowardennan and only campers, caravanners and picnickers use it. From near Balmaha you can look out over the wooded islands which stud the southern half of the loch and watch the pleasure boats pottering round them. There are numerous coves, walks and picnic places and energetic souls set out here to walk the long-distance **West Highland Way**, which runs up Loch Lomond, eventually to finish at Fort William. Ben Lomond, which rises over 3,000 feet above the loch on this

a blow of his battle-axe, the English appear to have withdrawn for the night into the boggy ground near the bank of the Forth, the worst possible terrain for the English heavy cavalry.

On seeing this the next day, Bruce went over to the attack, using his few cavalry to neutralise the opposing archers and his infantry to confine the English within a constricted and marshy space. The sheer size of the English army, and its inability to manoeuvre in such unfavourable conditions, caused chaos. The battle, hard fought for most of the day, seems to have reached a turning point with the appearance of Scottish reinforcements – traditionally thought to be only the camp-followers – who appeared over the skyline at a moment critical for English morale. The battle turned to rout. Edward II fled, first to Stirling and then, hotly pursued, to Dunbar and Berwick.

The spoils of Bannockburn were huge, enabling Bruce to ransom members of his family whom Edward had been holding hostage in England. Yet the battle did not lead at once to English recognition of Scotland as an independent kingdom, as Bruce had hoped. That had to wait until the treaty of Northampton in 1328, just before the death of King Robert the Bruce.

shore, is easily climbed from Rowardennan. On a clear day you can see the coast of Ireland and the peak of Ben Nevis.

Dunblane Cathedral

(HS, open in summer; call 0131-668 8800 to arrange a visit)
Before March 1996, the small town of Dunblane, north of Stirling and by-passed by the A9, was the kind of pleasant place you might have stopped at for a coffee but would otherwise have ignored. That would have been a mistake for the cathedral is not to be missed. Then came the massacre of a class of five- and six-year olds in their school gym, etched now in the national memory. The cathedral has thus become even more worth visiting as perhaps the most suitable place to remember the children.

After 300 years of ruin, a restoration programme, started in 1889, lavishly re-crafted the interior. The period of restoration coincided with the revival of craftsmanship in stained glass and wood, and continued to embrace the finer agonies of expression which came during and after World War I. The result is an ancient, weather-beaten building containing some of the finest modern wood-carving and stained glass in the country. The windows, with austere, beautiful faces subtly worked in lilacs and palest blue, shine behind the eroded pillars of the nave, with contributions by the artists Kempe, Strachan, Davis (the lovely *Nunc Dimittis* windows) and Webster. The carving of the pews, the screen and the choir stalls was mostly designed by Sir Robert Lorimer, and repays close scrutiny by revealing a Noah's ark-full of animals crouching in the choir stalls, while every pew in the nave is carved with a different flower.

The modern work fits well into the simple Gothic fabric of the building, which is seen at its best from the outside, especially if you look at the west front (which Ruskin adored) and the south side, where a pinkish Norman bell-tower seems grafted on to the thirteenth-century walls behind.

Doune Castle

(HS, standard times; closed Thur pm and Fri in winter)
From Dunblane you can veer west to join the A84, the main route to the Trossachs, at **Doune**. This village was once a centre for the manufacture of pistols and produced beautifully crafted weapons. Nearby, the stronghold of Doune Castle above the River Teith was built by one of the most powerful and unscrupulous men in medieval Scotland, Robert Stewart, first Duke of Albany.

As the younger son of one weak king (Robert II) and brother of another (Robert III), it did not take Albany, elected as Guardian of Scotland in 1388, long to achieve something approaching supreme power. Only the two sons of Robert III, David and James, stood between him and the throne. David died in Albany's 'safe keeping' at Falkland in 1402, and is widely believed to have been deliberately starved to death. Then the 11-year-old James, on his way to France for his own safety, was conveniently waylaid by English 'pirates' and taken to the English court, where he was to remain for 18 years. Albany, on the other hand, died in his bed in his eighties. Whatever history's assessment of him, there is no doubt what the captured James felt: on his eventual return to Scotland as king, one of his first acts was to eradicate the Albany family for high treason. Four of them were beheaded at Stirling, and Doune castle was forfeited to the crown.

Doune Castle was designed to be both strong and imposing, and, since a lot of it remains, it is an awe-inspiring place, with severe curtain walls and a massive gate-tower. Domestic arrangements are quite sophisticated, with corbelled 'free drop' latrines, three different halls, extensive kitchens and enough enormous fireplaces to remove at least some of the chill from the air. Extensive restoration in 1883 led to some rather peculiar refurbishing of the biggest rooms (banners, heavy dark wood and flagstoned floors).

Near Doune

Just to the north of Doune is the **Doune Motor Museum** (open end Mar to end Nov, daily 10 to 5), a collection for the enthusiast rather than for the whole family. The Earl of Moray's assembly of polished thoroughbreds stands in gleaming ranks, with all the famous names represented. The museum is also a centre for motor-racing hill climbs and other events.

To the south of Doune, **Blair Drummond Safari and Leisure Park** (open Apr to early Oct, daily 10 to 5.30) is the only conventional safari park in Scotland.

THE TROSSACHS

Strictly speaking the Trossachs is the short, rocky pass between Loch Achray and Loch Katrine, but the name now generally refers to the rugged country lying between Callander and Loch Lomond. It is easy enough to see why the Trossachs sprang to fame, for in the days before luxury coaches and double-track roads visitors could reach this part of the Highlands without difficulty, while the legends and the scenery were given a huge puff by Sir Walter Scott in *The Lady of the Lake* and were everything that Romantic taste might desire.

It is harder to see why the Trossachs remains so popular. Much of the scenery has been swathed in conifer plantations; Loch Katrine has been raised 17 feet and turned into a reservoir for Glasgow, and Scott's poetry is no longer in fashion. Yet the coaches and caravans go on rolling in. True, the Trossachs has the advantage of being easily accessible to much of Scotland's population and there is plenty of fine scenery left, despite the afforestation, especially if you take to your feet. For an extended holiday you will probably be better off elsewhere, but for a day-trip taste of the Highlands in miniature the Trossachs is a reasonably good bet.

Callander

On the road here from Doune, the views become more extensive, the hillsides barer, the ground gradually rockier. But any idea of wild desolation is rapidly dispelled once you reach Callander itself, for the town fairly seethes on summer weekends. It is far from being the quiet rural community pictured in that most famous of Scottish soap-operas, *Dr Finlay's Casebook*, for which it acted as the setting. Dr Cameron and Janet would be lost among the gift shops and tea rooms.

Among all the activity, you will find the **Trossachs and Rob Roy Visitor Centre** (For opening times, call 01877 330342). This purpose-built attraction is set up in an old kirk, well placed to pull in the crowds. In lists of genuinely heritage-worthy Scots, Rob Roy McGregor must rank pretty low but – thanks largely to Sir Walter Scott – he found a place in the myth of Romantic Scotland, and Callander is exploiting it. Consequently, there are two separate exhibitions devoted to the exploits of this glorified cattle-thief. A 'talking head' mutters to itself about the joys of cattle-stealing, while there is an audio-visual on the life and times of Rob Roy.

The Trossachs proper

A laugh was on every face when William said we were come to see the Trossachs; no doubt they thought we had better have stayed at our own homes. (Dorothy Wordsworth, 1803)

It is a short run beside Loch Venacher and Loch Achray

(both very attractive in autumn when the rowan-berries are at their best) to the branch road which leads off to the foot of Loch Katrine. The road plunges briefly through a gorge and emerges at a large car park and a pier. All the most scenic parts of Loch Katrine are out of sight, so you will need either to walk or else wait for the next sailing of the *Sir Walter Scott*, which runs from here up to Stronachlachar on the west bank, in order to see much. Notices forbidding any pollution of Glasgow's water supply add an unwelcome touch of officialdom to the scenery, but this is made up for by a fine, small exhibition about the construction of the Loch Katrine aqueducts in 1859 and the importance of this newly piped-in water in helping to alleviate Glasgow's terrifying infant mortality.

Aberfoyle

As it climbs over the Duke's Pass, the A821 runs mostly through conifers. The forests have been amalgamated into the **Queen Elizabeth Forest Park**, and the Forestry Commission is doing its best to suggest they are attractive by widespread provision of walks, picnic places and even the **Loch Achray Forest Drive** (for which they charge you). However, better walks are to be had by striking out for the summits of Ben Venue or Ben Ledi, both relatively gentle mountains (though you will still need proper equipment) or by seeking out a low-level walk by a river or loch, such as the path to the Bracklinn Falls just to the north of Callander.

On the far side of the Duke's Pass you come down to Aberfoyle, a quieter centre than Callander, but busy in summer all the same. From here, the narrow B829 past Loch Ard towards Loch Arklet and the east bank of Loch Lomond is worth exploring, its only disadvantage being that you must return the way you went. Queen Victoria was luckier; she climbed on board the *Prince Consort* for a sail on Loch Lomond: 'A pleasant idea that that dear name should have carried his poor little wife, alas! a widow, and children on their first sail on the beautiful lake.'

From Aberfoyle you can return to Stirling on the A873, which flanks the old marshes of **Flanders Moss**. Most of them have been transformed into fertile farmland, but for many years they were part of Stirling's natural defences.

Inchmahome Priory

(HS, standard times; closed winter)

The ruins stand a short distance south of the A873 on an island in the middle of the Lake of Menteith, one of the few expanses of water in Scotland that are not called lochs. There is no arcane tradition behind the name, merely a mistake by a Dutch surveyor helping to drain Flanders Moss. To get to the island you must embark on Historic Scotland's ferry, which is summoned by turning a semaphore board on the end of the jetty.

Inchmahome is an important place for followers of Mary Queen of Scots, for it was here that the young Queen came in 1547. Like many other Scottish religious houses before the Reformation, the priory had passed into the hands of commendators, who were royal appointees usually more interested in income than in religion. In this case, the commendators were the Erskine family, and Lord Erskine was the guardian of the young Mary. She was hidden here briefly after the Scots had been defeated by the English at the battle of Pinkie. The following year she set sail for France and marriage to the Dauphin. She was not to return for 12 years.

The priory ruins are simple and reasonably well preserved, especially the east window of the church with its five lancets. In the old Chapter House lie the heavily weathered remains of a double effigy of a thirteenth-century Earl and Countess of Menteith. It is an affectionate memorial: she rests her hand on his shoulder and they lie turned towards each other. Around the ruins and the careful lawns, paths wander over the island under redoubtable old trees. Mary's Bower, Mary's Garden and Mary's Tree remain as memories of the island's most famous visitor, but since the Queen was only four, and spent only three weeks here, she probably did not do much gardening. The custodian's hut is roomy enough to shelter in on a wet day while you are waiting for the return boat.

THE OCHIL HILLS

Stirling to Dollar

The A91 runs eastward from Stirling, close underneath the steep escarpment of the Ochil Hills. These rounded, grassy half-mountains run north-eastward to Newburgh on the Tay, diminishing gradually in size as they go, with fine views north and south to reward those few visitors who climb to explore their tops. Small mill towns (collectively called the Hillfoots) were built to take advantage of the water rushing down the steep glens on their southern side and the road passes through this old industrial landscape, which is more attractive than the power stations and refineries which fringe the Firth of Forth. The Hillfoots were once an important weaving centre and there are still a few mills nearby where you can hunt for tweed or tartan. There are a few curiosities here but nothing to compare with Culross down on the banks of the Forth, and that is where you should go first if you are short of time.

As you travel east from Stirling, **Blairlogie** is pretty, **Menstrie** has a restored but undistinguished sixteenth-century tower-house with connections to Nova Scotia, while **Alva** has the beautiful Strude Mill (now put to other uses) and a visitor centre where the story of a child worker introduces you to the social history of the old mills.

A detour south on the A908 to **Clackmannan** reveals the remains of a sixteenth-century tolbooth and a fourteenth-century tower on the outskirts of the little town. The chief curiosity here is the Clach of Mannan, by the tolbooth. This is a large stone on a modern plinth, which may or may not be sacred to a pre-Christian sea-god, and may or may not be very old indeed. It sits contentedly with lorries rumbling past, and may well outlast everything round about it.

Castle Campbell and Dollar Glen

Dollar is a comfortable residential town and a good place to seek out lunch before tackling Castle Campbell (HS, standard times; closed Thur pm and Fri in winter). From the car park up in the hills behind the town, a path descends into Dollar Glen (NTS, open all year). If you are not fit enough for this steep and sometimes slippery route there is a more straightforward but very narrow and steep road leading on from the car park.

At the bottom of Dollar Glen, the Burn of Care and the Burn of Sorrow meet in a tangle of rock faces and tumbled slabs. Cleverly engineered walkways lead through impossibly narrow gaps between lichen-encrusted slabs while the water hisses beneath. Few gorges have such a fascinating labyrinth at their bottom. Eventually, steep steps lead you from the depths of the Burn of Care and you see the walls of Castle Campbell above you.

Many things have been said about the Campbells, most of them bad, but at least they changed the name of their castle, which, in keeping with all the Care and the Sorrow, used to be called Castle Gloom. Gloomy it is not. It has splendid views across the Forth Valley to the Pentland Hills, and the custodian has planted flowers wherever there is room. The grim fifteenth-century tower at the castle's centre is virtually intact, with its four rooms on four floors linked by a wheel stair. Around it, the remains of later buildings are less overtly designed for defence, and there is even a tiny two-arched loggia tucked into a sunny corner of the courtyard where you can imagine it may occasionally have been pleasant to sit.

The castle was the Lowland stronghold of the Earls (later Dukes) of Argyll, and a symbol of the increasing Campbell influence which was at its greatest during Scotland's long conflict with Charles I, Charles II and James VII. John Knox stayed and preached here, though he probably never used the rock called Knox's Pulpit.

Rumbling Bridge

A small compensation for days of rain is that Scotland's waterfalls and gorges are at their best. The gorge at Rumbling Bridge is one of the most magnificent, though you might never guess it was there, since the road (A823 south, beyond Dollar) leaps it without a dip. Keep a sharp look-out for the signposted car park just to the north of the bridge, and walk to the edge of the chasm which the River Devon has carved from a fault in the rock. This was a favourite sight for visitors in the last century, and recently all the walkways and balconies down the precipitous sides have been restored. The Deil's Mill, where a horrible rumbling rises out of the depths, is especially worth stopping at. The nineteenth-century bridge which now carries the road over the gorge was built directly above its predecessor, which remains slung underneath it, creating a peculiar effect. The old bridge had no parapet, and must have taken steely nerves to cross on horseback.

Kinross

Although the town's Tourist Information Centre has been banished to a wooden chalet in the middle of a motorway service area (at Junction 6 of the M90), this does not mean Kinross has nothing worth looking at.

If you come in summer, on no account miss the gardens of **Kinross House** (open May to Sept, daily 10 to 6). The house was built by the architect Sir William Bruce in 1686 and it is one of his best, for he built it for himself. It is not open but you can admire the grey classical frontages, which are perfectly complemented by the garden. At its centre, a formal design directs the eye towards Loch Leven Castle seeming to float on the loch beyond, while the scents and colours of the herbaceous border and shrubbery fill the air under the enclosing walls.

Green-jacketed anglers in deerstalker hats are a common sight where the waters of Loch Leven lap at the lower edge of the town, for the wild, pink-fleshed trout that inhabit the loch are famous for their number and their flavour. It is relatively easy to find space in one of the dozens of boats lined up by the shore (ring 01577 863407 as far in advance as possible).

The bird-watchers you meet will have been to **Vane Farm** on the south side of the loch, where the RSPB has a visitor centre. Telescopes have been set up for visitors, through which you can gaze at geese and duck foraging among the clumps of rushes by the shore. The best time to see the thousands of autumn migrants is from mid-October onwards.

Fishermen and bird-watchers are few in number compared to those who visit Loch Leven because of Mary Queen of Scots. To follow her trail, you need to find the pier where two cheerful custodians take turns in ferrying you out to Loch Leven Castle.

Loch Leven Castle

(HS, standard times; closed in winter)

Here, under a load of misery which might have staggered a mind more masculine than hers, Mary exerted the potent witchery of her charms upon the heart of young Douglas, who, intoxicated with a romantic passion and ambitious hopes, sacrificed his duty and family interests at the shrine of all-powerful love. (The Scottish Tourist, 1827)

The first thing worth noting is that the trees, the carefully cut grass, the wooden benches and the overall air of pastoral contentment that pervades the island on which the castle stands would not have been what Mary Queen of Scots experienced here during her 11 months' imprisonment. The level of the loch was higher, the island smaller, the castle damp and old-fashioned and, in contrast to Historic Scotland's patient custodians, Mary's gaolers seem to have been coldly hostile to the point of cruelty.

MARY QUEEN OF SCOTS

It is hardly surprising that tragedians have found inspiration in the reign of Scotland's most famous queen: her life seems to belong more to the stage than to the pages of history. Widowed by the death of her husband François II of France, she returned to Scotland in 1561 at a time when the country was poised between France and England (which was nothing new), and between the forces of Roman Catholicism and Protestantism.

Her very existence posed threats or offered opportunities to half of Europe. Her marriage to a Catholic prince would be a blow struck for the Counter-Reformation and would help to isolate Protestant England. She was, in the eyes of many Catholics, already the legitimate Queen of England, and certainly had a strong claim to the succession should Queen Elizabeth I die childless. Within Scotland, the Protestant lords and ministers (especially John Knox) regarded her with deep suspicion, while the Catholics expected her to re-instate the old church and reverse the Scottish Parliament's decision to adopt Protestantism. Moreover, the young queen found no substitute among the self-interested Scottish nobility for the steady counsel she had become used to from her Guise relatives in France.

It is Mary's tolerance and humanity in the midst of this political mire which have so appealed to nineteenth- and twentieth-century sensibilities. Yet they were inappropriate qualities in a sixteenth-century ruler. Mary's far more ruthless and devious cousin, Elizabeth of England, was a less likeable person but a more successful Queen.

The beginning of Mary's reign in Scotland was a success. It was her marriage to the featherbrained Lord Darnley in 1565 that sealed her fate. An immediate rebellion against the couple was put down, but as Mary herself became disillusioned with Darnley the opportunities for those who desired to destabilise her rule increased. The murder of her secretary, Riccio, with Darnley at the head of the killers, is one of the many distasteful episodes of Mary's reign. Darnley, arrogant, foolish and resentful that he had not been granted the crown matrimonial, was provoked into an attempted coup through an easy arousal of his jealous suspicions of Riccio. Whether or not there was also a direct intent to murder the Queen, or at least pose a threat to her unborn child, is less clear, though the purpose of the conspiracy seems to have been to hold her powerless at

Stirling. The coup might well have succeeded if Mary had not managed to swing the unstable Darnley behind her again in the course of a night and to escape from Holyrood.

The murder of Darnley in Edinburgh in 1567, when the house in which he was sleeping was blown up (though Darnley himself was found strangled in the garden), cast a taint of suspicion on the Queen from which she was never to recover. Her marriage to the Earl of Bothwell, who was closely involved in the plot to kill Darnley, took place a bare three months later – a scandalous union.

Many of the nobles who immediately took up arms against Bothwell and the Queen had given Bothwell their secret approval only a month before. This may have helped him persuade the Queen into marriage, but it did him no good now. At Carberry Hill near Edinburgh the rebellious nobles outfaced the smaller army of Bothwell and the Queen. Mary submitted herself to the safe conduct of the nobles, who included many of the conspirators in the murder of Riccio.

Safe conduct turned out to mean imprisonment at Loch Leven and an enforced abdication in favour of the infant James. When the Queen escaped, the speed with which she gathered an army showed her support still to be strong. Her defeat at Langside was followed by the rash decision to seek shelter in England. Mary seems always to have hoped for Elizabeth's friendship, but the latter perceived her as a threat and so held the Scottish Queen in detention in England. Meanwhile, Scotland was split into further factions. During the 19 years that Mary was an exile in England, four separate regencies governed in the name of the young King James VI.

The threat posed by Mary as a centrepiece of Catholic plotting eventually became too great for the English government to bear. In 1586 she was secretly tried on the charge of conspiring to assassinate Elizabeth. The evidence against her seems largely to have been fabricated. Her inevitable execution – at Fotheringhay Castle in Northamptonshire – followed, despite Elizabeth's initial hesitation in signing the death warrant.

The questions which remain are numerous. How closely was Mary implicated in Darnley's murder? Was her marriage to Bothwell a matter of policy or a matter of the heart? Why did she flee to England after Langside? Did she really plot against Elizabeth? The life of Mary Queen of Scots continues to fascinate those who love historical puzzles.

By the time Mary came here as a prisoner in 1567 the castle already had a long history. The island may have been fortified during the English occupation under Edward I and captured by Wallace and/or Robert the Bruce, later resisting renewed attempts by the English to take it. As a place to isolate an important prisoner from her supporters and to wring from her an enforced abdication, Loch Leven was perfect. On top of this, Mary suffered a miscarriage here, and she was far from well afterwards. Yet she escaped. The manner in which she did so has all the elements of a good thriller – the loyalty of the orphan Willie Douglas, whom she persuaded to help her, the careful stealing of the keys, the holing of all the boats except the one needed for escape, and finally the moment of highest drama as the Queen crossed the courtyard in disguise, fearing last-minute discovery.

The thriller has no happy ending. In spite of the fact that supporters flocked to her, Mary's army was fatally beaten at Langside 11 days after her escape in May 1568. She fled south and decided to cross the Solway and seek help in England. Instead she was to find further imprisonment and eventual execution, 19 years later.

Come to Loch Leven Castle on a day without much wind (boats do not run if it is rough), and preferably with some sun, for there is nowhere much to shelter. Arm yourself with Antonia Fraser's *Mary Queen of Scots* but don't be lulled by the peace of the island – it was not always this way.

Kinross to Perth

The M90 swings over the eastern end of the Ochils into Strathearn. Castle-lovers should break at Junction 7 to see **Burleigh Castle**, a beautiful tower-house in two sections, built a century apart. Sir James Balfour, who built the later of the towers, had a hand in the nastier events of the sixteenth century. He helped murder Cardinal Beaton in 1546, served on the French galleys with John Knox, and was one of those who is thought to have signed the bond agreeing to the murder of Darnley, Mary Queen of Scots' second husband.

Abernethy (Junction 9) is only a small village now, but it was once the hub of a Pictish kingdom and an important centre for the Celtic church. An eleventh-century round tower standing by the churchyard is the only reminder of this long-vanished importance, but it is a lofty and impressive one none the less. At Abernethy, Malcolm Canmore (the same Malcolm who ends as King of Scots in Shakespeare's *Macbeth*) paid homage to William the Conqueror in 1072. This unfortunate act was to give birth to the perennial English idea that Scotland was part of the English feudal domain, and led indirectly to all the agonies of the Wars of Independence.

You can buy Abernethy biscuits in the village, but they actually originate from the parish of Abernethy on Speyside. They are certainly palatable, if not local.

PERTH

Ecce Tiber! Ecce Campus Martius! shouted Agricola's Roman soldiers on first seeing the green hollow in the hills by the dark River Tay where Perth was to be founded. The resemblance to Rome is not that close, but it makes a good story. The Romans built a camp near here and Perth has not looked back since. It gained from being close to Scone Abbey, the traditional coronation spot of Scottish kings, and had several religious houses of its own until John Knox's fiery sermons of 1559 inflamed the mob to pillage them all. In one of the monasteries, Blackfriars, James I came to a grisly end at the hand of an assassin in 1437. He had made one enemy too many among his powerful relatives.

In 1396 North Inch, by the bank of the Tay, was the scene of a ritual combat between Clan Chattan and Clan Kay, with 30 champions on each side bloodily settling their differences in front of King Robert III. This battle is the centre-piece of Sir Walter Scott's novel *The Fair Maid of Perth*. At the edge of this park today you will find the **Black Watch Museum,** a comprehensive regimental museum with a strong family feeling to it, situated in a much-reconstructed tower-house.

Perth is not short of places to stay, though they are scattered. There are several guesthouses and small hotels on the east side of the Tay and numerous hotels in the town centre, one of which, the Salutation, accommodated Charles Edward Stuart. The green spaces of North and South Inch beside the Tay are ideal for a stroll and for watching Perth's citizens taking the air, while the grid pattern of shopping streets – perhaps an inheritance from the Romans – allows for a convenient morning's browsing.

In and near Perth

• **Perth Art Gallery and Museum** (open Mon to Sat 10 to 5, also Sun 1 to 5 in May Arts Festival; enquiries 01738

632488). Crowds flock to see the heavily touted **Fair Maid's House**, which is a tea room with some medieval parts, but they virtually ignore this museum, which lies a few yards away and is far more interesting. It is a splendid, no-nonsense town museum with some good ideas about presentation, and interesting displays, notably the local Perth silverwork.

● **Church of St John** The church is small and plain, but it has witnessed plenty of history. Edward I worshipped in it during his 1296 campaign of conquest, while John Knox preached here the inflammatory sermons of 1559 which were to lead to so much destruction. The most recent re-modelling was in 1926, by Sir Robert Lorimer, whose gentle touch softens the fifteenth-century stonework. There is a beautiful window by Strachan at the east end.

● **Lower City Mills** (open Apr to Oct, Mon to Sat 10 to 5) A lovely Georgian grain mill has been fully restored west of the city centre. A huge water wheel now powers banks of elevators and millstones. It is an informative place, but there are a lot of stairs.

● **Branklyn Garden** (NTS, open Mar to end Oct, daily 9.30 to sunset) Essential visiting for keen gardeners, this is a large town garden with peat-loving plants. It lies on the east side of the Tay at the end of a street of large villas, and it is signposted from the A85 towards Dundee. The garden is made to feel larger than it is by clever design; wandering round the beds of primula and meconopsis can take much longer than you might imagine. The newly replanted rock garden and the small alpine house contain some rarities. Get to the garden early; it can become overcrowded by mid-morning.

● **Fairways Heavy Horse Centre** (open daily 10 to 5) This is the place to see the magnificent Clydesdale horses which are Scotland's best-known breed of working horse. To entertain visitors, they pull carriages or ploughs and give rides. The centre is east of Perth, off the A85.

● **Huntingtower Castle** (HS, standard times; winter closed Thur pm and Fri) A bland castle in an uninspiring setting on the very edge of the A85 to Crieff, Huntingtower has a curious structure of two fifteenth-century towers linked by a seventeenth-century wing. It is worth stopping there to see some of the earliest painted ceilings to be found in Scotland.

In the sixteenth century Huntingtower was in the possession of the Ruthvens (Earls of Gowrie), who were notorious and unpleasant conspirators. They were at the forefront of the plot to murder Riccio, Mary Queen of

Scots' secretary, helped with the imprisonment of Mary on Loch Leven, and here at Ruthven Castle (as it was then called) kidnapped the young James VI in 1582 and held him for ten months. He got his revenge in 1600 when another plot involving the Gowries seems to have gone wrong. Two members of the family died in a fracas at Perth, and the King hunted the others ruthlessly.

The castle does have a romantic legend too: the 'maiden's leap' between the two towers refers to the action of the first Earl's daughter, who was forced to leave her lover's bed in a hurry on hearing her mother's approach and made this perilous jump.

Scone Palace

(Open early Apr to mid-Oct, daily 9.30 to 5)
Approached from the A93 north of Perth, this huge mansion has ample space for tour coaches and hence gets more attention than it warrants. The neo-Gothic architecture may be described as restrained, but it is not restrained enough. Experts on ivories and French furniture will enjoy the interior, but for others the grounds will be the best part. The site of Scone Abbey, where so many Scottish Kings were crowned, can be seen, although there is nothing left of it. The Stone of Destiny on which the King sat for the ceremony was removed by Edward I to Westminster Abbey in 1296 – though you will doubtless hear that he was fobbed off with an imitation – and there it remains despite a brief outing in 1950–51 when it was taken by Scottish Nationalists and brought to Arbroath Abbey.

David Douglas, who discovered the Douglas fir, worked at Scone Palace as gardener. For a botanist, he suffered a sticky end – while in America he fell into a pit dug to catch bison. Unfortunately, a bison was already inside.

WEST OF PERTH

Strathearn

The wide valley of the Earn is gentle, arable land, with blue hills always lining the distance. The small sights of its eastern end cover a long period of time and a variety of interests. The Romans recognised the virtues of Strathearn as a line on which to establish military outposts. The chief of these was **Ardoch Roman Camp**, just outside Braco, which guarded the road south through Strathallan. Its extensive earthworks remain.

The Picts have left their mark too, in the shape of a weathered cross-slab outside St Bean's Church at **Foulis Wester**, east of Crieff. Inside the church there is a piece of MacBean tartan which went on an Apollo mission to the moon and another Pictish stone showing Jonah and the whale, a story which obviously much pleased the Picts, as it is a common theme. At **Muthill**, the pointed arches of a fifteenth-century church are attached to a square twelfth-century tower, while **Tulliebardine Chapel**, an easily overlooked barn-like building on the corner of a minor road off the A823 near Auchterarder, is actually a fifteenth-century collegiate chapel with an interior almost unaltered.

In summer the formal Italian gardens of **Drummond Castle**, where you can see one of the huge ornate sundials much fancied by the Scottish nobility, are open every afternoon. If you are fond of books you should visit **Innerpeffray Library** (open Apr to end Sept, Mon to Sat 10 to 12.45, 2 to 4.45; Oct to Mar, 2 to 4, closed Thur), south of Crieff on the B8062; the oldest library in Scotland, it houses a collection of rare books which is the more astonishing for being in such a tiny place.

Crieff and the Sma' Glen

Crieff used to hold one of the biggest trysts (cattle fairs) in Scotland until Falkirk became the centre for these long-vanished events. Today it is an easy-going little market town taking advantage of its position on the very edge of the Highlands to gather tourists into its shops and its tiny museum. The visitor centre just to the south of town is really a sales pitch for locally made products, including pottery and paperweights.

There are a number of hotels in Crieff which date from its days as a nineteenth-century resort, among them the massive Crieff Hydro. Numerous guesthouses are also to be found if you want to stay for a night or two.

The **Sma' Glen** is the usual name given to the route which runs northwards from Crieff to Amulree at the foot of Glen Quaich, though the glen itself is only a short stretch beside the River Almond. There is a salmon leap a little further downstream at **Buchanty Spout**, and a good, long walk westwards up towards the head of Glenalmond. In August the bell heather on the moors round Amulree turns the whole landscape rosy lilac.

Comrie

'The Shakey Toun' lies right on the edge of the Highland Boundary Fault, and owes its nickname to the earth tremors which occasionally rattle teacups. The world's first ever seismometers were set up here and you can still visit Earthquake House and look at the equipment.

The **Scottish Tartans Museum**, which used to be here, has now closed and is in search of a new home at the time of writing. **Auchingarrich Wildlife Centre** (open Apr to Oct, daily 10 to dusk) has animals, local and exotic, and makes a good diversion for children.

For an attractive drive or walk, try nearby **Glen Lednock**.

St Fillans

The village is named after the sixth-century missionary from Ireland, who is associated not only with Loch Earnside but with Glen Dochart and Strath Fillan as well (see Killin later in this chapter). Robert the Bruce insisted that the relics of the saint were carried into battle at Bannockburn. St Fillans is lucky in its setting at the gentle eastern end of Loch Earn, and is a centre for watersports, with a comfortable hotel. There are some good short walks on the hillsides near the village, particularly around Glen Tarken (get hold of a leaflet about it from Crieff Tourist Information Office).

At the western end of the loch you reach Lochearnhead, which is largely a water-skiing and water sports centre, much busier than St Fillans. Here you join the A84 which runs northwards from the Trossachs towards Killin.

THE ROAD NORTH TO PITLOCHRY

North of Perth the main A9 to Pitlochry passes through the rugged scenery of the Tay and Tummel valleys. Unfortunately, the terrible design of this road, with short stretches of dual carriageway alternating with long curves where it is never quite safe to overtake slow lorries or caravans, is at its worst here, and trying to split your time between watching the traffic and watching the scenery is not sensible. The Tummel is not quite the river it was before the huge hydro-electric network of tunnels and dams was built, but the Tay – deep, black and swirling in the strath where it sweeps past Birnam and Dunkeld – is the sort of river to haunt dreams and inspire legend.

289

For once the forests here improve rather than spoil the landscape; much is the result of careful work by various Dukes of Atholl. Many of the plantings are venerable, especially the larches of Dunkeld and the trees of Birnam Wood, though the latter will not be the same ones that Shakespeare wrote about. Fragments of mixed woodland break up the conifers, while the craggy hills rising above the trees give fresh texture and colour to the scenery. Bright blue lupins have established themselves on shingle banks by the Tay.

At Bankfoot, the **Perthshire Visitor Centre** is worth stopping at to see the Macbeth Experience, which puts Shakespeare's tragic hero into his historical context, and to browse through the excellent selection of books.

Dunkeld

When the Vikings drove St Columba's monks from Iona in about 729, it was to Dunkeld that they came. Its religious importance was further established by the cathedral, which dates from the twelfth century. After the battle of Killiecrankie in 1689, Dunkeld was the scene of a further battle, in which the Highland forces, dispirited by the death of their leader, Dundee, were defeated. In the process, medieval Dunkeld was thoroughly burnt.

What you see today, apart from the remains of the cathedral, is therefore eighteenth-century at its oldest, and very attractive it is too, for the short Cathedral Street, very like a cathedral close, is lined by harled cottages restored by the National Trust for Scotland. A similar one in the Square is now the Tourist Information Centre, while another contains the military Museum of the Scottish Horse.

Behind the houses lie the remnants of the cathedral – the nave roofless, the choir still serving as parish church. The interior will probably still be under restoration, but take a wander round the outside to look at the fifteenth-century windows with their elaborate tracery. At the back of the building, the huge scraggy larch tree is the 'parent larch', possibly the first grown in Scotland. It was planted in 1737 and is the ancestor, no doubt, of millions more. If you are fond of larches, drive up the east bank of the Tay to Dunkeld House and persuade someone at the hotel to show you the pot-grown larch in the grounds. This huge specimen started life in an eighteenth-century greenhouse before being planted out, and its enormous roots still faithfully reproduce the shape of the pot in which it was grown.

Loch of Lowes

This is one of a series of glacial lochs east of Dunkeld which run in a chain towards Blairgowrie and are known as the Stormont lochs after the district they lie in. Loch of Lowes is the largest, and is a nature reserve. From a hide you may be able to watch the ospreys which spend part of the year here. Even if there are none, the visitor centre will have information on what other kinds of bird you are likely to see.

The Hermitage

(NTS, open all year)
A mile-long walk by the River Braan, west of Dunkeld and signposted from the A9, is ideal for stretching your legs after too long in a car. It runs through ancient woodland to a folly, built in 1758, called Ossian's Hall or the Hermitage. Beyond lies Ossian's Cave – another piece of artifice. The whole walk, with its waterfall, gorge and little bridge, reflects the late eighteenth-century taste for the picturesque. It is still utterly charming, with only a faint hint of the ridiculous.

NORTH-EAST OF PERTH

Glenshee

Whether you travel up Glen Isla on the B954 (the pleasanter road), or stick to the A93 north from Blairgowrie, you rapidly leave the fertile Lowlands behind and drive into increasingly wild country. The hills on either side of the Glenshee road are unshapely great mounds which become higher and more barren as you penetrate deeper into them, with scree streaking the upper slopes of Creag Leacach and the Cairnwell at the head of the pass.

Spittal of Glenshee, a watering hole for skiers, is the last village you pass before heading up the steep stretch of road to the Cairnwell pass. This road used to be notorious for the Devil's Elbow – a steep hairpin bend which was the bane of buses and was frequently blocked by snow. Now the road is straight, graded and anonymous, though the disintegrating remains of the old hazard lie just beyond the fence.

At the lip of the pass, the **Cairwell Chairlift** will take you effortlessly up the mountain, summer or winter. Beyond the pass, the road drops rapidly towards Braemar and Deeside (see the chapter on the North-East).

Strathmore

This fertile valley runs from the junction of the Rivers Isla and Tay right over to the east coast. Strathmore is Scotland's soft fruit country, responsible for the best raspberries in the world. Tractors here look like giant insects from a horror film, built tall and narrow for straddling rows of canes. There are many pick-your-own farms.

Blairgowrie is the centre for the western end of the valley, a place somewhat bedevilled by traffic. Three miles south, at **Meikleour**, stands one of those useless curiosities which brighten the traveller's day: a beech hedge planted in 1746 and now 110 feet high. It is trimmed every ten years.

Meigle Museum

(HS, standard times; closed winter)
Long before raspberries were domesticated, the Picts had made Strathmore a centre of population. At the village of Meigle, the old school has been converted into a museum to house thirty Pictish carved stones and four fragments, dating from the seventh to the tenth centuries. The custodian needs to open the building for you, but a visit is worthwhile.

The room is dominated by three great stone cross-slabs, almost entirely covered in intricate carving. One shows Daniel in the lions' den, the lions pawing at him like overgrown cats while Daniel pats their heads. Beautiful interlaced patterns shroud the edges of another slab, and on the rear are examples of most of the enigmatic symbols – disc, Z-rod, 'swimming elephant' and mirror and comb – which appear on many Pictish stones, and whose meaning is lost to us. The stones are full of movement, curves and knots, and obviously belong to a culture very different from the Anglo-Norman society which was to become dominant in Lowland Scotland.

PITLOCHRY

At first sight, Pitlochry is a place which appears to have bred hotels, gift shops and tour coaches to the exclusion of all else. It is nevertheless a mistake to write the town off as a ghastly tourist trap and move on without delay. It is certainly crowded, and neither beautiful nor historic, but it has managed somehow to retain the leisurely atmosphere of the old-fashioned mountain resort which it has been since the coming of the railway in 1863. There is no shortage of places to stay, ranging from large Victorian hotels in spa style to simple guesthouses. Prowl until you find a place to suit you and remember to check the menu, for the town is short of decent restaurants if your hotel disappoints.

Pitlochry is an excellent place for gentle walks, especially along the banks of **Loch Faskally**. Many other Scottish lochs have suffered from the raising of their levels for hydro-electric needs, but this entirely man-made stretch of water is a resounding success in the landscape. You can walk as far as the pass of Killiecrankie should you wish, but there are plenty of shorter round trips. Boats can also be hired. The old village of **Moulin** on the outskirts of Pitlochry makes another good stroll, with a pleasant pub at its end, while a stiffer walk beyond the golf course up the hill of **Craigower** (NTS) rewards you with fine views.

At the **Pitlochry Festival Theatre** you can now see eight plays in six days in season. The tent-like interior of the foyer recalls the marquee in which the theatre started in 1951. A short distance upstream, beneath the massive dam and power station, thick glass windows allow you to peer into the swirling waters of the **Fish Pass**, a series of ascending pools by the side of the dam allowing salmon upstream to spawn. Although there is often nothing but an empty tank to look at, a random visit will occasionally find a salmon or sea trout poised inside the glass. An electronic recorder counts the fish passing up the ladder but none exists to count the visitors, who must far outnumber them.

While at the dam, don't miss the **Hydro-Electric Visitor Centre** (open end Mar to end Oct, daily 9.40 to 5.30) – not so much to see the power station, which just hums away without any visible action, but the series of excellent exhibitions, films and electronic displays which show the workings of the station, describe the Tummel Valley Hydro-Electric scheme, or tell you about the life-cycle of the salmon.

Edradour Distillery, up the hill to the east of Pitlochry, is the smallest distillery in Scotland, but there seems to be enough room for all the visitors. It is free and friendly but a little plagued by wasps.

LOCH TAY

Ballinluig to Aberfeldy

Five miles south of Pitlochry, the A827 strikes across the Tummel and points you in the direction of Aberfeldy, Crianlarich, Oban and the sea. By following the south bank you pass the minor road to **St Mary's Church** at Grandtully. The church, dating back at least to 1533, looks like a barn attached to the neighbouring farm. Inside, however, there is a ceiling richly decorated with medallions and heraldic crests, probably done around 1636. It is the pleasure of finding a small hidden treasure which makes a visit here rewarding.

Aberfeldy

Aberfeldy is an unrushed place, little more than a large village with an attractive square and a few shops. If you do not want to stay in the bustle of Pitlochry, Aberfeldy is just as well situated for touring and a great deal more peaceful.

Aberfeldy is distinguished by General Wade's bridge across the Tay. This is widely seen as the road-building General's tour de force. He brought in William Adam to design it, and it took two years to build. With its pinnacles and steep arches, it is certainly the most imposing bridge in the Highlands. Beside it stands the **Black Watch Monument**, a memorial to that most famous of Highland regiments, which was raised in 1739.

Aberfeldy Water Mill is a carefully restored oatmeal mill, driven by the waters of the Moness Burn. The process looks simple, but as you listen to the technical details it becomes obvious that there is more to milling than meets the eye. Porridge-freaks and oatcake-addicts will travel miles for stone-ground oatmeal of different grades such as is sold here.

The local beauty spot, the **Birks (birches) o' Aberfeldy**, owes its fame to a poem by Burns and the walk up the miniature glen behind the town to the Falls of Moness is pretty enough if you feel like a stroll.

Castle Menzies

(Open Apr to mid-Oct, Mon to Sat 10.30 to 5, Sun 2 to 5) This creepy-looking pile across the Tay from Aberfeldy and beyond the tiny village of Weem was derelict for years. Clan

Menzies got hold of it in the nick of time and it has now been restored as a Clan Centre, but also as rather more than that, for it is a splendid example of a 'Z-plan' fortification (a castle with a tower on diagonally opposite sides of the main wing). There is not much to see inside, apart from a few intriguing objects found behind the old walls, which include a single green satin eighteenth-century lady's shoe.

Fortingall

Follow the River Lyon up behind Drummond Hill and you reach this cluster of houses – an unlikely place to find the oldest living thing in Europe and the alleged birthplace of one of the most vilified characters in history.

The former is a yew tree. It does not look 3,000 years old at first glance, but once you have peered over the railings that keep you away from it and have seen that all the fragments of wood were once one huge trunk, whose circumference in 1776 was 65 feet, the timescale begins to sink in. The poor old tree has suffered much, from souvenir hunters, bow-makers and festival bonfires, but it still lives on.

The vilified character was Pontius Pilate. The story goes that he was the son of a local woman (maybe a Menzies) and a Roman envoy sent by Caesar Augustus, who went back to Rome with the baby once his mission was completed. How true the tradition is is anybody's guess, and the village does not exactly celebrate its infamous son, even now.

Taymouth Castle

This mammoth nineteenth-century folly of a mock castle stands hidden by trees at Kenmore, by the foot of Loch Tay. It was completed just in time for Queen Victoria's visit, and she was thrilled: 'The firing of the guns, the cheering of the great crowd, the picturesqueness of the dresses . . . formed one of the finest scenes imaginable . . . It was princely and romantic.' It is all very different now, for the castle stands empty and the yellow flags of the local golf course flutter on the lawn. You cannot go inside the castle, but it makes a pleasant diversion to peer at it from the outside and imagine Queen Victoria's enjoyment.

Glen Lyon

This is the longest glen in Scotland, running almost across to Glenorchy. It is not quite a cul-de-sac, since a road winds out across the shoulder of Ben Lawers down to Loch Tay, making one of the best round trips from Aberfeldy. Glen Lyon was populous Campbell territory for many years; now it is almost deserted, apart from the odd 'big hoose' or large farm. The outlawed Macgregors were here too, persecuted by the Campbells of Glenorchy and Lawers (who bred a bloodhound suckled by a Macgregor woman, so that the dog would know the smell of its enemy).

The entrance to the glen beyond Fortingall is half-hidden and dramatically steep. Then the scenery relaxes, the river broadens and becomes good for picnics and the glen opens up into an attractive valley between the steep slopes of Ben Lawers on the left and Carn Gorm on the right.

As you penetrate to the end of the road the glen becomes wilder and the encroaching mountains more persistent, until finally you come to the dam which doubled the size of Loch Lyon behind it. Beyond, all is pathless wilderness.

Ben Lawers

A road runs on either side of Loch Tay to Killin. The main A827 is fast and undemanding, with good views of the loch, but of little else. The back road on the southern shore is narrow and slow, but you have the advantage of being able to look across the water to the peak of Ben Lawers.

For a closer look at Ben Lawers (which has been a National Nature Reserve since 1975), head for the road which runs over its shoulder to Glen Lyon (see above). On the flank of the mountain you will find a visitor centre (NTS, open Apr to late Sept, daily 10 to 5; centre may close for 30 mins between 1 and 2), with the usual facilities and information – quite a good introduction to the hill. Various walks are suggested, but your chances of spotting the rare alpines for which Ben Lawers is famous are remote unless you know exactly what you are looking for. Ben Lawers is a friendly sort of mountain for a hill walk, and correspondingly popular. If you want mountainous solitude, go somewhere else.

Killin

A small village at the head of Loch Tay, Killin is busy with walkers and those who have stopped to look at the **Falls of Dochart**, tame rapids easily visible from the road. The **Breadalbane Folklore Centre** tells the story of St Fillan, one

of the earliest missionaries to Sc...
to have been carried into the...
healing stones remain at Killin; h...
under the guardianship of heredita...
relics) have now ended up in the F...
in Edinburgh. In Killin, Shutters re...
lunchtime halt, especially in the rair...
up Glen Lochay to get away from the...

LOCHS TUMMEL AND ...OCH

The B8019 branches west from the A9 three miles north of Pitlochry to take you into the glacial gouge which holds these two lochs. You can also get here over the hill from Aberfeldy. The beauty spot of **Queen's View** at the foot of Loch Tummel, with its long vista over the water to the pyramid peak of Schiehallion on the opposite shore, remains unspoilt but the rest of Loch Tummel has been ruined by the dense conifers clothing the hills on its northern shore. All colours other than spruce green have been expunged.

Luckily, Loch Rannoch beyond is a different story. Beyond Kinloch Rannoch, the last evidence of tourism is a time-share enterprise, but then you are alone with the loch. The drive round is excellent. On the northern shore, birch forest comes down to the lake edge, dusty gold in autumn, silver-green in spring, with the aquamarine or slate grey of the water seen through the trunks.

On the southern shore, and worth all the drive to see, is the **Black Wood of Rannoch**. This pine forest contains some of the few gnarled survivors of the great Caledonian forest, and a beautiful place of light and air it is, with great lumps of moss and heather as its floor, and pines of all ages, alder and birch growing in profusion.

If you continue west beyond Bridge of Gaur towards Rannoch Station, the landscape changes. The woodland of Loch Rannoch lies behind as the road climbs towards Rannoch Moor, that great seed-bed of Ice-Age glaciers. At this eastern end the land is not beautiful, for the glacial rubble is like a gargantuan overgrown building site and hydro-electric man has not disguised his work very carefully. Push on to **Rannoch Station**, where, beside the isolated railway at the end of the road, under suddenly wide skies, you will find a single white hotel, a cottage, and a silence such as you have seldom heard before.

S Visitor Centre, open Apr to late Oct, daily 10 to 5.30)
*The tourist enters the celebrated Pass of Killiecrankie with a feeling
approaching to terror.* (The Scottish Tourist, 1827)

Killiecrankie lost much of its wild grandeur when the
River Garry gave up most of its water for the sake of elec-
tricity. The **Soldier's Leap** across the narrowest part of the
gorge, where a fleeing Englishman jumped to save his skin
from the Highlanders hard on his heels, does not now look
quite such a desperate feat. However, the steepness of the
pass, its link with a famous battle won by an all-out charge
of the clans and the general loveliness of the surrounding
woodlands make Killiecrankie much visited.

The battle of Killiecrankie was the climax of the Jacobite
uprising of 1689. James Graham of Claverhouse, objecting
to the way in which James VII had been forced into
exile and the Scottish crown offered to William of Orange,
had gathered a Highland army to dispute the cause. The
charge of the clans at the head of this narrow gorge put the
Williamite army to flight. Dundee, however, was fatally
wounded in the battle, and without his leadership the
uprising fizzled out after the Highland army was blocked at
Dunkeld (page 290). Dundee (Bonnie Dundee of the song)
owes his romantic reputation to Killiecrankie, but is the
same man whose ruthless persecution of the Covenanters
after the restoration of Charles II gave 'The Killing Times'
to Scottish history.

The visitor centre has a detailed account of the battle and
is signposted from the A9. In summer, there are ranger-led
walks.

Blair Atholl

This is a modest village, by-passed by the A9, and is the
place to look for somewhere to stay (although there is not
too much choice) if you want to do some of the long walks
that thread through the lumpy mountains of the district of
Atholl to the east. The restored **Blair Atholl Mill**, like the
one at Aberfeldy, will grind the oatmeal for your porridge
with a great rumbling of grindstones and rattle of boxed-in
elevators carrying the oats or cracked grain to the floor
above.

The next stretch of the A9 northwards will serve to introduce General Wade, who chose this route for one of his many roads. Sent to Scotland in 1724 in the aftermath of the 1715 Jacobite rising, he built roads and bridges through the Highlands which, to a great extent, still define what you can see from your car today and what you cannot. These roads, a network of military communication where none had previously existed, were built to keep the Highlands pacified. Ironically, they were put to use by Charles Edward Stuart during his campaign in 1746. Now they are mostly hidden beneath tarmac, though many of his bridges remain, notably at Aberfeldy. Some stretches (marked 'military road' on OS maps) are left where modern road-makers have chosen a different route. Perhaps the most remarkable is at the Corrieyarrick pass (built 1735), which runs between Laggan and Fort Augustus. 'If you had seen these roads before they were made, you would get down on your knees and bless General Wade,' runs the old saying.

Before the coming of the General, two alternative routes northwards ran up **Glen Tilt** over to the River Dee and up **Glen Bruar** over the pass called Minigaig down as far as Glen Feshie and Speyside. These old routes now make two of the finest medium-distance walks in Scotland, through country which is about as remote from modern life (and from rescue) as it is possible to get in Britain. Even if you do not want to make the full crossing, for which you must be adequately prepared, exploring the start of both walks is enjoyable. Although this country is deserted now, it was not always so; you will find the remains of shielings up both glens, where cattle used to be pastured in summer before the days of depopulation.

Blair Castle

(Open Apr to late Oct, daily 10 to 6)
Home of the Duke of Atholl, Blair Castle is historically the mustering ground of his private army, the only one allowed in Britain. The Atholl Highlanders were the product of a moment's romantic weakness by Queen Victoria, who visited the castle in 1844.

The panelled entrance hall to this pleasing mixture of castle and stately home is garnished by pretty patterns of muskets, bayonets and swords — unusual wall-coverings. Unusual too was the practice of keeping large stags in the grounds and gluing their shed antlers on to the skulls of dead deer to make the estate's trophies look outstanding (there are ranks of them in the ballroom).

Blair Castle is old, turreted and white, and there is a lot of it. It is not easy to tell from the outside what is thirteenth-century and what is Victorian, though the castellations most certainly are the latter. The best parts of the interior are the Georgian conversions of older rooms, the drawing-room ceiling being especially elaborate and beautiful. Rank upon rank of family portraits cover the walls and there is often an accompanying family tree to show you who was who. The most eccentric and fascinating collection in the castle is the Victorian miscellany on the lowest floor, which has everything from old balldresses and reticules to mourning brooches. Innocuous-looking walking canes conceal a sword, an airgun, a blowpipe and a collapsible fishing rod.

There is a family connection to the 1745 rising, for Lord George Murray, Prince Charles' one competent commander, was brother to the Duke of Atholl. Consequently, there are a number of Jacobite relics, including the Chevalier's gloves and lockets with his miniature inside. Knotty, hoary seventeenth-century furniture is scattered around, and objects in glass cases, from snuff-boxes to fragments of flag, are everywhere; by the time you progress to the collection of china, you are beginning to wonder whether you will ever reach the end. A gift shop rounds off the experience.

The castle grounds are both ducal and welcoming, which means specimen trees, picnic benches, few restrictions on where you walk and a car park which, for once, is not a half-mile trudge in the drizzle. This is primarily a stately home for lovers of odds and ends; you cannot help wondering where all the junk was kept through the years before it went on display.

Drumochter

After Blair Atholl the A9 leaves the southward-flowing river valleys and heads up Glen Garry to this bleak pass at the top of a great barrier of peat bog and sour hillside which separates the districts of Atholl and Badenoch. On one side lies the mountainous hump of the Sow of Atholl, mirrored by the Boar of Badenoch on the other. It always seems to be raining on Drumochter, no matter how clear the skies are elsewhere.

In the fourteenth-century this would have been a long,

wet journey on horseback, with the followers of the Wolf of Badenoch lying in wait. The Wolf was Alexander, Earl of Buchan and Ross, who was a bastard son of King Robert II, and struck fear into Lowland hearts. Nominally justiciary of the north, he made the central Highlands into a fastness, whence his predatory raids, notably that on Elgin, gave him, and this part of the world, an unenviable reputation.

WHERE TO STAY

£ – under £70 per room per night, incl. VAT
££ – £70 to £110 per room per night, incl. VAT
£££ – over £110 per room per night, incl. VAT

ABERFELDY
Farleyer House
Aberfeldy PH15 2JE
TEL (01887) 820332
FAX (01887) 829430
A sixteenth-century croft and dower house furnished in bright and airy country-house style with a golden-walled drawing-room and swagged curtains. The formal restaurant menu shows imagination and modern flair; simpler dishes in the bistro, decorated in Black Watch tartan. Bedrooms are a restorative mix of antique and new furnishings.
£££ All year; 11 rooms; drying-room; golf; croquet; putting (See Where to Eat)

Guinach House
By the Birks, Aberfeldy PH15 2ET
TEL (01887) 820251
FAX (01887) 829607
Reassuringly traditional hotel a short walk from the town centre, set in three acres of garden. Scattered rugs and a paisley border give the lounge a comfortable air. Food served in the dining-room is appetising and skilfully prepared.

Some bedrooms are bright with chintz and old furniture, others more homely.
££ All year exc Chr; 7 rooms; drying-room

Letterellan
Fearnan, by Aberfeldy PH15 2NY
TEL (01887) 830221
Restored hunting lodge now an impressive bed and breakfast on the north shore of Loch Tay, with fishing rights for guests on its own loch. Family treasures and photographs brighten the sitting-room and bedrooms are comfortable and well equipped.
£ Easter to Oct; 3 rooms; drying-room; sauna; fishing; shooting; credit cards not accepted

Tigh' n Eilean
Taybridge Drive, Aberfeldy PH15 2BP
TEL (01887) 820109
Welcoming private house with pretty decoration and attractive china on display in the dining-room. Evening meals are home-made and traditional; pine and wicker furniture and floral soft furnishings give the bedrooms a light and airy feel.
£ All year; 3 rooms; credit cards not accepted

USEFUL DIRECTORY

Main tourist offices
Argyll, the Isles, Loch Lomond, Stirling & Trossachs Tourist Board
41 Dumbarton Road
Stirling FK8 2QQ
(01786) 475019

Perthshire Tourist Information Centre
45 High Street
Perth PH1 5TJ
(01738) 638353

Tourist Board publications Annual *Visitor's Guide* lists everything
from sight opening times to boat trips and Perthshire crafts; quarterly
events guides. Special interest: guides on fishing, golf, walking,
cycling. Postal or phone orders to the above addresses.

Local tourist information centres
Aberfeldy (01887) 820276
Aberfoyle (01877) 382352 (Apr to Oct)
Alva Mill Trail Visitor Centre (01259) 769696
Auchterarder (01764) 663450
Blairgowrie (01250) 872960/873701
Callander (01877) 330342
Crief (01764) 652578
Dunblane (01786) 824428 (May to Sept)
Dunkeld (01350) 727688 (Mar to Oct)
Killin (01567) 820254 (Mar to Sept)
Kinross (01577) 863680
Pitlochry (01796) 472215/472751
Tyndrum (01838) 400246 (Apr to Oct)

Local Transport
Scotrail Stirling (01786) 473763
National Rail Enquiries (0345) 212282
Brave Heart Bus Station, Stirling (all local services, plus National
Express & Citylink) (01786) 813384
Tayside Transport (01382) 201121

Ferries and cruises
East Loch Lomond (Balmaha) (01360) 870214 (Inversnaid) (01877)
386223 (Rowardennan) (01360) 870273
Loch Katrine 0141-355 5333

Watersports
Loch Tay (boating centre) (01887) 830291
(watersport centre) (01887) 830236

AUCHTERARDER
Auchterarder House
Auchterarder PH3 1DZ
TEL (01764) 663646
FAX (01764) 662939
A first-class country-house hotel where the formal elegance of the interior is studiously in keeping with the Scots baronial turrets and gables. A delightful art nouveau drawing-room and landscape-lined dining-room epitomise the style of the house. Good food in the classic tradition and bedrooms of individual design with flair.
£££ All year; 15 rooms (See Where to Eat)

Gleneagles
Auchterarder PH3 1NF
TEL (01764) 662231
FAX (01764) 662134
The grandee of Scottish hotels, with unmatched facilities and luxury service in the gentle Perthshire hills. Gleneagles is built on a grand scale; room enough for corporate executives to exist happily alongside honeymooners and golfing weekenders. There are battle scene murals in the tartan-draped drawing-room and the Strathearn restaurant is bright in sky-blue. Bedrooms vary in size and sumptuousness but all are appreciably comfortable and well appointed.
£££ All year; 234 rooms; drying-room; games room; golf; tennis; horse-riding; solarium; sauna; swimming-pool; gym; crèche

BALLINLUIG
Tulliemet House
Ballinluig, by Pitlochry PH9 0PA
TEL (01796) 482419
FAX (01796) 482617
Built in 1820 as part of the Atholl Estate, this former hunting lodge exudes a happy and informal air.

The drawing-room is comfortable and well proportioned; evening meals may be booked in advance. Commodious bedrooms.
£ All year exc sometimes at Chr; 2 rooms; credit cards not accepted

BALQUHIDDER
Monachyle Mhor
Balquhidder, Lochearnhead FK19 8PQ
TEL (01877) 384622
FAX (01877) 384305
A four-mile journey along a single track by Loch Voil leads to this traditional farmhouse where a roaring fire blazes in the popular bar. The pink walls of the dining-room and the floral drapes continue the country theme. Food is well priced and imaginative; meals are also served in a conservatory with views out over the loch. Pleasant bedrooms, quiet and stylish courtyard conversions.
£ All year; 12 rooms, most with shower/wc; drying-room; fishing

BLAIRGOWRIE
Kinloch House
by Blairgowrie PH10 6SG
TEL (01250) 884237
FAX (01250) 884333
Superb hotel extended in Edwardian times with imposing panelling and a sweeping staircase. The character of that lively period remains pre-eminent. A good base for outdoor sporting pursuits, although the welcoming public rooms invite one to linger. Food is imaginative and accomplished with skilful use of local ingredients. Bedrooms are bright and harmonious.
£££ All year exc 15-30 Dec; 21 rooms; drying-room (See Where to Eat)

CALLANDER
Arran Lodge

Leny Road, Callander FK17 8AJ
TEL (01877) 330976
A Victorian bungalow with a riverside garden and a verandah. Inside, the lounge is light and airy with white leather sofas and an Adam-style fireplace. The welcome is warm and generous, the menus traditional. The bedrooms are immaculate with a modern feel.
£ All year exc mid-Nov to end Jan; 4 rooms; fishing

Leny House

Leny Estate, Callander FK17 8HA
TEL/FAX (01877) 331078
The history of this house stretches back 1,000 years; it played a role in the Jacobite rising as secret meeting-place and arms store. The original small fortress has been enlarged and is now a graceful manor house with elegant rooms. Breakfast only is served, and self-catering lodges are available.
£ Easter to end Sept; 4 rooms, 2 with bath/shower

The Roman Camp

Callander FK17 8BG
TEL (01877) 330003
FAX (01877) 331533
A former hunting lodge full of charm and character. Past the pink-harled exterior are an imposing reception hall, a classically furnished drawing-room and a host of nooks and crannies to search out. Food is exciting and good value with prime ingredients and fresh flavours. Bedrooms vary in size and are individually decorated.
££-£££ All year; 14 rooms; drying-room; fishing

DENNY
Lochend Farm

Carronbridge, Denny FK6 5JJ
TEL (01324) 822778
A working sheep farm with views over 700 acres of moorland grazing and across Loch Coulter. Two comfortable bedrooms share a bathroom. A pleasant TV lounge is downstairs. Breakfast only served.
£ Easter to Oct, or by arrangement; 2 rooms with wash-basin; credit cards not accepted

DRYMEN
Dunleen

Milton of Buchanan, Drymen G63 0JE
TEL (01360) 870274
Modern bungalow about a mile from Loch Lomond, with a large lounge-cum-breakfast room. Bedrooms are comfortable and spotlessly clean.
£ May to Oct; 2 rooms with wash-basin; credit cards not accepted

DUNKELD
Kinnaird

Kinnaird Estate, Dunkeld PH8 0LB
TEL (01796) 482440
FAX (01796) 482289
This fine eighteenth-century house exudes sparkling style and cultivated comfort at every turn, harking back to wonderful Edwardian house-party pleasures. Most memorable of the public rooms is the dining-room where delicate panels depict pastoral scenes rivalled only by the glorious views of the Tay itself. Culinary expertise and wonderful food presentation are very much in evidence. Modish and extravagant bedrooms match the splendour of their surroundings.
£££ Closed Mon to Wed during Jan to Mar; 9 rooms; drying-room; games room; fishing; tennis (See Where to Eat)

Stakis Dunkeld House
Dunkeld PH8 0HX
TEL (01350) 727771
FAX (01350) 728924
Edwardian house built by the Duke
of Athol and now a superior chain
hotel, charmingly managed. Public
rooms are modern and fairly bland
but refurbished bedrooms offer real
character and comfort.
*££ All year; 86 rooms; games
room; swimming-pool; sauna; steam
room; gym; table tennis; putting;
tennis; fishing; clay pigeon shooting;
4x4 driving*

DUNNING
Garvock House
Dunning, Perthshire PH2 9BY
TEL (01764) 684287
Bright and welcoming Georgian
country house with delightful
service and comfortable, relaxing
rooms. Dinner is by arrangement
and designed to resemble an
informal supper party. Excellent
Scottish breakfasts add to the
attractions. Bedrooms are tastefully
decorated.
*£ All year; 3 rooms; croquet; credit
cards not accepted*

GARTOCHARN
Ardoch Cottage
Gartocharn G83 8NE
TEL (01389) 830452
Cheerful, welcoming cottage with a
comfortable sitting-room. Evening
meals are served in the dining-
room; packed lunches are available.
Pretty bedrooms.
*£ All year; 3 rooms; credit cards not
accepted*

KILLIECRANKIE
Killiecrankie Hotel
Killiecrankie, by Pitlochry PH16 5LG
TEL (01796) 473220
FAX (01796) 472451
This whitewashed house kindles a
dream of the very essence of

Scotland. Hunting pictures, antlers
and stuffed birds set a traditional
tone in the public areas, although a
lighter touch prevails in the
conservatory. Food in the formal
dining-room is an inventive and
gastronomic delight. Bedrooms
have specially crafted pine furniture
and harmonious soft furnishings.
*££ Closed Jan to Feb; 10 rooms;
drying-room (See Where to Eat)*

KILLIN
Fairview Guest House
Main Street, Killin FK21 8UT
TEL (01567) 820667
Guesthouse in the middle of Killin
village with views over the Ben
Lawers, Loch Tay and the
Breadalbane Hills. Inside the
accommodation is warm and
welcoming. The lounge is on the first
floor and evening meals are served on
pine tables in the dining-room.
Packed lunches can be provided.
*£ All year exc Chr; 7 rooms, most
with bath/shower*

KINBUCK
Cromlix House
Kinbuck, by Dunblane FK15 9JT
TEL (01786) 822125
FAX (01786) 825450
An atmospheric and impressive
country-house hotel. The reception
hallway provides baronial splendour
while the morning-room is light
and comfortable. Delicious food
and an excellent Scottish
cheeseboard; early suppers available
for children. Bedrooms are large,
many with coronet drapes or half-
testers; some remain a little old-
fashioned but still well equipped.
*£££ All year exc Jan; 14 rooms;
fishing; tennis; croquet*

KINCLAVEN
Ballathie House
Kinclaven, by Stanley PH1 4QN
TEL (01250) 883268
FAX (01250) 883396
At the end of a long drive, this
sporting hotel in peaceful
countryside has good facilities.
Good, traditional cooking with
super vegetables. Floral soft
furnishings brighten the bedrooms.
*£££ All year; 28 rooms; fishing;
shooting; tennis; croquet (See Where
to Eat)*

KINLOCH RANNOCH
Cuilmore Cottage
Kinloch Rannoch, Pitlochry PH16 5QB
TEL/FAX (01882) 632218
A tiny creeper-clad croft. The neat
little sitting-room has pine-clad and
slate walls. Rural motifs abound
with an old-fashioned range and a
rocking chair in the dining-room.
The no-choice dinner is
thoughtfully presented. Upstairs
bedrooms are a mix of pine,
modern and antique furniture.
*£ Closed Nov to Jan; 2 rooms;
drying-room*

KIRKTON OF GLENISLA
Glenisla Hotel
Kirkton of Glenisla, by Alyth
PH11 8PH
TEL/FAX (01575) 582223
See full description in Fife and
Angus chapter.
£ All year exc Chr; 6 rooms

MEIKLEOUR
Tay Farm House
Meikleour, Perth PH2 6EE
TEL (01250) 883345
Neat and plainly decorated house in
a lovely country location. Evening
meals can be requested and
barbecues are highlights here in
summer. Fishing on good local
beats can be organised. Bedrooms
with floral soft furnishings have

pine furniture and views over the
fields.
*£ All year; 2 rooms; fishing; credit
cards not accepted*

PERTH
Achnacarry Guest House
3 Pitcullen Crescent, Perth PH2 7HT
TEL (01738) 621421
FAX (01738) 444110
A warm and friendly guesthouse ten
minutes' walk from Perth city
centre. There is a small lounge and
evening meals are available by
arrangement in the dining-room.
Bedrooms are small and neat.
£ All year; 4 rooms

Kinneard Guest House
5 Marshall Place, Perth PH2 8AH
TEL (01738) 628021
FAX (01738) 444056
Small Georgian terraced bed and
breakfast not far from the centre of
town, with a sitting-room for guests
and homely, neat bedrooms.
Evening meals are home-cooked
and traditional.
£ All year; 7 rooms

Park Lane Guest House
17 Marshall Place, Perth PH2 8AG
TEL (01738) 637218
FAX (01738) 643519
Welcoming and friendly bed and
breakfast in a Georgian terrace near
Perth town centre, facing a park.
En-suite bedrooms are cosy with
pine furniture, pretty lamps and
mirrors.
£ All year; 6 rooms

PITLOCHRY
Arrandale House
Knochfarrie Road, Pitlochry PH16 5DN
TEL (01796) 472987
Built last century as a manse for
Pitlochry East Church, this stone-
built house enjoys splendid views
over the valley to the hills. There is
no lounge but the spacious bedrooms

have their own sitting areas. Breakfast only is served in the dining-room.
£ *Mar to Nov; 6 rooms; credit cards not accepted*

Craigroyston House
2 Lower Oakfield, Pitlochry
PH16 5HQ
TEL (01796) 472053
Welcoming house on a quiet residential street within easy walking distance of the town centre. Cheerfully decorated with light, floral en-suite bedrooms. Good, home-cooked evening meals by arrangement.
£ *Mar to early Dec; 8 rooms; credit cards not accepted*

East Haugh House
East Haugh, Pitlochry PH16 5JS
TEL (01796) 473121
FAX (01796) 472473
Fishing predominates here, the decoration of this guesthouse happily proclaiming the fact. The atmosphere is friendly and warm with an air of welcome and open fires; evening meals in the restaurant feature local game and seafood from the Western Isles. Neat bedrooms with fishing prints.
££ *All year exc Chr and first 2 weeks Feb; 8 rooms; fishing; shooting; stalking*

ST FILLANS
Four Seasons Hotel
St Fillans, by Crieff PH6 2NF
TEL/FAX (01764) 685333
At the edge of Loch Earn, this is a friendly and cheerful hotel with rustic furnishings and a homely atmosphere. The menu in the pretty dining-room is firmly Scottish-centred and the ingredients local and fresh. The dramatic colours of the loch can be seen from bedrooms at the front of the main house. There are hillside chalets on the slope behind.

£-££ *Closed mid-Dec to early Mar; 18 rooms; drying-room; fishing*

SOUTH LOCH TAYSIDE
The Ardeonaig Hotel
South Loch Tayside, Perthshire
FK21 8SU
TEL (01567) 820400
FAX (01567) 820282
Comfortable hotel in a picturesque setting by the loch. The small bar is welcoming and a bright open fire burns in the sitting-room. Traditional food is served in the dining-room and the Scottish cheeseboard is good. Lovely views from bedrooms with new pine furniture.
££ *All year (with limited service from Nov to Mar); 14 rooms; fishing; stalking; credit cards not accepted*

STIRLING
Forth Guest House
23 Forth Place, Riverside, Stirling
FK8 1UD
TEL (01786) 471020
FAX (01786) 447220
Cheerful house in a sombre street of Georgian terraces in central Stirling. A pretty dining-room overlooks the small garden and breakfast is served in the small sitting area at the back of the room. Evening meals can be arranged. Bedrooms are small and well equipped. The two top-floor rooms can connect to make a family suite.
£ *All year exc Chr and New Year; 6 rooms*

The Heritage Hotel
16 Allan Park, Stirling FK8 2QG
TEL (01786) 473660
FAX (01786) 449748
Characterful hotel on a leafy, residential street close to the city centre with pleasant public rooms and good food. Bedrooms are comfortable with modern bathrooms.
£ *All year; 4 rooms; drying-room*

Ravenscroft
21 Clarendon Place, Stirling FK8 2QW
TEL (01786) 473815
Cosy bed and breakfast a few
minutes from the centre of town.
The decor is stylish and comfortable
with a few antique pieces. Well-
equipped bedrooms.
£ *Mar to Oct; 2 rooms; credit cards
not accepted*

Stirling Highland Hotel
Spittal Street, Stirling FK8 1DU
TEL (01786) 475444
FAX (01786) 462929
A former boys' school, now a
business hotel with certain character
and lots of good leisure facilities.
Standard bedrooms.
££ *All year; 76 rooms; swimming-
pool; sauna; solarium; spa; turkish
baths; squash; gym; snooker*

STRATHYRE
Creagan House
Strathyre, Perthshire FK18 8ND
TEL (01877) 384638
FAX (01877) 384319
Traditional, family-run restaurant-
with-rooms in a lovely wooded
setting. A homely and relaxing
atmosphere; French-influenced
cooking is served in the rather
grand baronial-style, wooden-
floored dining-room. Bedrooms are
warm and comfortable.
£ *All year exc Feb and 1 week Oct;
5 rooms*

TUMMEL BRIDGE
Kynachan Lodge
Tummel Bridge, by Pitlochry
PH16 5SB
TEL (01882) 634214
FAX (01882) 634316
A happy combination of traditional
and unusual elements makes for a
distinctive decorating scheme in this
former sporting lodge, where
Samurai swords, antlers and
mythological figurines enliven
public areas. The dining-room is
more traditional and the menu
follows suit with well-prepared,
classical dishes. Bedrooms are
tasteful and polished.
£ *Closed Nov to Mar exc
Hogmanay; 6 rooms; drying-room;
fishing*

WHERE TO EAT

Key: A ★ marks a place that is
particularly good value for money

ABERFELDY
Farleyer House
by Aberfeldy PH15 2JE
TEL (01887) 820332
FAX (01887) 829430
Good eating options at this historic
Tayside house with Scottish bistro,
lounge and set-price format
restaurant. Informed modern
cooking, excellently handled
seafood and clever puddings; wine
prices rather steep.
*Restaurant all week 7.30 for 8, one
sitting; bistro all week 12 to 2.30, 6
to 9.30; restaurant closed Nov to Apr,
Mon to Thur (See Where to Stay)*

ABERFOYLE
Braeval Old Mill
by Aberfoyle FK8 3UY
TEL (01877) 382711
FAX (01877) 382400
Inspired cooking at miniature mill
with lively repertoire of prime
produce, delightful sauces and
perfect textures. Excellent puddings
on the limited-choice menu and a
short, quality wine list.
Sun 12.30 to 1.30; Tue to Sat

7.30 to 9.30; closed 1 week
Oct/Nov, 1 week Feb, 1 week June

ALYTH
Drumnacree House
50 St Ninians Road, Alyth PH11 8AP
TEL/FAX (01828) 632194
Informal country-house hotel with
a winningly relaxed cooking style
and varied menu. Local produce
includes splendid wild mushrooms
and prime game. Standard wine list.
Tue to Sat only (all week for
residents) 7 to 9.30; closed 15 Dec-
31 Mar

AUCHTERARDER
Auchterarder House
Auchterarder PH3 1DZ
TEL (01764) 663646
FAX (01764) 662939
Generous three-course lunches and
a choice of dinner menus including
'A Taste of Auchterarder House'.
Well-cooked Scottish produce and
excellent no-nonsense puddings.
Claret-based, fairly priced wine list.
All week 12 to 3, 6 to 9.30 (See
Where to Stay)

BLAIRGOWRIE
Kinloch House
by Blairgowrie PH10 6SG
TEL (01250) 884237
FAX (01250) 884333
Outstanding fish and game cookery
in a beautiful setting overlooking
Loch Marlee. Vegetables are treated
royally and puddings are sublime.
Strongly French wine list, fairly
priced, with a choice of half-bottles.
All week 12.30 to 2, 7 to 9.15 (See
Where to Stay)

COMRIE
Deil's Cauldron
27 Dundas Street, Comrie PH6 2LN
TEL (01764) 670352
Good value snack and platter lunches
with 'Fisherman's' and 'Farmer's'
assortments; dinner is more formal.
Realistically priced wines and a good

selection of half-bottles.
Mon, Wed to Sat 12 to 2, 6.30 to
8.30, Sun 12.30 to 2, 7 to 8.30

DRYMEN
Clachan Inn ★
2 Main Street, Drymen G63 0BG
TEL (01360) 660824
Hearty fare in local pub setting;
stalwart options include casseroles,
fish and chips and fudge sundaes.
Children's menu available.
All week 12 to 4, 6 to 10, Sun 5
to 10

DUNKELD
Kinnaird
Kinnaird Estate, by Dunkeld PH8 0LB
TEL (01796) 482440
FAX (01796) 482289
A most luxurious setting for classy
country-house style cooking.
Delicious, exciting dishes from a
top chef combine prime local
ingredients and modern British flair.
An excellent cellar well supplied
with half-bottles and prime clarets.
All week 12.30 to 1.45, 7 to 9.30;
closed Mon to Wed from Jan to Mar
(See Where to Stay)

GLENFARG
Bein Inn ★
Glenfarg PH2 9PY
TEL (01577) 830216
A comfortable bar with a bargain
three-course lunchtime menu. Good
value plain cooking, crunchy chips
and decent coffee. Extensive wine list.
All week 12 to 2, 5 to 9.30, winter
Sun 6-9.30

KILLIECRANKIE
Killiecrankie Hotel
Killiecrankie, by Pitlochry PH16 5LG
TEL (01796) 473220
FAX (01796) 472451
Confident cooking with tip-top
produce. The fixed-price menu
offers fine contrasting flavours,
distinctive and delightful puddings
and superb Scottish cheeses. Good

half-bottle selection on the
reasonably priced wine list.
*All week 7 to 8.30; closed Jan and
Feb (See Where to Stay)*

KILMAHOG
Lade Inn ★
Trossachs Road, Kilmahog, by
Callander FK17 8HD
TEL (01877) 330152
A pub to watch, with ambitious
aspirations for both lunchtime and
evening menus. The wine list is
extensive.
*Open for food Mon to Sat 12 to 3, 6
to 9, Sun 12.30 to 5; restaurant all
week 7 to 9, Fri and Sat 7 to 9.30*

KINCLAVEN
Ballathie House ★
Kinclaven, by Stanley PH1 4QN
TEL (01250) 883268
FAX (01250) 883396
Thoroughbred service at the heart
of a sporting estate where premier
Scottish ingredients contribute to
straightforward lunches and
memorable fixed-price dinners.
Vegetarians fare well here.
International wine list.
*All week 12.30 to 2, 7 to 9 (See
Where to Stay)*

KINNESSWOOD
Lomond Country Inn ★
Kinnesswood, by Loch Leven
KY13 7HN
TEL (01592) 840253
Good home cooking and a simple
bar menu at this Victorian country
inn near Loch Leven. Facilities

include three family rooms and an
outdoor play area.
*Mon to Fri 12 to 2.30, 6 to 9, Sat
and Sun 12 to 11*

KIPPEN
Cross Keys ★
Main Street, Kippen FK8 3DN
TEL (01786) 870293
Jaunty pub located in the middle of
the conservation village. Scottish
regional recipes feature; generous
portions, carefully prepared.
*Open for food 12 to 2 (Sun 12.30
to 2) 7 to 8.45*

PERTH
Number Thirty Three
33 George Street, Perth PH1 5LA
TEL (01738) 633771
Specialises in sparklingly fresh
Scottish seafood with delicious
accompanying sauces. Vegetables
get special treatment, and puddings
are good.
*Tue to Sat 12.30 to 2.30, 6.30 to
9.30; closed 25-26 Dec, last 2 weeks
Jan*

WEEM
Ailean Chraggan
Weem, by Aberfeldy PH15 2LD
TEL (01887) 820346
Pretty inn where tourists, fishermen
and hikers enjoy consistently good
food. The menu is strong on freshly
caught and cooked fish. Traditional
puddings and a decent wine list
with half-bottle choices.
*All week 12-2, 6.30 to 9.30,
weekdays in winter 6.30 to 8.30*

FIFE AND ANGUS

- Golfing country – Carnoustie and St Andrews
- Ancient ports and fishing villages, a royal palace and some fine stately homes
- Gentle, fertile landscapes, with the isolation and grandeur of the Angus glens to the north as well

St. Andrews Cathedral

THE peninsula of Fife lies between the twin firths of Forth and Tay. North of the Tay, the Grampian mountains rise above the fertile countryside of Strathmore, bounding the district of Angus. Fife and Angus are rich farming country for the most part, and the inland scenery, except where the Angus glens penetrate the Grampian massif, is unspectacular, though wherever you find a hill you will usually find first-class views to go with it. It is the coast which draws most visitors − either to see the ancient trading ports and fishing villages along the coast of Fife, or else to play the renowned golf courses on the links.

Before the Forth and Tay bridges were built, Fife was effectively cut off from the rest of Scotland by the long estuaries. In the Dark Ages it may have had its own king − locals still like to refer to the Kingdom of Fife. In 1975, Fife was the only part of Scotland to mount a successful resistance against plans to partition it between neighbouring regional authorities. Even today, most of the visitors who arrive by car must pay to get into the region, for both Forth and Tay bridges carry tolls. St Andrews, on the eastern fringe, was once the religious and academic centre of pre-Reformation Scotland. Modern-day pilgrims go there to see the spot thought of as the home of golf.

Dundee, on the north bank of the Tay, is the fourth largest

THE PICTS

The *picti*, or painted ones, was the name given by the Romans to the inhabitants of the land beyond Hadrian's Wall. In the third century AD, most of what is now Scotland was under Pictish rule, but 700 years later, after the unification of Picts and Scots under Kenneth MacAlpine in AD 843, they appear to have been either absorbed or subjugated.

For a race which left behind it such graphic monuments in stone and silver, frustratingly little is known about the Picts. Although Pictish kings began to be converted to Christianity as early as the sixth century, during St Columba's lifetime, we have no identifiable manuscripts from Pictish monasteries to rank with those from Anglo-Saxon England (though the famous *Book of Kells* may be a

city in Scotland. Famous for the three Js of jute, jam and journalism, it also has a long history as a trading, ship-building and whaling port. It is not a beautiful town but gives life and energy to the agricultural surroundings of both Fife and Angus.

The Eastward look

The ports up and down this coastline (especially after the loss of Berwick to the English) provided Scotland's trading link with the rest of Europe. Before the trade with America from Glasgow shifted Scotland's industrial energies towards the west, merchants from the coasts of Fife and Angus were busy importing and exporting to the Baltic, to the Hanseatic ports and to the Low Countries. Timber, cloth, fish and wool were the staples of this trade, and the long history of weaving in the small towns of Angus is linked to it. You can also find echoes in the Baltic timber that lines the rooms of old houses, and in the distinctive domestic architecture of places like Culross, Pittenweem or Crail, with hints of Holland or Lübeck. Whaling was an important industry in the nineteenth century, the oil used to soften jute. It was in Dundee, too, that the ship was built which took Captain Scott to the Antarctic for the first time.

Pictish manuscript). We have no knowledge of what language the Picts spoke – where we find the Ogam script carved on stones it is unintelligible – while Latin records are confined to a list of Pictish kings and a few inscriptions. Nor, apart from what we can see on their carved monuments or interpret from the remains of their houses, do we know much about what they looked like (at one time they were thought to have been pigmies but evidence from burials shows otherwise), how they lived, or how their society worked, although the historian Bede claimed that they practised matrilineal succession.

What we do have are the symbol stones which once must have existed in hundreds or even thousands over the land. These enigmatic and elaborately beautiful works of art (see later in the chapter) show us glimpses of a culture of which it would be a joy to know more.

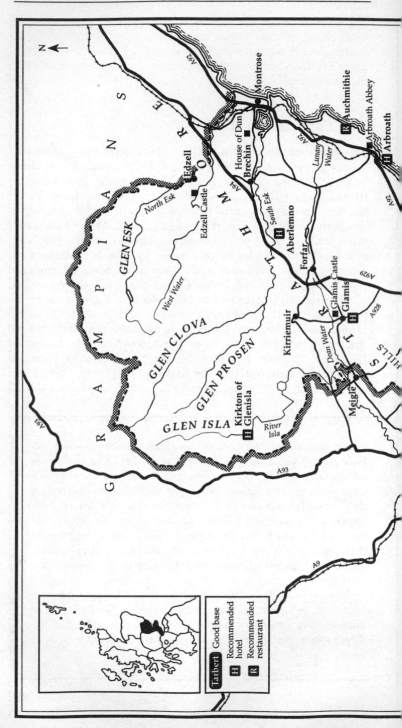

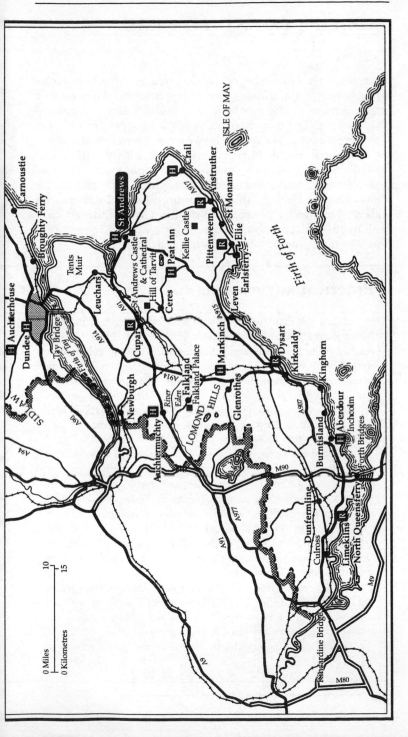

THE FIFE COAST TO CRAIL

Culross

Lost among a landscape of cooling towers, the sixteenth-century burgh of Culross survives intact in the industrialised upper estuary of the Forth. It was rescued and restored by the National Trust for Scotland over a 50-year period. It is a showpiece and, like other showpieces, gets crowded. Four or five steep cobbled streets are lined with pantiled and harled cottages; a small square has a replica mercat cross and a seventeenth-century tolbooth which now acts as the visitor centre. Luckily, there is nothing twee about the old village. Despite its photogenic qualities it has the air of a well lived-in place, though there is little now to suggest that this was once one of Scotland's major trading ports.

Practical suggestions

If you are a golf fiend, or if you want to be beside the sea, Fife and Angus should be among your choices for a Scottish holiday. Lovely beaches are to be found round these coasts, while the golf courses rival those of Ayrshire or East Lothian. A further reason for coming to this area is to explore the glens of Angus. They are off the tourist trail and there is plenty of variety among them, whether you are driving or exploring on foot. Finding good accommodation there may be difficult – many of the people you meet will be the self-sufficient type who prefer tents.

The most rewarding way to see Fife and Angus is to wander slowly through the area from the south, with Aberdeen as your eventual goal. Culross, Falkland, the East Neuk of Fife and St Andrews are the obvious stopping points. St Andrews is important and attractive enough to be worth the effort of getting to, even if you do not wish to spend longer in Fife. If you do, climb the Lomond Hills for views, go to the folk museum at Ceres and the Deer Centre near Cupar, visit Falkland Palace and wander the long sandy coastline at Tents Muir.

The Tay road bridge takes you straight to Dundee, from where you can either go up the coast to Arbroath with its abbey, or head north to Strathmore to visit the Iron Age and Pictish remains, the pick-your-own farms and the old weaving towns.

Accommodation is plentiful in the coastal towns and villages of

At the top of the steep hill behind the village are the remains of **Culross Abbey** (HS, access from keykeeper; details at site). The old choir and tower are now the site of the parish church, and there is little left of the rest. Nevertheless, it is worth the climb for the peaceful surroundings and the views over the Forth.

Even if you are not there on the occasions when the **Study** (NTS, open mid-Apr to early Oct, daily 1.30 to 5), with its panelling and painted ceiling is open, do not miss the **Palace** (NTS, open mid-Apr to early Oct, daily 11 to 5), the grandest house in the village and the best place in Scotland to see how prosperous merchants of the seventeenth century lived. Sir George Bruce made his money from coal and salt panning. He also had fingers in foreign trade, for he used Baltic timber and Dutch tiles to decorate his palace. You wander through the three different

---

both Fife and Angus, though you may have very much less selection inland.

Good bases
● **St Andrews** has few rivals in the region. The ruins of its cathedral and its castle mark its previous importance, while the Royal and Ancient Golf Club on the sandy links is the symbol of its modern claim to fame. It has the oldest university in Scotland to lend life to the streets, a wide choice of hotels and guesthouses to stay in, and some magnificent beaches within easy striking distance.

● **Earlsferry and Elie** These two burghs form the nicest resort on the north Forth coast. They are blessed with a long sea front with rocks, golf and caravans at one end and sand and a lighthouse at the other. The burghs are old, and there are attractive houses to see. Earlsferry and Elie do not draw quite the same crowds as the more picturesque villages of Anstruther and Pittenweem to the east. Accommodation is mostly of the seaside guesthouse type, but there is plenty of it.

● In **Angus**, Arbroath, though less interesting than St Andrews, is a possible seaside base for a night or two. Inland, the small towns of Angus – Forfar, Kirriemuir and Brechin – are not especially lively places to stay. There is more to be said for staying briefly in Dundee – it may seem like many another industrial city, but it has a humour and accent all its own.

ranges of the palace by a circuitous route which makes you feel it is much larger than it is. There are spiral stairs and corner rooms, old fireplaces and a fireproof and burglar-proof strongroom. The panelling and the decorative painting are the high points. The Allegory ceiling has 16 worthy scenes, each with a motto, painted on the pine barrel-vaulting. 'Mens pleasures fond do promeis only joyes. Bot he that yeldes at lengthe him self destroyes' reads one – a suitable reflection if you are tempted into the village pub for lunch. The National Trust for Scotland has filled the house with sixteenth- and seventeenth-century furniture and has restored the neat garden to reflect horticulture of the same period.

East of Culross, **Charlestown** and **Limekilns** are also ancient, though very much less compact than Culross; they do not receive the same flood of visitors.

North Queensferry

The northern terminal for the old ferry across the Forth (and now for the bridges) is little more than a cluster of houses. But, nearby, **Deep Sea World** (open Apr to Oct, 10 to 6; Nov to Mar, 10 to 4; weekends 10 to 6) was created from a deliberately flooded quarry. A moving walkway crosses the 'ocean floor' with fish of all descriptions swimming above and alongside. It is enthralling for children, and a good spot to know of for a wet day.

Dunfermline

Back in the reign of Malcolm Canmore (1005–1034), Dunfermline was the site of a royal palace. The abbey was founded by David I, and the royal burgh remained a favourite among Scottish kings. The old ballad *Sir Patrick Spens* starts with the King sitting 'in Dunfermline toun, drinking the bluid-red wine', before despatching Patrick Spens on an ill-fated voyage to Norway.

Edward I of England found an excuse for burning the abbey in 1303; the Scots, he said, had turned it into a den of thieves by holding their rebellious parliaments there. The zealots of the Reformation who destroyed more of it required no such justification. Yet the abbey (HS, standard times; closed Thur pm and Fri in winter) is enjoyable as much for its history as for its beauty, for this is where the Scottish kings were buried after Iona had become vulnerable to Norse raiders. This is where Scotland's saintly Queen Margaret, fleeing from the Norman Conquest of England, married Malcolm Canmore, and proceeded to establish a priory on the site of an old Celtic church. This too is where she was buried, her shrine in the old Lady Chapel becoming a place of pilgrimage.

Dunfermline's most famous burial is signalled from afar. The words 'King Robert the Bruce' are woven in stone on the balustrade of the tower of the nineteenth-century parish church, which was built on the site of the abbey's choir. In 1818, while the foundations for the church were being dug, the remains of the Bruce were unearthed. A plaster cast was taken of his skull, and he was left to lie in peace.

The magnificent Norman nave is really the only part of the old abbey church worth careful study. There are huge pillars and a substantial west door flanked by towers. Most of the domestic buildings of the monastery were pillaged long ago, but the remains of the refectory are palatial – you can see why a thirteenth-century chronicler stated that two monarchs with all their retinue would have room and some to spare. Even less is left of the old royal palace – one wall only.

Dunfermline was the birthplace of Andrew Carnegie, the American steel magnate whose philanthropic bequests ran into millions. There is a museum about his life at the cottage where he was born (open Apr to end Oct, Mon to Sat 11 to 5, Sun 2 to 5; Nov to Mar, daily 2 to 5), but his most eloquent memorial here is the beautiful park of **Pittencrief Glen**, which he bought and gave to the town. Dunfermline's linen industry is remembered in the **Dunfermline Museum** (open Mon to Sat 11 to 5), which has samples of fine damask and a hand-loom. **Abbot House** (open daily 10 to 5) is a small heritage centre in a medieval building with displays on the history of Dunfermline.

Aberdour

The town's castle stands almost next door to the sunny old-fashioned railway station with its beds of flowers, where families once poured off the train (most now come by car) and headed for the Silver Sands beach – perhaps the same beach where Sir Patrick Spens was walking when he got the King's fatal letter telling him to put to sea. Aberdour is the nicest resort on this part of the coast – a solid, dignified-looking place with views over the Forth to Edinburgh.

Aberdour Castle (HS, standard times, closed Thur pm

and Fri in winter) was a Douglas stronghold, and for a crucial period the residence of the Earls of Morton. When Mary Queen of Scots' secretary, Riccio, was murdered in Holyrood Palace (see box, page 282) in 1566, the Earl of Morton was one of the principal conspirators and had to leave for England in a hurry. He was soon back however, helped to force Mary to abdicate, and eventually became Regent, before being executed on the charge of having had a hand in the death of Darnley, Mary's second husband.

The castle's heart is a very ancient tower – possibly the earliest remains are eleventh-century. This part is badly ruined, so the sixteenth- and seventeenth-century extensions are more interesting to wander around. The gardens are by far the best part of the castle – the seventeenth-century walled garden is filled with colour, and the terraces beneath the castle are also delightful.

East of Aberdour lie **Burntisland** and **Kinghorn** – the former with extensive sand, the latter notable as the place where Alexander III, the last of Scotland's Celtic kings, was thrown off a cliff by his horse in 1286. He was apparently hurrying, heedless of advice to the contrary, to rejoin his second bride, the sensuous Yolande of Dreux. His death marked the end of Scotland's golden age.

His successor was his grand-daughter, Margaret, the Maid of Norway, who was declared Queen at the age of three. For a moment all seemed to be going well, for a treaty was signed in 1290 which agreed to marry Margaret to the son of Edward I of England, thus solving at a stroke the problems which existed between Scotland and Norway and Scotland and England. But the little girl, sent from Norway when she was only eight, died in Orkney – from seasickness, it is said. With her went Scotland's last hope, for there were now 13 claimants to the throne; the only person in a position to adjudicate was Edward I of England, and he – as became clear – expected feudal obedience in return for his decision.

Kirkcaldy

The curious scent of linseed oil and twine which used to hang over Kirkcaldy came from the manufacture of linoleum, for which this town was famous. Kirkcaldy is not attractive – traffic schemes ruin its dignity and its modern architecture is undistinguished – but it may be worth running the gauntlet of the town centre if you want to see the collection of paintings by McTaggart and Peploe, who are particularly well represented in the Museum and Art Gallery here (due to open late spring 1996 after refurbishment, Mon to Sat 10.30 to 5, Sun 2 to 5), along with the pottery for which the town was also known. The industrial section will initiate you into the secrets of linoleum-making.

Elie and Earlsferry

Strung out around a bay between a rocky headland and a sandy one, these two burghs have gradually merged into one large seafront village – although when walking or driving from one end to the other, you pass through two distinctively different old centres. Elie, at the eastern end of the bay, is where the sand is and where the harbour lies tucked under the lighthouse. Earlsferry has a rocky headland and some prosperous and substantial houses.

Although it fills up on fine weekends, the resort seldom gets really crowded. It is a gentle, respectable sort of place, where you can play on the sands or go golfing or sailing, but where there are not many opportunities for raucous self-indulgence. Elie's best-known bather was Lady Janet Anstruther, who used to make her servants ring a bell when she was about to go in for a dip, so that the populace would know to keep away. Earlsferry is said to be the place where Macduff, in flight from Macbeth, was ferried across the Forth. He managed to get the town made a royal burgh as a result, with the stipulation that the inhabitants should always convey any fleeing criminal over the Firth, and should not allow any other vessels to put to sea until the fugitive had got halfway across. All the town's charters were burnt in an Edinburgh fire, so it is not worth putting this to the test.

St Monans and Pittenweem

From the west, St Monans' T-shaped fourteenth-century church seems to be standing on its own. However, steep wynds leading down to the cottage-lined harbour lie beyond it and there is more modern housing on top of the hill. The church's tower and short spire give it a solid, reassuring appearance; inside the church, a model ship hanging from the roof emphasises the community's reliance on the sea, and you can even hear the waves on the rocks outside.

Pittenweem, the next fishing town to the east along the stretch of coast known as the East Neuk, is a more substantial place. The 'weem' part of the name refers to the cave in the village (Cove Wynd, key from the Gingerbread Horse shop), said to have been the retreat of St Fillan. The cave is still a shrine, though the entry is through a building that looks more like a harled public convenience. A stone altar stands on one side, and there is a blocked-off staircase once used by smugglers. Pittenweem was once the twelfth richest town in Scotland, and the substantial seventeenth-century houses are a mark of that prosperity. The prettiest part is down by the harbour, where piles of orange or green nets dry in the sun, and seagulls wheel above the fishing boats. Many of the red pantiled cottages with their crow-step gables bear small National Trust markers, for the towns of the East Neuk are where the National Trust for Scotland's 'Little Houses' restoration scheme has probably had its greatest impact.

Kellie Castle

(NTS, castle open mid-Apr to end Oct, daily 1.30 to 5.30; garden and grounds all year, daily 9.30 to sunset)
This castle is well worth the short diversion from the coast, even if you only have time to look at the exterior. Two fifteenth-century towers are linked by a later sixteenth-century building, and the result is a curious T shape. A walk round the outside reveals contrasting architecture, from the four-square simplicity of the eastern tower to the turrets, corbelling and crow-step gables of the south-west one.

The story of its nineteenth- and twentieth-century 're-discovery' and restoration by one of Scotland's most talented families gives Kellie a touch of romance lacking in its previously prosaic history. Professor Lorimer, father of the architect Robert Lorimer, took over the tenancy of what was becoming a crumbling ruin in 1878, and the preservation and revitalising of the house is largely as a result of the efforts of three generations of a family who loved the place. You can sense this as you wander through the interior, for it is adorned by their work and governed by their taste. The ancient painted panelling and the fine seventeenth-century plaster ceilings are complemented by paintings, fabrics and furniture which are often Lorimer in inspiration or design. One room is given over to the work of Robert Lorimer, but it is mostly the achievements of his daughter-in-law, Louise, that have turned Kellie Castle into a genuinely homely place. The garden too is largely a Lorimer production.

Anstruther

This is the biggest and the most touristy of the East Neuk towns. People come here for the Scottish Fisheries Museum (open Apr to Oct, Mon to Sat 10 to 5.30, Sun 11 to 5; Nov to Mar, Mon to Sat 10 to 4.30, Sun 2 to 4.30), which has an extensive collection of creels, models and old photographs, some lovely paintings by local artist John McGhie, the reconstructed sitting-room of a fisherman's house, and a mini-aquarium whose contents provoke squeals from visiting school parties.

In the strung-out harbour, families dodge amongst the cars along the harbour-front, gazing into the gift shops and licking ice-creams. There is a small sandy beach.

Anstruther is the starting point for trips to the **Isle of May**, which lies some five (often choppy) miles out into the Forth. Birds are the draw here, especially the puffins. Boats run between May and end September, and depend on the tide; with a 30–40 minute crossing either way, and one to three hours on the island, the trip takes four or five hours. Warm clothes and a picnic are essential – call (01333) 310103 for information. Three-hour fishing trips with rods and bait supplied are also available.

Crail

The most compact and the prettiest of the East Neuk towns has a winning combination of a broad High Street, a delicate golden-brown harbour with steep wynds running down to it, a crescent of sand backed by cliffs and a strong smell of fish to prove authenticity. There is a tiny town museum (open Easter week, June to Sept, Mon to Sat 10 to 1, 2 to 5, Sun 2 to 5; mid-Apr, Sun 2 to 5; May, daily 2 to 5) and a harbour-master with a forceful personality ('To steal this life-belt shows your own value of human life'). A short walk along the coastal path will give you the best of the views of the Bass Rock and North Berwick Law on the far side of the Forth. The church goes back to the thirteenth century and has an earlier Pictish cross slab. While there is nothing particularly special to pick out Crail from the other towns on the coast, it is the best to see if you have time only for one.

ST ANDREWS

If you stand in the middle of the scanty remains of the cathedral of St Andrews, you are at medieval Scotland's spiritual heart. What is now an unassuming university town and seaside resort was once as influential as Edinburgh or Stirling, while the men who ruled here as bishop or arch-bishop – Lamberton, Beaton, Sharp – were often as power-ful as Scotland's kings. St Andrews owed its ecclesiastical pre-eminence to the tradition that the Greek monk Regulus landed here with relics of the apostle Andrew in the year 345. St Andrew became patron saint of Scotland, and his relics remained here until they were lost at the Reformation.

In fact, the earliest Christian settlement at St Andrews is more likely to date from the eighth century, and to have been more closely connected to Northumbria than to Greece. Whatever the case, St Andrews grew increasingly important, and became an archbishopric in 1472.

It is hardly surprising that the cruellest dramas of the Scottish Reformation were played out here. The reformer Wishart was burnt beneath the castle walls, and his per-secutor, Cardinal Beaton, was murdered in his turn (his body thrown into the castle's dungeon and covered in salt to preserve it). John Knox studied and preached here and was taken forcibly from the castle after a year's siege to serve on the French galleys. In the seventeenth-century religious convulsions, the Archbishop of St Andrews was waylaid and butchered by Covenanters a few miles away.

St Andrews has the third oldest university in the United Kingdom, founded in 1411, where three of Scotland's fifteenth-century poets – Dunbar, Douglas and Lindsay – studied, where the reflector telescope was invented, and where Mary Queen of Scots planted a thorn tree. Its stu-dents wear red gowns – legend has it that they could be more easily recognised entering brothels if thus clad. The best way of seeing the university's ancient buildings is to take one of the organised tours, which run twice daily from July to September.

Most foreign visitors come to St Andrews because of golf, for, although it is not the oldest golf club in the country, the Royal and Ancient Golf Club is now recognised as the ruling body of the sport, and St Andrews with its four courses draws enthusiasts from all over the world. Almost all the golfing activity takes place at the north-western corner of the town, where the Royal and Ancient Club House stands. Here are the big (and pricey) golfing hotels, and the museum of golf.

However, if your interest lies elsewhere, you can ignore the sport entirely and still find much to please you. The burgh has an untouched medieval street pattern, with North, South and Market Streets fanning out from the cathedral; it is a pleasing combination of university town, classy resort and shopping centre for a large rural area. Very little architectural vandalism has taken place, and there are many buildings from the eighteenth century and earlier. If you come to the town during the Lammas Fair on the second Monday and Tuesday in August (a medieval survival), you will find the centre packed with stalls and amusements.

To the north of the town lies the West Beach, a long, dune-backed stretch of sand pounded and furrowed by the breakers of the North Sea. The further you venture along here, the more you will have it to yourself. A second beach, less attractive but more accessible, lies just to the east of the town, and there is the old harbour (built from the stones of the cathedral and castle) to fish in as an alternative. St Andrews still thrives as a family seaside resort, of the gentle, slightly old-fashioned, donkey-riding kind, and if you are lucky enough to hit a spell of fine weather you are unlikely to be disappointed by it.

As far as accommodation goes, you have a choice between the big hotels, where there will be golf balls on sale at reception, and the large numbers of guesthouses, many of which are well used to sandy children. The Byre Theatre is one source of evening entertainment, but if you visit the city in term time you will find a wide range of events.

The main sights

• **St Andrews Cathedral and Precinct** (HS, standard times, joint entry ticket with St Andrews Castle available) Not much remains of what was once the greatest church in Scotland, but luckily what the Reformation mob and the stone-quarriers left behind is striking. The great east front stands alone and unsupported by prop or buttress, looking as though the next gale will blow it flat like a domino. At the opposite end of what was once the nave, the single remaining spike of the western front hangs above the small houses of Market Street like a spiritual lightning conductor. Round these, the foundations, sections of arcaded wall, a few thirteenth-century windows and the stumps of great pillars

325

are all that remain of a building which was started in 1160 and consecrated in 1318 in the presence of Robert the Bruce.

Although it must once have been dwarfed into insignificance by the cathedral which stood beside it, the twelfth-century **Church of St Regulus**, or St Rule, has re-emerged into the light with the cathedral's ruin. A single square tower, over 100 feet high, rises almost alone from a forest of gravestones, with a small Saxon choir at its base. This was the predecessor of the cathedral. Climbing the tower in the constrictions of the tiny spiral stair can be claustrophobic and dizzying, but the view of the town from the top is worth the effort. From here you can see how all the cathedral precinct was enclosed by a strong wall (the fourteenth-century gateway into it called the Pends is now traversed by cars rather than canons). Outside the wall lie the foundations of the even earlier Celtic church, **St Mary of the Rock**, whose clergy were gradually displaced in favour of Augustinian canons under the remodelling of the Scottish church on Roman Catholic lines carried out by Queen Margaret and Malcolm Canmore.

Do not leave the cathedral precinct without looking at the **museum**, where among the collection of early Christian sculptured stones is a sarcophagus, a blend of Pictish and Anglian work, with David killing a lion, surrounded by all kinds of vividly carved animals running full pelt.

● **St Andrews Castle** (HS, standard times) The castle, strikingly poised on the sea's edge, was in fact the bishop's palace – and a notable prison for reformers. It was from here that Cardinal Beaton watched Wishart being burnt beneath the walls, and from here that his own murdered body was displayed to the crowd. Although there is not much left of the building, two fascinating features remain. One is the bottle dungeon, carved 24 feet down into the rock and narrowing towards the trap-door at the top, through which prisoners and food were dropped alike. Of all Scotland's nasty dungeons, this is the one in which it would be easiest to despair. The other relic of the castle's history is the mine and counter-mine. When the reformers (disguised as masons) broke into the castle and murdered Beaton in 1546, they held the place for a year against all efforts to take them. One such effort was a mine – a tunnel from outside the walls – against which the chosen defence was an opposing tunnel – the counter-mine – driven to meet it. You stumble down the narrow counter-mine to the spot where besieged and besiegers met in an underground clash, pedestrians scurrying along the pavement above your head. A joint entry ticket to the castle and cathedral is available.

● **British Golf Museum** (open mid-Apr to mid-Oct, daily 10 to 5.30; mid-Oct to mid-Apr, 11 to 3, closed Tue and Wed) This high-tech venture will tell you all you ever wanted to know about golf. As well as exhibits of golfing memorabilia, there are endless audio-visual gadgets – tapes, touch-screen computers and videos – that allow you to test your own knowledge of the game or to watch the winning shot of the 1974 Open. Enthusiasts will happily spend a day here, while there are curiosities to interest the non-golfer too, such as the history of golf ball making, from the days of the leather-and-feather ball onwards, or the fact that James II banned the game – it was keeping people from archery practice.

Other things to see

Of the university buildings, **St Salvator's College**, founded in 1450, retains its fifteenth-century church and tower, **St Mary's College** has a sixteenth-century range, and **St Leonard's Chapel** has been well restored to recreate its old medieval lay-out. **St Andrews Preservation Trust Museum** (open Easter, June to Sept, daily 2 to 5) in North Street has relics of old St Andrews, mostly from Victorian times. The **West Port**, at the head of South Street, is a rare survival of an old burgh gateway, still holding up the traffic. The **Burgh Kirk** – Holy Trinity – is fifteenth-century in origin, but heavily restored. Inside is a grotesquely decorated marble memorial to the slaughtered Archbishop Sharp. Only scanty fragments of **Blackfriar's Chapel** remain from another of St Andrews' once-thriving religious foundations.

In College Street, spare a thought for one of Scotland's more peculiar lovers, Pierre de Châtelard. This French gallant seems to have contracted a passionate obsession for Mary Queen of Scots, to the extent of twice intruding into her bed-chamber. The second occasion was once too many – the cross in the street marks the spot of his execution. His last words were 'Adieu the most beautiful and most cruel princess of the world.'

Round St Andrews

If you are keen on church architecture, drive up the unattractive estuary of the Eden, past the smelly paper mill at Guardbridge and through the outskirts of the huge base at

RAF Leuchars to **Leuchars Church**, where the chancel and apse are outstanding in twelfth-century Norman style. It is a pity that the surroundings are not more attractive, but the church is certainly worth discovering. If you are travelling by train you will have the chance to test the platforms at Leuchars station, which are said to be the windiest in Scotland.

North of Leuchars, reached from the B945, the great stretch of beach, dunes and pine forest called **Tents Muir** extends from the northern bank of the Eden estuary almost as far as Tayport at the mouth of the Tay. Two nature reserves are to be found here, as well as networks of coastal or inland walks and picnic sites. Although a very popular spot for fine weekends, Tents Muir is too big for you to feel cramped by over-organisation, and is thoroughly recommendable for a day by the sea (though swimming may be hazardous because of currents).

INLAND FIFE AND THE NORTH COAST

Falkland Palace

(NTS, open Apr to end Oct, Mon to Sat 11 to 5.30, Sun 1.30 to 5.30)
This was once the favourite hunting lodge of the Stewart kings. At one time there was to have been a courtyard surrounded by buildings, but there was never a west range and only the south and east ranges remain. It was James IV and James V who were responsible for most of what you see today, and the result is a Renaissance building, owing much to the French. The frontages are decorated with pillar buttresses, medallions and ornate dormer windows, and some crafty work has been done on the south range to give an impression of a symmetry which does not in fact exist.

Falkland was the scene of James V's death. Afflicted by despairing melancholy after the defeat at Solway Moss in 1542 (see page 36), he was not consoled by the news of his daughter's birth. 'It came wi' a lass and it'll gang wi' a lass,' he exclaimed, referring to the Stewart dynasty; but his daughter, Mary Queen of Scots, enjoyed the hunting here.

The restoration of the interior of the south range is entirely thanks to the efforts of the Crichton Stuart family, who became hereditary keepers of the palace in 1887. The rooms here are done as far as possible in the style of the seventeenth century, with exact reproductions of furniture and painted ceilings. Among many ancient pieces, look out for the ornate James VI bed and the magnificent tapestries. Two rooms in the east range have also been restored as bed-chambers, one as the 'King's Room' containing the seventeenth-century Golden Bed of Brahan, made in the East Indies.

Falkland Palace has two further points of interest – the tennis court and the garden. The tennis court (royal or 'real' tennis, of course) is the oldest in Britain. Unless you are lucky enough to see a game being played (a local club plays on summer weekends), you will probably be left unenlightened about exactly what happens, despite the efforts of the guidebook to explain the obscure rules. The garden is easier to appreciate. Laid out after World War II to complement the frontage of the palace rising behind it, it is a mass of herbaceous colour from May onwards, while its subtle design only gradually reveals itself as you walk round. Do not leave Falkland without wandering round the old burgh, where there are some well-preserved and photogenic old houses.

Ceres and around

Ceres, midway between Falkland and St Andrews, is a small, quiet, attractive village, worth going to for the sake of the **Fife Folk Museum** (open Easter weekend, mid-May to end Oct, daily 2 to 5, closed Fri), which is housed in the old Weigh House and a couple of weavers' cottages. What raises this folk museum above the many similar ones is the strong sense of community involvement demonstrated by the book of donations – some items even come from Canadian emigrants. This manages to give life and unity to the collection of domestic utensils, scales, milk churns and relics of the weaving industry. Ceres is just about large enough for an hotel and an antique shop or two. If you want a really quiet village to stay in, you might consider this one.

Not far north, **Hill of Tarvit** (NTS, house open Easter, May to end Oct, daily 1.30 to 5.30; garden and grounds all year, daily 9.30 to sunset) forms a fascinating comparison with Hill House near Helensburgh, and it is almost worth the drive across central Scotland to see the two in sequence. Both houses were designed by renowned Scottish architects – Lorimer and Mackintosh respectively – for wealthy industrialists. In 1902, at Hill House, Mackintosh had to compromise with his client's taste; in 1906, at Hill of Tarvit, Lorimer had to design (or, strictly, remodel) a house round the collection of paintings, furniture and porcelain amassed by the Dundee jute manufacturer Frederick Sharp. In both houses, the smallest details of design are governed by the imagination of the architect.

At Hill of Tarvit, Lorimer's public rooms provide 'correct' settings for the collections they were designed to hold, without descending into pastiche. Thus the entrance hall, panelled in oak, looks baronial enough to show off the Flemish tapestries which hang there, but is none the less original. The drawing-room, filled with French furniture, is, in its plasterwork and woodwork, pure eighteenth-century France, while the magnificence of the Palladian-style dining-room sets off the Georgian furniture which fills it.

Of the many things to look at, the collection of Dutch paintings, the silverwork and the Chinese porcelain are all good. Do not ignore the more modern side to the house with its Wizard vacuum cleaner with continuous suction and the shower with its ascending spray. Do not miss the gardens either – another Lorimer design.

Finally, a few miles away, the **Scottish Deer Centre** (open Easter to end Oct, daily 10 to 5) is much less tacky than the initial impression of souvenir shop, restaurant and ice-cream kiosk might suggest. In fact, once you have seen the excellent audio-visual, and taken a tour round the fields to look at and learn about deer, you come away both well informed and well satisfied.

DUNDEE

Of the three Js that made Dundee, it was jute that turned it into a flourishing industrial town (look for the chimney known as Cox's Stack which is said to be wide enough for a taxi to drive round the top). The jam and the journalism have had more influence on the rest of the country, however, for Dundee is where marmalade, using Seville oranges, was first invented, and it is the home of the *Beano* and other publications from the D.C. Thomson stable.

One of the most idiosyncratic is the *Sunday Post*, a newspaper with a curious stuck-in-the-1950s mixture of homely gossip and sentimental patriotism which has become a staple of popular Scottish culture. All Scots will recognise 'Oor Wullie' – the spiky-haired comic-strip urchin whose seat is an upturned bucket. The *Sunday Post* is heartily loathed by those trying to awaken Scotland to the modern world, but many a Scot in exile will fall upon a chance copy with cries of joy all the same.

Dundee is not a pretty place, but equally it is a city without artifice, with plenty of humour and plenty of life. It suffered from constant sackings during Scotland's many wars, from Edward I's burning in 1296 to Monck's effective pillaging during the Cromwellian invasion of 1651. It may be that the habit of rebuilding their town became so ingrained in Dundonians that they could not give it up. Little survives from before the nineteenth century, and much of the city centre is entirely modern, though sculptures and murals brighten it up. Dundee is busy sprucing up its tourist attractions – a new visitor centre down by the docks is one example. Don't leave town without buying a Dundee cake.

Drive up to the top of **Dundee Law**, a volcanic plug sticking out of the city centre. Beneath you, the Tay road bridge runs apparently diagonally across the estuary. The rail bridge lies a little further upstream, and you may be able to pick out the stumps of its predecessor beside it – a reminder of the disaster of 1879 when it collapsed as a train was crossing it. The famous elegist of the disaster is the poet William McGonagall, who lived in Dundee for much of his life. Widely hailed as the worst poet in Scotland if not the world, and subject of endless parodies, McGonagall has now become something of a cult figure:

So the train mov'd slowly along the Bridge of Tay
Until it was about midway,
Then the central girders with a crash gave way
And down went the train and passengers into the Tay
The Storm Fiend did loudly bray
Because ninety lives had been taken away
On the last Sabbath day of 1879,
Which will be remembered for a very long time.

Sights in Dundee

● *Discovery* **and** *Unicorn* The ship in which Captain Scott voyaged to the Antarctic in 1901 returned to Dundee, where she was built, in 1986. Now *Discovery* (open Apr to end Oct Mon to Sat 10 to 5; Nov to Mar, Sun 11 to 4) has been restored apart from her engines and populated with realistic models. The visitor centre at **Discovery Point** uses brilliant audio-visual techniques to tell the story of the ship and her captain, and introduces you to the minutiae of arranging an Antarctic expedition. The *Unicorn* (open daily 10 to 5) berthed nearby, looks more of a hulk than a warship from the outside, for she has no masts. Launched in 1824, she is one of the oldest warships still afloat. Below decks, long rows of guns sit on their carriages, and there are various exhibits about nineteenth-century naval life.

• **McManus Art Gallery and Museum** (open Mon 11 to 5, Tue to Sat 10 to 5) Partly built as a memorial to Prince Albert, this museum is a shrine to Victoriana. A high-ceilinged gallery contains collections of over-elaborate china, glass and silver-gilt which once graced Victorian dinner tables, while the Victorian gallery is expertly hung and displays ranks of sentimental paintings with titles like 'Funeral of the First Born'. There are also good displays on Dundee's history and its industries. Great fun.

THE COAST TO MONTROSE

East of Dundee, you arrive at **Broughty Ferry**, a fishing village which developed into a suburb of Dundee when the 'jute princes' built their houses here. Castle enthusiasts should delve into the estates on the north-western side of the town to find **Claypotts Castle** (for access arrangements call 01786 450000), which is a complete example of a sixteenth-century Z-plan castle. The practice of squaring off and corbelling a tower to provide an extra room at the top is here carried to such extremes that the whole castle seems in danger of overbalancing.

On the far side of Buddon Ness, which juts sandily into the Tay but is mostly occupied by the military, **Carnoustie** is renowned for its championship golf course, but is also a small seaside resort, with fine sand. East Haven, a little further along the coast, is a much smaller beach, half-hidden by the cliffs on both sides.

Arbroath

It is difficult to know whether Arbroath is more famous for its 'smokies', its abbey, or the declaration of Scotland's freedom from English overlordship which was signed here in 1320. It is a solid red sandstone town with the ruins of the abbey squarely at the centre and a working harbour and rows of fishermen's cottages beneath. Down by the harbour, every second house has a sign offering fresh smokies, and it is senseless not to sample this smoked haddock while you are here. Boat trips run from the harbour to visit local caves and cliffs or to go sea fishing.

The Signal Tower Museum gives an insight into the local fishing and jute industries, with careful explanations of how smokies are produced.

Arbroath Abbey

(HS, standard times)

A satisfactory amount is left of the great red thirteenth-century abbey church – certainly enough to see that it must once have been a splendid place, lit by the huge round window in the western gable – of which only the lower half remains – and the remarkable lancets in the transepts. There is plenty for architecture enthusiasts – notably the variety of the patterns of the arcades – while the fifteenth-century sacristy and abbot's house are sufficiently complete to give a good impression of at least a part of the monastic life. The gatehouse which once led into the walled precinct of the monastery remains intact.

The Declaration of Arbroath, which was signed here on 6 April 1320, confirmed the Scottish nobility's support for the kingship of Robert the Bruce, and was taken to the Pope at Avignon. It was an important step in Scotland's intense diplomatic effort after Bannockburn to gain international recognition for the independence won on the battlefield. The declaration was probably drafted by the abbot of the time, Bernard de Linton. If so, he had a good line in rhetoric, as the ringing phrases of the document's most famous passage (in translation from the Latin) prove: 'For, so long as one hundred remain alive, we will never in any degree be subject to the dominion of the English. Since not for glory, riches or honours do we fight, but for freedom alone, which no good man loses but with his life . . .'

St Vigeans

By driving past an industrial estate on the northern outskirts of Arbroath, you arrive at a cul-de-sac where a small red church stands on a high mound, surrounded by low cottages. The tiny village is named after a seventh-century Irish saint, and has the atmosphere of an ancient sacred site. In one of the cottages you can see the collection of Pictish stones found (HS, for access arrangements call 01786 450000).

Although not quite so inspiring as the collection at Meigle they are more than worth the brief excursion.

Lunan Bay

The cliffs north of Arbroath are suddenly broken by the sweep of this classically beautiful beach, found on many a postcard but often deserted for all that. Above the sand there is the gaunt ruin of a red sandstone castle, while at either end of the bay rocky headlands jut into the sea.

Montrose

With its tidal basin behind it and the sea to its front, Montrose seems almost cut off by the sea; it looks like a town from a Dutch painting as you approach it from the south. Apart from being the birthplace of the famous Marquess of Montrose, it has had remarkably little share in Scottish history, and remains a peaceful, rather sleepy place, with a broad High Street. The museum – purpose-built in 1842 – has prints, paintings, boxes of shells and stones and curious pieces of historical flotsam, such as a bicorn hat, said to be Napoleon's. There is also an evocative message found in a bottle: 'No water on board, provisions all gone. Ate the dog yesterday, 3 men left alive . . .'

PICTISH STONES

The majority of carved Pictish stones are concentrated in eastern Scotland, especially around Strathmore in Tayside, the fertile areas of Moray, Banff and Aberdeenshire, and the Tain and Dornoch peninsulas. A couple of hundred have survived, and many more may lie buried or built into houses. These stones seem to have been carved between the sixth and ninth centuries, and vary from unshaped slabs of stone with designs incised into them, to elaborate monuments or Christian cross-slabs with intricate patterns and figures carved in relief. The stones are remarkable enough for the scale and beauty of their carving, but what must intrigue even the most casual onlooker is the meaning of the symbols with which many of them are embellished. Mirror and comb, double disc, Z-rod, serpent, crescent and the curious beast known as the 'swimming elephant' are the most common, and they appear on

Behind the town, **Montrose Basin** is almost landlocked, and at low tide it becomes a great pool of mud. Attractive it is not, but for naturalists it is one of the best places to see duck and waders in huge numbers.

INLAND ANGUS

Reekie Linn

Follow the B954 north from near Alyth to **Bridge of Craigisla** for Reekie Linn, one of Scotland's best waterfalls: the river plunges suddenly into a deep gorge. From the car park there is little warning of what is to come, but a very short walk brings you to the top of this 'smoking fall'. There is an even better viewpoint on top of a jutting cliff a little further on. Wild broom clouds the whole place yellow in early summer. The urgent warnings to take care are justified – there is no protection.

Glamis Castle

(Open Apr to end Oct, daily 10.30 to 5.30; tours run every 10 to 15 mins and last 50 to 60 mins)
Royal and literary connections draw the crowds here. The

---

their own, as part of a secular scene, or on a Christian cross-slab alike. Furthermore, they are common to all of Pictland, their use cutting across boundaries between tribes or kingdoms.

What these symbols meant to the people who used them (and they were not just carved on stones but on humbler objects too) is unknown. One theory is that the stones are memorials to people or events denoted by the symbols. Another is that they are property markers, with the symbols representing different genealogies. Neither of these interpretations seems entirely satisfactory when you are confronted by the detail of the carved symbols themselves.

Pictish stones were mostly free-standing uprights. Many remain in their original positions in open countryside, and it can be quite a job to track them down. Others are to be found in churchyards to which they have been moved. The best indoor collections are at Meigle in Tayside, St Vigeans in Angus, St Andrews in Fife, Dunrobin Castle in Sutherland and in the Royal Museum of Scotland in Edinburgh.

multi-turreted pinkish pile of Glamis Castle is not only the traditional scene of Macbeth's murder of Duncan, but also the home of the Queen Mother's family – the Bowes-Lyons, Earls of Strathmore and Kinghorne. The grounds surrounding the castle were remodelled in best eighteenth-century style: as you approach down a long, straight avenue flanked by trees, the conical turret caps reveal themselves, followed by a village-worth of chimneys and towers. Although the core of the castle is fifteenth-century or earlier, its present appearance is largely a result of late seventeenth-century work.

At the busiest times, tours through the sequence of grand rooms turn into one of those delicately balanced affairs whereby as soon as one group leaves a room, another files in behind it. This puts pressure on the time-keeping of the guides, who none the less manage to sustain a serious and thorough commentary. The highlights are the painting of the third Earl dressed in what looks like see-through armour, the jester's outfit (he got the sack for making a pass at a lady in waiting) and the plaster ceilings of the drawing-room and billiard-room. The chapel is decorated with seventeenth-century painted panels by Jacob de Wet (see also Holyrood) on walls and ceiling. It is said he was so outraged by his low pay (£90 for four years' work) that the night before he finished, he endowed his 'Christ mistaken for a gardener' with a floppy hat and gave St Simon a pair of spectacles. Look too for the gloomy St Andrew obviously wondering how the two fishes he carries can possibly feed five thousand. The chapel has a ghost – that of Lady Janet Douglas, burnt for witchcraft. The royal apartments, arranged as a suite after the Queen Mother's marriage into the royal family, are simultaneously homely and ornate. From the comfort of these rooms you come to Duncan's Hall, in the oldest part of the castle, where, standing beneath a large stuffed bear, the guide explains the Shakespeare connection. The family exhibition contains a wide variety of curiosities from a violin-playing monkey to the Old Pretender's watch (stolen by the maidservant who cleaned his room when he stayed here in 1715).

Glamis has a noticeably relaxed and pleasant restaurant to end up in, and plenty of space in the grounds to stroll through. An extremely complicated sundial stands beside the castle, precisely three degrees west of Greenwich.

Angus Folk Museum

(NTS, open Easter to early Oct, daily 11 to 5, early to end Oct, Sat and Sun 11 to 5)
In the village of Glamis, and making a very good counterpoint to the splendours of the castle, this museum is housed in a number of old cottages and stuffed with artefacts from the everyday life of the nineteenth and early twentieth centuries. The cottages are themed so that you move from a laundry to a weaving room, kitchen, schoolroom and nursery. A well-put-together and well-laid-out place.

Kirriemuir, Forfar and Brechin

J. M. Barrie, creator of Peter Pan, was born in Kirriemuir. His birthplace, 9 Brechin Road (NTS, open Easter, May to end Sept, Mon to Sat 11 to 5.30, Sun 1.30 to 5.30; Oct, Sat 11 to 5.30, Sun 1.30 to 5.30), is easily missed if you are not keeping a close watch. Exhibits in this small museum are a mixture of furnishings such as Barrie's writing desk, accounts of theatrical performances, photographs and newspaper cuttings. For our salacious era, the various cuttings suggesting that Barrie was more than just a friend to the Llewellyn boys he eventually adopted make intriguing reading.

Forfar, an old weaving town, lies six miles south-east of Kirriemuir. Go into the town if you want to see the horrible Forfar bridle, used to restrain witches as they were burnt. It is in the local museum, **The Messan** (open Mon to Sat 10 to 5), which takes you back to Forfar's past with old shops and re-created sounds and smells.. Otherwise, take the B9113 eastward to see the remains of the twelfth-century **Restenneth Priory** (HS, access from keykeeper; details at site), or follow the B9134 to **Aberlemno** to see the Pictish carved stones here. There are four of them, the best, with its entwined beasts and its battle scene, being in the churchyard.

On top of the nearby **Finavon Hill** are the remains of one of the most accessible vitrified forts in the country. There are still wrangles over whether the fused stonework of these Iron Age defences was created by deliberate burning of fires round them, or whether it was the result of enemy assault. If you wish to see more of the Iron Age remains, head north-east for the twin Iron Age forts at **Caterthun** up behind Brechin, which are again very accessible. A lot of stonework can still be seen, and the outline is clear.

Most people pause in the steep little town of Brechin to

look at the round tower (HS, access from keykeeper; details at site), which like the one at Abernethy dates from the tenth century and is similar to those found in Ireland. It stands beside the little cathedral, much of which was either restored or rebuilt at the beginning of the century, although parts are thirteenth-century.

The Angus glens

The glens running north from Strathmore into the Grampians make an attractive contrast to the lowlands of Angus. The hills surrounding them are not of the dramatic, craggy kind, but are high, rounded lumps, often heather-covered, which merge into the high plateaux which separate Strathmore from Deeside. It is not until you get further east into Grampian region that roads manage to penetrate through the massif, though a network of old tracks and drove roads radiates from the head of the Angus glens, notably from **Glen Clova** and **Glen Doll**. For exploring by car, both **Glen Clova** and **Glen Prosen**, with roads on either side, allow round trips, while you can travel furthest into the mountains up **Glen Esk**.

At the westward side of the district, the upper stretches of Glen Isla and the tributaries of Glen Finlet and Glen Taitney can all be explored easily enough on foot, though there are a lot of trees about. Glen Prosen is more open, and the woods more attractive. Glen Clova is where Scott planned his expedition to the Antarctic, and a memorial stands by the foot of the glen. This is probably the most popular of the Angus glens – if you want more solitude, try the road which runs up beside West Water behind Brechin, from Bridgend to Waterhead. Glen Esk, up behind Edzell, is a long haul through rolling scenery. Loch Lee, at the head of the glen, is a good spot for walking if you like a watery backdrop. **Glenesk Folk Museum** (open Easter to end May, Sat to Mon 12 to 6; June to mid-Oct, daily 12 to 6) diverts you en route.

Unless you are bent on doing some strenuous walking through to Deeside or across the tops, the Angus glens are best sampled as slow excursions on a fine day, with time to stop beside the rivers or just to look at the views. The midges may, as usual, put paid to any idea of evening picnics – otherwise the country looks its best at this time of day.

Edzell Castle

(HS, standard times closed Thur pm and Fri in winter)

On a warm day there are few more pleasant spots than this. Historic Scotland's curator will be mowing the grass or planting seedlings in the grounds of the ruined red castle, an elegant affair built by the Lindsays in the sixteenth century. However, it is not so much the ruins as the castle's pleasance which charms. This is a tiny walled garden, created in 1604 in that short period between the union of the crowns and the outbreak of the civil and religious wars when it seemed that Scotland had time at last for a few luxuries. The walls are set with *bas reliefs* of improving subjects such as the Cardinal Virtues and the Liberal Arts, and the niches between them spill white and blue flowers over the red stone. In the centre, formal parterres are surrounded by a box hedge which picks out the Lindsay motto. In one corner stands a summer house (there used to be a bath house in another). The best view of the garden is to be had from the upper floors of the castle: here you can best see the perfection of the layout.

House of Dun

(NTS, house open mid–Apr to end June, Sept, daily 1.30 to 5.30; July to end Aug, daily 11 to 5.30; Oct, Sat and Sun 1.30 to 5.30; garden and grounds open all year, daily 9.30 to sunset)

Newly restored by the National Trust for Scotland, this William Adam mansion is primarily for lovers of elaborate plasterwork, for the huge trophies and emblems by Joseph Enzer which decorate the public rooms are extraordinary. Dun was an Erskine holding from the fourteenth century, though the house itself dates from 1730. The Earl of Mar (called 'Bobbing John' after his political vacillations) was in exile after his failed Jacobite rising in 1715 but seems to have influenced the design of the place nevertheless, for he was always writing to his kinsman, David Erskine, with suggestions for the new house, and the elaborate plaster-work certainly contains cryptic Jacobite symbolism. However, the design of the house is unmistakably Adam, with its slightly severe façade, its first-floor library and its chimney-pieces and fireplaces.

The second character of influence to the house, as becomes plain from the awe in which the guides seem to hold

USEFUL DIRECTORY

Kingdom of Fife Tourist Board
6/7 Hanover Court, North Street
Glenrothes KY9 5SB
(01592) 750066

Angus & City of Dundee Tourist Board
4 City Square, Dundee DD1 3BA
(01382) 434664

Tourist Board publications Angus and City of Dundee *Visitor's Guide*, Kingdom of Fife Holiday Guide (planned for 1997) – listings include main sights, sports, accommodation plus What's on Guide. Special interest: guides on golf (St Andrews & NE Fife, Kirkcaldy). Postal or phone orders from the above addresses.

Local tourist information centres
Anstruther (01333) 311073 (Apr to Sept)
Arbroath (01241) 872609
Brechin (01356) 623050 (Apr to Sept)
Burntisland (01592) 872667
Carnoustie (01241) 852258 (Apr to Sept)
Crail (01333) 450869 (Easter to Sept)
Cupar (01334) 652874 (Easter to Sept)
Forfar (01307) 467876 (Apr to Sept)
Kirriemuir (01575) 574097 (Apr to Sept)
Kirkcaldy (01592) 267775
Leven (01333) 429464
Montrose (01674) 672000 (Apr to Sept)
St Andrews (01334) 472021

Local transport
For Dundee, Kirkcaldy and Leuchars rail services (0345) 212282
Edinburgh British Rail central booking (0131) 556 2451
Fife Scottish Omnibuses (01334) 474238
Moffat & Williamson Bus Co. (01382) 22155
Strathay Scottish Omnibuses (01382) 228054

Other useful information
Boat trips to Isle of May daily from Anstruther Harbour, May to Sept, also fishing trips (01333) 310103
To find out about playing golf at St Andrews, phone the Links Management Committee (01334) 475757
For weather conditions in the Angus Glens area of the Grampians phone (0891) 500442 (pre-recorded information)

her, was Lady Augusta, an illegitimate daughter of King William IV, who married into the family in 1827. She was responsible for most of the fine needlework, including that which decorates the huge four-poster given to her as a wedding present by her father. She also did a lot of work in the gardens, collecting plants from the surrounding country-side on outings in her yellow carriage.

One of the best curiosities at Dun (though it does not belong to the house) is 'Mr Riach's Performing Theatre of Arts', a miniature child's theatre, with about 200 cut-out characters. A video shows how it was used. Even if nothing else in the house charms you, this will.

WHERE TO STAY

£ – under £70 per room per night, incl. VAT

££ – £70 to £110 per room per night, incl. VAT

£££ – over £110 per room per night, incl. VAT

ABERLEMNO
Wood of Auldbar Farmhouse
Aberlemno, near Brechin DD9 6SZ
TEL (01307) 830218
This Victorian stone house is part of a working mixed farm. Dinners are served in the sun room; children's helpings and packed lunches can be arranged. Neat bedrooms.
£ *All year exc Chr and New Year; 3 rooms; credit cards not accepted*

ARBROATH
Rosely Country House Hotel
Arbroath DD11 3RB
TEL/FAX (01241) 876828
Intriguing country house built for a wealthy jute merchant in 1845 still full of fascinating paraphernalia. Good home-cooked evening meals served. Some antique beds come from local castles.
£ *All year; 14 rooms; credit cards not accepted*

AUCHTERHOUSE
Old Mansion House
Auchterhouse, by Dundee DD3 0QN
TEL (01382) 320366
FAX (01382) 320400
Atmospheric baronial house on the river a short drive from Dundee. The vaulted entrance and the coffered ceiling of the library bar hint at the extravagant ornamentation of the dining-room and Jacobean fireplace. The menu here leans towards traditional Scottish favourites. All bedrooms are comfortable, the best lavish.
££ *All year exc 24 Dec to 4 Jan; 6 rooms; tennis; outdoor heated swimming-pool; squash court; croquet*

AUCHTERMUCHTY
Ardchoille Farm
Dunshalt, Auchtermuchty KY14 7EY
TEL/FAX (01337) 828414
Farmhouse with views of the Lomond Hills. Vegetarian choices are offered at dinner and packed lunches may be arranged. Small bedrooms, thoughtfully stocked with extras. Bunks can be added for children.
£ *All year exc Chr and New Year; 3 rooms*

CRAIL
Selcraig House
47 Nethergate, Crail KY10 3TX
TEL (01333) 450697
A 200-year-old stone house near
Crail harbour, with Edwardian-
themed decoration throughout.
Dinner is served in the pretty
dining-room; excellent breakfasts.
Pleasantly furnished bedrooms.
£ *All year; 5 rooms with wash-
basin; credit cards not accepted*

DUNDEE
Hillside Guest House
43 Constitution Street, Dundee
DD3 6JH
TEL (01382) 223443
Merchant's house with a mix of
antiques and good furniture. Breakfast
is served in the conservatory. Pastel
bedrooms; the best overlook the river.
£ *All year; 4 rooms; credit cards not
accepted*

GLAMIS
Castleton House
by Glamis, Forfar DD8 1SJ
TEL (01307) 840340
FAX (01307) 840506
Small country-house hotel with
smart, cultivated décor and ambitious
food. Leather club chairs and a gilt
mirror furnish the bar, and the
conservatory restaurant is bright with
green-grained tables and a terracotta-
tiled floor. Floral drapes decorate the
formal main restaurant. Comfortable,
well-furnished bedrooms.
££ *All year; 6 rooms; drying-room*

HAWKCRAIG
Hawkcraig House
Hawkcraig Point, Aberdour,
Burntisland KY3 0TZ
TEL (01383) 860335
The downstairs sitting-room of this
homely, ferryman's cottage is
charming while one upstairs has a fine
china collection and views over the
Isle of Inchcolm. Food in the dining-

room is wholesome. Trim bedrooms.
£ *Closed Nov to mid-Mar; 2 rooms;
credit cards not accepted*

KIRKTON OF GLENISLA
Glenisla Hotel
Kirkton of Glenisla, by Alyth
PH11 8PH
TEL/FAX (01575) 582223
Seventeenth-century coaching inn
stylishly renovated, now a
comfortable hotel. Food in the pine-
floored dining-room is good and
involves local produce. Bedrooms
are simple yet sophisticated.
£ *All year exc Chr; 6 rooms*

MARKINCH
Balbirnie House
Balbirnie Park, Markinch, Glenrothes
KY7 6NE
TEL (01592) 610066
FAX (01592) 610529
This graceful neo-classical Georgian
mansion is a top-flight country-
house hotel. The Long Gallery with
trompe l'oeil cherubs and the public
rooms are polished and shining.
Overlooking the gardens, the main
restaurant serves ambitious food.
The bedrooms are distinctive, the
bathrooms superb.
£££ *All year; 30 rooms; drying-
room; games room; golf (See Where
to Eat)*

PEAT INN
Peat Inn
Peat Inn, Cupar KY15 5LH
TEL (01334) 840206
FAX (01334) 840530
A restaurant-with-rooms with
sublime food and enchanting
accommodation. Accomplished
cooking, marrying French
technique and Scottish ingredients.
Split-level bedrooms offer plenty of
space. Glamorous bathrooms.
£££ *All year; 8 rooms; restaurant
closed Sun and Mon eves (See Where
to Eat)*

ST ANDREWS
Glenderran Guest House
9 Murray Park, St Andrews KY16 9AW
TEL (01334) 477951
FAX (01334) 477908
Elegant Victorian terraced house in
the middle of town. The lounge is
decorated with care and bedrooms
are well equipped. Packed lunches
are available.
£ All year; 5 rooms

Rufflets
Strathkinness Low Road, St Andrews
KY16 9TX
TEL (01334) 472594
FAX (01334) 478703
Delightful gardens hide behind the
exterior of this creeper-clad hotel.
Inside, the reception is bright and
the bar stylish; comfy plaid sofas fill
the sitting-room. Traditional food is
served in the Garden Restaurant.
Well-equipped bedrooms.
*££-£££ All year; 26 rooms;
drying-room*

St Andrews Old Course Hotel
St Andrews KY16 9SP
TEL (01334) 474371
FAX (01334) 477668
Adjacent to the 17th Road Hole of
the famous links, the Old Course
Hotel is a star in its own right.
Excellent leisure facilities enhance
the showcase public areas, and
relaxed designer country-house style
abounds. Menus in the Roadhouse
Grill acknowledge a North
American clientele and food is
accomplished. Bedrooms are
glamorous with swanky bathrooms.
*£££ All year; 125 rooms; golf;
gym; sauna; solarium; swimming-pool*

WHERE TO EAT

Key: A * marks a place that is
particularly good value for money

ANSTRUTHER
Cellar
24 East Green, Anstruther KY10 3AA
TEL (01333 310378)
FAX (01333 312544)
Exceptional local seafood and
shellfish in this Fife fishing village.
Freshness and quality shine in every
dish; the simple cooking style and
presentation succeed every time.
Good puddings. Classy and
interesting wine list.
*Tue to Sat 12.30 to 1.30, 7.30 to
9; closed Chr, New Year*

AUCHMITHIE
But 'n' Ben *
Auchmithie DD11 5SQ
TEL (01241) 877223
Family-run restaurant with good
cooking; strong on fish and
shellfish, meat alternatives always
on offer. The Scottish high tea is
held in high esteem here. Good
value for money with warm
service; brief wine list.
*Wed to Mon 12 to 2.30, high tea 4
to 5.30; Mon and Wed to Sat
dinner 7 to 9.30*

CUPAR
Ostlers Close
25 Bonnygate, Cupar KY15 4BU
TEL (01334 655574)
Sample fresh local produce, home-
made preserves and pickles here.
Menus change daily but understated
simplicity rules. Good puddings;
interesting wine list, reasonably priced.
Tue to Sat 12.15 to 2, 7 to 9.30

DYSART
Old Rectory ★
West Quality Street, Dysart KY1 2TE
TEL (01592 651211)
Civilised inn above the harbour. A
distinctive Scottish flavour runs
through dishes on offer both in the
bar and in the more formal restaurant
where evening meals are served.
*Open for food Tue to Sun 12 to
2.30, Sun 12.30 to 2.30, Tue to
Sat 6.30 to 9.30*

ELIE
Ship Inn ★
The Toft, Elie KY9 1DT
TEL (01333 330246)
This busy quayside pub serves good
food based on traditional recipes.
Daily-changing menus in both the
pub and the restaurant. A good
selection of real ales and a short
wine list.
*Bar food 12 to 2.30, 6 to 9.30;
restaurant Mon to Sat 7 to 9.30*

LIMEKILNS
Ship Inn ★
Halketts Hall, Limekilns KY11 3HJ
TEL (01383 872247)
Bargain prices at this friendly pub
on the Forth. Fried haddock is a
favourite; filling cream teas.
Impressive choice of real ales and
house wine by the glass.
*Open for food 12 to 2, Sat and Sun
12 to 2.30; credit cards not accepted*

MARKINCH
Balbirnie House
Balbirnie Park, Markinch, Glenrothes
KY7 6NE
TEL (01592) 610066
FAX (01592) 610529
Attractive Georgian mansion set in a
landscaped park with golf course. The
food is ambitious and great things are
anticipated from the new chef.
*All week 12 to 2, 7 to 9 (See Where
to Stay)*

PEAT INN
Peat Inn
Peat Inn KY15 5LH
TEL (01334) 840206
FAX (01334) 840530
Cooking of the highest order, with
simplicity and freshness at the heart
of some excellent menus. Flavours,
textures and a delicate touch create
excellent dishes. Seafood and game
are royally treated; gorgeous
puddings also shine. Impeccable
wine list, good service.
*Tue to Sat 12.30 for 1, 7 to 9.30;
closed 25 Dec, 1 Jan (See Where to
Stay)*

THE
NORTH-EAST

- A country of contrasts – flat lowlands, rocky coastline and desolate mountains
- The most rewarding area of Scotland for castle-visiting
- The ancient, oil-prosperous city of Aberdeen

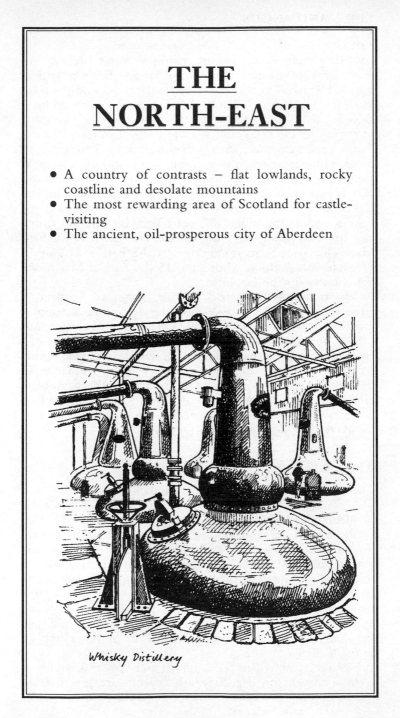

Whisky Distillery

THE Grampian mountains, rising to their highest and most desolate in the Cairngorm range, form a largely impassable massif in the centre of Scotland. Round them on three sides run the lowlands of Kincardine, Aberdeenshire, Buchan, Banff and Moray. In the past, some of the most powerful men in the country – the Earls of Moray, Huntly, Buchan and Mar – had their power base here. Too far north to be within easy reach of Edinburgh or Stirling, the great families up here were inclined to go their own way and did not always take kindly to events further south. In the eleventh-century, the men of Moray were in constant rebellion against the king; 300 years later Robert the Bruce had to break the power of the Comyn Earls of Buchan. Mary Queen of Scots fought against the Earl of Huntly in the sixteenth-century, while in 1715 the Earl of Mar raised the country for the Jacobites.

The traditional industries of this corner of Scotland – farming, fishing and whisky-distilling – have been supplemented in the last decades by oil. This turned Aberdeen into a boom town and brought much-needed business to the east coast. Three things draw visitors: the whisky distillery country of lower Speyside, the scenery and the romance of 'Royal Deeside' and the great castles of Aberdeenshire. However, there is more to enjoy than these, including two coastlines and several secret corners, such as the valleys of the River Findhorn and the River Don.

The castles

The North-East has a superabundance of castles and fine country houses. There are ruins of great fortresses (Kildrummy, Huntly) and Georgian mansions (Haddo, Duff), but the area is renowned for its beautiful tower-houses. The Scottish tower-house developed from the defensive fortress by building upwards and outwards from a thick-walled core. The medieval habit of placing rooms one above the other and linking them by a spiral stair was retained, but lateral space was created by corbelling out the upper storeys and adding turrets, towers or gabled rooms, so the houses grow larger and more intricate as you climb up through them.

Several reasons for the appearance of this style of architecture in the late sixteenth-century are given, from the continuing need for a castle that could be defended to the relative abundance of stone and the expense of good wood. The beauty of these fortress houses was recognised by the Victorians, and the nineteenth-century revival of Scottish baronial style can be seen everywhere, but there is no comparison with the originals, and the North-East is the place to see the best of them.

To avoid a surfeit, it is sensible to be selective. Our first choices would be Crathes (superb combination of house and garden), Fyvie (extravagant architecture and fine paintings), Craigievar (perfect architecture, but apt to be crowded), Huntly (romantic ruin with good architecture), Corgaff (for setting and good restoration), and Fasque (untouched Victoriana, and a different experience from all the above).

SOUTH OF ABERDEEN

Fasque

(Open May to Sept, daily 11.30 to 5.30; June, July and Aug, 11.30 to 8)

The Grampian mountains gradually pinch the valley of Strathmore into a narrow strip of countryside between the sea and the hills. This is the Howe of the Mearns, a stretch of difficult farming land, made famous as the setting for Lewis Grassic Gibbon's trilogy of rural life, *A Scots Quair.* Where the B974 breaks north through the declining hump of the mountains you come to the village of **Fettercairn**, marked by a triumphal arch in memory of a visit by Queen Victoria, and then to Fasque, the family home of W.E. Gladstone, four times Prime Minister before retiring in 1894.

Fasque is a neglected, damp-ridden, rotting white elephant of a house, abandoned – or so it seems – at the height of its splendour around 1914, and left undisturbed ever since. As such, it is a welcome antidote to the carefully restored and highly polished castles further north. In the servants' hall, ranks of chairs stand covered in dust, waiting for domestic staff who will never return. Cupboards open on heaps of rust-covered candlesticks and boot-trees; in the laundry, ranks of flat irons stand on the long-unkindled stove. A double staircase of wonderful proportions leads you up from the quiet hallway to the drawing-room above, where again, everything – portraits, furniture, china – waits suspended in its slow decay. The only moving things are the deer cropping the grass beyond the windows. One small room holds relics of the great Prime Minister – a collection

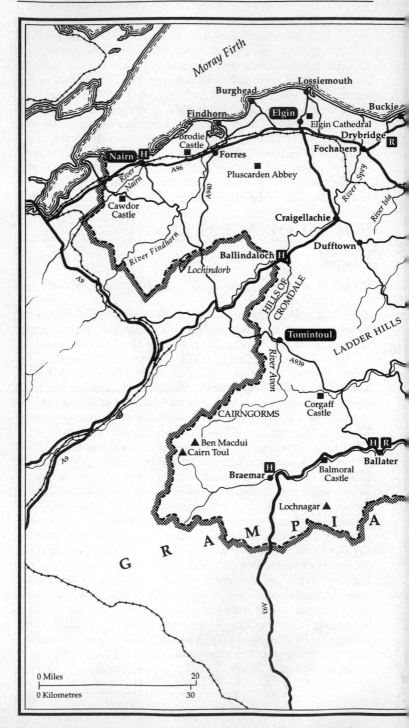

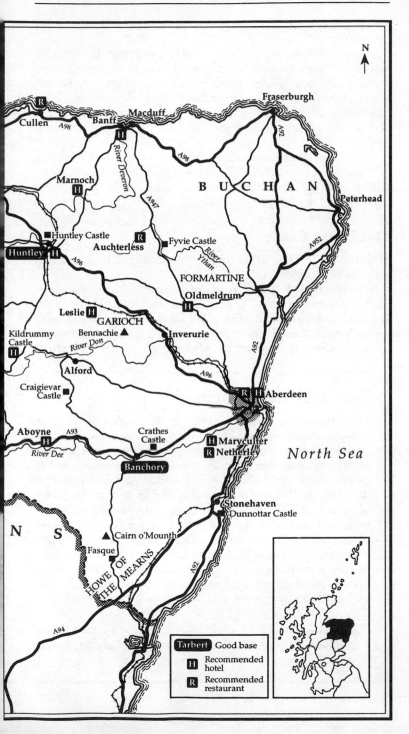

of cuttings, small gifts from constituencies, addresses from admirers.

Despite the damp, the closed-off rooms, the weak light-bulbs and the smudged handwritten notices that guide you round, this is a house which recalls a bygone way of life more potently than any of the burnished Victorian kitchens elsewhere in the country. Reason says it cannot continue – it will either decay completely or else be restored – so see it before it is lost.

North of Fasque, the road continues up the side of Cairn o' Mount, running through lonely moorland with extensive views before descending into the valley of the Feugh and arriving at Banchory.

Dunnottar Castle

(Open Mar to Oct, Mon to Sat 9 to 6, Sun 2 to 5; Nov to Feb, Mon to Fri 9 to dusk)
The coastal road (A92) from Montrose to Stonehaven is more interesting than the dual carriageway which links Dundee and Aberdeen, with good views out to sea and small villages tucked into the steep shore. There is an extensive coastal nature reserve at **St Cyrus**, while the church at

Practical suggestions

For a family seaside holiday, head for the beaches of Nairn or Lossiemouth; for Highland scenery and tough walking, Braemar and Deeside are the best areas. For gentler but still strenuous walking, try the area round Tomintoul. For fishing, unless you can afford to pursue salmon on the Dee or the Spey, start your researches with the Avon, the Don or the Ythan. For touring, head for the valley of the Don, although the coastal trail along the Moray Firth would be a good alternative. For castles, the area north and west of Aberdeen is the place to start. Golfing is good all along the north coast; naturalists should head for the east coast. If you want to bury yourself in local life, go to the farmlands of the Mearns or of Buchan. Spend at least a day in Aberdeen. A taste of all of these would probably provide the most satisfactory holiday of the lot.

Good bases
• **Tomintoul** A small village high on the edge of the Grampians,

Kineff was the hiding place for the regalia of Scotland, which were smuggled out of Dunnottar Castle during the Cromwellian invasion. The ruin of this great castle, just south of Stonehaven, is the most important stopping point.

In about 1382 Sir William Keith, Great Marischal of Scotland, came into possession of the massive crag which is almost split from the mainland. It is hardly surprising that he considered the site more suited to a castle than to the church which shared it with earlier fortifications. In demolishing the church he got himself excommunicated, but in exchange built himself a virtually impregnable fortress, for it is a steep climb over the narrow neck of land which is the castle's only point of approach.

A litter of buildings from different periods covers the crag, dominated by the fifteenth-century keep. When living conditions there came to be regarded as too primitive, a large, comfortable mansion was built in the sixteenth and seventeenth centuries. The restored drawing-room here allows superbly contrasting views of angry sea and peaceful courtyard.

Dunnottar was especially important in the period of the Scottish civil and religious wars. It was from here that the seventh Earl Marischal watched his land being burnt in 1645

---

very well placed for walking in the hills, for dropping down to visit the Speyside distilleries or for touring the valley of the Don.

● **Nairn** A friendly, quiet seaside town on the Moray Firth, with sandy seashore close by and the wooded Findhorn valley to explore. Inverness is within easy reach.

● **Elgin** An old town which grew up around its medieval cathedral and is now the shopping centre for the rich countryside around. The beach at Lossiemouth is close, as are the distilleries of Speyside, and there are a number of historic sights nearby.

● **Huntly** An elegant town with a ducal atmosphere, thanks to the remains of Huntly Castle which dominate the place. It is very quiet and off the tourist trail, but a good place from which to explore the north-east corner of the region.

● **Banchory** Of the small towns on the River Dee, Banchory is best placed for castle-visiting and is within easy reach of Aberdeen. It is a smart place, with enough business trade from Aberdeen to push accommodation prices up a little, and it is also a popular stopping place on tours of the Dee valley.

by his one-time ally, Montrose, while Andrew Cant, one of the Covenanting ministers to whom he had given refuge, told him: 'Trouble not, for the reek will be a sweet-smelling incense in the nostrils of the Lord.' It was here too that the Scottish regalia were sent for safety during Cromwell's invasion and occupation, to be smuggled out again during the eight months' siege in 1651 which ended in the castle's final capitulation; and in the sorry chapter of persecution which followed the restoration of Charles II, 167 Covenanters were crammed into a dungeon (the Whig's Vault) at Dunnottar.

Stonehaven and beyond

The old fishing town of Stonehaven, despite the fact that its beach is more shingle than sand, remains a popular resort. The oldest part is by the harbour, with the newer, predominantly Victorian town stretching up the hill behind. It is a gentle, old-fashioned sort of place – douce rather than raucous, and more suited to brisk strolls around the harbour than to getting a suntan on the beach. It comes to life on Hogmanay, with a fire festival all of its own. The old Tolbooth on the harbour's edge is Stonehaven's most venerable building, now a small museum and tearoom.

Beyond Stonehaven, a series of fishing villages lie squeezed into crannies in the cliffs, reached by short detours from the dual carriageway road. Where herring boats were once hauled bodily out of the water and the fish loaded into creels, Aberdeen commuters now return from a hard day in the office. **Findon**, one of these tiny places, has given its name to the ubiquitous Finnan haddie – the smoked haddock (which should really be peat-smoked, but seldom is) found on most Scottish hotel menus.

DEESIDE

If Queen Victoria had not bought Balmoral and turned it from a pleasant country house into a monstrosity, the River Dee and its valley would not have half the draw they do today, for 'Royal Deeside' is where the monarch has her very own self-catering property, and half the fun of travelling along the river is being able to cast an eye over the boundary fence. Balmoral apart, a trip over Glenshee and down the Dee with lunch at Braemar and tea at Banchory provides a worthwhile taste of Highland country. There is, however, something slightly packaged about the Deeside scenery, as if Nature had deliberately produced an assemblage of heather, pine forest and mountainside designed to appeal to manufacturers of biscuit boxes and picture postcards. The River Don, to the north, has a more subtle attraction.

The waterfall (more a series of rapids and a narrow gut) at **Linn of Dee** is as far up the river as you can get by road, and is the starting point for a series of medium-distance walks through the heart of the Grampians. The best-known of these is the one through the mountain trench of the Lairig Ghru to Rothiemurchus and the Spey Valley. Another route runs southwards to Glen Tilt with a branch to Glen Feshie. All these walks take you deep into the wilderness and should not be undertaken without suitable preparation, but you can explore a little further up the Dee without trouble.

Braemar

This small town lies at the bottom of the road descending from the Cairnwell pass. Because of its position it is a centre for walkers, climbers and skiers, though at 1,100 feet above sea level it is scarcely a balmy resort. It is also a popular stop for coach tours, so there are plenty of shops and places for tea. The Braemar Gathering, held in September, has the highest snob-value of all Highland Games, since the royal family usually puts in an appearance. The Gathering is also one of the largest and best, noted for the piping. If you miss the real thing, the **Braemar Highland Heritage Centre** (open daily 10 to 6) has a model of a beefy hammer-thrower and a film with plenty of royal footage.

Balmoral

Between Braemar and Balmoral the Deeside scenery is at its best, with the river plunging along beside the road and Scots pines outlined against the ridges of hills rising towards the lovely mountain of Lochnagar. From May to July the grounds and a couple of rooms of **Balmoral Castle** are open to the public (provided the royal family is not in residence – Mon to Sat 10 to 5). Walking here, you can appreciate (or not) Prince Albert's talent as castle-designer, for there seems little doubt that he played a large part in the rebuilding that went on after the royal family bought the estate in 1852. Signs embellished with Queen Victoria's head lead you to other royal sights throughout the region.

Ballater

The town started its life as a spa when an old woman bathing in a nearby peat bog cured herself of scrofula and her discovery was exploited by the local Jacobite laird, who had just been reprieved from execution. If this does not sound auspicious, Ballater is nevertheless quite a good stopping point on the road downstream, being less crowded than Braemar and not quite so refined as Banchory. It is also the place from which to explore the road up Glen Muick – a favourite for those on the trail of Queen Victoria, but also worth a detour in its own right. One good reason for coming up here is to climb Lochnagar: it is a relatively easy ascent, but quite a dangerous mountain, with numerous vertical cliffs dropping abruptly from its summit. Views from the top on a clear day are the best in the eastern Highlands. Various walks also lead from near Ballater over the Mounth to Glen Esk in Angus. Arranging some way of getting back is usually the hardest part of such expeditions.

Five miles downstream of Ballater, the flat expanse of **Dinnet Moor** is peppered with lochans, scrub birch and Scots pine. The landscape was formed after the last Ice Age, and is now a nature reserve.

Banchory

Banchory is sufficiently close to Aberdeen to be commutable, as well as making an excellent place for the entertaining of business clients. Consequently, you are apt to find that the posher hotels have helicopter pads and plenty of room for salmon rods. The fishing on the Dee in this area is renowned (and correspondingly pricey). Even if you are not in the helicopter league, Banchory's shops and tearooms are worth a stroll. An exploration of the valley of the **River Feugh**, which joins the Dee here, takes you into peaceful woodland, where in autumn the crimson rowan, russet bracken and pale yellow birch are as well coordinated as if an interior designer had arranged them.

Crathes Castle

(NTS, castle opens Apr to late Oct, daily 11 to 5.30; other times by appointment; garden and grounds open all year, daily 9.30 to sunset)

This is the very best of the Aberdeenshire sights, combining as it does a sixteenth-century tower-house, which is second only to Craigievar in the balanced elegance of its architecture, with a twentieth-century garden which will be enthralling to keen gardeners. Leave yourself at least two hours to explore.

The main part of the house was finished in 1596. Its heart is an L-shaped building with narrow slits of windows. At about third-floor level the house starts growing outwards. A smooth wall bulges and throws out a half-column, which rises for a further two floors until a sudden lateral corbelling allows space for a tiny rectangular room before a further forward corbel supports the battlemented parapet. Elsewhere the sequence is reversed, with the rounded corners of the main walls abruptly squared off, corbelled, and crowned with a round pepper-pot turret or a square gabled tower. The word organic could be applied to this architecture – its shape is reminiscent of a huge beech tree.

Crathes is famous for its painted ceilings, which are among the best in Scotland. Three remain, with a whole gallery of characters, emblems, mottoes, grotesques and patterns taking up every cranny of the awkward spaces around the beams. Unfortunately, little of the decoration in the vaulted High Hall has survived, though there is enough to show how pretty it must have been. The ghost at Crathes is well documented (a good ghost apparently adds to visitor numbers), while a more tangible relic of the castle's antiquity is the Horn of Leys, given by Robert the Bruce to an early member of the Burnetts, the family who owned and lived in Crathes for more than 350 years. The finest room in the castle is the Long Gallery right at the top, which has a beautiful oak-panelled ceiling and views over the gardens below.

The gardens at Crathes are the work of the thirteenth baronet and his wife, Sybil. In the walled garden and among the venerable eighteenth-century yew hedges in front of the castle they planted a remarkable series of colour gardens, by and large following the designer Gertrude Jekyll's principles, but with the addition of their own considerable originality. The current gardens were started around 1926. The most unusual border is the Colour Garden, where yellow, red and bronze combine superbly. The Golden Garden, developed by the National Trust after Lady Burnett's idea, is another inspiring section. Among the shrubs, keep an eye open for the *Eucryphia glutinosa* which covers itself in white flowers in the shelter of the great yews, and for the many interesting viburnum, cornus and berberis varieties. If you still have the energy, there is a further wild garden among the trees beyond the old wall. The plant sales area is good evidence of the skill and interest of the gardening staff.

Drum Castle

(NTS, house open mid-Apr to late June and Sept, daily 1.30 to 5.30; July to end Aug, daily 11 to 5.30; Oct, Sat and Sun 1.30 to 5.30; grounds open mid-Apr to late Oct, daily 10 to 6)

This castle stands about five miles downstream of Crathes and is a very different building, for here an early seventeenth-century mansion has been tacked on to a square thirteenth-century keep. This old tower is actually the more interesting part for it survives almost intact, with the exception of the former Great Hall of the keep, which was turned into a library and incorporated into the newer house. The storeroom, the upper hall and the battlements demonstrate what an impregnable (if uncomfortable) fortress Drum used to be. Views from the battlements are worth the steep climb. The interior of the mansion house has been heavily Victorianised, but a few of the older features remain. There are good portraits of, and plenty of detail about, the Irvine family, who held Drum from the time of Robert the Bruce. A small arboretum in the grounds provides a pleasant short walk.

THE LECHT AND THE RIVER DON

Tomintoul

Tomintoul squats on the very edge of inhabitable country at the top of Strath Avon. The rolling plateaux of the Ladder Hills start just beyond the village, while the great tops of the Cairngorms lie to the south. Despite its height of 1,160 feet, this is not the highest village in Scotland – that honour goes to Wanlockhead in Dumfries and Galloway. Tomintoul looks strange in its isolated setting, for it is a planned village, created from scratch in 1779 with its long street and central square. The main road east jinks sideways out of the village – if you do what comes naturally and follow the main street to its end, you end up on a track.

In the country round Tomintoul there is a choice of medium-distance highish-level walks, while the Glenlivet

Estate (owned by the Crown) to the north of the village has an abundance of waymarked routes, some of which are suitable for mountain biking. Pony-trekking is available in summer and cross-country skiing in winter (the ski slopes of the Lecht are also in easy reach). Accommodation is not abundant, but it should be possible to find somewhere to stay. Tomintoul has a small **museum** of local life (open Apr, May and Oct, Mon to Sat 10 to 5; June and Sept, Mon to Sat 10 to 6, Sun 2 to 5; July and Aug, Mon to Sat 10 to 7, Sun 2 to 5), with a well-conceived reconstruction of an old smithy.

The Lecht Road (A939) running between Tomintoul and Strath Don is a splendid piece of eighteenth-century engineering; it was largely built by the military after the 1745 rising. It is still one of the first roads in Scotland to be blocked by snow and as you travel over the pass through the Ladder Hills it is easy to see why, for expanses of windswept moorland stretch in all directions, a blaze of purple when the heather is in bloom. The climb up the pass from Tomintoul is relatively gentle but the road rushes in recently improved sweeps down the other side until, in a suddenly green strath just beyond the few scattered houses of Cock Bridge, you reach the River Don and Corgaff Castle.

Corgaff Castle

(HS, standard times; Sat and Sun in winter)
Thanks to an enthusiastic curator and an excellent restoration by Historic Scotland, a visit to Corgaff Castle is well worth the short climb up from the car park. It is a miniature sixteenth-century white tower surrounded by a curious star-shaped wall and, despite its isolation, has an eventful history. This started with a nasty massacre during a patch of local rivalry when James VI was a child, and continued with an occupation by Montrose in 1645. At the time of the Jacobite uprisings, Corgaff, thanks to its isolated position, acted as a rallying point and weapon store. After Culloden, the Hanoverians turned it into a stronghold – part of the network of watch-posts on the Highlands – and it is this period that produced the exterior fortification against musketry and that the interior restoration represents. Life for the garrison was not exactly comfortable – five or six double beds fill the small rooms. Corgaff lingered on as a military post until 1831, although by then the soldiers were watching for illicit stills rather than Jacobites.

Glenbuchat Castle

(HS, access at all reasonable times)
Follow the River Don along the A944 and A97 for the next two castles. Glenbuchat is easily missed, for it stands directly above the road, but the ruined, unfrequented, sixteenth-century Z-plan castle is worth a stop. There is easily enough left to give you a good impression of what it was like to live here – rather comfortable by the look of things. The last Laird, 'Old Glenbucket', is one of the tragic figures of the Jacobite years. Having already fought in the rising of 1715, he returned to the field at the age of 68 to take part in the desperate retreat from Derby and was with Prince Charles at Culloden in 1746. Thereafter, with a price on his head, he was forced, like so many others, to spend months living rough and dodging the Redcoats before eventually escaping from Scotland by sea. He died in poverty in Boulogne in 1750.

Kildrummy Castle

(HS, standard times; closed in winter)
Only a few miles beyond Glenbuchat, Kildrummy is a very different kettle of fish. It was once a huge medieval fortress, seat of the Earls of Mar, and symbolic of that noble family's power and status.

Edward I of England may have supervised some of the building work which raised Kildrummy's four towers and produced its imposing gatehouse. He no doubt regretted this during the Wars of Independence, for Kildrummy became a Bruce stronghold, and held out against the English until the garrison was betrayed from inside – in this case a treacherous blacksmith set fire to the store of grain in return for as much gold as he could carry. His reward was paid in the form of molten metal poured down his throat. Kildrummy's second claim to fame is as the place where much of the plotting for the 1715 Jacobite uprising occurred, for it was the sixth Earl of Mar who raised the standard for that revolt.

Kildrummy is now ruined – only the foundations of the gatehouse and of the Snow Tower remain, and the rest has been much used as a stone quarry. However, enough remains to show how strong the place must once have been.

Kildrummy Gardens

(Open Apr to late Oct, daily 10 to 5)
A certain Colonel Ogston bought Kildrummy Castle in

1898 and built a new castle (now an hotel) nearby. Needing a garden to go with it, he commissioned a Japanese firm to make a water garden in the 'Back Den', the ravine which provided the defensive cover for the back of the old castle. Among the rocks of the old quarry on the fringes of the Den, an alpine garden was constructed. Since the colonel's time the gardens have gone through periods of neglect, but are now well re-established under a trust. The primary appeal of the planting is in the old quarry, where acers and rhododendrons are blended skilfully in the tumbled rock. The water garden, apart from some magnificent gunneras and a good collection of *Primula florindae*, is less interesting. There are some fine specimen trees. This is less a garden for specialists than Crathes but is a stimulating example of naturalistic planting, and, especially in autumn, makes for a colourful and peaceful stroll.

Craigievar Castle

(NTS, open end Apr to early Oct, daily 1.30 to 5.30; grounds all year, 9.30 to sunset)
From Mossat the A944 follows the Don eastward to Alford, the landscape becoming flatter but dominated by the shapely peak of **Bennachie**, a mountain of no great height yet visible from every quarter. Four miles to the south of Alford on the A980 stands Craigievar, a castle widely held to be the apotheosis of the tower-house.

Craigievar was not built for the convenient shepherding of bus-loads of visitors, and the National Trust has been keen to discourage the mass tourism which has been damaging the building, so you won't find many references to it in tourist literature. But the castle is still open, and well worth finding, for the architecture is fascinating. The solid L-shaped trunk of the house blossoms effortlessly into a whole village-worth of gables, balustrades and bartizans. It is worth walking slowly round the outside looking at the constantly changing perspectives of the roofs.

Internally, Craigievar is very different from Crathes. William Forbes of Menie, who had 'made a goodly pile merchandising at Danzig' was obviously keen to impress. Quite what his contemporaries made of his taste is unrecorded, but time has dulled the excesses and it is possible to admire Danzig Willie's medieval-style hall, complete with its vaulted ceiling, musicians' gallery and massive coat of arms, without suffering the temptation to giggle.

Decorative plasterwork is Craigievar's forte: there is scarcely a room without a superb moulded ceiling. The one in the Queen's Room (apparently named in hope of a visit rather than as the result of one) is the best of these. At the very top of the house, the Long Room runs the entire width of the castle and is plain and beautiful with its small alcoves.

Alford

Montrose won a victory over the Covenanters near this large village, which is now home to the **Grampian Transport Museum** (open all year, Mon to Sat 10 to 5), a large, if antiseptically displayed, collection of ancient vehicles. A narrow-gauge steam railway is part of the set-up and there is also a heritage centre. From Alford, side roads follow the Don through the Garioch district, dotted with small havens like the villages of Monymusk and Oldmeldrum, as well as less attractive spots, such as Inverurie. Seek out the **Maiden Stone** near the hamlet of Chapel of Garioch – this is the best of the many Pictish stones in the area and shows Jonah and two whales along with a Z-rod symbol and the 'swimming elephant'. If what you are looking at does not have these carvings, but is instead shaped like a nubile girl, you have been sidetracked by a rival maiden – a modern sculpture of Primavera, who stands almost opposite. The village of Oyne, close to the Chapel of Garioch, is the site for a new exhibition which will explain the history of the region's stone circles and sculptured stones. This, the **Archaeolink**, is scheduled to open in 1997.

Castle Fraser

(NTS, castle open mid–Apr to end June and Sept, daily 1.30 to 5.30; July to end Aug, 11.30 to 5.30; Oct, Sat and Sun 1.30 to 5.30; grounds all year, daily 9.30 to 6)
The appearance of the castle at the end of its avenue is distinctly French, thanks largely to the conical turrets which grace the corners of the Z-plan structure and the wings of the courtyard with their capped half-dormer windows. Although the central tower is really quite small, Castle Fraser looks a lot less compact than Crathes and less graceful than Craigievar. Nevertheless, it is actually a subtle, harmonious building, despite numerous alterations and rebuildings.

Most of the furnishings are nineteenth-century and on

the scanty side, though they give an excellent idea of how such a castle was lived in at that time. The grounds of the castle (best appreciated from the roof) have more antiquity about them – they bear the stamp of eighteenth-century landscaping. The walled garden is certainly worth a look on the way back to your car, for it is sheltered and colourful.

ABERDEEN

The Silver City has come in for a lot of flak over the past decades for having become the poodle of the oil industry – the Houston of the north – with accusations of high prices, a brash attitude and a generally unpleasant boom-town atmosphere. This is a gross exaggeration, though the city looks and feels prosperous, and some prices are geared more to expense accounts than to humble tourists. However, to avoid the city would be foolish, especially since it contains a first-class art gallery. The granite from which much of it is built really does glisten silver in the sun, though on a cloudy day, Aberdeen looks as grey as anywhere else.

Aberdeen is a mixture of St Andrews and Glasgow, with the academic atmosphere and the seascapes of the former and the bustle and some of the planning mistakes of the latter. It lies spreadeagled between the mouths of the Don and the Dee, without seeming quite certain whether its heart is the tranquil, academic area round the former or the busy seaport of the latter. Although it has a magnificent stretch of curving shoreline, Aberdeen is a riverside, not a seaside, city. The links behind the beach and the esplanade remain undeveloped, providing an open aspect in the heart of the city and a good blow of sea air for the inhabitants.

Aberdeen is also renowned for its parks. You are most likely to go to Seaton Park near the cathedral, or Duthie Park with its Winter Gardens and its beds of roses, but there are plenty more to discover.

The centre is a mixture of architecture – a few elegant Georgian buildings, plenty of Victorian, one or two hideous pieces of Post-War Municipal and modern buildings dating from the oil boom, all rather haphazardly scattered along streets which are longer than they seem to be before you start walking; a bus map will be useful. Most of the activity happens on or around the ruler-straight Union Street, especially at its eastern end by Castle Street, where the seventeenth-century mercat cross stands. The modern Bon

Accord Centre has chain stores under cover, tourist information is to be found in Broad Street, and the streets running towards and round the harbour make the best area for casual wandering. Aberdeen has a relaxed attitude to people who enjoy watching ships, and you can poke around the quays without being harassed. There is usually something going on: sea-going barges laden with drilling pipes, supply vessels for the rigs, fishing boats, and the 'North Boats' to Kirkwall and Lerwick coming or going. The fish market is already stirring into life at about 4.30am.

Walk along the northern edge of the quays towards the sea to discover the tiny planned fishing village of Footdee (or Fittie) clustered at the tip of Aberdeen harbour, with the esplanade and Aberdeen beach stretching away north of it. Fittie consists of three little squares of cottages, and is still a self-contained living community, so there is some excitement in discovering it, counteracted by the sensation that you are intruding.

Old Aberdeen

This is the area of the city up by the mouth of the River Don, containing the city's most venerable buildings. Start by wandering across the **Brig o'Balgownie**, unless you happen to be an only son riding a mare's only foal (Thomas the Rhymer predicted the bridge would fall in these circumstances, and Lord Byron – as an only son – remembered the 'awful proverb which made me pause to cross it'). This is Scotland's oldest bridge, built in the early fourteenth century, and a very beautiful single-arched structure it is.

Walk back through Seaton Park to **St Machar's Cathedral**. Only the nave and aisles remain of this largely fifteenth-century building, so it appears unbalanced from every angle except at the west front. It is imposing all the same, with twin spires and a magnificent heraldic roof in the interior, which dates from 1520. The 48 shields that compose the ceiling provide a kind of visual guide to the spiritual and secular hierarchies of sixteenth-century Scotland and Europe.

Once you have dodged the traffic on St Machar Drive, you come to a section of pedestrianised tranquillity in the High Street. This is the university quarter of Aberdeen, and is dominated by the crowned tower of **King's College** which was founded in 1495 and now comes complete with a visitor centre. It is worth exploring to have a glimpse of the chapel. The High Street has a veneer of ancient houses on either side, behind which the modern university buildings rear their heads.

Central Aberdeen

Make your way from Union Street to Schoolhill to visit the excellent **Aberdeen Art Gallery** (open Mon to Fri 10 to 5, Thur 10 to 8, Sun 2 to 5). The collection is magnificent and beautifully displayed; the slight austerity of the building is countered by a lively shop and café, and the tone varies from the formal melancholy of the War Memorial Court to the bright spaciousness of the upper rooms.

The gallery's strength lies primarily in its collection of British painting through three centuries, but the decorative arts section is almost as good – the collection of locally worked silver and of modern enamel and ceramic work on the ground floor is full of gleaming objects.

The wide range of paintings and drawings includes Blake's *Raising of Lazarus*, Piper's *Dunnottar Castle*, Millais' wonderful portrait of a self-confident young girl, entitled *Bright Eyes*, Paul Nash's windswept *Wood on the Downs*, Augustus John's sensuous *The Blue Pool*, and, among local painters, James Cowie's *Two Schoolgirls* and James McBey's simple and precise capturing of *Ythan Mouth*. Look out also for the ridiculously melodramatic *Flood in the Highlands* by Landseer.

Close to the tourist office in Broad Street stands **Provost Skene's House** (open Mon to Sat 10 to 5), the oldest domestic house in Aberdeen with title deeds dating from 1545, although most of the building is seventeenth-century. It has been restored and turned into a museum of domestic life from Cromwellian to Victorian times; as you move from room to room, you shift from one period to the next. One room has a seventeenth-century painted ceiling, over-flowing with religious imagery, showing how slow the full force of the Reformation was to catch on in these parts. To counteract the silent furniture, a rather well-acted audio-visual brings to life some of the characters who made their mark on the house over the years. A further museum is located in the **Old Tolbooth** on Union Street (open Apr to Sept, Tue, Wed, Fri and Sat 10 to 5, Thur 10 to 8, Sun 2 to 5). Here Aberdeen's civic history is lovingly explained against the background of the cells of the former prison.

You cannot miss **Marischal College**, also in Broad Street, for its frontage is a rippling maze of granite ribs, like a complicated root system or a fishing net. The college was founded in 1593, but the frontage was built in 1906 and the buildings behind are only slightly earlier.

In Shiprow, a street running down to the harbour, **Aberdeen Maritime Museum** (open Mon to Sat 10 to 5) is housed in another ancient building – Provost Ross's House. The museum traces Aberdeen's history as a port, from the building of the harbours to the advent of the oil industry. There are plenty of pictures, photographs and models to look at (and a National Trust for Scotland shop), and you can glean information about what is going on in the North Sea. The museum is currently being expanded to about seven times its current size.

DUFFTOWN AND HUNTLY

There are names on the map in this area which ring bells, notably Glen Livet and Glen Fiddich. For this is Speyside whisky country, and the characteristic pagoda caps and breath of malty steam of the distillery are an inescapable part of the scenery.

The landscape, where the Grampians peter out towards the coast of the Moray Firth, consists of low heather-covered hills, which flatten out towards the east into the plains of Buchan. **Strath Avon** is the prettiest of the tributary valleys of the Spey, with peaty water pouring through steep stretches under the Hills of Cromdale. **Glen Livet**, which joins it a short distance before it reaches the main river, is smaller and gentler. The first distillery here was founded in 1824, replacing an estimated 200 illicit stills.

Below Bridge of Avon the Spey is at its most beautiful, with dark swirling pools haunted by oystercatchers and by salmon fishermen, whose cars with attached rod-clips stand outside the hotels of **Aberlour** and **Craigellachie**. The road running down Strathspey towards Elgin is apt to be busy, and to see the river you really need to take to your feet. The long-distance **Speyside Way** runs by the river from Spey Bay to Ballindalloch (leaflet from tourist offices), and sections of this make excellent short walks.

Just south of Craigellachie, **Speyside Cooperage** (open Mon to Fri 9.30 to 4.30; Easter to Sept, Sat 9.30 to 4.30) gives you a glimpse of a different side of the distilling business. From a gallery you can watch oak casks being painstakingly restored – ready to be filled with whisky. You can buy miniture barrels in the gift shop.

Dufftown and around

This is another of the many planned villages in the area, laid out in 1817 in the form of a cross, at the very centre of distillery country. The **Glenfiddich Distillery** (open all year, Mon to Sat 9.30 to 4.30; Sun 12 to 4.30) on the edge of the village has an extremely popular and extremely slick visitor centre and tour, and this is Dufftown's main attraction. If you like ruins, however, visit **Balvenie Castle** (HS, standard times; closed in winter), which is half-hidden by the steam from the distilleries. This was once the seat of Robert the Bruce's rivals, the Comyn Earls of Buchan, but most of what remains dates from the sixteenth century.

Half a mile south of Dufftown, **Mortlach Church** is thought to be one of the earliest places of Christian worship in the north of Scotland. The building itself has some twelfth-century work, but tradition has it that an existing church was extended in 1010, after Malcolm II won a battle against Norse invaders. Two very old carved stones – the Battle Stone and the Elephant Stone, with inscribed Christian symbols – suggest that there may be something to the story that the church was founded by St Moluag in AD 566.

Huntly

The broad square, the great archway spanning the street to the north and the careful layout all speak of an eighteenth- and nineteenth-century town deliberately designed to reflect the magnificence of the local magnate. In this case, the local magnates were the Gordon family – Earls and later Marquesses of Huntly before they became Dukes of Gordon.

Huntly is a quiet agricultural town in the middle of wooded countryside, safely by-passed by the main A96. Its convenient position for touring Speyside and the Banff coast makes it a good place to stop for a night or two. For recreation there is a newly refurbished swimming-pool, a golf course, and opportunities to fish the Bogie, the Isla and the Deveron.

Huntly Castle

(HS, standard times; closed Thur pm and Fri in winter)
This is a magnificent ruin of a sixteenth-century palace, but

the fortifications on the steep bank of the River Deveron go back much further than that and it is easy enough to see the motte and bailey of the first timber castle that stood here in the time of Robert the Bruce. The fragmentary remains of the tower-house which succeeded it are also visible. The palace, with its round tower, oriel windows and unique heraldic doorway, remains reasonably intact. The doorway still achieves its purpose: as you approach it, you are confronted by the arms of Huntly, the royal arms of Scotland, the five wounds of Christ and finally the risen Christ in Glory – all mounting in sequence above your head and instilling a proper sense of your own lowliness. The Covenanters who occupied the castle during the Civil War studiously defaced the more 'popish' elements, but the rest remains untouched.

The castle is at its most impressive from the outside, for the oriel windows, French in inspiration and probably craftsmanship too, jut out high over the south front. Above and beneath them runs a giant frieze, inscribed – with what you will find is a characteristic lack of modesty – with the

WHISKY DISTILLERIES

Of all Scottish industries, the whisky industry flaunts itself most openly to the public. In almost every region covered by this book there is at least one distillery you can visit. Whisky – 'the water of life' in the Gaelic – has been made to seem as typically Scottish as tartan or the bagpipes, and distillery-visiting is often promoted as an unmissable part of the Scottish experience. This is nonsense, for you can perfectly well appreciate Scotland without knowing anything about whisky.

That said, visiting distilleries can be great fun, and, while the process is the same in all of them, there is a lot of variety in the way they present themselves to visitors. In the distilleries of the more famous brands there may be kilted guides and batteries of audio-visuals. In smaller and more out-of-the-way places you are likely to be taken round by someone in overalls. At Dallas Dhu (page 378) you go round by yourself. Take your pick, but remember that if you are asked to pay for anything, plenty of competitors will show you round free.

The process of distilling is simple – one of the reasons illegal

names of the first Marquess and his wife in letters a couple of feet high.

The interior of the castle has some further examples of heraldry – this time it is the mantelpieces above the elaborate fireplaces which remind you firmly whose home you are in. The wall walk on top of the great round tower gives you a bird's-eye view of Huntly and the Deveron valley beneath. Up here you find the most human feature of the palace – a tiny turret room built above the main staircase where the first Marquess liked to escape from all his magnificence and enjoy the view.

Leith Hall

(NTS, house open mid–Apr to early Oct; daily 1.30 to 5.30; grounds all year, daily 9.30 to sunset)
South of Huntly, off the A97, Leith Hall makes a interesting contrast to the great castles such as Crathes or Castle Fraser. It started life as a simple laird's house, its oldest section dating from 1650, and was gradually extended around its

stills existed for so long in the Highlands. Barley is allowed to germinate and is then dried over a peat fire (malted) before being ground and added to hot water in a huge vessel called a mash tun. Here yeast is added and the mixture is left to ferment. Malt whisky, made from malted barley alone, is then distilled twice in huge copper stills, and put into oak casks to mature. Grain whisky, which includes other cereals, is continuously distilled, and is much less dependent on geographical location for its flavour. The best-known brands of Scotch are blends, containing many different malt and grain whiskies. The more expensive 'single malts' are the product of a single distillery. Their distinctively different flavours depend on a number of factors, including the source of the water, the shape of the stills and the nature of the casks used for maturing. You will hear plenty about what makes each whisky unique as you visit the distilleries.

All the best distillery tours offer you a free dram at the end. If you are driving, some will give you a miniature bottle instead, but you may have to put up with orange juice. The Scotch Whisky Association (01716 294384), produces a useful map of distilleries which welcome visitors

courtyard over the following centuries until it reached substantial proportions. The Leith (later Leith-Hay) family lived in the house right up to the time it was given to the National Trust for Scotland, and the history of the house is really the history of the family who lived there. There are fine parts of the house – notably the Georgian rooms, with lots of family portraits and one or two good pieces of furniture – but nothing of exceptional interest. The garden is good (at its best when the long herbaceous border is full of colour).

BUCHAN AND FORMARTINE

East of Huntly, the land suddenly flattens. This is Buchan – an isolated countryside consisting of small farms, winding back roads and big skies. As you approach the sea, the trees dwindle away and the wind rises. It is a countryside which can seem bleak, especially in the dead winter months; it seems far removed from the forests and moors which lie only a few dozen miles westward. The best area to explore is round the valley of the Ythan, a river famed for its sea trout and whose deep estuary is a relic of a past geological era, when a much larger stream poured over what is now the North Sea to meet the Rhine.

Fyvie Castle

(NTS, castle open Apr to end June and Sept, daily 1.30 to 5.30; July to end Aug, 11 to 5.30; early to late Oct, Sat and Sun 1.30 to 5.30; grounds all year, daily 9.30 to sunset)
No one can accuse Fyvie of lacking character, though whether you love it or hate it depends on your taste. It is a Z-shaped mixture of palace and castle, which straggles across its surrounding lawns like a snake which has swallowed a carpenter's rule. It has five towers (rather too many), each named after a family that owned Fyvie – Preston, Seton, Meldrum, Gordon and Leith. The fantastic roofscape of turrets, dormers and finials is largely the responsibility of Sir Alexander Seton, who bought the place in 1596. The south front, where the original gatehouse with its drum towers (perhaps going back to the time of Edward I) has been modified into a five-storey archway with flanking turrets, shows off the architecture at its grandest.

Internally, the castle bears the stamp of Alexander Forbes-

Leith (who became Lord Leith in 1905). Having married an American heiress and made a fortune in the Illinois Steel Company, he bought Fyvie in 1889 and proceeded to pour money into refurbishing and extending it in his own inimitable style. This is seen to best effect in the astonishing Gallery, a room in the 'modern antique' mode. One end of it is taken up by a gargantuan self-playing organ, installed in 1906, while seventeenth-century tapestries clothe the walls, a massive French Renaissance fireplace juts out into the room and a Tiffany lamp sits by the leaded window.

Not all of Fyvie was Edwardianised. Several magnificent plaster ceilings remain from earlier periods, as does Fyvie's most beautiful feature, the great wheel stair. Its ten-foot-wide pinkish stone steps rise for four floors.

Whatever you think of Lord Leith's taste in armour, tapestry or furniture, there is no doubt about the quality of the pictures, especially the portraits, that he assembled at Fyvie. In this he was building on a collection established by the previous Gordon owners, which included Fyvie's most famous painting, Batoni's portrait of William Gordon, a Byronic figure poised with drawn sword against a classical background. Yet it is the Raeburn portraits which are the most striking in number and quality, and these were almost all acquired by Lord Leith – he was especially fond of tracking down portraits of his Aberdeenshire connections. The portraits of Mrs Gregory and of John Stirling of Kippendavie and his daughter are worth the whole journey to Fyvie to see.

Fyvie has its mysteries – notably the secret vault below the Charter Room, which has never been opened because of an unpleasant curse. Attempts to gain entry are supposed to result in the death of the laird and the blindness of his wife – and this has twice occurred.

Haddo House

(NTS, house open mid-Apr to end June and Sept, daily 1.30 to 5.30; July to end Aug, 11 to 5.30; Oct, Sat and Sun 1.30 to 5.30; grounds open all year, daily 9.30 to sunset)
A little further down the Ythan, off the B9005, Haddo House was another Gordon property, and makes a good contrast to Fyvie (with which there appears to be a little quiet rivalry – Haddo has a Batoni portrait, which according to the guides is 'rather more natural than the one at Fyvie', for example). Haddo is an Adam mansion, its Palladian style

and austere, symmetrical façade very different from the spikes and turrets of older tower-houses. Unfortunately, much of the interior is Adam revival from 1880 rather than the real thing (papier-mâché ceiling mouldings and 'Adam-style' fireplaces, for example), but the effect is still splendid. Haddo House has a guided tour, and you can get pretty befuddled by the Gordon family tree after hearing about the activities of the owners of Haddo for almost an hour. One of them was Prime Minister in 1852, but the others tend to become a blur, despite the guides' best efforts.

Haddo is furnished with comfortable clutter rather than suits of armour. There is a chapel, with some Burne-Jones designs. The nineteenth-century library at the end of one of the wings is too like a gentlemen's club to be very interesting, but tempts you to take down the odd volume and sink into one of the old leather armchairs. Keep an eye open too for the Queen's Bedroom, which contains a portrait of Queen Victoria aged four, where she looks even more like a large plum than she did in her old age.

Haddo is well established as a cultural centre for the neighbourhood. Operas, choral concerts and plays take place in a Canadian-style hall built near the house, and there are usually other activities throughout the season. (Call the Arts Trust Office, 01651 851770, for information.)

Pitmedden Garden

(NTS, open end Apr to early Oct, daily 10 to 5.30)
If you like intricate seventeenth-century formal gardens in French style, then Pitmedden, east of Oldmeldrum, is unmissable. It was created by Sir Alexander Seton around 1675, but had to be re-created from scratch in the 1950s – it had become a kitchen garden. This has been done with some panache, with the planting of four great parterres, three of which follow seventeenth-century designs for the gardens at Holyrood in Edinburgh.

The garden is surrounded by a retaining wall and is sunk beneath the level of the ground to the west, for it is essential to see all the patterns from above. Two small pavilions and a double stone staircase break up the smooth expanse of terrace. Beneath you, there is a maze of box hedges and 40,000 colourful annuals, from which the designs and lettering are created. The sound of rooks in the nearby trees fills the garden, and all is elegance and peace.

A small agricultural museum is here too – largely a

collection of farm implements, but with an interesting example of an Aberdeenshire farm-worker's bothy. The museum still has a long way to go in other respects.

THE COAST
NORTH OF ABERDEEN

The east coast of Aberdeenshire alternates between swathes of sandy beach and rocky headlands. It is an exposed seashore, with nothing much to restrict the wind as it scours inland. Small fishing villages with inadequate harbours dot the shore. You can be alone as much as you want here — and on the rare still day of sunshine it can be very beautiful. However, if your time is limited the coast of the Moray Firth is more scenic.

Among the dunes and rough heath of the Ythan estuary is the **Sands of Forvie Nature Reserve**, a stopping point for both bird-watchers and botanists. Huge numbers of eider duck concentrate here in the breeding season. **Cruden Bay** is the next place worth a halt. Although a major oil pipeline runs ashore here, the bay — with its high dunes and semi-circle of sand — is unspoilt. At the northern end a tiny harbour and a few cottages make it positively photogenic. An enormous hotel was once built here, with tennis courts, croquet lawns and a golf course, for in the railway age Cruden Bay was to be the resort to beat them all. Alas, it was just too far away, and the project was a mammoth flop; nothing remains save the golf course, which is still going strong.

The ruins you see against the horizon just north of Cruden Bay are the remains of **New Slains Castle**. A short puddle-strewn walk from the road takes you into its tumble-down, labyrinthine interior. The castle dates from 1598 and, although most of the best stonework has been robbed, some fine pieces of granite remain to show how well constructed it must have been. The cliff-edge situation impressed Dr Johnson in 1773, and the waves still slap against the cliff foot with suitably dramatic force.

At the **Bullers of Buchan**, two miles further north, a car park by the edge of the road signals that this is a beauty spot. In fact it is more of a terror spot, for the Bullers (boiler) is a collapsed sea cave, with a chasm over 200 feet deep. A narrow arch of rock separates it from the sea. A legend goes that a local laird, when drunk, won a bet by galloping around the chasm on horseback, but contemplation of this feat, once he had sobered up, was enough to make him die of shock. The Bullers is at its best in rough weather, but worth the short walk at any time. Dr Johnson insisted on exploring the place by boat. It is unlikely that you will want to imitate him.

Peterhead

This is a big, rather grim, fishing town built largely of granite. Peterhead's harbour and fish market bustle, and, if you like watching fishing boats come and go, or getting up at four in the morning to watch boxes of fish being haggled over, this is an excellent place. A small museum (open Mon to Sat, 10 to 5, Wed 10.30 to 1) takes you back to Peterhead's heyday as a whaling and then a herring port.

If you prefer country matters, the **Aden Country Park and North East of Scotland Agricultural Heritage Centre**, a few miles west of the town, is not quite as impressive as its title, but makes a good introduction to the old Aberdeenshire farming life for all that (park open daily dawn to dusk; centre late Apr, daily 12 to 4.30; May to Sept, daily 11 to 4.30). **Deer Abbey** (HS, access at all reasonable times) close by is famous as the source of a ninth-century manuscript with twelfth-century Gaelic annotations – the earliest example of written Gaelic. Now the abbey is reduced to scanty ruins, only of interest to the enthusiast.

North of Peterhead, the sand starts again. On this shifting, exposed section of coast, the villages are huddled against the elements. One (Rattray, by the Loch of Strathbeg) has vanished altogether. There are golf courses round here, and some attempts to suggest that holiday-makers come – they must be a hardy breed. Finally, where the coastline turns abruptly west, the fishing town of Fraserburgh stands, offering a haven from the wind, but not much else.

However, at **Kinnaird Head**, directly north of the town, Scotland's first ever lighthouse has been turned into a **museum** (open Nov to Mar, Mon to Sat 10 to 4, Sun 12.30 to 4; Apr to Oct, Mon to Sat 10 to 6, Sun 12.30 to 6), which tells the story of Scottish lighthouses, and in particular of Robert Louis Stevenson's family, who designed so many of them. There are huge lenses on display, knowledgeable ex-lighthouse keepers to guide you, and a tea-room where you can eat fresh fish from the adjacent smokehouse.

THE MORAY COAST

If Scotland were Cornwall this coast would be crowded throughout the season, for its combination of cliff scenery, sandy beaches and ancient towns is just as attractive as that of the West Country. Since Scotland is not Cornwall it is largely neglected, despite its well-signed coastal trail, by all except golfers and those Scots who discovered its charms some time ago. For those who love wild seashores, two or three days spent near this coast are likely to pay dividends.

Nairn

Nairn is a small, genteel seaside resort, though to call itself the Brighton of the North may be stretching things. Certainly its sandy beach is more comfortable to lie on. It is a restrained town, where the back streets are lined with substantial stone villas, each with its own rose garden, and where every second house does bed and breakfast. There are also a substantial number of hotels (plus plenty of farmhouse accommodation in the surrounding country), so you are unlikely to have difficulty in finding somewhere to stay. If it is a day or two by the seaside you are looking for, Nairn is more sheltered and better set up for families than its competitors (though Findhorn is better for small boats, and Lossiemouth has the best beach).

South of Nairn

Cawdor Castle

(Open May to mid-Oct, daily 10 to 5.30)
The late Lord Cawdor's guide to his castle remains the wittiest introduction to any sight in Scotland. Not only that, the castle is a joy to visit; its history is leavened with home-liness, its dignity modified by mild eccentricity. To add to the bargain, the garden is a delight. Forget *Macbeth* – this is a place well worth travelling to for its own sake.

It starts with a legend. An early Thane of Cawdor, wanting a new castle, had a dream in which he was told to load a donkey with gold, let it wander around for a day and watch where it lay down, for this would be the best spot for his new castle. He did this, and the donkey proceeded to lie down under a thorn tree. The tree still stands (long defunct) in the middle of the vaulted guardroom of the fourteenth-century tower and carbon-dating has shown it to be older

373

than the surrounding castle (although holly rather than thorn). This same room contains a dungeon which was discovered only in 1979. It is typical that everything found in this dungeon is displayed without regard to its worthiness – there are sawn-off bits of moulding, bones of chicken and horse, pieces of crab and lead.

On a more cultivated level, the paintings are especially worth looking at – both the portraits (brought to life by Lord Cawdor's notes: '. . . the handsome lady in the saucy brown hat is Mrs Jane Philips, affectionately nicknamed Aunt Glum . . .') and the more serious pieces such as several by John Piper and a Stanley Spencer, not to mention some fine watercolours. The tapestries are also good, helped again by suitable (or unsuitable) notes on their subjects.

It is hard to know what to pick out from the rest. The tour takes you through the Modern Kitchen ('the object on the table is not a thumbscrew, it is a French duck-press') as well as the old one, past the collections of Victoriana, the Pet's Corner ('Albert passed away untimely after drinking a gallon of red-lead paint primer'), the Stones, a model of the castle, a model of a man-o'-war, not to mention the drawing-room, several bedrooms and various cubby-holes. After all this, the garden may seem a haven of normality. It is, and very colourful with it.

The Findhorn Valley and Lochindorb

The Findhorn River drains the wilderness of the Monadhliath Mountains south of Inverness. Where it runs south of Nairn it flows black and powerful in the confines of its wooded gorges. To drive on the minor roads round the villages of Ferness, Dulsie and Relugas is to enter a secret countryside, hidden in the pines of the Darnaway Forest. There are walks, rides and one or two things to see, such as **Ardclach Bell Tower** (HS, access at all reasonable times), a fortified belfry of 1665, perched high above the church it served.

The A939 to Grantown-on-Spey climbs from the Findhorn River over the ridge of a stony moor which separates Strathspey from the fertile lands round Nairn – one of the most attractive routes in this part of Scotland. At the top (a short diversion from the road) is the bleak expanse of **Lochindorb**, a stretch of water notable for having been the strategic lair of the Wolf of Badenoch (see page 301) around 1372, from which he mounted his raid to burn Elgin Cathedral. His old castle, taking up every spare foot of an island in the loch, was demolished on James II's orders (the old yett can be seen in Cawdor Castle), but you can still make out the walls. Lochindorb is a grim place to this day.

Nairn to Elgin

At **Auldearn**, the site of one of Montrose's victories over the Covenanters in 1645, you can climb up to Boath Doocot, where a plan shows how the battle was fought in and around the small village below you. It is worth the short diversion from the main road as a viewpoint rather than a battlefield site.

Brodie Castle

(NTS, castle open mid-Apr to late Sept, Mon to Sat 11 to 5.30, Sun 1.30 to 5.30; early to late Oct, Sat 11 to 5.30, Sun 1.30 to 5.30; other times by appointment; grounds all year, daily 9.30 to sunset)
There have been 25 Brodies of Brodie since the thirteenth century, and Brodies have been living at Brodie Castle since 1567. Today they share it with the National Trust for Scotland.
   With care you can disentangle the outline of the original sixteenth-century Z-plan tower-house from the later additions. Internally it is not so easy, for much of the old house was 'improved' in Victorian times and the Renaissance pillars in the entrance hall turn out to have been carved in the 1840s. The same period produced the cosy library and the spectacularly successful Gothic fireplace in the red drawing-room. The other star piece in the interior is the seventeenth-century plasterwork on the ceiling of the dining-room − a riot of mermaids, fruit and flowers. The collection of twentieth-century paintings (notably water-colours) assembled by the twenty-fourth Brodie should be seen, while the same laird's interest in daffodils turns the well-landscaped grounds into a picture in spring.

Forres

If civic pride is measured in colourful flowerbeds Forres is the peacock of the region, and the list of awards won for its floral displays must daunt less dedicated municipalities. On the outskirts of this otherwise unremarkable town, and perilously close to the by-pass, stands Sueno's Stone, one of the best Pictish stones in Scotland. It is over 20 feet high and is covered on one side with a huge battle scene, dotted with footmen, cavalry and headless bodies.

Findhorn

The B9011 past RAF Kinloss takes you to this exposed village on the edge of Findhorn Bay, a stretch of water which is attractive when the tide is in, but not when it is out. It is almost the only refuge for small sailing boats on this coast, however, so there are dinghies to lend colour, and a small water-sports centre beside the few cottages sufficiently far out of the wind to look relaxed. Behind the village, the dunes reach aridly into the hinterland.

Findhorn has achieved notoriety as the place where 'they grow giant cabbages' – 'they' being the Findhorn Foundation, a community founded in 1962, dedicated to building 'a spiritually based, holistic planetary culture'. In so far as it anticipated the popularity of Gaian theories by half a generation, the Findhorn Foundation has some reason to feel pleased with itself; it reveals itself to visitors as a stable, slightly self-conscious place. If you hang about looking lost for long enough, someone will show you around the palatial

JAMES GRAHAM, MARQUESS OF MONTROSE (1612–1650)

In the confused tangle of the Scottish civil wars of the seventeenth century, the figure of Montrose stands out as the single personality whom it has been possible to cast in a romantic light, thanks to his loyalty to his king, Charles I, his abilities as a leader of men in the tradition of Wallace or Bruce, and his death in the hands of his Covenanting enemies.

Montrose was among the first to sign the 1638 Covenant, and for the first years of the confrontation between King Charles and the Scots was firmly on the Covenanting side. However, as the Covenanters increasingly began to demand the subordination of king to kirk and parliament, Montrose, who perceived only anarchy in this course of events, became increasingly alienated. It was the signing of the Solemn League and Covenant in 1643, by which the Scots agreed to join the English armed rebellion against King Charles, which seems to have made up Montrose's mind for him. In early 1644 King Charles commissioned him lieutenant-general of the royal forces in Scotland – not that there were any at that time. Montrose's entry into Scotland, with two companions and no troops, was not auspicious.

community centre, though not many giant cabbages are in evidence.

On the far side of the mouth of Findhorn Bay, a forest now covers the famous Culbin Sands – huge dunes six miles long and two miles wide, known as the Scottish Sahara. These sands are supposed to have buried a whole estate in 1694, and it is said that the steeple of the old church occasionally emerged from the dunes as they shifted. Now the whole area has been stabilised by tree-planting – a triumph for the Forestry Commission, but less romantic for the rest of us.

Burghead

This is a substantial nineteenth-century town of single-storey fishermen's cottages laid out in a grid plan over a blunt peninsula. It is a place that has been battered by generations of winds, and has, metaphorically speaking, all its hatches permanently battened down. Do not dismiss it

His luck turned when he met Alasdair Macdonnell, who had come with a small force from Antrim in the king's cause. Montrose won his first victory against the Covenanters at Tippermuir in August 1644, sacked Aberdeen and disappeared into the Highlands. In the winter, he descended on Argyll with a force of clansmen happy to pillage the lands of Clan Campbell. In January 1645, by an astonishing flank march through the snow-bound glens beside Loch Ness, he took the pursuing force of Campbells by surprise at Inverlochy. Throughout the spring of 1645 Montrose was in Aberdeenshire, beating the Covenanters at Auldearn and Alford, and, when he finally descended on the Lowlands, he shattered another Covenanting army at Kilsyth. But it could not last. The Scottish troops in England hurried home, yet Montrose got no support from the weakened king. In September he was outmanoeuvred for the first time, and his army routed at Philiphaugh. At the beginning of 1646 Montrose was still trying to continue his campaign, but on 25 April King Charles surrendered to his enemies and Montrose was forced abroad.

He returned in 1650, commissioned by King Charles II, raised troops in Orkney, but was soundly defeated at Carbisdale in Sutherland and captured a few days later. Taken to Edinburgh, Montrose was tried, condemned and executed on 21 May.

for its superficial unattractiveness, for this unlikely spot appears to have been the centre of a large Pictish settlement, of which one remarkable relic remains. This is **Burghead Well** (HS, access at all reasonable times), and you find it by squeezing round the gable ends of grey cottages on the sea's edge and seeking out the custodian. A flight of steps leads you down into a chamber hewn out of solid rock, where a still pool of water lies. The well may have been some kind of ritual centre, perhaps even built by followers of St Columba in the sixth-century. Burghead is one of three Scottish towns (see also Lerwick and Stonehaven) which has a New Year fire ceremony – in this case the Burning of the Clavie (a tar barrel) on 11 January. West of Burghead, a beautiful creamy bay of sand and wild seas fades into the spume, and reaches almost as far as Findhorn.

Lossiemouth

Until you see the beach, it is hard to imagine that this grey, grid-plan fishing town can be a much-loved holiday resort, for Lossiemouth, like other towns and villages along this coast, bears the utilitarian stamp of a place that expanded in a hurry to cope with a boom industry – in this case the nineteenth-century herring rush. Apart from some of the quainter cottages with gable ends facing the sea and a half-buried look about them, Lossiemouth is ugly. Its attractions are not enhanced by the rumble of aircraft from the nearby RAF base.

Yet the beach redeems the place, as does the golf course, the flourishing harbour where seine-netters lumber out on the tide, and the cram-full little **museum** (open Easter to late Sept, Mon to Sat 10 to 5) down by the piers, complete with a reconstruction of Ramsay Macdonald's study – for Lossiemouth has produced a British prime minister. If you hit a fine spell and want to build sand-castles, this place is worth remembering.

Dallas Dhu

(HS, standard times; closed Thur pm and Fri in winter)
Deep in the country to the south of the A96 – you may need a good map to find it – lies a distillery which has been turned into a museum by Historic Scotland, allowing visitors more time than they would have on a guided tour, and also allowing children under eight (not allowed by law

into some parts of working distilleries) to see what happens.

The distillery has been very well arranged to let you poke and prod at your leisure, with a clear leaflet to explain the process, a trail of painted footmarks to follow, and some good human models which suddenly come to life and start explaining their job (keep an eye open for the customs officer). It comes as close to the real thing as a museum possibly could, and would make either an excellent introduction to distillery-visiting or a fitting finale.

Pluscarden Abbey

(Open daily 4.45am to 8.45pm)
In bald terms, this is a thirteenth-century monastery which is now owned and being restored by a community of Benedictine monks. Yet Pluscarden is more than this: it is an ancient piece of Scotland's religious tradition which has been resurrected from decay, and is being made beautiful once more.

Parts of the abbey do look like a building site for the monks have a long way to go, though what has been achieved since 1948 when the fraternity took up residence is impressive. The choir, the transepts and the tower of the old church have been fully restored. The nave exists merely at foundation level.

Pluscarden is a mish-mash of architectural styles and of rejiggings of existing work. One side of the choir, for example, is lit by large windows with fine tracery, while the other has only a few small lights, the outline of the larger arches being firmly blocked in. Curious half-arches are to be seen on the exterior walls too, as if the architect had changed his mind half-way up. The glory of the place lies in its modern stained glass, much of it done in the abbey workshops. It is difficult to forget the searing reds which illuminate the chancel, setting the ancient walls alight all over again. The abbey is lucky in its setting – nothing disturbs the peace of the valley it sits in, apart from the birdsong.

Elgin

A self-confident, ancient royal burgh, Elgin acts as the natural market-town for the fertile coastal strip of Moray. It has a High Street which contains some ancient arcaded houses, a municipal park of some splendour, suitable shops and monuments, a small museum, and a good scattering of hotels and guesthouses – nothing exceptional perhaps, but everything in the right proportions and the right place. It is a larger and livelier place than either Nairn or Huntly, and makes an ideal base in which to stay for exploring both coastal and inland regions.

All the same it is a far cry from the days when Elgin was the cathedral city of the north, rivalled only by St Andrews. The story of Elgin's thirteenth-century **cathedral** (HS, standard times; winter closed Thur pm and Fri) shows Scotland at its best and at its worst – on the one hand the raising of a building which in scale, elaboration and beauty could compete with any in medieval Europe; on the other, the wanton destruction by piracy, religious fervour, avarice and neglect which left the building a wreck.

For all this, it is still possible to catch something of the scale and magnificence of what used to be the 'Lanthorn of the North', either by contemplating the well-preserved chapter house with its jerky vaulting and ceiling bosses (look for the dragon with folded wings) or by gazing at the splendour of the western doorway. In the middle of the ruin, a single Pictish cross-slab stands, older by far than all this folly.

East of Elgin

Seven miles beyond Elgin lies **Fochabers**, which owes its position beside the road to the desire of the Dukes of Gordon to have some privacy at their nearby castle – the village was shifted wholesale in the eighteenth century. It still has the look of an estate village, and many of the houses are attractive. The **Fochabers Folk Museum** (open daily 9.30 to 1, 2 to 5.30) is well worth a look, not just for its collection of old coaches but for the heaps of ancient domestic objects which clutter the place. However, the main attraction near Fochabers is a factory: **Baxters Visitor Centre** (open daily 10 to 5.30; no factory tours at weekends or during factory holidays). The story of Baxters – producers of fine Scottish foods to the gentry – is a folksy tale to bring tears of joy to the eyes of the marketing department. George Baxter, gardener to His Grace the Duke of Gordon in the nineteenth century, had a wife whose home-made jams found favour with all who sampled them. From grocery shop to factory by the banks of the Spey, helped on its way by the philanthropic Duke, the Baxter enterprise expanded, and continues to expand.

Tours of the factory (weekdays only) are slickly handled

and fun, though you may have to wait on busy days. The inevitable audio-visual is followed by a visit to the canning line, where thousands of the silvery objects rattle round conveyor belts at high speed. The day's 'menu' is chalked up, so that you know what delicacies are in production (though if it is beetroot, you will be able to tell the moment you arrive). Is there any truth in the old story that the choicest raspberries are picked out with a reverential murmur of 'The Queen', before being packed off to Balmoral?

The fishing towns

From Spey Bay, where the river joins the Moray Firth amongst great shingle banks, the coast begins to change character. Gone are the sand dunes and inland woods; in their place rise cliffs of reddish rock. In every indentation lie fishing villages and towns – often surprisingly large for such a difficult coast. Some are jammed with fishing boats and container lorries; others lie quiet. Almost all have their 'seatown', a cluster of the oldest cottages, gable end to the sea and the street, which was the heart of the fishing community.

The Scottish fishing industry remains poised on the edge of precipitous decline and you are likely to hear bitter words about quotas and the arbitrary rules about who can fish where and for what – while you can sense, all along the coast, that times are hard. The following is just a choice of the towns and villages worth exploring; there are more.

● **Buckie** is a grey, industrious fishing town, full of seafood processing factories, fish-selling agencies, container lorries, ice-factories, ship chandlers and repair yards. All the action is down by the harbour, although you might take a break in the new museum, **The Buckie Drifter** (open Apr to end Oct, Mon to Sat 10 to 6, Sun 12 to 6) where there is a reconstructed steam drifter, a lifeboat, and plenty of information about herring. This is the place to book harbour tours (call 01542 834646 well in advance) to get an inside view of the industry.

● **Findochty and Portknockie** are typical of the quiet fishing burghs whose inhabitants now work out of Buckie. Look for the rather fine modern statue of the fisherman in Findochty. There is dramatic cliff scenery between the two.

● **Cullen** gave its name to an excellent smoked haddock soup. It is not an attractive town but it is blessed with a long stretch of sand and a fine golf course, both of which draw visitors. The old church is fourteenth-century.

USEFUL DIRECTORY

Main tourist offices
Aberdeen and Grampian Tourist Board
Migvie House
North Silver Street
Aberdeen AB1 1RJ
(01224) 848848

Highlands of Scotland Tourist Board
Tourist Information Centre
Castle Wynd
Inverness IV2 3BJ
(0990) 143070

Tourist Board publications Very useful: *What to See and Where to Go in Grampian Highlands and Aberdeen*; also annually updated *Visitor's Guide*. Special interest booklets include ones on the Castle Trail, the Malt Whisky Trail and the Victorian Heritage Trail, and cover activities such as fishing, hillwalking and golf.

Local tourist information centres
Aberdeen (01224) 632727
Aboyne (013398) 86060 (Easter to late Sept)
Alford (019755) 62052 (late Mar to Sept/weekends in Oct)
Ballater (013397) 55306 (Easter to late Oct)
Banchory (01330) 822000
Banff (01261) 812419 (Apr to Oct)
Braemar (013397) 41600

● **Portsoy** exudes a greater air of antiquity down by its harbour than neighbouring villages, with some of the houses going back to the early eighteenth century. There is a leaflet to guide you round. Portsoy marble is a species of locally quarried serpentine. It once provided two chimneypieces for the palace at Versailles; now it provides pretty souvenirs, on sale by the harbour.

Banff

For lovers of eighteenth-century architecture, Banff is something of a treasure trove. In those days, the landed gentry from much of the surrounding country were accustomed to abandon their draughty seats in the winter and congregate somewhere where they could enjoy each other's company. Banff was the chosen spot, and the result is a number of

Buckie (01542) 834853 (May to Sept)
Crathie (013397) 42414
Cullen (01542) 840757 (May to Sept)
Dufftown (01340) 820501 (Easter to Oct)
Elgin (01343) 542666
Ellon (01358) 720730
Forres (01309) 672938 (mid-May to Oct)
Fraserburgh (01346) 518315 (Apr to Oct)
Huntly (01466) 792255 (late Apr to Sept)
Inverurie (01467) 620600 (late Apr to Sept)
Keith (01542) 882634 (May to Sept)
Nairn (01667) 452753 (Apr to Oct)
Peterhead (01779) 471904 (Apr to Oct)
Stonehaven (01569) 762806 (Easter to Oct)
Tomintoul (01807) 580285 (Easter to Oct)
Turriff (01888) 563001

Local transport
Aberdeen Airport Information (01224) 722331
Inverness Airport Information (01463) 232471
Scotrail Aberdeen (01224) 594222
National Express bus and coaches (0990) 808080
Bluebird bus and coaches (01224) 212266

Other useful numbers
P&O Aberdeen for information on boats to Orkney & Shetland
(01224) 572615
Aberdeen 'What's On Line' (01224) 636363

substantial houses. The town retains much of the dignity of earlier centuries, and is a complete contrast to the raucous hive of maritime activity in **Macduff**, across the Deveron estuary. The silting up of its harbour put a stop to Banff's days as a fishing town, though old fishers' cottages remain.

Dr Johnson, who had already eaten 'a vile meal' in Elgin, found the Black Bull Inn here 'indifferent'. Standards have changed for the better, and you should find a choice of reasonable places to stay.

Duff House

(Open mid-Apr to end Sept, 10 to 5, closed Tue; Oct to end Mar, Thur to Sun 10 to 5)
This great baroque mansion which dominates the outskirts

of Banff has been rescued from a state of decay and turned into an art gallery. Ornate plasterwork has been restored, and the building now looks much as it did in its heyday.

William Adam started building Duff House for the first Earl of Fife in 1735, and, although their relationship degenerated into a legal wrangle and the second Earl avoided all contact with the Adam family as he continued the house, William left behind a magnificent block with a façade ornamented by pilasters with Corinthian capitals, and a wealth of detail. The paintings (from the national collection) include a fine El Greco and some good Dutch seascapes.

Gardenstown and Pennan

Gardenstown is squeezed onto what is almost a cliff face, and the road down is on the precipitous side of steep. The cottages at the bottom are so jammed together that there is scarcely room for two cars to pass on the street. If you survive the descent, spare a minute or two to wander round the harbour and observe how many modern facilities this place manages to cram into its tiny space. Further round the bay, tucked under the cliffs of Troup Head, lies the even more dramatically situated **Crovie**. Don't even think of trying to get your car there – walk instead. Beyond the headland lies **Pennan**, the one village on the coast that starts tourist literature off on superlatives. If you saw the film *Local Hero* you will immediately recognise the red telephone box and the pub. Pennan is not so much a village as a single row of cottages squeezed on to a shelf between a gnarled, over-hanging cliff and the sea, leaving so little room that washing has to be dried on the very edge of the breakwater. There is absolutely nothing to do here except walk from one end of the street to the other and to take photographs, though if you do want to spend a romantic night in the inn listening to the beat of the waves on the shingle you will find that prices have been inflated only a little by celluloid fame.

WHERE TO STAY

£ – under £70 per room per night, incl. VAT

££ – £70 to £110 per room per night, incl. VAT

£££ – over £110 per room per night, incl. VAT

ABERDEEN

Aberdeen Springdale Guesthouse

404 Great Western Road, Aberdeen AB1 6NR

TEL (01224) 316561

FAX (01224) 210773

Victorian house with large rooms and ornate ceilings, on a main road into Aberdeen. Breakfast only is served in the dining-room; packed lunches are available. Warm bedrooms, some sharing bathroom facilities.

£ All year; 6 rooms, credit cards not accepted

The Marcliffe at Pitfodels

North Deeside Road, Aberdeen AB1 9YA

TEL (01224) 861000

FAX (01224) 868860

Utilitarian modern frontage hides a desirable country-house style interior, given character and charm by old furniture and paintings. Polished sideboards and silver gleam in the small dining-room. Large, comfortable bedrooms.

££ All year; 42 rooms; drying-room; games room

ABOYNE

Hazlehurst Lodge

Ballater Road, Aboyne AB34 5HY

TEL (01339) 886921

The rose-granite watchman's lodge of Aboyne Castle is an endorsement of modern Scottish arts and crafts. Original montages adorn rooms and commissioned chairs deck the minimalist dining-room. There are colourful sofas in the sitting-rooms. Scottish country cooking is prepared with continental style for the daily changing menu. White bedrooms with cherrywood furniture.

£ Closed Dec to Feb; 5 rooms; drying-room; art gallery

Struan Hall

Ballater Road, Aboyne AB34 5HY

TEL/FAX (01339) 887241

Surrounded by coniferous woodland, Struan Hall was moved to its present site stone by stone in 1904 from a spot some five miles distant. Well settled in its new location, it is now a comfortable and welcoming place.

£ Mar to end Oct; 3 rooms

BALLATER

Balgonie Country House

Braemar Place, Ballater AB35 5RQ

TEL/FAX (01339) 755482

A balustraded turn-of-the-century house with striking interiors and sensational cooking by a former royal chef. The clean-cut modern white-and-cream interior includes space for anglers' rod racks. Paisley and stained glass enliven the dining-room, where the menu is exciting and progressive. Bedrooms are a happy blend of old and new; bathrooms up-to-the-minute.

££ Closed mid-Jan to mid-Feb; 9 rooms; drying-room (See Where to Eat)

Craigendarroch Hotel

Braemar Road, Ballater AB35 5XA

TEL (01339) 755858

FAX (01339) 755447

At the centre of a timeshare development, this child-friendly, Scottish-style sandstone hotel combines excellent sports facilities and grand country living. Portrait-lined walls and panelled halls happily co-exist with a state-of-the-art leisure centre. Food in the major restaurant is innovative and ambitious. Suites are lavish, standard rooms pleasant and comfortable.

£££ All year; 44 rooms; drying-room; 2 games rooms; tennis; solarium; sauna; 2 indoor heated swimming-pools; children's swimming-pool; gym; aerobics; archery; gliding; clay pigeon shooting; health and beauty salon; crèche

Darroch Learg
Braemar Road, Ballater AB35 5UX
TEL (01339) 755443
FAX (01339) 755252
Old-fashioned hotel with a friendly welcome and good food. Though public rooms are a little worn, the dining-room is brightened by a conservatory extension. Food is the main attraction; cooking features game and local produce. Very pleasant bedrooms.

££ All year exc Jan; 19 rooms; drying-room (See Where to Eat)

Tullich Lodge
Ballater AB35 5SB
TEL (01339) 755406
FAX (01339) 755397
Crenellated baronial lodge with elaborate Victorian interior and food fit for a king. Imperial splendour in the first-floor lounge and stately panelled dining-room. The beautifully balanced no-choice menu is rich, earthy and flavoursome. Striking coloured furnishings decorate the grand bedrooms where comfort is a priority.

£££ Closed Nov to Mar; 10 rooms; drying-room (See Where to Eat)

BALLINDALLOCH
Delnashaugh Inn
Ballindalloch AB37 9AS
TEL (01807) 500255
FAX (01807) 500389
A dapper sporting hotel where blazing fires and satisfying fare refresh the tired traveller and chilled

angler. Flower prints and fresh-cut blooms brighten the lounge. Set dinners involve top-class local ingredients, prepared with dexterous culinary skill. Jaunty fabrics in the well-equipped bedrooms.

££ Closed 5 Nov to 4 Mar; 9 rooms; drying-room; rod room; fishing; shooting

Raemoir House
Banchory AB31 4ED
TEL (01330) 824884
FAX (01330) 822171
Delightful service distinguishes this noble eighteenth-century mansion. The bar, fashioned from an ornate four-poster bed, typifies the eclectic feel of the house which exudes friendliness and warmth in a traditional setting. Hearty food in the well-proportioned dining-room. Bedrooms are filled with luxuriant soft-furnishings and intriguing antiques.

££ All year exc first 2 weeks in Jan; 29 rooms; drying-room; tennis; golf; sauna; gym

BANFF
Eden House
by Banff AB45 3NT
TEL (01261) 821282
FAX (01261) 821283
Classical with a porticoed entrance, Eden House was restored from a ruin in 1988. The large drawing-room has hand-painted wallpaper. There is a smaller sitting-room, a billiard room and basement games room. Meals are served in the dining-room.

£ All year exc Chr and New Year; 5 rooms; games room; credit cards not accepted

BRAEMAR
Clunie Lodge
Clunie Bank Road, Braemar AB35 5YP
TEL (01339) 741330
A former manse on the edge of the town, Clunie Lodge has lovely views of the glen and the river.

Evening meals are served in the pine-clad dining-room. Spacious, simply furnished bedrooms.

£ All year exc Chr, 2 weeks Nov and 2 weeks Mar; 7 rooms; drying-room; credit cards not accepted

HUNTLY
Faich-Hill Farmhouse

Gartly, nr Huntly AB54 4RR
TEL (01466) 720240

Granite farmhouse in an isolated location with views over the hills. There is a cosy lounge and meals are served by arrangement in the evening. Pleasantly furnished bedrooms.

£ Easter to Oct; 3 rooms; credit cards not accepted

KILDRUMMY
Kildrummy Castle

Kildrummy, Alford AB33 8RA
TEL (01975) 571288
FAX (01975) 571345

Archetypal Scottish baronial mansion with a lavish interior, the highlight is a superb lion-flanked staircase. Hunting prints and antlers embody masculine tradition, but the Wedgwood-blue drawing-room is altogether lighter. Rich, satisfying food with winning use of fresh local produce. Pleasant, classic country-house style bedrooms.

£££ All year exc 4 Jan-10 Feb; 16 rooms; drying-room; games room

LESLIE
Leslie Castle

Leslie, by Inch, Aberdeen AB52 6NX
TEL (01464) 820869
FAX (01464) 821076

Atmospheric turreted castle where flag floors and diamond windows remain intact despite the welcome addition of modern heating and conveniences. Custom-made Jacobean-style furniture, flags and a collection of owls compound the impression of living history. Hearty food is served. Light, generously

sized bedrooms contain commissioned furniture.

£££ All year; 4 rooms; drying-room

MARNOCH
Old Manse of Marnoch

Bridge of Marnoch, by Huntly AB54 5RS
TEL/FAX (01446) 780873

Extended Georgian manse with a restful atmosphere on the banks of the River Deveron. Objects gathered during years of travelling are elegantly displayed within. Many of the meals feature home-grown ingredients. Stunning antique beds and wardrobes dominate bedrooms well supplied with thoughtful extras.

££ All year exc 2 weeks in Nov; 9 rooms; drying-room

MARYCULTER
Maryculter House Hotel

South Deeside Road, Maryculter, Aberdeen AB1 0BB
TEL (01224) 732124
FAX (01224) 733510

Anglers and oil executives mix easily in this white-harled house whose heritage dates back 600 years to the times of the Knights Templar. Tasty food in the popular bar; the Priory Restaurant moves up a culinary level with an ambitious menu. Chintzy, light bedrooms.

££-£££ All year; 23 rooms

NAIRN
Clifton House

Viewfield Street, Nairn IV12 4HW
TEL (01667) 453119
FAX (01667) 452836

A theatrical and extravagant grand hotel on the Moray Firth. Public rooms are stagey and dramatic with eclectic collections of antiques and objets d'art. Every winter, plays are performed in what is also the main restaurant. The delicious food is suitably classic, with a menu in French. Bedrooms contain antiques and personal extras.

££ Closed Dec and Jan; 12 rooms; drying-room (See Where to Eat)

Greenlawns
13 Seafield Street, Nairn IV12 4HG
TEL (01667) 452738
Guesthouse near the sea-front and the golf course, with a large gallery lounge where the work of local artists is displayed. Breakfast only is served; packed lunches are available. Comfortable bedrooms.

£ All year exc Chr; 6 rooms

OLDMELDRUM
Cromlet Hill
South Road, Oldmeldrum, nr Inverurie
AB51 0AB
TEL (01651) 872315
FAX (01651) 872164
Georgian house to which an Italianate wing was added in Victorian times, set in secluded gardens. Guests use an elegant lounge. Four-course meals are available by prior arrangement. Spacious bedrooms.

£ All year exc Chr; 3 rooms; credit cards not accepted

WHERE TO EAT

Key: A ★ marks a place that is particularly good value for money

ABERDEEN
Courtyard on the Lane
1 Alford Lane, Aberdeen AB1 1YD
TEL (01224) 213795
FAX (01224) 212961
Bustling, ground-floor bistro with a transatlantic-stlye blackboard menu. Upstairs, in calmer surroundings, eating is a more restrained, serious business. Traditional puddings. Up-to-date wine list.

Tue to Sat 12 to 2.15, 6.30 to 9.45; closed 2 weeks mid-July

Faraday's
2-4 Kirk Brae, Cults, Aberdeen AB1 9SQ
TEL/FAX (01224) 869666
Converted hydro-electric station now running on candlepower serving plain, wholesome cooking. Dinners are more adventurous than the lunchtime menu. Mostly French wines.

Tue to Sat 12 to 1.45, Mon to Sat 7 to 9.45; closed 26 Dec to 6 Jan

Silver Darling
Pocra Quay, North Pier, Aberdeen
AB2 1DQ
TEL (01224) 576229
FAX (01224) 626558

Restaurant next to the lighthouse at the harbour entrance, with appropriately fish- and seafood-based cuisine. Inventive sauces accompany generous main dishes. A silver darling is a herring but to date none feature on the menu. Adventurous puddings.

Mon to Fri 12 to 2, Mon to Sat 7 to 10; closed 23 Dec to 6 Jan

AUCHTERLESS
Towie Tavern ★
Auchterless AB53 8EP
TEL (01888) 511201
Popular dining pub with daily changing menus based on fresh produce, especially fish and game. Steaks and grills lead the way in the restaurant. Good malt whiskies.

Open for food 12 to 2 (Sun 2.30), 6 to 9.30

BALLATER
Balgonie Country House
Braemar Place, Ballater AB35 5RQ
TEL (01339) 755482
Excellently prepared local produce served in a light white dining-room. The chef once worked down the road at Balmoral, and copes effortlessly with game and fish. Good Scottish cheeses are an alternative to fairly traditional

puddings. Forthright wine list.
*All week 12.30 to 2, 7 to 9,
booking essential; closed mid-Jan to
mid-Feb (See Where to Stay)*

Darroch Learg
Braemar Road, Ballater AB35 5UX
TEL (01339) 755443
FAX (01339) 755252
The conservatory dining-room is a
pretty place in which to eat in
summer. A new chef is installed and
the menu includes local game. Very
reasonable wine list prices.
*Sun 12.30 to 2; all week 7 to 8.30,
Sat 7 to 9; closed Jan (See Where to
Stay)*

Green Inn ⋆
9 Victoria Road, Ballater AB35 5QQ
TEL (01339) 755701
Emphatically Scottish menu with
skilled and sensible cooking of rural
produce. A flavour of the
Mediterranean is also perceptible.
Good puddings and Scottish
cheeseboard; straightforward wine list.
*Sun 12.30 to 2, all week 6 to 9;
closed Sun Nov to Mar, 2 weeks Dec*

Tullich Lodge
Ballater AB35 5SB
TEL (01339) 755406
FAX (01339) 755397
The no-choice menu offers
beautifully balanced dining and
flavourful, distinctive cooking.
Mostly French wine list, good
choice of malts.
*All week 7.30 to 9; closed end Oct
to end Mar (See Where to Stay)*

CULLEN
Bayview Hotel ⋆
57 Seafield Street, Cullen AB56 2SU
TEL (01542) 841031
Restaurant overlooking the harbour
and the Moray Firth whose short
menu includes an unrivalled
fisherman's pie and local dishes
including Cullen Skink. Good

blackboard specials. Delicious
puddings. Brief wine list.
*All week 12 to 1 .45, 6.30 to 9
(phone to check in winter)*

DRYBRIDGE
Old Monastery
Drybridge AB56 2JB
TEL (01542) 832660
The spring that supplied
Benedictine monks still flows; their
chapel is now the main dining-
room and cloisters form part of the
bar. The straightforward cooking
here stresses quality. Creative
puddings. Good wine list with
decent half-bottles.
*Tue to Sat 12 to 1.30, 7.45 to 9.30;
closed 3 weeks Jan, 2 weeks Nov*

NAIRN
Clifton House
Nairn IV12 4HW
TEL (01667) 453119
FAX (01667) 452836
French provincial cooking in a
dramatic but delightfully unaffected
setting. Absolute freshness is evident
in the clean and exciting flavours.
Puddings are more traditional. High
quality, accessible wine list;
impressive malts.
*All week 12.30 to 1, 7 to 9.30;
closed early Nov to end Mar (See
Where to Stay)*

NETHERLEY
Lairhillock Inn ⋆
Netherley, nr Stonehaven AB3 2QS
TEL (01569) 730001
Isolated eighteenth-century pub on
a back road between Stonehaven
and Aberdeen. The menu takes a
culinary world tour, using good
local produce as a base. Evening
meals served in the beamed
restaurant; vegetarians well catered
for. Real ale taken seriously.
*Open for food 12 to 2, 6 to 9.30,
Fri and Sat 6 to 10; restaurant Sun
12 to 2, all week 7 to 9.15*

THE CENTRAL
AND NORTHERN
HIGHLANDS

- Mountain scenery and empty wilderness in abundance
- The outdoor holiday centres of Strathspey and the Great Glen

Urquhart Castle

FOR many visitors, the real Scotland begins beyond Drumochter Pass or Rannoch Moor. Further south, it seems, the landscape is tame, the way of life effete and the midges mere shadows of the great biters of the Great Glen. The central and northern Highlands are marked by a change of scale – mountainous country becomes more extensive, roads fewer, the glens longer and the population sparser. It can be a mysterious, sometimes awesome country: wild, bleak and beautiful in fine weather, a dismal hell in the rain. Parts of this landscape are tamed – Speyside and the Great Glen bustle with holiday-makers. Parts are not – the rust-coloured bogs of Sutherland contain scarcely a house. Parts – the gentle country of Easter Ross, for example – are outposts of Lowland countryside in the middle of the Highlands.

The emptiness of the countryside is comparatively recent. The glens were once full of settlements, whose crumbled remains are marked by heaps of bracken-covered stone. The Clearances, when people were evicted from their houses to be replaced by sheep, were only a part of the long-running process of depopulation which swelled the Lowland cities and forced so many families onto the emigrant ships. Over 22,000 Scots went to Nova Scotia between 1815 and 1838; by 1840, Glasgow had absorbed more than 30,000 Highlanders.

The sheep that replaced the Highlanders in the glens eventually proved equally unprofitable. The sheep farms gave way to the deer forests, and huge tracts of once-populated land became the province of the deer, the ghillie, and the gentleman with the rifle. Much of the Highlands remains divided into sporting estates covering several thousand acres and the big Edwardian shooting-lodges still stand, surrounded by sheltering trees and game larders. The subject of land ownership in the Highlands is a touchy one, and you get drawn into an argument about it at your peril.

Another characteristic building of the northern Highlands is the croft house. A croft, famously defined as a piece of land surrounded by legislation, is a smallholding, the house usually ringed by a couple of fields. Few crofters have enough land from which to make a full-time living, and most supplement their income by fishing, forestry or from tourism.

Stamping ground of the clans

Before the coming of the sheep or the shooting-lodge, Highland life, deep in the mountains, centred around the extended family – the clan. The chieftain was father to his clansmen, possessing a power over them verging on the absolute, but with an equally absolute responsibility for their welfare. Where the hierarchies of Lowland society were defined by rank or wealth, the clansman defined himself by his genealogy. He might acknowledge a difference in seniority to others in his clan, but none in quality.

The truth of what clan life was like has become so obscured by romance that it is difficult to gain a clear picture. It was certainly bloody: feuds between clans were continuous, and the 'tail' of fighting men that a chieftain could raise was the most important measure of his power. Life was also pastoral, revolving around the rearing of black cattle, but there was always poverty, and raiding the neighbouring clan or joining a Lowland struggle in the hope of plunder were popular ways of relieving it. The clansman was always his own man, and one of the frustrations of generals from Montrose to Prince Charles Edward was the tendency of their Highland allies to return home when they had amassed enough loot or when it was time for the harvest.

Highland culture was, and in a few places still is, subtler than the bagpipes-and-Highland-games spectacular which is happily thrust at tourists. The history of the clan was in the custody of bards who transmitted it orally from one generation to the next, and of the piper whose duty it was to inspire the clan to battle or recall its dead in sonorous laments. Before the Battle of Culloden in 1746 there were few outsiders to record this Gaelic culture, and afterwards its mainspring had been broken. It lives on in the work of modern Gaelic poets, of whom Sorley Maclean is the most renowned, in the expertise of pipers, and in the festivals of song and music called 'Mods'.

After two centuries of emigration, the clans are now dispersed in a worldwide diaspora. Yet beneath the fashion for clan gatherings, clan museums, clan tartans, or tracing ancestors – which a cynic may see as an attempt to glue together something which is irrevocably broken – there are echoes of old loyalties which refuse to die away.

SPEYSIDE

As you travel north over the Drumochter Pass from Glen Garry and Blair Atholl, the network of glens and lochs making up the Tay river system is replaced by the single broad strath of the Spey, bleak here in its upper stretches, with two great mountain massifs — the Monadhliath to the west and the Cairngorms to the east — on the horizons. The Monadhliath are a featureless jumble of hills little frequented by visitors, but the Cairngorms, with many of the highest tops in Scotland among them, are beautiful. They are a constant presence beside the Spey valley, sometimes sinister in the lurid light preceding a blizzard, sometimes alluring in the purples and greens of summer.

The tourist industry has expanded over the 30-odd years since Lord Fraser conceived a purpose-built resort at Aviemore, and now covers most of Speyside from Newtonmore to Grantown. Thanks to the ski slopes on Cairn Gorm, to the opportunities for sailing and wind-surfing on Loch Insh and Loch Morlich, and to the endless tough or easy walks in the area, this is one of the few parts of Scotland to have a genuine year-round tourist season.

At **Dalwhinnie**, whose lonely distillery is the first sign of the great whisky industry of Speyside, there is a glimpse of the top of Loch Ericht, a deep trench scooped out by glaciers running north-east from Rannoch Moor, with the gloomy shoulder of Ben Alder hanging over it. The A889 branches off here to join the A86 which runs down Glen Spean to Fort William.

Newtonmore is the first of the series of small towns lining Speyside to have been given a new lease of life by tourism, and is one of the more peaceful. This is Macpherson territory (the clan museum is here) and also a stronghold of shinty — a game like hockey but even more vicious — which has fanatical adherents throughout the Highlands, but especially on Speyside. The place to learn about shinty is at the **Highland Folk Park** (open July to Sept, Mon to Sat 10 to 5) which has an exhibition about the game, as well as hands-on demonstrations of crofting life, like butter-churning for example.

Like so many of the planned villages in the Highlands, **Kingussie** consists of a single long street with a few side streets off it. Busier than Newtonmore, Kingussie's major attraction is the **Highland Folk Museum** (open Apr to late Oct, Mon to Sat 10 to 6, Sun 2 to 6; Nov to Mar, Mon to Fri 10 to 3) which is less interactive and has rather more to see than its Folk Park sister at Newtonmore. A visit will make you see both the ingenuity of the people living in a land with few resources and uncertain climate, and the grinding poverty which so many of them endured. With a

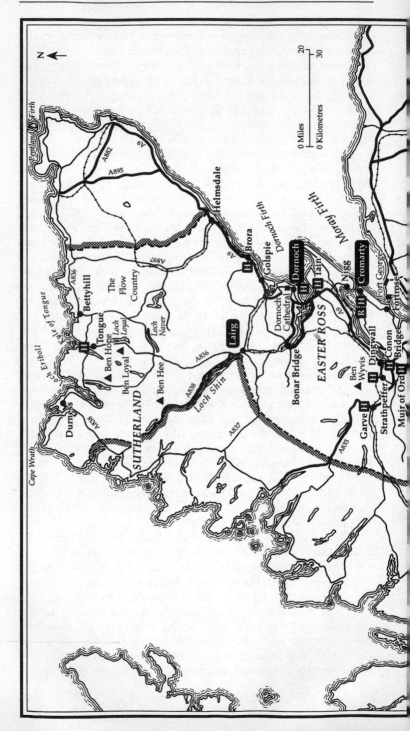

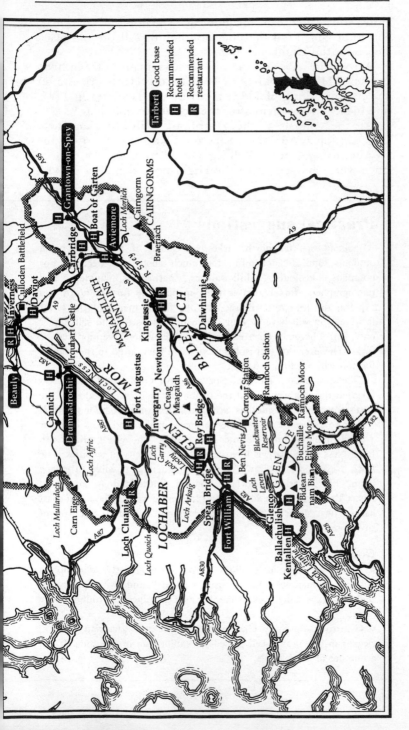

little effort you can imagine the squalor and the mal-nutrition which led the poet Southey to call the old black houses of the Highlands 'men-styes'.

Across the A9 are the shattered remains of Ruthven barracks (HS, always open), built by the Hanoverians after the Jacobite rising of 1715, taken by the Jacobites in 1746, and blown up by them after the defeat at Culloden.

All the animals at the **Highland Wildlife Park** near Kincraig (open Apr, May, Sept and Oct, daily 10 to 4; June to Aug, daily 10 to 5; well signposted from the A9) are, or once were, indigenous to the Highlands, including wolves,

Practical suggestions

A holiday this far north makes sense only if you enjoy being outdoors, and do not mind too much about the weather. For botanists, geologists, hill-walkers, naturalists, anglers and photographers, this region is tailor-made. The further north you explore, the less you will see of your fellow man and the fewer facilities you will have at your command. Shops tend to sell staples only, petrol becomes more expensive and television reception may be fuzzy. However, for real isolation you will have to go to the islands, for you will not find it here.

The two great valleys of Speyside and Glen More (the Great Glen) at the southern end of the region are the focus for most of the area's tourism. Speyside has Scotland's first purpose-built resort at Aviemore and some of the finest scenery in the land. It is ideal for a family holiday, both summer and winter. The Great Glen, with Loch Ness at its heart, is less scenic, but has plenty of facilities. The Loch Ness Monster draws crowds though it is possible to escape them. For deserted moorland, central Sutherland is matchless. Easter Ross is the place for golf and for gentle walks. The north coast has its own stark beauty of cliffs, knobbly headlands and bays of silvery sand.

Good bases

● **Aviemore** Speyside's 1960s purpose-built resort, Aviemore is bustling, sometimes vulgar, usually lively, and with plenty of activities. It is not for everyone, but is a genuine year-round family resort.

● **Grantown-on-Spey** Grantown is sedate and Victorian in tone, elegant in layout and well placed for exploration of Speyside. It has a number of solid hotels.

deer and wildcats. Part of the park is drive-through, part walk-through, and it is informative and sensibly organised (there is a free kennel for your dog, for example).

Nearby **Loch Insh** is a pretty, round loch — really a widening of the Spey. It is a good place to watch birds (there is an RSPB reserve at Insh marshes) and you may see an osprey if you are fortunate. Gardeners should head for Jack Drake's Inshriach Nursery, on the back road (B970) to Aviemore, which is famous for alpines.

● **Fort William** The excellence of the location and the proximity of first-class mountain country go some way to counteract this town's fundamental dreariness. There is a large range of guesthouse accommodation and reasonable facilities.

● **Drumnadrochit** The village itself is bedevilled by traffic and by 'Nessie' souvenir tat, but it is centrally placed for touring round Loch Ness and for penetrating the glens to the west. Staying in one of several smaller communities spread up Glen Urquhart will shield you from the worst of the main road.

● **Beauly** This very small, red sandstone town to the west of Inverness is ideal if you do not want to get bogged down in the city itself. The position is good for exploration of Glen Affric and Easter Ross. There is not a huge choice of accommodation.

● **Cromarty** Isolated on the tip of the Black Isle, Cromarty is a handsome burgh which has so far avoided the worst effects of tourism, while managing to provide a choice of places to stay. It is too far away from the through-routes to be a sensible centre for touring, but would be ideal if you wanted a few days in a small town by the sea.

● **Dornoch** This is a very pretty small town, famous for its golf course and for its good sands. The old cathedral in its centre is beautiful. Dornoch is a seaside resort of a quiet and restrained kind. It is ideal in a spell of good weather, and not badly placed for touring either.

● **Lairg** The position of Lairg makes it the obvious place from which to wander the desolate expanses of Sutherland. It lies at the foot of Loch Shin and is the centre of a network of bus routes. Not a great deal happens in the village itself, but there is a fair choice of accommodation.

Aviemore

The bones of a small, grim railway town are buried in what is now almost entirely a tourist resort. At its heart lies the Aviemore Centre, or 'Aviemore Mountain Resort' in its most recent incarnation, a complex of hotels, ice-rink, cinema, shops and arcades. The complex has recently been taken over by new owners, and there are plans for extensive refurbishment. But meanwhile, the buildings, despite being firmly 1960s in style, have worn well, thanks to the good sense of the original design. Nevertheless, it is a shock to come across what might well be a package-holiday resort on a Mediterranean coast in the middle of the Scottish Highlands, and it is certainly no place for those who hate lively and occasionally noisy entertainment. Aviemore also has plenty of accommodation outside the Centre.

The resort's huge advantage is that there is always something going on, even on the wettest of days. In winter, the ski shops are crowded, and minibuses covered in ski racks fill the car parks. In summer the same shops sell rucksacks and anti-midge cream, while the minibuses are full of families setting off on ranger-led walks. In both seasons mountaineers abound, though the high tops of the Cairngorms can be Arctic in temperament and climate. They should deter all but the expert in winter, and will punish the foolhardy at any time of year.

Most outdoor activities take place in nearby Glen More. Loch Morlich is home to sailing and windsurfing; you can fish the Spey (not one of its best stretches) or the various stocked lochs set up to cater for learners. You can visit Scotland's reindeer herd, learn rock-climbing, or go cross-country skiing. Information about all these activities and more can be found at the Tourist Information Centre in Aviemore, the Forestry Commission Centre by Loch Morlich or the Rothiemurchus Visitor Centre at Inverdruie.

Glen More

The great bowl which extends eastwards from Aviemore to the foot of Cairn Gorm is part forest park and part nature reserve (the reserve extends over much of the Cairngorm range). At its heart lies Loch Morlich, fringed by beaches of coarse granite sand. The pines of Rothiemurchus form one of the largest remaining fragments of the old Caledonian forest to be found in Scotland, and are now being carefully husbanded. It is one of the last strongholds of the rarer species of Scottish wildlife – the capercaillie, the blackcock, the pine marten, the red squirrel and the wild cat.

The walks range from gentle strolls through the silence of the forest – perhaps round **Loch an Eilein** to strenuous expeditions. The most famous of these is through the **Lairig Ghru** pass down to Linn of Dee, and leads you under the shoulders of Braeriach and Ben Macdui (whose summit is haunted by a dimly perceived grey man) right through the heart of the Cairngorms. If you insist on standing on top of a mountain without too much effort, the Cairn Gorm chair-lift (reached by the road up to the ski slopes of Coire na Ciste and Coire Cas) will get you within striking range. In

THE GLEN COE MASSACRE

In the 'Glorious Revolution' of 1688, the Catholic James VII of Scotland and II of England fled the country to avoid being deposed. The English Parliament offered the crown of England to the Protestant William of Orange. The Scots, after some hesitation, offered the Scottish crown too. The rising in support of James, started by Graham of Claverhouse (Bonnie Dundee), petered out after Dundee's death at the Battle of Killiecrankie but certain clans remained in opposition. All chiefs were required to take an oath of loyalty to King William by 1 January 1692, but it was not until the last minute that the chief of the MacDonalds of Glen coe went to sign at Fort William. No one there was authorised to receive his oath, and he had to go to Inveraray, which put him technically in breach of the deadline.

The purpose of the orders which were thereafter issued to Campbell of Glenlyon, telling him to 'fall upon the Rebells, the McDonalds of Glenco, and putt all to the sword under seventy' was simply '*pour encourager les autres*'. The orders reached Campbell on 12 February 1692, after he and his 128 men had been billeted on the MacDonalds for two weeks, and the massacre began at five the following morning. Some 40 MacDonalds were slain.

Queen Victoria piously hoped that King William had known nothing about it. This seems unlikely, although the chief agent in the massacre was Sir John Dalrymple, Master of Stair. There was an inquiry, but although the Scottish parliament agreed that the killing had been murder, Stair suffered only dismissal and the involvement of King William was glossed over.

winter, the slopes here are dotted with figures weaving their way downhill, the car parks are full, and you must go else-where for wilderness.

Boat of Garten and Carrbridge

Boat of Garten is the terminus for the small steam railway which runs in season from Aviemore. Nearby is Loch Garten, one of the most popular nature reserves in Scotland, made famous as the breeding site of the first ospreys to begin the recolonisation of the Highlands.

Carrbridge lies where the road to Inverness curves out of the Spey Valley and begins its climb up the Monadhliath to the Slochd summit. The village is almost as full of guest-houses and ski schools as Aviemore, but is a more peaceful place. The **Landmark Highland Heritage and Adventure Park** (open Nov to Mar, daily 10 to 5; Apr to mid-July 9.30 to 6; mid-July to end Aug, 9.30 to 8; Sept to late Oct, 9.30 to 5.30) provides visitors with a carefully tended stretch of old pine forest, equipped with boardwalks to stop your feet getting wet and a treetop trail to carry you to the upper storeys of the pines. There is a small nature trail, an adven-ture playground, and an audio-visual about the history of man in the Highlands, if it is wet.

Grantown-on-Spey

Grantown has the air of a place that was a well-established holiday town when Aviemore was a collection of shacks. It is a little too far from the slopes of Cairn Gorm to be able to capitalise on the skiing boom, so has to make do with its traditional clientele – those who come to fish on the Spey and those who prefer gentle walks by the river to flogging through the mountains. Grantown is staid and Victorian in its architecture, with a large central square and a long street of shops. If you intend to explore the Spey, Grantown is better placed than Aviemore, and the immediate surroundings are more enticing.

RANNOCH MOOR TO FORT WILLIAM

From Tyndrum the A82 to Fort William runs north-west into the hills, flanked by the scree-littered cone of Ben

Dorain. Across the expanse of Loch Tulla you look at the mountains which run down the south-eastern side of Glen Etive. A lonely path runs through Glen Kinglass to Loch Etive; otherwise the hills are trackless. Here, as you approach the West Highlands, there is a stepping up in the scales of grandeur and roughness of the scenery.

Most travellers get their first glimpse of **Rannoch Moor** after driving up the steep ascent above Loch Tulla. The over-whelming impression is of a watery desolation – mile upon mile of peat hag, cut by networks of small burns and lochans, with cotton grass ruffling in the wind. This hollow among the hills was filled with ice as recently as 10,000 years ago.

Nowadays, it is Scottish bog at its most uncompromising – trying to walk across its squelchy expanse without a compass in bad conditions is potentially lethal. The most sensible track, sticking to dry ground, runs along the shore of Loch Laidon and eventually ends up at Rannoch Station (catch a train back to Bridge of Orchy). Great stumps jutting from the peat hags like the bones of dinosaurs show that this area, like so much of what is now treeless wilderness, once carried a forest.

Rannoch Moor is best seen from the train. Between 2,000 and 5,000 men took almost five years to build the railway which crosses the very heart of the wilderness – it runs for miles without sight of house or road. Corrour Station, near the foot of Loch Ossian, lies entirely on its own – you can walk from here back to Rannoch Station.

Glen Coe

At the head of Glen Coe stands one of Scotland's best-known mountains, **Buachaille Etive Mòr**, the Great Shepherd of Etive. For rock-climbers, it is a landscape of beloved gullies and buttresses; for the rest, it is a shapely triangle of precipitous rock, gleaming with ice in winter, pearly grey in summer, which stands like a lighthouse on the western extremity of Rannoch Moor.

Behind it the road begins to drop into Glen Coe. The glen is famous for its notorious massacre, which, unlike the many massacres which took place in the ceaseless feuds between clans, was inspired by politics, and it is this, and the abuse of hospitality that went with it, that has made it notorious.

The road runs parallel with the jagged height of the Aonach Eagach ridge on one side and passes the three massive buttresses of Bidean nam Bian, known as the Three Sisters, on the other. When cloud hangs on the tops and the serried slabs of the buttresses are glistening with rain, Glen Coe is at its most sinister and oppressive.

Most of the mountains here are the province of the experienced walker only, but a summer expedition into the 'Lost Valley' of Coire Gabhail is demanding but less dangerous. The hanging valley between two of the Three Sisters is approached by a steep path up from the River Coe, which winds among great tangles of boulders and trees. The open expanse at the top comes as a welcome surprise after the constricted path; on a still day, this is a sheltered spot, with only echoes from the surrounding cliffs to disturb the peace.

Glen Etive, which branches off south-west just before Glen Coe, is a greener, brighter and less threatening glen to explore if you have time. The narrow road winds beside the River Etive down to a lonely pier at the head of the loch. There are plenty of grassy spaces for picnics (though beware midges). A fine day's ridge walking is to be had along the great nose of Aonach Mór to the peak of Stob Ghabhar overlooking Loch Tulla, but the usual precautions about map and compass apply stringently.

At the foot of Glen Coe, the **National Trust Visitor Centre** (NTS, open Apr to late May and early Sept to late Oct, daily 10 to 5; late May to late Aug, daily 9.30 to 6) has information about flora, fauna and history, plus ranger-led walks in summer, while **Glencoe** village has a simple memorial to the massacre and a small museum. Beyond **Ballachulish**, once famous for its slate quarries, the road north swings over Loch Leven and heads for Fort William.

Fort William

Squashed between Loch Linnhe and the mass of Ben Nevis, Fort William's location at the crossroads of the only through-routes in this part of the world, together with its easy access to Glen Nevis and Loch Ness, has turned the town from a military outpost into a holiday resort. Fort William is neither attractive nor particularly historic, and is often drenching wet into the bargain. Even so, the gift shops and tea-rooms do a thriving trade in summer, while model 'Nessies' of every shape and size line the shop windows.

There are two good reasons for basing yourself here. The first is that, short of Oban, Inverness, Aviemore or Portree, you will not find anywhere else with as many shops or so much choice of places to stay or eat. The second reason is that Fort William makes an obvious base for exploring the Ben Nevis range, which has some of the best hill-walking in the country, and now skiing at the Aonach Mór/Nevis Range complex nearby (the gondola system will take you up the mountain in summer too).

Much the most interesting sight in Fort William is the **West Highland Museum** (due to partially open May 1996 after refurbishment; call 01397 702169 for details). It is serious, modest and deliberately rather old-fashioned. The Jacobite section's star offering is a secret portrait of Charles Edward Stuart, which looks like a splodge of paint until you hold a curved mirror to it. There are also many local stories, including one describing the first ascent of Ben Nevis by car in 1911.

Ben Nevis

The great hump-backed mountain rising behind Fort William is, at 4,406 feet, Britain's highest. Streams of visitors have been making their way up it since the nineteenth century, and nowadays its top is the object of an annual race. The views are wonderful, but the summit is rather bleak. The great precipice which rings the mountain's north-eastern flank provides some of the finest rock-climbing ground in Britain, and for the experienced walker there is wonderful ridge-walking on the Mamores, the Aonachs and the range known as the Grey Corries. These hills have some of the heaviest rainfall in Scotland, so go well prepared.

Glen Nevis

Because it is so close to Fort William this glen sees a lot of visitors. It is worth persisting along the road to the car park at the end, from where the walk beside a deep gorge to the Steall waterfall is relatively easy, if rough. The track continues beyond the falls right through to Corrour Station in the middle of Rannoch Moor, about 14 miles from the car park.

GLEN SPEAN

Glen Spean is the only route to link Speyside with the southern part of the Great Glen. It is not the prettiest of glens, for fluctuating water levels caused by the dam below Loch Laggan often leave exposed patches of shingle or mud.

Spean Bridge, at the foot of the glen, is a popular stopping point because of the large woollen mill shop here and the memorial to the Commandos who trained in the nearby mountains during the World War II. This aggressive monument, with three stern figures gazing over the hills, is much photographed. At Roy Bridge a narrow road with scanty passing places winds northwards up the hill into **Glen Roy**. This otherwise ordinary, lonely glen has been made famous by the 'Parallel Roads of Glen Roy', a geological freak which you see clearly as the road turns into the upper glen. Three level stripes follow the contours of the hills about 600 feet above the floor of the glen, looking exactly as if someone had carved roads in the side of the mountains. These were once the shorelines of the deep loch that filled Glen Roy at the end of the last Ice Age; the water was unable to escape because of an ice dam in Glen Spean. The three levels reflect different stages in the melting of the ice.

Glen Roy was also the scene of the forced march by Montrose over the hills in the depths of winter. During his 1645 campaign in support of King Charles I, Montrose found his tired troops pinned in the Great Glen between an army of Campbells near Fort William and other hostile troops at Inverness. With about 1,500 men and little food apart from oatmeal, he marched south-east up Glen Tarff from the shore of Loch Ness, over passes choked by snow and down Glen Roy before inflicting a terrible defeat on Argyll and his Campbells at Inverlochy.

Creag Meagaidh, the mountain which rises on the northern shore of Loch Laggan, is not shapely, but has a corrie of considerable grandeur. The path leads in from Aberarder (boggy but not difficult) to the depths of Corie Ardair, surrounded by cliffs and with a calm lochan in the middle. The whole area is a nature reserve and it is well worth the walk to see.

At Laggan, close by the junction of the A86 and the A889, the minor road heading west is General Wade's old road (1735) over the Corrieyairack pass to the Great Glen. The road peters out into a track fairly rapidly, and makes a good walk.

THE GREAT GLEN

Glen More, also known as Glen Albyn or the Great Glen, is the remarkable geological fault which almost severs

Scotland. Running from Loch Linnhe in the south-west to Inverness in the north-east, this ruler-straight declivity is filled by deep lochs, linked by Telford's Caledonian Canal. The glen has long been the most important through-route in the north of Scotland, and inspiring or shameful things have happened in its depths. But it is the supposed presence of a monster in the dark profundities of Loch Ness that draws visitors here. A whole branch of the tourist industry thrives on this legend (or as-yet-unproven fact), which was first voiced by St Columba's biographer.

Looked at dispassionately, the Great Glen is monotonously straight, its hillsides tree-clad and uniform, and its lochs interchangeably similar in the mind's eye. Military strategy, not beauty of setting, lies behind the location of its small towns. Yet the Great Glen has advantages. It is a fine place for watery activity, from sailing to boat trips; the glens off it to the west are beautiful and distinct, and Strath Errick and Strath Nairn behind the hills to the east contain further good landscape.

North from Spean Bridge

The A82 rushes you to Inverness if you are in a hurry. Roads branch into the westward-leading glens, all of which carry you into the isolated mountainous territory lying between Loch Ness and the sea, though forestry blights the scenery in places. What would otherwise be excellent walking country west of **Loch Arkaig** is especially badly affected, and both here and at the eastern end of **Glen Garry** you need to get up above the trees to see the views. The road running along **Loch Quoich** is recommended for its isolation and its views of distant mountains. It eventually brings you to Kinloch Hourn, where you have the satisfaction of being on the edge of nowhere before making the 21-mile return trip.

A shorter expedition involves taking the A87 up to Loch Cluanie and returning down **Glen Moriston**. A viewpoint on the way up allows you a marvellous panorama of Loch Garry and the hills beyond, while Glen Moriston, with its brawling river running beneath wooded banks, is beautiful. A memorial beside the A887 commemorates Roderick Mackenzie, who drew pursuit away from Prince Charles Edward Stuart after Culloden and was shot in mistake for him.

Seven miles north of Invergarry at the foot of Loch Ness is **Fort Augustus**, built after the rising of 1715 and named after William Augustus, Duke of Cumberland – later to be called 'Butcher' after the Battle of Culloden. What remains of the fort is incorporated into the buildings of the Benedictine Abbey (open daily 9 to 6), a foundation set up in 1867 by monks from Ratisbon and now host to the local heritage centre. Fort Augustus is a sleepy sort of place today.

Just south of Drumnadrochit, the ruins of **Urquhart Castle** (HS, standard times), the most substantial fortress on Loch Ness, are essential viewing for most passers-by, as much for the drama of the site as for the interest of the castle. The ruin stands on a promontory jutting into the loch, and its walls drop sheer into the water. This stretch of the loch is where numerous sightings of the monster have been made, so the walls are manned by hopeful monster-gazers. For much of the castle's history it figured as a bastion against the western clans, especially Macdonald Lords of the Isles. During the period of the Jacobite troubles, some of the castle was blown up to prevent it from falling into 'rebel' hands. Thereafter, stone-robbers and the weather continued the destruction.

Drumnadrochit

If you are not put off by the traffic and the 'monster' tat which fills the place, Drumnadrochit is excellently situated for exploration of Loch Ness, Inverness, and the glens of Cannich and Affric. The main village stands at the head of a sheltered inlet of Loch Ness but scattered houses extend up Glen Urquhart, which rises gently behind, and if you can find somewhere to stay here it is far enough away from the loch shore to be peaceful.

By the main road, the **Loch Ness Monster Exhibition Centre** (open Easter to end May, daily 9.30 to 5.30; June, Sept, 9.30 to 6.30; July, Aug, 9 to 8.30; Oct, 9.30 to 6; Nov to Easter, 10 to 4) is housed in a substantial building. Forget any forebodings for the exhibition is well presented, and almost dispassionate. It is a walk-through audio-visual experience – rooms come to life in turn, with lights and commentary to highlight the photographs, statistics and scientific gadgets used in the hunt for the monster. A lot of money has been spent to this end – a whole fleet of boats making a sonar trawl, for example – but nothing has been proved. While the technology is impressive, it seems even more impressive that all the electronic wizardry of the twentieth century has been unable to penetrate the murky depths of Loch Ness precisely enough to reveal more (or less) than a few ambiguous traces.

In Glen Urquhart, the heap of stones which forms the prehistoric **Corrimony Chambered Cairn** (HS, always open) is surrounded by 11 standing stones. A passage, part of which is still roofed, leads to the central chamber.

Glen Affric, Glen Cannich and Strathfarrar

The road up Glen Urquhart to the modern village of Cannich is the quickest way into the scenery of these lengthy westward-running glens. The return trip down Strath Glass and round by Beauly makes a good outing. This is large-scale landscape: the glens stretch for miles to the west, with high mountains bunched in an untidy tangle around their heads. For the hill-walker, this is an area for long, hard days alone with the deer.

Strathfarrar is the northernmost of the three glens, and is accessible only on foot. It is a long 14-mile plod to Loch Monar at the top. Glen Cannich is more enclosed and not so beautiful as Glen Affric, the road up it winding over hummocks of rough ground and through woods of birch and alder to arrive at the dam behind which toss the waters of Loch Mullardoch. Glen Affric, despite hydro-electric works, has that particular combination of water, hillside and ancient pine forest which is unmatchable on a fine day. The road up is narrow and winding, but there are parking places, often with walks striking off from them into the old pine woods. Dog Fall is a popular spot – it got its name after a shepherd tried to dispose of his old dog here, but was later woken by her pathetic scratching at his door. Remorse overcame him and he allowed her to live out her days in peace. Loch Affric has been left in its natural state, and is a suitably beautiful climax to the drive.

Strath Errick and Strath Nairn

This hidden piece of country lies between the slopes of the hills bordering the eastern edge of Loch Ness and the western edge of the Monadhliath mountains. It is the country of Clan Fraser. The watershed between the two straths is barely noticeable, and the whole area forms a single open upland valley, dotted with craggy outcrops and small lochs. Away from the narrow horizons of the Great Glen, this seems a light and airy region, though the heavy afforestation will spoil much of it when the trees are taller.

Down on the shores of Loch Ness itself runs General Wade's old military road, the B852. It is much quieter than the A82 on the opposite bank, and has picnic spots along the shore. At **Foyers** the waterfall used to be a great draw (a spot praised by Burns), but it is now emasculated by hydro-electric needs, except in spates. It is still worth stopping for, though, as is the narrow gorge at **Inverfarigaig** a little further north.

INVERNESS

All the main routes through the Highlands pass through Inverness sooner or later, making it almost impossible to avoid. For the inhabitants of Sutherland, Caithness and the Northern Isles, Inverness is the great southern metropolis. If you come from anywhere else, you will find it a small, rather ordinary town — a bit of industry here and there, quiet residential estates and a compact centre with unexceptional shops (apart from James Thin, one of the best bookshops north of Edinburgh) and a good example of a covered market. The influx of summer visitors colours the

THE BATTLE OF CULLODEN

The aura of tragedy which surrounds Culloden is the result of the inevitability of the Jacobite defeat. After its long and dispiriting retreat from Derby, a half-starved, under-strength army, exhausted after an abortive night march on Nairn, faced a body of disciplined troops on ground which its most experienced officer considered utterly unsuitable.

In such circumstances, the charge of the clans was a gamble almost bound to end in failure. For half an hour they had suffered under an artillery bombardment to which they were powerless to reply. The charge, when it came, was an ill-coordinated act of courage, its only chance of success being to break the opposing troops by its ferocity. At Prestonpans and Falkirk, the Hanoverians had broken; at Culloden, sustained by their artillery and by their three ranks of bayonets, they held. At times the clansmen, powerless

streets, but Inverness can be dull off-season, while on Sundays nothing stirs.

Like Dundee, Inverness has not treated its older buildings with respect, and a number of vile modern buildings intrude into the Victorian architecture. The oldest houses are to be found in **Church Street**, notably Abertarff House, which dates from 1592. The Victorian Gothic cathedral of St Andrew is worth a glance on a wet day, while the modern Eden Court contains a theatre and gallery. Next door to the battlemented nineteenth-century mock castle, **Inverness Museum** (open Mon to Sat 9 to 5) has a comprehensive regional collection – the silver is especially worth seeing. The castle itself is the scene for **The Castle Garrison Encounter** (open Easter to Nov, 10.30 to 5) where the life of the eighteenth-century soldier is portrayed by actors, backed by a few exhibits. New recruits (you) are conducted through the Quartermaster's Store and are introduced to the Sergeant of the Guard and a female camp follower before being let loose in the Garrison shop.

Culloden Battlefield

The ground where the 1745 Jacobite rising was snuffed out is well signposted from all the southern and eastern

---

to reach the redcoats with their broadswords, were reduced to throwing stones.

All along the line, the Jacobite front rank was thrown back – the Macdonalds on the left, Clan Chattan, Frasers, Camerons and Stewarts of Appin on the right. Hanoverian casualties were given as 50 dead; well over 1,000 of the Highland army died and Prince Charles Edward was led from the field to begin months of fugitive existence before he made his final escape to France.

The aftermath was savage – most of the wounded were killed where they lay, and the prisoners, being 'rebels', were ill-treated. But the real savagery was to come. The victorious Duke of Cumberland, recognising, perhaps rightly, that this military defeat was not enough to put an end to Jacobite dreams, resolved to make an example of the Highlands. Burnings and summary arrests were followed by the banning of Highland dress. For his deeds, it is said that the English named the garden flower Sweet William after him – the Scots equivalent is the weed called Stinking Willie.

approaches to Inverness. The National Trust has restored Drumossie Moor to something nearing its state on 16 April 1746. With flags fluttering above the barren ground, and the wind whipping over the heather, the field of Culloden is by far the most evocative of Scotland's battlefields.

The visitor centre (NTS, open Apr to Oct, daily 9 to 6; Feb, Mar, Nov, Dec daily 10 to 4) is the obvious starting point and has an audio-visual introduction to the battle which is both beautifully scripted and movingly narrated. Thereafter, paths lead over the moor to the headstones which bear the names of all the clans who fought in the battle. Over 1,000 of the Jacobite Highlanders fell on this ground, and few of the wounded were spared. The restored cottage of Old Leanach marks the spot where 30 Highlanders were burnt alive.

Culloden is at its best on a day of cold sleet carried on the wind – the conditions under which the battle was fought.

Clava Cairns

Three stone chambered cairns stand in a wood not far from Culloden. Although they are open to the skies, their size and the huge number of stones used to build them show what impressive structures they were in the third millennium BC. Standing stones ring them. Oddly enough their setting adds to their air of mystery – if your experience of prehistoric monuments is linked to open barren moorland, try these cairns for a contrast.

Fort George

No enthusiast of military architecture can afford to miss this completely intact example of an eighteenth-century stronghold (HS, standard times). Fort George was started in 1748, with the aim, after Culloden, of ensuring an impregnable base in the Highlands (earlier forts had proved too vulnerable to attack). The result is a network of glacis, ditches, ravelins and bastions on the neck of a small peninsula jutting into the Moray Firth by Ardersier to the east of Inverness. You can test its impregnability by walking round the outside and imagining how you might get in under fire.

Through the gateway, the eighteenth-century barracks with their parade-ground in front look much like an upmarket housing estate. There was room for two battalions. Some rooms have been reconstructed to show standards of accommodation in 1780 and 1868. Fort George contains the Regimental Museum of the amalgamated Seaforth, Cameron and Gordon Highland regiments. It is filled with some fine displays.

EASTER ROSS

North of Inverness, three firths push inland towards the mountains, enclosing two isolated peninsulas. The countryside at their heads where the Rivers Beauly, Conon and Oykel flow down from the glens is hilly and wooded. It seems a manageable, tame landscape, yet the bulk of Ben Wyvis rising above it is a reminder that you are still in the Highlands.

Oil has wrought changes here, visible in the platform fabrication yards of Nigg. On the whole, the changes are for the better, injecting some much-needed prosperity into the small towns and villages, and leaving few unsightly messes behind.

Beauly

'*Quel beau lieu*', Mary Queen of Scots is reputed to have said, looking at this small russet town 14 miles west of Inverness. Beauly has a couple of hotels, an old-fashioned woollen and tweed shop (Campbell and Company) with a country-wide reputation, and a pleasant, wide main street. It also has the ruins of a beautiful thirteenth-century priory, with notable windows.

The Black Isle

This used to be secret country before the Beauly Firth was bridged and the A9 driven through its centre. Few people stop to explore, even now. Much of the Black Isle is farmland or forest, though some patches of oakwood and bog remain. It is on the coast that the most interesting places are found.

Drive east on the A832 and look out for a flash of garish colour by the side of the road. This is a clootie well, a spring whose waters have healing or magic properties. Those who drink hang pieces of bright cloth (or the occasional plastic bag) from nearby branches to mark their visit. There is another such well near the village of **Avoch**, a pronunciation trap (the 'a' and 'v' are silent) with a pretty harbour.

411

The A832 brings you to **Fortrose**, where copper beeches and yew trees stand by the fragmentary remains of the cathedral, and substantial Victorian villas with ball and spike finials on their gables line the quiet streets. The cathedral (HS, always open) dates from the thirteenth century but now only the south aisle and the sacristy remain. Still, the warm, buttery sandstone and the simplicity of the early Gothic vaulting are exceptional.

On the eastern side of the small headland of Chanonry Point (the result of a glacial moraine) lies the little resort of **Rosemarkie**. The beach is not appealing. Go instead to the museum at **Groam House** (open Easter to Oct, Mon to Sat 10 to 5, Sun 2 to 4.30; Oct to early May, open weekends only 2 to 4), which has a fine Pictish symbol stone as well as videos about the Black Isle and the Brahan Seer. This famous local came to a sticky end in a barrel of boiling tar on Chanonry Point for being rather too frank with the Countess of Seaforth about what her absent husband was up to. Chanonry Point is also the place to try to see the Moray Firth's school of bottle-nosed -dolphins. You will find more information about them at the **Dolphin and Seal Centre**, which is on the A9 two miles north of Inverness.

Cromarty

The ancient royal burgh at the tip of the Black Isle is still not much larger than a village, but contains some of the most beautiful late eighteenth-century buildings in Scotland. Cromarty's prosperity was due to the imagination of George Ross, who bought the town in 1772 and supplemented the Scandinavian trade with a variety of small industries. Substantial red sandstone houses line some of the streets and old fishermen's cottages cling to the shore. There is a quiet little church with three separate lofts, and the restored buildings of an old rope works. The new **Cromarty Courthouse** (open Easter to end Oct, daily 10 to 6; Nov to Easter, l2 to 4) explains the history of the town.

Two men from Cromarty achieved renown in very different fields. One, Sir Thomas Urquhart, is remembered for his translation of Rabelais, for his eccentricity, and for the fact that he died laughing when he heard of Charles II's restoration in 1660. The other, Hugh Miller, early nineteenth-century stonemason, naturalist, philosopher and writer, is little read now, but his researches into the local old red sandstone still bring geologists to trace his footsteps. His house is now open as a simple museum (NTS, open late Apr to early Oct, Mon to Sat 10 to 1, 2 to 5.30, Sun 2 to 5.30).

Beyond the town, a narrow lane leads up to the top of **South Sutor**, one of the twin precipitous headlands guarding the narrow entrance to the Cromarty Firth. From the rubble of old military emplacements here, the view stuns. Northward, white-streaked cliffs and a green sea; southward, on a clear day, the whole of the Moray coast stretching into the haze.

Dingwall and around

The Munros hold much of the land round here, on condition that they furnish a snowball in mid-summer to their overlord if required to do so, some poor retainer being despatched to the northern corries of Ben Wyvis for the purpose. Dingwall itself is a small town, by-passed by the traffic, and a place to stock up on necessities if you are venturing into the wild. The **museum** (open May to end Sept, Mon to Sat 10 to 5) contains a good selection of local relics, including a monstrous clock mechanism.

Not far west, on the A834, **Strathpeffer** is said to be Scotland's answer to Bavarian mountain resorts. Its outcrop of Germanic-looking hotels and villas denotes that the place was once a spa, with a branch railway line from Dingwall (the restored station is now a craft centre). In keeping with the spa atmosphere there are plenty of undemanding walks in the surrounding countryside. One such leads to the **Eagle Stone**, a Pictish monument on the outskirts of the town. It is said (by the Brahan Seer) that ships will moor to it if it falls three times. It has fallen twice so far.

Garve, on the A832, is barely more than a hamlet by a road junction, but there are plenty of parking places and picnic spots in the woods nearby, while the **Falls of Rogie** are popular, largely because they are close to the road. The railway running through Garve towards Kyle of Lochalsh (the subject of many a closure scare) is lauded as one of the most attractive lines in Britain. So it is, in its last few miles by Loch Carron, but the long run down Strath Bran and Glen Carron cannot hold a candle to the line from Fort William to Mallaig.

The Tain Peninsula

More people have heard of Glenmorangie than of Tain, for that whisky is certainly the best-known product of the area.

Flat and unlovely in parts, and with the industry of Invergordon and Nigg on its southern shore, the hammer-headed peninsula sandwiched between Dornoch and Cromarty firths is not immediately appealing but retains the capacity to surprise, occasionally.

One such surprise is the **Black Rock Gorge**. With its inauspicious beginning near the caravan site at the back of Evanton, this takes a bit of finding among the trees which fringe it (try the third track to your left). The cleft is so deep and narrow that it is almost impossible to see the bottom without taking foolish risks, and there are no paths or barriers. Mosses and ferns dangle in the chasm like a hairy fringe, and the River Glass hisses in the depths.

Take the B9175 towards the North Sutor headland and explore the minor road behind Nigg for its views. At Nigg, see the fine Pictish cross-slab in the church. A further Pictish stone stands near the roadside by the coastal village of Shandwick, covered with hunting and battle scenes.

Near the tip of Tarbat Ness, **Portmahomack** is one of the oldest planned villages in Scotland, dating from the early eighteenth century. It is a tiny seaside resort with a little golf course, a semi-circle of sand, some rocks to climb over and a couple of streets of cottages. On a fine day, it is perfect. The old church here has a slightly oriental-looking dome instead of a spire – it was possibly once used as a lighthouse.

The solid, self-confident sandstone town of **Tain** is a burgh of great antiquity, but of no great beauty. The turreted tolbooth dominating the High Street looks like a product of Victorian baronial tastes, but is early eighteenth-century. Elizabeth de Burgh, wife of Robert the Bruce, fled to St Duthus Chapel for sanctuary in 1307. The Earl of Ross did not give a fig for such niceties and handed her over to Bruce's enemies.

Strathcarron

Not to be confused with the better known Glen Carron to the west, this gentle valley runs down to join the Kyle of Sutherland opposite Bonar Bridge. Roads run on either side of the light, open strath, while fragments of old pine forest remain up towards its head. The combination of river and heathery scenery is very fine.

In the churchyard of **Croik**, where the road ends, people from neighbouring Glencalvie took shelter after being evicted from their homes in May 1845. Scratched on the glass of the church windows are the graffiti which are their only memorial.

SUTHERLAND

North of the Dornoch Firth lies Sutherland, a huge tract of the bleakest wilderness in Scotland. Only a few tour coaches battle their way up the east coast to Dunrobin Castle and John o' Groats. The west coast is a jumble of rock; the straths of the centre are empty of people and the small settlements of the east and north cling to the rough coasts. Sutherland is the province of the angler, the bird-watcher and the forester.

Strath Oykel

Flocks of wading birds feed on the mudflats of the Dornoch Firth, and salmon fishermen line the Kyle of Sutherland above the cheerful village of Bonar Bridge. The River Oykel, which empties into this estuary, has its source by Ben More Assynt close to the west coast, and its valley forms a convenient route to Ullapool.

Drive up the Oykel from Bonar Bridge and turn up **Glen Cassley** to see the Cassley Waterfall, which plunges into a rocky pool surrounded by pine trees and boulders. There will probably be salmon fishermen, up to their chests in waders, to watch for entertainment. Just beneath the falls lies an old graveyard with tombstones under the pines.

As far as Oykel Bridge, the road dips in and out of conifer plantations, and there is not much to be said for it, but as it climbs over the watershed, towards Ledmore, the eastern peak of **Suilven** rears into view. This is far the best way to approach Scotland's most remarkable mountain, for it appears like an unscalable alpine peak over the horizon.

Lairg and Loch Shin

The River Shin pours into the Oykel by the power station at Inveran. Take the B864 from here through Achanay Glen to visit the **Falls of Shin**. These form the best salmon leap in the country, and there is a large car park for visitors and a well-maintained path down through the trees to a platform above the falls. The river plunges in a peat-coloured chute into a black pool, from which the salmon hurl themselves upwards into the force of water. An early evening in summer when there is plenty of water is said to give you the best chance of seeing them – take anti-midge precautions.

Lambs from all over the north are brought to the sales at **Lairg**, a sunny village by the foot of Loch Shin which is also the connecting point between the railway and the network of post buses which wind over Sutherland's isolated roads. For its size, Lairg has a reasonable sprinkling of hotels and guesthouses, a network of gentle walks, and a number of hill lochs containing trout. There is also a small countryside centre with information about Sutherland landscapes.

The A838 beside the long, narrow **Loch Shin** is monotonous at first, but eventually emerges into bleak and mountainous terrain by Loch Merkland and Loch More, where the broken quartzite on the tops of Foinaven and Arkle is easily mistaken for the shimmer of ice. Beyond, the scenery changes to the fragmented, knobbly country typical of Sutherland's west coast. When the rain is lashing down, this is the sort of landscape where you hope your car was properly serviced; even on fine summer days it seems stark and primeval.

The northern routes from Lairg

From Lairg, the A836 to **Altnaharra** emerges gradually from the spruce forests which suffocate the views for the first few miles. From now on, the forests – always present and always spreading – are merely irritating patches on the great tawny blankets of bog which stretch in all directions, except where the rounded humps of Ben Klibreck heave themselves skywards. Altnaharra is little more than a few cottages, but a renowned centre for anglers. The salmon rivers flowing northwards are famous – getting a day on one of them is nearly impossible – but there is trout fishing in abundance in the isolated lochs or burns.

From Altnaharra, the route that takes you through the most isolated country is the B873 down Loch Naver to Syre and on the B871 to Kinbrace on the River Helmsdale. This skirts patches of the **Flow Country** – that quaking blanket bog, half-water, half-land, which is (or was, before the tree-planting started) an untouched quagmire whose intact community of plants, birds and animals is unique. The best way of seeing it without spending a day up to your knees in peat mire is to visit the RSPB's visitor centre at Forsinard (open Easter to Oct, daily 9 to 6) on the A897 north from

Kinbrace (in the railway station). There is a short path out into the bog with an explanatory leaflet. There are occasional guided walks further afield. Call 01641 571225 for information. Another, unsurpassable, way of seeing the Flow Country is to take the train, for the railway which runs up the Strath of Kildonan loops eastward from Forsinard towards Wick, running over mile after mile of wilderness.

A more mountainous round trip from Altnaharra involves driving down Strath More under the shadow of Ben Hope and returning via Tongue past Lettermore and Loch Loyal. One of the attractions of this route is the well-preserved broch of Dun Dornaig.

The shallow valley of Strath Naver running down to Bettyhill is a less attractive route, but interesting for its relics of the Clearances. At **Rossal**, just before you emerge from the forest at Syre, the remnants of a pre-Clearance village lie in a clearing. Here you can see the layout of a typical settlement, from which the inhabitants were summarily turfed out and told to start making their living at Bettyhill.

The East Coast

Dornoch

Golf is the biggest draw here, but Dornoch is also blessed with an excellent sandy beach. There are a number of golfing hotels fronting the links, as well as one or two in the town itself and plenty of guesthouse accommodation. Dornoch is a handsome old burgh, with a little cruciform cathedral, greenery and flowers. The **cathedral** (open dawn to dusk) was started in 1224 by Gilbert de Moravia, and the bishop's palace (now an hotel) rose alongside. The cathedral was burnt in 1570 during a clan feud and restored (with much butchering) by William Burn in 1835. A better restoration in 1924 has left it a very beautiful church indeed: the thirteenth-century work at the crossing – all in deep red sandstone – is wonderful. Do not miss the gargoyles peering from the eaves.

Dunrobin Castle

(Open Easter to end May and early to mid-Oct, Mon to Sat 10.30 to 4.30, Sun 1 to 4.30; June to end Sept, Mon to Sat 10.30 to 5.30, Sun 12 to 5.30; July and Aug, 10.30 to 5.30) As the only stately home north of Inverness regularly open to the public, and as one of the very few sights in Sutherland or Caithness, Dunrobin Castle gets more attention than it really warrants. The castle, to which the 'fairy-tale' epithet is often attached, is in fact a ponderous nineteenth-century version of a French château with Scottish baronial overtones, and something is not quite right about the proportions of the Renaissance-style windows. Buried in the depths of Sir Charles Barry's work are the remains of a much older castle, while Sir Robert Lorimer remodelled much of the interior following a fire in 1915.

Dunrobin has passed through hard times since the days when the wealth of the Dukes of Sutherland drove the railway north (the Duke's private station can still be seen). Few traces remain of its period as a school, but the furniture has that aura of having been stored away and not used for years. The best things are the paintings – some fine portraits of diaphanously clad duchesses and some Canalettos. Wander down to the gardens for the best view of the castle, and go to the museum to see the Pictish stones.

THE HIGHLAND CLEARANCES

'. . . the entire population were then compressed into a space of three thousand acres of the most barren land in the parish, and the remaining one hundred and thirty thousand acres were divided among six sheep farmers.' (Evidence to the Napier Commission, 1883)

There are few corners of Scottish history as emotionally and politically charged as the Clearances. Throughout the nineteenth century, landlords evicted Highland tenants from their homes, replacing the pattern of marginal smallholdings with extensive sheep farms. It was not until 1886, in the face of growing civil disobedience such as the Battle of the Braes on Skye, that the Napier Commission's report resulted in the passing of the Crofting Act. This gave crofters security of tenure and brought the Clearances to an end, but did nothing to restore land already cleared.

The methods of eviction were often harsh, in some cases involving violence, and certainly the burning of croft houses. Some of those evicted from their homes were resettled by the sea to work in the kelp industry, to take up fishing, or to try to wrest a new living from even more marginal land. But many thousands more emigrated. The Clearances were the most significant factor in the depopulation of the Highlands, but not the only one. Not every ruin you see has an eviction behind it.

Helmsdale and Kildonan

Helmsdale, at the foot of a steep ravine, was a fishing settlement for displaced crofters which boomed during the herring years in the second half of the nineteenth century. A new bridge sweeps you through the town, but it is worth turning off and exploring the old harbour, with buildings going back to the heyday of the herring fleet. Helmsdale also has the **Timespan Heritage Centre** (open Easter to Oct, Mon to Sat 10 to 5, Sun 2 to 5; July and Aug 10 to 6, Sun 2 to 6) where, among a well-mounted display of local history (including the Clearances), you will also find the Barbara Cartland room – for the romantic novelist is a regular visitor. If your taste for incongruity needs further sharpening, have a snack in 'La Mirage', a café with a difference.

The River Helmsdale, one of the best and most exclusive salmon rivers in Scotland, runs down the **Strath of**

The left-wing view of the Clearances is to see them as part of a capitalist drive to maximise gain at the expense of the people. Much the best popular expression of this interpretation remains John McGrath's 1973 play *The Cheviot, the Stag and the Black, Black Oil.* The right-wing view sees the Clearances as an unnecessarily harsh but inevitable process, justified at the time by the fashionable theory of political economy (satirised by Dickens in *Hard Times*) and in retrospect by the success of many of the emigrants' descendants. The view today's visitor gets is most likely to be the fashionable 'heritage' approach to the topic, which concentrates clearly on the dispersed communities and their lifestyle, but is apt to simplify the underlying issues.

The first Duke of Sutherland is a key figure in the demonology of the Clearances. Sir Ian Moncrieff (quoted in the guide to Dunrobin Castle) sums him up as a man willing 'to dedicate his life and fortune to making other folk do something they found desperately disagreeable for the sake of what he believed to be their future good'. On the other hand, Rob Donn, the Gaelic poet (quoted by John McGrath in *As an Fhearann*) wrote: 'First Duke of Sutherland, for your deviousness and collusion with the Lowlanders, the depths of hell are what you deserve. I would rather have Judas by my side than you.' The Duke's statue stands on Ben Vraggie; its subscribers include his 'grateful tenants'.

USEFUL DIRECTORY

Main tourist office
Highlands of Scotland Tourist Board
Tourist Information Centre
Aviemore
Inverness-shire PH22 1PP
Tel (0990) 143070
Fax (01479) 811063

Tourist office publications Annual visitor's guides. Special interest leaflets include Loch Ness Monster Trail, A9 Trail and Ski Scotland.

Local tourist information offices
Aviemore (01479) 810363
Ballachulish (01855) 811296 (Apr to Oct)
Bettyhill (01641) 521342 (Mar to Sept)
Carrbridge (01479) 841360 (May to Sept)
Daviot Wood (01463) 772203 (Apr to Oct)
Dornoch (01862) 810400
Durness (01971) 511259 (late Mar to Oct)
Fort Augustus (01320) 366367 (Apr to Oct)
Fort William (01397) 703781
Grantown-on-Spey (01479) 872773 (Apr to Oct)
Helmsdale (01431) 821640 (late Mar to Sept)
Inverness (01463) 234353
Kingussie (01540) 661297 (May to Sept)
Lairg (01549) 402160 (late Mar to Sept)
North Kessock (01463) 731505
Ralia (Newtonmore) (01540) 673253 (Apr to Oct)
Spean Bridge (01397) 712576 (Apr to Oct)
Strathpeffer (01997) 421415 (Apr to Oct)

Public transport
For Inverness, Fort William and Aviemore rail services (0345) 212282
Inverness Airport (01463) 234471
Wick Airport (01955) 602215
Highland Bus and Coach (01463) 233371
Cromarty-Nigg ferry (regular daily summer service, weekdays only winter, check) (01862) 851324
Corran ferry, Loch Linnhe (frequent crossings) (01855) 841243
Durness-Cape Wrath ferry (May to end Sept three to eight times per day) (01971) 511376

Aviemore information

Aviemore Mountain Resort (01479) 810624

Aviemore – Boat of Garten steam railway (01479) 810725

Cairngorm ski information (01479) 861261

Forestry Commission Centre, Loch Morlich (01479) 861220

Glen Coe Chairlift (01855) 851226

Glen Coe Mountain Rescue (01855) 811258

Glen More area mountain rescue (01479) 810150

Local mountain weather information: Grampian and Highlands weather line (0891) 505324

Rothiemurchus Estate (farm tours, estate safaris, fishing, clay pigeon shooting) (01479) 810858

Recreation

Boat trips on Loch Ness (01456) 450395

Boat trips on Loch Ness and Caledonian Canal (01463) 233999

Cruise Loch Ness (01320) 366277

Dolphin Ecosse (dolphin watching trips, booking essential) (01381) 600323

Moray Firth cruises (from Inverness), (01463)717900

Nevis Range Aonach Mór information (01397) 705825 (skiing, gondola, cable cars, walks); (01397) 704008 (mountain bikes)

Kildonan. This is well known for its prehistoric remains, and as the scene of the 'Kildonan gold rush', when a whole shanty town sprung up at Baile an or, the town of the gold.

The North coast

The north coast of Scotland, confronting the turbulent waters of the Pentland Firth, is a remote place, and the narrow road skirting it is slow, winding and unfrequented. The steep cliffs are broken here and there by perfect beaches, and by the long fingers of sea – the Kyles of Durness and Tongue, and Loch Eriboll – that reach inland. Those who come here are rewarded by the short summer nights, the wildness of the sea and the dunes, and the relaxed pace of life in the small communities.

Cape Wrath

Getting to the most north-westerly tip of mainland Britain is an adventure. There is no road from the south, and no bridge across the Kyle of Durness. Instead, a ferry shuttles across, connecting with a minibus on the far side (to no particular timetable). When the Kyle is too rough, the operation comes to a halt. Once across the Kyle, the minibus bumps along ten miles of deserted track – the whole of this area is a naval bombardment range – until the lighthouse at Cape Wrath comes into view. You look at the cliffs to the east and the cliffs to the south, and at the skerries of the Pentland Firth being creamed by the waves. If it rains you take shelter in the old engine room of the lighthouse among some ancient diesels. And that is it – a far cry from the tourist trappings of John o' Groats.

Durness

There is a café and gift shop in Durness called 'The Last Resort', which sums the place up. Hardy caravanners come here, and others drawn by the magnificent beaches and sand dunes around Faraid Head; regulars will tell you of the pleasure of swimming from Balnakeil sands with only seals for company. A limestone outcrop at Durness turns the country green, and explains the quality of the local trout lochs. The geology, and much else, is explained in the excellent visitor centre (open Apr, late Sept and early Nov, Mon to Sat 10 to 5; May, Mon to Sat 10 to 6; June, Mon to Sat 9.30 to 6, Sun 10 to 4; July to early Sept, Mon to Sat 9 to 6.30, Sun 10 to 4; early to mid–Sept, Mon to Sat 9.30 to 5.30 or 6, Sun 10 to 4), with liberal illustrations by local schoolchildren. **Balnakeil Craft Village** is a group of vile concrete blocks, marked on windy days by colourful kites, where you can buy candles, knitwear and so on. The buildings were once an early warning station; later an enterprising council let them to craftspeople at peppercorn rents.

Smoo Cave

This cavern, east of Durness, is another result of the limestone. A steep path leads down to the entrance, out of which rushes a small burn. The cave's outer chamber is massive, and the drips fall at speed. The roar of a waterfall comes from an inner chamber, which you penetrate on a neat wooden bridge, deafened by noise and blinded by spray where the burn plunges 70 feet from the sinkhole above. If there is not too much water, a rubber inflatable will take you into a further chamber. An unusual form of graffiti is the rule here: visitors leave their messages picked out in stones on the slope in front of the cave.

Loch Eriboll to Bettyhill

Loch Eriboll is a very beautiful sea loch, which you have plenty of time to admire as the road winds round it. It was here that the Norse ships gathered before sailing south to their defeat at Largs in 1263 and here, in 1945, that the remnants of the German U-boat fleet surfaced to surrender.

As you come over the rise beyond Loch Eriboll, the multi-peaked Ben Loyal lies before you, and will dominate the view henceforth.

A causeway crosses the **Kyle of Tongue**, which is pleasant when the tide is in, but very muddy when it is out. Just before you cross it, a road northwards takes you to the small township of Melness. This area of indented coastline, with a little pier, offshore rocky islets and rumours of Jacobite gold, may tempt you into staying. Tongue itself, a semi-rural town with a ruined castle rising above it, is a good alternative.

The settlement of **Bettyhill**, 12 miles east, was established for evicted crofters at the time of the Clearances, and was named after the first Duchess of Sutherland. It is windblown, but there is beautiful seashore nearby. Part of Torrisdale Bay is a nature reserve, especially good for botanists, while Farr Bay to the east has a lovely beach. The **Strathnaver Museum** (open Apr to end Oct, Mon to Sat 10 to 1, 2 to 5; open during winter but check times beforehand, call 01641 521330) is in the old church at Bettyhill, and is the place to absorb the history of the locality. The sections on the Clearances and on post-Clearance life are particularly strong.

WHERE TO STAY

£ – under £70 per room per night, incl. VAT

££ – £70 to £110 per room per night, incl. VAT

£££ – over £110 per room per night, incl. VAT

AVIEMORE
Alvie Manse

Aviemore PH22 1QB
TEL (01479) 810248
Near the loch, this building shares a driveway with the church. The drawing and dining-rooms have antique furniture. Packed lunches are available. Bedrooms are all top floor.
£ All year; 3 rooms with wash-basin; credit cards not accepted

BALLACHULISH
Ballachulish Home Farm
Ballachulish PA39 4JX
TEL (01855) 811792
A modern building on the south
shore of Loch Leven, with good
views. Breakfast only is served in
the dining-room. Comfortable,
good-sized bedrooms.
£ *All year exc Chr; 3 rooms; credit
cards not accepted*

Ballachulish House
Ballachulish PA39 4JX
TEL (01855) 811266
FAX (01855) 811498
Eighteenth-century family home
surrounded by glorious Highland
countryside. The large drawing-
room is smart, the dining-room
formal with equine prints. The
menu features local ingredients.
Bedrooms range from homely to
enormous.
£-££ *All year exc Chr and New
Year; 6 rooms*

BOAT OF GARTEN
Moorfield House
Deshar Road, Boat of Garten PH24 3BN
TEL (01479) 831646
Comfortable Victorian house next to
the church. Home-cooked meals
served in a dining area adjacent to the
lounge; packed lunches are available.
Simply furnished bedrooms.
£ *All year exc 25 Dec; 4 rooms;
credit cards not accepted*

Old Ferryman's House
Boat of Garten PH24 3BY
TEL (01479) 831370
Welcoming house just outside the
village; new arrivals are given tea
and flapjacks. A cosy sitting-room
has cane furniture. Home-cooked
meals are served in the dining-
room. Neat bedrooms.
£ *Variable opening periods; 4 rooms
sharing a bathroom and wc; credit
cards not accepted*

BRORA
Tigh Fada
Golf Road, Brora KW9 6QS
TEL/FAX (01408) 621332
Guesthouse on the edge of town
with uninterrupted views of the
hills and sea. With four-hole pitch
and putt course and croquet green,
the garden provides access to a golf
course and sandy beach. Breakfast is
served in the dining-room; tea and
cakes are provided in the evening.
Comfortable bedrooms.
£ *All year exc Chr and New Year;
3 rooms; credit cards not accepted*

CARRBRIDGE
Féith Mho'r Country House
Station Road, Carrbridge PH23 3AP
TEL (01479) 841621
A small Victorian house with views
overlooking the hills. Pre-dinner
drinks are sipped in front of a log
fire in the lounge; home-cooked
food is served in the dining-room.
Comfortable bedrooms.
£ *All year exc 26 Dec to 1 Jan; 6
rooms; credit cards not accepted*

CONON BRIDGE
Kinkell House
Easter Kinkell, Conon Bridge IV7 8HY
TEL/FAX (01349) 861270
Small family-run hotel. Spruce
sitting-rooms are pretty in pink; the
conservatory and dining-room are
spotless. Traditional British food.
Bedrooms have pine and antique
furnishings.
£ *4 rooms; closed Jan to Feb*

CROMARTY
Royal Hotel
Marine Terrace, Cromarty IV11 8YN
TEL/FAX (01381) 600217
Hospitable pebble-dash waterfront
inn. The blue-toned lounge is
comfortable; the lively bar
decorated with local prints. No-
nonsense cooking in a formal

dining-room. Pretty fabrics enliven the bedrooms.

£ All year; restaurant closed Sun eves; 10 rooms; fishing (See Where to Eat)

DAVIOT
Daviot Mains Farm
Daviot, nr Inverness IV1 2ER
TEL/FAX (01463) 772215
Mixed working farm near Culloden Moor. A wood-burning stove cheers the lounge and dining-room; dinner is by arrangement. A steep staircase leads to the homely bedrooms.

£ All year exc 24 to 25 Dec; 3 rooms

DORNOCH
Trevose Guest House
Cathedral Square, Dornoch IV25 3SD
TEL (01862) 810269
Trevose stands near the Cathedral, overlooking the village green. The cosy dining-room has a bar. Comfortable lounge.

£ Mar to mid-Oct; 5 rooms, some with bath-shower; credit cards not accepted

DRUMNADROCHIT
Glenkirk
Drumnadrochit, Inverness IV3 6TZ
TEL (01456) 450802
A simply furnished converted chapel. The lounge on the half-landing retains the original chapel window; there is a ground-floor breakfast room. Neat bedrooms.

£ All year exc 10 Jan to 20 Feb; 4 rooms with wash-basin; credit cards not accepted

Polmaily House Hotel
Drumnadrochit, Inverness IV3 6XT
TEL (01456) 450343
FAX (01456) 450813
Plenty to do at this cheerful hotel. The comfortable sitting-room and upstairs library provide places to sit and read; outdoors are woodland walks and a play area. Food is

traditional and slightly uninspiring. Smart bedrooms.

£-££ All year; 11 rooms; drying-room; tennis; horse-riding; heated swimming-pool; fishing; canoeing; croquet

FORT AUGUSTUS
Old Pier House
Fort Augustus PH32 4BX
TEL (01320) 366418
FAX (01320) 366770
This whitewashed building on Loch Ness is attached to a riding centre and has its own Highland cattle. A large patio area overlooks the loch and an open fire burns in the lounge. Evening meals are by arrangement and served in the kitchen-cum-dining-room; packed lunches are available. Ground floor bedrooms are simple.

£ Apr to Oct; 4 rooms; boating; canoeing; cycling; credit cards not accepted

FORT WILLIAM
Ashburn House
1 Achintore Road, Fort William
PH33 6RQ
TEL/FAX (01397) 706000
Guesthouse with views over Loch Linnhe. Inside, stripped-pine adds character. The conservatory lounge has books and board-games and the breakfast-room overlooks the water. Spacious, bedrooms.

£ Feb to end Nov; 7 rooms

The Factor's House
Torlundy, Fort William PH33 6SN
TEL (01397) 705767
FAX (01397) 702953
Edwardian estate manager's house and retreat at the foot of Ben Nevis. Books, maps and sailing photographs decorate the public rooms. The contemporary dining-room forms an ideal setting for adventurous cooking. Modern-style, large bedrooms.

£££ Closed 5 Jan to 1 Mar;

restaurant closed Sun and Mon eves; 5 rooms; tennis

Glenlochy Guest House

Nevis Bridge, Fort William PH33 6PF
TEL (01397) 702909
Built in 1930 for a distillery manager, Glenlochy is immaculate. The lounge is comfortable; breakfast only is served in the dining-room. Small, functional bedrooms; two adjacent self-catering units.
£ *All year exc Chr; 12 rooms*

The Grange

Grange Road, Fort William PH33 6JF
TEL (01397) 705516
Victorian house in a quiet road above town with views over Loch Linnhe. Guests are welcomed with sherry in an elegant cream drawing-room; breakfasts are served in the dining-room. Spacious bedrooms.
£ *Mar to Nov; 3 rooms*

Inverlochy Castle

Torlundy, Fort William PH33 6SN
TEL (01397) 702177
FAX (01397) 702953
Without peer among Scottish country-house hotels, Inverlochy Castle offers superb service and sublime cuisine. An air of grandeur and elegance pervades this baronial castle where guests' comfort is paramount. The gold drawing room overlooks Loch Linnhe. The dining-room is traditional, the adventurous food a *tour de force*. Large, luxurious bedrooms.
£££ *Closed Dec to Feb; 17 rooms; drying-room; games room; fishing; tennis (See Where to Eat)*

GARVE
Inchbae Lodge

Garve IV23 2PH
TEL (01997) 455269
FAX (01997) 455207
Unprepossessing roadside inn with a comfortable feel. The hub of the place is a small bar; the lounge is well stocked with books and board-games. The delicious menu uses local game and fish. Bedrooms in the main house have modern soft-furnishings. Chalet rooms used in summer only.
£ *All year exc 25 to 26 Dec; 12 rooms; drying-room; fishing*

GRANTOWN-ON-SPEY
Culdearn House

Woodlands Terrace, Grantown-on-Spey PH26 3JU
TEL (01479) 872106
FAX (01479) 873641
An exemplary guesthouse. Seascapes and antique maps decorate the neat lounge and malts and liqueurs line the sideboard in the pretty dining-room. Enjoyable food. Bedrooms are fresh and smart with thoughtful touches.
££ *Nov to Feb; 9 rooms; drying-room*

Kinross House

Woodside Avenue, Grantown-on-Spey PH26 3JR
TEL (01479) 872042
FAX (01479) 873504
A Victorian stone house, a short walk from the centre of town. A log fire burns in the sitting-room; traditional evening meals are served in the dining-room. Ample bedrooms are bright and smart.
£ *Apr to end Oct; 6 rooms; credit cards not accepted*

INVERNESS
Clisham House

43 Fairfield Road, Inverness IV3 5QP
TEL/FAX (01463) 239965
Formerly the Bishop's house, this guesthouse is in a quiet road. The lounge is comfortable and breakfast only is served in the dining-room. Large, airy bedrooms.
£ *All year; 4 rooms; credit cards not accepted*

Craigside Lodge

4 Gordon Terrace, Inverness IV2 3HD
TEL (01463) 231576
FAX (01463) 713409
A Victorian residence with views
over the castle and river. Breakfast
is served in the lower ground-floor
dining-room and packed lunches
are available. The bedrooms have
been recently decorated.
£ All year; 6 rooms

Culduthel Lodge

14 Culduthel Road, Inverness IV2 4AG
TEL/FAX (01463) 240089
Fresh flowers give this Georgian
house elegance. Pre-dinner drinks
are served in the comfortable
lounge; the dining-room is
attractive. Appetising home
cooking; packed lunches available.
Bedrooms are individually
decorated.
£ All year exc Chr; 12 rooms

Dunain Park

Inverness IV3 6JN
TEL (01463) 230512
FAX (01463) 224532
Luxurious Georgian villa on the
outskirts of Inverness. Family
photographs and curios add a
personal touch in the public rooms;
the elegant green drawing-room has
robust leather chesterfields and
fragile Doulton figurines. Cooking
is skilful and polished. Lots of extras
in the individually designed
bedrooms.
£ Closed Jan to Feb; 12 rooms, 2
cottages; drying-room; indoor
swimming-pool; sauna; croquet,
badminton (See Where to Eat)

Sealladh Sona

3 Whinpark, Muirtown, Inverness IV3
6NQ
TEL (01463) 239209
About 15 minutes' walk from
town, this renovated cottage beside
the Caledonian canal has views over

houses to open countryside. Its
entrance opens into a sitting-room.
Evening meals are available by
arrangement as are packed lunches.
Prettily decorated bedrooms.
£ All year; 3 rooms

KENTALLEN
Ardsheal House

Kentallen, Appin PA38 4BX
TEL (01631) 740227
FAX (01631) 740342
Atmospheric mansion now an
elegant country-house hotel;
retained features include an imposing
staircase and stately panelling. A
blue-and-gold lounge is enticing
while the warm library has views
over Loch Linnhe. Traditional food
with modern touches in the dining-
room or conservatory. Antiques and
personal extras in the bedrooms.
££ All year; 13 rooms; tennis (See
Where to Eat)

KINGUSSIE
Homewood Lodge

Newtonmore Road, Kingussie
PH21 1HD
TEL (01540) 661507
Homely accommodation with
views of the Cairngorms. The
dining-room has a heather colour
scheme; food is good value.
Thoughtful extras in the simple,
spacious bedrooms include electric
blankets for chilly Strathspey nights.
£ All year; 4 rooms with shower/wc;
drying-room; credit cards not accepted

Osprey Hotel

Ruthven Road, Kingussie PH21 1EN
TEL/FAX (01540) 661510
Cheerful, comfortable granite hotel
overlooking the Memorial Gardens.
There are two cosy lounges and
cooking in the plaid-clad dining-
room is good. The carpet running
through the house depicts an
osprey. Spruce, small bedrooms.
£ All year; 9 rooms

MUIR OF ORD
The Dower House
Highfield, Muir of Ord IV6 7XN
TEL/FAX   (01463) 870090
Essentially a restaurant-with-rooms, the Dower House has style. Bold patterns in the small lounge; inventive cooking. Sumptuous bedrooms combine brass, pine and antiques. Excellent bathrooms with Victorian fittings.
£-££ *All year; 5 rooms; drying-room (See Where to Eat)*

ROY BRIDGE
Station House
Roy Bridge, nr Inverness PH31 4AG
TEL   (01397) 712285
Quiet old station-master's house set in a colourful garden. The lounge doubles as the dining-room where evening meals are served by arrangement. Good-sized bedrooms.
£ *Apr to Oct; 3 rooms with wash-basin; credit cards not accepted*

SPEAN BRIDGE
Corriegour Lodge
Loch Lochy, nr Spean Bridge PH34 4EB
TEL   (01397) 712685
FAX   (01397) 712696
This Victorian hunting-lodge with views over Loch Lochy leads down to a lochside beach with jetty. A boat and fishing reels are available. A log fire burns in the sitting-room and the bar is cosy; there is a conservatory-style dining area. Large, smartly furnished bedrooms.
£ *Mar to end Oct; 9 rooms; fishing*

Invergloy House
Spean Bridge PH34 4DY
TEL   (01397) 712681
Former stables with views and free fishing on the loch. Evening meals are available by arrangement in the dining-room, equipped with a grand piano. Bedrooms are attractive; new bathrooms are planned.
£ *All year; 4 rooms; fishing; rowing boats; tennis; credit cards not accepted*

Old Pines
Gairlochy Road, Spean Bridge
PH34 4EG
TEL   (01397) 712324
FAX   (01397) 712433
Early 1980s long, low Scandinavian-style house built almost entirely of wood with some stone additions. The public rooms are light and bright with log-burning fires. Freshly delivered local produce on the menu; vegetarian options always available. Bedrooms simply furnished in pine.
££ *All year exc 2 weeks Nov; 8 rooms; play room*

Riverside
Invergloy, Spean Bridge PH34 4DY
TEL/FAX   (01397) 712684
Close to shore with stunning views over the water, Riverside occupies the east side of Loch Lochy. Breakfast is served in an eating area off the lounge; packed lunches are available. Large, comfortable bedrooms. Three chalets in the grounds.
£ *All year exc Chr; 2 rooms; 3 chalets; credit cards not accepted*

STRATHPEFFER
Craigvar
The Square, Strathpeffer IV14 9DL
TEL   (01997) 421622
Built in 1839 when Strathpeffer was a Victorian spa village, Craigvar overlooks the Square. The building retains many original features. There is a fire in the lounge and breakfast is served in the dining-room. Attractive bedrooms.
£ *Easter to Oct; 3 rooms*

Inver Lodge
Strathpeffer IV14 9DL
TEL (01997) 421392
Guesthouse on a quiet road with lovely views of wooded hills. Fresh local produce, home-baked desserts and cakes are features of evening meals served in the dining-room. Comfortable, simple bedrooms.
£ *Mar to Dec; 2 rooms with wash-basin*

TAIN
Morangie House
Morangie Road, Tain IV19 1KY
TEL (01862) 892281
FAX (01862) 892872
Attractive stained glass illuminates this turn-of-the-century mansion at the north end of Tain. Good food in the dining-room with its smart red-and-gold carpet; traditional at lunchtime, more adventurous in the evening. Pleasant bedrooms with thoughtful extras.
£ *All year; 26 rooms; drying-room*

TONGUE
Ben Loyal Hotel
Tongue, by Laird IV27 4XE
TEL/FAX (01847) 611216
Plain hotel in the centre of the village with outstanding views over hills around the Kyle of Tongue. Old prints and photographs brighten the lounge. A Scottish menu uses local ingredients. The main house boasts smart, modern bedrooms; those in the annexe share a bathroom and lounge.
£ *Mar to end Oct; 18 rooms; drying-room; games room; fishing*

WHERE TO EAT

Key: A * marks a place that is particularly good value for money

CROMARTY
Royal Hotel *
Marine Terrace, Cromarty IV11 8YN
TEL (01381) 600217
Seafood stars at this family-run waterfront inn; more traditional Scottish dishes including haggis and game play supporting roles.
Open for food all week 12 to 2, Sat and Sun 12 to 2.30, Sun to Thur 5.30 to 9, Fri and Sat 5.30 to 9.30; restaurant all week 12 to 2, Mon to Sat 6.30 to 8.30 (See Where to Stay)

Thistles *
20 Church Street, Cromarty IV11 8XA
TEL (01381) 600471
Wholesome food in a simple setting. Vegetarians well looked after; friendly service and down-to-earth prices.
Open 12 to 2, 7 to 9; closed Sun eve and Mon

FORT WILLIAM
Crannog *
Town Pier, Fort William PH33 7NG
TEL (01397) 705589
FAX (01397) 705026
A converted bait store with views over Loch Linnhe and exceptionally fresh seafood. Langoustines travel from the proprietor's own boat to the table in fine style; delicacies from the Crannog smokehouse also supply the Edinburgh branch. Fine puddings; good value wine list.
All week 12 to 2.30, 6 to 10 (9 in winter); closed 25 Dec, 1 Jan

Inverlochy Castle
Torlundy, Fort William PH33 6SN
TEL (01397) 702177
FAX (01397) 702953
Eating becomes a theatrical experience at this grand Scottish castle where wonderful food exonerates the highly priced set menus. Service is attentive and

puddings are sensational; the serious wine list is priced accordingly.
All week 12.30 to 1.45, 7 to 9.30; closed Dec to Feb (See Where to Stay)

INVERNESS
Culloden House
Inverness IV1 2NZ
TEL (01463) 790461
FAX (01463) 792181
A Palladian mansion on a grand scale with a similarly adventurous menu. Scottish- and French- influenced dishes, with Mediterranean touches enhancing prime Highland fare. The international wine list is reasonably priced.
All week 12.30 to 2, 7 to 9

Dunain Park
Inverness IV3 6JN
TEL (01463) 230512
FAX (01463) 224532
Refreshing contemporary cooking at this Georgian house whose own kitchen gardens provide ingredients. Excellent home baking plus a carefully chosen wine list and comprehensive malt selection.
All week 12 to 1.30, 7 to 9; closed 3 weeks Jan to Feb (See Where to Stay)

KENTALLEN
Ardsheal House
Kentallen, Appin PA38 4BX
TEL (01631) 740227
FAX (01631) 740342
This shoreside hotel makes a convivial setting for good cooking with its wonderful outlook over Loch Linnhe. Interesting dishes on the short menu. Service is professional and friendly; the wine list chosen for quality and value with a decent choice of half-bottles.
All week 12 to 1.45, 8.30 one sitting (See Where to Stay)

KINGUSSIE
The Cross
Tweed Mill Brae, Ardbroilach Road,
Kingussie PH21 1TC
TEL (01540) 661166
FAX (01540) 661080
Delightful Scottish food in a sympathetically converted tweed mill. Canny cooking techniques and quality ingredients ensure superb flavours; wine recommended by the knowledgeable proprietor is sure to suit. Reasonable prices.
Wed to Mon 7 to 9; closed 1 to 26 Dec, 8 Jan to 28 Feb

LOCH CLUANIE
Cluanie Inn ★
Loch Cluanie, Glen Moriston IV3 6YW
TEL (01320) 340238
Isolated inn providing good home-cooked staples for walkers with hearty appetites. Fixed-price dinners in the restaurant.
Open for food 12 to 2.30, 6 to 9, Nov to Mar 6 to 8.30

MUIR OF ORD
The Dower House
Highfield, Muir of Ord IV6 7XN
TEL/FAX (01463) 870090
Leisurely, relaxed eating and splendid food. The four-course no-choice menu changes daily; the varied wine list includes a good selection of half-bottles.
All week 7.30 to 9; closed Chr, 1 week Mar, 1 week Oct (See Where to Stay)

SPEAN BRIDGE
Letterfinlay Lodge Hotel ★
Spean Bridge PH34 4DZ
TEL (01397) 712622
Traditional Scottish fare makes this restaurant a firm favourite with walkers and anglers. Snacks served in the lounge bar, formal fixed-price dinners in the restaurant (booking necessary).
Open for food 12 to 2, 6.30 to 8.30, July and Aug 12 to 2.30, 6.30 to 9; restaurant all week 7 to 9

THE
NORTH-WEST

- The best that Scotland has to offer in mountains and sea lochs
- Skye and the Small Isles
- Inverewe Gardens

Suilven

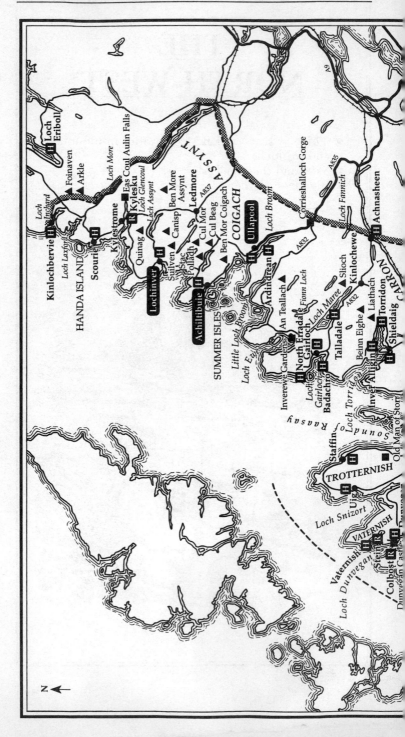

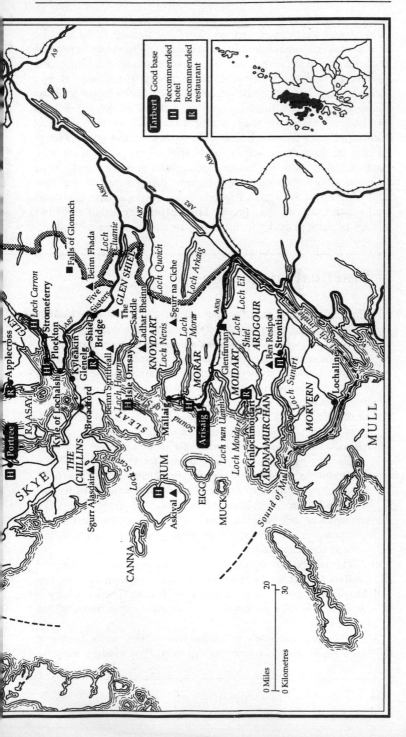

IN a spell of clear, warm weather, the beauty of Scotland's north-western coastline is unrivalled. The interlacing of mountains, islands and sea becomes a study in blues and greens, picked out in a pure, northern light. Geological up-heavals have left the coast broken by sea lochs from Mull to Kinlochbervie, and have created mountains unlike any others in Scotland. From the map, it might seem laborious or mono-tonous country for touring, but this is not so: the complexities of the geology have left a landscape where vegetation and rocks change radically between one area and the next, from oak woods where mosses and lichens proliferate, to the bare gneiss desert of Sutherland, where bog myrtle, coarse grass and bell heather are all that grow. The shapely peaks of the Five Sisters of Kintail and the humped, isolated masses of Suilven

Practical suggestions

The best way to explore the North-West is to take a long, leisurely tour through it, leaving time for expeditions to Skye or the Small Isles, and being prepared to stop for a night or two in any area that you like. This is also a particularly good region for self-catering – your chances of having good scenery beyond the windows are high, there is masses of space for children to roam in and few main roads to worry about. If you want to stay put in a particular area there is much to be said for choosing Skye, Kintail, the Torridon area, Ullapool or Achiltibuie, all of which are within easy reach of outstanding scenery and are relatively well provided with facilities for visitors.

Climbers will probably make a beeline for the Black Cuillin on Skye, while experienced hill-walkers are embarrassed by the choice here, and merely have to decide whether the mountains of Kintail, of Torridon or of Sutherland are most to their taste. The inexperienced hill-walker is better off elsewhere, for most of the mountains are precipitous, but there are plenty of tough, low-level walks as compensation.

This is great country for the angler who is happy to pursue wild 'brownies' in remote lochs. Sea-trout fishing is often available too, though opportunities to catch salmon are limited. There is plenty of sea-fishing, with expeditions easily arranged from most of the harbours.

If you are interested in natural history, the nature reserve at Beinn Eighe should be your starting point. Bird-watchers make for

or Cul Mór are mountains from different geological eras, utterly distinct. Even the sea lochs have individual characters, from the gloomy waters of Loch Hourn to the sunny openness of Loch Torridon. Many are dotted with the rafts of salmon farms, which slightly spoil their appearance, but are of vital importance to the local economy.

For many people, the charm of the North-West lies in the remote places where single-track roads wind round stony outcrops to end in tiny crofting townships on rocky shores, or in the wilderness altogether untouched by the car, where you must still carry all that you need to survive on your back. It is in the North-West that you are most aware of how thinly populated the Highlands now are. With the exception of Ullapool there are no towns, and even the larger villages seldom run to more than a few rows of houses

---

Handa Island in the breeding season. Geologists are drawn to the Moine Thrust. Perhaps the most interesting area of this convulsive pressure zone is Assynt, north of Ullapool.

Island-lovers may be disappointed in Skye, which has none of the remoteness they may seek. But isolation is possible on Eigg, Muck, Rum, Canna and Raasay. Mallaig is the crossroads for ferry traffic, and a particularly useful place for those relying on public transport.

Good bases

● **Portree** Skye's 'capital' is a neat little town built around its sheltered harbour. It can get busy with visitors, but never quite loses its peacefulness. Well located for touring Skye, it has plenty of accommodation and is very much the centre of the island's life.

● **Ullapool** This friendly fishing town was planned in the eighteenth century and has worn well. Boat trips and fishing expeditions are popular and there is plenty of accommodation.

● **Achiltibuie** This straggling township is blessed with superb views, a nearby sandy beach, some fishing, and easy access to the Sutherland mountains. It is a slow drive to or from it and there are few facilities, so it is especially suited to stay-put self-catering holidays.

● **Lochinver** The village itself is rather ordinary, but the surrounding country is splendid, with sandy beaches to the north and mountains to the east.

● **Arisaig** Good beaches and a variety of boat trips make this small village worth considering.

and a simple shop or two.

Then there is Skye. This is the most popular of all the Scottish islands, sold as heavily for its romantic connections with Flora Macdonald and Bonnie Prince Charlie as for its scenery of mountain and sea. The romance is overdone but the scenery is hard to beat, for the serrated peaks of the Cuillins, black and bare against a blue sky, are unforgettable. To experience Scotland at its best, you should travel on a steam train from Fort William to Mallaig, and then cross the Sound of Sleat to Armadale, with the mountains of Knoydart blue on one side and the outlines of Eigg and Rum rising from the sea on the other.

The weather is not always good, for the mountains on this coast attract the heaviest rainfall in the British Isles. When the clouds close in and the midges come out, the whole area descends into a kind of grey misery in which even the most determined optimists can find it hard to keep their spirits up. Then you need to be able to scrap your plans for outdoor expeditions and turn to books or indoor games instead. When planning a holiday up here, it is vital to think how you will stay happy if the weather turns against you.

FROM MORVERN TO KNOYDART

Morvern, Ardgour and Ardnamurchan

The barrier of Loch Linnhe leaves the districts of Morvern, Ardgour and Ardnamurchan isolated. Few visitors come; those who do mostly travel to Lochaline for the ferry to Mull through inland scenery desolate except where patches of scrub oak and birch woodland add splashes of colour. All the beauty is to be found on the coasts. On the eastern side you look across to the hump of Ben Nevis with the blue spikes of the Glencoe hills rising behind, while to the west there are wave-lashed rocks and a string of the white sandy beaches for which the coast is renowned.

Morvern is bounded by Loch Sunart to the north and the Sound of Mull to the south. The prettiest road here is the B8043, which leads you down a rocky stretch of coast to sudden greenery round Camasnacroise. **Lochaline** is the only village of any size, with some pleasant greenery round it and two ancient castles at Ardtornish Point and Kinlochaline, the former once belonging to the Lord of the Isles, and the latter (a MacInnes stronghold) in a good state of preservation.

Ardtornish gave its name to the unlikely-sounding Treaty of Ardtornish-Westminster (1461). This was a plot to divide Scotland between the Lord of the Isles and the exiled Earl of Douglas, under the overlordship of Edward IV of England – a fairly typical example of the sort of conspiracy faced by the medieval Stewarts.

Ardgour is more rugged than Morvern, its fastnesses penetrated by three long glens. It is bounded by Loch Shiel, Loch Linnhe and Loch Sunart. **Strontian** is the main settlement, a tiny village which gave its name to the element strontium, which was isolated from ore found here. The old mines behind the village are sited above a vein of mineral-rich rock running down from Ben Resipol. This beautifully isolated peak dominates the western fringe of Ardgour, and the views of the Hebrides from its top are wonderful. Moss and lichen flourish in Ariundle Wood in Strontian Glen, where the humidity and the purity of the air make for a riot of unlikely growths.

Ardnamurchan is a low, bare peninsula of blue-white skies, ochre ground and the vestigial remains of volcanoes, with the westernmost point of mainland Britain at its end. It is blessed with some beautiful beaches but is otherwise an exposed and windswept place, wonderful if you like wind on your face, but not everyone's cup of tea.

The drive along the shore of Loch Sunart beyond Salen, on a typical West Highland road pinned between hill and seashore, shows this peaceful loch at its best, rippled by flotillas of duck. A short way beyond Glen Beg, a walk will take you to a pillar of great age, carved with a cross and a dog, thought to be in memory of St Ciarin and possibly dedicated by St Columba.

Mingary Castle, a thirteenth-century stronghold that is more impressive from a distance than close to, rises out of the sea near Kilchoan. In 1588, a Spanish galleon from the Armada was wrecked on Mull, and its crew was enlisted by Maclean of Duart for an attack on Mingary. Even with this help he did not succeed in taking it. A car ferry runs between Kilchoan and Tobermory on Mull, making a very pleasant day trip if the sea is calm.

Sanna Bay is the most renowned of Ardnamurchan's beaches (so not the most deserted). Further pretty coves lie along the northern coast, the grassy areas round the shore a feast of clover, buttercup and thyme.

Moidart

Moidart is almost cut off from its neighbours by the great trench of Loch Shiel, best seen from the monument at Glenfinnan. Those intent on following Charles Edward Stuart's footsteps should go to Dalilea at the southern end. From here he was rowed up to Glenfinnan to meet the gathering clansmen.

Loch Moidart, cutting inland from the sea, is island-studded, heavily wooded and may have seals lying on its skerries. It is a picture of loveliness at high tide in fine weather, and desolate at low tide in the rain. The best way to see it is to branch left beyond Acharacle to the little township of Cul Doirlinn. On a small island (accessible except at very high tide) are the ruins of **Castle Tioram**. This, the impregnable stronghold of Macdonald of Clanranald, survived for four centuries until it was burnt by the fourteenth chief, as he set off for the 1715 uprising, to prevent his Campbell enemies from occupying it.

Glenfinnan

The monument at the head of Loch Shiel commemorates the raising of Prince Charles Edward Stuart's standard on 19 August 1745. The monument, which looks like a lighthouse from a distance, is cared for by the National Trust for Scotland, and in the visitor centre (NTS, open Apr to mid-May, early Sept to late Oct, daily 10 to 1, 2 to 5; late May to late Aug, daily 9.30 to 6) there is a first-class explanation of the complex events leading to the '45, including a clear chart of Stewart genealogy which makes it plain why the 'Old Pretender' was the legitimate claimant to the throne of Britain. Once you have grasped the background, climb the tower for the view.

Loch nan Uamh

This sea loch on the way to Arisaig is where the French ship *Du Teillay* landed Prince Charles Edward and his seven companions on 25 July 1745 to start their attempt to raise the Jacobite clans. On 20 September 1746, the fugitive prince, his army shattered and with a price of £30,000 on his head, embarked from this same loch on another French ship. Diligence will lead you to the beach where he landed (by the Glen Borrodale burn) and to the cairn which marks the spot where he re-embarked.

Arisaig

A small cluttered harbour and a small village at the head of Loch nan Ceall, a knobbly peninsula to the south and a lather of reefs and skerries offshore make up this ill-defined district. The village of Arisaig itself has a number of places to stay, and there are further guesthouses in nearby crofting townships. The area makes a good base for two reasons: the lovely (though exposed) silver sand beaches to the north and the variety of boat trips, especially to the Small Isles, which run from the harbour here and from Mallaig to the north.

Many of the beaches near Arisaig have caravan sites beside them, but there is no lack of space. The best views are seaward, where the Cuillins of Skye and Rum puncture sunsets with jagged outlines. The bay by the township of Back of Keppoch is particularly well situated for this view. By walking a short distance away from the beaches closest to the road, you should find peace and quiet. **Loch Morar** is a geological freak, for it is far deeper than the sea which lies a quarter of a mile distant, a tribute to the erosive power of ice channelled between mountains. The Loch is said to have a monster whose appearance foretells the death of a Macdonald of Clanranald. The western end of the loch is studded with wooded islands. The scenery gets bleaker if you walk eastward along its northern shore towards Tarbet, on the southern shore of Loch Nevis (roughish going). Careful study of the timetable may enable you to catch the thrice-weekly mail ferry from Tarbet to Mallaig.

Mallaig

This is a utilitarian ferry and fishing port, with little charm as a place to stay in but plenty as a place to visit. In summer, Mallaig is crowded with cars waiting for ferries, passengers from steam excursions on the railway, fish lorries, and tourists who have simply arrived at the end of the road and are wondering what to do next.

On a fine day, wandering around Mallaig's quay watching the cosmopolitan traffic or perhaps trying to pick up a bucketful of prawns cheaply from one of the small fishing boats is a pleasant way of passing an hour or two. On a wet day, Mallaig is dismal, and there are barely enough pubs and cafés to contain the crowds seeking shelter. Raucous seagulls seem to mock their discomfort.

Mallaig is a natural junction for island-hoppers, hikers

and those using public transport. Motorists wishing to go further north must cross to Skye, or return all the way to Fort William. Foot passengers, juggling the complexities of crossings from Mallaig and Arisaig, can reach Eigg, Rum, Muck, Canna, Skye or Kyle of Lochalsh. Those bent on getting into the wilds of Knoydart without having to trek over the mountains can catch the thrice-weekly mail ferry to Inverie. It gives you a little time ashore without having to rough it overnight. Both Mallaig and Arisaig have boats available for charter, allowing you either to supplement the official timetables, cruise the coasts or go fishing.

Knoydart

The mass of rugged country lying between Loch Nevis and Loch Hourn was once home to over 1,000 people. Now its population is minuscule. Few visitors penetrate through the 'rough bounds' of the mass of craggy peaks which fringe the heads of the lochs. To get into Knoydart you must abandon wheeled transport and be self-sufficient, for apart from a small hostel at the tiny settlement of Inverie, the only accommodation is mountain bothies. For hill-walkers, the ridges of Ladhar Bheinn make excellent walking, with marvellous seaward views to the Small Isles and Skye when the rain holds off.

KINTAIL AND GLENELG

Glen Shiel

The great trench running westward from Loch Cluanie is the smoothest and fastest route west from the Great Glen to Skye, and thunders with tour coaches bound for the Skye Bridge. The glen is hemmed in on either side by high ridges and peaks, and the modern road plunges between them towards the glitter of Loch Duich at the foot. The mountains themselves are better seen from further away, but their steep, grass-clad slopes, silvered with rocky outcrops and spouting rivulets after rain, are enough to make the hill-walker itch to pull on boots.

Glen Shiel was the scene of the culminating battle of one of the lesser Jacobite uprisings – that of 1719. It was little more than a nuisance raid, mounted by a force of Spaniards in alliance with the local Mackenzies. The Jacobites' base at

Eilean Donan Castle was bombarded by English frigates, and the Spaniards and the Mackenzies were rapidly defeated by a force from Inverness.

At the foot of Glen Shiel, the river widens into a small loch, and here the tiny village of **Shiel Bridge** acts as a base for campers and caravanners, sells chocolate and gives out information to visitors stretching their legs before the drive down Loch Duich.

Glenelg

The steep zigzag pass of **Mam Ratachan** from Shiel Bridge is the course of the old military road to the Hanoverian barracks at Glenelg. It was also the drove road for the cattle crossing from Skye by the Kyle Rhea narrows. Once spectacular, the road is now blighted by forestry but the viewpoint near the summit is still first-class. You look back up Glen Shiel with the peaks of the **Five Sisters of Kintail** rising on the northern side in sequence. Owned by the National Trust for Scotland, these mountains are marvellous for hill-walkers, being easily reached from all sides and allowing expeditions of varying length and complexity.

Beyond the pass, the road drops to **Glen More**, a sheltered valley studded with small farms. At its foot, you turn right to reach the Kyle Rhea ferry to Skye. This summer crossing is worth knowing about but call 01599 511302 to make sure it is operating, or ask at Shiel Bridge.

The houses of Glenelg stand close to Bernera Barracks, a utilitarian ruin. A short distance south, **Gleann Beag** hides two of the best-preserved brochs on the mainland – **Dun Telve** standing on flat ground on the right of the road, and **Dun Troddan**, rather more fragmentary, on a hillside a little further up the glen. The walls of the former rise to 33 feet, and the double skin of the wall and the series of galleries passing between the two skins are clearly visible. If you have been disappointed in making the trek to brochs which turn out to be little more than rubble, these two come as a revelation.

The house Gavin Maxwell wrote about as 'Camusfearna' was at **Sandaig**, on the coast a mile or two south of Glenelg village. Many of those who have read *Ring of Bright Water* and its sequels attempt to make their way here, only to be frustrated by the dense conifer plantations which line the road and make the place difficult to get to. If you do persist through the trees down to the shore, you will find a bay of the haunting loveliness that Maxwell describes. However, it is a melancholy place – nothing remains of the house but rubble.

By continuing south to the end of the road you penetrate the fastness of **Loch Hourn**, a brooding, shadowy sea loch, at its best when silvered by the evening sun. Behind the pretty lochside village of Arnisdale, the scree slopes of Beinn Sgritheall rise into the mists that usually crown its top.

Loch Duich

The most peaceful way to watch this loch is to take the road along the southern shore. It is a dead end, but if you explore along it you are rewarded by the remains of a broch, hidden among the trees beyond Totaig. From Totaig, the view out over the meeting of three lochs (Duich, Long and Alsh) is splendid – Eilean Donan Castle lies almost opposite, and tide races churn the waters into swirls of colour.

BROCHS

Brochs are a type of fortress unique to Scotland. They were tall, circular towers, not unlike modern cooling towers in shape. They had no windows and the walls were double to allow galleries and stairways to run between the inner and outer skins. The interior of the broch was open to the sky, but roofed galleries probably ran round the walls, allowing the inhabitants some shelter.

The remains of about 500 brochs are visible, many of them close to the sea. For many years arguments raged about who built them and what they were used for. The Picts were popular candidates at first, but it now seems certain that brochs are Iron Age constructions, dating from around 100 BC. The skill of the construction can be seen in the better-preserved examples: the inner and outer walls are pinned together by stone cross-slabs, stairways run up towards vanished parapets, and doorways have impressive lintels. The need for such fortresses seems to have disappeared by about AD 200. Thereafter, old brochs often became the centre of a small settlement, perhaps with little houses being built inside. The best-preserved broch of all is to be found at Mousa on Shetland (page 514); those in Glenelg come a close second.

The A87 beyond Shiel Bridge bends round the head of Loch Duich. If you want to walk, turn off to Morvich. The most popular low-level walk from here is to the **Falls of Glomach**, the second highest waterfall in Britain. The start – through conifers – is not attractive, but the views improve as you approach the saddle of Bealach na Sroine. From here it is a quick downhill lope to the falls. Unless you are blessed with a head for heights, you will have to make do with the view of the upper part of the falls as they plunge 500 feet into a narrow ravine.

If you are not hooked on waterfalls, try the path up Gleann Choinneachain to the windswept pass of Bealach an Sgairne, from which you look down on the boggy beginnings of Glen Affric.

Eilean Donan Castle

(Open Apr to late Oct, daily 10 to 6; Nov to Mar by request, call 01599 555202)

The subject of countless photographs and paintings, Eilean Donan Castle has been used so extensively to sell Scotland that you are bound to recognise its familiar outline. It is ironic that the building is a total restoration, completed only in 1932, though a very successful one. It is an obligatory stop on the road to Skye, its setting being the main attraction, though several rooms and an extensive souvenir shop are open to visitors, with more facilities promised.

The castle's history goes back to the thirteenth century. Its Mackenzie owners entrusted it to the Macraes (a clan who proudly styled themselves 'Mackenzie's shirt of mail'), and it was a Macrae who undertook the restoration two centuries after the castle had been destroyed by Hanoverian bombardment during the 1719 uprising.

Eilean Donan's modern incarnation as the film director's ideal backdrop is actually more interesting than its history. Chat to the custodians on a quiet day and you will hear gossip about who came to advertise what, and how the rain and the midges drove everyone crazy.

LOCH ALSH AND LOCH CARRON

Since the opening of the bridge which now links Skye to the mainland, **Kyle of Lochalsh** has become a lot quieter. The ferries which used to ply from here to Kyleakin have gone, but the shops and tearooms remain for the present. It is useful as a stopping point on the road north, but it is not the prettiest of places.

Loch Carron marks a divide in the landscape. North of here the tangles of rhododendron thickets become sparser and the land harsher. The mountains change radically: the jumbled peaks and ridges give way to isolated mountains of red sandstone, often topped with shining quartzite, whose sides drop in precipitous terraces gouged with gullies. The damp, quasi-tropical lushness turns to a starker and less fertile seaboard where outcrops of grey-white gneiss, scraped clean by glaciers, thrust through thin coverings of peat and grass.

Built on the edge of a sheltered bay of Loch Carron, and with spindly palm trees to prove that Scotland is sub-tropical after all, **Plockton** is the kind of village that artists settle down to paint. Here they wear midge-repellent. Plockton is tranquil and beautiful of an evening; during the day its craft shops can get crowded.

East of Plockton a road wide enough for three tour coaches whisks you up the southern shore of the loch, with various viewpoints from which to look over to the tangle of low hills on the far side. If you are continuing north, double round the head of Loch Carron and down to the village of the same name, where there is a nature reserve in a dangerous and spectacular gorge.

From here the road crosses a low neck of land to **Loch Kishorn**, once the scene of oil-platform construction, and with a certain amount of industrial clutter still visible. You then have the choice of heading across moorland to Shieldaig, or of taking the long diversion round the Applecross peninsula.

APPLECROSS AND TORRIDON

The road that runs west from Loch Kishorn into Applecross is the closest thing to an alpine pass in Britain. It wriggles up a corrie between walls of rock and scree to a series of hairpins beneath the col at Bealach na Ba. The black cliffs of Beinn Bhàn and Sgurr a' Chaorachain loom over the approach, suggesting a rugged wilderness beyond the pass, but at the top there is only undulating moor, sloping gently down to the sea.

Applecross was once a monastery, founded in 673 by St Maelrubha, and second only to Iona in importance. It was destroyed by the Norsemen, and virtually nothing remains. The village has a pub, a telephone box and a few houses. Southward, a lonely cul-de-sac road runs to Toscaig, with coves to explore and clear views to Skye. Northward, the road was opened only in 1976, too late to save many of the tiny townships along the shore. The landscape of Applecross itself is uninspiring – all the interest lies in the views seaward, where the islands of Raasay and Rona half hide the hills of Skye behind.

Shieldaig, where the road across Applecross rejoins the main route, is an early nineteenth-century planned village, as lovely as Plockton but less obviously postcard material. Offshore views are blocked by an island which is a sanctuary for a stand of ancient Caledonian pines. Sheep munch grass on Shieldaig's little waterfront.

Eastward from Shieldaig, a modernised road speeds you to the head of Loch Torridon. An older road, now a quiet track, runs beneath it by the water's edge, making a gentle walk with views over the loch and surrounded by venerable trees. Now the scale of the Torridon mountains makes itself felt. Three great mountains tower above **Glen Torridon** – Beinn Alligin, Liathach and Beinn Eighe. Liathach is the queen, its castellated ridge running parallel to the glen 3,400 feet beneath, dwarfing the cottages of Torridon into insignificance. On a grey day, with the clouds hiding the battlements of the ridge, Liathach loses little, for then the layered terraces of stone and grass disappear into the grey swirl, to unguessable heights.

Drop into the **visitor centre** (NTS, May to end Sept, Mon to Sat 10 to 5, Sun 2 to 5) at the head of Loch Torridon to learn the extent and nature of the Torridon estate.

Do not ignore the **deer museum** (NTS, open all year) here either – it was set up by a local man with a lifetime's experience of deer management, and explains, with little sentimentality but much sympathy, the life of the red deer on the Scottish hills. There are also gruesome photographs of what can be done to deer by poachers or careless visitors.

Bordering the Torridon estate to the east lies the **Beinn Eighe National Nature Reserve**. Beinn Eighe does not loom above the road as menacingly as Liathach, but its southern face, streaked with quartzite screes, is forbidding enough to deter thoughts of a casual climb. However, an exceptional low-level walk strikes up the cleft of the Coire Duibh Mhoir burn between Liathach and Beinn Eighe. On reaching the northern side of these mountains, you see them in a different aspect – hollowed by enormous, echoing corries. You can make for Loch Coire na Caime under the highest tops of the Liathach ridge, which is spectacular enough, or you can contour round the flank of Beinn Eighe to Loch Coire Mhic Fhearchair. This corrie is second only to the Toll an Lochan beneath An Teallach (page 448) in drama. Screes rise steeply above the dark lochan, and a sheer triple buttress, split by dark gullies, looms above the far end.

LOCH MAREE AND GAIRLOCH

Loch Maree, with the peak of Slioch reflected in its silver-blue, island-dotted waters, is rivalled for beauty only by Loch Lomond. The A832 runs along the south-western shore; much of the north-eastern shore can be explored on the path leading through Letterewe Forest. North of Slioch lies a tract of remote deer forest, bog and precipitous mountain, empty of human habitation and savage in bad weather.

Just north-west of Kinlochewe village is the **Visitor Centre** for the Beinn Eighe National Nature Reserve (open Easter to mid-Sept, daily 10 to 5), a vital port of call if you want to learn about the natural history of the area. Further west, you arrive at the parking place for two nature trails on the lower slopes of Beinn Eighe. The low-level walk leads you through the old pine forest around which the reserve was established. The mountain trail is extremely steep, and quite beautifully crafted, with a minimum disturbance of the land. If you do not want to penetrate the remote hinterland of the reserve, these walks are an excellent alternative. Useful 'breathing points' are spaced along the trail, each with a feature of natural history picked out for you to contemplate.

Boats containing intent fishermen drift on Loch Maree, for it is a renowned sea-trout loch. Ask at the Loch Maree Hotel about fishing possibilities.

At the western end of the loch, the road runs down to the River Kerry to the coast. Turn left on the minor road to Redpoint through a secluded landscape of water, birch and oak. **Badachro** is a tiny village by the shore, its pub ideally situated on the sea's edge, with views of rocky islets in the bay. Continue south to get to three beaches of reddish sand (one accessible only on foot). They are all fairly exposed, so do not expect to do much basking in the sun.

After miles of sparsely populated country, the holiday

resort of **Gairloch** comes as a surprise. The Mackenzies of Gairloch resisted the fashionable nineteenth-century trend for turfing people off the land, and this has left the coasts of Gair Loch sprinkled with cottages. Gairloch is popular because of the sandy beaches in the area, and there are numerous guesthouses and caravan sites. Stop here to see the **Gairloch Heritage Museum** (open Apr to Sept, Mon to Sat 10 to 5; Oct to end Mar by appointment, call 01445 712287) which has a splendid collection of objects salvaged from houses and cottages in the area, including an illicit still. It gives an excellent impression of West Highland life.

LOCH EWE TO LOCH BROOM

Inverewe Gardens

(NTS, gardens open Apr to late Oct, daily 9.30 to 9; late Oct to late Mar, daily 9.30 to 5, visitor centre and shop open Apr to late Oct, daily 9.30 to 5.30; guided walks Mon to Fri 1.30).

That a sub-tropical garden exists on the same latitude as Siberia is thanks to the mild climate created by the North Atlantic Drift, and to the efforts of one man – Osgood Mackenzie – to transform a barren patch of ground on which only a single stunted willow grew. The project was started in 1862 with shelter belts to protect the site from the salt-laden gales. Estate workers carried in soil in creels and the first plantings were made. By the time Inverewe was given to the National Trust for Scotland in 1952 by Osgood Mackenzie's daughter, it was already famous. The size of the coach and car park testifies to its popularity.

Inverewe is a woodland garden, its winding paths dotted with rarities from the southern hemisphere and China. It has an enormous *Magnolia stellata*, superb rhododendrons, primulas and azaleas. At its heart lies a sheltered rockery full of interesting plants. All the time you sense what a fragile place this is, for its luxuriance is surrounded by boggy moorland and distant mountains. Inverewe is at its most colourful in spring, but also has superb autumn colouring. July and August do not find it at its best, except for the hydrangeas, but there is always something to admire. Plant lovers should aim to spend the better part of a day here. Seeds are on sale.

Gruinard Bay

Over the neck of the Rubha Mór peninsula, Gruinard Bay, with its famous pink sands, forms a shallow bite out of the coast. If you are in search of a peaceful spot in the sun, take the minor road up the western side to Mellon Udrigle, where there is a sandy beach, a cluster of cottages, a camp-site and a lovely view. Even if the mountains to the east are being rained on, it may well be fine out here and on other coastal peninsulas.

Gruinard Island, a heather-clad lump in the bay, was used during the World War II to conduct experiments in biological warfare, and was infected with anthrax. For years after the war the island remained contaminated – something of a local scandal. However, a massive decon-tamination programme was put into effect a few years ago, and Gruinard is now pure once again.

Little Loch Broom and Loch Broom

A further neck of land separates Gruinard Bay from the tranquil waters of Little Loch Broom. At its top, you gaze out to the scattered **Summer Isles** in the sea to the north-west. Up Little Loch Broom, the A832 runs wide and straight along the shore, putting the local sheep in hazard of their lives. Once past the sudden spout of the waterfall at Ardessie and the hotel at Dundonnell you can stop for a strenuous walk up to Loch Toll an Lochain underneath the peaks of **An Teallach**. The precipices and tumbled screes of the mountain are faithfully reflected in the black water cupped under its cliffs. It is an awesome place, surrounded on three sides by bare rock or steep grass.

From the head of Little Loch Broom, the A832 winds up the narrow valley of the peaty-yellow Dundonnell River and debouches on to bare open moorland at the top – a spectacular and lonely drive, at its best from west to east – where you gaze into the tangle of mountains above Loch Fannich. This is the best-known of several Destitution roads in the West Highlands, built at the time of the potato famines in the mid-nineteenth century by the labour of those whose only alternative was starvation. They were financed from a Destitution Fund – hence their name – and it is worth remembering the road's origin as you stop to tuck into a picnic. Just when this road seems to be running straight into the mountains it takes a dog-leg north-east along a small glen scented with bog myrtle and joins the A835 from Garve to Ullapool at the head of the Corrieshalloch Gorge.

Corrieshalloch Gorge

This is among the most accessible of Scotland's gorges, and purist gorge-lovers may sneer at its slightly touristy atmosphere. A torrent pouring from a melting ice-cap on the Fannich mountains cut the Corrieshalloch at the end of the last Ice Age. Now a quick walk down a wooded path takes you to the chasm, spanned by a bouncy suspension bridge. There is a nasty drop to today's rather pathetic little river enclosed between vertical walls of black rock, on which ranks of exotic ferns thrive in such footholds as they can find. The Falls of Measach at the head of the gorge are more a chute than a waterfall proper and provide appropriate thunder only in heavy spate. The trout at the bottom of the ravine are of course reputed to be of grand size and fearsome fighters.

On the road to Ullapool, **Lael Forest Gardens** are actually a scruffy plantation of conifers, not worth your time.

ULLAPOOL

A real town, and a genuinely pleasant one, Ullapool was established in 1788 by the British Fisheries Society to take advantage of the huge catches of herring which were taken in Loch Broom. The rectangular grid-plan of streets lined by cottages and the neat lochside frontage show the benefits of eighteenth-century town planning, ruined in some places by the less inspired ideas of the twentieth century. The huge shoals of herring are long gone but fishing is still important to Ullapool, although in summer the town seems entirely given over to tourism. Europeans of all nationalities wander the streets and, on a warm evening, an informal procession of Italian and French couples can give the town's little promenade in front of the harbour a Mediterranean atmosphere. This is about the only place north of Stirling where you can enjoy watching the street life. Much of it centres round the excellent Ceilidh Place – a combination of coffee shop, folk club, bookshop and hotel – but it extends down to the sea front, where groups gather to study the posters advertising boat trips to the Summer Isles or sea-fishing expeditions. A heavy smell of fish and chips occasionally drifts over the streets if the wind is wrong. The car park for the ferry to Stornoway is sometimes used by a pipe band or Highland dancers when not occupied by queues for the Western Isles.

Ullapool Museum (open Easter to Oct, Mon to Sat 10 to 6; July, Aug, 10 to 6, 7.30 to 9.30; Nov to Easter, 10 to 4) is situated in a refurbished kirk, where many of the town's relics such as photographs, quilts and tapestry are supplemented by electronic gadgets, putting everything into context. Elsewhere, a second small museum lurks in a room behind a bookshop. Here geological specimens vie for pride of place with scruffy stuffed birds and a curious collection of historical flotsam. This includes Lord Nelson's razor and a scented pastille found in the pocket of Charles I's coat after his execution.

ULLAPOOL TO KINLOCHBERVIE

North of Ullapool, the west-coast scenery becomes even more the stuff of fantasy. Isolated dull red or silvery mountains rear out of a wilderness of grey-white tumbled rock. Cotton grass, bog myrtle and bell heather cover the peat, except where it has been trenched for drainage or dug for fuel. On still evenings, you can scent the peat-smoke from the tiny communities clinging to the coastline.

This land is too much of a desert for some visitors, for walking through the hummocks of bare rock and picking your way around the boggy lochans can be work rather than pleasure, while the steepness of the mountains may deter thoughts of casual hill-walking. For others, the far North-West corner of Scotland is pure magic.

Coigach

This is the district between Loch Broom and Cam Loch, which marks the boundary between the old counties of Ross and Sutherland. The fast A835 runs through it to the Ledmore junction, where the A838 provides an escape route back to Lairg and the east coast, but these are boring routes. Instead, once you are past the severe bulk of **Ben Mor Coigach**, take the minor road at Drumrunie and head west to the **Inverpolly National Nature Reserve**. Two of the reserve's three peaks, **Cul Beag** and **Stac Pollaidh**, hide the inner sanctuary from the road. Cul Beag is not easy to admire from close quarters, but Stac Pollaidh, as it comes into view by Loch Lurgainn, is one of the most remarkable sights in the area. At just over 2,000 feet it is barely a mountain, but its ridge, eroded into a fantasy of sandstone pinnacles and towers, belongs to some airy alpine peak. The mountain is reflected photogenically in Loch Lurgainn, but this is not a good road for stopping on, and it is better to persist to the car park underneath the path up to the ridge.

To penetrate the interior of Inverpolly forest, go back a mile to the cottage at Linneraineach and take the track north a short way beyond. This is a wonderful low-level walk, leading you into a cirque of peaks, floored by lochs with sandy beaches. **Cul Mór** rises above Loch an Doire Duibh, round which you can walk before returning. Climbing Cul Mor, either from here or from the duller approach from Knockan, back on the main road, reveals the full beauty of the pattern of lochs, notably Loch Sionascaig and Loch Veyatie. You can gaze southward to the peaks of An Teallach and westward across the Minch to the mountains of Harris.

Achiltibuie

Beyond Inverpolly the road continues west past Loch Osgaig (which is likely to be sprinkled with anglers) and the stunning sandy beach at Achnahaird to arrive at the straggling crofting township of Achiltibuie. It is not the immediate surroundings but the wonderful views south and south-west to all the tangled mountains of Ross, with the Summer Isles lying on the sea in the foreground, that make Achiltibuie popular.

If the weather is fine there are few better places on the coast for an outdoor family holiday, with trout in the lochs, the beach at Achnahaird, the mountains of Inverpolly, and the rocky coastline along to Reiff to explore. There are sea-fishing opportunities, and trips to the Summer Isles. Achiltibuie is well supplied with self-catering properties, some bed-and-breakfasts, and the Summer Isles Hotel, whose bar is a refuge even if you do not stay there.

Achiltibuie's chief curiosity is the **Hydroponicum**, now called the **Summer Isles Garden of the Future** (open Apr to late Sept, daily, 90-minute tours at 10, 12, 2, 5). This huge greenhouse surrounded by clutter lies beneath the Summer Isles Hotel. Careful ventilation and control of the light create several different sub-tropical zones and a variety of exotic plants are grown without the aid of soil. Liquid nutrient trickles along channels filled with strawberry plants or drips on to the roots of banana trees. Oranges, lemons and figs compete with maidenhair ferns for space on the upper floor. Downstairs, apples and peaches ripen, and courgettes grow in fat ranks. The Hydroponicum still has to solve pest and algae problems, but the sight of what can be grown is enough to tempt you to buy the miniature jars, pots and packets of nutrient on sale.

Assynt

The coastal road north from Achiltibuie winds tortuously through a labyrinth of rocky hummocks and river valleys. It is not a road to take a caravan on, nor is it a road for careless drivers. By the time you arrive at **Inverkirkaig**, you are in need of a break. The tiny village fronts a broad, seaweedy bay, with the River Kirkaig running into it.

Assynt's chief village, **Lochinver**, is a mixture of grubby fishing harbour and clean, cottage-lined street. Tucked into a sheltered inlet, Lochinver suffers from lack of views but is the only place for miles with a decent choice of accommodation or anywhere much to eat. It also has the **Assynt Visitor Centre** (open all year, Mon to Sat, Sun in peak season – for times, contact the Tourist Office) which, with displays on local bird life, marine life, flora, fauna and the crofting tradition, provides a good introduction to the whole area. Lochinver is also the best place from which to climb Suilven and Canisp. You reach these mountains by the long walk past Glencanisp Lodge, which is made less wearisome by the increasingly spectacular sight of Suilven's western peak rearing above the intervening ridges.

As well as mountains, the Lochinver area has beaches. These are to be found on the Stoer peninsula, where the best sand is at Achmelvich, Clachtoll and Clashnessie. There are also small coves to explore, while a boggy walk will take you to the sea-stack of the Old Man of Stoer at the northernmost tip of the peninsula. Campsites and bed and breakfast accommodation are to be found by the main beaches. On the north coast, **Drumbeg**, with its loch and its view, is worth pausing at, and **Nedd**, a little further on, is also attractive.

The stubby ruins of **Ardvreck Castle** sit on a little headland in Loch Assynt, easily reached from the A894. There is not much of it left, but it has gone down in history as the place where Montrose was finally captured after his defeat at

Invershin. A small beach nearby on the loch shore makes a good spot from which to contemplate the ruin.

A bridge now sweeps the road over the Kylesku narrows, replacing the last ferry crossing on the road north. The old village of **Kylestrome** on the far bank is colourful with flowers, and lobster boats putter around in Loch Cairnbawn. The favourite occupation for visitors here is to take a boat trip up Loch Glencoul to see the highest waterfall in Britain. The **Eas Coul Aulin** is four times higher than Niagara, but somehow has not managed to achieve the same reputation.

Scourie

This sheltered village at the head of a cove is the centre for trout fishermen who like nothing better than to pursue their quarry through the myriad lochans that dot the gneiss desert inland. Scourie is nothing much, but it has an hotel, a rocky coastline to explore, and is generally a haven in a wilderness. Off the coast to the north lies **Handa Island**. This is the north-west coast's seabird city, though after early August you may not see much. Ornithologists are drawn to Handa in considerable numbers, and information about boat trips is to be found by the cottage at Tarbet. The 350-foot Stack of Handa stands 80 feet from the cliff's edge.

Kinlochbervie

North of Laxford Bridge the road from Lairg joins the route north, after traversing the length of Loch Shin. The scenery here is bleak in the extreme, for the mountains of Ben Stack, Arkle and Foinaven are massive lumps of inhospitable scree and rock, glimmering in the sunshine like snow. Do not be surprised to meet the odd fish lorry (though the heaviest traffic is at night), for Kinlochbervie has now become one of Scotland's chief fishing ports. The town sits in the middle of bleak scenery, with its little housing estate looking extremely incongruous. The modern port is enthralling if you are around when the catch is being landed.

Holidaymakers come for the sake of the beaches rather than the fish. The most famous of these is Sandwood Bay – everyone's ideal beach, with its long curve of empty white sand, a small river and a loch. It is empty because access is difficult. Even if you subject your car to three miles of extremely rough track, you will still have to walk a mile or so to reach it. In fine weather it is worth every step. Other, more frequented, but still beautiful beaches lie under the small township of Oldshore More. Beyond Sandwood Bay the coast is trackless right up to Cape Wrath (page 421).

SKYE

Skye exerts a hypnotic appeal, reflected in the number of coach tours that have the island as their destination. On a clear windy day, with the ridges of the Black Cuillin exposed under the sun in all their starkness and the Sound of Raasay dotted with white combers, the island is magical. However, few parts of Scotland are so disappointing in the rain or sea mist, when the mountains vanish, the treeless moors become soggily hostile and the sea turns a sullen grey. If the weather turns against you on your way to Skye (and the island has a notoriously fickle climate), change your plans if possible and try again later. This is an island which needs fair weather to be enjoyed.

As Scottish islands go, Skye is well endowed with facilities for visitors and, although there are few tourist sights as such, they are all sold hard. The island has plenty of places to stay, and you even have a choice of shops and places at which to eat. So, while Skye only occasionally feels overcrowded, do not expect to find yourself alone. If you need some solitude, you only have to make the short crossing to Raasay.

The best walks are long, difficult, or both, while the Black Cuillin is the preserve of the rock-climber or experienced rock-scrambler. However, if you are neither fit nor experienced, there are several enjoyable short walks, usually by the coast. The tourist office in Portree has a first-class selection of leaflets on walks.

Many visitors come to Skye because of its associations with the flight of Charles Edward Stuart after Culloden, and in particular because of Flora Macdonald, the girl who brought him, disguised as her maid, from Benbecula in the Western Isles to Portree. From there he went to Raasay, back to Skye, and eventually to a cave near Elgol where the Mackinnons gave him a banquet and a boat to Mallaig. It is easy enough to visit the scenes of these adventures, less easy perhaps to avoid the retrospective sentimentality that turned Flora Macdonald into a legend even in her own lifetime.

Sleat

If you cross to Skye from Mallaig, your first impression of the island will be of a richly wooded, sheltered shore. Close to the ferry pier at Armadale, the **Clan Donald Centre** (open Mar to Oct, daily 9.30 to 5.30; garden open all year) is more than just another clan centre, for there is an excellent exhibition and audio-visual outlining the history of the Lordship of the Isles. The loose confederation of clans under the Clan Donald Lords of the Isles took over from their Norse predecessors in ruling the Hebrides more or less independently of the Scottish kings. Their ambitious attempts to extend their power eastward reached their climax in the drawn Battle of Harlaw in 1411, but it was not until 1493 that the power of the Lords of the Isles was broken, and 'Without Clan Donald, there is no joy' turned from motto to lament. Armadale Castle, where the exhibition is mounted, is surrounded by fine woodland, and there are ranger-led walks further afield.

Sleat has numerous hotels and guesthouses lining its eastern coast, most of them with fine views over to the mainland. By driving over to the west coast from Kilbeg, you pass immediately into a bleaker and less frequented landscape.

Kyleakin to Portree

Kyleakin, which used to be the terminal for the ferry from Kyle of Lochalsh, is a nondescript village, but studded with tearooms and craft-shops, which will prove invaluable if the rain has set in. There is a small creeper-covered ruin of a castle to look at.

After the straggling village of **Broadford** the road to Portree negotiates the fringes of the Red Hills. These mountains lie adjacent to the Black Cuillin but they are entirely different, being large, rounded mounds of pinkish granite with scree-covered flanks. Both are the product of the ancient volcanic activity which makes the scenery of Skye so different from the neighbouring mainland.

At **Luib**, by the side of the main road, there is the first of the Skye folk museums (open Apr to Oct, daily 9 to 6). This one – just an old croft house with a few utensils and a smoky peat fire – is atmospheric and well worth a halt if there are not too many visitors there already. Of particular interest is the collection of fading newspaper cuttings about crofters' grievances – Skye was the setting for some of the most intense fight-backs by crofters threatened with eviction during the Clearances. A cairn on the B883 commemorates the 'Battle of the Braes', when police were confronted by stone-throwing crofters, and there is a memorial to the Glendale Land League at Colbost. Government over-reaction (troops and marines were stationed on Skye) eventually led to the enquiry which resulted in the Crofting Act of 1886.

Portree

Skye's little capital bustles with visitors on a hot summer's day, to the extent that you begin to wonder whether there are any local people left. It is an attractive place, set above the shore of a perfect blue-green inlet of the sea, and the row of painted cottages by the harbour beautifully offsets the elegant main square. Apart from the Royal Hotel where Prince Charles Edward Stuart said goodbye to Flora Macdonald, there is not much to see although the nearby **Aros Heritage Centre** (open all year, daily 9 to 6; Jun, July and Aug 9 to 9) may help in filling out the island's history with its models and storyboards. However, with its pubs, shops, banks and selection of places to eat, Portree is a natural hub if you are in need of some facilities. It is also the starting point for many of the island's bus services and for most of its bus tours.

Elgol and Loch Coruisk

At Broadford, the road to Elgol branches off. This is a cul-de-sac well worth exploring for the combination of sea and mountain scenery on the way, and with the added attraction of a boat trip into the heart of the Black Cuillin at its end. The boats to Loch Coruisk run from Elgol in season (call 01471 866244). As you cross Loch Scavaig, the black basalt and gabbro of the mountains closes in on either side, while the main ridge reveals itself as a great jagged circuit of teeth and pinnacles. A short walk from the boat brings you to Loch Coruisk. Enthralled nineteenth-century painters, inspired by Scott's *Lord of the Isles*, came to Coruisk and left impressions of a gloomy Gothic sanctuary whose over-whelming scale diminished man to a mere speck. It is not quite like that, though the wilderness of tumbled scree and layers of bare glaciated slabs beneath sheer cliffs cut by gullies leave an indelible impression.

Loch Harport and Glen Brittle

The drive down Glen Brittle gives you another excellent view of the Black Cuillin on the western side of their semi-circle. Emerging from forestry plantations, you gaze straight into the black recesses of Coire a' Mhadaidh. The road runs on down the glen, with splendid views of the mountains until you reach the campsite and shore at the bottom. This is a hive of activity for climbing expeditions, and there is a lot of entertainment to be had from watching the climbers loading up.

Further west, off the B8009, the **Talisker Distillery** runs very slick and informative tours during the summer season. At **Bracadale**, near the foot of Loch Harport, Skye's best preserved broch – Dun Beag – is on a hillside above the main road. From Bracadale, the B885 crosses Skye's lonely and boggy interior back to Portree.

Dunvegan Castle

(Open late Mar to late Oct, daily 10 to 5.30; other months by appointment, call 01470 521206)

The large car park and the numerous coaches signal that this, Skye's only substantial tourist sight, is extremely pop-ular. It is pricey if all you want to do is visit the castle, but if you take advantage of the fine gardens and grounds for a walk it becomes better value. The castle is the seat of Macleod of Macleod and has been continuously inhabited for about 750 years.

The castle's exterior belies its age, for the Victorians added pepper-pot turrets and a battlemented gatehouse. The antiquity reveals itself in the interior, where the old barrel-vaulted kitchen goes back to 1360, and where there is an unpleasant dungeon. The various stages in the building are well explained in the leaflet. The castle just about manages to retain the atmosphere of a lived-in home; the ancestral portraits in the dining-room and the drawing-room are comprehensive and rather fascinating. There are Jacobite relics which once belonged to Flora Macdonald, a portrait of Dr Johnson, who stayed here, and a very beautiful fifteenth-century silver cup. There is also Rory Mor's horn, a massive drinking vessel, which the chief's heir must drain to the dregs 'without setting down or falling down', when it is filled with claret (about one and a half bottles).

The greatest curiosity in Dunvegan is the 'Fairy Flag'. Enclosed in protective glass, this almost colourless piece of fabric looks like a dishcloth in the last stages of decay. It has been dated to between the fourth and seventh centuries, while its silk is of Near-Eastern origin. This banner, Am Bratach Sith, was given to a MacLeod chief by a fairy and it has the power to ensure victory for the clan in battle. It is known to have been used twice successfully. Popular boat trips to see seals run from near the castle.

Glendale and Vaternish

A 'visitor route' is signposted westward from just before Dunvegan village, and leads along the shores of Loch Dunvegan and over the neck of the peninsula beyond. The small sights include a crofting museum at Colbost, a restored watermill built into a steep rocky cleft, the memorial to the Land Leaguers who fought back against the Clearances, and even a toy museum. The most unusual, though, is the tiny **MacCrimmon Piping Heritage Centre** (open early Apr to late May, daily 12 to 5.30, closed Mon; late May to late Aug, daily 11 to 5.30; Sept to early Oct, daily 11 to 5.30, closed Mon) at Boreraig, which is something of a shrine to the famous Macrimmons, who were traditionally pipers to the Chief of the MacLeods. This is a serious place, where you will receive an enthusiastic reception.

The peninsula of Vaternish beyond Dunvegan is the place to go to watch the sun setting in a blaze of red over the Outer Hebrides, which line the horizon like dream islands. If there is no sunset, there is Skye's oldest pub at Stein to enjoy.

Trotternish

The north-east peninsula of Skye provides one of the best round trips from Portree, with a few sights worth stopping for and some amazing rock scenery. **Uig** is the attractive ferry port for North Uist and Harris, and most of the town's business revolves round ferry timetables.

At **Kingsburgh**, the refugee Prince Charles Edward sought shelter, and Dr Johnson not only slept in his bed (rather later on) but met Flora Macdonald here. The house where all this happened is long gone. In the cemetery north of **Kilmuir**, there is an austere memorial to Flora Macdonald, inscribed with Dr Johnson's tribute: 'A name that will be mentioned in history, and if courage and fidelity be virtues, mentioned with honour'. Nearby is the **Skye**

Musem of Island Life (open Apr to Oct, Mon to Sat 9.30 to 5.30, closed Sun), another folk museum, this time in a cluster of restored cottages and buildings, with the usual collection of domestic artefacts.

The east coast of Trotternish is where the rock scenery for which the peninsula is famous is to be found. A slow-motion landslip, caused by basalt lava on top of less stable rock sliding gradually downhill, has resulted in an escarpment of sheer cliffs, with broken-off fragments as outriders. The **Quiraing** is the best known of the strange formations, and is easily reached by a path from the minor road which crosses from Uig to Staffin. The various rock features of the Quiraing – the Prison, the Table and the Needle – can be appreciated only on foot. Eroded to curious squares and pinnacles, these rocks farrowed from the main cliffs lie in picturesque confusion.

Kilt Rock, a sea cliff nearby, gets its name from the vertical columnar basalt strata overlying horizontal ones beneath, the result bearing only the most fanciful relationship to tartan. The sea-cliffs in this area of Staffin are especially spectacular, as is the nearby waterfall which plunges vertically over them into the sea. Further south, the **Old Man of Storr** is a cigar-shaped pinnacle which has detached itself from the cliffs of the Storr behind. It is a laborious, though short trek up to its base, but unless you are a first-class rock-climber you will not make much further progress.

It is worth noting that the inhabitants of this corner of Skye observe Sundays very strictly, and some guesthouses will not take weekend guests for that reason. Check with the tourist office before booking.

RAASAY

The island of Raasay lies off Skye's eastern coast. It is secluded and gentle, even when Skye is bustling. Its lack of mountains is made up for by the excellent sea views and there are coastal walks, some quite strenuous, with the cliff scenery of the east coast rivalling that of Trotternish. The curious flat-topped Dun Caan is a volcanic hill, made famous as the place where Boswell danced a 'Highland Dance', while visiting the island with Dr Johnson in 1773. Raasay was the birthplace of Scotland's best-known modern Gaelic poet, Sorley Maclean. His poems (many of which he translated into English himself) contain many references to Raasay.

USEFUL DIRECTORY

Main tourist office
Highlands of Scotland Tourist Board
Tourist Information Centre
Aviemore
Inverness-shire PH22 1PP
Tel (0990) 143070
Fax (01479) 811063

Tourist Board special interest publications: guides on fishing include *Where to fish in Ross & Cromarty*, factsheets on river fishing and trout lochs on Skye, and *Fishing in Sutherland*; walks and drives, including Wester Ross coastal route; pony trekking; golf

Local tourist information centres
Broadford (01471) 822361 (Apr to Oct)
Dornoch (01862) 810400
Gairloch (01445) 712130
Kyle of Lochalsh (01599) 534276 (Apr to Oct)
Lochcarron (01520) 722357 (Easter to Oct)
Lochinver (01571) 844330 (late Mar to Oct)
Mallaig (01687) 462170 (Apr to Oct)
Portree (01478) 612137
Sheil Bridge (01599) 511264
Strontian (01967) 402131 (Apr to Oct)
Uig (Skye) (01470) 542404 (Easter to Oct)
Ullapool (01854) 612135 (Apr to Nov)

Local transport
For Mallaig and Fort William rail services (0345) 212282
Kyle of Lochalsh Railway Station (0345) 212282
Highland Bus and Coach (covers region) (01463) 233371
Skyeways buses (Skye and mainland routes) (01599) 534328
Wester Bus (Gairloch area) (01445) 712255

There are many small curiosities to be found on the island: the old iron ore mine at Suisnish that was worked by German prisoners during World War I, and the mermaids lying outside the perilously dilapidated Raasay House (now an outdoor centre), whose cost drove the last MacLeod chief into bankruptcy. Brochel Castle, a vegetatious ruin, stands picturesquely on the east coast, and makes a good goal for a short drive. Beyond, the road to Arnish was built

Car ferries
Ardgour-Corran (frequent daily crossings) (01855) 841243
Glenelg-Kylerhea (Apr to Oct, Mon to Sat, frequent service; plus
Sun May to Oct) (01599) 511302
All ferries below are run by Caledonian MacBrayne (01475) 650100:
Kilchoan-Tobermory (mid-Apr to mid-Oct, Mon to Sat, up to seven
sailings daily)
Lochaline-Fishnish (frequent service Mon to Sat, also Sun late May
to Aug)
Mallaig-Armadale (passenger service only, Oct to early Apr)
Sconser-Raasay (Mon to Sat, up to six sailings daily)
Ullapool-Stornoway (Mon to Sat, up to three sailings daily)
Uig-Lochmaddy (Mon to Sat, also Sun late Apr to mid-Oct, one or
two sailings daily)
Uig-Tarbet (Mon to Sat, one or two sailings daily)

Passenger ferries
Arisaig-Eigg-Muck-Rum (daily service May to mid-Sept) (01687)
450224/450678
Mallaig-Eigg-Muck-Rum-Canna (daily sailings) (01475) 650100
Mallaig-Inverie (two sailings three days/week) (01687) 462320
Mallaig-Kyle of Lochalsh (Apr to Oct, Fri only) (01475) 650100
Mallaig-Tarbet, Loch Nevis (two to three sailings a week) (01687)
462320

Other boat trips
Dunvegan-seal islands (01470) 521206
Elgol-Loch Coruisk (01471) 866244
Kylesku-Eas Coul Aulin waterfalls (01571) 844446
Mallaig-Loch Coruisk (01687) 462320 (summer only)
Trips out of Arisaig (01687) 450224/450678

Mountains
Kintail mountain rescue (01599) 5324222
Skye mountain rescue (police station, Portree) (01478) 612888

single-handedly by a local crofter over ten years from 1966,
after the local authority declined to do the job itself.

THE SMALL ISLES

The Small Isles, part of the Inner Hebrides group, fill the sea
between Skye and the Peninsula of Ardnamurchan. Of all

the islands clustered around Scotland these four are the most tempting to visit, for the jagged outline of Rum and the curious profile of Eigg seen over an aquamarine sea from the Moidart coast suggest places of almost tropical beauty. However, these islands, with their small and precarious populations and difficult communications, are not for people who need extensive facilities, and accommodation is limited. Short visits are possible, especially in the summer months when the year-round ferry service from Mallaig is supplemented by cruises from Arisaig, but the timetables are apt to leave you with either too little time on each island, or else too much.

Rum and Canna

Often spelt Rhum to avoid alcoholic associations, Rum is a wet, mountainous island and is at its most attractive from a distance for all except the naturalist and the walker, although those who enjoy eccentric hotels should make a special pilgrimage here. The island's population was unceremoniously forced off to Canada during the nineteenth century, and Rum became an uninhabited deer forest for sporting millionaires. It was the last of these, the Lancastrian industrialist George Bullough, who built the extravagant fantasy of Kinloch Castle, importing stone from Arran and craftsmen from Lancashire to create a bizarre combination of Scottish castle, Tudor mansion and Italian palazzo. This gross but charming folly is now an hotel; its interior remains as it was – a memorial to conspicuous consumption in an unlikely setting. Apart from this hotel, accommodation on Rum is limited to bothies and a campsite in Kinloch.

Rum is owned and managed by Scottish Natural Heritage as a huge outdoor research centre. Red deer form one of the most important areas of their work, but the island is also the scene of the experimental reintroduction of the sea eagle to Scotland. Access to parts of the island is restricted – ask the warden before exploring away from the marked nature trails. One interesting walk runs across the island to Harris Bay, where the Bullough family's mausoleum – a Doric temple surmounted by crosses – stands incongruously beside the sea. Rum's midges are notorious.

Canna is owned by the National Trust for Scotland, after years of benevolent stewardship by the Gaelic scholar Dr John Lorne Campbell. It is a small island, only five miles long, bounded by cliffs and with bright fertile patches fringing its rugged interior – a good place for birdwatchers and botanists and a very quiet refuge. Accommodation is extremely limited.

Eigg and Muck

Eigg always seems to be about to be bought or sold, and is one of those places at the focus of the land ownership debate in Scotland. In recent years it has been steered towards quiet tourism, so there is more accommodation here than on the other islands and a welcome for people who are happy to enjoy the island's peace. Eigg is dominated by the strange peak of An Sgurr, a flat-topped volcanic outcrop with precipitous sides. There are also singing sands at the Bay of Laig, which whisper underfoot in the right conditions. The most gruesome sight on Eigg is Macdonald's Cave, where 400 members of that clan were summarily suffocated by raiding MacLeods, who lit a fire at the entrance.

Flat and fertile, tiny **Muck** has just over a mile of road and a beautiful shell beach. It is really too small to stay on for long (there are two small hotels, camping and holiday cottages), but the ferry from Arisaig allows you to explore it inside a day on three days a week.

WHERE TO STAY

£ – under £70 per room per night, incl. VAT

££ – £70 to £110 per room per night, incl. VAT

£££ – over £110 per room per night, incl. VAT

ACHILTIBUIE
Summer Isles Hotel
Achiltibuie, Ullapool IV26 2YG
TEL (01854) 622282
FAX (01854) 622251
A 16-mile single-track road leads to Achiltibuie. Spectacular views of the Summer Isles from the lounge; fine local landscapes decorate the smart dining-room. Food is especially good with the cheeseboard and breakfast highly praised. Bedrooms are a pleasing combination of antique and homely.
££ Closed mid-Oct to Easter; 12 rooms; drying-room (See Where to Eat)

ACHNASHEEN
Loch Torridon Hotel
by Achnasheen IV22 2EY
TEL (01445) 791242
FAX (01445) 791296
Huge red sandstone hotel on the shore of the loch with central clocktower and glorious mountain views. Traditionally decorated in country-house style. Large bedrooms with thoughtful extras.
££ All year; 22 rooms; drying-room

ARDINDREAN
Taigh Na Mara Vegetarian Guesthouse
The Shore, Ardindrean, Loch Broom, nr Ullapool IV23 2SE
TEL/FAX (01854) 655282

A steep walk down from the car park, this guesthouse sits above a shingle beach on the west shore of Loch Broom. The vegetarian and vegan food is excellent. Early dinners for children; packed lunches are available. Guests can use a well-equipped kitchen and boats and bikes are on loan. Two bedrooms have skylights and views of the loch, the third is in a converted boatshed.

£ *All year; 3 rooms, one with bath/shower*

ARISAIG
Arisaig House
Beasdale, by Arisaig PH39 4NR
TEL (01687) 450622
FAX (01687) 450626
Behind the austere façade of this distinguished country house lies a welcoming interior. The gleaming central carved staircase is oak; floral prints in the drawing-room and a cherrywood-panelled dining-room. Impressive food. Attractive bedrooms, some with colourful patchwork quilts.

£££ *Closed Nov to Mar; 14 rooms; drying-room; games room (See Where to Eat)*

Old Library Lodge
Arisaig PH39 4NH
TEL (01687) 450651
FAX (01687) 450219
A converted barn, this restaurant-with-rooms enjoys splendid views. Home-cooked local fish, meat and game. Bedrooms in the main house have sea views, those in the extension small patios overlooking the garden.

£ *Easter to end Oct; 6 rooms*

BADACHRO
Harbour View
Badachro, Gairloch IV21 2AA
TEL (01445) 741316
Cosy fisherman's cottage with lovely views over a small bay. The comfortable sitting-room and cheerful sun room are filled with knick-knacks. Dinner always includes a vegetarian dish; packed lunches are available. Three bedrooms in the main house and a double room chalet at the top of the garden.

£ *Mar to Oct; 4 rooms; credit cards not accepted*

DUNVEGAN
Harlosh House
Dunvegan, Isle of Skye IV55 8ZG
TEL/FAX (01470) 521367
From the modest beamed lounge of this extended crofthouse, dramatic views of the Cuillins can be spied. The main attraction here, however, is the food. An inspiring repertoire mostly uses fresh local produce. Bedrooms are chintzy and bright with fresh flowers.

££ *Closed mid-Oct to 1 week before Easter; 6 rooms (See Where to Eat)*

GAIRLOCH
Strathgair House
Gairloch, Wester Ross IV21 2BT
TEL (01445) 712118
Built in 1790, this Church of Scotland manse is hospitable and traditionally run. Oriental rugs decorate the house. Bedrooms share a bathroom and two showers.

£ *Easter to end Sept; 4 rooms with wash-basin; credit cards not accepted*

INVER ALLIGIN
Grianan
Inver Alligin, Torridon IV22 2HB
TEL (01445) 791264
Neat bungalow reached by a scenic road from Torridon. Spectacular views over the loch. Breakfast and dinner are served in a pleasant lounge, dinner by arrangement. Packed lunches are available. Bedrooms are on the ground floor and share a shower-room.

£ *Apr to Sept; 2 rooms; credit cards not accepted*

ISLE ORNSAY
Hotel Eilean Iarmain
Sleat, Isle of Skye IV43 8QR
TEL (01471) 833332
FAX (01471) 833275
Bristling antlers, a plaid carpet and Highlander prints set a proud tone at this traditional, patriotically decorated hotel. Good cooking in the panelled drawing-room, the ingredients evidently local and fresh. Bedrooms decorated with taste and care; many have excellent bathrooms.
££ All year; 12 rooms

Tawny Croft
Isle Ornsay, Sleat, Isle of Skye IV43 8QS
TEL/FAX (01471) 833325
This whitewashed croft outside the village has a large lounge and sunny conservatory. Here a wood-burning stove and a telescope for watching local wildlife ensure that guests linger in comfort. Evening meals are served in the dining-room. Bedrooms look out over the Sound and are equipped with binoculars.
£ All year (minimum 2-day stay); 2 rooms; credit cards not accepted

KILMUIR
Kilmuir House
Kilmuir, by Uig, Isle of Skye IV51 9YN
TEL (01470) 542262
This gracious, relaxed family house overlooking Loch Snizort was once a derelict manse. Home-grown vegetables and free-range eggs used in cooking of dinners and breakfasts. First-floor bedrooms have beautiful views and there is a family room on the ground floor.
£ All year exc Chr; 3 rooms; credit cards not accepted

KINLOCHBERVIE
Old School Restaurant
Inshegra, Kinlochbervie, by Lairg IV27 4RH
TEL (01971) 521383
This village schoolhouse still has old children's slates with simple sums and maps, and the dreaded strap – but guests don't have to sit up straight or pay attention. Instead, the atmosphere is friendly and relaxed and the meals a far cry from school dinners. Bedrooms in the annexe bungalow decorated in pastel colours with good furniture.
£ All year exc 25 Dec; 6 rooms, most with shower/wc; drying-room

LOCH ERIBOLL
Port-na-Con House
Loch Eriboll, by Altnaharra, Lairg IV27 4UN
TEL/FAX (01971) 511367
Once the customs house and harbour store, Port-na-Con has its own small beach on the west side of Loch Eriboll. The lounge has books and maps on the locality and a balcony. Dinner makes use of locally caught seafood; packed lunches are available. The small bedrooms look over the loch.
£ Mid-Mar to mid-Oct; 4 rooms

LOCHCARRON
A'Chomraich
Lochcarron IV54 8YD
TEL (01520) 722225
A stone-built house in the village of Lochcarron with views across the loch. There is a cosy lounge. Breakfast is served in the dining-room. Simple, attic-style bedrooms.
£ Easter to end Oct; 2 rooms with wash-basin; credit cards not accepted

LOCHINVER
Inver Lodge Hotel
Lochinver, Lairg IV27 4LU
TEL (01571) 844496
FAX (01571) 844395
These rather plain buildings provide a wonderful view over the harbour. The bright and modern lodge leads to a smart bar and fine dining-room. The menu is progressive and ambitious. Bedrooms have

co-ordinated furnishings and good reproduction furniture.

£££ Closed Nov to Mar; 20 rooms; drying-room; games room; solarium; sauna

The Albannach
Baddidarroch, Lochinver IV27 4LP
TEL/FAX (01571) 844407
Guesthouse in a very peaceful spot, with splendid views from the conservatory across the bay to the mountains of Assynt. The panelled dining-room is candlelit for four-course evening meals. Comfortable, well-equipped bedrooms.

£ Mar to Chr; 4 rooms

NORTH ERRADALE
Little Lodge
North Erradale, Gairloch IV21 2DS
TEL (01445) 771237
A working croft on a wild moorland peninsula, with a quietly welcoming interior. An open fire warms a sitting-room with exposed stone walls. Good home-cooking served in the sun room. Comfortable bedrooms.

£ Apr to Oct; 3 rooms; credit cards not accepted

PLOCKTON
Haven Hotel
Plockton IV52 8TW
TEL (01599) 544223
FAX (01599) 544467
Victorian merchant's house, now a friendly hotel run according to traditional values of comfort, value and service. Food on the short table d'hôte menu in the dining-room is well cooked and satisfying. Bedrooms not particularly stylish but comfortable and well equipped.

££ Closed 20 Dec-1 Feb; 13 rooms, most with shower/wc; drying-room

The Shieling
Plockton IV52 8TL
TEL (01599) 544282
A footpath on top of a causeway leads to this low, narrow building. There are views of the hills and Duncraig Castle. Meals served either in the dining-room or the light-filled lounge. Packed lunches are available. Bedrooms are on the ground floor.

£ Apr to Oct; 3 rooms, 1 with bath/shower; credit cards not accepted

PORTREE
Viewfield House
Portree, Isle of Skye IV51 9EU
TEL (01478) 612217
FAX (01478) 613517
Delightful house-party feel at this atmospheric house with gracious public rooms and romantic bedrooms. Ornate carving and old books abound in the large sitting-room. Ancestral portraits stare from the walls in the dining-room, where food is flavoursome and well presented. Antiques and period detailing in the bedrooms.

£-££ Mid-Apr to mid-Oct; 11 rooms

RUM
Kinloch Castle
Isle of Rum PH43 4RR
TEL/FAX (01687) 462037
Remote island offering a unique and lively experience. This guesthouse built of red sandstone is still full of furnishings and chattels dating from its heyday as a turn-of-the-century hunting lodge. Food is good and fresh and dining provides the occasion for a house-party. Budget hostel rooms in the old servants' quarters; grander eccentric and palatial rooms in the castle proper. Fantastic Victorian bathrooms.

£££ Closed Oct to Mar; 9 rooms sharing 4 bathrooms; drying-room; games room; credit cards not accepted

SCOURIE
Minch View
Scouriemore, Scourie, Lairg IV27 4TG
TEL (01971) 502010
A simple whitewashed building
overlooking the water. Evening
meals are available by arrangement
in the large sitting-room. Small,
plain bedrooms.
£ *Mar to Oct; 3 rooms, 2 with*
wash-basin; credit cards not accepted

Scourie Hotel
Scourie, Lairg IV27 4SX
TEL (01971) 502396
FAX (01971) 502423
An angler's delight, this old-
coaching inn has fifty beats and a
boat on Loch More. Fishing
associations continue in a decorating
scheme involving weighing scales
and catch display cases in the
cocktail bar. Food is traditional and
wholesome. Bedrooms are well
equipped and homely.
£-££ *Closed mid-Oct to Apr; 20*
rooms; drying-room; fishing

SHIELDAIG
Tigh an Eilean
Shieldaig, Strathcarron IV54 8XN
TEL (01520) 755251
FAX (01520) 755321
Whitewashed waterfront hotel
looking over to the island in the sea
loch which gives it its name.
Endearing hospitality makes stays
here pleasurable. Small-scale, stylish
public rooms. Memorable food
with excellent local seafood;
marvellous breakfasts with home-
made rolls. Packed lunches are
available. Neat bedrooms.
££ *Closed late Oct to Easter; 11*
rooms; drying-room (See Where to Eat)

STAFFIN
Flodigarry Country House
Staffin, Isle of Skye IV51 9HZ
TEL (01470) 552203
FAX (01470) 552301

Gloriously-situated, restful country
house with views over Staffin Bay.
The public bar is popular with
Gaelic-speaking locals. Cooking in
the graceful restaurant is delightful
and makes exemplary use of fresh
produce. Exquisite antiques in Flora
MacDonald's genteel cottage, and in
some bedrooms in the main house.
£ *All year; 23 rooms; drying-room*

STRONTIAN
Kilcamb Lodge
Strontian PH36 4HY
TEL (01967) 402257
FAX (01967) 402041
A country house on the shores of
Loch Sunart. The main sitting-
room has rich floral drapes and
fleur-de-lys walls; another is
comfortable with guidebooks and a
jigsaw table. The cooking is good
and the dinner menu pleasant.
Good Scottish cheeseboard.
Bedrooms have gorgeous fabrics
teamed with reproduction furniture.
££ *Closed Nov to Mar; 9 rooms;*
fishing; water sports (See Where to Eat)

TALLADALE
Loch Maree Hotel
Loch Maree IV22 2HL
TEL 01445) 760288
Shoreside hotel with smartly
decorated public areas and inviting
bedrooms. The dining room is light
and bright and the lounge
welcoming with comfortable sofas
and plenty of books and magazines.
Pleasingly furnished bedrooms,
some with glorious loch views.
££ *Mid-Mar to end Oct; 23 rooms;*
drying-room; fishing

TORRIDON
Upper Diabaig Farm
by Torridon, Achnasheen IV22 2HE
TEL (01445) 790227
Farm in a remote and wild spot, a
steep and winding eight-mile drive
from Torridon. The house is

modern and comfortable and the views are marvellous. Home-cooking is served. Bedrooms all have heaters and share a bathroom.
£ *Apr to Sept; 3 rooms; credit cards not accepted*

ULLAPOOL
Altnaharrie Inn
Ullapool IV26 2SS
TEL (01854) 633230
Travellers are enveloped by unhurried style and elegance at Altnaharrie Inn, across Loch Broom by private launch. Thoughtfully placed antiques and small art treasures in the comfortable public rooms. Food is a magnificent gourmet adventure. Charming and delightful small bedrooms.
£££ *Closed Nov to Easter; 8 rooms, 2 cottages (See Where to Eat)*

The Shieling Guest House
Garve Road, Ullapool IV26 2SX
TEL (01854) 612947
A modern, comfortable house on the edge of town with views across Loch Broom. Both the lounge and the dining-room look over the water. Packed lunches are available. Bedrooms are small and bright.
£ *All year exc Chr and New Year; 7 rooms; drying-room; sauna; fishing*

VATERNISH
Lismore
Vaternish, Isle of Skye IV55 8GE
TEL (01470) 592318
One of the best vistas on Skye. Memorable sunsets can be viewed from the lounge, where meals are served. Vegetarian options available, as are packed lunches. Simple bedrooms on the ground floor.
£ *Apr to Oct; 2 rooms with wash-basin; credit cards not accepted*

WHERE TO EAT

Key: A ★ marks a place that is particularly good value for money

ACHILTIBUIE
Summer Isles Hotel
Achiltibuie IV26 2YG
TEL (01854) 622282
FAX (01854) 622251
Delightful, straightforward cooking and excellent use of local fish and shellfish at this isolated culinary outpost. Good cheese and commendable concoctions on the pudding trolley. Plenty of half-bottles on the good wine list.
All week 8, one sitting; closed 10 Oct to Easter (See Where to Stay)

APPLECROSS
Applecross Inn ★
Shore Street, Applecross
TEL (01520) 744262
Remote inn reached over the highest mountain pass in Britain. The atmosphere is convivial and good food includes fresh seafood and excellent traditional puddings.
Open for food summer, all week 12 to 9; winter Tue to Sun 12 to 12.30, Mon to Sat 5 to 9; restaurant all week 6.30 to 8.45 (exc Sun Nov to Mar)

ARISAIG
Arisaig House
Beasdale, by Arisaig PH39 4NR
TEL (01687) 450622
FAX (01687) 450626
A straightforward selection of accurately cooked dishes. Lunch is light but the cooking moves up a gear in the evening. Traditional

puddings. The conservative wine list is rather expensive.
All week 12.30 to 2, 7.30 to 8.30; closed 31 Oct to 31 Mar (See Where to Stay)

COLBOST
Three Chimneys
Colbost, by Dunvegan, Isle of Skye IV55 8ZT
TEL (01470) 511258
Freshness and simplicity reign supreme here. Light lunches and home-baked teas served; grand evening meals involve wonderful seafood and delicious sauces. A vegetarian menu is also available. Fair-priced bottles on the astutely selected wine list.
Mon to Sat 12.30 to 2, 7 to 9; light meals and afternoon tea 10.30 to 12, 2 to 4.30; closed Nov to late Mar

DUNVEGAN
Harlosh House
Dunvegan, Isle of Skye IV55 8ZG
TEL (01470) 521367
Sensible set-price, four-course dinners produced to high standards. Menus based around fish, shellfish, game and duck. Efficiently selected and well-priced wines.
All week 7 to 8.30; closed mid-Oct to Easter (See Where to Stay)

GLENELG
Glenelg Inn ★
Glenelg, by Kyle of Lochalsh
TEL (01599) 522273
Boat trips and free use of a motor yacht are attractions at this lochside inn. Local smoked salmon and a variety of seafood at the heart of the menu.
Open for food Mon to Sat 12.30 to 2, 6.30 to 9; restaurant Mon to Sat 7.30 to 9; credit cards not accepted

KINLOCHMOIDART
Kinacarra ★
Kinlochmoidart PH38 4ND
TEL (01967) 431238
Fresh produce, keen flavours and generous portions combine at this long stone cottage near Loch Moidart. New and old cooking styles enliven the menu; rich and scrumptious puddings. Brief wine list, fairly priced.
Tue to Sun 12 to 2, 7 to 9; closed end Oct to Easter; credit cards not accepted

KYLESKU
Kylesku Hotel ★
Kylesku, by Lairg IV27 4HW
TEL (01971) 502231
FAX (01971) 502313
Sturdy culinary skills in a small hamlet where the catch is unloaded from boats in the afternoon. Seafood features along with good game and duck, and a display of pudding choices. Excellent breakfasts.
All week 12 to 2.30, 6 to 9.45; closed Nov to Feb

SHIELDAIG
Tigh an Eilean
Shieldaig, by Strathcarron IV54 8XN
TEL (01520) 755251
FAX (01520) 755321
Restrained and classical cooking in a lovely country house with views over the Isle of Pines. Seafood heads the menu; other options are equally delicious. Excellent, sustaining breakfasts.
All week 7 to 8.30; closed late Oct to Easter (See Where to Stay)

STEIN
Loch Bay
1-2 Macleod Terrace, Stein, Vaternish, Isle of Skye IV55 8GA
TEL (01470) 592235
Gem of an inn with a dedicated seafood menu and *au naturel*

cooking using sparklingly fresh ingredients. Look out for daily specials which vary depending on the catch. The wine list includes very drinkable Highland brews from silver birch sap, elderflowers and brambles.

Sun to Fri 12 to 3, 6 to 9; closed Oct to Easter

STRONTIAN
Kilcamb Lodge
Strontian PH36 4HY
TEL (01967) 402257
Lively and unstuffy country lodge on the shores of Loch Sunart whose kitchen deals expertly with the very best of British produce. A memorable four-course dinner menu, presented with finesse.

Puddings are rich and delicious or fruity and refreshing. Good wine list.

All week 7.30, one sitting; closed mid-Nov to mid-Mar (See Where to Stay)

ULLAPOOL
Altnaharrie Inn
Ullapool IV26 2SS
TEL (01854) 633230
This luxurious island inn provides a composed and tranquil setting in which to enjoy superb cooking. Dishes are effortlessly produced with unique attention to detail and exquisite flavours; puddings simply dazzle. An unsurpassed experience from start to finish.

All week 8, one sitting; closed Nov to Easter (See Where to Stay)

THE WESTERN ISLES

- Remote islands which are the last stronghold of the old Highland way of life
- Superb beaches and wild flowers
- Excellent fishing

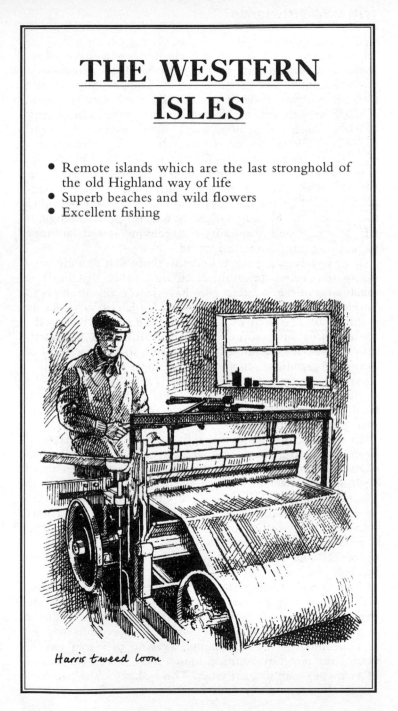

Harris tweed loom

THE islands of the Outer Hebrides (or Western Isles), which run for 130 miles parallel to Scotland's north-west coast, are unlike anywhere else in the country. Superficially they share many of the features of the north-west mainland – there are mountains, fertile coastal strips, magnificent beaches, desolate peat bogs and endless lochans. However, the Western Isles, despite the aircraft and the ferries which serve them, are remote, and for the inhabitants to climb into a car and head for the bright lights is easier said than done. Because of this, they remain in many ways the last strong-hold of old Highland life. Communities are closely bound to the sea and to the soil; Gaelic is widely spoken; religious faith is strong, and hospitality is as genuine as you can hope to find in a tourist-infested world.

It is, however, a grave mistake to think that you are ven-turing into some unsophisticated outpost of Britain. The inhabitants of the Western Isles have seen many attempts to 'modernise' them, from those efforts by James VI to set up a colony of Fife men on Lewis in 1598 to the twentieth-century efforts of Lord Leverhulme to turn Lewis and Harris into the base for a huge fishing industry, so they are wary of outsiders' grandiose schemes to transform their way of life. They are equally aware of how easy it is for the islands to be neglected – the Western Isles did not even have their own local government until 1974. Consequently, opinions are strongly held out here.

In religion, the islands are split between the Presbyterian Lewis, Harris and North Uist, and the predominantly Roman Catholic South Uist and Barra. Benbecula has adherents of both doctrines. On Lewis and Harris, the Free Presbyterian Church of Scotland and the Free Church of Scotland (the Wee Frees) are both strong, and Sundays are very strictly observed. It is worth remembering that public transport will not be running and shops and petrol stations will not be open. On the Roman Catholic islands, things are more relaxed.

Fishing and crofting are the islanders' main occupations, and island life outside Stornoway revolves around the rhythm of the seasons and of the tides. Almost every islander will have more than one occupation – work on the croft may be supplemented by lobster-fishing, weaving of Harris tweed, driving the post-bus, running a guesthouse or any number of other money-spinning activities. This makes for a network of relationships where everyone knows everyone else.

For visitors, especially those who have roots in the islands, the Western Isles exert a fascination which is difficult to justify to those who have not yet been there. The landscape of the interiors is mostly unrelenting rock, bog or water, and the long, straggling, crofting communities by the shore, where the functional croft houses are linked by wires and telephone poles, have no similarity to conventionally pretty villages. An outbreak of (subsidised) fencing has left many of the crofts surrounded by wire. Stray sheep may be better confined, but wind-blown litter trailing from the fence posts can get pretty unsightly. Even the superb beaches have their drawbacks, smelly seaweed being the commonest. Yet these are not the images that endure. Instead, it may be the blanket of wild flowers on a Uist machair, a shower clearing over the hills of Harris, a riotous evening in a Stornoway bar or simply the scent of burning peat drifting over the islands that you will remember.

LEWIS

The interior of Lewis is bare of people and bare of trees. The northern half is a flat, deserted moorland of rain-washed skies and distant horizons, where the only signs of human activity are the trenches and embankments of peat-cuttings, often marked by piles of plastic sacks. These excavations are everywhere, for peat is the universal fuel of the island and every croft house will have its peat stack, where the neat piles of dried black turf stand ready for the fire. The scent of peat smoke hangs over Lewis, an aroma which seems compounded of whisky, grass bonfires and a hint of coffee.

All the inhabitants of Lewis live by the sea, approximately 8,000 of them in Stornoway on the east coast, the only town on the islands. On the west coast, a long string of crofting townships runs the 34 miles from Ness to Carloway. Further south, settlements become sparse as rocky hills bulge out of the moor and long sea-lochs cut into the coast.

Lewis was once dominated by the MacLeods, said to be descendants of early settlers from Iceland. During the reign of James VI, when attempts to colonise Lewis with 'civilised' Lowlanders took place, Mackenzies managed to gain possession of the island. Cromwell demolished Stornoway Castle during a punitive expedition in 1653. In 1844, Lewis was sold to Sir James Matheson, who built

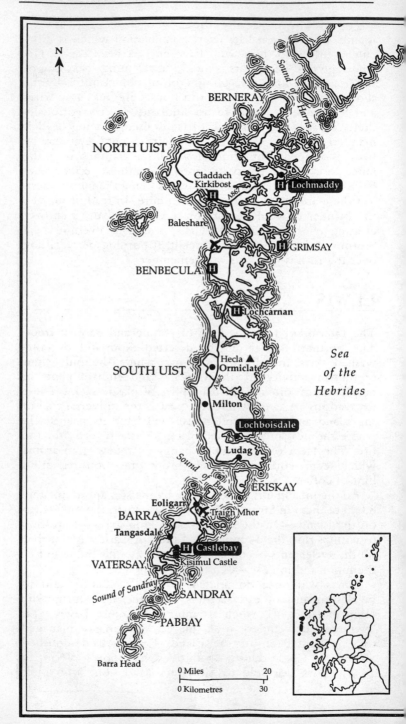

N

BERNERAY

NORTH UIST

Claddach
Kirkibost
H
A865
H Lochmaddy

Baleshare

H GRIMSAY

BENBECULA H

H Lochcarnan

Hecla ▲
Ormiclate

SOUTH UIST

A865

Milton

Lochboisdale

Ludag

Sea
of the
Hebrides

Sound of Barra
ERISKAY

Eoligarry
BARRA Traigh Mhor

Tangasdale

H Castlebay
VATERSAY Kisimul Castle

Sound of Sandray
SANDRAY

PABBAY

Barra Head

Sound of Harris

0 Miles 20
0 Kilometres 30

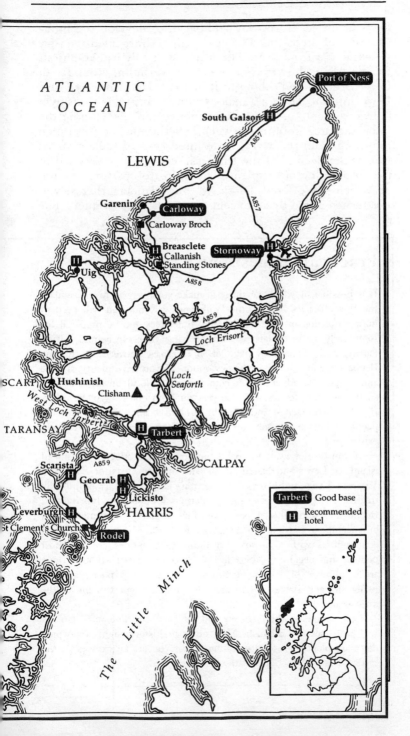

Lews Castle in Stornoway and began to develop the infra-structure of the island. He also set up a short-lived industry to extract tar from peat. The man who really had ambitions for the island, however, was Lord Leverhulme, founder of Lever Brothers, who bought it in 1918. He planned to turn Lewis into the base for a major fishing industry, with its own railway system, and he poured money into developing the infrastructure. Conflict between Leverhulme and local men returning from the war who wanted land of their own, as well as the decline of the fishing industry, eventually led to the abandoning of his plans. The magnate's parting gesture, in which he offered Lewis to the islanders themselves, was turned down by all except the Stornoway Council. The

Practical suggestions

It is possible, if you have time, to make your way from one end of the Western Isles to the other with your car, but you will need to master Caledonian MacBrayne ferry timetables and be prepared for some early starts or late arrivals. Leaving your car behind, hiring locally, and taking advantage of air services between Stornoway, Benbecula and Barra is an easier option. If you have plenty of time and a spirit of adventure, a combination of local buses, taxis and small passenger ferries will also get you from one end to the other. If you find yourself stranded, asking around locally will often unearth people willing to help get you from A to B where no formal transport exists.

If you do not want to spend time on ferries, stick to the linked islands of Lewis and Harris, Benbecula and the Uists, or Barra and Vatersay. Lewis and Harris – not separate islands, but always quirkily treated as such – are for wilderness-lovers and hill-walkers. Benbecula and the Uists are for anglers, naturalists and beachcombers. Barra and Vatersay are for those who like small island communities with a bit of everything. Guesthouses are the most popular and usually the best form of accommodation, though there are a number of hotels in Stornoway, the ferry ports, and on Benbecula and Barra. There are self-catering properties on all the main islands.

Conventional sights are few and far between. The most famous are the stones of Callanish. Most other prehistoric sights (of which there are plenty) are disappointing unless you are an expert. Of the castles, Kisimul on Barra is the best preserved.

island was split into estates and sold, and almost 1,000 people emigrated.

Stornoway

Clustered at the end of an eastward-thrusting peninsula, Stornoway is a small fishing town which also happens to be the only settlement of any size in the Western Isles – hence it is the administrative centre. There is not a great deal to see once you have bought any necessities you need (opportunities to do this will be limited elsewhere on the island), but a walk around the harbour will prove worthwhile if fishing boats are unloading. The **Museum nan**

The Western Isles Island Council has adopted a policy of using Gaelic place names on road signs, except in Stornoway and Benbecula, where they are bilingual. Most maps still use the English names, however. To help you find your way round, we recommend using a map (such as the one available from the Western Isles Tourist Board) which shows both names.

Place names

Balivanich	Baile a Mhanaich
Barra	Barraigh
Benbecula	Beinn na Faoghla
Butt of Lewis	Rubha Robhanais
Carloway	Carlabhagh
Castlebay	Bagh a Chaisteil
Eriskay	Eiriosgaigh
Harris	Na Hearadh
Lewis	Eilean Leodhais
Lochboisdale	Loch Baghasdail
Lochmaddy	Loch nam Madadh
Ness	Nis
Newtonferry	Port nan Long
North Uist	Uibhist a Tuath
Rodel	Roghadal
South Uist	Uibhist a Deas
Stornoway	Steornabhagh
Tarbert	Tairbeart
Vatersay	Bhatarsaigh

Eilean (open Mon to Fri 10 to 1, 2 to 5) offers background on local history, and perhaps walk in the grounds of **Lews Castle** (now a college), where the woods and shrubs would be unremarkable elsewhere, but, in the Western Isles, are exceptional. The tiny art gallery of **An Lanntair** is the most rewarding of Stornoway's places to visit. Exhibitions here are refreshing and radical.

The west coast of Lewis

From Stornoway, the A859 and A858 carry you westward across the interior of Lewis to the road junction at Garynahine. From here, the B8011 leads to the south-west corner, a country of gneiss and granite with a tiny population. The best beach on Lewis is here, at **Uig**, where in 1831 a crofter dug up the Lewis Chessmen, 78 pieces of Scandinavian origin, carved from walrus ivory and dating from the twelfth century. The kings glower, the queens look as if they are suffering an attack of the vapours, and the pawn-warriors bite their shields in frustration. You can buy reproductions on Lewis; the originals are split between museums in Edinburgh and London.

By continuing on the A858, you arrive at the **Callanish Standing Stones** (HS, always open). Set on a lonely small peninsula that is unlikely to be spoilt by crowds, the 53 stones form a pattern like a Celtic cross, with an inner circle and four arms. They date from 3000 BC and are thus older than Stonehenge. Their function is unknown, but a lunar observatory is a popular explanation. A recently built visitor centre explains such facts as are known.

A short distance north, the remains of **Carloway Broch** stand close to the road on a hillside overlooking the sea. The broch is very well preserved; part of the wall is still 30 feet high. Collapsing stonework has exposed the interior galleries and stairs. At **Garenin**, a little further on, detour from the main road to see the ruins of a village of 'Black Houses' (see below).

The next place to stop is **Shawbost** (open Mon to Sat at all reasonable times), where a folk museum, started as a project by local schoolchildren, has blossomed into a fascinating, if ramshackle, collection of artefacts and junk collected from all walks of Hebridean life.

Arnol is the place to see how the people of Lewis used to live. The **Black House Museum** (HS, standard times; closed Fri and Sun in winter) is a conserved example of a type of housing once common throughout the Highlands and Islands. Thick, low, double walls packed with peat for insulation support a roof thatched with heather and straw and weighed down with stones. Often there is only one door, used by both cattle and humans, and the interior is split between byre and living quarters. A peat fire smoulders on a central hearth. There is no chimney and the smoke filters out through the thatch. At first glance such living conditions may seem unbearably primitive but, in a land desperately short of everything but stone and heathery peat, and with a vile climate, the black house represented an extremely effective use of available material. It was energy-efficient in the best modern tradition: the double walls for insulation, the cattle for a renewable source of heat, the soot-impregnated roof to be used as fertiliser on the fields, and the absence of heat loss through windows. Black houses were inhabited until the 1960s (some modernised ones still are).

From Barvas, the A857 returns across the moors of Lewis to Stornoway, but if you are determined to explore further, a 15-mile drive on the coast road will bring you to the district of Ness and the Butt of Lewis. The tiny Port of Ness will provide you with tea before you make your way to the lighthouse on the very tip of Lewis, a wild and windy spot. Glance at the tiny twelfth-century **St Moluag's Church**.

HARRIS

Where Lewis is predominately flat moorland, Harris is largely mountain and rock. As you drive south from Stornoway on the A859, you will see the mountains rising in a barrier before you, with cloud probably hanging over their peaks. On the left, the narrow ribbon of Loch Seaforth eats deep into the coast; the land to its east is without road or habitation. At Tarbert, beyond the mountain barrier, Harris is almost split by the sea. On the west coast, south of here, wonderful sandy beaches suddenly turn the desolation silver.

The separation of Harris from Lewis goes right back to Norse times, when the island was divided between the two sons of Leod. Harris remained in MacLeod hands until 1834. Lord Leverhulme (see Lewis) also hoped to make Harris part of his ambitious schemes, and he concentrated his energies here when his plans for Lewis came to nothing. His death in 1925 brought an end to his plans for Harris also, and little remains of his work apart from the roads and the small harbour at Leverburgh. The latest project proposed for Harris is the opening of a quarry on the east coast. If it ever gets started, it will be the biggest in Europe. Needless to say, the whole scheme is highly controversial.

North Harris, the land lying north of Tarbert, is the country for hill-walkers. None of the mountains here are as high as those on the Scottish mainland, but they are steep, rocky in places, and views from them can be marvellous. **Clisham**, the highest peak, is relatively easy to get to from the A859. The B887 runs along the coast westward to a dead end in Husinish Bay (with a small sandy beach), passing the turreted shooting lodge of Amhuinnsuidh Castle on the way.

Tarbert is a tiny place, but as it is the ferry port for Harris it has more facilities (such as a bank and a restaurant) than anywhere else. Ask at the Tourist Information Centre or the Harris Hotel if you want to fish for sea trout. East of the village, a ten-mile drive takes you through scattered

MACHAIR

Machair is the name given to the strips of land lying behind the beaches of west Scotland and the islands. These strips are notable for their fertility, in contrast to the poor, acid peat of the interior. In summer they are a blaze of wild flowers, and provide good grazing. The explanation lies in the shell sand, with its rich content of calcium, which is carried inshore from the beaches by the wind and neutralises the acidity of the peaty soil. The very best land lies a little inland from the beaches, where the soil is neither too sandy nor too peaty, and this area will be where the crofters have their small fields. During the Clearances, many families were forced off this good land and were given plots of infertile peat instead. Their only way to grow crops was then to create the so-called 'lazy beds', patches which were made fertile by laborious application of seaweed, and raised slightly above the surrounding ground to give some drainage. The machair, meanwhile, was given over to sheep. The machair today is prized for the variety of flowers it produces – primroses, buttercup, vetch, orchid and gentian. In damper patches (wet machair) clumps of wild iris provide favoured shelter for corncrakes. Rabbits are the greatest menace to the machair, for their burrowings allow the wind to get at the sandy soil beneath the surface.

communities to Carnach, where a car ferry crosses to
Scalpay. Fishing keeps the population going on this remote
piece of land, which makes a good destination for an
expedition from Tarbert.

You should certainly drive right round **South Harris**, for
the change in landscape between east and west is fascinating.
The road down the west coast passes the firm sandy beaches
of Luskentyre and Scarista, and everywhere there are patches
of fertile machair. At **Leverburgh** you can see the remains of
Lord Leverhulme's building works for his projected fishing
port, but the village itself is just a row of houses. The passenger ferry for North Uist runs from here. Carry on to
Rodel, at the very end of the A859, to see **St Clement's
Church** (HS, always open). This beautifully crafted twelfth-
century church is a remarkable find in such a far-away spot.
Inside, the tomb of Alexander MacLeod, who died in 1547,
is even more remarkable. Its carvings, showing a hunting
scene, a castle and many religious images, repay a close look.

The single-track road up the east coast of Harris winds
amongst outcrops of rock, bare of any vegetation. Crofts
cling to tiny patches of level ground by the shore and boats
are tied up in the many inlets. Along the road, especially
near the township of **Plocrapool**, are several places where
you can stop to watch Harris tweed being woven. The
crofters are sent materials and patterns from Stornoway, and
make up the lengths of tweed on clattering looms in small
sheds beside their houses. You can sometimes see packets of
cloth left by cottage gateways for collection, where it will be
taken to Stornoway for finishing. If the tweed is not hand-
woven, dyed and finished in the Western Isles, it cannot be
stamped with the orb symbol which marks Harris tweed.

It was thanks to the Countess of Dunmore, who started
the fashion for it in 1842, that Harris tweed became sought
after. It was given its trademark in 1909. About one and a
half million yards of Harris tweed are produced annually by
about 400 weavers.

BENBECULA AND THE UISTS

These three islands are linked by causeways which cross the
shallow inlets of the sea between them. The sea creeps inland
in so many arms and there are so many fresh-water lochs that
it is difficult to know which island you are on. In fact, there
is almost as much water as land on these islands, and one of

the delights of flying over them is to watch the light reflected back at you from the hundreds of lochs, as if someone had shattered mirrors over a green and brown carpet. Sit on the east-facing side of the aircraft for the best view.

These are the islands to come to for sandy beaches, for sand runs almost the full length of their west coasts. Magnificent beaches they are too, catching the full force of the Atlantic as it piles on to the shore, haunted by crying seabirds and backed by sheets of wild flowers in early summer. The eastern side of the islands is where the lochs are – you can fish for trout and sea-trout until your arm drops off, but still fail to cover more than a fraction of the available water. The only respectable hills are on the east of North and South Uist – worth climbing to have your feet on dry ground or to catch new views of this bizarre landscape of rock and water (especially fine from **Eaval** on North Uist if you can ever pick your way across to it).

BONNIE PRINCE CHARLIE (1720–1788)

When Charles Edward Stuart, the son of 'The Old Pretender', or James VIII as his Scottish supporters knew him, set foot on the Hebridean island of Eriskay on 23 July 1745, his attempt to restore his father to the throne of Britain seemed doomed. Three previous efforts (1707, 1715 and 1719) had come to nothing; French support was lukewarm at best, while the strength of Scottish and English support was uncertain. The young prince persisted in the face of initial discouragement, sailing to the mainland and raising his father's standard at Glenfinnan on 19 August. If he had not personally persuaded Cameron of Lochiel to raise his clan, little might have come of his effort, for many of the Highland chiefs on whom he relied had refused to join him.

Despite its initial success in defeating the Hanoverian troops at Prestonpans and in occupying Edinburgh, the rising of 1745 was faced with failure from the moment it became clear that there was going to be no general uprising in England. Prince Charles' youth, optimism and charm created devoted followers for him, but a distrust of his father's Catholicism and an unwillingness to hazard life and limb in an uncertain cause deterred many others, even if they had no love for the Hanoverian kings.

The Jacobite army had reached Derby before military discretion caused its leaders to choose withdrawal. The Prince was outraged, but could do nothing. The recall of seasoned Hanoverian troops

North Uist

The ferry docks at **Lochmaddy**, a village so girdled with lochs that it almost floats. Again, the Tourist Information Centre here is the place to ask about fishing, or try at the Lochmaddy Hotel. Lochmaddy makes a good base for anglers, and is the largest settlement on the island. There is a small museum of local history too.

There is not much by way of sights on North Uist – the numerous prehistoric remains are fun to track down, but there is usually little to see when you reach them. The charms of the island lie in its beaches, especially those on its north coast, and in its birds. The **Balranald Nature Reserve** is a breeding site for duck and waders and an RSPB reserve. This is one of the places in Scotland where you really do have a chance of seeing an otter, and in summer you may hear the call of the corncrake, a bird that is

from the war against France diminished the hopes of success, and the Battle of Culloden in 1746 put an end to them. Some have judged Prince Charles' decision to return to France after that battle as premature, if not a betrayal, but it was little more than a recognition of reality.

After Culloden, the story of the charming, headstrong Prince takes on a tinge of genuine heroism. With a price of £30,000 on his head, and with soldiers combing Scotland for him, the royal refugee wandered the Highlands and Islands for five months. Sleeping rough or in crude bothies and in constant fear of discovery, he dodged from Arisaig to the Western Isles, guided and supplied by men and women who never dreamed of betraying him. Disguised as a maidservant, he was brought back over the sea to Skye by Flora Macdonald and eventually reached Mallaig and the hills above Loch Quoich and Loch Arkaig, where he was sheltered by the 'Seven men of Glenmoriston', who may have been brigands, but were devoted to the Prince. On 19 September, in company with Cameron of Lochiel with whom he had begun the whole desperate venture, he finally boarded a French ship in Loch nan Uamh and returned to exile.

His plea to Louis XV for 20,000 men went unheard, and eventually he was expelled from France. Wandering Europe, still in search of support, the Prince increasingly gave way to stubborn despair and to drink. He died in Italy in 1788. His marble tomb in Rome was partly paid for by the Hanoverian George III. With the death of his brother, the line of the exiled Stuart kings came to an end.

now extremely rare everywhere in Britain except among the crofts of the Western Isles, where traditional agricultural methods provide shelter for it.

Benbecula

Benbecula was linked to North Uist by causeway only in 1960. Before that, the only way to pass between the islands on foot was by fording the tidal sands between the islands. It is a relatively fertile island, and less beautiful than its neighbours, being flat and dotted with rather ugly crofts.

At **Balivanich** the army base adds to the utilitarian feeling, but compensation is to be found in the relatively large number of shops and other amenities. Here, too, is the airport. There are worries that the base may be run down or closed, which could devastate the local ecenomy.

Benbecula's sandy beaches are lovely, but subject, like other westward-facing beaches, to having malodorous piles of seaweed deposited on them by storms. A huge forest of kelp grows off the west coast of the islands; it was once extensively used in making glass and provided income for numerous communities. It is still occasionally collected and dried, as a valuable source of fertiliser.

At **Liniclett**, in the south of the island, the new community school has extensive facilities, including a library and small museum. It is also the site of various entertainments which are open to visitors. The school was the subject of a rare spat between the religious communities when it opened, the Presbyterians wishing it to be closed on Sundays and the Catholics seeing no reason why it should be.

It was from Benbecula that the refugee Prince Charles Edward set off with Flora Macdonald over the sea to Skye. He was disguised as her maid, a fact that the famous song does not mention.

South Uist

The history of South Uist, like that of its neighbours to the north, has been a turbulent one. The Norsemen were succeeded by the Lords of the Isles (this is Macdonald territory), and after them, on the forfeiture of the Lord of the Isles, the Campbell Earl of Argyll was made King's Lieutenant. After the Battle of Culloden, Prince Charles Edward spent much time hiding in the islands before his escape to Skye and France. The introduction of the potato increased the population, but the failure of the crop in 1846 brought famine. Clearance and emigration followed, and the population of South Uist dropped by 2,000 in 20 years.

You are welcomed into South Uist from the north by the statue (1957) of Our Lady of the Isles, which stands on the side of a low hill above the road. **Loch Bee**, which you cross just before reaching the statue, is the haunt of mute swans, while the next large loch, **Loch Druidibeg**, is a nature reserve, with a large colony of greylag geese, many breeding waders and some stretches of machair too. Beyond, the A865 runs down the spine of the island, with lochs and hills to the east, crofts, machair and Atlantic beaches to the west. You can divert to **Ormiclete** to see the ruins of a castle, or to **Milton**, where a cairn, surrounded by sheep pens, marks Flora Macdonald's birthplace. There is a local museum at nearby Kildonan. **Lochboisdale**, South Uist's ferry port and chief settlement, is set on a sea-loch of singular beauty whose imposing entrance between two sloping hills opens out into an island-dotted bay. There is even a ruined castle on an island to greet you if you arrive by ferry.

BARRA AND VATERSAY

From the map, Barra may look too small to be worth bothering with, but this is a mistake. On this self-contained island you will find a compendium of all the best parts of the Western Isles – beaches, machair, small crofting communities, and peat-smothered hills. Only the lochans are missing down here – otherwise Barra makes a perfect taster for Hebridean life.

Castlebay is a sheltered harbour with, right in its centre, a castle on a rocky shoal. **Kisimul Castle** (accessible by boat, call Barra tourist office 01871 810336 for opening times), is the ancient home of the MacNeil chiefs. On days when it is open, you are rowed out to it for a close-up of the fifteenth-century walls, but it is just as rewarding to gaze at it from the harbour-front of Castlebay.

Barra has one circular road (A888), and driving or bicycling slowly round this is one of the island's two diversions. The west coast is the nicest area, with the best beach (at Tangusdale) and a small valley of crofts – good for a gentle stroll – at Borve.

Detour north from the main road to see the beach of **Tràigh Mhór**, the 'cockle strand' which once provided 100 to 200 cartloads of the shellfish a day. This beach is also Barra's airport — a small shelter stands by it where families wait to pick up relatives who have been shopping in Glasgow. At low tide, the aircraft buzzes in, its wheels kicking up a fine spray from the sand as it touches down.

By the beach, stands the house that was once the home of Compton Mackenzie, author of *Whisky Galore*, among other novels. He spent much of his later middle-age on Barra, and briefly made the island a literary centre.

The second of the island's diversions is to drive across the

USEFUL DIRECTORY

Main tourist office
Western Isles Tourist Board
26 Cromwell Street
Stornoway, Lewis PA87 2DD
(01851) 703088

Tourist Board publications Annual Western Isles accommodation and tourist guide (sights, boat trips, crafts, cycle hire etc.); also *Harris Gazetteer* (routes around islands, places of interest); bilingual English/Gaelic *Western Isles Tourist Map*; angling leaflet. Order by post or phone from address above.

Local tourist information centres
Barra, Castlebay (01871) 810336 (Easter to Oct)
Harris, Tarbert (01895) 502011 (Easter to Oct)
North Uist, Lochmaddy (01876) 500321 (Easter to Oct)
South Uist, Lochboisdale (01878) 700286 (Easter to Oct)

Public transport
Stornoway airport (01851) 702256
British Airways/British Airways Express (flights to Stornoway from Glasgow and Inverness, to Benbecula from Glasgow and inter-island services between Stornoway, Barra and Benbecula) (0345) 222111
Stornoway bus station (01851) 704327
Post-bus timetables available from tourist information centres or Royal Mail (01463) 256200

new causeway to the island of **Vatersay**. There is nothing here apart from crofts, two beautiful beaches and some superb machair full of wild flowers, but on a clear day you can see the string of now uninhabited islands to the south – Sandray, Pabbay, Mingauly and Berneray.

Other islands

• **Berneray** The island is reached by ferry from Harris or North Uist. Its chief attraction are the beaches on the western side, their machair a wonderful place for wild flowers.

• **Eriskay** Reached by ferry from South Uist, this tiny

Mainland ferries

Car ferries from the mainland to the Western Isles are run by Caledonian MacBrayne (01475) 650100

Oban-Castlebay (5 hrs, up to four sailings a week)

Oban-Lochboisdale (5 hrs, up to six sailings a week, in winter three or four)

Uig-Lochmaddy (1 hr 45 mins, Mon to Sat, also Sun late Apr to mid-Oct, one or two sailings daily)

Uig-Tarbert (1 hr 45 mins, Mon to Sat, one or two sailings daily)

Ullapool-Stornoway (2 hrs 45 mins, Mon to Sat, up to three sailings daily, in winter one or two)

Inter-island ferries

Berneray-Leverburgh-North Uist car ferry (Mon to Sat, at least three sailings daily) (01475) 650100

Eriskay-South Uist-Barra passenger ferry (May to Sept, Mon to Sat four sailings a day, Oct to Apr, two a day) (01878) 720233

Harris-North Uist car (summer only) and passenger ferry (Mon to Sat in summer, three days a week in winter) (01876) 540230

Harris-Scalpay car ferry (Mon to Sat, frequent service) (01475) 650100

North Uist-Berneray car ferry (three or four sailings daily; Mon, Wed, Sat in winter) (01876) 540230

South Uist-Barra car ferry (up to four sailings a week) (01475) 650100

South Uist-Eriskay car ferry (Mon to Sat) (01878) 720261

Other

National Trust for Scotland boat cruises, also conservation working parties on the island of St Kilda; ring 0131-226 5922, or write to NTS, 5 Charlotte Square, Edinburgh EH2 4DU.

island supports about 200 people. Most visitors come to see the place where Prince Charles Edward first set foot in Scotland in 1745, or to catch a glimpse of the wreck of the *Politician*, which went down in 1941 carrying 20,000 cases of whisky. Compton Mackenzie's novel *Whisky Galore* and the subsequent film did much to make Eriskay famous.

● **St Kilda** Forty miles west of the Western Isles, the stark rocks of St Kilda rear from the Atlantic. The community was evacuated in 1930, and only the army maintains an occasional presence here.

WHERE TO STAY

£ – under £70 per room per night, incl. VAT
££ – £70 to £110 per room per night, incl. VAT
£££ – over £110 per room per night, incl. VAT

BREASCLETE
Eshcol Guest House
Breasclete, Isle of Lewis HS2 9ED
TEL (01851) 621357
Within walking distance of the Callanish stones and overlooking Loch Roag, the island of Great Bernera and the Uig and Harris hills. Accommodation is comfortable and home-cooking is good. Full board is available on Sundays and packed lunches can be arranged.
£ Mar to Oct; 3 rooms; credit cards not accepted

CASTLEBAY
Tigh-na-Mara
Castlebay, Isle of Barra H59 5XD
TEL (01871) 810304
This comfortable stone house looks across the bay to an old castle. Breakfast and evening meals are served and there is a small lounge for guests. Packed lunches are available.
£ Apr to Oct; 5 rooms; credit cards not accepted

CLADDACH KIRKIBOST
Sealladh Traigh
Claddach Kirkibost, North Uist HS6 5EP
TEL (01876) 580248
FAX (01876) 510257
A friendly and welcoming modern house close to the sandy beaches of North Uist. Home-cooked dinners are served in the pleasant lounge; packed lunches are available. Small and bright bedrooms. The owners also run the pub next door.
£ All year; 5 rooms with wash-basin

GRIMSAY
Glendale
7 Kallin, Grimsay, North Uist
HS62 5HY
TEL (01870) 602029
Glendale stands above the tiny fishing harbour of Kallin on the small island of Grimsay. The owner's fishing boat catches shrimp, crab and lobster to be freshly cooked for guests. Packed lunches are available. Comfortable bedrooms.
£ All year; 3 rooms; credit cards not accepted

HOUGHARRY
Sgeir Ruadh
Hougharry nr Lochmaddy, North Uist
HS6 5DL
TEL (01876) 510312

A modern house in the Balranald Bird Reserve, a perfect spot for families and birdwatchers. Breakfast and evening meals are served in a large lounge/diner which overlooks the beach; packed lunches available. *£ All year; 3 rooms; credit cards not accepted*

LEVERBURGH
St Kilda House
Leverburgh, Isle of Harris HS3 3UB
TEL (01859) 520419
This delightful small guesthouse was a ruined schoolteacher's house in 1992; plans are now afoot to transform the adjoining ruined schoolroom into a restaurant. Overlooking the sea is a tiny dining-room; cooking is traditional and generous, bread and yoghurt home-made. Packed lunches available. Comfortable bedrooms. *£ All year; 2 rooms; credit cards not accepted*

LICKISTO
Two Waters
Lickisto, Isle of Harris HS3 3EL
TEL (01859) 530246
On a narrow inlet of Harris' rocky coast, this modern bungalow is warm and hospitable. The owner is a keen fisherman and guests sittng around the large dining table are likely to feast on his catch, much of which is home-smoked for breakfast. Delicious four-course dinners feature rich puddings and home-smoked Cheddar. Welcoming extras such as home-made biscuits in the pretty floral bedrooms. *£ Closed Oct to end Apr; 4 rooms; drying-room; fishing*

LOCHCARNAN
Orasay Inn
Lochcarnan, South Uist HS8 5PD
TEL (01870) 610298
FAX (01870) 610390

Simple accommodation at this low building, a good base for exploring North and South Uist and Benbecula. The dining-room specialises in seafood and offers views across the Minch to the mountains. Packed lunches available. *£ All year; 8 rooms*

MUIR OF AIRD
Lennox Cottage
Muir of Aird, Isle of Benbecula PA88 5LA
TEL (01870) 602965
Warm and friendly cottage with an open fire in the lounge. Good home-cooked meals are served in the kitchen and packed lunches can be provided. Comfortable bedrooms. *£ All year; 3 rooms; credit cards not accepted*

SCARISTA
Scarista House
Scarista, Isle of Harris HS3 3HX
TEL (01859) 550238
FAX (01859) 550277
White Georgian manse on a deserted sandy beach on the island's west side. Fine furniture and a well-stocked library contribute to the charm of the place. The no-choice five-course dinner is a delicious affair. Damask curtains in the white-walled bedrooms. *££ Closed Oct to mid-May; 8 rooms; drying-room; credit cards not accepted (See Where to Eat)*

SOUTH GALSON
Galson Farm Guesthouse
South Galson, Isle of Lewis PA86 0SH
TEL/FAX (01851) 850492
Open all year on the north-west corner of the island, Galson Farm is especially warm and welcoming on a wild winter night. The two cosy lounges have blazing peat fires and comfy chairs. Home-cooked dinners must be ordered in advance;

breakfasts are plentiful and satisfying.
£ All year; 3 rooms with shower/wc;
drying-room

STORNOWAY
Ardlonan
29 Francis Street, Stornoway, Isle of
Lewis HS1 2NF
TEL (01851) 703482
Genuine Scottish hospitality at this
well-established guesthouse.
Breakfast only is served, but tea and
delicious home baking are provided
in the evenings.
£ All year exc Chr and New Year;
6 rooms with wash-basin; drying-
room; credit cards not accepted

TARBERT
Allan Cottage
Tarbert, Isle of Harris HS3 3DJ
TEL (01859) 502146
An old telephone exchange five
minutes' walk from the ferry with
views over the harbour and to the
mountains of Skye. An open fire

warms the lounge and the home-
cooked dinners are good; packed
lunches are available. Bedrooms are
very well equipped.
£ Apr to Sept; 3 rooms; credit cards
not accepted

UIG
Baile-na-Cille
Timsgarry, Uig, Isle of Lewis HS2 9JD
TEL (01851) 672242
FAX (01851) 672241
On the edge of a long sandy west-
coast beach, this whitewashed
manse occupies an enviable position
in a splendid remote setting. Simple
and friendly, it is a popular place
suited to families. First-rate cooking
makes use of fresh local produce
and the home baking is delicious.
Bedrooms are colourful and bright;
small bunk-bedrooms for children.
£ Closed 15 Nov to 1 Mar; 13
rooms; drying-room; games room;
fishing (See Where to Eat)

WHERE TO EAT

Key: A ★ marks a place that is
particularly good value for money

SCARISTA
Scarista House
Scarista, Isle of Harris HS3 3HX
TEL (01859) 550238
FAX (01859) 550277
Fresh fish and superbly prepared
vegetables are highlights at this
remote house. Garden-grown salad
and farmhouse cheese also feature
and the substantial breakfasts are
excellent.
All week 8, one sitting; closed Oct to
mid-May; credit cards not accepted
(See Where to Stay)

UIG
Baile-na-Cille
Timsgarry, Uig, Isle of Lewis PA86 9JD
TEL (01851) 672242
FAX (01851) 672241
A tiny hotel bounded by silver
beaches on the far side of the Outer
Hebrides. In this kitchen vegetables
are stars in their own right and the
home-baking is scrumptious. Set
three-course dinners; excellent
breakfasts.
All week 7.30, one sitting; lunch by
arrangement; closed 7 Oct-15 Feb
(See Where to Stay)

CAITHNESS, ORKNEY AND SHETLAND

- Scotland's far north: gales, cliffs, seas and islands
- Superb prehistoric sights
- Seabird cities and endless other birds

Puffins

A GLANCE at a map will show the link between Caithness and the island groups to the north. The Gaelic place names of the Highlands are replaced by a new vocabulary – peerie, geo, wick and voe. These names are relics of the time when Caithness, Orkney and Shetland were part of Norway, not of Scotland.

The Norse jarldom based on Orkney lasted more than 500 years (rather less in Caithness), and it was only in the nineteenth century that the last Norse-speaking inhabitant of Shetland died. The Scandinavian influence is still strong but the Norsemen were far from the first inhabitants of the islands. Nowhere else in Britain is there such a density of prehistoric sites, many dating from 3500 BC. Their remains survive together with the settlements of the Bronze Age, the brochs of the Iron Age, the houses of the Picts and the occasional Norse long house. At Jarlshof in Shetland the remains of houses spanning 2,500 years lie exposed.

History is not all that these areas have in common. In Caithness, Orkney and especially Shetland, the sensation that parts of Scotland are closer to the Arctic than to the south of England becomes inescapable. This has little to do with the temperature, which is mild for a part of the world on the same latitude as southern Greenland and Alaska. It has more to do with the absence of trees, the short summer nights, the teeming birdlife, the hissing gales and the feeling that you are on the edge of the unbridled north.

Caithness

Most visitors pass through Caithness on their way to John o'Groats, or to the Orkney ferry from Scrabster. Yet the district has a distinctive character, worth a little exploration. After the sodden moors of Sutherland, the green fields of the north-eastern tip of Scotland seem strange and exotic, the more so since there are no trees to block the views. Instead of trees, you see flagstones. Beneath the soil lie layers of horizontally bedded sedimentary rock, which splits perfectly into thin slabs. Roofs, walls, fences and floors are made from this stone (so are the pavements of many of Britain's cities), and where the sea washes against cliffs of it you find extraordinary effects, from half-finished flights of giant stairs to sea-stacks like carefully balanced towers of biscuits.

The moors lap all around. The blanket bogs of Sutherland extend into Caithness, their unique bird life and desolate beauty threatened by afforestation. The controversy over the spread of the trees has been well publicised, but until you have stood by the Grey Cairns of Camster and seen how the conifers wash up to them like an algae-ridden tide, you are unlikely to appreciate the full extent of the tragedy.

Orkney

It is Orkney's good fortune to be prosperous, beautiful and endowed with world-class sights at the same time as being far enough away from major population centres for there to be little threat from the unpleasant side-effects of mass tourism. Deserted beaches are two-a-penny, custodians have time to chat to you, the wildlife is undisturbed and tour coaches are rarely bigger than minibuses.

Mostly flat and mostly fertile, the Orkney islands are cattle-farming country. Neat fields run down to rocky or sandy beaches; offshore skerries are populated by seals and birds; small boats weave between the islands to set lobster pots. In Orkney, evidence of the far-distant past lies everywhere. The standing stones of Stenness and Brodgar, the chambered cairn of Maes Howe and the Neolithic village of Skara Brae would be worth journeying to see anywhere, but their setting against the stark sea or sky of Orkney adds hugely to their appeal.

Shetland

According to Tacitus, the Romans sighted Shetland on their expedition round Britain and named it Thule after the mythical island on the edge of the world. And this is what it feels like. Shetland is an acquired taste, for to spend money coming to a climate that is, at best, uncertain and to a landscape which has little of the welcoming fertility of Orkney may seem an act of sheer folly. Yet Shetland can be addictive in much the same way as strong black coffee. A draught composed of Arctic wind, luminous skies and tearing seas can stimulate and revivify when you are feeling creative, or misanthropic, or overdosed on stress. If all you want is to relax in comfort in the sun, leave it well alone.

In early summer Shetland's cliffs teem with seabirds, while rare waders breed on its lochs and desolate moorlands. To come to Shetland without doing a spot of birdwatching is a waste, even for those whose closest contact with feathers is normally their duvet. The seabird colonies in the full

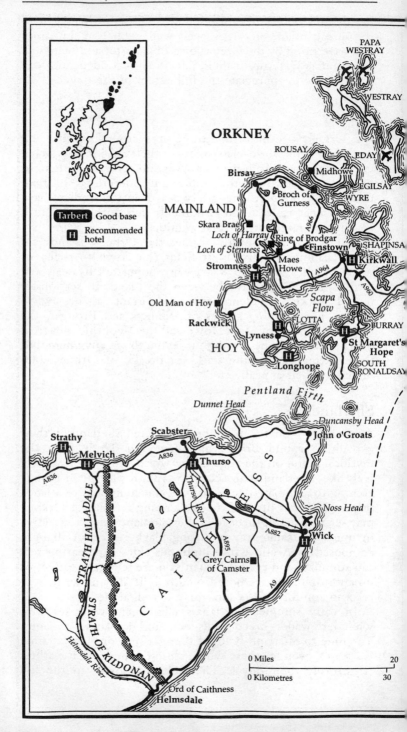

PAPA
WESTRAY

WESTRAY

ORKNEY

ROUSAY   EDAY
Midhowe
Birsay   EGILSAY
Broch of   WYRE
Gurness

MAINLAND

Skara Brae
Loch of Harray   Ring of Brodgar
Loch of Stenness   **Finstown**   SHAPINSAY
Maes   **H** **Kirkwall**
Stromness   **H** Howe   *A964*

*Scapa
Flow*
Old Man of Hoy   FLOTTA   BURRAY
Rackwick   **H**
Lyness   **H**   **St Margaret's
Hope**
HOY   SOUTH
H   RONALDSAY
Longhope

Pentland Firth
Dunnet Head   *Duncansby Head*

Strathy   **Scabster**   **John o'Groats**
H
Melvich   *A836*   **H** **Thurso**
H   *Noss Head*
A836   STRATH HALLADALE   Thurso River
A882
CAITHNESS   **H** **Wick**
Grey Cairns   *A895*
STRATH OF KILDONAN   of Camster
A9
Helmsdale River

Ord of Caithness
Helmsdale

Tarbert Good base

H Recommended
hotel

0 Miles   20

0 Kilometres   30

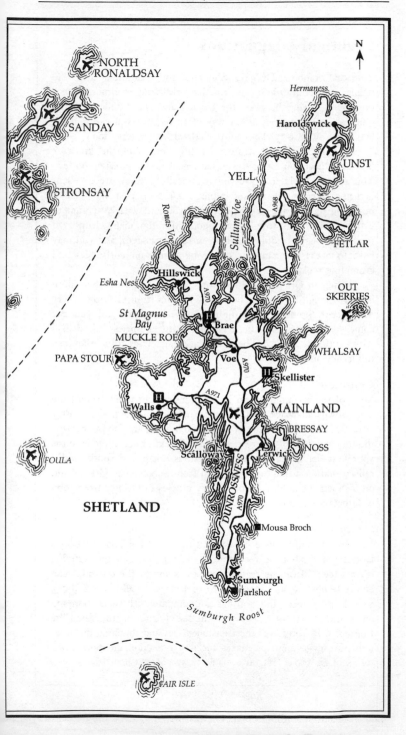

Practical suggestions

You can combine Orkney, Shetland and Caithness into one holiday, but both Orkney and Shetland really deserve more than a brief visit. Flying between the islands and the mainland is the quickest and most convenient way of travel, but you can journey between Caithness, Orkney and Shetland by car ferry too.

Wind is a constant feature of life here, and the knitwear industry thrives on tourists who have packed one sweater too few. You are not likely to regret buying locally – there are excellent bargains. Wellies are indispensable: ankle-deep peat sludge or a minefield of cowpats may lie between you and what you want to explore. Waterproof trousers are a good idea, too: many chambered tombs have large puddles in their entrance passages, and you may have to crawl. Be cautious of strong winds on cliff-edges and crumbling rock.

Getting to Orkney, Shetland or Caithness from further south is easy, though it may not be cheap. Flights from Glasgow (every day except Sunday) and Edinburgh are frequent, and you can come via Inverness or Aberdeen too. With enquiries, call British Airways (0345) 222747. There are daily car ferries from Aberdeen to Orkney and Shetland.

Caithness

Most of the accommodation in Caithness is clustered around the chief towns of Wick and Thurso, neither of them desperately attractive places. A couple of good hotels make up for the run-of-the-mill standard of the rest. Bed-and-breakfast accommodation is your best bet. Wick has air connections north and south, and a railway station, while car ferries run from Scrabster to Orkney and on to Shetland and a passenger ferry crosses to Orkney from John o' Groats in summer.

Orkney

You can happily spend all your time on Mainland (Orkney's largest island), but we recommend visiting some of the outlying islands too. All can be reached by sea (some of the crossings can be pretty bouncy) and there are ro-ro services to all but two (book a week in advance), but nothing can compare with island-hopping on British Airways Express' eight-seater aircraft (operated by Loganair). Buzzing over the translucent sea and touching down on miniature grass airstrips makes for wry reflection on more usual forms of air travel. If you are not fussy about which islands you go to, British Airways Express have good-value three-flight deals on a stand-by basis; call (01856) 873452. Flights run to the minute: do not get stranded.

Kirkwall is Orkney's capital and makes a convenient base for exploration and for shopping. The most renowned prehistoric sights are on Mainland, but enthusiasts should plan to visit Rousay, Hoy, Sanday and Papa Westray too. Anglers should base themselves near the lochs of Stenness and Harray, which are the most famous fishing waters, while birdwatchers make for Westray, Papa Westray or North Ronaldsay (for migrants). Sub-aqua enthusiasts dive to see the remains of the scuttled German High Seas Fleet in Scapa Flow. Other wartime relics are to be found on Hoy.

There is a reasonable choice of accommodation on Mainland, Hoy and Rousay, farmhouse bed-and-breakfasts being especially common, and you can just about get around Mainland by bus. On most outlying islands there is no public transport, and accommodation is much sparser. However, thanks to the entre-preneurial inhabitants, you will usually be able to find a car or bicycle to hire and somewhere to stay, even in spots which the Kirkwall tourist office claims are bare of facilities. On Sanday a bus service meets the ferry in summer and on Westray a bus conveys passengers from the ro-ro to the village; on Rousay limited service exists. Telephone the local community centres (some of which double as guesthouses) on the islands to be pointed in the right direction.

Shetland

In Shetland there is little need to stray from Mainland (again the largest island), though you should visit Fair Isle if you possibly can. A car is almost essential on Shetland, though there are coach outings to some remote spots and the bus network is reasonable. For details, call John Lease Transport (01595) 693162. Fly-drive deals are available or you can bring your own car from Caithness via Orkney, or from Aberdeen. Roads on Shetland are excellent. Lerwick, the capital, has good shops and plenty of atmosphere; the finest scenery is in the north and west of Mainland, the best sights in the south. The seabird cities on the islands of Unst or Noss are relatively easy to reach and worth seeing, while Fair Isle and Fetlar also draw birdwatchers. For really remote island communities to visit, Foula and Out Skerries have few rivals.

All the outlying islands can be reached by sea, but you cannot take your car to Foula, Fair Isle or Papa Stour (nor would you want to). Frequent car ferries run to Yell, Unst, Fetlar, Whalsay and Bressay. You should book in advance in summer. British Airways Express operates regular flights from Tingwall airport, slightly north of Lerwick, to Unst and Fair Isle Mon to Fri. Between Mar and Oct British Airways Express runs reasonably regular flights and day trips to Foula, Out Skerries, Papa Stour and Fair Isle. For details, call (01595) 840246, inter-island flights only.

A few of Shetland's hotels leave rather a lot to be desired since they were built rapidly at the beginning of the oil boom and act as staging posts for oil workers, sailors or helicopter pilots rather than as havens for the holidaymaker. Others have recently been upgraded, so the general situation is improving. It is still advisable not to book without seeing what you are getting. If you are bent on self-catering base yourself within striking distance of Lerwick, so that you can stock up on essentials without having to drive too far.

cacophony of the breeding season are not lightly forgotten. Nor is being dive-bombed by skuas, harassed by aggravated terns, or simply sitting watching the puffins at their burrows. Bring binoculars.

CAITHNESS

The East Coast

. . . the inciville and barbrous behaviour of the most part of oure subjectis in Caithness . . . (James VI, 1611)

Beyond Helmsdale, a ridge of hills which form part of the massif of Scaraben runs to the coast, providing a barrier between Caithness and Sutherland. The coastal road now climbs easily over the **Ord of Caithness**, but it used to be quite a motoring adventure. Caithness Sinclairs still avoid crossing the Ord on a Monday, for it was on this day that 300 men set out under Earl William to take part in the Battle of Flodden, where they were wiped out.

A little way beyond the Ord, signs point over a heathery ridge to the Clearance village of **Badbea**. The few humps of bracken-covered stone at the far end of the short path drive home the human suffering of the Clearances with great clarity. This was the sort of place where communities were forced to settle after being evicted from inland straths. Right on the edge of the cliffs (legend goes that the village children had to be tethered, like goats), with no shelter and little fertile land, people eked out some sort of living. The village was finally deserted when the last of its folk emigrated to New Zealand. It is hard to imagine, picking among the ruins of the crofts, or looking at the names inscribed on the memorial that stands over them, how anyone managed to exist in such a place.

By the side of the road a few miles further north **Lhaidhay Croft Museum** (open Easter to end Oct, Mon to Sat 10 to 5) is a well-preserved long croft house, furnished in nineteenth-century style. This is an excellent small museum, full of curiosities, most donated by local people. There are box beds, beautiful linen nightshirts and even a primitive washing machine. The lasting impression is of a snug comfort, both for the inhabitants and their beasts in the adjacent byre – quite a contrast to Badbea.

If you turn north on the minor road out of Clyth, the three huge stone piles of the **Grey Cairns of Camster** become visible among the young trees which surround them. These chambered cairns date from around 2500 BC. The three entrance passages are each guarded by a little gate to keep the sheep out, and it is worth the damp crawl into the biggest cairn at least, for the interior chamber is a spacious and sombre place (despite its concrete roof).

Back on the main road, the **Hill O' Many Stanes** is a very peculiar prehistoric site. On a patch of level ground on a hillside just off the main road, 22 rows of small upright stones form a fan shape. They are mostly under knee height, and there are more than 200. No one is sure of their purpose.

By the village of **Ulbster** is Whaligoe harbour, the most unlikely landing place on the fierce east coast of Caithness. Almost 365 vertiginous steps are needed to climb down the cliff to the pier beneath. Not surprisingly, the harbour has long gone out of use, but its very existence is testimony to the wealth to be had from the herring boom; 24 boats once operated from this harbour, and the catch was carried up those terrible steps on the backs of the fishermen's wives.

Wick

In 1589, when Wick became a royal burgh, it was a small village with a harbour scarcely worth the name. By 1862, 1,122 boats were fishing for herring from Wick and a whole new town and harbour had been built for the industry. The town was packed with the seasonal workers – gutters, packers and coopers – needed to get the fish from boat to barrel as quickly as possible. Today, Wick is quiet again, the herring gone, the fishing fleet much reduced in number. The herring industry comes to life again in the **Wick Heritage Centre** (open June to end Sept, Mon to Sat 10 to 5), one of the most detailed fishing museums on the coast.

Wick is a grey stone town – stark, like many another Scottish fishing port, as if its energies were focused entirely on the sea beyond the harbour wall. If you are interested in town planning, a stroll across the river brings you to 'Poltney' or Pultneytown, planned and laid out by Thomas Telford.

A port of call for most visitors is **Caithness Glass** (glass-blowing and shop open Oct to May, Mon to Fri 9 to 5; June to Sept, Mon to Fri 9 to 5, Sat 9 to 1, Sun 11 to 5), where, in a remarkably informal factory where furnaces roar and red-hot glassware is carried back and forth, you can follow the making of glass from ingredients to finished article.

North of Wick

Out beyond Wick airport (beware, the road crosses the runway), on the edge of Noss head, the remaining masonry of **Castle Sinclair** and **Castle Girnigoe** (one is a later extension of the other) rises out of the haze like a factory chimney. The castles stand on the narrowest of promontories, with the sea sucking at stacked layers of flagstone beneath. George Sinclair, fourth Earl of Caithness, threw his son into a dungeon here on suspicion of treachery, first starved him, then fed him on all the salt beef he could eat, and finally left him to die of thirst.

After this grisly tale, there is no better place to go than nearby **Duncansby Head**. This is the true north-eastern tip of Scotland, and is adorned by the Stacks of Duncansby – rock spires which rise straight out of the sea. There is also a lighthouse, two long geos, a cave, the Rispie tide-race, wheeling seabirds and short turf full of wild flowers.

The North coast

John o' Groats

Rainy rainy rattlestanes, dinna rain on me. Rain on Johnny Groats hoose, far across the sea (Nursery rhyme)

John o' Groats is a curious place for a tourist trap, for there is nothing here apart from an hotel and a scattering of gift shops. Still, it is being here that counts, and for as long as John o' Groats is considered to be 'opposite' Land's End in

Cornwall, long-distance walkers, cyclists or fund-raising bed-pushers will continue to make it their starting or finishing point, and the coaches will fill the car park.

Jan de Groot was a Dutchman, whom James IV employed in 1496 to start a ferry to the recently acquired territory of Orkney. He is said to have built an octagonal house with eight internal doors to solve problems of family precedence. The house is long gone, but the hotel sports an octagonal tower in its memory.

John o' Groats is not the northernmost point of mainland Britain. For that you must visit **Dunnet Head** to the west, a peninsula of humpy moorland, with good views of Orkney and the Pentland Firth on a clear day.

Thurso

This town used to be Scotland's chief trading port with Scandinavia, though you would never think so today. It is still the largest town on the mainland north of Inverness, its economy considerably boosted by the nearby Dounreay nuclear research station. Much of the town was planned by Sir John Sinclair ('Agricultural Sir John'), one of the best-known 'Improvers' of the eighteenth century. Thurso is a slightly scruffy place with little to linger for, apart from the **Thurso Folk Museum** (open June to mid-Sept, Mon to Sat 10 to 1, 2 to 5), where there are Pictish stones and the collection left by the Victorian naturalist Robert Dick, whom the locals thought to be daft.

Just north of Thurso lies **Scrabster**, the terminal for the car ferry to Stromness in Orkney, and a good place to arrange sea angling.

The road west runs past the attractive River Forss to **Dounreay**, where the dome of Britain's prototype fast reactor (now being decommissioned) stands out against the blue of the sea. The clutter of buildings round it mars the striking effect. There is a small exhibition centre.

ORKNEY

Kirkwall

Orkney's capital has been in existence since the eleventh century, so has the restrained dignity of a small town with a lot of history under its belt. Beside the magnificent red sandstone twelfth-century cathedral old houses line the single main street, while the ruined Bishop's Palace and Earl's Palace add Renaissance grandeur. Pottering around the shops and looking at the silverwork inspired by Norse designs does not take long, and a day will serve to cover the sights. Nevertheless, Kirkwall makes a congenial base. Roads radiate from it all over Mainland, and there is a distillery to visit, a small theatre and a swimming-pool.

Sights in Kirkwall

• **St Magnus Cathedral** (open Apr to Sept, Mon to Sat 9 to 6, Sun 2 to 6; Oct to Mar, Mon to Sat 9 to 1, 2 to 5, Sun services only) That a building of such size and splendour should exist so far out on the periphery of Scotland may seem surprising until you remember that when it was built, Orkney was the seat of a powerful Norse earldom. By the twelfth century, Orkney's inhabitants had stopped pillaging monasteries on the coasts of Britain and had turned Christian themselves. The cathedral bears the name of Orkney's own martyr, St Magnus.

Magnus was co-Earl of Orkney with his cousin, Haakon. After a series of disputes, the two met in 1117 on the island of Egilsay for a reconciliation. Haakon, however, broke the agreed terms and arrived with a large body of men, making it apparent that execution, not negotiation, was on the agenda. After Haakon's standard-bearer had refused to kill Magnus, his cook, Lifolf, eventually did the deed. The skull of Magnus, found in the cathedral in 1919, bears a great gash, very much as the fatal axe blow is described in the verse chronicle of early Orcadian history, the *Orkneyinga Saga*. The cathedral was founded by Magnus' nephew, Rognvald in 1137. It is constructed of a lucent red sandstone with occasional interleavings of yellow, and propped by massive nave columns like sea stacks. The Gothic clerestory pours light into the building, so that on sunny days it seems to glow throughout its interior.

• **Earl's Palace** (HS, standard times; closed in winter) This is the ruin of a magnificent Renaissance building which speaks of power and luxury. Huge oriel windows once flooded it with light, and enormous fireplaces held promise of roaring warmth. Yet its owner was a ruthless tyrant who needed a bodyguard of 50 men when he went to the cathedral only a few yards away, and whose eventual execution had to be postponed until he had been taught the Lord's

Prayer. This was Patrick Stewart, Earl of Orkney, the son of one of James V's bastards. His palace was constructed by what amounted to slave labour. The ground floor is evidence of the Earl's priorities, for it consists of a series of enormous vaulted storerooms, and a giant kitchen. Upstairs, the hall's beautiful windows are complemented by some severely practical loopholes for muskets. The Palace can be visited on a joint ticket which also admits you to the Bishop's Palace, Broch of Gurness, Maes Howe and Skara Brae.

● **The Bishop's Palace** (HS, standard times; closed in winter) This building, just over the road from the Earl's Palace and accessible on a joint ticket with its grander neighbour, is in places contemporary with the cathedral, though it was remodelled a number of times. It is a much more complicated building than the Earl's Palace, and a less obviously beautiful one, though there is plenty to interest those who like tracing architectural developments.

● **Tankerness House Museum** (open all year, Mon to Sat 10.30 to 12.30, 1.30 to 5; also Sun 2 to 5, May to Sept; out of season, call 01856 873191) Close to the cathedral, this museum makes a good starting point for learning about pre-historic Orkney, best seen before visiting the sites. The permanent exhibition leads you round the life and times of Orkney's earliest settlers, via pottery, carved stones, reconstructions of stone furniture and rows of skulls. Tankerness House has many of Orkney's best finds; keep an eye open for the delicate and beautiful bone combs, and do not be so distracted by the exhibits that you fail to notice the age and elegance of the house itself.

The Churchill Barriers and Lamb Holm

On top of a foundation of giant, haphazardly piled concrete blocks, a ribbon of road links Mainland to the islands of Lamb Holm, Glimps Holm, Burray and South Ronaldsay. The rusting remnants of sunken ships poke from the water beside the causeway. The concrete and the wrecks are the results of attempts to block the entrances from the North Sea to **Scapa Flow**, the sheltered anchorage which became a major naval base in the two world wars. The blockships proved unable to prevent an enterprising German U-boat from slipping into Scapa Flow on 14 October 1939 and torpedoing the battleship *Royal Oak* with the loss of 800 lives, so the concrete Churchill Barriers were installed with the labour of 550 Italian POWs.

The prisoners left a reminder of their stay in the shape of

the **Italian Chapel** (always open) on Lamb Holm. The Mediterranean façade of this tiny church, with its columned portico and surmounting belfry, seems incongruous in the steely northern light. The prisoners put it together from two Nissen huts, moulded concrete and whatever scrap came to hand. Inside, a Madonna and Child is painted above the altar, and there is an elaborate wrought-iron rood screen.

Isbister Chambered Cairn

(Open Apr to end Oct, daily 10 to 8; Nov to Mar, daily 10 to 12; out-of-season visitors should call 01856 831339)
Past the peaceful village of St Margaret's Hope and hidden among the hilltop farmsteads of the island of South Ronaldsay lies the Neolithic chambered cairn popularly known as the Tomb of the Eagles, from the many bird carcasses found in the 4,000-year-old burial chamber. The site is family-run (a most unusual occurrence), for the tomb lies on land belonging to farmer Ronald Simison. Even more unusually, he excavated the site himself. At Liddel Farm, you are taken on a most entrancing journey back in time. You are handed a prehistoric axe, which moulds perfectly into your hand, then a shiny black ring (the two halves found ten years apart) and then the cool, smooth skulls of a woman and a man, dead at 35 and 26. You will also encounter a row of wellies ready for visitors on the porch, and a trolley, knee patches and torch by the tomb entrance.

The north coast of Mainland

There are prehistoric remains to whet your appetite as you head west from Kirkwall, notably the chambered cairn on Wideford Hill, but unless you are keen on a roughish walk it is probably better to save your energies for the **Broch of Gurness** (HS, standard times; closed in winter) on the shore opposite the island of Rousay. The broch lies beyond the Sands of Evie, where oystercatchers and curlews strut in the shallows, at the narrowest part of the Eynhallow Sound. It is a complicated site (though much of it has vanished into the sea) with a jumble of Iron Age houses surrounding the substantial remains of the broch at their centre, a surrounding ditch and rampart and the relocated remains of a Pictish house and what may have been a Norse hall. Explanations are clear and convincing, and artists' impressions help to give you an idea of what it was once like.

Birsay

The ecclesiastical centre of the islands before St Magnus Cathedral was built, Birsay is now an exposed straggle of a village. It is dominated by the austere remains of the **Earl's Palace** (HS, always open), another work of the deplorable Stewart earls. Off the coast lies the **Brough of Birsay**. Brough is the word for tidal island, and this one is reached across a slippery causeway. The sea can sneak up behind you, so keep your eyes peeled. Check the tide tables in the *Orcadian* before coming: Birsay is one hour before Kirkwall.

Much of the ancient settlement on the brough has been lost to the sea, but what is left is the most substantial complex of Norse buildings on the islands. The Norsemen were not the first inhabitants, for the shattered remains of a Pictish stone were found scattered over the graveyard of the little twelfth-century church. A copy is now in place, showing two dignified warriors marching behind their chief.

Maes Howe

(HS, standard times; closed Wed and Thur am in winter)
Of the four great prehistoric sights grouped by the Loch of Stenness, Maes Howe is the most fabulous. It is a giant chambered cairn standing on a levelled platform with a rock-cut ditch running round it. The entrance passage and much of the interior of the tomb are built from gigantic slabs of stone, slotted together with the neatness of a Lego building.

A long stooping shuffle through the entrance passage takes you into the dim central chamber, where the custodian gradually brings up the lights to show you the details of the ceiling corbelling, the three side-cells and the massive block-stones which would have closed upon the last remains of the deceased. You are told how, on the shortest night of the year, a shaft of light from the setting sun will turn the entrance passage to gold and throw a splash of light on to the back wall of the chamber.

Attention then shifts to the graffiti. These were left in the twelfth century by Norsemen who seem to have broken into the tomb more than once (the *Orkneyinga Saga* records that two men went mad here while sheltering from a snowstorm). The scratchings of the Norsemen's runes show up under the custodian's torch: there is a lion and what could be a walrus. In translation, the runes are generally no more interesting than modern graffiti, but some talk of 'a great treasure', an idea sniffily dismissed by archaeologists. Maes

Howe was empty when excavated. It is curious to think of those Norse warriors scratching on the walls only 800 years ago, while the time that separated them from the people who dragged the massive slabs over the moors to build this astonishing place was closer to 4,000 years.

The Stones of Stenness and the Ring of Brodgar

Only four great monoliths survive out of the original 12 which made up the stone circle of Stenness, poised where the Loch of Harray flows into the Loch of Stenness. Grey, gaunt and lonely in the middle of farmland, the huge slabs seem to have been frozen in place. It is easy to imagine them lumbering down to drink at the loch on some midsummer's night, and indeed one seems to have been caught in the act, for as you cross the causeway, a single menhir – the Watch Stone – stands on the very edge of the water.

At Bamhouse, just beside the stones, recent exavations have uncovered houses and ritual buildings which must have been linked with the stones. A short walk from the road brings you to the partially reconstructed remains.

The time to be at the nearby Ring of Brodgar is at sunset, preferably when the sky boils with cloud and burning light. The 27 stones (there were once 60) stand still and lonely in a perfect circle silhouetted against the hills of Hoy, with water on both sides and a great sweep of sky above.

The lochs on each side of the ring, Stenness and Harray, are the best-known fishing lochs of Orkney. Stenness is unusual in that you can catch sea fish as well as fresh-water fish. This is because of the loch's narrow outlet to the sea, which leaves the water sufficiently fresh to hold trout, but which can bring in pollock, herring, plaice and sea trout.

Corrigall and Kirkbister Farm Museums

(Open Mar to end Oct, Mon to Sat 10.30 to 1, 2 to 5, Sun 2 to 7)

Between them, these old Orkney farms give a clear impression of life in the last century. While conditions were less spartan than in one of the black houses of the Hebrides, they were hardly luxurious. At Kirkbister, you will find an unaltered example of an old Orkney kitchen, with its freestanding hearth, smoke hole in the roof and tiny bed built into the thickness of the wall. Corrigall is more fully restored, complete with implements, hens and cheese but, while there is more to see, it is rather less evocative.

Skara Brae

(HS, standard times)

This is Orkney's second extraordinary prehistoric sight. It is a complete Neolithic village, buried for millennia in the sand until unearthed by a freak storm in 1850. It is hard to see until you are standing almost on top of it, for the village was semi-subterranean, built deliberately in the middle of a great heap of decayed household refuse – the midden. Skara Brae is 5,000 years old, yet its state of preservation, right down to the furniture and the drainage system, is such that a great effort is needed to realise that it is older than the Egyptian pyramids or Stonehenge.

Skara Brae lies right at the edge of the sea, where the Bay of Skaill takes a great bite out of Mainland's rugged west coast. The waves lash the edge of the site, and much of it may have been lost to erosion in previous centuries. This curious little community, where cramped, tortuous passages lead between spacious houses, with the local stone-working workshop set a little apart, irresistibly recalls a suburban housing estate. All the houses have the same design, with little cupboards, stone-sided beds and central hearths, and all have stone dressers arranged opposite the doorways, perhaps so that *objets d'art* could be displayed with maximum effect to the neighbours. All that is missing is the television.

Current theories suggest that Skara Brae was a self-sufficient, egalitarian community of farmers and fishermen. Everything they had was made from stone, bone, wood or skin – there is no evidence of metal or cloth. Yet some of the things they produced – especially the intricately carved and decorated stone objects of unknown purpose – and some of their building techniques – notably the strong possibility that the village had a sanitation system flushed by running water – make it impossible to dismiss the inhabitants of Skara Brae as primitive. For six centuries or so they lived in their village, then abandoned it – no one knows why.

When you have gazed enough, the foreshore of the Bay of Skaill is good for a gentle stroll. On the other hand, if there is a wind blowing, travel down the coast to **Yesnaby**, where the sea beats against cliffs and shelves of flagstone and cormorants perch on half-submerged rocks, their out-stretched wings giving them the appearance of scarecrows.

A new, unobtrusive visitor centre is planned for Skara Brae; at the moment, the custodian is more than happy to answer questions.

Stromness

Only the gulls and the arrival of the ferry from Scrabster disturb the quiet of this town. It was once a far livelier place, for the Hudson Bay Company's ships called in regularly on their fur-trading run to northern Canada, and Stromness supplied both men and stores for the Davis Strait whalers. The main street meanders for a mile between the seafront and the steep slope of Brinkie's Brae. At the start of Victoria Street, the complex of buildings by the pier has been converted into the **Pier Arts Centre** (open Tue to Sat 10.30 to 12.30, 1.30 to 5; July and Aug, also Sun 2 to 5). Displayed here is a permanent collection of twentieth-century works by Barbara Hepworth, Ben Nicholson, Naum Gabo and Eduardo Paolozzi which was donated to Orkney by Margaret Gardiner; there are also temporary exhibitions, children's workshops, lectures and poetry readings.

Stromness Museum (open Oct to end Apr, Mon to Sat 10.30 to 12.30, 1.30 to 5, May to end Sept, daily 10 to 5) was founded in 1837 and is showing its age, but the wonderful clutter of photographs and objects, mostly donated by local people, can absorb you for hours. The most fascinating story told here is that of the scuttling of the German fleet in Scapa Flow in 1919. The fleet had been interned at the end of World War I to await the terms of the peace treaty, its sailors cold and dispirited. On 21 June a group of children from Stromness went on a cruise which turned out to be the most exciting school outing ever: all around them huge warships suddenly started to sink, deliberately scuttled in a final act of defiance. Seventy-four ships went to the bottom. The subsequent salvage operation was extremely complicated. Three battleships and four battle-cruisers remain on the sea bed and they form an excellent sight, in clear waters, for scuba-divers.

Hoy

The island of Hoy is unlike the rest of Orkney, being hilly, peat-covered and sparsely populated. It has the finest cliff scenery in the islands, culminating in the huge precipices of St John's Head, and in the Old Man of Hoy, the most famous of Scotland's sea-stacks. This is also the place to see relics of Orkney's wartime base, which is in the south of the island.

Lyness

The car ferry from Houton docks under the shadow of the rusting naval guns which stand watch over the visitor centre (open mid-Apr to mid-Oct, Mon to Fri 9 to 4.30; mid-May to mid-Sept, Sat 10.30 to 3.30, Sun 10 to 4; July, Aug, Sun 9 to 6.15) at the end of the pier. Much of the display has been salvaged from the depths of Scapa Flow, including an old aircraft engine, and there is a mass of information about wartime Orkney. The enormous propellor and drive shaft of *HMS Hampshire*, which went down off Marwick Head in 1916 taking Lord Kitchener with her, is the largest exhibit. An old oil storage tank now makes a spendid echoing tap-dancing arena.

The hillsides are studded with the rotting foundations of bunkers, hutments and emplacements, but little else is left of a base that once held more than 60,000 personnel. If you explore the crumbling road that leads up the hillside, you come to the mouth of a tunnel leading deep into the rock where fuel oil was stored out of reach of the bombs, and the area still smells of it. At the base of the hill lies a windswept cemetery, containing the dead of two world wars.

The Dwarfie Stane and Rackwick

Hoy's only chambered tomb, and a remarkable one, lies off the road that leads across the north of the island to Rackwick. The neat path that leads away from the road ought to get you dry-shod to the huge block of sandstone that contains the tomb. This, complete with two side cells, has been hollowed out of the solid rock. Only stone tools were used and there cannot have been room for more than two people to work at a time. Why did they go to this enormous effort? No one knows.

At the end of the road lies **Rackwick**, held by some to be the most beautiful spot on Orkney. It is also the starting point for the walk to the **Old Man of Hoy**. Rackwick is a sheltered green breach in a rampart of red sea-cliffs. It would be perfect if it had a sandy beach, but alas there are only boulders.

The path to the Old Man of Hoy goes uphill round the headland east of Rackwick. At first you see only the green top of the Old Man level with the cliff edge, but as you draw near the plunging layers of rock which make up the stack become apparent. It is a substantial walk to reach the cliffs of St John's Head further along the coast, and the view from the Stromness to Scrabster ferry is just as good.

Rousay

Next to Mainland, this is the best island for prehistoric remains, and there is some accommodation if you want to take more than a day over them. The single road runs around the perimeter and the chief sights are close to it, so hiring a bicycle is probably the best way of getting around if you have not brought a car. A small interpretation centre by the pier provides an introduction to island life.

The **Midhowe Chambered Cairn** (HS, always open), like Maes Howe, is about 5,000 years old, but of a very different design. Whereas Maes Howe has a central chamber with cells built into the walls, Midhowe has a long passage partitioned by pairs of upright slabs, resembling a byre as much as anything, and known as a stalled cairn. It is housed in a modern hangar, which has a gantry allowing you to walk above the tomb and look down into it. Deep silence hangs over this age-old burial ground, and it can be a relief to get out into the wind again.

Only a short walk away is one of the best brochs in Orkney. Much of the surrounding settlement has dissolved into the ocean, but **Midhowe Broch** still stands 13 feet high. One of the interesting features is the ground-level gallery (most brochs have their galleries higher up), and if you have a torch you may be tempted to explore the dark, narrow passage. Two smaller stalled cairns, **Knowe of Yarso** and **Blackhammer**, lie on the way to Midhowe. Neither lives up to Midhowe in scale. Even if you ignore these, the chambered cairn called **Traversoe Tuick** is worth a visit, for here two separate tombs were built one on top of the other and you can explore both.

Westray

Westray is a large, solid island with a long flat tail stretching to the south-east, a range of low hills to the west, the bird cliffs of **Noup Head** to the north-west and an area of sand dunes and machair in the north. **Pierowall**, quite a substantial village, is strung out round the edge of an attractive bay, and it is here that you will arrive if you have come by boat or hitched a ride in from the airstrip. Birdwatchers will probably set out for Noup Head without delay (it is a longish walk), but the first sight for most visitors will be **Noltland Castle** (HS, access from keykeeper; details at site), half a mile's stroll from the village. This splendid sixteenth-century Z-plan fortress is studded with gunloops, and is a place of extraordinary strength for such a remote location. It was built by an incomer from Fife, of dubious reputation, called Gilbert Balfour. It is not just a grim, damp fortress, for the main staircase with its great stone newel at its head is a spacious and beautiful piece of building (take a torch to see it at its best). North of Noltland, Westray's golf course lies on the flat links leading down to the sea. A walk across the sandy turf reveals wild flowers – and hosts of rabbits (many of them black), for there are no ground predators. By making a few inquiries in Pierowall, you should be able to see the holding tanks full of lobsters (usually with some gigantic specimens) in the centre of the village.

Papa Westray

You can get here by boat, but if you are coming from Westray it may prove irresistible to splash out on the shortest scheduled flight in the world. It takes two minutes. Papa Westray is small, and uninhabited at its northern end, where the fields give way to maritime heath. This is **North Hill**, now a nature reserve inhabited by bonxies (skuas) and thousands of arctic terns. The former will buzz you ferociously if you intrude. A stout hat is a good idea for protecting your head against skua strikes.

More or less in the centre of the island, through an extremely muddy farmyard, a track leads you down to the **Knap of Howar**, the oldest standing house in north-west Europe. If you have visited Skara Brae, you will recognise the structure you find here – a semi-subterranean house built into a midden. Unlike Skara Brae, this is not a village but an independent farmhouse, complete with a barn next door.

The east coast is a good place to see seals, both common and grey, which haul themselves up on to the reefs at low tide and bask with head and flippers in the air, looking as if they were doing an aerobics exercise. This is also the side of the island to make for in order to get a boat to the islet **Holm of Papa**, which has an excellent chambered cairn. You may be able to arrange this on the spot by asking at the island's shop, or ask at the tourist office at Kirkwall.

Sanday

This is a big, low-lying island, shaped like a pterodactyl in flight. If you want to explore it thoroughly you will need a car, unless you are a very fit cyclist. A minibus meets the ferry, which arrives at the south of the island, and will take you to the village of Kettletoft, where someone will give you advice.

Sanday is ideal for beach-lovers. The coastline is indented with one bay after another – sandy, weedy, rocky, calm or full of hissing waves. They face enough different directions for you to be certain of finding shelter. The **Bay of Lopness** with miles of dunes is one of the best, and the beaches on either side of the Els Ness peninsula are also good. You are certain to see seals somewhere as you prowl the coastline. The views from the small hill in the south-west of the island – prosaically called the Wart – encompass much of Sanday, Stronsay to the south and the cliffs of Calf of Eday.

Sanday is good for birds, especially terns, and the marshy areas round the Loch of Langamay and North Loch in the north-east tip of the island are the places to look. At Tafts Ness, one of the biggest prehistoric sites in Europe remains unexcavated. Over 500 burial mounds dot the landscape. However, the best prehistoric sight on Sanday is **Quoyness chambered cairn** (HS, standard times). This is the same type of tomb as Maes Howe, and, although not on the same scale, it is an impressive piece of work. Part of the attraction is its isolation – you need not worry about crowds here. The tomb lies near the extremity of Els Ness, half a mile beyond the end of a sand-covered track.

Other islands

• **Eday** has much more heather moorland than most of the islands, and used to export peat widely. The outstanding monument is the prehistoric Stone of Setter, a standing stone fully 15 feet high, superbly situated.
• **Egilsay** If you look over Rousay Sound towards Egilsay, the prominent round tower on the church could easily be mistaken for a factory chimney. It in fact belongs to the twelfth-century St Magnus Church, which stands on the site where St Magnus is supposed to have prayed the night before his murder.
• **Flotta** Orkney's oil island is dominated by the oil terminal, and best viewed from a distance.
• **North Ronaldsay** This is the smallest and most remote of the northern islands. The seaweed-fed sheep are a unique

breed and roam the shore in a communal flock, confined by a dry-stone dyke. There is the much-ruined Broch of Burrian by the shore to visit and rare migrant birds to spot.

● **Shapinsay** Shapinsay is a flat, gentle island dominated by the Victorian pile of Balfour Castle, which it is possible both to tour and stay in. Its accessibility (a 25-minute ferry ride from Kirkwall) makes up for a lack of striking sights.

● **Stronsay** If you want to leave fellow tourists behind, Stronsay is probably the least visited of all the islands, with neither outstanding sights nor outstanding scenery.

● **Wyre** This tiny arrow-shaped island has the remains of Scotland's oldest stone castle on it. There is also a partly restored twelfth-century chapel.

SHETLAND

Sumburgh

The long, thin ridge of land that forms the tail of Shetland ends in the cliffs of **Sumburgh Head**. If you have just arrived by air, spend some time exploring the area before setting off on the journey north. From Sumburgh Head itself you look out over the tide-race of Sumburgh Roost to the angular profile of Fair Isle on the horizon. There is a colony of seabirds, and a cluster of sandy beaches. Within the shadow of the airport lies the most important archaeological site in Shetland.

Jarlshof

(HS, standard times; closed in winter)
Walter Scott coined the name in his novel *The Pirate*, long before the existence of a Norse settlement here was confirmed. Jarlshof was inhabited from prehistoric times right down to the seventeenth century, so there is a profusion of buildings dating from the late Neolithic period onwards. From the Bronze Age there is a metal-worker's workshop; from the Iron Age, earth houses and the remains of a broch. The best-preserved houses, however, are wheel houses from the third to the eighth centuries. These are comfortable-looking designs, with a series of individual rooms radiating round a central hearth, giving everyone privacy and warmth in equal measure. The Norse settlement would seem to have spanned the next 500 years, and the foundations of a

number of long houses remain. Then there is a medieval farmstead and finally the shell of a seventeenth-century house. A platform here gives an aerial view of the jumble of buildings. In the background, helicopters from the oil rigs shuttle in and out of the Sumburgh airport.

Dunrossness

Oil wealth is responsible for the fine road which runs up the eastern side of Dunrossness (Da Ness) towards Lerwick. It is easy enough to speed along it, but exploring the side roads to either side leads you immediately into more typical Shetland scenery: clusters of small modern croft houses, small fields, and boats drawn up at the edge of shallow bays.

The **Shetland Croft House Museum** (open May to end Sept, daily 10 to 1, 2 to 5) near Boddam on the east coast shows how things have changed since the last century. Almost all the furniture in the house is made from driftwood, for Shetland has no trees to speak of and even the cabbages have to be salt-resistant. The old farmstead has its separate water mill and corn-drying kiln, well restored.

On the west side of the peninsula there is a restored watermill in **Quendale,** and the **Loch of Spiggie** which is a shallow patch of water famous for its whooper swans and ducks. A little further north on the back roads is **St Ninian's Isle**. This is a place of remarkable beauty where a small near-island is linked to the mainland only by a double oxbow of white shell sand, like two parentheses back to back. This unusual formation is known as a tombolo, and this is the only sandy one in Britain. The island is the site of a ruined twelfth-century church where a treasure of silver objects from the eighth or ninth centuries was found buried beneath a slab. There are replicas in the Lerwick museum.

Mousa Broch

This is the best-preserved broch (see page 442) in Scotland. It stands on the edge of the island of Mousa, opposite Sandwick on the east coast. The broch is just visible from the main road, but to see it properly you must take the boat from Sandwick, run by Tom Jamieson (call 01950 431367 in advance) during the summer months. The walls stand 45 feet high, probably to within a few feet of the original top, and, from inside, the impression is of standing in the base of an enormous chimney. Galleries run up the middle of the massively thick walls, and you can get to the top of the tower via one of them. Mousa (or Moseyjarborg, as the Norsemen called it) leapt into written history in the *Orkneyinga Saga* as the scene of an elopement: the absconding couple took refuge in the broch from their pursuer, Earl Harald, and forced him to negotiate.

Lerwick

Shetland's capital, sheltered by the offshore island of Bressay, exists by and for the sea. In the narrow Bressay Sound, ships of every description lie at anchor while their crews roam the shops. You will hear northern languages at every step – Russian, Polish and Norwegian in particular. Lerwick is the closest shopping centre for Norwegians who want to escape their own high prices.

Consequently, Lerwick's shops are a step up on Kirkwall's, despite being much further north. A pleasant half-day's shopping is to be had here, fingering the knitwear (though the best shop for this is in Scalloway), thumbing through the books about Shetland – look especially for short stories in the local dialect – or simply window-shopping along with half the visiting mariners. All the action takes place on Commercial Street, a flagstoned alleyway which runs parallel to the seafront. Some of the houses rise straight out of the water.

The hill behind Commercial Street is topped by **Fort Charlotte** (HS, standard times), the only intact Cromwellian fortress in Britain. The pentangle of walls and gunports were put in place to deter the Dutch, by whom the fort was burnt in 1673. Nearby, the **Shetland Museum** (open Mon, Wed, Fri 10 to 7, Tues, Thur, Sat 10 to 5) is old-fashioned but lovingly kept, with masses of material about fishing, finds from ancient sites, geological specimens, and curiosities enough to keep anyone happy. The **Up-Helly-Aa exhibition** (open mid-May to mid-Sept, Tue 2 to 4, 7 to 9, Fri 7 to 9, Sat 2 to 4) is in a shed off St Sunniva Street.

Suburban Lerwick surrounds the fortified settlement of **Clickhimmin Broch** (HS, standard times), which stands in the centre of a small loch. The broch does not match that on Mousa, but its walls still stand 18 feet thick and 15 feet high. Together with the broch and the muddle of walls from various periods around it, there is a remarkable 'blockhouse', probably an intimidating Iron Age gateway.

Scalloway and west Mainland

Scalloway used to be Shetland's capital before Lerwick, but now it is small in comparison. Attractively situated on the edge of a curving bay looking over to the island of Trondra, it is a town of narrow streets and ancient cottages. The ruins of Earl Patrick's castle loom over the town. It was built in 1600 by labour exacted from the locals, but the castle was abandoned when the notorious Stewart earl was executed.

A drive south from Scalloway over the bridges to the islands of Trondra, West Burra and East Burra leads you through a tangle of sea lochs (called voes in Shetland) with some fine views. Just before the bridge to Burra, you can wander among Shetland sheep, ponies and cattle on the **Borland Croft Trail** (open Mon to Sat 11 to 6). A tour north-west from Scalloway to Walls takes you through scenery which grows ever wilder as you head west. Bleak moorland gives way to patches of green as you loop round the head of the voes. White cottages stand out against the dazzling sea or vanish into the grey gloom of heavy showers. Shetland sheep are everywhere, their colours ranging from deep chocolate to pure white, their knowing, pinched faces gazing at you with goat-like intensity. Their wool used to be gathered by plucking rather than shearing, and the finest Shetland shawls could be drawn through a wedding ring. Shetland ponies graze beside the road, and star in many rolls of film. In the past they were bred as pit ponies, their small stature making them ideal for underground work.

There are a few distractions on this journey – the view from Wormadale Hill on a clear day, for one. Silverwork and knitting workshops are clearly signposted. Often you will find knitwear for sale in the front room of small croft houses while the knitting machines chatter in the back. At the sea's edge you will come across the characteristic Shetland yoals – small boats pointed at each end derived from ancient Norse designs.

Beyond Walls, the road heads out to the tiny village of Melby, a sudden haven of green fertility, with the island of Papa Stour a short distance offshore. A longish walk southwards along the coast takes you to some fine cliff scenery.

North of Lerwick

Like the rest of Shetland, north Mainland is a country of sheep, birds, cottages, sea and wind. However, there is one difference: oil. Sullom Voe terminal is the biggest in

Europe, but also the least conspicuous. The effect on land-scape and wildlife has been minimal. Only the flickering flares at night, like something from Norse mythology, or the huge tankers threading their way between islands, tell you that it is there.

A diversion east takes you to **Lunna Ness**, where Lunna House was the headquarters of the Norwegian resistance in World War II. **Brae** is a village which has expanded with the coming of the terminal; there is a swimming-pool here. A trip across the bridge to the island of **Muckle Roe** is worthwhile for views and beach walks. A little further north, at **Mavis Grind**, the land is pinched into an isthmus between (somewhat fancifully) the North Sea and the Atlantic. After this, head west again, looking out for the spiny sea-stacks called **the Drongs**, half-hidden in spray, the oldest pub in Shetland at **Hillswick** (now a vegetarian restaurant), the natural arch off the coast beyond **Brae Wick**, and finally the cliffs at **Esha Ness**, where the road ends beside the chasm of Caldersgeo.

Outer islands

Shetland's inhabited outer islands divide into the big three (Unst, Yell and Fetlar), the smaller nearby ones (Bressay,

---

Up-Helly-Aa

Shetland's new year festival takes place on the last Tuesday of January (though 'the Helly' means the weekend) and reaches its climax in the burning of a Viking-style longship. The festival may have originated in pagan Yule but it is more of a nineteenth-century tradition, now tamer than it was when blazing tar barrels were rolled through the streets of Lerwick and 40 special constables had to be enrolled. Guisers dressed as Vikings sing rousing choruses – 'We are the sons of mighty sires, whose souls were staunch and strong; We sweep upon our serried foes, the hosts of Hate and Wrong'. If you cannot go to Shetland in the last week of January, the Up-Helly-Aa exhibition will give you a flavour. As well as a longship, there are samples of the shields, costumes and torches used by the celebrants, and plenty of photographs. If your enthusiasm for the Vikings mounts, you can take a trip round the harbour in season on a replica longship, the *Dim Riv*.

Noss, Whalsay and Papa Stour) and the really isolated ones (Foula, Out Skerries and Fair Isle). If your ambition is to get to the northernmost point of Britain (and why not, now you are here?), a day trip to Unst is easy.

Yell and Fetlar

Yell is an island of desolate peat hag and rusting cars dumped behind crofts whose charms for visitors are hidden very deep. The Loch of Lumbister, an RSPB reserve, is the best area for wildlife. **Fetlar** is a different matter: small, largely green, and full of interesting nooks and crannies. Snowy owls nested on the island between 1967 and 1975, and although they no longer breed, one or more females can sometimes be seen at the RSPB reserve at Vord Hill. The rare red-necked phalarope, red-throated divers and whimbrel are all also found on Fetlar (the Loch of Funzie at the east of the island is the place to look). The Wick of Trests has a lovely beach, bounded by the reddish moor-topped cliffs of Lamb Hoga where stormy petrels come ashore at night to breed.

Unst

Up here, where summer nights are never dark (the long twilight is called *simmer dim*), it is easy to persuade yourself that this is the edge of the world. Unst is not quite tundra country, but often looks or feels arctic. The most scenic part of this rather bleak island is the far north-west corner, and here too is the seabird colony of Hermaness (notable for puffins), at the edge of an extensive reserve of maritime heath. From the cliffs at Hermaness, you can gaze out on the rock islet of Muckle Flugga, the last piece of land before the Arctic Circle. There is a visitor centre, with information about the reserve, and a warden to answer questions, in the old lighthouse buildings at Burrafirth.

Haroldswick is a scattered cluster of houses where the northernmost post office in the United Kingdom will stamp your letters with a special postmark. The **Unst Boat Haven** (open May to Sept, 2 to 5) is the place to go to see traditional Shetland boats. Among the collection, a Welsh coracle is a distinct outsider. **Muness Castle**, in the south-east of Unst, is also the northernmost British castle.

Fair Isle

Rising out of the sea, more or less half-way between Orkney and Shetland, Fair Isle is paradoxically more isolated than Shetland's other outliers yet more accessible. It is a place which is well used to visitors, but which has retained all its genuine hospitality. The residents put it simply – by the end of winter they are longing for some new faces, and then, just when they are getting fed up with visitors, they all go away and they are left to themselves again. It is birds – especially those rare migrants – which bring most visitors to Fair Isle, and in spring or autumn your fellow guests are likely to be 'twitchers'. The enthusiastically run **Bird Observatory**, which doubles as a comfortable guesthouse, can be intimidating if you cannot tell a blackbird from a thrush, but there is no need to join in if you do not want to.

Fair Isle is just the right size to wander around in a day, with enough variety in its scenery, inland as well as round its wild coast, to keep you happy for longer. The locals are happy to chat, and you can poke round the little museum in the **George Waterston Memorial Centre**, join half the island in waiting for the Good Shepherd IV on its voyage from Mainland, or track down Fair Isle sweaters.

The other islands

- **Whalsay** is an important base for part of Shetland's fishing fleet, which explains its comparatively large population and the size of the harbour at Symbister. It has always been an important place of trade. Hanseatic merchants from the north German coast had booths here in the Middle Ages, and one has been fully restored, with an explanation of the trade between Bremen, Hamburg and Whalsay.
- **Bressay and Noss Bressay** lies offshore of Lerwick, and apart from having good views of the town is of little special interest except as a stepping stone to Noss (it is about an hour's walk across the island so it may be worth taking your car). Noss is the home of one of Shetland's biggest seabird cities, and is a National Nature Reserve. It is not open on Monday or Thursday, but at other times you can be ferried across the narrow Noss Sound from Bressay in a perilous-looking inflatable.
- **Papa Stour** is an island of caves and flowers with a population of around 40. Ferries leave from West Burra Firth, or you can fly.
- **Out Skerries** This cluster of three tiny islands, two of them linked together by a bridge, still supports a community of over 80, largely dependent on fishing. Few visitors make it out here, so you can be certain of a friendly welcome. Out

USEFUL DIRECTORY

Main tourist offices
Highlands of Scotland Tourist Board
Whitechapel Road, Wick KW1 4EA
(01955) 602596

Orkney Tourist Board
6 Broad Street
Kirkwall, Orkney KW15 1NX
(01856) 872856

Shetland Islands Tourism
Market Cross, Lerwick
Shetland ZE1 0LU
(01595) 693434

Tourist Board publications Annual visitor's and accommodation
guides (all three tourist boards), also *Shetland Official Tourist Guide*
(very useful, £5.00), and leaflets on individual Orkney islands with
main sights, services etc. Special-interest leaflets include cruising,
archaeology and fishing (Shetland); walks, birds, fishing and golf
(Highlands). Order by post or phone from above addresses.

Local tourist information centres
Helmsdale (01431) 821640 (late Mar to Sept)
John o' Groats (01955) 611373 (Apr to Oct)
Stromness (01856) 850716
Thurso (01847) 892371 (Apr to Oct)

Local transport
British Airways Express/Loganair (services to Kirkwall, Unst,
Lerwick and Wick, from Fair Isle) (0345) 222111; also inter-island
flights around the Orkney (01856 872494) and Shetland islands
(01595 840246)
Wick Railway Station (01955) 602131
Bus from Kirkwall–Houton for Hoy ferry (01856) 872866

Ferries
P&O routes:

Aberdeen–Lerwick	Aberdeen–Stromness
Scrabster–Stromness	Stromness–Lerwick

Skerries are good for migratory birds; otherwise carpets of
flowers in spring and the sense of being miles from anywhere are the attractions.

Aberdeen–Lerwick–Bergen (summer only)
P&O information: (01595) 694848/695252

Houton–Hoy–Flotta (up to five sailings daily; not Sun in winter)
(01856) 811397
John o' Groats–Burwick, South Ronaldsay (passenger only, end Apr
to Sept, four sailings daily) (01955) 611353/611342
Kirkwall–Eday–Stronsay (one or two sailings daily; not Sun in
winter) Orkney Ferries (01856) 872044
Kirkwall–Sanday–Westray–Papa Westray–North Ronaldsay (three
sailings daily in summer, Sunday sailings all islands; in winter one
sailing a day Mon to Sat; North Ronaldsay Sat only) Orkney Ferries
(01856) 872044
Kirkwall–Shapinsay (up to five sailings daily; not Sun in winter)
(01856) 872044
Laxo–Whalsay (frequent daily service) (01806) 566259
Lerwick–Bressay (frequent daily service) (01595) 744850
Lerwick–Out Skerries (twice a week) (01595) 692042
Stromness–Moaness, Hoy (passenger only, June to Sept, three
sailings on weekdays, two at weekends; two a day, weekdays only
winter) (01856) 850624
Sumburgh–Fair Isle (passenger only, up to three times a week in
summer, once a week in winter) (01595) 760222
Tingwall–Rousay–Egilsay–Wyre (up to six sailings daily; not Sun in
winter) (01856) 751360
Toft–Yell and Yell–Unst–Fetlar (frequent daily services) (01957)
722259/722268
West Burrafirth–Foula (passenger only, once or twice a week)
(01595) 873232
West Burrafirth–Papa Stour (passenger only, three or four times a
week) (01595) 744850
Westray–Papa Westray (school terms and summer, passenger only)
(01857) 677216
Vidlin–Out Skerries (three times a week) (01595) 692042

Other
Fair Isle Lodge and Bird Observatory (01595) 760258
Scottish Natural Heritage (information on reserves, plus ferry to
Noss) (01595) 693345
Go-Orkney (round coach tour) (01856) 874260

• **Foula** Scarcely populated, wild and mountainous, Foula sees
few visitors. The sea crossing is rough and the island often gets
cut off.

WHERE TO STAY

£ – under £70 per room per night, incl. VAT

££ – £70 to £110 per room per night, incl. VAT

£££ – over £110 per room per night, incl. VAT

BRAE
Busta House
Busta, Shetland ZE2 9QN
TEL (01806) 522506
FAX (01806) 522588
Busta House has panoramic views. The menu emphasises fish. Well-equipped bedrooms.
££ All year exc 20 Dec to 4 Jan; 22 rooms; drying-room; fishing

KIRKWALL
Briar Lea
10 Dundas Crescent, Kirkwall, Orkney KW15 1JQ
TEL (01856) 872747
Homely Victorian stone house. Breakfast and packed lunches served. Simple bedrooms.
£ All year; 4 rooms; credit cards not accepted

Foveran Hotel
St Ola, Kirkwall, Orkney KW15 1SF
TEL (01856) 872389/872337
FAX (01856) 876430
Modern hotel. Watch otters and seabirds while dining. Small bedrooms.
£ Closed Jan; 8 rooms; drying-room

LONGHOPE
Burnhouse Farm
Longhope, South Walls, Orkney KW16 3PA
TEL (01856) 701263
Friendly old farmhouse. Children's and vegetarian meals available. Ground-floor bedrooms.
£ All year exc Chr; 2 rooms with wash-basin; credit cards not accepted

LYNESS
Stoneyquoy Farm
Lyness, Hoy, Orkney KW16 3NY
TEL (01856) 791234
Farmhouse above Longhope Bay. Packed lunches available. Simple bedrooms.
£ All year exc Chr and New Year; 2 rooms; credit cards not accepted

MELVICH
The Sheiling
Melvich KW14 7YJ
TEL (01641) 531256
FAX (01641) 531356
A family home with sea views. Ground-floor bedrooms.
£ Apr to Nov; 3 rooms; credit cards not accepted

ST MARGARET'S HOPE
Bellevue Guest House
St Margaret's Hope, South Ronaldsay, Orkney KW17 2TL
TEL (01856) 831294
Guesthouse serving evening meals and packed lunches. Large bedrooms.
£ All year; 3 rooms all with wash-basin; credit cards not accepted

Blanster House
St Margaret's Hope, South Ronaldsay, Orkney KW17 2TG
TEL (01856) 831549
Guesthouse with TV lounge. Packed lunches available. Spacious bedrooms.
£ All year; 3 rooms, 2 with wash-basin; credit cards not accepted

SKELLISTER
The Knowles
Skellister, South Nesting, Shetland ZE2 9PP
TEL (01595) 890204
Comfortable family home in a beautiful spot. Evening meals and packed lunches are available.

£ All year; 3 rooms with wash-basin; sauna; credit cards not accepted

STRATHY
Catalina
Aultivullin, Strathy Point, Strathy
KW14 7RY
TEL/FAX (01641) 541279
Comfortable guesthouse on a wild headland. Evening meals available.
£ All year; 2 rooms; credit cards not accepted

STROMNESS
Millburn
Sandwick by Stromness, South Ronaldsay, Orkney KW16 3JB
TEL (01856) 841656
A modern house in grounds above Loch Harray. Breakfast and packed lunches available. Guests may use a boat.
£ Feb to Nov; 3 rooms; credit cards not accepted

THURSO
Forss House
by Thurso KW14 7XY
TEL (01847) 861201
FAX (01847) 863101

Welcoming house frequented by fishermen. Good old-fashioned dishes served. Spacious bedrooms.
££ All year; 10 rooms, 2 cottages; drying-room; fishing

WALLS
Burrastow House
Walls, Shetland ZE2 9PB
TEL (01595) 809307
FAX (01595) 809213
Elegant and remote Georgian house. Dinners involve local seafood. Boat excursions.
£££ Closed Jan to mid-Mar; restaurant closed to non-residents Mon eve; 6 rooms; fishing; water sports; credit cards not accepted (See Where to Eat)

WICK
Bilbster House
Bilbster, nr Wick KW1 5TB
TEL (01955) 621212
Friendly house in a woodland setting. Excellent value.
£ Easter to end Sept; 3 rooms; credit cards not accepted

WHERE TO EAT

Key: A ★ marks a place that is particularly good value for money

ST MARGARET'S HOPE
The Creel
Front Road, St Margaret's Hope, South Ronaldsay, Orkney KW17 2SL
TEL (01856) 831311
Waterfront inn serving local seafood, wonderful puddings.
May to end Sept, all week 7 to 9, Oct to Feb, Fri to Sun 7 to 9 (ring to check first); closed Jan and occasionally low season

WALLS
Burrastow House
Walls, Shetland ZE2 9PB
TEL (01595) 809307
FAX (01595) 809213
Remote house with a sparkling menu. Traditional European dishes. Good wine list.
Tue to Sun 12.30 to 2.30, 7.30 to 9; closed Jan to Mar; credit cards not accepted (See Where to Stay)

INDEX

Bold entries refer to boxed sections on, for example, Robert the Bruce and the Edinburgh Festival.